Frommer's®

BATH

W9-BMB-915

POSTCARDS

FROM

LONDON

Tower Bridge is one of London's most celebrated landmarks. See chapter 6. © Michel Friang Photography.

Sometimes the most memorable sights are simply chance encounters on the street. © Yellow Dog Productions/ The Image Bank.

Westminster Abbey, where English kings have been crowned for a thousand years. See chapter 6. Photo above © Markham Johnson/Robert Holmes Photography; photo opposite © Kelly/ Mooney Photography.

Trafalgar Square is a major landmark in central London, a focal point for Christmas and New Year's celebrations, and a venue for street performers year-round. See chapter 6. © Kindra Clineff Photography.

For our favorite pubs, see chapters 5 and 9. Both images © Dave Bartruff Photography.

NEW LONDON THEATRE

Trafalgar Sq. Westminster
Elephant New Cross **53**
Blackheath Woolwich

PLUMSTEAD STN VIA PLUMSTEAD COMMON

HER MAJEST
THEATR

PAY DRIVER

Leyland

The world's most famous timepiece, housed in the clock tower of the Houses of Parliament. (The name "Big Ben" refers not to the clock tower itself, but to the largest bell in the chime, which weights almost 14 tons.) See chapter 6. © Andrea Pistolesi Photography.

Perhaps the most famous department store in the world, Harrods is especially noted for its spectacular Food Halls. See chapter 8. © Hilary Wilkes/International Stock.

Portobello Market was once known largely for its produce, but has now become synonymous with antiques. See chapter 8. Photo above © Jan Butchofsky-Houser Photography; photo opposite © Kelly/Mooney Photography.

History comes alive at the Tower of London, where you can see the Crown Jewels and a collection of ancient armor, like this suit, which dates from the days of Henry VIII. © Catherine Karnow Photography.

The Yeoman Warders, "Beefeaters," keep watch at the Tower of London, where famous prisoners such as Anne Boleyn, Lady Jane Grey, and Sir Thomas More lost their lives. © Catherine Karnow Photography.

A full English breakfast is a hearty, lavish affair. In chapter 4, we've noted which hotels offer breakfast in their room rates. © Dave Bartruff Photography.

When Londoners speak of "The City," they mean the original square mile that's become the British version of Wall Street. © Lisl Dennis/The Image Bank.

Two London "bobbies" at St. James's Palace. © Dave Bartruff Photography.

Wimbledon is the most prestigious Grand Slam event on the pro tennis tour; spectators enjoy strawberries and cream while watching the world's best players compete. See chapter 2. © Nik Wheeler Photography.

Hyde Park, with adjoining Kensington Gardens, covers 615 acres of central London. See chapter 6. © Robert Holmes Photography.

The Houses of Parliament are in the former royal palace of Westminster. See chapter 6 for details on how to attend a session and sit on a civilized but freewheeling debate. Photo above © Catherine Karnow Photography; photo below © Jan Butchofsky-Houser.

Frommer's® 2000

London

**by Darwin Porter
and Danforth Prince**

with Online Directory by Michael Shapiro

MACMILLAN • USA

ABOUT THE AUTHOR

Authors **Darwin Porter** and **Danforth Prince** share their love of their favorite European city in this guide. Porter, a bureau chief for The Miami Herald at 21 who later worked in television advertising, wrote the first-ever book to London for Frommer's. He's joined by Prince, formerly of the Paris bureau of the *New York Times*. Together, they're the authors of several best-selling Frommer's guides, notably to England, France, the Caribbean, Italy, and Germany.

MACMILLAN TRAVEL

Macmillan General Reference USA, Inc.
1633 Broadway
New York, NY 10019

Find us online at **www.frommers.com**

ISBN 0-02-863064-5
ISSN 1096-6439

Editor: Alice Fellows
Production Editor: Suzanne Snyder
Photo Editor: Richard Fox
Design: Michele Laseau
Digital Cartography: Ortelius Design
Staff Cartographer: Roberta Stockwell
Page Creation: Pete Lippincott and Linda Quigley

SPECIAL SALES

Bulk purchases (10+ copies) of Frommer's and selected Macmillan travel guides are available to corporations, organizations, mail-order catalogs, institutions, and charities at special discounts, and can be customized to suit individual needs. For more information write to Special Sales, Macmillan General Reference, 1633 Broadway, New York, NY 10019.

Manufactured in the United States of America

5 4 3 2 1

Contents

6 **Exploring London   186**

7 **London Walks   240**

8 **Shopping   259**

9 **London After Dark   283**

List of Maps

AN INVITATION TO THE READER

In researching this book, we discovered many wonderful places—hotels, restaurants, shops, and more. We're sure you'll find others. Please tell us about them, so we can share the information with your fellow travelers in upcoming editions. If you were disappointed with a recommendation, we'd love to know that, too. Please write to:

Frommer's London
Macmillan Travel
1633 Broadway
New York, NY 10019

AN ADDITIONAL NOTE

Please be advised that travel information is subject to change at any time—and this is especially true of prices. We therefore suggest that you write or call ahead for confirmation when making your travel plans. The authors, editors, and publisher cannot be held responsible for the experiences of readers while traveling. Your safety is important to us, however, so we encourage you to stay alert and be aware of your surroundings. Keep a close eye on cameras, purses, and wallets, all favorite targets of thieves and pickpockets.

WHAT THE SYMBOLS MEAN

✪ Frommer's Favorites

Our favorite places and experiences—outstanding for quality, value, or both.

The following abbreviations are used for credit cards:

AE	American Express	EURO	Eurocard
CB	Carte Blanche	JCB	Japan Credit Bank
DC	Diners Club	MC	MasterCard
DISC	Discover	V	Visa
ER	EnRoute		

FIND FROMMER'S ONLINE

Arthur Frommer's Budget Travel Online (**www.frommers.com**) offers more than 6,000 pages of up-to-the-minute travel information—including the latest bargains and candid, personal articles updated daily by Arthur Frommer himself. No other Web site offers such comprehensive and timely coverage of the world of travel.

The Best of London

As London prepares to welcome some 30 million visitors at the millennium, the city on the Thames is dusting off its monuments and launching new attractions. The Dome at Greenwich (see box in chapter 6) will spearhead the millennium celebrations. This is the most ambitious project ever undertaken for visitors, and the Dome will highlight Britain's past achievements and its surprises for the future in the way of products and developments. But with or without a Millennium Dome, London is called the Futura 2000 of cities. Its giddy energy and cutting-edge style have made it the new-wave capital of trendsetting chic. Many view the year 2000 and beyond as the point where the past of Britain will meet the future.

The Dome will contain major educational facilities such as multi-media shows, as well as displays and exhibitions on the environment, society, and culture—all with an eye to what's coming up in the 21st century. The Dome is the largest structure of its kind in the world—it alone could house 13 Albert Halls or two Wembley Stadiums.

The British Airways London Eye in the heart of the capital is a giant Millennium Ferris Wheel to open in December 1999 on the South Bank. The world's largest observation wheel, it will give you a perspective of the British capital and a sweeping view of a skyline usually reserved for planes or birds.

There's more. The Tate Gallery of Modern Art is establishing a new national gallery. The British Museum's Great Court is being turned into a dramatic new public space. Construction is proceeding rapidly on the Millennium Bridge at Southwark, along the banks of the Thames, the first pedestrian-only bridge to be built across the Thames in the 20th century, linking St. Paul's Cathedral with the new Tate when it eventually opens.

The British capital is more eclectic and electric than it's been in years. There's almost a feeding frenzy setting out to prove that London is the most pulsating, vibrant city on the planet, even rivaling New York for sheer energy, outrageous art, trendy restaurants, and a nightlife equal to none. *Newsweek* hailed London as a "hip compromise between the non-stop newness of Los Angeles and the aspic-preserved beauty of Paris—sharpened to New York's edge." *Wine Spectator* proclaims more modestly that "The sun is shining brighter in London these days."

The sounds of Brit-pop and techno pour out of Victorian pubs; experimental theater is taking over stages that were built for Shakespeare's plays, upstart chefs are reinventing the bland dishes

Central London

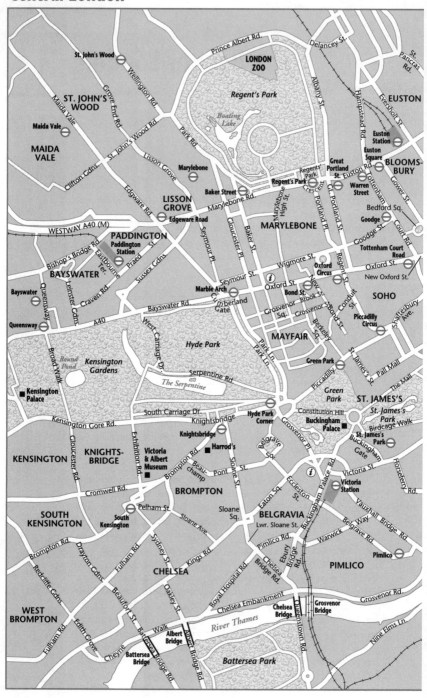

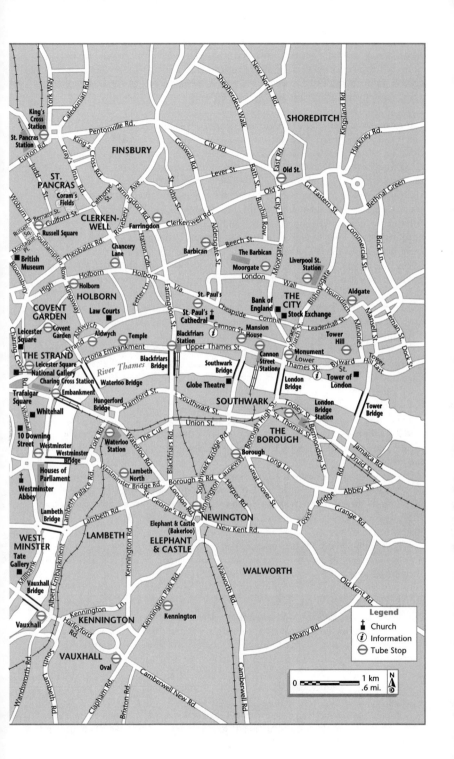

3

British mums made for generations into a new and inventive cuisine, and for the first time ever, Brits are even running the couture houses of Dior and Givenchy. In food, fashion, film, pop music, the visual arts, and just about everything else, London stands at the cutting edge again, just as it did in the 1960s.

If you just don't give a hoot about the new London—if this sea of change worries you more than it appeals—rest assured: Traditional London still lives, basically intact under the veneer of hip. This ancient city has survived a thousand years of invasion, from the Normans to the Blitz, so a few scenesters moving in isn't going to change anything fundamental. From high tea at Brown's to the changing of the guard at Buckingham Palace, the city abounds with the culture and charm of days gone by.

Discovering London and making it your own can be a bit of a challenge, especially if you have just a little time. Even in the 18th century, Daniel Defoe found London "stretched out in buildings, straggling, confused, out of all shape, uncompact and unequal; neither long nor broad, round nor square." London is a city that has never quite made up its mind about its own size. The City of London proper is merely one square mile of very expensive real estate around the Bank of England. All the gargantuan rest of the city is made up of separate villages, boroughs, and corporations—Westminster, Chelsea, Hampstead, Kensington, and many more—each with its own mayor and administration ready to fight for its independent status at the drop of an ordinance. Together, however, they add up to a mammoth metropolis, once the largest on the globe.

Luckily, whether you're looking for Dickens' house or the Dr. Marten's Superstore, only a minute fraction of London's huge territory need concern you. The heart of this behemoth is one of the most fascinating areas on earth, and for about a century, one-quarter of the world was ruled from central London. With almost every step you take, you'll come across signs of the tremendous influence this city has exerted over our past, both in thought and action.

London is a mass of contradictions. On the one hand, it's a decidedly royal city, studded with palaces, court gardens, coats-of-arms, and other regal paraphernalia. Yet it's also the home of the world's second-oldest parliamentary democracy. (Iceland was the first.)

Today, London is growing less English and more international. The gent with the bowler hat has long gone out of fashion; today's Londoner might arrive in a turban. It's becoming easier to find a café au lait and a croissant than a scone and a cup of tea. Increasingly, the city is home to immigrants and refugees, both rich and poor, from all reaches of the world.

What's really amazing is that this city—ancient and modern, sprawling and compact, stolidly English and increasingly multicultural—works as well as it does. Come, and discover.

1 Frommer's Favorite London Experiences

- **Watching the Sunset at Waterloo Bridge:** Waterloo Bridge is the ideal place for watching the sun set over Westminster, to the west. From here, you can see the last rays of light bounce off the dome of St. Paul's and the city spires in the East End, too.
- **Enjoying a Traditional Afternoon Tea:** Nothing is more typically British. Try the Hotel Goring, dating from 1910. From the lounge, you'll look out on a small garden as you enjoy finger sandwiches (often watercress or cucumber), the hotel's special Ceylon-blend tea, scones and clotted cream, and the chef's famous light fruitcake offered from a trolley.

- **Cruising London's Waterways:** In addition to the Thames, London has an antique canal system, complete with towpath walks, bridges, and wharves. Replaced by the railroad, the canal system remained forgotten until recently, when it was rediscovered by a new generation. Now, in a process of urban renewal that's been called "industrial archaeology," the old system has been restored, bridges painted and repaired, and towpaths cleaned up. See "Sightseeing & Boat Tours Along the Thames" in chapter 6.
- **Spending Sunday Morning at Speakers' Corner:** At the northeastern corner of Hyde Park, near Marble Arch, a 19th-century British tradition carries on. Speakers sound off on any subject they wish, and "in-your-face" hecklers are part of the fun. You might hear everything from denunciations of the monarchy to anti-gay rhetoric. Anyone can get up and speak. The only rules: You can't blaspheme, be obscene, or incite a riot. The tradition began in 1855—before the legal right to assembly was guaranteed in 1872—when a mob of 150,000 gathered to attack a proposed Sunday Trading Bill. Orators from all over Britain have been taking advantage of this spot ever since.
- **Studying the Turners at the Tate:** Upon his death in 1851, J. M. W. Turner bequeathed his personal collection of 19,000 watercolors and some 300 paintings to the people of Britain. He wanted his finished works, some 100 paintings, displayed under one roof. Today at the Tate, you see not only Turner, but also glimpses of the Thames through the museum's windows. How appropriate—the artist lived and died on its banks in Chelsea and painted the river in its many changing moods.
- **Strolling Through Covent Garden:** George Bernard Shaw got his inspiration for *Pygmalion* here, where the character Eliza Doolittle sold violets to wealthy operagoers and became a household name around the world. The old fruit and vegetable market, with its Cockney cauliflower peddlers and butchers in bloodsoaked aprons, is long gone. What's left is just as interesting: Covent Garden today is London's best example of urban renewal and one of its hippest shopping districts. In the footsteps of Chippendale and Dickens, you can wander about and discover colorful street stalls, an array of boutiques, shops selling one-of-a-kind merchandise, and all the while enjoy the city's best sidewalk entertainment. There's an antiques market in the piazza on Monday and a crafts market Tuesday through Saturday. When you're parched, plenty of pubs in the area will quench your thirst, like the Nag's Head, an Edwardian pub that'll serve you a draft Guinness and a plate of pork cooked in cider.
- **Treasure Hunting for Antiques:** Some 2,000 antiquarians live within the city limits of London. Check with the tourist office to see if a major antiques fair is on at the time of your visit; the Dorchester Fair and Grosvenor House Fair take place in June. If a fair isn't being held while you're in London, head for one of the following antiques centers; they sell everything from plain old junk (mugs with Prince Philip's face on them) to rare bric-a-brac. The best ones are **Gray's and Gray's** in the Mews, 58 Davies St. (Tube: Bond Street); **Chelsea Antiques Market,** 245A-53 King's Rd. (Tube: Sloane Square); and **Alfie's Antique Market,** 13-25 Church St. (Tube: Edgware Road).
- **Shopping Harrods:** Regardless of how many times you visit London, it's hard to resist a visit to this vast Knightsbridge emporium. Spread across 15 acres, Harrods proclaims as its motto *Omnia Omnibus Ubique* or "everything for everyone, everywhere." They mean it, too: Someone didn't believe the claim, and in 1975 called Harrods at midnight and ordered that a baby elephant be delivered to the

home of the governor of California and his first lady—Mr. and Mrs. Ronald Reagan in Sacramento. The animal arrived safely, albeit a bit bewildered. (Nancy even sent a "thank-you" note.) The food halls are our favorite section, with some 500 different cheeses and some 163 brands of whiskey among zillions of other goodies. It's estimated that at Christmas, Harrods sells 100 tons of Christmas puddings. You can even arrange your funeral at the store.

- **Rowing on the Serpentine:** When the weather's right, we always like to head to this 41-acre artificial lake dating from 1730. A stream was dammed to create the artificial lake, whose name derives from its winding, snakelike shape. At the Boathouse, you can rent (they call it "hire") a boat by the hour. With the right companion, it's one of the most idyllic ways to spend a sunny London afternoon. Renoir must have agreed; he depicted the custom on canvas.

- **Making a Brass Rubbing:** Re-create all those costumed ladies and knights in armor from England's age of chivalry. One good place to make your very own brass rubbing is the crypt of St. Martin-in-the-Fields in Trafalgar Square; the staff there will be happy to show you how.

- **Getting to Know North London on a Sunday:** Begin by looking for some smart fashion at Camden Market, a Sunday affair in the northern reaches of Camden High Street where stallholders hawk designer jewelry and clothing. Next, walk up to Hampstead Heath off Well Walk and take the right fork, which will lead you to an open field with a panoramic view of London. If you walk long and hard enough, you'll be ready for a traditional Sunday lunch at Jack Straw's Castle at North End Way. Cap your meal with a visit to the Freud Museum, which is open on Sunday until 5pm.

- **Dining at Rules:** Rules, at 35 Maiden Lane (WC2), was first established as an oyster bar in 1798; it may, in fact, be the oldest restaurant in London. Long a venue for the theatrical elite and literary beau monde, it still serves the same dishes that delighted Edward VII and his mistress, Lillie Langtry. They always began with champagne and oysters behind a closed door upstairs. Charles Dickens liked the place so much that he had a regular table. Over the years, everyone from William Thackeray to Clark Gable has enjoyed its pheasant and grouse. Where else can you get a good purée of parsnips these days, anyway? If you're looking for unreconstructed British cuisine, finish off with the treacle sponge or apple suet pudding—how English can you get?

- **Spending a Night at the West End Theater:** London is the theatrical capital of the world. The live stage offers a unique combination of variety, accessibility, and economy—and perhaps a look at next year's Broadway hit.

- **Crawling the London Pubs:** Americans bar hop; Londoners do a pub crawl. With some 5,000 pubs within the city limits, you would be crawling indeed if you tried to have a drink in each of them. Enough traditional ones remain, especially in central London, to make it worthwhile to go on a crawl. While making the rounds, you can partake of that peculiarly British fare known as "pub grub," which might include everything from a ploughman's lunch (a hunk of bread, cheese, and a pickle) to a plate of shepherd's pie. However, if you go to the right places, some of that pub grub today tastes better than most fare served in many restaurants. More about this later.

- Here's our favorite crawl, which gives you a chance to see several of London's districts: Begin at **Dickens Inn** by the tower on St. Katharine's Way (E1), and then go on to **Ye Olde Cheshire Cheese,** Wine Office Court, 145 Fleet St. (EC4), before making your way to **Cittie of Yorke** at 22-23 High Holborn (WC1). Then it's off to **Old Coffee House** at 49 Beak St. (W1) in Soho, before descending on **Red Lion,** 2 Duke of York St. (SW1). If you're still standing, rush to **Shepherd's Tavern,** 50 Hertford St. (W1) in Mayfair, before the publican rings the bell for "final call."

2 Best Hotel Bets

- **Best Historic Hotel:** Founded by the former manservant to Lord Byron, stylish **Brown's Hotel,** 29-34 Albemarle St., W1 (☎ **0171/493-6020**), dates back to Victorian times. It's one of London's most genteel hotels, from its legendary afternoon tea to its centenary Times clock in the reception area.
- **Best for Business Travelers:** For wheeling and dealing, head to the **Langham Hilton,** 1 Portland Place, W1 (☎ **0171/636-1000**), Hilton's flagship hotel in Europe. At times it seems that all the world's business is conducted from this nerve center. It can sound like the Tower of Babel, but it's humming along just fine.
- **Best for a Romantic Getaway: The Gore,** 189 Queen's Gate, SW7 (☎ **800/637-7200**), has been sheltering lovers both on and off the record since 1892. The place is eccentric and a lot of fun, and the staff doesn't bother you unless you need something. For nostalgia-accented romance, request the Venus Room—its bed was once owned by Judy Garland.
- **Best Trendy Hotel: The Lanesborough,** 1 Lanesborough Place, Hyde Park Corner, SW1 (☎ **800/999-1828**), is a sumptuous temple of luxury—$1.7 million was spent on each guest room. Not surprisingly, it attracts glitterati galore.
- **Best Lobby for Pretending that You're Rich: The Dorchester,** 53 Park Lane, W1 (☎ **800/727-9820**), has a long promenade with London's largest floral display and rows of faux-marble columns with ornate gilt capitals. Even if you can't afford to stay at this citadel of luxury, come by for the traditional afternoon tea.
- **Best Lobby for Celebrity Spotting:** If you sit in the lobby long enough at the **Halcyon Hotel,** 81 Holland Park Ave., W11 (☎ **800/595-5416**), you're sure to spot a famous face checking in. It might even be Faye Dunaway—but you might get RuPaul, Snoop Doggy Dogg, or Sting instead. Brad Pitt always stays here when he's in town. The address of this celebrity favorite gets passed around a lot in Hollywood and New York. Many of the rooms are like stage sets for movies, making stars feel quite at home.
- **Best Newcomer of the Year:** You don't normally think of Smithfield as a hotel district of London, but **The Rookery,** 12 Peter's Lane, Cowcross St., EC1 (☎ **0171/336-0931**), is luring some of London's most discerning visitors. It's quirky and fun, and loaded with atmosphere in its individually decorated bedrooms of great charm and comfort. Even the bathrooms still retain their Victorian cast-iron fittings. The owners combed London's antiques stores and flea markets to create the place's decor.
- **Best Grande Dame:** The **Park Lane Hotel,** Piccadilly, W1 (☎ **800/325-3535**), is English to the core. It evokes the grand old days of debutante balls; the suites still have their 1920s styling and art deco bathrooms. No wonder the producers of *Brideshead Revisited* filmed part of their series here.
- **Best Shabbily Genteel Hotel:** Not afraid to be old-fashioned, the **Wilbraham Hotel,** 1-5 Wilbraham Place, SW1 (☎ **0171/730-8296**), remains true to itself: floral-print wallpaper, old-world English politeness, and stately Victorian style. They're so old-timey here they still call their lounge the "Bar and Buttery."
- **Best for Showing Off:** Anouska Hempel's luxurious **Blake's Hotel,** 33 Roland Gardens, SW7 (☎ **800/926-3173**), is personalized, elegant, and fun, with

beautiful bathrooms in marble, opulent accessories, and a restaurant packed with London glitterati. This is the place to show off—and wait until later to worry about how much you spent.

- **Best for Thoroughly British Ambience:** In a gaslit courtyard in back of St. James's Palace, **Dukes Hotel,** 35 St. James's Place, SW1 (☎ **800/381-4702**), has a nearly unsurpassed dignity. From the bread-and-butter pudding served in the clubby dining room to the impeccable service, it's the epitome of what Britain used to be.

- **Best Re-creation of an English Country House:** Tim and Kit Kemp are hoteliers of charm, taste, and sophistication. They were in top form when they combined two Georgian town houses into the **Dorset Square Hotel,** 39-40 Dorset Sq., NW1 (☎ **0171/723-7874**). They've made an English country house right in the heart of the city: Gilt-framed paintings, antiques, tapestry cushions, and mahogany bathrooms make you feel warm, cozy, and elegantly refined.

- **Best Service: 22 Jermyn Street,** SW1 (☎ **800/682-7808**), does more for its guests than any other hotel in London. The owner, a technology buff, even offers Internet services. He also diligently informs you of the hottest and newest restaurants, along with old favorites, the best shopping buys, and even what's hot in theater. The staff won't deny any reasonable request—they even grant some unreasonable ones.

- **Best Location:** Creaky, quirky **Fielding Hotel,** 4 Broad Court, Bow Street, WC2 (☎ **0171/836-8305**), is hardly London's finest hotel, but oh, the location! It's in an alleyway in the dead center of Covent Garden. You're in the heart of the real excitement of London, almost opposite the Royal Opera House, and with pubs, shops, markets, and restaurants, even street entertainment, just outside your door. Stay here, and London is yours.

- **Best Health Club & Pool: The Savoy,** The Strand, WC2 (☎ **800/263-SAVOY**), has a unique health club and large swimming pool, built atop the historic Savoy Theatre, overlooking the heart of London. For guests looking to tone up or wind down, it's the best gym in central London; the views make it extra special. There is also a massage room, plus state-of-the-heart health and beauty treatments.

- **Best Hotel Restaurant:** The **Connaught Restaurant,** in the Connaught Hotel, Carlos Place, W1 (☎ **0171/499-7070**), is what hotel dining is all about: discreet elegance, top-notch food, and a traditional ambience. Unbent by fad or fashion, it dispenses its array of turbot, truffles, foie gras, and lobster as if the English still ruled an empire. Wait until you sample its new-season lamb sweetened on Welsh grass. See chapter 5 for a complete review.

- **Best View:** Sometimes the best way to view a great city is from a distance. From the **Sandringham Hotel,** 3 Holford Rd., NW3 (☎ **0171/435-1569**), a top-notch little hotel in North London—near the Hampstead Heath so beloved by John Keats—rooms open onto panoramic views of England's capital.

- **Best Boutique Hotel: Franklin Hotel,** 28 Egerton Gardens, SW3 (☎ **0171/584-5533**), is a gem of a hotel that's sure to charm. Personal service and tranquillity combine to form a winning choice, a private but not snobbish place halfway between Harrods and the center of South Kensington. Even patrons of Claridge's and the Dorchester have deserted those citadels to check into the Franklin.

- **Best Moderately Priced Hotel:** Housed in three historic homes on Soho Square, **Hazlitt's 1718,** 6 Frith St., W1 (☎ **0171/434-1771**), was a fashionable address two centuries ago—and so it is again today. One of London's best small hotels, it's a favorite with artists, actors, media people, and models. Many bedrooms have four-poster beds.

- **Best Inexpensive Hotel:** Known for the wacky themes of its bedrooms, **The Pavilion,** 34-36 Sussex Gardens, W2 (☎ **0171/262-0905**), is theatrical and a bit outrageous, attracting many fashion models and music industry buffs. They check into their temporary room—that is, rooms ranging in decor themes from oriental bordello to "Honky-Tonk Afro." In this price category, it's hard to be chic in London, but The Pavilion fits the bill.

- **Best for Families Who Don't Want to Break the Bank:** Hailed by some as one of the top B&Bs in London, **James House/Cartref House,** 108 and 129 Ebury St. (☎ **0171/730-6176**), are two houses filled with charm that face each other across a street in the section of London near Victoria Station. Each house deserves its accolades. Some of the large accommodations have bunk beds that make them ideal for families.

- **Best B&B: Vicarage Private Hotel,** 10 Vicarage Gate, W8 (☎ **0171/229-4030**), fits the bill if you want old-fashioned English charm and hospitality—all at affordable prices. Close to Kensington High Street, the family-run B&B charges only a modest price for a cozy nest in Kensington—that is, if you can forego a private bath.

- **Best Value:** Savvy hotel shoppers seek out **Aston's Budget Studios,** 39 Rosary Gardens, SW7 (☎ **0171/590-6000**). The accommodations here range widely in price, and well they should: They vary from basic lodgings to designer suites.

3 Best Dining Bets

- **Best for Romance:** Either on or off the record, **Mirabelle,** 56 Cruzon St., W1 (☎ **0171/499-4636**), is the place to go. The waitstaff is very discreet. When Jeremy Irons wanted to have a private moment alone with the late Princess Di, and with all of London as their choice, he chose Mirabelle. London's most outstanding chef, Marco Pierre White, now runs this elegant retreat, and when you can take your eyes off your partner, you can concentrate on his viands.

- **Best Place for a Business Lunch:** Instead of some noisy City tavern serving up bangers and mash, impress your clients by taking them to **Poons in the City,** 2 Minster Pavement, Minster Court, Mincing Lane, EC3 (☎ **0171/626-0126**). This fabled Chinese restaurant is elegantly outfitted with furniture and accessories from China, and the menu is wide ranging enough to please most clients. After a taste of the finely chopped wind-dried meats or the crispy aromatic duck, it'll be a snap to seal the deal.

- **Best Spot for a Celebration:** There's no spot in all of London that's more fun than **Quaglino's,** 16 Bury St., SW1 (☎ **0171/930-6767**). On some nights, as many as 800 diners show up at Sir Terence Conran's gargantuan Mayfair eatery to dine, laugh, and gossip. It's the best place in London to celebrate almost any occasion— and the food's good, too. There's live jazz on Friday and Saturday nights.

- **Best Wine List:** The renowned wine list at the **Tate Gallery Restaurant,** in the Tate Gallery, Millbank, SW1 (☎ **0171/887-8877**), reads like a who's who of famous French châteaux. So does the one at Le Gavroche—but this one is affordable. The Tate offers the city's best bargains on fine wines; the management keeps the markups between 40% and 65%, as opposed to the 100% to 200% that most restaurants add to the price of a bottle.

- **Best Newcomer of the Year:** One of London's most talked about new restaurants, **Rhodes in the Square,** Dolphin Square, Chichester St., SW1 (☎ 0171/ 798-6767), is the domain of celebrated chef, Gary Rhodes. In a discreet residential district, this chef—a media darling—continues to win new friends and please old palates with his take on giving a new twist to staid British cuisine. He's always innovative, always filled with good surprises.
- **Best Value:** Cheap and cheerful **Simply Nico,** 48A Rochester Row, SW1 (☎ 0171/630-8061), grand Chef Nico Ladenis' "moment of whimsy," offers some of the best value fixed-price meals in London. This isn't the fabled haute cuisine Nico serves on Park Lane, but quality ingredients are beautifully prepared into some of the best French food in central London. Breast of guinea fowl with lentils and other specialties will keep you coming back for more.
- **Best Traditional British Cuisine:** No restaurant, not even Simpson's-in-the-Strand, is quite as British as **Wiltons,** 55 Jermyn St., SW1 (☎ 0171/629-9955). As other British restaurants loosen up, Wiltons remains fiercely entrenched in tradition—or, as one London diner put it, "Wiltons refuses to unclench its upper-class buttocks." It serves the same menu it did to the 18th-century nobs of St. James's. We're talking grilled plaice, steaks, chops, kidneys, whitebait (a Victorian favorite), and game dishes such as roast widgeon (a wild fish-eating river duck).
- **Best Modern British Cuisine:** In a former smokehouse just north of Smithfield Market, **St. John,** 26 St. John St., EC1 (☎ 0171/251-0848), has a modern interpretation of British cuisine that's like none other in town. The chefs here believe in offal—after all, why use just parts of the animal when you can use it all? Although some diners are a bit squeamish at first, once they get past the first bite, they're usually hooked on the viands—and they keep coming back for more; so book ahead.
- **Best Pub Grub:** Tom Conran, son of super-restaurateur Sir Terence Conran, is attracting all of London to **The Cow,** 89 Westbourne Park Rd., W2 (☎ 0171/ 221-0021)—even people who haven't been in a pub for years. Leading the revolution in upgrading pub cuisine, The Cow somehow manages to secure the biggest and juiciest oysters in town. Ox tongue poached in milk? Don't knock it 'til you've tried it. Proof that the London pub scene has changed radically: The hip young staff even serves finger bowls to its even hipper clientele.
- **Best Continental Cuisine:** Le Gavroche, 43 Upper Brook St., W1 (☎ 0171/ 408-0881), was the forerunner of the modern French approach to cuisine in London, and it's lost none of its appeal over the years. If you want to know why, order *pigeonneau de Bresse en vessie aux deux celeris:* The whole bird is presented at your table, enclosed in a pig's bladder; the pigeon is skillfully removed, and then carved and served on a bed of braised fennel and celery. Trust us—it's fabulous.
- **Best Indian Cuisine:** London's finest Indian food is served at **Café Spice Namaste,** in a landmark Victorian hall near Tower Bridge, 16 Prescot St., E1 (☎ 0171/488-9242). You'll be tantalized with a bewildering array of spicy southern and northern Indian dishes. What we especially like about this place is its strong Portuguese influence; the chef, Cyrus Todiwala, is a former resident of Goa (a Portuguese territory absorbed by India long ago), where he learned many of his culinary secrets.
- **Best Italian Cuisine: The River Café,** Thames Wharf, Rainville Rd., W6 (☎ 0171/381-6217), remains seriously chic, and for good reason: Foodies flock to this Thameside restaurant (designed by Sir Richard Rogers, who also did the

Lloyd's building and Paris's Pompidou Centre) for cuisine that's been likened to that served in the best private homes in Italy. The freshest of ingredients from all over the world are brought here, where waiting chefs transform them into culinary art.

- **Best American Cuisine:** Like a traditionally British gentlemen's club, **Joe Allen,** 13 Exeter St., WC2 (☎ 0171/836-0651), has only a small brass plaque marking its entrance. But the food here will be more familiar: Maryland crab cakes, spinach salad, black-bean soup, chili, Caesar salad, and that famous pecan pie. On our last visit, we spotted movie legend Lauren Bacall digging into a sirloin steak (rare) with sautéed red onions and steak frites—just like she used to cook for Bogie.

- **Best Japanese Cuisine:** Robert de Niro and his gang have generated much excitement about **Nobu,** in the Metropolitan Hotel, 19 Old Park Lane, W1 (☎ 0171/447-4747), and all other Japanese restaurants fear the challenge—rightly so. The kitchen staff here is as brilliant and innovative as at their New York father restaurant. The sushi chefs don't create just sushi, but gastronomic pyrotechnics. They do exceedingly well with the other dishes, too.

- **Best Chinese Cuisine:** If you'd like to dine on such dishes as "The Whims and Fancies of the Empress" or "Buddha Jumps Over the Wall," head for **Kay Mayfair,** 65 S. Audley St., W1 (☎ 0171/493-8988). It's one of London's glitziest Chinese restaurants, lying near the American Embassy. Chefs wander the Orient for culinary inspiration, and succeed in serving some of the city's zestiest Chinese fare, like bang-bang chicken in a nut sauce.

- **Best Desserts: Nico Central,** 35 Great Portland St., W1 (☎ 0171/436-8846), is the place to satisfy your sweet tooth. The "puddings" menu is extremely limited, but is it ever choice: The caramelized lemon tart is the best we've ever had in London. The nougat ice cream with a strongly flavored blackberry coulis was worth a return visit, as was the walnut and Armagnac parfait. Other unforgettable desserts accompanying memorable meals here have included a velvety smooth warm chocolate mousse with pear sorbet, and a poached pear sablé made even more delectable with a caramel ginger sauce.

- **Best Late-Night Dining:** Most London restaurants open after 10:30pm aren't worth the trouble. There's one notable exception, however: **Bombay Brasserie,** adjacent to Bailey's Hotel, Courtfield Rd., SW7 (☎ 0171/370-4040). Not only is it one of the best Indian restaurants in London (where the competition is stiff), it also serves the same well-prepared dinners at midnight (last order) that it does at 7:30pm.

- **Best People Watching:** In Karl Marx's former apartment house, **Quo Vadis,** 26-29 Dean St., W1 (☎ 0171/437-9585), is a joint venture of London's *enfant terrible* chef, Marco Pierre White, and Damien Hirst, the artist who wowed the London art world with his cow carcasses in formaldehyde. With a pedigree like this, it's no wonder this is the hottest see-and-be-seen circuit in town. If Goldie Hawn should come to London, this is where you'd find her. And the food's not bad, either.

- **Best Afternoon Tea:** While everyone else is donning fancy hats and heading for the Ritz (where, chances are, they won't be able to get a table), you should retreat to the **Palm Court at the Waldorf Meridien,** Aldwych, WC2 (☎ 0171/836-2400), in the grand 1908 Waldorf Hotel. The Sunday tea dances here are legendary: Originating with the famous "Tango Teas" of the 1920s and 1930s, they've been going strong ever since, interrupted only by war and a few other inconveniences.

- **Best Pre-Theater Menu:** Opposite the Ambassador Theatre, **The Ivy,** 1-5 West St., WC2 (☎ **0171/836-4751**), is popular for both pre- and après-theater dining. The brasserie-style food reflects both traditional English and modern continental influences. You can try longtime favorites such as potted shrimp or tripe and onions, or more imaginative dishes such as butternut pumpkin salad or a wild mushroom risotto.

- **Best Decor:** There's no more beautiful dining room in all of London than the **Oak Room/Marco Pierre White,** in Le Méridien Piccadilly, 21 Piccadilly, W1 (☎ **0171/734-8000**). It's the best of the *fin-de-siècle* era, with walls of limed oak paneling inlaid with towering gilded mirrors, gargantuan crystal chandeliers hanging from the ornate plaster ceiling, and Chinese vases bursting with flowers. And, best of all, the fabulous French cuisine of Marco Pierre White more than holds its own in the spectacular setting.

- **Best View: Ship Hispaniola,** River Thames, Victoria Embankment, Charing Cross, WC2 (☎ **0171/839-3011**), is a ship-turned-restaurant permanently moored to a quay beside the Thames. Tables are set up on two different levels to take full advantage of the grand views. You'll enjoy a seasonal menu as a harpist or pianist sets the mood and the river traffic passes by.

- **Best For Kids:** After you and the kids have visited the Tower of London, take them to **Dickens Inn by the Tower,** St. Katharine's Way, E1 (☎ **0171/ 488-2208**), an old spice warehouse turned three-floor restaurant with sweeping views of the Thames and Tower Bridge. Dickens Inn serves tasty well-stuffed sandwiches, platters of lasagna, and steaming bowls of chili. One whole floor is devoted to serving pizza.

- **Best Fast Food:** Instead of noshing on greasy fish-and-chips while you're exploring the City (or a hamburger with meat from God knows where), take a break from sightseeing at **Poons in the City** (see above). This famous Chinese restaurant serves top-notch Chinese fast food in its bar, the Express. The cookery is homestyle and the recipes original, and the menu still includes Poons's specialty, wind-dried meats.

- **Best Pizza:** Although many will dispute this accolade, **Pizzeria Condotti,** 4 Mill St., W1 (☎ **0171/499-1308**), consistently serves up some of London's most savory pies—with an array of hot, bubbling, and delectable toppings. In attractive, rather expensive-looking surroundings, the restaurant serves pizzas on thin, crisp crusts. All are prepared to order and taste fresh from the oven. Each is a meal unto itself.

- **Best Picnic Fare:** If you'd like to prepare a picnic fit for a queen, go to **Fortnum & Mason, Ltd.,** 181 Piccadilly, W1 (☎ **0171/734-8040**), the world's most famous grocery store. You'll find a wide array of foodstuffs to take away to your favorite park. (For details, see "The Department Stores," chapter 8.)

- **Best Pub Atmosphere:** On leave from fighting Napoléon, the Duke of Wellington's officers downed many a pint of lager at the **Grenadier,** 18 Wilton Row, SW1 (☎ **0171/235-3074**). It comes complete with a ghost (allegedly that of an officer flogged to death for cheating at cards) and a very British restaurant. Bloody Marys are a Sunday tradition.

- **Best English Breakfast:** The **Fox and Anchor,** 115 Charterhouse St., EC1 (☎ **0171/253-4838**), is a longtime favorite among early-morning pub crawlers and club trawlers who fancy a pint and a bite to get them going for the day. One local called the array of breakfast goodies here "gut-busting"—everything from black pudding to fried bread and baked beans. After the "full house" breakfast at this Smithfield Market pub, you won't be ready to eat again until the following morning.

• **Best Fish-and-Chips:** The best place to introduce yourself to this trad British dish is **North Sea Fish Restaurant,** 7-8 Leigh St., WC1 (☎ **0171/387-5892**). Unlike the overcooked frozen fish served at those joints around Leicester Square, North Sea's fresh cod comes perfectly prepared: crisp batter on the outside, moist and tender fish inside. The haddock is equally delectable—and what a big platter it is.

2

Planning a Trip to London

This chapter tackles the hows of your trip to London—those issues required to get your trip together and take it on the road, whether you're a frequent traveler or a first-timer.

1 Visitor Information

Before you go, you can get information from the following **British Tourist Authority** offices: 551 Fifth Ave., Suite 701, New York, NY 10176-0799 (☎ **800/462-2748** or 212/986-2200); 111 Avenue Rd., Suite 450, Toronto M5R 3J8, Canada (☎ **888/VISIT-UK** or 905/405-1840); Level 16, Gateway, 1 Macquarie Place, Sydney, NSW 2000, Australia (☎ **02/9377-4400**); and Suite 305, Dilworth Bldg., at Customs and Queen streets, Auckland 1, New Zealand (☎ **09/303-1446**). The British Tourist Authority maintains a Web page at **www.visitbritain.com**.

For a full information pack on London, write to the **London Tourist Board,** Glenn House, Stag Place, London SN1E 5LT (☎ **0171/932-2000**). You can also call the recorded-message service, **Visitorcall** (☎ **01839/123456**), 24 hours a day. This number cannot be dialed outside Britain. Various topics are listed; calls cost 50p (85¢) per minute.

Time Out, the most up-to-date source for what's happening in London, has joined the Net, so you can also log on for current information; you'll find the weekly magazine at **www.timeout.co.uk**. You can also pick up a copy at any international newsstand.

London Guide (**www.cs.ucl.ac.uk/misc/uk/london.html**) is run by London's University College and has practical information on cheap dining and accommodations in the Bloomsbury area close to the university. There are also travelogues and tips for theatergoers.

To book accommodations by credit card (MasterCard or Visa), call the London Tourist Board Booking Office at ☎ **0171/932-2020,** or fax them at 0171/932-2021. They're available to make bookings Monday to Friday from 9:30am to 5:30pm (London time). There is a £5 ($8.25) fee for booking.

2 Entry Requirements & Customs

DOCUMENTS

Citizens of the United States, Canada, Australia, New Zealand, and South Africa require a passport to enter the United Kingdom, but no

---

London Area Code Change

Note that in mid-year 2000, London area codes will change. The old 171 and 187 codes will change to 20, followed by an eight-digit telephone number. See the box in chapter 3 for details.

---

visa. Irish citizens and other members of European Union countries need only an identity card. The maximum allowable stay for visitors is 6 months. Some Customs officials will request proof that you have the means to eventually leave the country (usually a round-trip ticket) and visible means of support while you're in Britain. If you're planning to fly on from the United Kingdom to a country that requires a visa, it's wise to secure the necessary visa before your arrival in Britain.

Your valid driver's license and at least one year's driving experience is required to drive personal or rented cars.

PASSPORT INFORMATION

Safeguard your passport—if you should lose it, visit your nearest national consulate as soon as possible for a replacement. Passport applications are downloadable from the Internet sites listed below.

FOR U.S. RESIDENTS   If applying for a first-time passport, you need to go in person to one of 13 passport offices throughout the U.S.; a major post office (call the number below to find out which ones accept applications); or a federal, state, or probate court. You must present a certified birth certificate as proof of citizenship, and it's wise to bring along your driver's license, state or military ID, and Social Security card as well. You also need two identical passport-sized photos (2 in. by 2 in.), taken at any corner photo shop (not, however, from a photo-vending machine).

For people over 15, a passport is valid for 10 years and costs $60 ($45 plus a $15 handling fee); for those 15 and under, it's valid for 5 years and costs $40. If you have a valid passport that was issued within the past 12 years, you can renew it by mail and bypass the $15 handling fee. Allow plenty of time before your trip to apply; processing normally takes 3 weeks, but can take longer during busy periods (especially spring). For general information, call the **National Passport Agency** (☎ **202/647-0518**). To find your regional passport office, call the **National Passport Information Center** (☎ **900/225-5674**; http://travel.state.gov).

FOR RESIDENTS OF CANADA   You can pick up a passport application at one of 28 regional passport offices or most travel agencies. The passport is valid for 5 years and costs $60. Children under 16 may be included on a parent's passport, but need their own to travel unaccompanied by the parent. Applications, which must be accompanied by two identical passport-sized photographs and proof of Canadian citizenship, are available at travel agencies throughout Canada or from the central **Passport Office, Department of Foreign Affairs and International Trade,** Ottawa K1A 0G3 (☎ **800/567-6868**; www.dfait-maeci.gc.ca/passport). Processing takes 5 to 10 days if you apply in person, or about 3 weeks by mail.

FOR RESIDENTS OF IRELAND   You can apply for a 10-year passport, costing IR£45, at the **Passport Office,** Setanta Centre, Molesworth Street, Dublin 2 (☎ **01/ 671-1633**; www.irlgov.ie/iveagh/foreignaffairs/services). Those under age 18 and those over 65 must apply for an IR£10 3-year passport. You can also apply at 1A South Mall, Cork (☎ 021/272-525) or over the counter at most main post offices.

FOR RESIDENTS OF AUSTRALIA   Apply at your local post office or passport office or search the government Web site at www.dfat.gov.au/passports/. Passports for adults are A$126 and for those under 18 A$63.

FOR RESIDENTS OF NEW ZEALAND   You can pick up a passport application at any travel agency or Link Centre. For more info, contact the **Passport Office,** P.O. Box 805, Wellington (☎ **0800/225-050**). Passports for adults are NZ$80 and for those under 16 NZ$40.

CUSTOMS

WHAT YOU CAN BRING INTO THE U.K.   Visitors (17 and older) coming to England from a non-European Union (EU) country or bringing in goods bought tax-free within the EU may bring in 200 cigarettes (or 50 cigars or 250 grams of loose tobacco), 2 liters of table wine, 1 liter of liquor (over 22% alcohol content) or 2 liters of liquor (under 22%), and 2 fluid ounces of perfume. Visitors entering England from a European Union country may bring in goods bought tax-paid in the EU as follows: 800 cigarettes, 200 cigars, and 1 kilogram of loose tobacco; 90 liters of wine, 10 liters of alcohol (over 22%), and 110 liters of beer; plus unlimited amounts of perfume.

Sorry, but you can't bring your pet to England. Six months' quarantine is required before a pet is allowed into the country. An illegally imported animal is liable to be destroyed.

WHAT YOU CAN BRING HOME   Returning **U.S. citizens** who have been away for 48 hours or more are allowed to bring back, once every 30 days, $400 worth of merchandise duty-free. You'll be charged a flat rate of 10% duty on the next $1,000 worth of purchases. Be sure to have your receipts handy. On gifts, the duty-free limit is $100. You cannot bring fresh foodstuffs into the United States; tinned foods, however, are allowed. For more information, contact the **U.S. Customs Service,** 1301 Constitution Ave. (P.O. Box 7407), Washington, D.C. 20044 (☎ **202/ 927-6724**) and request the free pamphlet *Know Before You Go.* It's also available on the Web at www.customs.ustreas.gov/travel/kbygo.htm.

For a clear summary of **Canadian** rules, write for the booklet *I Declare,* issued by **Revenue Canada,** 2265 St. Laurent Blvd., Ottawa K1G 4KE (☎ **613/993-0534**). Canada allows its citizens a Can$500 exemption, and you're allowed to bring back duty free 200 cigarettes, 2.2 pounds of tobacco, 40 imperial ounces of liquor, and 50 cigars. In addition, you're allowed to mail gifts to Canada from abroad at the rate of Can$60 a day, provided they're unsolicited and don't contain alcohol or tobacco (write on the package "Unsolicited gift, under $60 value"). All valuables should be declared on the Y-38 form before departure from Canada, including serial numbers of valuables you already own, such as expensive foreign cameras. Note: The $500 exemption can only be used once a year and only after an absence of 7 days.

The duty-free allowance in **Australia** is A$400 or, for those under 18, A$200. Personal property mailed back from England should be marked "Australian goods returned" to avoid payment of duty. Upon returning to Australia, citizens can bring in 250 cigarettes or 250 grams of loose tobacco, and 1.125 liters of alcohol. If you're returning with valuable goods you already own, such as foreign-made cameras, you should file form B263. A helpful brochure, available from Australian consulates or Customs offices, is *Know Before You Go.* For more information, contact **Australian Customs Services,** GPO Box 8, Sydney, NSW 2001 (☎ **02/9213-2000**).

The duty-free allowance for **New Zealand** is NZ$700. Citizens over 17 can bring in 200 cigarettes, or 50 cigars, or 250 grams of tobacco (or a mixture of all three if their combined weight doesn't exceed 250 grams); plus 4.5 liters of wine and beer, or 1.125 liters of liquor. New Zealand currency does not carry import or export restrictions. Fill out a certificate of export, listing the valuables you are taking out of the country; that way, you can bring them back without paying duty. Most questions are answered in a free pamphlet available at New Zealand consulates and Customs offices: *New Zealand Customs Guide for Travellers*, Notice no. 4. For more information, contact **New Zealand Customs,** 50 Anzac Ave., P.O. Box 29, Auckland (☎ **09/359-6655**).

3 Money

POUNDS & PENCE   Britain's decimal monetary system is based on the pound sterling (£), which is made up of 100 pence (written as "p"). There are now £1 coins (called "quid" by Britons), plus coins of 50p, 20p, 10p, 5p, 2p, and 1p. Even though the 0.5p coin has been officially discontinued, it will be around for a while. Banknotes come in denominations of £5, £10, £20, and £50.

As a general guideline, the price conversions in this book have been computed at the rate of £1 = $1.65 (U.S.). Bear in mind, however, that exchange rates fluctuate daily.

ATM NETWORKS   Check with your bank to find out if you need a new personal ID number (PIN) to use in automatic teller machines (ATMs) overseas.

The most popular ATM networks are **Cirrus** (☎ **800/424-7787;** www.mastercard.com/atm/) and **Plus** (☎ **800/843-7587;** www.visa.com/atms); check the back of your ATM card to see which network your bank belongs to. You can use the 800 numbers to locate ATMs in your destination or ask your bank for a list of overseas ATMs.

Note that many banks impose a fee every time a card is used at their ATM from a different city or bank.

CREDIT CARDS   Credit cards are a safe way to carry money and provide a convenient record of all your expenses. You can also withdraw cash advances from your credit cards at any bank (though you'll start paying hefty interest on the advance the moment you receive the cash, and you won't receive frequent-flyer miles on an airline credit card). At most banks, you don't even need to go to a teller; you can get a cash advance at the ATM with your PIN number. If you don't know your PIN number, call the phone number on the back of your credit card and ask the bank to send it to you. It usually takes 5 to 7 business days, though some banks will provide the number over the phone if you pass a security clearance.

TRAVELER'S CHECKS   Traveler's checks are becoming something of an anachronism from the days before the 24-hour ATMs made cash accessible at any time. However, traveler's checks are as reliable as currency, unlike personal checks, and can be replaced if lost or stolen.

You can get traveler's checks at almost any bank. **American Express** offers denominations of $10, $20, $50, $100, $500, and $1,000. You'll pay a service charge ranging from 1 to 4%. You can also get American Express traveler's checks over the phone by calling **800/221-7282;** by using this number, Amex gold and platinum cardholders are exempt from the 1% fee. AAA members can obtain checks without a fee at most AAA offices.

Visa offers traveler's checks at Citibank locations nationwide, as well as several other banks. The service charge ranges between 1.5 and 2%; checks come in denominations of $20, $50, $100, $500, and $1,000. **MasterCard** also offers traveler's checks. Call **800/223-9920** for a location near you.

Be sure to keep a record of your traveler's checks' serial numbers—separate from the checks of course—so that you're ensured a refund in an emergency.

The U.S. Dollar & the British Pound

Note: The rate of exchange at press time was approximately $1.65 U.S. to £1, and was used to compile this chart. Because rates change almost daily, however, check the current value of the pound in a newspaper or at a bank.

U.S.$	U.K. £	U.S.$	U.K. £
0.25	0.15	15	9.15
0.50	0.31	20	12.20
0.75	0.46	25	15.25
1.00	0.61	50	30.50
2.00	1.22	75	45.75
3.00	1.83	100	61.00
4.00	2.44	150	91.50
5.00	3.05	200	122.00
6.00	3.66	250	152.50
7.00	4.27	300	183.00
8.00	4.88	350	213.50
9.00	5.49	400	244.00
10.00	6.10	500	305.00

THEFT   Almost every credit card company has an emergency 800 number that you can call if your wallet or purse is stolen. They may be able to wire you a cash advance off your credit card immediately, and in many places, can deliver an emergency credit card in a day or two. The toll-free information directory will provide the number. Visa's emergency number is **800/336-8472** in the U.S. or **410/581-9994** outside the U.S. American Express cardholders and traveler's check holders should call **800/221-7282** for all money emergencies. MasterCard holders should call **800/307-7309** in the U.S. or call **collect 525/326-2566** outside the U.S.

Odds are that if your wallet is gone, the police won't be able to recover it. However, it is still worth informing them; your credit card company or insurer may require a police report number.

CURRENCY EXCHANGE   It's wise to exchange enough money before departure to get from the airport to your hotel. This way, you avoid delays and the lousy rates at the airport exchange booths.

When exchanging money, you're likely to obtain a better rate for traveler's checks than for cash. London banks generally offer the best rates of exchange; they're usually open Monday to Friday from 9:30am to 3:30pm. Many of the "high street" branches are now open until 5pm; a handful of central London branches are open until noon on Saturday, including **Barclays,** 208 Kensington High St., W8 (☎ **0171/441-3200**). Money exchange is now also available at competitive rates at major London post offices, with a 1% service charge. Money can be exchanged during off-hours at a variety of bureaux de change throughout the city, found at small shops and in hotels, railway stations (including the international terminal at Waterloo Station), travel agencies, and

What Things Cost in London	U.S.$
Taxi from Heathrow Airport to central London	74.25
Underground from Heathrow Airport to central London	16.50
Local telephone call	15–30¢
Double room at The Dorchester (Very expensive)	486.75
Double room at Sanctuary House (Moderate)	119.65
Double room at Edward Lear (Inexpensive)	99.00
Lunch for one at The Ivy (Expensive)	35.00
Lunch for one at Ye Olde Cheshire Cheese (Inexpensive)	20.00
Dinner for one, without wine, at Bibendum/ The Oyster Bar (Expensive)	80.00
Dinner for one, without wine, at Odin's (Moderate)	39.00
Dinner for one, without wine, at Porter's English Restaurant (Inexpensive)	26.00
Pint of beer	3.35
Coca-Cola in a cafe	1.90
Cup of coffee	2.15
Roll of ASA 100 color film, 36 exposures	8.00
Admission to the British Museum	Free
Movie ticket	8.00-14.00
Theater ticket	24.00–96.00

airports, but their exchange rates are poorer and they charge high service fees. Examine the prices and rates carefully before handing over your dollars, as there's no consumer organization to regulate the activities of privately run bureaus de change.

In a recent *Time Out* survey of various exchange facilities, **American Express** came out on top, with the lowest commission charged on dollar transactions. They're at 6 Haymarket, SW1 (☎ **800/221-7282** or 0171/930-4411) and other locations throughout the city. They charge no commission when cashing traveler's checks. However, a flat rate of £2 ($3.30) is charged when exchanging the dollar to the pound. Most other agencies tend to charge a percentage rate commission (usually 2%) with a £2 to £3 ($3.30 to $4.95) minimum charge. Other reputable firms are **Thomas Cook,** 45 Berkeley St., W1A 1EB (☎ **800/223-7373** or 0171/408-4218), branches of which can also be found at Victoria Station, Marble Arch, and other city locations; and, for 24-hour foreign exchange, **Chequepoint,** at 548 Oxford St., W1N 9HJ (☎ **0171-723-1005**) and other locations throughout London (hours will vary). Try not to change money at your hotel; the rates they offer tend to be horrendous.

4 When to Go

CLIMATE
Charles Dudley Warner (in a remark most often attributed to Mark Twain) once said that the trouble with the weather is that everybody talks about it but nobody does anything about it. Well, Londoners talk about weather more than anyone, but they have

also done something about it: air-pollution control, which has resulted in the virtual disappearance of the pea-soup fogs that once blanketed the city.

A typical London-area weather forecast for a summer day predicts "scattered clouds with sunny periods and showers, possibly heavy at times." Summer temperatures seldom rise above 78°F, nor do they drop below 35°(F) in winter. London, being in one of the mildest parts of the country, can be very pleasant in the spring and fall. Yes, it rains, but you'll rarely get a true downpour. The rain is heaviest in November, when it reaches $2^1/_2$ inches on average.

The British consider chilliness wholesome and usually try to keep room temperatures about 10°F below the American comfort level.

London's Average Daytime Temperature & Rainfall

	Jan	Feb	Mar	Apr	May	June	July	Aug	Sept	Oct	Nov	Dec
Temp. (°F)	40	40	44	49	55	61	64	64	59	52	46	42
Rainfall (")	2.1	1.6	1.5	1.5	1.8	1.8	2.2	2.3	1.9	2.2	2.5	1.9

CURRENT WEATHER CONDITIONS In the United States, you can dial ☎ 1/900-WEATHER, and then press the first four letters of the desired foreign city—in this case, LOND for London—for the time of day in that city, plus current temperatures, weather conditions, and forecasts. The cost is 95¢ per minute. Another good way to check conditions before you go is on the Weather Channel's Web site: **www.weather.com.**

HOLIDAYS

In England, public holidays include New Year's Day, Good Friday, Easter Monday, May Day (first Monday in May), spring and summer bank holidays (last Monday in May and August, respectively), Christmas Day, and Boxing Day (December 26).

London Calendar of Events

January
- **London Parade,** from Parliament Square to Berkeley Square in Mayfair. Bands, floats, and carriages. Procession starts around 2:45pm. January 1.
- **January sales.** Most shops offer good reductions. Many sales now start as early as late December to perk up the post-Christmas slump. The most voracious shoppers camp overnight outside Harrods to get in first.
- **London International Boat Show,** Earl's Court Exhibition Centre, Warwick Road. The largest boat show in Europe. Call ☎ 01784/473377 for details. Early January.
- **London Contemporary Art Fair** at the Business Design Centre, Islington Green. Call ☎ 0171/359-3535 for exact dates and details. Mid-January.
- **Charles I Commemoration.** Anniversary of the execution of King Charles I "in the name of freedom and democracy." Hundreds of cavaliers march through central London in 17th-century dress, and prayers are said at the Banqueting House in Whitehall. Free. Last Sunday in January.

February
- **Chinese New Year.** The famous Lion Dancers in Soho. Free. Either in late January or early February (based on the lunar calendar).

- **Great Spitalfields Pancake Race.** Teams of four run in relays, tossing their pancakes. At Old Spitalfields Market, Brushfield Street, E1. To join in, call ☎ **0171/375-0441.** At noon on Shrove Tuesday (last day before Lent).

March

- **St. David's Day.** A member of the Royal Family usually presents the Welsh Guards with the principality's national emblem, a leek; call ☎ **0171/414-3291** for location and further information. March 1 (or nearest Sunday).
- **Chelsea Antiques Fair,** a twice-yearly gathering of England's best dealers, held at Old Town Hall, King's Road, SW3 (☎ **01444/482-514**). Mid-March (and again in mid-September).
- **Oranges and Lemons Service,** at St. Clement Danes, Strand, WC2. As a reminder of the nursery rhyme, children are presented with the fruits during service, and the church bells ring out the rhyme at 9am, noon, 3pm, and 6pm; call ☎ **0171/242-8282** for more information. March 3.
- **Abbey Choir** performs at Westminster Abbey on Holy Week Tuesday; call ☎ **0171/222-5152** for information.

April

- **Easter Parade,** around Battersea Park. Brightly colored floats and marching bands; a full day of Easter Sunday activities. Free. Easter Sunday.
- **Harness Horse Parade,** a morning parade of heavy working horses in superb gleaming brass harnesses and plumes, at Battersea Park. Call ☎ **01733/234-451.** April 5.
- **Boat Race, Putney to Mortlake.** Oxford and Cambridge University eights battle upstream with awesome power. Park yourself at one of the Thames-side pubs along the route to see the action. Early April; check *Time Out* for exact dates and times.
- **London Marathon.** 30,000 competitors run from Greenwich Park to Buckingham Palace; call ☎ **0161/703-8161** for information. Mid- to late April.
- **The Queen's Birthday** is celebrated with 21-gun salutes in Hyde Park and on Tower Hill at noon by troops in parade dress. April 21.
- **National Gardens Scheme.** More than 100 private gardens in Greater London are open to the public on set days until October, and tea is sometimes served. Pick up a current copy of the NGS guidebook for £4.50 ($7.45) from most bookstores for schedule information, or contact the National Gardens Scheme Charitable Trust, Hatchlands Park, East Clandon, Guildford, Surrey GU4 7RT (☎ **01483/211-535**). Late April to early May.

May

- **Shakespeare Under the Stars.** If you want to see *Macbeth, Hamlet,* or *Romeo and Juliet* (or any other Shakespeare play), our advice is to bring a blanket and a bottle of wine to watch the Bard's works performed at the Open Air Theatre, Inner Circle, Regent's Park, NW1. Take the Tube to Regent's Park or Baker Street. Previews begin in late May and last throughout the summer. Performances are Monday to Saturday at 8pm, Wednesday, Thursday, and Saturday also at 2:30pm. Call ☎ **0171/935-5756** for more information.
- **May Fayre and Puppet Festival,** Covent Garden. Procession at 10am, service at St. Paul's at 11:30am, then Punch and Judy shows until 6pm at the site where Pepys watched England's first show in 1662; call ☎ **0171/375-0441.** Second Sunday in May.
- **FA Cup Final.** England's showpiece soccer match is held at Wembley Stadium in mid-May; for exact date and details, call ☎ **0181/902-8833.**

- **The Royal Windsor Horse Show** is held at Home Park, Windsor Castle (☎ **01753-860633**); you might even spot a royal. Mid-May.
- **Chelsea Flower Show,** Chelsea Royal Hospital. The best of British gardening, with displays of plants and flowers of all seasons. Tickets are available through TicketMaster (☎ **0171/344-4343**). The show runs from 8am to 8pm on May 20; tickets are £25 ($40). On May 28, the show runs from 8am to 5:30pm, and tickets are £24 ($39.60). Call ☎ **0171/630-7422** for more information. Ticket sales must be made in advance. There are no event-day sales.
- **Glyndebourne Festival Opera Season,** Sussex. Exclusive performances in a beautiful setting, with champagne picnics in between performances. Since the completion of the Glydnebourne opera house, one of the world's best, tickets are a bit easier to come by (☎ **01273/813813**). It runs from mid-May to late August.

June

- **Vodafone Derby Stakes.** Famous horse-racing event at Epsom Racecourse, Epsom, Surrey. The "darby" (as it's called here) is the best-known event on the British horse-racing calendar and a chance for men to wear top hats and women, including the queen, to put on silly millinery creations. Grandstand tickets range from £18 to £22 ($29.70 to $36.30). Call ☎ **01372/470047** for more information. June 4 to 6.
- **Grosvenor House Art and Antique Fair,** Grosvenor House. A very prestigious antiques fair. Call ☎ **0171/495-8743** for information. Second week of June.
- **Kenwood Lakeside Concerts,** ☎ **0181/348-1286.** Annual concerts on the north side of Hampstead Heath. Fireworks displays and laser shows enliven the premier musical performances staged here. Music drifts to the fans from a performance shell across the lake every Saturday in summer from early July to early September.
- **Royal Academy's Summer Exhibition.** This institution, founded in 1768 with Sir Joshua Reynolds as president and Thomas Gainsborough as a member, has sponsored summer exhibitions of living painters for some 2 centuries. Visitors can both browse and make art purchases, many of them quite reasonable in price. Exhibitions are presented daily at Burlington House, Piccadilly Circus, W1. Call ☎ **0171/439-7438** for details. From early June to mid-August.
- **Royal Ascot Week.** Ascot Racecourse is open year-round for guided tours, events, exhibitions, and conferences. There are 24 race days throughout the year with the feature race meetings being the Royal Meeting in June, Diamond Day in late July, and the Festival at Ascot in late September. For further information, contact **Ascot Racecourse,** Ascot, Berkshire SL5 7JN (☎ **01344/622211**).
- ✪ **Trooping the Colour,** Horse Guards Parade, Whitehall. The official birthday of the queen. Seated in a carriage (no longer on horseback), the royal monarch inspects her regiments and takes their salute as they parade their colors before her. A quintessential British event religiously watched by the populace on TV. The pageantry and pomp are exquisite. Depending on the weather, the young men under the bearskins have been known to pass out from the heat. Held on a designated day in June (not necessarily the queen's actual birthday). Tickets for the parade and two reviews, held on preceding Saturdays, are allocated by ballot. Those interested in attending must write to apply for tickets between January 1 and the end of February, enclosing a stamped, self-addressed envelope, or International Reply Coupon—exact dates and ticket prices will be supplied later. The ballot is held in mid-March, and successful applicants *only* are informed in April. For details, write to **HQ Household Division,** Horse Guards, Whitehall, London SW1X 6AA, enclosing a self-addressed envelope with an International Reply Coupon.

○ **Lawn Tennis Championships,** Wimbledon, Southwest London. Ever since the players in flannels and bonnets took to the grass courts at Wimbledon in 1877, this tournament has drawn a socially prominent crowd. Although the courts are now crowded with all kinds of tennis fans, there's still an excited hush at Centre Court and a certain thrill in being here. Savoring the strawberries and cream is part of the experience. Tickets for Centre and Number One courts are handed out through a lottery; write to **All England Lawn Tennis Club,** P.O. Box 98, Church Road, Wimbledon, London SW19 5AE (☎ **0181/ 946-2244**), between August and December. A certain number of tickets are set aside for visitors from abroad, so you may be able to purchase some in spring for this year's games; call to inquire. Outside court tickets are available daily, but be prepared to wait in line. Late June to early July.

- **City of London Festival.** Annual arts festival throughout the city. Call ☎ **0171/ 377-0540** for information about the various programs and venues. Held in June and July.

July

- **City of London Festival.** Classical concerts at various venues throughout the City, including St. Paul's Cathedral; for details, call ☎ **0171/377-0540.** Early July.
- **Hampton Court Palace Flower Show,** East Molesey, Surrey. This widely acclaimed 5-day international show is eclipsing its sister show in Chelsea; here, you can actually purchase the exhibits. Call ☎ **0171/834-4333** for exact dates and details. Early July.
- **Royal Tournament,** Earl's Court Exhibition Centre, Warwick Road. British armed forces put on dazzling displays of athletic and military skills, which have been called "military pomp, show biz, and outright jingoism." For information and details about performance times and tickets, call ☎ **0171/244-0244.** Ticket prices range from £6 to £26 ($9.90 to $42.90). July 21 to August 2.
- **The Proms.** "The Proms"—the annual Henry Wood Promenade Concerts at Royal Albert Hall—attract music aficionados from around the world. Staged almost daily (except for a few Sundays), these traditional concerts were launched in 1895 and are the principal summer venue for the BBC Symphony Orchestra. Cheering, clapping, Union Jacks on parade, banners, and balloons create summer fun. Mid-July to mid-September.

August

- **Notting Hill Carnival,** Notting Hill. One of the largest street festivals in Europe, attracting more than a half-million people annually. Live reggae and soul music combine with great Caribbean food. Free. Call ☎ **0181/964-0544** for information. Two days in late August (usually the last Sunday and Monday).

September

- **Chelsea Antiques Fair,** Chelsea Old Town Hall, King's Road, SW3. Mid-September (see Mar above, for details).
- **Open House,** a 1-day event during which members of the public have access to normally closed buildings of architectural significance. Call ☎ **0181/341-1371** for schedule and further information. Mid-September.
- **Horse of the Year Show.** At Wembley Arena, outside London, this event is the premier equestrian highlight on the English calendar. Riders fly in from all continents to join in this festive display of horseflesh (much appreciated by the queen herself). The British press call it "an equine extravaganza." For more information, call ☎ **0181/902-8833.** End of September to early October.

- **Raising of the Thames Barrier,** Unity Way, SE18. Once a year, a full test is done on this miracle of modern engineering; all 10 of the massive steel gates are raised against the high tide. Call ☎ **0181/854-1373** for exact date and time.

October

○ **Opening of Parliament,** House of Lords, Westminster. Ever since the 17th century, when the English cut off the head of Charles I, the British monarch has had no right to enter the House of Commons. Instead, the monarch opens Parliament in the House of Lords, reading an official speech that is written by the government of the day. The monarch rides from Buckingham Palace to Westminster in a royal coach accompanied by the Yeoman of the Guard and the Household Cavalry. The Strangers' Gallery is open to spectators on a first-come, first-served basis. First Monday in October.

- **Judges Service,** Westminster Abbey. The judiciary attends a service in Westminster Abbey to mark the opening of the law term. Afterward, in full regalia—wigs and all—they form a procession and walk to the House of Lords for their "Annual Breakfast." You'll have a great view of the procession from behind the Abbey. First Monday in October.

- **Quit Rents Ceremony,** Royal Courts of Justice, WC2. An official receives token rents on behalf of the queen; the ceremony includes splitting sticks and counting horseshoes. Call ☎ **0171/936-6131** for free tickets. Late October.

November

- **Guy Fawkes Night.** Commemorating the anniversary of the Gunpowder Plot, an attempt to blow up King James I and his Parliament. Huge organized bonfires are lit throughout the city, and Guy Fawkes, the plot's most famous conspirator, is burned in effigy. Free. Check *Time Out* for locations. Early November.

○ **Lord Mayor's Procession and Show,** from the Guildhall to the Royal Courts of Justice, in the City of London. This impressive annual event marks the inauguration of the new lord mayor of the City of London. The queen must ask permission to enter the City's square mile—a right that has been jealously guarded by London merchants from the 17th century to this very day. You can watch the procession from the street; the banquet is by invitation only. Second week in November.

December

- **Caroling Under the Norwegian Christmas Tree.** There's caroling most evenings beneath the tree in Trafalgar Square. Early December.

- **Harrods After-Christmas Sale,** Knightsbridge. Call ☎ **0171/730-1234** for exact dates and hours. Late December.

- **Watch Night,** St. Paul's Cathedral, where a rather lovely New Year's Eve service takes place on December 31 at 11:30pm; call ☎ **0171/236-4128** for information.

5 Health & Insurance

STAYING HEALTHY

You'll encounter few health problems while traveling in England. The tap water is safe to drink, the milk is pasteurized, and health services are good. The crisis over Mad Cow Disease appears over. When a probable link was discovered between British beef and versions of degenerative brain disease, Britain—a nation of beef eaters—was plunged into turmoil. British beef is now back on the menu, although some very cautious people still avoid British beef just to be on the safe side. London's Hard Rock

Cafe is no longer having to import foreign beef for its burgers. Other than that, traveling to London doesn't pose any health risk.

WHAT TO DO IF YOU GET SICK AWAY FROM HOME

It can be hard to find a doctor you can trust when you're in an unfamiliar place. Try to take proper precautions the week before you depart, to avoid falling ill while you're away from home. Amid the last-minute frenzy that often precedes a vacation break, make an extra effort to eat and sleep well—especially if you feel an illness coming on.

If you need a doctor, your hotel can recommend one, or you can contact your embassy or consulate. Outside London, dial **100** and ask the operator for the local police, who will give you the name, address, and telephone number of a doctor in your area. Also see "Fast Facts: London" in chapter 3. *Note:* U.S. visitors who become ill while they're in England are eligible only for free *emergency* care. For other treatment, including follow-up care, you'll be asked to pay.

If you worry about getting sick away from home, you may want to consider **medical travel insurance** (see the section on travel insurance later in this chapter). In most cases, however, your existing health plan will provide all the coverage you need. Be sure to carry your identification card in your wallet.

If you suffer from a chronic illness, consult your doctor before your departure. For conditions like epilepsy, diabetes, or heart problems, wear a **Medic Alert Identification Tag** (☎ **800/825-3785**; www.medicalert.org), which will immediately alert doctors to your condition and give them access to your records through Medic Alert's 24-hour hot line. Membership is $35, plus a $15 annual fee.

Pack prescription medications in your carry-on luggage. Carry written prescriptions in generic, not brand-name form, and dispense all prescription medications from their original labeled vials. Also bring along copies of your prescriptions in case you lose your pills or run out. If you wear contact lenses, pack an extra pair in case you lose one.

Contact the **International Association for Medical Assistance to Travelers (IAMAT)** (☎ **716/754-4883** or 416/652-0137; www.sentex.net/~iamat). This organization offers tips on travel and health concerns in the countries you'll be visiting, and lists many local English-speaking doctors. The United States **Centers for Disease Control and Prevention** (☎ **404/332-4559**; www.cdc.gov) provides up-to-date information on necessary vaccines and health hazards by region or country (by mail, their booklet is $20; on the Internet, it's free). When you're abroad, any local consulate can provide a list of area doctors who speak English. If you do get sick, you may want to ask the concierge at your hotel to recommend a local doctor—even his or her own. This will probably yield a better recommendation than any 800 number would. If you can't find a doctor who can help you right away, try the emergency room at the local hospital. Many emergency rooms have walk-in clinics for emergency cases that are not life threatening. You may not get immediate attention, but you won't pay the high price of an emergency room visit in the U.S.

INSURANCE

There are three kinds of travel insurance: trip cancellation, medical, and lost luggage coverage. **Trip cancellation insurance** is a good idea if you have paid a large portion of your vacation expenses up front. The other two types of insurance, however, don't make sense for most travelers. Rule number one: Check your existing policies before you buy any additional coverage.

Your existing health insurance should cover you if you get sick while on vacation (though if you belong to an HMO, you should check to see whether you are fully covered when away from home). If you need hospital treatment, most health-insurance plans and HMOs will cover out-of-country hospital visits and procedures, at least to some extent. However, most make you pay the bills up front at the time of care, and you'll get a refund after you've returned and filed all the paperwork. Members of **Blue Cross/Blue Shield** can now use their cards at select hospitals in most major cities worldwide (☎ 800/810-BLUE or www.bluecares.com/blue/bluecard/wwn for a list of hospitals). For independent travel health-insurance providers, see below. Your homeowner's insurance should cover stolen luggage. The airlines are responsible $9.07 per pound, or a total of $634.90 per bag, if they lose your luggage; if you plan to carry anything more valuable than that, keep it in your carry-on bag.

The differences between travel assistance and insurance are often blurred, but in general the former offers on-the-spot assistance and 24-hour hot lines (mostly oriented toward medical problems), while the latter reimburses you for travel problems (medical, travel, or otherwise) after you have filed the paperwork. The coverage you should consider will depend on how much protection is already contained in your existing health insurance or other policies. Some credit card and charge card companies may insure you against travel accidents if you buy plane, train, or bus tickets with their cards. Before purchasing additional insurance, read your policies and agreements over carefully. Call your insurers or credit/charge card companies if you have any questions.

Some credit cards (American Express and certain gold and platinum Visa and MasterCards, for example) offer automatic flight insurance against death or dismemberment in case of an airplane crash.

If you do require additional insurance, try one of the companies listed below. But don't pay for more than you need. For example, if you need only trip cancellation insurance, don't purchase coverage for lost or stolen property. Trip cancellation insurance costs approximately 6 to 8% of the total value of your vacation. Among the reputable issuers of travel insurance are the following:

> **Access America,** 6600 W. Broad St., Richmond, VA 23230 (☎ 800/ 284-8300)
>
> **Travel Guard International,** 1145 Clark St., Stevens Point, WI 54481 (☎ 800/ 826-1300)
>
> **Travel Insured International, Inc.,** P.O. Box 280568, East Hartford, CT 06128 (☎ 800/243-3174)
>
> **Columbus Travel Insurance,** 279 High St., Croydon CR0 1QH (☎ 0171/ 375-0011 in London; www2.columbusdirect.com/columbusdirect)
>
> **International SOS Assistance,** P.O. Box 11568, Philadelphia PA 11916 (☎ 800/523-8930 or 215/244-1500), strictly an assistance company
>
> **Travelex Insurance Services,** P.O. Box 9408, Garden City, NY 11530-9408 (☎ 800/228-9792)

Medicare only covers U.S. citizens traveling in Mexico and Canada. For Blue Cross/Blue Shield coverage abroad, see "Insurance" above. Companies specializing in accident and medical care include the following:

> **MEDEX International,** P.O. Box 5375, Timonium, MD 21094-5375 (☎ 888/ MEDEX-00 or 410/453-6300; fax 410/453-6301; www.medexassist.com)
>
> **Travel Assistance International (Worldwide Assistance Services, Inc.),** 1133 15th St. NW, Suite 400, Washington, D.C. 20005 (☎ 800/821-2828 or 202/828-5894; fax 202/828-5896)

6 Tips for Travelers with Special Needs

TIPS FOR TRAVELERS WITH DISABILITIES

Many London hotels, museums, restaurants, and sightseeing attractions have wheelchair ramps. Persons with disabilities are often granted special discounts at attractions and, in some cases, nightclubs. These are called "concessions" in Britain. It always pays to ask. Free information and advice is available from **Holiday Care Service,** Imperial Building, 2nd Floor, Victoria Road, Horley, Surrey RH6 7PZ (☎ **01293/774535;** fax 01293/784647).

Bookstores in London often carry *Access in London* (£8 ($13.20), a helpful publication listing facilities for persons with disabilities, among other things.

The transport system, cinemas, and theaters are still pretty much off-limits, but **London Transport** does publish a leaflet called *Access to the Underground,* which gives details of elevators and ramps at individual Underground stations; call ☎ **0171/918-3312.** And the **London black cab** is perfectly suited for those in wheelchairs; the roomy interiors have plenty of room for maneuvering.

London's most visible organization for information about access to theaters, cinemas, galleries, museums, and restaurants is **Artsline,** 54 Chalton St., London NW1 1HS (☎ **0171/388-2227;** fax 0171/383-2653). It offers free information about wheelchair access, theaters with hearing aids, tourist attractions, and cinemas. Artsline will mail information to North America, but it's even more helpful to contact Artsline once you arrive in London; the line is staffed Monday to Friday from 9:30am to 5:30pm.

An organization that cooperates closely with Artsline is **Tripscope,** The Courtyard, 4 Evelyn Rd., London W4 5JL (☎ **0181/994-9294;** fax 0181/994-3618), which offers advice on travel in Britain and elsewhere for persons with disabilities.

There are more resources out there than ever before for travelers with disabilities. *A World of Options,* a 658-page book of resources for travelers with disabilities, covers everything, even biking trips. It costs $35 ($30 for members) and is available from **Mobility International USA,** P.O. Box 10767, Eugene, OR 97440 (☎ **541/343-1284,** voice and TDD; www.miusa.org). Annual membership for Mobility International is $35, which includes their quarterly newsletter, *Over the Rainbow.* In addition, **Twin Peaks Press,** P.O. Box 129, Vancouver, WA 98666 (☎ **360/694-2462**), publishes travel-related books for people with disabilities.

The Moss Rehab Hospital (☎ **215/456-9600**) has been providing friendly and helpful phone advice and referrals to disabled travelers for years through its **Travel Information Service** (☎ **215/456-9603**; www.mossresourcenet.org).

You can join **The Society for the Advancement of Travel for the Handicapped (SATH),** 347 Fifth Ave. Suite 610, New York, NY 10016 (☎ **212/447-7284;** fax 212-725-8253; www.sath.org) for $45 annually, $30 for seniors and students, to gain access to their vast network of connections in the travel industry. They provide information sheets on travel destinations, and referrals to tour operators that specialize in traveling with disabilities. Their quarterly magazine, *Open World for Disability and Mature Travel,* is full of good information and resources. A year's subscription is $13.00 ($21 outside the U.S.).

Travelers with disabilities may also want to consider joining a tour that caters specifically to them. One of the best operators is **Flying Wheels Travel,** 143 West Bridge (P.O. Box 382), Owatonna, MN 55060 (☎ **800/535-6790**). They offer various escorted tours, with an emphasis on sports, as well as private tours in minivans with lifts. Other reputable specialized tour operators include **Access Adventures** (☎ **716/ 889-9096**), which offers sports-related vacations; **Accessible Journeys** (☎ 800/ **TINGLES** or 610/521-0339), for slow walkers and wheelchair travelers; **The Guided Tour, Inc.** (☎ 215/782-1370); **Wilderness Inquiry** (☎ 800/728-0719 or 612/379-3858); and **Directions Unlimited** (☎ 800/533-5343).

You can obtain a copy of *Air Transportation of Handicapped Persons* by writing to Free Advisory Circular No. AC12032, Distribution Unit, U.S. Department of Transportation, Publications Division, M-4332, Washington, D.C. 20590.

Vision-impaired travelers should contact the **American Foundation for the Blind,** 11 Penn Plaza, Suite 300, New York, NY 10001 (☎ 800/232-5463), for information on traveling with Seeing-Eye dogs.

TIPS FOR GAY & LESBIAN TRAVELERS

London has one of the most active gay and lesbian scenes in the world; we've recommended a number of the city's best gay clubs (at least as of press time) in chapter 9, "London After Dark." For up-to-the-minute information on activities, we recommend the monthly *Gay Times* (London) for £2.50 ($4.15).

The **International Gay & Lesbian Travel Association (IGLTA),** (☎ 800/ **448-8550** or 954/776-2626; fax 954/776-3303; www.iglta.org), links travelers up with the appropriate gay-friendly service organization or tour specialist. With around 1,200 members, it offers quarterly newsletters, marketing mailings, and a membership directory that's updated quarterly. Membership often includes gay or lesbian businesses but is open to individuals for $150 yearly, plus a $100 administration fee for new members. Members are kept informed of gay and gay-friendly hoteliers, tour operators, and airline and cruise-line representatives. Contact the IGLTA for a list of its member agencies, who will be tied into IGLTA's information resources.

General gay and lesbian travel agencies include **Family Abroad** (☎ 800/999-5500 or 212/459-1800, gay and lesbian); **Above and Beyond Tours** (☎ 800/397-2681, mainly gay men); and **Yellowbrick Road** (☎ 800/642-2488, gay and lesbian).

There are also two good, biannual English-language gay guidebooks, both focused on gay men but including information for lesbians as well. You can get the *Spartacus International Gay Guide* or *Odysseus* from most gay and lesbian bookstores, or order them from **Giovanni's Room** (☎ 215/923-2960), or **A Different Light Bookstore** (☎ 800/343-4002 or 212/989-4850). Both lesbians and gays might want to pick up a copy of *Gay Travel A to Z* ($16). The **Ferrari Guides** (www.q-net.com) is yet another very good series of gay and lesbian guidebooks. A new guide is the recently published *Frommer's Gay & Lesbian Europe.*

Out and About, 8 W. 19th St. #401, New York, NY 10011 (☎ 800/929-2268 or 212/645-6922), offers guidebooks and a monthly newsletter packed with good information on the global gay and lesbian scene. A year's subscription to the newsletter costs $49. *Our World,* 1104 North Nova Rd., Suite 251, Daytona Beach, FL 32117 (☎ 904/441-5367), is a slicker monthly magazine promoting and highlighting travel bargains and opportunities. Annual subscription rates are $35 in the U.S., $45 outside the U.S.

Lesbian and Gay Switchboard (☎ 0171/837-7324) is open 24 hours a day, providing information about gay-related activities in London, or advice in general. The **Bisexual Helpline** (☎ 0181/569-7500) offers useful information, but only on Tuesday and Wednesday from 7:30 to 9:30pm, and Saturday between 9:30am and noon. London's best gay-oriented bookstore is **Gay's the Word,** 66 Marchmont St., WC1 (☎ 0171/278-7654; Tube: Russell Square), the largest such store in Britain. The staff here is really friendly and helpful and will offer advice about the ever-changing gay scene in London. It's open Monday to Wednesday, Friday, and Saturday 10am to 6pm, Thursday 10am to 7pm, and Sunday 2 to 6pm. At Gay's the Word as well as other gay-friendly venues, you can also pick up a number of publications, many of which are free, including the most popular, *Boyz.* Another free publication is *Pink Paper* (this one has a good lesbian section); and check out *9X,* which is filled with data about all the new clubs and the hottest escorts (if you want what Londoners call "a rent boy").

TIPS FOR SENIORS

Many discounts are available to seniors. Be advised, however, that in England you often have to be a member of an association to obtain discounts. Public-transportation reductions, for example, are available only to holders of British Pension books. However, many attractions do offer discounts for senior citizens (women 60 or over and men 65 or over). Even if discounts aren't posted, you might ask if they're available.

If you're over 60, you're eligible for special 10% discounts on **British Airways** through its Privileged Traveler program. You also qualify for reduced restrictions on APEX cancellations. Discounts are also granted for BA tours and for intra-Britain air tickets that are booked in North America.

British Rail offers seniors discounted rates on first-class rail passes for travel around Britain. See the discussion under "Getting There by Train" below.

Don't be shy about asking for discounts, but always carry some kind of identification, such as a driver's license, that shows your date of birth. Also, mention the fact that you're a senior citizen when you first make your travel reservations. For example, many hotels offer seniors discounts. In most cities, people over the age of 60 qualify for reduced admission to theatres, museums, and other attractions, and discounted fares on public transportation.

Members of the **American Association of Retired Persons (AARP),** 601 E St. NW, Washington, D.C. 20049 (☎ 800/424-3410 or 202/434-2277), get discounts not only on hotels but on airfares and car rentals, too. AARP offers members a wide range of special benefits, including *Modern Maturity* magazine and a monthly newsletter.

The National Council of Senior Citizens, 8403 Colesville Rd., Suite 1200, Silver Springs, MD 20910 (☎ 301/578-8800), a nonprofit organization, offers a newsletter six times a year (partly devoted to travel tips) and discounts on hotel and auto rentals; annual dues are $13 per person or couple.

Mature Outlook, P.O. Box 9390, Des Moines, IA 50306 (☎ 800/336-6330), began as a travel organization for people over 50, although it now caters to people of all ages. Members receive discounts on hotels and receive a bimonthly magazine. Annual membership is $19.95, which entitles members to discounts and, often, free coupons for discounted merchandise from Sears.

Golden Companions, P.O. Box 5249, Reno, NV 89513 (☎ 702/324-2227), helps travelers 45-plus find compatible companions through a personal voice-mail service. Contact them for more information.

The Mature Traveler, a monthly 12-page newsletter on senior-citizen travel is a valuable resource. It is available by subscription ($30 a year) from GEM Publishing Group, Box 50400, Reno, NV 89513-0400. GEM also publishes *The Book of Deals,* a collection of more than 1,000 senior discounts on airlines, lodging, tours, and attractions around the country; it's available for $9.95 by calling ☎ 800/460-6676. Another helpful publication is *101 Tips for the Mature Traveler,* available from Grand Circle Travel, 347 Congress St., Suite 3A, Boston, MA 02210 (☎ 800/221-2610 or 617/350-7500; fax 617/346-6700).

Grand Circle Travel is also one of the hundreds of travel agencies specializing in vacations for seniors (347 Congress St., Suite 3A, Boston, MA 02210 (☎ **800/ 221-2610** or 617/350-7500). Many of these packages, however, are of the tour-bus variety, with free trips thrown in for those who organize groups of 10 or more. Seniors seeking more independent travel should probably consult a regular travel agent. **SAGA International Holidays,** 222 Berkeley St., Boston, MA 02116 (☎ **800/343-0273**), offers inclusive tours and cruises for those 50 and older. SAGA also sponsors the more substantial "Road Scholar Tours" (☎ **800/621-2151**), which are fun-loving but with an educational bent.

If you want something more than the average vacation or guided tour, try **Elderhostel** (☎ 877/426-8056; www.elderhostel.org) or the University of New Hampshire's **Interhostel** (☎ **800/733-9753**), both variations on the same theme: educational travel for senior citizens. On these escorted tours, the days are packed with seminars, lectures, and field trips, and the sightseeing is all led by academic experts. **Elderhostel,** 75 Federal St., Boston, MA 02110-1941 (☎ **877/426-8056;** www.elderhostel.org), arranges study programs for those aged 55 and over (and a spouse or companion of any age) in the U.S. and in 77 countries around the world, including Asia, Africa, and the South Pacific. Most courses last about 3 weeks and many include airfare, accommodations in student dormitories or modest inns, meals, and tuition. Write or call for a free catalog, which lists upcoming courses and destinations. **Interhostel** takes travelers 50 and over (with companions over 40), and offers 2- and 3-week trips, mostly international. The courses in both these programs are ungraded, involve no homework, and often focus on the liberal arts. They're not luxury vacations, but they're fun and fulfilling.

Although all the **specialty books** on the market are U.S.–focused, three do provide good general advice and contacts for the savvy senior traveler. Thumb through *The 50+ Traveler's Guidebook* (St. Martin's Press), *The Seasoned Traveler* (Country Roads Press), or *Unbelievably Good Deals and Great Adventures That You Absolutely Can't Get Unless You're Over 50* (Contemporary Books). Also check out your newsstand for the quarterly magazine *Travel 50 & Beyond.*

TIPS FOR FAMILIES

On airlines, you must request a special menu for children at least 24 hours in advance. Bring your own baby food, though; you can ask a flight attendant to warm it to the right temperature.

Arrange ahead of time for such necessities as a crib, bottle warmer, and car seat (in England, small children aren't allowed to ride in the front seat). If you're staying with friends, you can rent baby equipment from **Chelsea Baby Hire,** 83 Burntwood Lane, SW17 OAJ (☎ **0181/540-8830**). The **London black cab** is a lifesaver for families; the roomy interior allows a stroller to be lifted right into the cab without unstrapping baby.

If you want a night out without the kids, you're in luck: London has its own children's hotel, **Pippa Popins,** 430 Fulham Rd., SW6 1DU (☎ **0171/385-2458**), which accommodates children overnight in a wonderful nursery filled with lots of toys and caring minders. Other recommendable baby-sitting services are **Babysitters Unlimited** (☎ **0181/892-8888**) and **Childminders** (☎ **0171/935-2049** or 0171/935-3000). Baby-sitters can also be found for you at most hotels.

To find out what's on for kids while you're in London, pick up the leaflet *Where to Take Children,* published by the London Tourist Board. If you have specific questions, ring **Kidsline** (☎ **0171/222-8070**) Monday to Friday 4 to 6pm and summer holidays 9am to 4pm or the **London Tourist Board's** special children's information lines (☎ **0839/123-425**) for listings of special events and places to visit for children. The number is accessible in London at 50p (85¢) per minute.

Several books on the market offer tips to help you travel with kids. Most concentrate on the U.S., but two, *Family Travel* (Lanier Publishing International) and *How to Take Great Trips with Your Kids* (The Harvard Common Press), are full of good general advice that can apply to travel anywhere. Another reliable tome, with a worldwide focus, is *Adventuring with Children* (Foghorn Press).

Family Travel Times is published 6 times a year by **TWYCH (Travel with Your Children; ☎ 888/822-4388** or 212/477-5524), and includes a weekly call-in service for subscribers. Subscriptions are $40 a year for quarterly editions. A free publication list and a sample issue are available by calling or sending a request to the above address.

Families Welcome!, 92 N. Main, Ashland, OR 97520 (☎ **800/326-0724** or 541/482-6121), a travel company specializing in worry-free vacations for families, offers "City Kids" packages to certain European cities, including London.

The University of New Hampshire runs **Familyhostel** (☎ **800/733-9753**), an intergenerational alternative to standard guided tours. You live on a European college campus for the 2- or 3-week program, attend lectures, seminars, go on lots of field trips, and do all the sightseeing—all of it guided by a team of experts and academics. It's designed for children (aged 8 to 15), parents, and grandparents.

TIPS FOR STUDENTS

The best resource for students is the **Council on International Educational Exchange,** or CIEE. They can set you up with an ID card (see below), and their travel branch, **Council Travel Service** (☎ **800/226-8624;** www.ciee.com), is the biggest student travel agency operation in the world. It can get you discounts on plane tickets, rail passes, and the like. Ask them for a list of CTS offices in major cities so that you can keep the discounts flowing (and aid lines open) as you travel.

From CIEE you can obtain the student traveler's best friend, the $18 **International Student Identity Card (ISIC).** It's the only officially acceptable form of student identification, good for cut rates on rail passes, plane tickets, and other discounts. It also provides you with basic health and life insurance and a 24-hour help line. If you're no longer a student but are still under 26, you can get a **GO 25 card** from the same people, which will get you the insurance and some of the discounts (but not student admission prices in museums).

In Canada, **Travel CUTS,** 200 Ronson St., Ste. 320, Toronto, M9W 5Z9 (☎ **800/ 667-2887** or 416/614-2887; www.travelcuts.com), offers similar services. **Campus Travel,** 52 Grosvenor Gardens, London SW1W 0AG (☎ **0171/730-3402;** www.campustravel.co.uk), opposite Victoria Station, is Britain's leading specialist in student and youth travel.

STA Travel, 86 Old Brompton Rd., SW7 3LQ (☎ **0171/361-6161;** Tube: South Kensington), is the only worldwide company specializing in student- and youth-discounted airfares. It's open Monday to Friday 8:30am to 7pm, Saturday 10am to 5pm, and Sunday 10am to 2pm.

The International Student House, 229 Great Portland St., W1 (☎ **0171/ 631-3223**), lies at the foot of Regent's Park across from the Tube stop for Great Portland Street. It's a beehive of student activity, such as discos and film showings, and rents blandly furnished, very institutional rooms for £29.50 ($48.70) single, £21 ($34.65) per person double, £17.50 ($28.90) per person triple, and £9.99 ($16.50) per person in a dorm. Laundry facilities are available, and a £10 ($16.50) key deposit is charged. Reserve way in advance.

University of London Student Union, 1 Malet St., WC1E 7HY (☎ 0171/664-2000; Tube: Goodge Street or Russell Square), is the best place to go to learn about student activities in the Greater London area. The Union contains a swimming pool, a fitness center, a gymnasium, a general store, a sports shop, a ticket agency, banks, bars, inexpensive restaurants, venues for live events, an office of STA Travel (see above), and many other facilities. It's open Monday to Thursday 8:30am to 11pm, Friday 8:30am to 1pm, Saturday 9am to 2pm, and Sunday 9:30am to 10:30pm. Bulletin boards at the Union provide a rundown on sponsored events, some of which you might be able to attend; others might be "closed door."

TIPS FOR WOMEN TRAVELERS

Several Web sites offer women advice on how to travel safely and happily. The Executive **Woman's Travel Network** (www.delta-air.com/womenexecs/) is the official women's travel site of Delta airlines and offers women tips on staying fit while traveling, eating well, finding special airfares, and dealing with many other feminine travel issues. **WomanTraveler** (www.womantraveler.com) is an excellent guide that suggests places where women can stay and eat in various destinations. The site is authored by women and includes listings of women-owned businesses such as hotels, hostels, and so on.

Several books on the market cater to the concerns of the female traveler. Look into the Virago Women's Travel Guides, $14.95. The series is excellent but new, and covers only three cities to date: London, San Francisco, and Amsterdam. *Safety and Security for Women Who Travel*, by Sheila Swan Laufer and Peter Laufer, is well worth $12.95.

TIPS FOR SINGLE TRAVELERS

Many people prefer traveling alone except for the relatively steep cost of booking a single room, which usually costs well over half the price of a double. **Travel Companion** (☎ 516/454-0880) is one of the nation's oldest roommate finders for single travelers. Register with them and find a trustworthy travel mate who will split the cost of the room with you and be around as little, or as often, as you like during the day.

Several tour organizers cater to solo travelers as well. **Experience Plus** (☎ 800/685-4565; fax 907/484-8489) offers an interesting selection of single-only trips.

Travel Buddies (☎ 800/998-9099 or 604/533-2483) runs single-friendly tours with no singles supplement. **The Single Gourmet Club** (133 E. 58th St., New York, NY 10022; ☎ 212/980-8788; fax 212/980-3138) is an international social, dining, and travel club for singles, with offices in 21 cities in the U.S. and Canada. There is, however, no longer an office in London.

You may also want to research the *Outdoor Singles Network* (P.O. Box 781, Haines, AK 99827). An established quarterly newsletter (since 1989) for outdoor-loving singles, ages 19 to 90, the network will help you find a travel companion, pen pal, or soul mate within its pages. A one-year subscription costs $45, and your own personal ad is printed free in the next issue. Current issues are $15. Write for free information or check out the group's Web site at **http://www.kcd.com/bearstar/osn.html**.

7 Getting There

BY PLANE

If given a choice, opt to land at Heathrow Airport, London's main airport. Gatwick Airport, where most charters land, requires a train trip into London.

FROM THE UNITED STATES **American Airlines** (☎ 800/433-7300; www.americanair.com) offers daily routes to London Heathrow Airport from five U.S.

gateways: New York's JFK (six times daily), Chicago's O'Hare and Boston's Logan (twice daily), Miami International and Los Angeles International (each once daily).

British Airways (☎ 800/247-9297; www.british-airways.com) offers mostly nonstop flights from 18 U.S. cities to Heathrow and Gatwick Airports. With more add-on options than any other airline, British Airways can make a visit to Britain cheaper than you might have expected. The 1993 union of some of BA's functions and routings with US Airways has opened additional North American gateways to BA, improved services, and reduced some of its fares. Of particular interest are the "Value Plus," "London on the Town," and "Europe Escorted" packages that include both airfare and discounted accommodations throughout Britain.

Continental Airlines (☎ 800/525-0280; www.flycontinental.com) flies daily to Gatwick Airport from Newark, Houston, and Cleveland.

Depending on day and season, **Delta Air Lines** (☎ 800/241-4141; www.delta-air.com) runs either one or two daily nonstop flights between Atlanta and Gatwick, near London. Delta also offers nonstop daily service from Cincinnati.

Northwest Airlines (☎ 800/447-4747; www.nwa.com) flies nonstop from both Minneapolis and Detroit to Gatwick, with connections possible from other cities, such as Boston and New York.

TWA (☎ 800/221-2000; www.twa.com) flies nonstop to Gatwick every day from its hub in St. Louis. Connections are possible through St. Louis from most of North America.

United Airlines (☎ 800/538-2929; www.ual.com) flies nonstop from New York's JFK and Chicago's O'Hare to Heathrow two or three times a day, depending on the season. United also offers nonstop service twice a day from Dulles Airport, near Washington, D.C., plus once-a-day service from Newark, Los Angeles, and San Francisco to Heathrow.

Virgin Atlantic Airways (☎ 800/862-8621; www.fly.virgin.com) flies daily to either Gatwick or Heathrow from Boston, Newark, New York's JFK, Los Angeles, San Francisco, Washington's Dulles, Miami, and Orlando.

From Canada For travelers departing from Canada, **Air Canada** (☎ 800/776-3000; www.aircanada.ca) flies daily to London Heathrow nonstop from Vancouver, Montreal, and Toronto. There are also frequent direct flights from Calgary, and Ottawa.

FROM AUSTRALIA Qantas (☎ 131211; www.qantas.com) flies from both Sydney and Melbourne daily. **British Airways** (☎ 02/92583300 or 03/96031133; www.british-airways.com) has five to seven flights weekly from Sydney and Melbourne.

FROM SOUTH AFRICA South African Airways (☎ 011/978-1111; www.saa.co.za) schedules two daily flights from Johannesburg and three weekly flights from Cape Town. From Johannesburg, both **British Airways** (☎ 0800/011747; www.british-airways.com) and **Virgin Atlantic Airways** (☎ 011/340-3400; www.fly.virgin.com) have daily flights to Heathrow. British Airways flies five times weekly from Cape Town.

FLYING FOR LESS: TIPS FOR GETTING THE BEST AIRFARES

Passengers within the same airplane cabin rarely pay the same fare for their seats. Business travelers who need to purchase tickets at the last minute, change their itinerary at a moment's notice, or get home before the weekend pay the premium rate, known as the full fare. Passengers who can book their ticket long in advance, who don't mind staying over Saturday night, or who are willing to travel on a Tuesday, Wednesday, or

Thursday after 7pm, will pay a fraction of the full fare. On most flights, even the shortest hops, the full fare is close to $1,000 or more, but a 7-day or 14-day advance purchase ticket is closer to $200 to $300. Here are a few other easy ways to save.

1. Periodically airlines lower prices on their most popular routes. Check your newspaper for advertised discounts or call the airlines directly and ask if any **promotional rates** or special fares are available. Of course, you'll almost never see a sale during the peak summer vacation months of July and August, or during the Christmas season. If your schedule is flexible, ask if you can secure a cheaper fare by staying an extra day or by flying midweek. (Many airlines won't volunteer this information.) If you already hold a ticket when a sale breaks, it may even pay to exchange your ticket, which usually incurs a $50 to $75 charge.

   Note, however, that the lowest-priced fares are often nonrefundable, require advance purchase of 1 to 3 weeks and a certain length of stay, and carry penalties for changing dates of travel.

2. **Consolidators,** also known as bucket shops, are a good place to find low fares. Consolidators buy seats in bulk from the airlines, and then sell them back to the public at prices below even the airlines' discounted rates. Their small, boxed ads usually run in the Sunday travel section at the bottom of the page. Before you pay a consolidator, however, ask for a record locator number and confirm your seat with the airline itself. Be prepared to book your ticket with a different consolidator—there are many to choose from—if the airline can't confirm your reservation. Also be aware that bucket shop tickets are usually nonrefundable or rigged with stiff cancellation penalties, often as high as 50% to 75% of the ticket price.

   Council Travel (☎ 800/226-8624; www.counciltravel.com) and **STA Travel** (☎ 800/781-4040; www.sta.travel.com) cater especially to young travelers, but their bargain-basement prices are available to people of all ages. **Travel Bargains** (☎ 800/AIR-FARE; www.1800airfare.com) was formerly owned by TWA, but now offers the deepest discounts on many other airlines, with a 4-day advance purchase. Other reliable consolidators include **1-800-FLY-CHEAP** (www. 1800flycheap.com); **TFI Tours International** (☎ 800-745-8000 or 212/ 736-1140), which serves as a clearinghouse for unused seats; or "rebators" such as **Travel Avenue** (☎ 800/333-3335 or 312/876-1116) and the **Smart Traveller** (☎ 800/448-3338 or 305/448-3338; www.smarttraveller@juno.com), which rebate part of their commissions to you.

3. Book a seat on a **charter flight.** Discounted fares have pared the number available, but they still can be found. Most charter operators advertise and sell their seats through travel agents, thus making these local professionals your best source of information for available flights. Before deciding to take a charter flight, however, check the restrictions on the ticket: You may be asked to purchase a tour package, to pay in advance, to be amenable if the day of departure is changed, to pay a service charge, to fly on an airline you're not familiar with (this usually is not the case), and to pay harsh penalties if you cancel—but be understanding if the charter doesn't fill up and is canceled up to 10 days before departure. Summer charters fill up more quickly than others and are almost sure to fly, but if you decide on a charter flight, seriously consider cancellation and baggage insurance.

4. Look into **courier flights**—although they are usually unavailable on domestic flights. Companies that hire couriers use your luggage allowance for their business baggage; in return, you get a deeply discounted ticket. Flights are often offered at the last minute, and you may have to arrange a pretrip interview to make sure you're right for the job. **Now Voyager,** open Monday to Friday from

10am to 5:30pm and Saturday from noon to 4:30pm (☎ 212/431-1616), flies from New York and sometimes has flights to San Francisco for as little as $199 round-trip. Now Voyager also offers noncourier, discounted fares, so call the company even if you don't want to fly as a courier.

5. Join a travel club such as **Moment's Notice** (☎ 718/234-6295) or **Sears Discount Travel Club** (☎ 800/433-9383, or 800/255-1487 to join), which supply unsold tickets at discounted prices. You pay an annual membership fee to get the club's hot-line number. Of course, you're limited to what's available, so you have to be flexible.

BY TRAIN

VIA THE CHUNNEL FROM THE CONTINENT   Queen Elizabeth and President François Mitterrand officially opened the Channel Tunnel in 1994, and the **Eurostar Express** began twice-daily passenger service between London and both Paris and Brussels. The $15-billion tunnel, one of the great engineering feats of all time, is the first link between Britain and the Continent since the Ice Age.

Rail Europe (☎ 800/94-CHUNNEL for information) sells tickets on the *Eurostar* direct train service between Paris or Brussels and London. A round-trip, first-class fare between Paris and London, for example, costs $438 ($298 in second class); but you can cut costs to $218 with a second-class, 14-day advance purchase (non-refundable) round-trip fare. In London, make reservations for *Eurostar* at **0990/300003;** in Paris, at **01-44-51-06-02;** and in the United States, at **800/EUROSTAR.** *Eurostar* trains arrive and depart from London's Waterloo Station, Paris's Gare du Nord, and Brussels' Central Station.

VIA BRITRAIL FROM OTHER PARTS OF EUROPE   If you're traveling to London from elsewhere in the United Kingdom, consider buying a **BritRail Classic Pass,** which allows unlimited rail travel during a set time period (8 days, 15 days, or 1 month). (Eurailpasses aren't accepted in Britain, although they are in Ireland.) For 8 days, a pass costs $400 in first class, and $265 in standard class; for 15 days, it's $600 and $400, respectively; for 22 days, it's $760 and $505; and for 1 month, it's $900 and $600. If a child age 5 to 15 is traveling with a full-fare adult, the fare is half the adult fare. Children under 5 travel free if not occupying a seat. Senior citizens (60 and over) qualify for discounts, but only on first-class travel: It's $340 for an 8-day pass, $510 for a 15-day pass, $645 for a 22-day pass, and $765 for a 1-month pass. Travelers between 16 and 25 can purchase a BritRail Classic Youth Pass, which allows unlimited second-class travel: $215 for 8 days, $280 for 15 days, $355 for 22 days, or $420 for 1 month.

You must purchase your BritRail pass before you leave home. Americans can secure BritRail passes at **BritRail Travel International,** 500 Mamaroneck Ave., Suite 314, Harrison, NY 10528 (☎ 800/677-8585 in the U.S., 800/555-2748 in Canada), or you can get booking information on the Internet at www.raileurope.com.

Travelers who arrive from France via ferry or hovercraft (see "By Boat" below) and pick up a BritRail train at Dover arrive at **Victoria Station,** in the center of London. Those journeying south by rail from Edinburgh arrive at **King's Cross Station.**

BY CAR

If you plan to take a rented car across or under the Channel, check carefully with the rental company about license and insurance requirements before you leave.

FERRIES FROM THE CONTINENT   There are many "drive-on, drive-off" car-ferry services across the Channel. The most popular ports in France for Channel crossings are Boulogne and Calais, where you can board Stena ferries or hovercraft

Cyber Deals for Net Surfers

It's possible to get some great deals on airfare, hotels, and car rentals via the Internet. Grab your mouse and surf before you take off—you could save a bundle on your trip. The Web sites highlighted below are worth checking out, especially since all services are free. Always check the lowest published fare, however, before you shop for flights online.

Arthur Frommer's Budget Travel (www.frommers.com)   Home of the Encyclopedia of Travel and *Arthur Frommer's Budget Travel* magazine and daily newsletter, this site offers detailed information on 200 cities and islands around the world, and up-to-the-minute ways to save dramatically on flights, hotels, car reservations, and cruises. Book an entire vacation online and research your destination before you leave. Consult the message board to set up "hospitality exchanges" in other countries, to talk with other travelers who have visited a hotel you're considering, or to direct travel questions to Arthur Frommer himself. The newsletter is updated daily to keep you abreast of the latest breaking ways to save, to publicize new hot spots and best buys, and to present veteran readers with fresh, ever-changing approaches to travel.

Microsoft Expedia (www.expedia.com)   The best part of this multipurpose travel site is the "Fare Tracker": You fill out a form on the screen indicating that you're interested in cheap flights from your hometown, and, once a week, they'll e-mail you the best airfare deals on up to three destinations. The site's "Travel Agent" will steer you to bargains on hotels and car rentals, and with the help of hotel and airline seat pinpointers, you can book everything right online. This site is even useful once you're booked. Before you depart, log on to Expedia for maps and up-to-date travel information, including weather reports and foreign-exchange rates.

Travelocity (www.travelocity.com)   This is one of the best travel sites out there, especially for finding cheap airfare. In addition to its "Personal Fare Watcher," which notifies you via e-mail of the lowest airfares for up to five different destinations, Travelocity will track the three lowest fares for any routes on any dates

---

taking you to the English ports of Dover and Folkestone. For details, see "Ferries & Hovercraft" under "Getting There by Boat," below.

LE SHUTTLE   You can take Le Shuttle (☎ 0990/353535) under the English Channel. The tunnel not only accommodates trains but passenger cars, charter buses, taxis, and motorcycles, under the English Channel from Calais, France, to Folkestone, England, or vice versa. It operates 24 hours a day, 365 days a year, running every 15 minutes during peak travel times and at least once an hour at night. With Le Shuttle, gone are weather-related delays, seasickness, and a need for reservations. Motorists drive onto a half-mile-long train and travel though an underground tunnel built beneath the seabed through a layer of impermeable chalk marl and sealed with a reinforced-concrete lining.

Before boarding Le Shuttle, you'll stop at a toll booth to pay, and then pass through Immigration for both countries at one time. During the ride, you'll stay in bright, air-conditioned carriages, remaining inside your car or stepping outside to stretch your legs. When the trip is completed, you'll simply drive off toward London. The total travel time between the French and English highway system is about 1 hour.

in minutes. You can book a flight right then and there, and if you need a rental car or hotel, Travelocity will find you the best deal via the SABRE computer reservations system (another huge travel agent database). Click on "Last Minute Deals" for the latest travel bargains, including a link to "H.O.T. Coupons" (www.hotcoupons.com), where you can print out electronic coupons for travel in the U.S. and Canada.

The Trip (www.thetrip.com)   This site is really geared toward the business traveler, but vacationers-to-be can also use The Trip's exceptionally powerful fare-finding engine, which will e-mail you every week with the best city-to-city airfare deals for as many as 10 routes. The Trip uses the Internet Travel Network, another reputable travel agent database, to book hotels and restaurants.

E-Savers Programs   Several major airlines offer a free e-mail service known as E-Savers, via which they'll send you their best bargain airfares on a regular basis. Here's how it works: Once a week (usually Wed), or whenever a sale fare comes up, subscribers receive a list of discounted flights to and from various destinations, both international and domestic. Here's the catch: These fares are usually only available if you leave the very next Saturday (or sometimes Friday night) and return on the following Monday or Tuesday. It's really a service for the spontaneously inclined and travelers looking for a quick getaway. But the fares are cheap, so it's worth taking a look. If you have a preference for certain airlines (in other words, the ones you fly most frequently), sign up with them first.

One caveat: You'll get frequent-flier miles if you purchase one of these fares, but you can't use miles to buy the ticket.

Smarter Living (www.smarterliving.com)   If the thought of all that surfing and comparison shopping gives you a headache, then head right for Smarter Living. Sign up for their newsletter service, and every week you'll get a customized e-mail summarizing the discount fares available from your departure city. Smarter Living tracks more than 15 different airlines, so it's a worthwhile time-saver.

The cost of moving a car on Le Shuttle varies, according to the season and the day of the week. Count on at least £84.50 ($139.40) each way. Discounts are granted to passengers who return to France with their cars within 5 days of their departure; otherwise, the round-trip fare is twice the price of the one-way fare.

Stores selling duty-free goods, restaurants, and service stations are available to travelers on both sides of the Channel. A bilingual staff is on hand to assist travelers at both the British and French terminals.

Hertz offers **Le Swap,** a service for passengers taking Le Shuttle. At Calais, you can switch cars for either a left-hand- or right-hand-drive vehicle, depending upon which country you're heading for.

BY BUS

If you're traveling to London from elsewhere in the United Kingdom, consider purchasing a **Britexpress Card,** which entitles you to a 30% discount on National Express (England and Wales) and Caledonian Express (Scotland) buses. Contact a travel agent for details.

Bus connections to Britain from the Continent are generally not very comfortable, although some lines are more convenient than others. One line with a relatively good reputation is **Euroways Eurolines, Ltd.,** 52 Grosvenor Gardens, London SW1W OAU (☎ **0171/730-8235**). They book passage on buses traveling two times a day between London and Paris (9 hours), three times a day from Amsterdam (12 hours), three times a week from Munich (24 hours), and three times a week from Stockholm (44 hours). On the longer routes, which employ two alternating drivers, the bus proceeds almost without interruption, taking occasional breaks for meals.

BY BOAT

CROSSING THE ATLANTIC   The **Cunard Line,** 6100 Blue Lagoon Dr., Suite 400, Miami, FL 33126 (☎ **305/463-3000** or 800/7-CUNARD), boasts that its flagship, *Queen Elizabeth 2,* is the only five-star-plus luxury ocean liner providing regular transatlantic service—some 18 voyages a year between April and December. Many passengers appreciate its graceful introduction to British mores, as well as the absolute lack of jet lag that an ocean crossing can provide.

Fares vary, based on the season and the cabin grade. During the super-value season (May 26 to June 21 and Dec 9 to 15), the fares for a 6-day crossing range from $1,601 to $6,405. During peak season (July 10 to Aug 28), fares for a 6-day crossing range from $1,777 to $7,112. All prices are per person, double occupancy; passengers also pay $250 port and handling charges. Many packages are offered, which include inexpensive airfare from your home city to the point of departure plus a return flight to your home city from London on British Airways.

FERRIES & HOVERCRAFT   For centuries, sailing ships and ferryboats have traversed the English Channel bearing supplies, merchandise, and passengers. Today, the major carriers are P&O Channel Lines, and HoverSpeed. Once you arrive in Dover, you can pick up a BritRail train to London (see "By Train," above).

CAR & PASSENGER FERRIES   **P&O Stena Lines** (☎ **0990/980980**) operates car and passenger ferries between Dover (England) and Calais (France) only. Trip time is 75 minutes. **P&O European Ferry** (☎ **0870/242-4999**) operates ferry service from Portsmouth (England) to Cherbourg (France). Depending on the vessel, this trip can take from 2 hours and 45 minutes to up to 5 hours.

HOVERCRAFT & SEACATS   Traveling by Hovercraft or Seacat cuts your journey time from the Continent to Britain. **HoverSpeed** operates at least 6 daily 35-minute hovercraft crossings, as well as slightly longer crossings via Seacat (a catamaran propelled by jet engines; these go four times daily and take about 50 minutes), between Boulogne and Folkestone. A Hovercraft trip is definitely a fun adventure, as the vessel is technically "flying" over the water. Seacats also travel from the mainland of Britain to the Isle of Wight, Belfast, and the Isle of Man. For reservations and information, call **HoverSpeed** at ☎ **0870/5240241.** Typical one-way fares are £15 to £20 ($24.75 to $33) per person.

Getting to Know London

3

Europe's largest city is like a great wheel, with Piccadilly Circus at the hub and dozens of communities branching out from it. Since London is such a conglomeration of sections, each with its own life and personality, first-time visitors may be intimidated until they get the hang of it. Many visitors spend all their time in the West End, where most of the attractions are located with the exception of that historic part of London known as the City, where the Tower of London stands.

This chapter will help you get your bearings. It provides a brief orientation and a preview of the city's most important neighborhoods and tells you what you need to know about getting around London by public transportation or on foot. In addition, the "Fast Facts" section covers everything from baby-sitters to shoe repairs.

1 Orientation

ARRIVING
BY PLANE

LONDON HEATHROW AIRPORT Located west of London in Hounslow (☎ **0181/759-4321** for flight information), Heathrow is one of the world's busiest airports, with flights arriving from around the world and throughout Great Britain. It's divided into four terminals, each relatively self-contained. Terminal 4, the most modern, handles the long-haul and transatlantic operations of British Airways. Most transatlantic flights of U.S.–based airlines arrive at Terminal 3. Terminals 1 and 2 receive the intra-European flights of several European airlines.

It takes 50 minutes by **Underground** and costs £3.40 ($5.60) to make the 15-mile trip from Heathrow to center city. You can also take the **Airbus,** which gets you into central London in about an hour and costs £6 ($9.90) for adults and £3 ($4.95) for children. A **taxi** is likely to cost at least £45 ($74.25). For more information about train or bus connections, call ☎ **0171/222-1234.**

The British Airport Authority now operates a **London-Heathrow Express** (☎ **0845/600-1515**), a 100-mile-an-hour train service running every 15 minutes daily from 5:10am until 11:40pm between Heathrow and Paddington Station in the center of London. Trips cost £10 ($16.50) each way in economy class, rising to £20 ($33) in first class. Children ages 5 to 15 go for half the fare (free for those 4 and under). The trip takes only 15 minutes each way between Paddington and Terminals 1, 2, and 3, or 20 minutes from Terminal 4. The trains have special areas for wheelchairs. From Paddington, passengers can connect to other trains or hail a taxi. You can buy tickets on the train or at self-service machines at Heathrow Airport (also available from travel agents). At Paddington, a bus link, Hotel Express, takes passengers from Paddington to a number of hotels in central London, costing £2.05 ($3.40) for adults, £1.05 ($1.75) children 5 to 15, and free for children under 4. This service has already revolutionized travel to and from the airport, much to the regret of London cabbies.

GATWICK AIRPORT   While Heathrow still dominates, more and more scheduled flights land at relatively remote Gatwick (☎ **01293/535353** for flight information), located some 25 miles south of London in West Sussex. From Gatwick, **express trains** leave for Victoria Station in London every 15 minutes during the day and every hour at night. The charge is £9.50 ($15.65) for adults, half price for children 5 to 15, free for children under 5. There's also an express bus from Gatwick to Victoria, **Flightline Bus 777,** every hour from 5am to 8pm and every hour from 8 to 11pm; the fare is £7.50 ($12.40) per person. A **taxi** from Gatwick to central London usually costs £60 ($99). However, you must negotiate a fare with the driver before you enter the cab; the meter doesn't apply because Gatwick lies outside the Metropolitan Police District. For further transportation information, call **0345/ 484950** in London only.

LONDON STANSTED AIRPORT   Located some 50 miles northeast of London's West End, Stansted, in Essex (☎ **01279/680500**), mostly handles flights to and from the European continent. From Stansted, your best bet to reach central London is the **Stansted Express** to Liverpool Street Station, costing £10.40 ($17.15) for adults and £5.20 ($8.60) for children under 15. Daily service runs every 30 minutes from 5:30am to 11pm. Trip time is 45 minutes.

LONDON CITY AIRPORT   London City Airport (☎ **0171/646-0000**) receives mainly short-haul flights from Britain and northern Europe, making it popular with business travelers.

From London City Airport, there are three ways to reach the center of London: First, the **blue-and-white bus** charges £4 ($6.60) each way to and from the Liverpool Street Station, where passengers can get rail and Underground transport to almost anywhere in England. The bus runs daily every 10 minutes, during open hours of the airport—roughly from 6:50am to 9:20pm (airport closes at 1pm Sat). Second, there's a **shuttle bus to Canary Wharf,** where trains from the Docklands Light Railway make frequent 10-minute runs to the heart of London's financial district, the City. Here, passengers can catch an Underground from the Bank Tube stop. Third, **London Transport bus no. 473** goes from the City Airport to East London, where passengers can pick up the Underground at the Plaistow Tube stop.

BY TRAIN

Each of London's train stations is connected to the city's vast bus and Underground network, and each has phones, restaurants, pubs, luggage-storage areas, and London Regional Transport Information Centres.

If you're arriving from France, the fastest way to get to London is by taking the HoverSpeed connection between Calais and Dover (see "Ferries & Hovercraft" under "By Boat," in chapter 2), where you can pick up a BritRail train into the city. If you prefer the ease of one-stop travel, you can take the Chunnel train directly from Paris to Waterloo Station in London.

BY CAR

Once you arrive on the English side of the channel, the M20 takes you directly into London. *Remember to drive on the left.* London is circled by two roadways: the A406 and A205 combination close in, and the M25 farther out. Determine which part of the city you wish to enter and follow signposts.

We suggest you confine driving in London to the bare minimum, which means arriving and parking. Because of parking problems and heavy traffic, getting around London by car is not a viable option. Once there, abandon it in a garage and rely on public transportation or taxis. Before arrival in London, call your hotel and inquire if it has a garage (and what the charges are), or ask the staff to give you the name and address of a garage nearby.

VISITOR INFORMATION

The **British Travel Centre,** Rex House, 4-12 Lower Regent St., London SW1 4PQ (Tube: Piccadilly Circus), caters to walk-in visitors who need information about all parts of Britain. Telephone service has been suspended; you must show up in person and often wait in a lengthy line. On the premises you'll find a British Rail ticket office, travel and theater-ticket agencies, a hotel-booking service, a bookshop, and a souvenir shop. It's open Monday to Friday 9am to 6:30pm, Saturday and Sunday 10am to 4pm, with extended hours on Saturday from June to September.

London Tourist Board's **Tourist Information Centre,** Victoria Station Forecourt, SW1 (Tube: Victoria Station), can help you with almost anything. The center deals chiefly with accommodations in all price categories and can handle the whole spectrum of travelers' questions. It also arranges tour-ticket sales, theater reservations, and offers a wide selection of books and souvenirs. From Easter to October, the center is open daily 8am to 7pm; November to Easter, it's open Monday to Saturday 8am to 6pm and Sunday 9am to 4pm.

The tourist board also has offices at **Heathrow** Terminals 1, 2, and 3, and on the Underground concourse at **Liverpool Street Railway Station.**

CITY LAYOUT

AN OVERVIEW OF THE CITY

While **Central London** doesn't formally define itself, most Londoners today would probably accept the Underground's Circle Line as a fair boundary. The city center is customarily divided into two areas, the **City** and the **West End.**

The City is where London began; it's the original square mile the Romans called Londinium, and still exists as its own self-governing entity. Rich in historical, architectural, and social interest, the City is now one of the world's great financial theaters.

The City and the West End are surrounded first by **Inner London** (which includes the East End), and then by the sprawling hinterland of **Outer London.** You'll find the greatest number of hotels in the west, in inner districts such as **Kensington, Chelsea,** and **Victoria,** and in the West End. Even though the City is jeweled with historic sights, it empties out in the evenings and on weekends.

In much the way that the City is a buffer to the east, so is the River Thames to the south. The Barbican Centre in the City and the South Bank Arts Centre across the river were conscious attempts to extend the geographical spread of central London's nocturnal life, but central London really fades in the City and only half-heartedly crosses the Thames. Still, the new urban development of Docklands, the tourist attraction of the new Globe Theatre, and some up-and-coming residential neighborhoods are infusing energy into the area across the river.

London's Neighborhoods

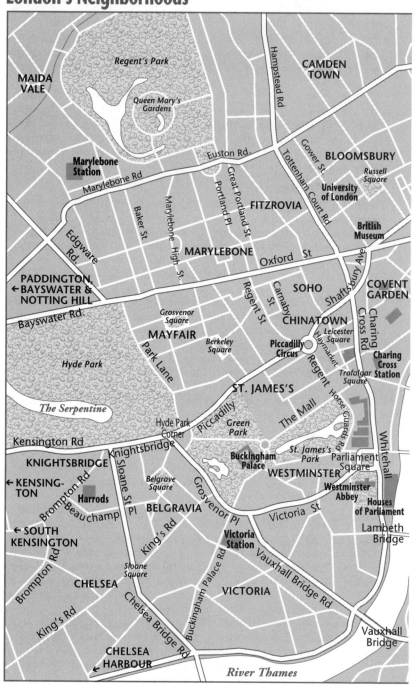

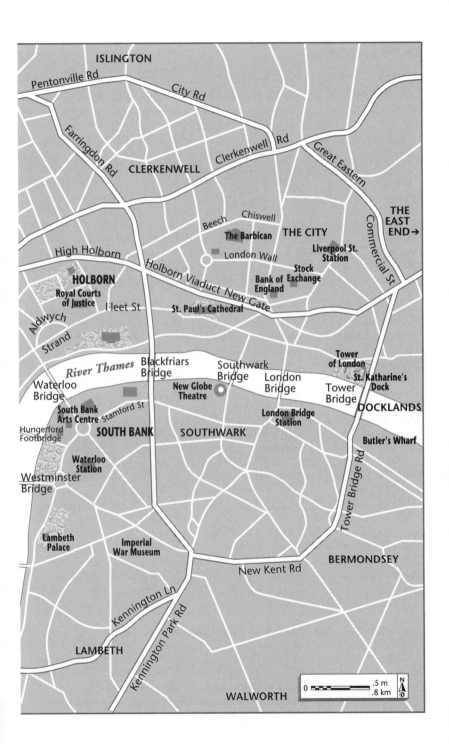

ISLINGTON

Pentonville Rd

City Rd

Farringdon Rd

Clerkenwell Rd

Great Eastern

CLERKENWELL

THE EAST END →

Beech
Chiswell

The Barbican

THE CITY

Commercial St

High Holborn

London Wall

Liverpool St. Station

HOLBORN

Holborn Viaduct New Gate

Bank of England

Stock Exchange

Royal Courts of Justice

Fleet St

St. Paul's Cathedral

Aldwych

Strand

River Thames

Blackfriars Bridge

Southwark Bridge

London Bridge

Tower of London

Waterloo Bridge

New Globe Theatre

St. Katharine's Dock

Tower Bridge

DOCKLANDS

South Bank Arts Centre

Stamford St

London Bridge Station

Hungerford Footbridge

SOUTH BANK

SOUTHWARK

Butler's Wharf

Waterloo Station

Westminster Bridge

Tower Bridge Rd

Lambeth Palace

Imperial War Museum

BERMONDSEY

New Kent Rd

Kennington Ln

Kennington Park Rd

LAMBETH

0   .5 m
     .8 km

N

WALWORTH

ORIENTING YOURSELF

There is—fortunately—an immense difference between the sprawling vastness of Greater London and the pocket-size chunk north of the River Thames that might be considered Prime Tourist Territory. This London begins at **Chelsea,** on the north bank of the river, and stretches for roughly 5 miles north to **Hampstead.** Its western periphery runs through **Kensington,** whereas the eastern boundary lies 5 miles away at Tower Bridge. Within these 25 square miles, you'll find all the hotels and restaurants and nearly all the sights that are of primary interest to visitors.

Make no mistake: This is still a hefty space to cover, and a really thorough exploration of it would take a couple of years. But it has the advantage of being flat and walkable, besides boasting one of the best public transportation systems ever devised.

The logical (although not geographical) center of this area is **Trafalgar Square,** which we'll take as our orientation point (see "London's Neighborhoods" map on pp. 42–43). If you stand facing the steps of the imposing National Gallery, you're looking northwest. That is the direction of **Piccadilly Circus**—the real core of central London—and the maze of streets that make up **Soho.** Farther north is **Oxford Street,** London's gift to moderate shopping; still farther northwest lies **Regent's Park,** home to the London Zoo.

At your back—that is, south—is **Whitehall,** which houses or skirts nearly every British government building, from the Ministry of Defence to the official residence of the prime minister at no. 10 Downing Street. In the same direction, a bit farther south, stand the Houses of Parliament and Westminster Abbey.

Flowing southwest from Trafalgar Square is the table-smooth **Mall,** flanked by magnificent parks and mansions and leading to Buckingham Palace, residence of the queen. Farther in the same direction lie **Belgravia** and **Knightsbridge,** the city's plushest residential areas, and south of them lie the aforementioned chic **Chelsea** and **King's Road,** the famous shopping boulevard.

Due west of Trafalgar Square stretches the superb and distinctly high-priced shopping area bordered by **Regent Street** and **Piccadilly** (the street, distinct from the Circus). Farther west lie the equally elegant shops and even more elegant homes of **Mayfair.** Then comes ritzy **Park Lane.** On the other side of Park Lane is **Hyde Park,** the biggest park in London and one of the largest in the world.

Charing Cross Road runs north from Trafalgar Square, past **Leicester Square,** and intersects with **Shaftesbury Avenue.** This is London's Theaterland. A bit farther along, Charing Cross Road turns into a browser's paradise, lined with shops selling new and secondhand books.

Finally, Charing Cross Road funnels into **St. Giles Circus.** This is where you enter **Bloomsbury,** site of the University of London, the British Museum, and some of London's best budget hotels; as well as the erstwhile stamping ground of the famed Bloomsbury Group, which included Virginia Woolf, E. M. Forster, and John Maynard Keynes.

Northeast of your position sprawls **Covent Garden,** known for its Royal Opera House and today a major—and very hip—shopping, restaurant, and cafe district.

Following the **Strand** eastward from Trafalgar Square, you'll come into **Fleet Street.** Beginning in the 19th century, this corner of London became the most concentrated newspaper district in the world (most of the papers have fled Fleet St. for the new Docklands development in the last decade or so). Where the Strand becomes Fleet Street stands Temple Bar, and only here do you enter the actual City of London, or **the City.** Its focal point and shrine is the Bank of England on Threadneedle Street, with the Stock Exchange next door and the Royal Exchange across the street. In the midst of all the hustle and bustle rises St. Paul's Cathedral, a monument to beauty and tranquillity. At the far-eastern fringe of the City looms the Tower of London, shrouded in legend, blood, and history, and permanently besieged by battalions of visitors.

FINDING YOUR WAY AROUND

It's not easy to find an address in London, as the city's streets—both names and house numbers—follow no pattern whatsoever. London is checkered with innumerable squares, mews, closes, and terraces, which jut into, cross, overlap, or interrupt whatever street you're trying to follow. And house numbers run in odds and evens, clockwise and counterclockwise—when they exist at all. Many establishments, such as the Four Seasons Hotel and Langan's Brasserie, don't have numbers, even though the building right next door is numbered.

Throughout this book, street addresses are followed by designations like SW1 and EC1. These are the postal areas. The original post office was at St. Martin-le-Grand in the City, so the postal districts are related to where they lie geographically from there. For example, Victoria is SW1 since it's the first area southwest of St. Martin-le-Grand; Covent Garden is west (west central), so its postal area is WC1 or WC2; Liverpool Street is east of there, so its postal area is EC1.

If you plan on exploring London in any depth, you'll need a detailed street map with an index, not one of those superficial overviews given away at many hotels or tourist offices. The best ones are published by Falk, and they're available at most newsstands and nearly all bookstores, including **W. & G. Foyle Ltd.,** 113-119 Charing Cross Rd., WC2 (☎ **0171/439-8501;** Tube: Leicester Square), which carries a wide range of maps and guides. And no Londoner is without a *London A to Z*, the ultimate street-by-street reference guide, available at bookstores and newsstands everywhere. Also, don't forget to check out the detailed foldout street map included with this book; you may find that it's all you need to find your way around.

London's Neighborhoods in Brief

West End & Central London Neighborhoods

Mayfair   Bounded by Piccadilly, Hyde Park, and Oxford and Regent streets, this is the most elegant, fashionable section of London, filled with luxury hotels, Georgian town houses, and swank shops. Grosvenor Square (*Grov*-nor) is nicknamed "Little America" because it's home to the American Embassy and a statue of Franklin D. Roosevelt; Berkeley Square (*Bark*-ley) was made famous by the song, whose mythical nightingale sang here. At least once you'll want to dip into this exclusive section. One of the curiosities of Mayfair is **Shepherd Market,** a tiny village of pubs, two-story inns, restaurants, and book and food stalls, all sandwiched within Mayfair's grandness. If you're seeking a sophisticated albeit expensive address, then Mayfair is for you. If Bond Street shopping, tony boutiques, and art galleries, along with tree-filled squares, warm the cockles of your heart, by all means check in.

Marylebone   Most first-time visitors head to Marylebone to explore Madame Tussaud's waxworks or walk along Baker Street in the make-believe footsteps of Sherlock Holmes. The streets form a near-perfect grid, with the major ones running north-south from Regent's Park toward Oxford Street. Architect Robert Adam laid out Portland Place, one of the most characteristic squares, from 1776 to 1780, and it was at Cavendish Square that Mrs. Horatio Nelson waited—often in vain—for the return of the admiral. Marylebone Lane and High Street still retain some of their former village atmosphere, but this is otherwise a rather anonymous area. Dickens (who seems to have lived everywhere) wrote nearly a dozen books when he resided here. At Regent's Park, you can visit Queen Mary's Gardens or, in summer, see Shakespeare performed in an open-air theater. Marylebone has a number of inexpensive to moderately priced B&B lodgings, often converted former town houses.

St. James's　Often called "Royal London," St. James's basks in its associations with everybody from the "merrie monarch" Charles II to Elizabeth II, who lives at its most famous address, Buckingham Palace. The neighborhood begins at Piccadilly Circus and moves southwest, incorporating Pall Mall, The Mall, St. James's Park, and Green Park; it's "frightfully convenient," as the English say, enclosing such addresses as American Express on Haymarket and many of London's leading department stores. In this bastion of aristocracy and royalty, a certain pomp is still evident—this is where the English gentleman seeks haven at that male-only bastion of English tradition, the gentlemen's club. Be sure to stop in at **Fortnum & Mason,** 181 Piccadilly, the world's most luxurious grocery store. Launched in 1788, the store sent hams to the duke of Wellington's army, baskets of tinned goodies to Florence Nightingale in the Crimea, and packed a picnic basket for Stanley when he went looking for Livingstone. If you want to live in the same section as the Queen, and have a real classy address, you can find a scattering of hotels here. The frugal hotel shopper will flee elsewhere, however, and come later just to look around.

Piccadilly Circus & Leicester Square　Piccadilly Circus, with its statue of Eros, is the heart and soul of London. The circus isn't Times Square yet, but its traffic, neon, and jostling crowds might indeed make "circus" an apt word here. Piccadilly, traditionally the western road out of town, was named for the "picadil," a ruffled collar created by Robert Baker, a 17th-century tailor. If you want a little more grandeur, retreat to the Regency promenade of exclusive shops, the **Burlington Arcade,** designed in 1819. The English gentry—tired of being mud-splashed by horses and carriages along Piccadilly—came here to do their shopping. Some 35 shops, housing a treasure trove of expensive goodies, await you. A bit more tawdry is **Leicester Square,** a center of theaters, restaurants, movie palaces, and nightlife. The square is no longer the chic address it was when William Hogarth or Joshua Reynolds lived here, Reynolds painting all of high society in his elegant salon. The square changed forever in the Victorian era, when four towering entertainment halls were opened (even Queen Victoria came to see a circus here on occasion). In time the old palaces changed from stage to screen; three of them are still showing films. The Café de Paris is no longer a chic cabaret—now it's a disco. This would be the London equivalent of staying in Times Square in New York.

Soho　A nightclubber's paradise, especially if you're gay, Soho is a confusing grid of streets and restaurants—a great place to stay, not necessarily to lodge in, although there is one hotel. These densely packed streets in the heart of the West End are famous for their gloriously cosmopolitan mix of people and trades. A decade ago, much was heard about the decline of Soho when the thriving sex industry threatened to engulf it; even the pub where Dylan Thomas used to drink himself into oblivion became a sex cinema. That destruction has now largely been halted. Respectable businesses have returned, and fashionable restaurants and shops prosper; it's now the heart of London's expanding gay life.

Soho starts at Piccadilly Circus and spreads out, more-or-less bordered by Regent Street, Oxford Street, Charing Cross Road, and the theaters of Shaftesbury Avenue. Carnaby Street, a block from Regent Street, was the center of the universe in the Swinging Sixties, but is now just a schlocky sideshow. Across Shaftesbury Avenue, a busy street lined with theaters, is London's **Chinatown,** centered on Gerrard Street.

It's small, authentic, and packed with excellent restaurants. But Soho's heart—with marvelous French and Italian delicatessens, fine butchers, fish stores, and wine merchants—is farther north, on Brewer, Old Compton, and Berwick streets; Berwick is also a wonderful open-air fresh food market. To the north of Old Compton Street, Dean, Frith, and Greek streets have fine little restaurants, pubs, and clubs, like Ronnie Scott's for jazz. The British movie industry is centered on Wardour Street.

Bloomsbury   This district, a world within itself, lies northeast of Piccadilly Circus, beyond Soho. It is, among other things, the academic heart of London; here you'll find the University of London, several other colleges, and many bookstores. Despite its student population, this neighborhood is fairly staid. Its reputation has been fanned by such writers as Virginia Woolf, who lived within its bounds (it figured in her novel *Jacob's Room*). The novelist and her husband, Leonard, were once unofficial leaders of a group of artists and writers known as "the Bloomsbury Group" (nicknamed "Bloomsberries"), which at times included Bertrand Russell.

The heart of Bloomsbury is Russell Square, whose outlying streets are lined with moderately priced to inexpensive hotels and B&Bs. It's a rather noisy but very central place to stay. Most visitors come to the neighborhood to visit the British Museum, one of the world's greatest repositories of treasures. The British Telecom Tower (1964) on Cleveland Street is a familiar landmark.

Nearby is **Fitzrovia,** bounded by Great Portland, Oxford, and Gower streets, and reached by the Goodge Street Tube. Goodge Street, with its many shops and pubs, forms the heart of the "village." Once a major haunt of artists and writers—this was the stamping ground of Ezra Pound, Wyndham Lewis, and George Orwell, among others—the bottom end of Fitzrovia is a virtual extension of Soho, with a cluster of Greek restaurants.

Clerkenwell   This was the site of London's first hospital and the home of several early churches before it evolved into a muck-filled 18th-century cattle yard that was home to cheap gin distilleries. By the 1870s, London's new socialist movement centered itself here: Clerkenwell was home to John Stuart Mill's London Patriotic Club in 1872 and William Morris's socialist press of the 1890s; Lenin lived and worked here editing *Iskra*. In later years, the neighborhood dwindled. However, it's recently been reinvented by the moneyed and groovy—a handful of hot new restaurants and clubs have sprouted up, and art galleries now line St. John's Square and the border of Clerkenwell Green. But lorries still rumble into Smithfield Market throughout the night, unloading thousands of beef carcasses, and the church of St. Bartholomew-the-Great, built in 1123, still stands as London's oldest church and the best piece of large-scale Norman building in the city. Farringdon is the central Tube stop.

Holborn   The old borough of Holborn (*ho*-burn), which abuts the City to the west, takes in the heart of legal London—the city's barristers, solicitors, and law clerks call it home. Still Dickensian in spirit, the area preserves the Victorian author's footsteps in the two Inns of Court and the Bleeding Heart Yard of *Little Dorrit* fame. A 14-year-old Dickens was once employed as a solicitor's clerk at Lincoln's Inn Fields. The Old Bailey has stood for English justice down through the years; Fagin went to the gallows from this site in *Oliver Twist*. Everything in Holborn seems steeped in history. Even as you're quenching your thirst with a half-pint of bitter at the **Viaduct Tavern,** 126 Newgate St. (Tube: St. Paul's), you learn the pub was built over the notorious Newgate Prison (which specialized in death by pressing) and was named after the Holborn Viaduct, the world's first overpass.

Covent Garden & the Strand   The flower, fruit, and "veg" market is long gone (since 1970), but memories of Professor Higgins and his "squashed cabbage leaf,"

Eliza Doolittle, linger on. **Covent Garden** now contains the city's liveliest group of restaurants, pubs, and cafes outside Soho, as well as some of the city's hippest shops—including the world's only Dr. Marten's Super Store. The restored marketplace with its glass and iron roofs has been called a magnificent example of urban recycling. Covent Garden is traditionally London's theater area, and Inigo Jones's St. Paul's Covent Garden is known as the actors' church; over the years it has attracted everybody from Ellen Terry to Vivien Leigh and is still attended by actors and artists. The Theatre Royal Drury Lane was where Charles II's mistress Nell Gwynne made her debut in 1665 and the Irish actress Dorothea Jordan first caught the eye of the duke of Clarence, later William IV. (She became not only his mistress, but also the mother of 10 of his children.) The place is not packed with hotel beds, but there are a few choice ones. In fact, if you want a fashionable address, but one not as obvious as Mayfair, make it Covent Garden. Your newly made London friends will compliment you on your taste and discretion.

Beginning at Trafalgar Square, the **Strand** runs east into Fleet Street and borders Covent Garden to the south. It's flanked with theaters, shops, first-class hotels, and restaurants. Ye Olde Cheshire Cheese pub, Dr. Johnson's House, rooms fragrant with brewing Twinings English tea—all these evoke memories of the rich heyday of this district. The Strand runs parallel to the River Thames, and to walk it is to follow in the footsteps of Charles Lamb, Mark Twain, Henry Fielding, James Boswell, William Thackeray, and Sir Walter Raleigh. The Savoy Theatre helped make Gilbert and Sullivan household names.

Westminster   Westminster has been the seat of the British government since the days of Edward the Confessor. Dominated by the Houses of Parliament and Westminster Abbey, the area runs along the Thames to the east of St. James's Park. **Trafalgar Square,** at the area's northern end and one of the city's major landmarks, remains a testament to England's victory over Napoléon in 1805, and the paintings in its landmark National Gallery will restore your soul. Whitehall is the main thoroughfare, linking Trafalgar Square with Parliament Square. You can visit Churchill's Cabinet War Rooms and walk down Downing Street to see no. 10, the world's most famous street address, home to Britain's prime minister. No visit is complete without a call at **Westminster Abbey,** one of the greatest Gothic churches in the world. It has witnessed a parade of English history, beginning when William the Conqueror was crowned here on Christmas Day, 1066.

Westminster also encompasses **Victoria,** an area that takes its unofficial name from bustling Victoria Station, known as "the gateway to the Continent." Because of Westminster's location near the rail station, many B&Bs and hotels have sprouted up here. It's not a tony address, but it's cheap to moderate in price for living, if you don't mind the noise and crowds.

The City & Environs

The City   When the Londoners speak of "the City" (EC2, EC3), they don't mean all of London; they mean the original square mile that's now the British version of Wall Street. The buildings of this district are known all over the world: the Bank of England, the London Stock Exchange, and the financially troubled Lloyd's of London. This was the original site of Londinium, as it was called by its Roman conquerors. Despite its age, the City doesn't easily reveal its past; much of it was swept away by the Great Fire of 1666, the bombs of 1940, the IRA bombs of the early 1990s, and the zeal of modern developers. Still, it retains its medieval character, and landmarks include St. Paul's Cathedral—the masterpiece of Sir Christopher Wren, which stood virtually alone among the rubble after the Blitz. Some 2,000 years of history unfold at the Museum of London and the Barbican Centre, opened by Queen Elizabeth in 1982, and hailed by her as a "wonder" of the cultural world. At the Guildhall, the first lord mayor of London was installed in 1192.

Fleet Street was London's journalistic hub since William Caxton printed the first book in English here. *The Daily Consort,* the first daily newspaper printed in England, was launched at Ludgate Circus in 1702. However, most of the London tabloids have abandoned Fleet Street for the Docklands development across the river.

The City of London still prefers to function on its own, separate from the rest of the city; in keeping with its independence, it maintains its own **Information Centre** at St. Paul's Churchyard, EC4 (☎ **0171/332-1456**).

Docklands   In 1981, the London Docklands Development Corporation (LDDC) was formed to redevelop Wapping, the Isle of Dogs, the Royal Docks, and Surrey Docks in the largest, the most ambitious scheme of its kind in Europe. The area is bordered roughly by Tower Bridge to the west and London City Airport and the Royal Docks to the east. Many businesses have moved here; Thames-side warehouses have been converted to Manhattan-style lofts; and museums, entertainment complexes, shops, and an ever-growing list of restaurants have popped up at this 21st-century river city in the making.

Canary Wharf, on the Isle of Dogs, is the heart of Docklands; this huge 71-acre site is dominated by an 800-foot-high tower, the tallest building in the United Kingdom, designed by Cesar Pelli. The Piazza is lined with shops and restaurants. On the south side of the river at Surrey Docks, the Victorian warehouses of **Butler's Wharf** have been converted by Sir Terence Conran into offices, workshops, houses, shops, and restaurants. Butler's Wharf is also home to the Design Museum.

To get to Docklands, take the Underground to Tower Hill and pick up the **Docklands Light Railway** (☎ **0171/363-9696**), which operates Monday to Friday from 5:30am to 12:30am, with selected main routes now offering weekend service from 6am to 12:30pm Saturday and 7:30am to 11:30pm Sunday.

The East End   Traditionally, this was one of London's poorest districts, and was nearly bombed out of existence in World War II. Hitler, in the words of one commentator at the time, created "instant urban renewal" here. The East End extends from the City Walls east encompassing Stepney, Bow, Poplar, West Ham, Canning Town, and other districts. The East End has always been filled with legend and lore. It's the home of the Cockney, London's most colorful character. To be a true Cockney, it's said that you must have been born "within the sound of Bow Bells," a reference to a church, St. Mary-le-Bow, rebuilt by Sir Christopher Wren in 1670. Many immigrants to London have found a home here.

South Bank   Although not officially a district like Mayfair, South Bank is the setting today for the **South Bank Arts Centre,** now the largest arts center in Western Europe and still growing. Reached by Waterloo Bridge or on foot by Hungerford Bridge, it lies across the Thames from the Victoria Embankment. Culture buffs flock to its many galleries and halls, including the National Theatre, Queen Elizabeth Hall, Royal Festival Hall, and the Hayward Gallery. It's also the setting of the National Film Theatre and the Museum of the Moving Image (MOMI). Nearby are such neighborhoods as Elephant and Castle and Southwark, home to grand Southwark Cathedral. To get here, take the Tube to Waterloo Station.

Knightsbridge   One of London's most fashionable neighborhoods, Knightsbridge is a top residential and shopping district, just south of Hyde Park. **Harrods** on Brompton Road is its chief attraction. Founded in 1901, it's been called "the Notre Dame of department stores"—they'll even arrange your burial. Right nearby,

Beauchamp Place (*Bee*-cham) is one of London's most fashionable shopping streets, a Regency-era boutique-lined little street with a scattering of restaurants. Shops include Bruce Oldfield at 27 Beauchamp Place, where the likes of Joan Collins come for evening wear. And, at the end of a shopping day, if Harrods' five restaurants and five bars haven't tempted you, retreat to Bill Bentley's at 31 Beauchamp Place for a dozen oysters, washed down with a few glasses of muscadet. If you're checking in, Knightsbridge, in spite of its commercial overtones, is still a swank address. Most hotels are deluxe or first class, although a few moderately priced ones exist in the neighborhood as well.

Belgravia   South of Knightsbridge, this area has long been the aristocratic quarter of London, rivaling Mayfair in grandness. Although it reached its pinnacle of prestige during the reign of Queen Victoria, it's still a chic address if you're looking for a hotel; the duke and duchess of Westminster, one of England's richest families, still live at Eaton Square. The area's centerpiece is Belgrave Square (1825–35). When town houses were built there, aristocrats followed—the duke of Connaught, the earl of Essex, even Queen Victoria's mother, the duchess of Kent. Chopin, on holiday in 1837, was appropriately impressed: "And the English! And the houses! And the palaces! And the pomp, and the carriages! Everything from soap to the razors is extraordinary."

Chelsea   This stylish Thames-side district lies south of Belgravia. It begins at Sloane Square, with Gilbert Ledward's Venus fountain playing watery music and flower sellers hustling their wares. The area has always been a favorite of writers and artists, including such names as Oscar Wilde (who was arrested here), George Eliot, James Whistler, J. M. W. Turner, Henry James, Augustus John, and Thomas Carlyle (whose former home can be visited). Mick Jagger and Margaret Thatcher (not together) have been more recent residents, and the late Princess Diana and her "Sloane Rangers" of the 1980s gave it even more fame. There are some swank hotels here and a scattering of modestly priced ones. The main drawback to living in Chelsea is inaccessibility. Except for Sloane Square, there's a dearth of Tube stops; and unless you like to take a lot of buses or expensive taxis, you may find getting about a chore.

Its major boulevard is **King's Road,** where Mary Quant launched the miniskirt in the 1960s and where the English punk look began. King's Road runs the entire length of Chelsea; it's at its liveliest on Saturday. The hip-hop of King's Road isn't typical of otherwise upmarket Chelsea, an elegant village filled with town houses and little mews dwellings that only successful stockbrokers and solicitors can afford to occupy.

On the Chelsea/Fulham border is **Chelsea Harbour,** a luxury development of apartments and restaurants with a private marina. You can spot its tall tower from far away; the golden ball on top moves up and down to indicate the tide level. Driving by the Chelsea Harbour Club in the mid-1990s you could often see paparazzi perched on ladders, trying to get a shot of the late Princess Di entering or exiting the exclusive gym.

Kensington   This Royal Borough (W8) lies west of Kensington Gardens and Hyde Park and is traversed by two of London's major shopping streets, Kensington High Street and Kensington Church Street. Since 1689, when asthmatic William III fled Whitehall Palace for Nottingham House (where the air was fresher), the district has enjoyed royal associations. In time, Nottingham House became Kensington Palace, and the royals grabbed a chunk of Hyde Park to plant their roses. Queen Victoria was born here. "KP," as the royals say, is still home to Princess Margaret (20 rooms with a view), Prince and Princess Michael of Kent, and the duke and duchess of Gloucester. It was also the residence of the late Princess of Wales. Kensington Gardens is now open to the public, ever since George II decreed that "respectably dressed" people would be permitted in on Saturday—providing that no servants, soldiers, or sailors came. In the footsteps of William III, Kensington Square developed, attracting artists and writers. Thackeray wrote *Vanity Fair* while living here. With all those royal associations, Kensington is a fashionable hotel address, although not necessarily for the bargain shopper. If you're a frugal traveler and would like to live in the area, head for South Kensington (see below) which has moderately priced hotels and B&B galore.

Southeast of Kensington Gardens and Earl's Court, primarily residential **South Kensington** is often called "museumland" because it's dominated by a complex of museums and colleges—set upon land bought with the proceeds from Prince Albert's Great Exhibition, held in Hyde Park in 1851—that includes the Natural History Museum, the Victoria and Albert Museum, and the Science Museum; nearby is Royal Albert Hall. South Kensington is also home to some fashionable restaurants and townhouse hotels, many converted to B&Bs. One of the district's chief curiosities is the Albert Memorial, completed in 1872 by Sir George Gilbert Scott; for sheer excess, the Victorian monument is unequaled in the world.

Earl's Court   Earl's Court lies below Kensington, bordering the western half of Chelsea. For decades a staid residential district, drawing genteel ladies between the wars who wore pince-nez, Earl's Court now attracts a new and younger crowd (often gay), particularly at night, to its pubs, wine bars, and coffeehouses. It's long been a popular base for budget travelers (particularly Australians, for reasons known only to them), thanks to its wealth of B&Bs and budget hotels, and its convenient access to central London: A 15-minute Tube ride will take you into the heart of Piccadilly.

Once regarded as "the boondocks," nearby **West Brompton** is seen today as an extension of central London. It lies directly south of Earl's Court (take the Tube to West Brompton) and directly southeast of West Kensington. Its focal point is the sprawling Brompton Cemetery, a flower-filled "green lung" and burial place of such famous names as Frederick Leyland, the Pre-Raphaelite patron who died in 1892. It also has many good restaurants, pubs, and taverns, as well as some budget hotels.

Notting Hill   Increasingly fashionable Notting Hill is bounded on the east by Bayswater and on the south by Kensington. Hemmed in on the north by West Way and on the west by the Shepherd's Bush ramp leading to the M40, it has many turn-of-the-century mansions and small houses sitting on quiet, leafy streets, plus a growing number of hot restaurants and clubs. Gentrified in recent years, it's becoming an extension of central London. Living in one of the few hotels in Notting Hill would brand you a hip hotel shopper.

On the north end, across Notting Hill Gate and west of Bayswater, is the hip neighborhood known as **Notting Hill Gate.** Portobello Road is home to one of London's most famous street markets. The area Tube stops are Notting Hill Gate, Holland Park, or Ladbroke Grove.

Nearby **Holland Park** is a chi-chi residential neighborhood visited chiefly by the chic guests of Halcyon Hotel, one of the grandest of London's small hotels.

Paddington & Bayswater   The **Paddington** section centers around Paddington Station, north of Kensington Gardens and Hyde Park. It's one of the major centers in London, attracting budget travelers who fill up the B&Bs in Sussex Gardens and Norfolk Square. After the first railway was introduced in London in 1836, it was followed by a circle of sprawling railway termini, including Paddington Station in 1838, which spurred the growth of this middle-class area, which is now blighted in parts.

Just south of Paddington, north of Hyde Park, and abutting more fashionable Notting Hill to the west is **Bayswater,** a sort of unofficial area also filled with a large number of B&Bs attracting budget travelers. Inspired by Marylebone and elegant

Mayfair, a relatively prosperous set of Victorian merchants moved in and built terrace houses around spacious squares.

Nearby is **Maida Vale,** a village that, like St. John's Wood and Camden, has been absorbed by central London. Maida Vale lies directly west of Regent's Park, north of Paddington, and next to the more prestigious address of **St. John's Wood** (home to the Beatles' Abbey Road Studios). The whole area is very sports oriented; if you take the Tube to Maida Vale, you'll find Paddington Recreation Ground, plus a smaller "green lung," Paddington Bowling and Sports Club. It's also home to some of the BBC studios.

Farther Afield

Greenwich   To the southeast of London, this suburb—ground zero for use in the reckoning of terrestrial longitudes—enjoyed its heyday under the Tudors. Henry VIII and both of his daughters, Mary I and Elizabeth I, were born here. Greenwich Palace, Henry's favorite, is long gone, though; today's visitors come to this lovely port village for nautical sights along the Thames, including visits to the 1869 tea clipper, *Cutty Sark,* and the tiny *Gipsy Moth IV,* a 54-foot ketch in which Sir Francis Chichester sailed solo around the world in 1966–67. Other attractions in the district include the National Maritime Museum. Because Greenwich was selected as the site of the Millennium Dome, it will be overwhelmed with visitors in the year 2000, many of whom will be flocking here even if they have to skip the British Museum and the Tower of London.

Hampstead   This residential suburb of north London, beloved by Keats and Hogarth, is a favorite excursion spot for Londoners on the weekend. Everybody from Sigmund Freud to D. H. Lawrence to Anna Pavlova to John Le Carré has lived here, and it's still one of the most desirable districts in the Greater London area to call home. It has very few hotels, however, and, of course, is quite far from central London so that if you lodge here, you may spend a great deal of time commuting. Its centerpiece is Hampstead Heath, nearly 800 acres of rolling meadows and woodland with panoramic views; it still maintains its rural atmosphere even though engulfed by cityscapes on all sides. The hilltop village is filled with cafes, tearooms, and restaurants, and there are pubs galore, some with historic pedigrees. Take the Northern Line to Hampstead Heath station.

Highgate   Along with Hampstead, Highgate in north London is another choice residential area, particularly on or near Pond Square and along Hampstead High Street. Once celebrated for its "sweer salutarie airs," Highgate has long been a desirable place to live, and Londoners used to flock to its taverns and pubs for "exercise and harmless merriment"; some still do. Today, most visitors come to see moody Highgate Cemetery, London's most famous cemetery—it's the final resting place of such famous figures as Karl Marx and George Eliot.

Hammersmith   Sitting on the north bank of the Thames, just to the west of Kensington, Hammersmith will fool you at first into thinking it's an industrial park, thanks to the stretch of factories between Putney and Hammersmith bridges. Actually, it's predominantly residential. Its most attractive feature is its waterfront, filled with boathouses, small businesses, some very good restaurants, and artists' studios. Beyond Hammersmith Bridge the neighborhood blossoms with balconied 18th-century homes behind lime and catalpa trees, more boathouses, and old pubs that use the warm weather as an excuse to spill out onto the riverbank.

Nearby is the delightful old village of **Barnes,** with its ironwork-decorated Barnes Terrace. Hammersmith Terrace, a favorite stamping ground of artists, adds color to the neighborhood, and another stretch of gracious homes lies along Chiswick Mall, curling into Church Street. This area deftly imitates an intimate English village before dumping you back into teeming London along Great West Road.

2 Getting Around

BY PUBLIC TRANSPORTATION

If you know the ropes, transportation in London can be easy and inexpensive. Both the Underground (the subway casually known as the "Tube") and bus systems are operated by London Transport.

Travel Information Centres are located in the Underground stations at Hammersmith, King's Cross, Oxford Circus, St. James's Park, Liverpool Street Station, and Piccadilly Circus, as well as in the British Rail stations at Euston and Victoria and in each of the terminals at Heathrow Airport. They take reservations for London Transport's guided tours and offer free Underground and bus maps and other information leaflets. A **24-hour information service** is available (☎ **0171/222-1234**). You can get information before you go by writing **London Transport,** Travel Information Service, 55 Broadway, London SW1H 0BD.

TRAVEL PASSES   London Transport offers **Travelcards** for use on bus, Underground, and British Rail services in Greater London. Sold in combinations of adjacent zones, Travelcards are available for a minimum of 7 days or for any period from a month to a year. A Travelcard allowing travel in two zones for 1 week costs adults £17.60 ($29.05), children £6.50 ($10.75). Travelcards must be used in conjunction with a Photocard (a photo ID used for identification by London Transport as well as by several other entities in London). A free Photocard is issued simultaneously with your Travelcard—bring a passport photo from one of the instant photo booths in London's train stations—when you buy your Travelcard at main post offices in the London area, the ticket window of any Tube station, or at the Travel Information Centres of London Transport (see above).

For shorter stays in London, consider the **One-Day Off-Peak Travelcard.** This Travelcard can be used on most bus, Underground, and British Rail services throughout Greater London Monday to Friday after 9:30am and at any time on weekends and bank holidays. The Travelcard is available from Underground ticket offices, Travel Information Centres, and some newsstands. For two zones, the cost is £3.80 ($6.25) for adults and £1.90 ($3.15) for children 5 to 15. Children 4 and under travel free.

Visitor Travelcard is worthwhile if you plan to travel a lot within Greater London. This card allows unlimited transport within all six zones of Greater London's Underground and bus network. You'll most likely travel within the first two zones of the network's boundaries, but you're able to travel as far as Heathrow during valid times. However, you must buy this pass in North America; it's not available in England. A pass good for 3 consecutive days of travel is $32 for adults, $14 for children 5 to 15; for 4 consecutive days of travel, it's $41 for adults, $16 for children; and for 7 consecutive days of travel, it's $63 for adults, $24 for children. Contact **BritRail Travel International,** 500 Mamaroneck Ave., Suite 314, Harrison, NY 10528 (☎ **800/ 677-8585;** 800/555-2748 in Canada).

Another pass is the 1-day **Family Travelcard.** It's a go-as-you-please ticket, allowing as many journeys as you wish on the Tube, buses (excluding night buses) displaying the London Transport bus sign, and even the Docklands Light Railway or any rail service within the travel zones designated on your ticket. The family card is valid Monday to Friday after 9:30am and all day on weekends and public holidays. It's available for families as small as two (one adult and one child) to as large as six (two adults and four children). The cost is £3 to £3.20 ($4.95 to $5.30) per adult, 60p ($1) per child. Yet a final discount pass is the **Weekend Travelcard,** which allows you 2 days of weekend transportation on the Underground or buses. The cost ranges from £5.70 to £6 ($9.40 to $9.90) for adults or £2.80 ($4.60) for children. These passes are available at all Underground stations.

You can now buy **Carnet** tickets, a booklet of 10 single Underground tickets valid for 12 months from the issue date. Carnet tickets are valid for travel only in Zone 1 (Central London), and cost £10 ($16.50) for adults and £5 ($8.25) for children (up to 15). A book of Carnet tickets gives you a savings of £2 ($3.30) over the cost of 10 separate single tickets.

THE UNDERGROUND

The Underground, or Tube, is the fastest and easiest way to get from place to place. All Tube stations are clearly marked with a red circle and blue crossbar. You descend by stairways, escalators, or huge elevators, depending on the depth. Some Underground stations have complete subterranean shopping arcades, and several have push-button information machines.

You pick the station for which you're heading on the large diagram displayed on the wall, which includes an alphabetical index. You note the color of the line (Bakerloo is brown, Central is red, and so on). Then, by merely following the colored band, you can see at a glance whether and where you'll have to change and how many stops are between you and your destination.

If you have British coins, you can get your ticket at a vending machine. Otherwise, buy it at the ticket office. You can transfer as many times as you like as long as you stay in the Underground. The flat fare for one trip within the Central zone is £1.40 ($2.30). Trips from the Central zone to destinations in the suburbs range from £1.40 to £4.70 ($2.30 to $7.75) in most cases.

Slide your ticket into the slot at the gate, and pick it up as it comes through on the other side and hold on to it—it must be presented when you exit the station at your destination. If you're caught without a valid ticket, you'll be fined £10 ($16.50) on the spot. If you owe extra money, you'll be asked to pay the difference by the attendant at the exit. The Tube runs roughly 5am to 11:30pm. After that you must take a taxi or night bus to your destination. For information on the London Tube system, call the **London Underground** at **0171/222-1234,** but expect to stay on hold for a good while before a live person comes on the line.

Scheduled for completion in late 1999 or early 2000, the **Jubilee Underground** line extension will open south of the river as well as into the East End, thus providing much-needed fast access from central London to both Greenwich, site of the Millennium Dome, and Docklands.

BUSES

The first thing you learn about London buses is that nobody just boards them. You "queue up"—that is, form a single-file line at the bus stop.

The comparably priced bus system is almost as good as the Underground and gives you better views of the city. To find out about current routes, pick up a free bus map at one of London Transport's Travel Information Centres, listed above. The map is available in person only, not by mail.

London still has some old-style Routemaster buses, with both driver and conductor: After you've boarded the bus, a conductor will come to your seat; you pay a fare based on your destination and receive a ticket in return. This type of bus is being phased out and replaced with buses that have only a driver; you pay the driver as you enter and you exit via a rear door. As with the Underground, the fares vary according to distance traveled. Generally, bus fares are 50p to £1.20 (85¢ to $2)—less than Tube fares. If you travel for two or three stops, the cost is 60p ($1); longer runs within Zone 1 cost £1 ($1.65). If you want your stop called out, simply ask the conductor or driver.

Buses generally run between about 5am and 11:30pm. There are a few night buses on special routes, running once an hour or so; most pass through Trafalgar Square. Keep in mind that night buses are often crowded (especially on weekends) and unable to pick up passengers. You may find yourself waiting a long time. Consider taking a taxi. Call the 24-hour **hot line** (☎ **0171/222-1234**) for schedule and fare information.

BY TAXI

London cabs are among the most comfortable and best-designed in the world. You can pick one up either by heading for a cab rank or by hailing one in the street (the taxi is available if the yellow taxi sign on the roof is lighted); once they have stopped for you, taxis are obliged to take you anywhere you want to go within 6 miles of the pick-up point, provided it's within the metropolitan area. For a **radio cab,** call **0171/ 272-0272** or 0171/253-5000.

The minimum taxi fare is £5 ($8.25), with the meter starting at £3.80 ($6.25), with increments of 20p (35¢) thereafter, based on distance or time. Each additional passenger is charged 40p (65¢). Passengers pay 10p (15¢) for each piece of luggage in the driver's compartment and any other item more than 2 feet long. Surcharges are imposed after 8pm and on weekends and public holidays. All these tariffs include VAT. Fares usually increase annually. It's recommended that you tip 10% to 15% of the fare.

If you call for a cab, the meter starts running when the taxi receives instructions from the dispatcher, so you could find £1.40 ($2.25) or more already on the meter when you step inside.

Minicabs are also available, and they're often useful when the regular taxis become scarce or when the Tube stops running. These cabs are meterless, so the fare must be negotiated in advance. Unlike regular cabs, minicabs are forbidden by law to cruise for fares. They operate from sidewalk kiosks, such as those around Leicester Square. If you need to call one, try **Brunswick Chauffeurs/Abbey Cars** (☎ **0181/969-2555**) in west London; **Greater London Hire** (☎ **0181/340-2450**) in north London; **London Cabs, Ltd.** (☎ **0181/778-3000**) in east London; or **Newname Minicars** (☎ **0181/472-1400**) in south London. Minicab kiosks can be found near many Tube or BritRail stops, especially in outlying areas.

If you have a complaint about taxi service, or if you leave something in a cab, contact the **Public Carriage Office,** 15 Penton St., N1 9PU (Tube: Angel Station). If it's a complaint, you must have the cab number, which is displayed in the passenger compartment. Call ☎ **0171/230-1631** with complaints.

Cab sharing is permitted in London, as British law allows cabbies to carry two to five persons. Taxis accepting such riders display a notice on yellow plastic, with the words "Shared Taxi." Each of two riders sharing is charged 65% of the fare a lone passenger would be charged. Three persons pay 55%, four pay 45%, and five (the seating capacity of all new London cabs) pay 40% of the single-passenger fare.

BY CAR

Don't drive if you don't have to. London is easy to get around without a car, traffic and parking are nightmares, and—to top it all off—you'll have to drive a car from what

Central London Bus Routes

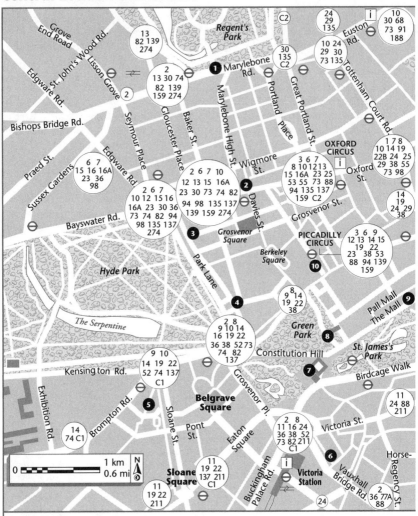

The map contains the following bus route circles:

Regent's Park area: C2; 24 29 135; i; 10 30 68 73 91 188

13 82 139 274; 10 24 29 30 73 135; 30 135 C2; Euston Rd.

2 13 30 74 82 139 159 274; ● 1 Marylebone Rd.

6 7 15 16 16A 23 36 98

2 6 7 10 12 13 15 16A 23 30 73 74 82 94 98 135 137 139 159 274; ● 3 Grosvenor Square

2 6 7 10 12 15 16 16A 23 30 36 73 74 82 94 98 135 137 274

OXFORD CIRCUS i; 3 6 7 8 10 12 13 15 16A 23 25 53 55 73 88 94 135 137 159 C2; Oxford St.

1 7 8 10 14 19 22B 24 25 29 38 55 73 98

14 19 24 29 38

PICCADILLY CIRCUS; 3 6 9 12 13 14 15 19 22 23 38 53 88 94 139 159; ● 10

9 8 14 19 22 38

2 8 9 10 14 16 19 22 36 38 52 73 74 82 137; ● 4

Green Park ● 8

Pall Mall The Mall 9

9 10 14 19 22 52 74 137 C1; ● 5 Kensington Rd.

St. James's Park; Birdcage Walk

Constitution Hill ● 7

14 74 C1; Belgrave Square

11 24 88 211

2 8 11 16 24 36 38 52 73 82 211 C1; ● 6 Victoria St.

11 19 22 137 211 C1; Sloane Square; i Victoria Station

11 19 22 211

2 36 77A 88

24

Legend
⊖ Tube Station
‡ British Rail Station

Scale: 0 — 1 km / 0.6 mi; N

Using the Map

London bus route numbers are shown in circles at places where routes cross. Locate where you are going and then follow the route circles back toward your starting point. This will show if and where you need to change buses and the bus route number or numbers for your trip.

MAJOR ATTRACTIONS

Admiralty Arch 9
Barbican Centre 25
British Museum 11
Buckingham Palace 7
Downing Street 16
Harrods 5
Horse Guards 15
Houses of Parliament 18
Imperial War Museum 20

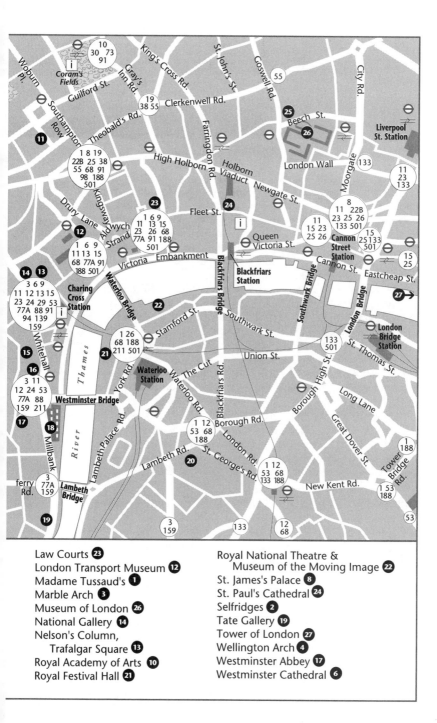

Law Courts **23**
London Transport Museum **12**
Madame Tussaud's **1**
Marble Arch **3**
Museum of London **26**
National Gallery **14**
Nelson's Column,
    Trafalgar Square **13**
Royal Academy of Arts **10**
Royal Festival Hall **21**

Royal National Theatre &
    Museum of the Moving Image **22**
St. James's Palace **8**
St. Paul's Cathedral **24**
Selfridges **2**
Tate Gallery **19**
Tower of London **27**
Wellington Arch **4**
Westminster Abbey **17**
Westminster Cathedral **6**

you normally consider the passenger seat on the wrong side of the road. It all adds up to a big headache.

RENTALS   Car rentals are relatively expensive, and London offers a large array of companies to choose from. Most will accept your U.S. or Canadian driver's license, provided you've held it for more than a year; no special British license is needed. Your passport and driver's license must be presented when you rent a car. There's also an age requirement: 23 for cars rented through Avis, or 25 for cars arranged through Budget Rent-a-Car, British Airways, and Hertz.

Many companies grant discounts to clients who reserve their cars in advance (usually 48 weekday hours) through the toll-free reservations offices in a renter's home country and rent for periods longer than a week. When renting, be sure to ask if the price quoted includes the $17^1/_2\%$ value-added tax (VAT), personal accident insurance (PAI), collision damage waiver (CDW), and other insurance options. If not, ask what these will cost because they can make a big difference in your bottom line.

As in the United States, the CDW and some added insurance are offered free by certain credit cards if you use them to rent a car. Check to see if you are covered by the credit card you use, thus avoiding the added expense.

Some of the major agencies—with North American toll-free numbers—are: **Avis** (☎ **800/331-2112;** www.avis.com), whose main office is in Mayfair at 8 Balderton St., London W1 (**0171/917-6700;** Tube: Bond Street); **Budget Rent-a-Car** (☎ **800/ 472-3325;** www.budgetrentacar.com), whose busiest office is at 89 Wigmore St., London W1 (☎ **0171/538-2228;** Tube: Marble Arch); and **Hertz** (☎ **800/ 654-3001;** www.hertz.com), whose main office is at 35 Edgware Rd., Marble Arch, London W1 (☎ **0171/402-4242;** Tube: Marble Arch). Two prominent European agencies are **Kemwel Holiday Auto** (☎ **800/678-0678;** www.kemwel.com) and **Auto Europe** (☎ **800/223-5555;** www.autoeurope.com).

British Airways (☎ **800/876-2200** or 800/AIRWAYS; www.british-airways.com) offers a relatively inexpensive way to rent a car in Britain through its reservations service. As the U.K.'s largest car renter, BA can offer discounted rates on Hertz rentals in the U.K. Understandably, these arrangements are offered only to passengers flying into Britain on BA. You must apply at least seven days in advance of your departure from the U.S. or Canada, and have your flight information ready to give the rental agent.

DRIVING RULES & REQUIREMENTS   In England, as you probably know, you drive on the left and pass on the right. Road signs are clear and the international symbols unmistakable. The prudent driver will secure a copy of the *British Highway Code,* available from almost any stationer or newsstand. Wearing of seat belts by both front- and rear-seat occupants is mandatory in the British Isles.

Warning: Pedestrian crossings are marked by striped lines (zebra striping) on the road; flashing lights near the curb indicate that drivers must stop and yield the right of way if a pedestrian has stepped into the zebra zone to cross the street.

PARKING   Driving around London is tricky business. The city is a warren of one-way streets, and parking spots are at a premium. In addition to strategically placed expensive garages, central London offers metered parking—but be aware that traffic wardens are famous for issuing substantial fines when the meter runs out. The time limit and the cost of metered parking are posted on the meter. Zones marked "Permit Holders Only" are for local residents. If you violate these sacrosanct places, your vehicle is likely to be towed away. A yellow line along the curb indicates "No Parking"; a double yellow line signifies "No Waiting." However, at night (meters indicate exact times), and on Sunday, you're allowed to park along a curb with a single yellow line.

GASOLINE (PETROL)   Gasoline, called "petrol" by the British, is usually sold by the liter, with 4.5 liters making an imperial gallon. Prices, incidentally, will be much higher than you're accustomed to paying, and you'll probably have to serve yourself. Many stations are closed on Sunday.

BREAKDOWNS   A membership in one of the two major auto clubs in England can be helpful: the **Automobile Association,** Norfolk House, Priestly Rd., Basingstoke, Hampshire RG24 9NY (☎ **0990/448866** for information, 0800/887766 for 24-hour breakdown service; www.theaa.com), and the **Royal Automobile Club,** P.O. Box 700, Spectrum, Bond St., Bristol, Somerset BS99 1RB (☎ **01454/208000** for information, **0800/828282** for 24-hour breakdown service; www.rac.co.uk). Membership in one of these clubs is usually handled by a car-rental agent; inquire when you book. Members in either club are entitled to free legal and technical advice on motoring matters, as well as a range of discounts on motor-related products and services.

All motorways are provided with special emergency phones connected to police traffic units. The police can also contact an automobile club on your behalf.

BY BICYCLE

With central London's heavy traffic, it is not advisable to use a bike for getting around. You can rent bicycles by the day or week from a number of firms, including **On Your Bike,** 52-54 Tooley St., SE1 (☎ **0171/378-6669;** Tube: London Bridge), open Monday to Friday 9am to 6pm, Saturday 9:30am to 5:30pm. The cost is £15 ($24.75) per day, and deposits are payable by MasterCard or Visa.

ON FOOT

London is too vast and sprawling to explore entirely on foot, but if you use public transportation for the long distances and your feet for the narrow crooked lanes, you should do fine. *Remember that cars drive on the left:* Always look both ways before stepping off a curb. Unlike in some countries, vehicles in London have the right of way before pedestrians, except in the zebra-striped zones mentioned above. When you step off the curb onto a zebra, the cars actually stop for you.

Fast Facts: London

American Express   The main AmEx office is at 6 Haymarket, SW1 (☎ **0171/ 930-4411;** Tube: Piccadilly Circus). Full services are available Monday to Friday 9am to 5:30pm and Saturday 9am to 4pm. At other times—Saturday 4pm to 6pm and Sunday 10am to 4pm—only the foreign-exchange bureau is open.

Area Code   London has two telephone area codes: 0171 and 0181. The **0171** area code is for central London within a 4-mile radius of Charing Cross (including the City, Knightsbridge, Oxford St., and as far south as Brixton). The **0181** area code is for outer London (including Heathrow Airport, Wimbledon, and Greenwich). Within London, you'll need to dial the area code when calling from one section of the city to the other, but not within a section. The country code for England is 44; see "Telephone" below for instructions on how to dial.

Warning: London area codes (but not the country code) are changing in the year 2000. See the following box.

Baby-sitters   Baby-sitting organizations provide registered nurses and carefully screened mothers, as well as trained nannies, as sitters. One such is **Childminders** (☎ **0171/935-3000** or 0171/935-2049; Tube: Baker Street). You pay £5.50 ($9.05) per hour in the daytime and £4 to £5 ($6.60 to $8.25) per hour at night.

There's a 4-hour minimum, and hotel guests pay a £8 ($13.20) booking fee each time they use a sitter. You must also pay reasonable transportation costs.

Business Hours   Banks are usually open Monday to Friday 9:30am to 3:30pm. Business offices are open Monday to Friday 9am to 5pm; the lunch break lasts an hour, but most places stay open during that time. Pubs and bars are allowed to stay open from 11am to 11pm on Monday to Saturday and from noon to 10:30pm on Sunday. London stores generally open at 9am and close at 5:30pm, staying open until 7pm on Wednesday or Thursday. Most central shops close on Saturday around 1pm. By law, most stores are closed on Sunday. Some service stores such as small groceries might remain open.

Car Rentals   See "Getting Around" earlier in this chapter.

Climate   See "When to Go" in chapter 2.

Currency Exchange   See "Money" in chapter 2.

Dentists   For dental emergencies, call **Eastman Dental Hospital** (☎ 0171/915-1000;** Tube: King's Cross).

Doctors   In an emergency, contact **Doctor's Call** (☎ 07000/372255). Some hotels also have physicians on call. **Medical Express,** 117A Harley St., W1 (☎ 0171/499-1991; Tube: Regent's Park), is a private British clinic; it's not part of the free British medical establishment. For filling the British equivalent of a U.S. prescription, there's sometimes a surcharge of £20 ($33) on top of the cost of the medications. The clinic is open Monday to Friday 9am to 6pm and Saturday 9:30am to 2:30pm.

Documents Required   See "Documents" in chapter 2.

Driving Rules   See "Getting Around," earlier in this chapter.

Drugstores   In Britain they're called chemist shops. Every police station in the country has a list of emergency chemists (dial "0" and ask the operator for the local police). One of the most centrally located chemists, keeping long hours, is **Bliss the Chemist,** 5 Marble Arch, W1 (☎ 0171/723-6116; Tube: Marble Arch), open daily 9am to midnight. Every London neighborhood has a branch of **Boots,** Britain's leading pharmacy.

Electricity   British current is 240 volts, AC cycle, roughly twice the voltage of the North American current, which is 115 to 120 volts, AC cycle. You'll probably not be able to plug the flat pins of your appliance's plugs into the holes of British wall outlets without suitable converters or adapters. Some (but not all) hotels will supply them for guests. Experienced travelers bring their own transformers. An electrical supply shop will also have what you need. Be forewarned that you'll destroy the inner workings of your appliance (and possibly start a fire as well) if you plug most American appliances directly into a European electrical outlet without a transformer.

Embassies & High Commissions   We hope you'll not need such services, but in case you lose your passport or have some other emergency, here's a list of addresses and phone numbers:

- **Australia**   The high commission is at Australia House, Strand, WC2
  (☎ 0171/379-4334; Tube: Charing Cross or Aldwych); it's open Monday
  to Friday from 10am to 4pm.
- **Canada**   The high commission is located at MacDonald House, 38
  Grosvenor Sq., W1 (☎ 0171/258-6600; Tube: Bond St.); it's open Monday
  to Friday from 8 to 4pm.

- **Ireland**   The embassy is at 17 Grosvenor Place, SW1 (☎ **0171/235-2171;** Tube: Hyde Park Corner); it's open Monday to Friday from 9:30am to 1pm and 2:15 to 5pm.
- **New Zealand**   The high commission is at New Zealand House, 80 Haymarket at Pall Mall, SW1 (☎ **0171/930-8422;** Tube: Charing Cross or Piccadilly Circus); it's open Monday to Friday from 9am to 5pm.
- **The United States**   The embassy is located at 24 Grosvenor Sq., W1 (☎ **0171/499-9000;** Tube: Bond St.). For passport and visa information go to the U.S. Passport & Citizenship Unit, 55-56 Upper Brook St., W1 (☎ **0171/499-9000,** ext. 2563 or 2564; Tube: Marble Arch or Bond St.). Hours are Monday to Friday from 8:30am to 5:30pm.

Emergencies   For police, fire, or an ambulance, dial ☎ **999.**

Holidays   See "When to Go" in chapter 2.

Hospitals   The following offer emergency care in London 24 hours a day, with the first treatment free under the National Health Service: **Royal Free Hospital,** Pond Street, NW3 (☎ **0171/794-0500;** Tube: Belsize Park), and University College Hospital, Grafton Way, WC1 (☎ **0171/387-9300;** Tube: Warren St. or Euston Sq.). Many other London hospitals also have accident and emergency departments.

Hot Lines   For police or medical emergencies, dial ☎ **999** (no coins required). If you're in some sort of legal emergency, call **Release** at ☎ **0171/729-9904,** 24 hours a day. The Rape Crisis Line is ☎ **0171/837-1600,** accepting calls after 6pm. Samaritans, 46 Marshall St., W1 (☎ **0171/734-2800;** Tube: Oxford Circus or Piccadilly Circus), maintains a crisis hot line that helps with all kinds of trouble, even threatened suicides. Doors open from 9am to 9pm daily, but phones are 24 hours. Alcoholics Anonymous (☎ **0171/833-0022**) answers its hot line daily from 10am to 10pm. The AIDS 24-hour hot line is ☎**0800/567-123.**

Information   See "Visitor Information" in chapter 2 and "Orientation" earlier in this chapter.

Libraries   Westminster Reference Library, 35 St. Martin's St., WC2 (☎ **0171/641-2036;** Tube: Leicester Sq.), is one of London's best general reference public libraries, specializing in business, art and design, official publications, performing arts, and periodicals. Open Monday to Friday 10am to 8pm and Saturday 10am to 5pm.

Liquor Laws   No alcohol is served to anyone under 18. Children under 16 aren't allowed in pubs, except in certain rooms, and then only when accompanied by a parent or guardian. Don't drink and drive; penalties for drunk driving are stiff, even if you're an overseas visitor. Pubs are open Monday to Saturday from 11am to 11pm and Sunday noon to 10:30pm. Restaurants are allowed to serve liquor during the same hours as pubs; however, only people who are eating a meal on the premises can be served a drink. A meal, incidentally, is defined as "substantial refreshment," and you have to eat and drink sitting down. In hotels, liquor may be served from 11am to 11pm to both residents and nonresidents; after 11pm, only residents may be served.

Mail   An airmail letter to North America costs 43p (70¢) for 10 grams and postcards require a 39p (65¢) stamp; letters generally take 7 to 10 days to arrive from the United States. See "Post Offices" below for locations.

Maps   See "Finding Your Way Around" under "Orientation," earlier in this chapter.

Money   See "Money," in chapter 2.

Newspapers/Magazines   *The Times, Daily Telegraph, Daily Mail,* and *Guardian* are all dailies carrying the latest news. The *International Herald Tribune,* published in Paris, and an international edition of *USA Today,* beamed via satellite, are available daily. Copies of *Time* and *Newsweek* are also sold at most newsstands. Magazines such as *Time Out, City Limits,* and *Where* contain lots of useful information about the latest happenings in London.

Police   In an emergency, dial ☎ **999** (no coins required). You can also go to one of the local police branches in central London, including New Scotland Yard, Broadway, SW1 (☎ **0171/230-1212;** Tube: St. James's Park).

Post Offices   The main post office is at 24 William IV St. (☎ **0171/ 484-9307;** Tube: Charing Cross). It operates as three separate businesses: inland and international postal service and banking (open Mon to Fri 8am to 8pm, Sat 9am to 8pm); philatelic postage stamp sales (open Mon to Sat 8am to 8pm); and the post shop, selling greeting cards and stationery (open Mon to Sat from 8am to 8pm). Other post offices and sub–post offices are open Monday to Friday 9am to 5:30pm and on Saturday 9am to 12:30pm. Many sub–post offices and some main post offices close for an hour at lunchtime.

Radio   There are 24-hour radio channels operating throughout the United Kingdom, including London. They offer mostly pop music and chat shows at night. Some "pirate" radio stations add more spice. So-called legal FM stations are BBC1 (104.8), BBC2 (89.1), BBC3 (between 90 and 92), and the classical station BBC4 (95). There is also the BBC Greater London Radio (94.9) station, with lots of rock, plus LBC Crown (97.3), with news and reports of "what's on" in London. Pop/rock U.S. style is heard on Capital FM (95.8), and if you like jazz, reggae, or salsa, tune in to Choice FM (96.9). Jazz FM (102.2) also offers blues and big-band music.

Rest Rooms   They're marked by "Public Toilets" signs in streets, parks, and Tube stations; many are automatic, which are sterilized after each use. The English often call toilets "loos." You'll also find well-maintained lavatories that can be used by anybody in all larger public buildings, such as museums and art galleries, large department stores, and railway stations. It's not really acceptable to use the lavatories in hotels, restaurants, and pubs if you're not a customer, but we can't say that we always stick to this rule. Public lavatories are usually free, but you may need a small coin to get in or to use a proper washroom.

Smoking   Most U.S. cigarette brands are available in London. Antismoking laws are tougher than ever: Smoking is strictly forbidden in the Underground (on the cars and the platforms) and on buses, and it's increasingly frowned upon in many other places. But London still isn't a particularly friendly place for the nonsmoker. Most restaurants have no-smoking tables, but they're usually separated from the smoking section by only a little bit of space. No-smoking rooms are available in the bigger hotels. While some of the smaller hotels claim that they have no-smoking rooms, we've often found that this means that the room is smoke-free only during our visit; if you're bothered by the odor, ask to be shown another room.

Taxes   To encourage energy conservation, the British government levies a 25% tax on gasoline ("petrol"). There is also a 17.5% national value-added tax (VAT) that is added to all hotel and restaurant bills, and will be included in the price of many items you purchase. This can be refunded if you shop at stores that

A Change in London's Area Code

The two London city codes (171 and 181) are changing in the year 2000. They will be replaced by **20**, followed by an eight-digit number beginning with **7** (for the old 171 numbers) or **8** (for the old 181 numbers). The seven digits of the present numbers will remain unchanged. When calling from inside the United Kingdom, but outside London, use 020 followed by the new eight-digit number. (Example: For a number now dialed as **0171/533-7000,** you will dial **020/7533-7000.**) In London, dial the eight-digit number only. At press time, our information was that this change would begin in the summer of 1999, but that the old numbers would be in effect as well until June 2000.

participate in the Retail Export Scheme (signs are posted in the window). See the "How to Get Your VAT Refund" box in chapter 8.

In October 1994, Britain imposed a departure tax: £10 ($16.50) for flights within Britain and the European Union or £20 ($33) for passengers flying elsewhere, including to the United States. Your airline ticket may or may not include this tax. Ask in advance to avoid a surprise at the gate.

Taxis   See "Getting Around" earlier in this chapter.

Telephone   For directory assistance in London, dial ☎ **142;** for the rest of Britain, **192.** To call London from the United States, dial 011 (international code), 44 (Britain's country code), 171 or 181 (London's area codes), and the seven-digit local phone number. Note that these area codes will change in 2000; see the box above.

There are three types of public pay phones: those taking only coins, those accepting only phonecards (called Cardphones), and those taking both phonecards and credit cards. At coin-operated phones, insert your coins before dialing. The minimum charge is 10p (15¢).

Phonecards are available in four values—£2 ($3.30), £4 ($6.60), £10 ($16.50), and £20 ($33)—and are reusable until the total value has expired. Cards can be purchased from newsstands and post offices. Finally, the credit-call pay phone operates on credit cards—Access (MasterCard), Visa, American Express, and Diners Club—and is most common at airports and large railway stations.

Phone numbers in Britain outside of the major cities consist of an exchange name plus telephone number. To dial the number, you'll need the code of the exchange being called. Information sheets on call-box walls give the codes in most instances. If your code isn't there, call the operator by dialing 100.

In London, phone numbers consist of the exchange code and number (seven digits or more). These digits are all you need to dial if you are calling from within the same city. If you're calling from elsewhere, you will need to prefix them with the dialing code for the city. Again, you'll find these codes on the call-box information sheets or by dialing the operator (100).

To make an international call from London, dial the international access code (00), then the country code, then the area code, and finally the local number. Or call through one of the following long-distance access codes: **AT&T USA Direct** (☎ 0800/890011), **Canada Direct** (☎ 0800/890016), **Australia** (☎ 0800/890061), and **New Zealand** (☎ 0800/890064). Common country codes are: **USA and Canada,** 1; **Australia,** 61; **New Zealand,** 64; **South Africa,** 27.

Time   England follows Greenwich Mean Time (5 hours ahead of Eastern Standard Time). Most of the year, including the summer, Britain is 5 hours ahead of the time observed on the East Coast of the United States. Because the U.S. and Britain observe Daylight Savings Time at slightly different times of year, there's a brief period (about a week) in autumn when Britain is only 4 hours ahead of New York, and a brief period in spring when it's 6 hours ahead of New York.

Tipping   In restaurants, service charges in the 15% to 20% range are usually added to the bill. Sometimes this is clearly marked; at other times, it isn't. When in doubt, ask. If service isn't included, it's customary to add 15% to the bill. Sommeliers get about £1 ($1.65) per bottle of wine served. There's no tipping in pubs. In cocktail bars, the server usually gets about 75p ($1.25) per round of drinks.

Hotels, like restaurants, often add a service charge of 10% to 15% to most bills. In smaller B&Bs, the tip isn't likely to be included. Therefore, tip for special service, such as for the person who served you breakfast. If several persons have served you in a B&B, many guests ask that 10% or 15% be added to the bill and divided among the staff.

It's standard to tip taxi drivers 10% to 15% of the fare, although a tip for a taxi driver should never be less than 30p (50¢), even for a short run. Barbers and hairdressers expect 10% to 15%. Tour guides expect £2 ($3.30), although it's not mandatory. Today petrol (gas) station attendants are rarely tipped and theater ushers don't expect tips.

Travel Information   For travel in London, call ☎ **0171/222-1234,** 24 hours a day.

Weather   Call ☎ **0171/922-8844** for current weather information, but chances are the line will be busy.

Accommodations 4

With the millennium upon London, hoteliers face a new century with a daunting challenge. Will London have enough beds for the anticipated invasion of 30 million visitors in the year 2000? In the past, 28 million visitors have filled to bursting the city's hotels, B&Bs, and short-term apartment rentals.

The London Tourist Board campaigned to secure another 10,000 hotel rooms by 2000. That target will be met, but with few exceptions the newly opened hotels are in districts far from the center and most of them are of the no frills, efficient budget chain variety.

Some hoteliers have wisely decided to adapt former public or institutional buildings rather than start from scratch. For example, the imposing County Hall building in the S1 district now boasts two chains—a more luxurious Marriott and a leaner, meaner Travel Inn where rooms are modest indeed. Another trend is a shift away from the West End as the traditional hotel stamping ground to such salubrious sections of London as Greenwich (now a virtual suburb of London), the Docklands, and even the City (London's staid financial district).

With all the vast improvements and upgrades in the 1990s, chances are you'll like your room. What you won't like is the price, and that's almost guaranteed. Even if a hotel remains scruffy and shabby, London hoteliers, operating in a seller's market, have little embarrassment about jacking up prices. Hotels in all categories remain vastly overpriced as European capitals go.

As London observer Christopher Reynolds put it, "Looking for a really good price on a hotel room? Try Arizona in August, Alaska in February, or New York in about 1962. But if it's London you want to see, brace yourself." Face it—you're just going to pay more than you'd like for a hotel room in London.

London boasts some of the most famous hotels in the world—hallowed temples of luxury like Claridge's and the Dorchester as well as recent-vintage rivals like the Four Seasons—and they're all superlative. The problem (and it's a serious one) is that there are too many of them and not enough of the moderately priced options so typical of other European capitals.

Even at the luxury level, you might be surprised at what you don't get at a London hotel. Many of these stately Victorian and Edwardian gems are so steeped in tradition that they still lack many of the modern conveniences that are standard in the luxury hotels of, say, New York. Some have gone to no end to modernize, but others remain at Boer

War vintage. London does have some cutting-edge, chintz-free hotels that seem shifted bodily from Los Angeles—complete with high-end sound systems and gadget-filled marble baths—but they're not necessarily superior; what the others lack in streamlining and convenience, they frequently make up in personal service and spaciousness. It all depends on what you like.

In the 1990s, the opening of a number of new boutique hotels generated lots of excitement; each one seemed to outdazzle the one before. With their charm, intimate scale, and attention to detail, they're an attractive alternative to the larger, stuffier established names. As London faces the millennium, the boutiquing of the hotel scene continues; the city is currently offering more personally run and privately operated boutique hotels than ever before. We've surveyed the best of them for this edition, concentrating on the reasonably priced choices.

If you're looking for reasonable options, don't despair. London does have some good-value places in the lower price ranges, of which we've included the best. An affordable way to go is to book a **bed-and-breakfast.** At their best, they're clean, comfortable, and friendly. Currently, however, good B&Bs are in short supply; don't reserve a room at one without a recommendation you can trust. The following services will arrange a B&B room for you: **Bed & Breakfast** (☎ **800/367-4668** or 423/690-8484), **Worldwide Bed & Breakfast Association** (☎ **800/852-2632** in the United States, or 0181/742-9123; fax 0181/749-7084), and **The London Bed and Breakfast Agency Limited** (☎ **0171/586-2768;** fax 0171/586-6567), another reputable agency that can provide inexpensive accommodations in selected private homes. Prices range from £18 to £40 ($29.70 to $66) per person a night, based on double occupancy, although some will cost a lot more.

You can almost always get a room at a deluxe hotel if you're willing to pay the price. But during certain peak periods, including the high season (roughly April to October) and during certain trade shows, seasonal events, and royal occasions, rooms in all kinds of hotels may be snatched up early. Book ahead. If you arrive without a reservation, begin your search for a room as early in the day as possible. If you arrive late at night, you may have to take what you can get, often at a much higher price than you'd like to pay.

A NOTE ABOUT PRICES   Unless otherwise noted, prices are published rack prices for rooms with a private bathroom. Many include breakfast (often continental instead of English) and a 10% to 15% service charge. The British Government also imposes a VAT (value added tax) that adds 17.5% to your bill. This is not included in the prices quoted in the guide. Always ask for a better rate, particularly at the first-class and deluxe hotels (B&Bs generally charge a fixed rate). Parking rates are per night.

Please note that the rates published in this guide were correct at the time of printing, but could change at any time, particularly if London is so bursting at the seams in 2000 that hoteliers start raising their prices dramatically. We recommend that you use the prices presented here only as a guide to rate category, and confirm the latest and always changing prices directly with the hotel of your choice.

RATE REGULATIONS   All hotels, motels, inns, and guest houses in Britain with four bedrooms or more (including self-catering accommodations) must display notices showing minimum and maximum overnight charges. The notice must be displayed in a prominent position in the reception area or at the entrance. The prices shown must include any service charge and may include VAT, and it must be made clear whether these items are included; if VAT isn't included, then it must be shown separately. If meals are provided, this must be made clear, too. If prices aren't standard for all rooms, then only the lowest and highest prices need be given.

Area Code Change

After June of 2000, London's area code will become **020.** The present seven-digit numbers will not change, but all 0171 numbers will add a "7" and all 0181 will add an "8." See the box in chapter 3 for more details.

A FEW REMINDERS

- Elevators are called "**lifts.**" Some of them predate Teddy Roosevelt's Rough Riders, and act it. They are, however, regularly inspected and completely safe.
- Hotel rooms are somewhat cooler than elsewhere; it's supposed to be more healthful that way. However, London has had some hot summers in the last few years. If you're coming in the summer months and expect hotter-than-usual weather, don't assume your hotel, even if you're booked at the luxury level, has central air; many have only partial A/C or none at all. Check if this is a concern for you.
- What's termed a **continental breakfast** consists of coffee or tea and some sort of roll or pastry. An **English breakfast** is a fairly lavish, traditionally hearty meal of tea or coffee, cereal, eggs, bacon, ham or sausage, toast, and jam.
- If you want to remain undisturbed, don't forget to hang the "Do Not Disturb" sign on your doorknob. English hotel service personnel—most of whom aren't English—have a disconcerting habit of bursting in simultaneously with their knock.

TIPS FOR SAVING ON YOUR HOTEL ROOM

The rack rate is the maximum rate that a hotel charges for a room. It's the rate you'd get if you walked in off the street and asked for a room for the night. Hardly anybody pays these prices, however, and there are many ways around them.

- **Don't be afraid to bargain.** Get in the habit of asking for a lower price than the first one quoted. Be aware that you may not get it, particularly in the busy summer season or during certain trade fairs, when practically every room in the city is booked. You can sometimes negotiate a 20 to 30% discount in winter. Most rack rates include commissions of 10% to 25% or more for travel agents, which many hotels will cut if you make your own reservations and haggle a bit. It never hurts to ask. Always ask politely whether a less expensive room is available, or whether any special rates apply to you. You may qualify for corporate, student, military, senior citizen, or other discounts. Be sure to mention membership in AAA, AARP, frequent flyer programs, or trade unions, which may entitle you to special deals as well. Sometimes hotels may offer "spot specials," which may be cheaper still.
- **Rely on a qualified professional.** Certain hotels give travel agents discounts in exchange for steering business their way, so if you're shy about bargaining, an agent may be better equipped to negotiate discounts for you. In most cases travel agents have access to wholesale rates which can be significantly less expensive than hotel rack rates.
- **Dial direct.** When booking a room in a chain hotel, call the hotel's local line, as well as the toll-free number, and see where you get the best deal. A hotel makes nothing on a room that stays empty. The clerk who runs the place is more likely to know about vacancies and will often grant deep discounts in order to fill up.
- **Remember the law of supply and demand.** Business hotels in downtown locations are busiest during the week; expect discounts over the weekend. Avoid

high-season stays whenever you can; planning your vacation just a week before or after official peak season can mean big savings.

- **Look into group or long-stay discounts.** If you come as part of a large group, you should be able to negotiate a bargain, since the hotel can then guarantee occupancy in a number of rooms. Likewise, when you're planning a long stay in town (usually from five days to a week) you'll qualify for a discount. As a general rule, you will receive one night free after a seven-night stay.
- **Avoid excess charges.** When you book a room, ask whether the hotel charges for parking. Most hotels have free, available space, but many urban hotels don't. Also, find out before you dial whether your hotel imposes a surcharge on local or long-distance calls. A pay phone, however inconvenient, may save you money.
- **Watch for coupons and advertised discounts.** Scan ads in your local Sunday travel section, an excellent source for up-to-the-minute hotel deals.
- **Consider a suite.** If you are traveling with your family or another couple, you can pack more people into a suite (which usually comes with a sofa bed), and thereby reduce your per-person rate. Remember that some places charge for extra guests; some don't.
- **Book an efficiency.** A room with a kitchenette allows you to grocery shop and eat some meals in. Especially during long stays with families, you're bound to save money on food this way.
- **Investigate reservation services.** These outfits usually work as consolidators, buying up or reserving rooms in bulk, and then dealing them out to customers at a profit. They do garner special deals that range from 10% to 50% off; but remember, these discounts apply to rack rates. You're probably better off dealing directly with a hotel, but if you don't like bargaining, this is certainly a viable option. Most of them offer online reservation services as well. Here are a few of the more reputable providers.

Accommodations Express (☎ 800/950-4685; www.accommodationsxpress.com); **Hotel Reservations Network** (☎ 800/96HOTEL; www.180096HOTEL.com); **Quikbook** (☎ 800/789-9887, includes fax-on-demand service; www.quikbook. com); and **Room Exchange** (☎ 800/846-7000 in the United States, 800/486-7000 in Canada).

At the inexpensive end, **Hostelling International/American Youth Hostels,** 733 15th St. NW, Suite 840, Washington, DC 20005 (☎ **800/444-6111** or 202/ 783-6161), offers a directory of low-cost accommodations around the country and abroad.

Online, try booking your hotel through **Arthur Frommer's Budget Travel** (www. frommers.com), and save up to 50% on the cost of your room. **Microsoft Expedia** (www.expedia.com) features a "Travel Agent" that will also direct you to affordable lodgings.

LANDING THE BEST ROOM

Somebody has to get the best room in the house. It might as well be you.

Always ask for a corner room. They're usually larger, quieter, and closer to the elevator. They often have more windows and light than standard rooms, and they don't always cost more.

When you make your reservation, ask if the hotel is renovating; if it is, request a room away from the renovation work. Many hotels now offer no-smoking rooms; if smoke bothers you, by all means ask for one. Inquire, too, about the location of the restaurants, bars, and discos in the hotel—these could all be a source of irritating noise. If you aren't happy with your room when you arrive, talk to the front desk. If they have another room, they should be happy to accommodate you, within reason.

1   West End Hotels

MAYFAIR
VERY EXPENSIVE

✪ **Brown's Hotel.** 29–34 Albemarle St., London W1X 4BP. ☎ **0171/493-6020.** Fax 0171/493-9381. www.brownshotel.com. E-mail: brownshotel@ukbusiness.com. 118 units. A/C MINIBAR TV TEL. £265–£285 ($437.25–$470.25) double; from £415 ($684.75) suite. AE, DC, MC, V. Off-site parking £32 ($52.80). Tube: Green Park.

Almost every year a hotel sprouts up trying to evoke an English country house ambience with Chippendale and chintz; this quintessential town-house hotel watches these competitors come and go, and always comes out on top. Brown's was founded by James Brown, a former manservant of Lord Byron's, who knew the tastes of well-bred gentlemen and wanted to create a dignified, club-like place for them. He opened its doors in 1837, the same year Queen Victoria took the throne.

Brown's, which occupies 14 historic houses just off Berkeley Square, is still a thorough realization of its founder's vision. The guest rooms vary considerably and are a tangible record of England's history, showing restrained taste in decoration and appointments; even the washbasins are antiques. Accommodations, which range in size from small to extra spacious, have such extras as voice mail, dual-phone lines, and data ports; each is equipped with a luxurious mattress, even if the bed is antique. Bathrooms come in a variety of sizes, but are beautifully equipped with robes, luxurious cosmetics, hair dryers, and a rack of fluffy towels. In keeping with the atmosphere of the rest of the hotel, the inviting lounges pay homage to the past: They include the Roosevelt Room (Theodore Roosevelt spent his honeymoon at Brown's in 1886), the Rudyard Kipling Room (the famous author was a frequent visitor), and the paneled St. George's Bar for the drinking of spirits.

Dining: The dining room has a quiet dignity and unmatched service. Afternoon tea is served in the **Albemarle Room.** See "Teatime," in chapter 5.

Amenities: 24-hour room service, dry cleaning and laundry service, baby-sitting, secretarial services, valet, men's hairdresser, tour desk, business center; health club nearby.

Claridge's. Brook St., London W1A 2JQ. ☎ **800/223-6800** or 0171/629-8860. Fax 0171/409-6335. E-mail: info@claridges.co.uk. 190 units. A/C MINIBAR TV TEL. £320–£335 ($528–$552.75) double; suites from £450 ($742.50). AE, DC, MC, V. Tube: Bond St.

This is *the* hotel for *Pax Britannia* nostalgists. Although other upper-crust addresses conjure up images of Empire, nobody does it better than Claridge's, which has cocooned royal visitors in an ambience of discreet elegance since the time of the Battle of Waterloo. This is stuffy British formality at its appealing best: As a reviewer once wrote, the "staff here will never try to be your friends"—as they might at, say, the Dorchester.

The hotel took on its present modest exterior in 1898. Inside, an art deco look was added in the 1930s; much of it still exists agreeably alongside antiques and TVs. The guest rooms are spacious, many with generous-size bathrooms complete with dressing rooms and other extras. About half the units are in a chic art deco style, the others more in a classic English vein. Tasteful fabrics and extremely comfortable beds with state-of-the-art mattresses and quality linens are in each unit, along with double glazing, private safes, call buttons, and mirrored closets, plus dual-line phones with

West End Hotels

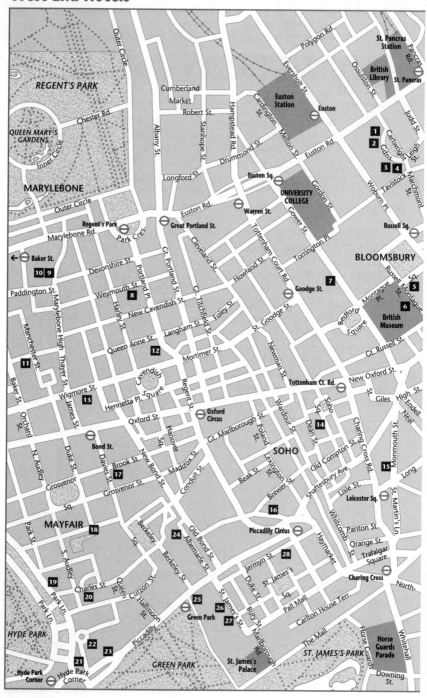

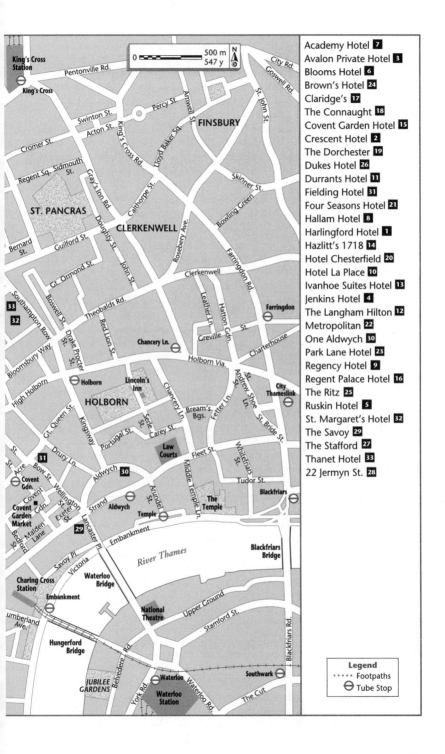

Academy Hotel **7**
Avalon Private Hotel **3**
Blooms Hotel **6**
Brown's Hotel **24**
Claridge's **17**
The Connaught **18**
Covent Garden Hotel **15**
Crescent Hotel **2**
The Dorchester **19**
Dukes Hotel **26**
Durrants Hotel **11**
Fielding Hotel **31**
Four Seasons Hotel **21**
Hallam Hotel **8**
Harlingford Hotel **1**
Hazlitt's 1718 **14**
Hotel Chesterfield **20**
Hotel La Place **10**
Ivanhoe Suites Hotel **13**
Jenkins Hotel **4**
The Langham Hilton **12**
Metropolitan **22**
One Aldwych **30**
Park Lane Hotel **23**
Regency Hotel **9**
Regent Palace Hotel **16**
The Ritz **25**
Ruskin Hotel **5**
St. Margaret's Hotel **32**
The Savoy **29**
The Stafford **27**
Thanet Hotel **33**
22 Jermyn St. **28**

Legend
····· Footpaths
⊖ Tube Stop

data ports. Most of the rooms are air conditioned. The combination shower and tub baths have been called "sybaritic," with tubs big enough for the late Churchill to float in, and water pressure with the force of a fire hydrant. Everything lush and plush is here from the thick towels to the deluxe toiletries, from the hair dryers to the big robes. The emphasis is on old-fashioned room layouts instead of modern comforts, so you may feel embarrassed if you check in without your valet, à la Prince Charles.

Dining: Excellent food is stylishly served in the intimacy of the **Causerie,** renowned for its lunchtime smorgasbord and pre-theater suppers, and the more formal **Restaurant,** with English and French specialties. The strains of the Hungarian Quartet, a Claridge's institution since 1902, can be heard in the adjacent foyer during lunch and dinner.

Amenities: 24-hour room service, valet, laundry service, baby-sitting, on-call physician, concierge, currency exchange, basic secretarial services, salon, travel and theater desk, health club.

The Connaught. Carlos Place, W1Y 6AL. ☎ **0171/499-7070.** Fax 0171/495-3262. www.savoy_group.co.uk. E-mail: info@the_connaught.co.uk. 90 units. A/C TV TEL. £335–£395 ($552.75–$651.75) double; from £630 ($1,039.50) suite. AE, DC, MC, V. Parking £32 ($52.80). Tube: Green Park.

This elegant hotel evoking an English country house and siting in the heart of May-fair is one of Europe's most prestigious addresses. Not the most glamorous, nor even the most fashionable hotel in London, it nonetheless coddles you in comfort and luxury, with a hospitality that's legendary and guarantees privacy even if you're a film star sex symbol. Near Grosvenor Square, this brick-built house is somewhat like a club, many repeat guests demanding their favorite room. You enter a world of fresh flowers, crystal chandeliers, Wedgwood, and antiques. There is something of an aura of aristocratic decay here, just as the country gentry like it.

Rooms range from medium to large, and are a world of antiques, chintz, tasteful appointments such as gilt-trimmed white paneling, and sumptuous beds with grand mattresses and the finest of Irish linen bed clothing. Marble fireplaces, ornate plasterwork, and oak paneling add to its allure. The large, old-fashioned baths are still intact, and are outfitted with robes, a hair dryer, and thick fluffy towels.

Dining/Diversions: The on-site **Grill Connaught Restaurant,** with its mahogany paneling, and the smaller Georgian-style **Grill Room** are among the premier dining venues of London. Under the guidance of chef Michel Bourdin, they both offer the same menu but may have different daily specials. Classical French dishes and old-fashioned English cookery are combined to entice tout London. Yes, they still serve Irish stew on Tuesday, but they can also dazzle with the finest haute cuisine of the Escoffier tradition. One loyal patron who comes here twice a week to dine told us, "I picked up the habit from my great-grandfather." The bar and lounges appear as if waiting for the arrival of an ambassador.

Amenities: Concierge, 24-hour room service, dry cleaning and laundry service, baby-sitting, access to nearby health club.

✪ **The Dorchester.** 53 Park Lane, London W1A 2HJ. ☎ **800/727-9820** or 0171/629-8888. Fax 0171/409-0114. E-mail: info@dorchesterhotel.com. 248 units. A/C MINIBAR TV TEL. £295–£325 ($486.75–$536.25) double; from £415 ($684.75) suite. AE, DC, MC, V. Parking £27 ($44.55). Tube: Hyde Park Corner or Marble Arch.

This is among the best of today's London hotels. It has all the elegance of Claridge's, but without the upper-crust attitude that can verge on snobbery. Few hotels have the time-honored experience of "The Dorch," which has maintained a tradition of fine comfort and cuisine since it opened its doors in 1931.

Breaking from the neoclassical tradition, the most ambitious architects of the era designed a building of reinforced concrete clothed in terrazzo slabs. Within you'll find a 1930s take on Regency motifs: The monumental arrangements of flowers and the elegance of the gilded-cage promenade seem appropriate for a diplomatic reception, yet convey a kind of comfort in which guests from all over the world feel at ease.

The Dorchester boasts guest rooms outfitted with Irish linen sheets on deluxe mattresses, plus all the electronic gadgetry you'd expect, and double- and triple-glazed windows to keep out noise, along with plump armchairs, cherrywood furnishings, and, in many cases, four-poster beds piled high with pillows. The large bathrooms are equally stylish, with mottled carrara marble and Lalique-style sconces, plus hair dryers, thick towels, makeup mirrors, and posh toiletries. The best rooms open onto views of Hyde Park.

Dining: The hotel's restaurant, **The Grill Room,** is among the finest dining establishments in London, and the **Dorchester Bar** is a legendary meeting place. The promenade, with its glorious lush sofas, is the ideal setting to enjoy afternoon tea and watch the world go by. The hotel also offers Cantonese cuisine at **The Oriental,** London's most exclusive—and expensive—Chinese restaurant.

Amenities: 24-hour room service, dry cleaning and laundry service, one of the best-outfitted health clubs in London, the Dorchester Spa, barbershop, hairdresser, tour desk, secretarial services, and baby-sitting.

Four Seasons Hotel. Hamilton Place, Park Lane, London W1A 1AZ. ☎ **800/332-3442** or 0171/499-0888. Fax 0171/493-1895. www.fshr.com E-mail: fshl@4seasons.com 247 units. A/C MINIBAR TV TEL. £305–£315 ($503.25–$519.75) double; £440 ($726) conservatory double; from £550 ($907.50) suite. AE, DC, MC, V. Parking £15 ($24.75). Tube: Hyde Park Corner.

This deluxe hostelry has captured the imagination of glamor-mongers the world over ever since it was inaugurated by Princess Alexandra in 1970; its clientele include heads of state, superstars, and top-brass business execs. The hotel sits behind a tastefully modern facade, at a premier location in one of the most exclusive neighborhoods in the world. It's directly opposite its major competitors, the London Hilton and the Inter-Continental—but it has better food, better rooms, more style, and more taste and refinement than either of its rivals. Inside, acres of superbly crafted paneling and opulent but conservative decor create the impression that the hotel is far older than it is. The guest rooms are large and beautifully outfitted with well-chosen chintz, reproductions, plush upholstery, and dozens of well-concealed electronic extras. Most rooms are medium size, although some are quite large, and maintained in state-of-the-art condition, with plenty of desk space, TV/VCRs, and often have tall windows opening to stand-up balconies. Mattresses are of the finest quality, as are the bed linens. Bathrooms are good size with thought-out extras such as hair dryers, robes, deluxe toiletries, and a big set of fluffy towels.

Dining/Diversions: Lanes Restaurant is modern, trendy, offering some fine hotel dining from an international menu. Tables are arranged for grand views of Park Lane. There is also a cocktail bar and a downstairs lounge where a traditional English tea is served.

Amenities: 24-hour room service, valet, laundry service, baby-sitting, quality shops, theater-reservations desk, Conservatory fitness club, with all the latest equipment, garden, car-rental agency, business services available around the clock.

Metropolitan. 19 Old Park Lane, London W1Y 4LB. ☎ **1071/447-1000.** Fax 0171/447-1100. www.metropolitan.co.uk. E-mail: sales@metropolitan.co.uk. 155 units. A/C MINIBAR TV TEL. £265–£300 ($437.25–$495) double; £320 ($528) studio suite; £340–£395

($561–$651.75) city studio suite; £445–£515 ($734.25–$849.75) park suite; £650–£1,200 ($1,072.50–$1,980) deluxe suite; £1,400–£1,700 ($2,310–$2,805) penthouse. AE, DC, DISC, MC, V. Tube: Hyde Park Corner.

The Metropolitan, smack dab between the Hilton and the Four Seasons, is the first hotel to open on Park Lane since the heady eighties. Unlike some of its opulent neighbors, minimalism is the word here. Designer Keith Hobbs believes in understatement, a style he perfected at Dublin's Clarence hotel. His staff uniforms are a far cry from the top hats and tails seen at some of the posh nests nearby.

The Metropolitan is graced with hardwood floors, marbles, and natural fabrics. Simple elegance is the code word for the bedrooms here, the most desirable of which open onto views of Hyde Park. Bedrooms have moleskin covers and cushions in soothing pastels, and wood furnishings—spare, functional, yet luxurious in a way. The good-size bedrooms have three dual-line phones with voice mail and data ports, twice-daily housekeeping, and king- or queen-size beds with deluxe mattresses, plus medium-size bathrooms with hair dryers, fluffy towels, robes, and luxurious toilet articles. Its owner Christina Ong is already a hotel legend in London, having opened, among other properties, the deluxe Halkin in 1991. Her clientele are the young and well heeled, patrons who value style and a lively atmosphere. The place is a relaxing retreat with wood and leather sofas, a carved stone clock in the pale marble lobby, and cool blue-patterned rugs.

Dining: An all-white skylit breakfast room, open to residents only, sets the tone for the day. The on-site Japanese restaurant and sushi bar, a twin to New York's **Nobu,** is one of the chic dining rendezvous of London. A late-night bar club has a modern-cum-fifties aura with frosted glass and metal tables.

Amenities: In-room fax machines, VCRs available on request, 24-hour room service, concierge, dry cleaning and laundry service, massage, baby-sitting, secretarial services, express checkout, health club.

✪ **Park Lane Hotel.** Piccadilly, London W1Y 8BX. ☎ **800/325-3535** or 0171/499-6321. Fax 0171/499-1965. www.sheraton.com. 305 units. A/C MINIBAR TV TEL. £260 ($429) double; from £360 ($594) suite. AE, DC, MC, V. Parking £28 ($46.20). Tube: Hyde Park Corner or Green Park.

The most traditional of the Park Lane mansions, and once the lone holdout against chain management, the Park Lane Hotel was sold in 1996 to the Sheraton Corporation, which upgraded it but maintained its quintessential Britishness. Launched in 1913 but kept empty for years, the Park Lane finally opened in 1924 under the leadership of Bracewell Smith, one of London's leading hoteliers. Today, its Silver Entrance remains an art deco marvel that has been used as a backdrop in many films, including the classic BBC miniseries *Brideshead Revisited.*

Designed in a U shape, with a view overlooking Green Park, the hotel offers luxurious accommodations that are a surprisingly good deal—they're among the least expensive on Park Lane. Many of the suites have marble fireplaces and original marble bathrooms. The rooms have benefited from an impressive refurbishment—they're larger, and the decor is lighter in tone. All have double-glazed windows to block out noise.

Some bedrooms are larger and better appointed than others, with higher ceilings and taller windows. In the more deluxe rooms, you get trouser presses and better views. The most tranquil rooms open onto the rear, but those opening onto the court are dark. Mattresses have been renewed and are deluxe. Bathrooms are generally spacious and well equipped with fluffy towels and hair dryers; many units also have robes.

Dining/Diversions: On-site is a **Brasserie,** serving French cuisine. A harpist plays in the **Palm Court Lounge** every Sunday and tea is served daily. For more information, see "Teatime" in chapter 5.

Amenities: 24-hour room service, concierge, dry cleaning and laundry service, baby-sitting, secretarial services, fitness center, beauty salon, business center, safety-deposit boxes, gift and newspaper shop, barbershop, women's salon, and Daniele Ryman Aromatherapy Shop.

EXPENSIVE

Hotel Chesterfield. 35 Charles St., London W18 LX. ☎ **0171/491-2622.** Fax 0171/491-4793. E-mail: reservations@chesterfield.viewinn.co.uk. 110 units. A/C MINIBAR TV TEL. £190 ($313.50) double; from £350 ($577.50) suite. AE, DC, MC, V. Tube: Green Park.

The owners of this Mayfair hotel take great pride and care in their decorative techniques: Each bedroom contains some form of rich-looking accessories, or an antique or two, or some kind of artifact which might remind you of what you'd find in a private, and rather stately, English home. The site that contains all this was composed in the early 1970s by interconnecting a trio of brick-fronted town houses, one of which functioned for many years as the London home of the Earl of Chesterfield. Inside, the plaster moldings of the building's original construction, the glossy paneling, the air of Victorian respectability, and the easy access to Berkeley Square form part of the allure. Upstairs, a labyrinth of carefully decorated hallways, each with crooks and angles that correspond to the latter-day linkage among the three buildings, leads to the well-decorated bedrooms. These small but comfortable bedrooms are traditionally styled with solid hardwood furniture and bright contemporary fabrics, including such extras as a trouser press in some units. Only a few have private safes. Bathrooms are well appointed with combination tub and shower, robes, sachets of potpourri, fluffy towels, and a hair dryer.

Dining/Diversions: Dickens would feel right at home in the dark, clubby bar. It has a glass-domed patio if you'd like more light. On every night except Sunday, you can listen to a pianist and a singer; there's even a small dance floor. There's a good restaurant on the premises, open daily for lunch and dinner, serving a British and continental cuisine.

Amenities: Room service, laundry, Internet access in every room.

INEXPENSIVE

Ivanhoe Suite Hotel. 1 St. Christopher's Place, Barrett St. Piazza, London W1M 5HB. ☎ **0171/935-1047.** Fax 0171/224-0563. www.scoot.co.uk/ivanhoe_suite_hotel. 8 units. MINIBAR TV TEL. £79 ($130.35) double; £89 ($146.85) triple. Rates include continental breakfast. AE, DC, MC, V. Tube: Bond St.

Born-to-shop buffs flock to this little hidden discovery located in a part of town off Oxford Street not known for its hotels. "It's like having my own little flatlet every time I come to London," one satisfied guest told us. "If you dare tell anybody about it, I might have to get out the old horse whip or at least scold you." Situated above a restaurant on a pedestrian street of boutiques and restaurants and close to the shop-flanked New and Old Bond streets, this town-house hotel has attractively furnished small and medium-size singles and doubles, each with a sitting area. Each stylish room has its own entry, security video, trouser press, and beverage-making facilities along with a fridge/bar, plus a wide selection of videotapes. Its bedrooms were redecorated in 1998, the mattresses renewed. The newly tiled baths are small—half with a shower, half with a tub-shower combination, plus hair dryers, and a rack of medium-size towels. Breakfast is served in a very small area at the top of the first flight of stairs, and you can stop off for a nightcap at the corner pub, a real neighborhood locale. The Ivanhoe offers a number of services including room service, baby-sitting, secretarial service, laundry, and sightseeing tour and theater reservations. *Note:* The four-floor hotel doesn't have an elevator.

MARYLEBONE

To locate these hotels, see the map, "Marylebone, Paddington, Bayswater & Notting Hill Gate Hotels" on pp. 108.

VERY EXPENSIVE

⚙ The Langham Hilton. 1 Portland Place, London W1N 4JA. ☎ **0171/636-1000.** Fax 0171/323-2340. www.hilton.com. 379 units. A/C MINIBAR TV TEL. £280 ($462) double; £365 ($602.25) executive room; from £670 ($1,105.50) suite. Rates include breakfast for executive room and suite. AE, DC, MC, V. Tube: Oxford Circus.

When this extremely well-located hotel was inaugurated in 1865 by the Prince of Wales, it was a suitably fashionable address for aristocrats seeking respite from their country estates. After it was bombed in World War II, it languished as dusty office space for the BBC until the early 1990s, when Hilton International took it over. Its restoration was painstaking; today, it's Hilton's European flagship. The Langham's public rooms reflect the power and majesty of the British Empire at its apex. Guest rooms are somewhat less opulent, but they're still attractively furnished and comfortable, featuring French provincial furniture and red oak trim. Major refurbishment to the bedrooms was carried out in 1999 to be ready for the millennium. Mattresses are of extremely high quality, and the small bathrooms contain hair dryers, robes, trouser presses, and an array of fluffy towels. And the location is still terrific: within easy reach of Mayfair and Soho restaurants and theaters and Oxford and Regent Street shopping; Regent's Park is just blocks away.

   Dining/Diversions: Vodka, caviar, and champagne flow liberally at the **Tsar's Russian Bar and Restaurant.** Drinks are served in the **Chukka Bar,** a re-creation of a private polo club. The most upscale restaurant is a high-ceilinged Victorian fantasy called **Memories,** featuring patriotic nostalgia and cuisine from the far corners of the British Commonwealth. Afternoon tea is served amid the potted palms of the Edwardian-style **Palm Court.**

   Amenities: 24-hour room service, concierge, health club, business center, beauty salon.

Landmark London. 222 Marylebone Rd., London NW1 6JQ. ☎ **800/457-4000** or 0171/631-8000. Fax 0171/631-8080. www.landmarklondon.co.uk. 302 units. A/C MINIBAR TV TEL. £290–£360 ($478.50–$594) double; from £360 ($594) suite. AE, DC, MC, V. Tube: Marylebone or Baker St.

Some hotels in London come with a ghost. This one just has a secret—it's the least expensive luxury hotel in London. Great corporate and promotional rates make it a real find for those in need of five-star luxury (almost nobody pays the rack rates here; ask, and you'll do better). It's also fabulously located, particularly if you're traveling with children: Madame Tussaud's is a half block away, and the Sherlock Holmes house is just a short walk.

   This was the finest Victorian railway hotel in England when it opened in 1899, and millions of dollars of renovations have recently restored it to its former glory. The rooms are some of London's largest, and they come with grand marble bathrooms, blond-wood furnishings, and modern paintings. The decor is on the level of the Four Seasons, with such extras as fax machines, plus king-size beds with high-quality mattresses. Most of the baths have combined shower stalls and tubs along with a hair dryer and fluffy towels. Half the rooms overlook a soaring eight-story central courtyard known as the Winter Garden, where you can dine amid palm trees.

   Dining/Diversions: The cuisine—international, with an emphasis at times on the Mediterranean or Far East—is most recommendable, served rather formally in **The**

Dining Room or casually in the **Winter Garden.** You can also come here for after-noon tea: It's not as good as the Ritz, but, chances are, you won't be able to get a reservation at the Ritz anyway. **The Cellar's Bar** is a favorite retreat for a pint.

Amenities: 24-hour room service, concierge, dry cleaning and laundry service, in-room massage, baby-sitting, express checkout, valet parking, large health club, indoor pool, access to tennis courts, business center, conference facilities, VCR on request.

EXPENSIVE

❂ **Dorset Square Hotel.** 39-40 Dorset Sq., London NW1 6QN. ☎ **0171/723-7874.** Fax 0171/724-3328. www.firmdale.com. E-mail: Dorset@afirmdale.com. 38 units. MINIBAR TV TEL. £130–£195 ($214.50–$321.75) double; suites from £215 ($354.75). AE, MC, V. Parking £25 ($41.25). Tube: Baker St. or Marylebone.

Situated in a lovely Regency Square steps away from Regent's Park, this is one of London's best and most stylish "house hotels," overlooking Thomas Lord's first cricket pitch. Hot hoteliers Tim and Kit Kemp have furnished the interior of these two Georgian town houses in a comfy mix of antiques, reproductions, and chintz that will make you feel like you're in an elegant private home. All the impressive guest rooms come with marble baths; about half are air-conditioned. All units are decorated in a personal yet extravagantly beautiful style—the owners are interior decorators known for their taste, which is often bold and daring. Eight offer crown-canopied beds, but all have firm and very high-quality mattresses. The baths are exquisite in taste with robes, hair dryers, and fluffy towels.

Dining: The menu at the **Potting Shed** changes seasonally and features the best of English cuisine as well as a wide selection of champagnes and wines. The restaurant occupies an old servants' hall, with a trompe l'oeil mural of a cricket pitch and a sisal-decked floor.

Amenities: 24-hour room service, baby-sitting, dry cleaning and laundry service, massage, and secretarial services. You can ride in the owner's chauffeured vintage Bentley for a fee; it'll make you feel like Norma Desmond in *Sunset Boulevard*.

The Leonard. 15 Seymour St., London W1H 5AA. ☎ **0171/935-2010.** Fax 0171/935-6700. E-mail: the.leonard@dial.pipex.com. 31 units. TV TEL. £180 ($297) double; £225–£390 ($371.25–$643.50) suite. AE, DC, MC, V. Tube: Marble Arch.

One of the newest boutique hotels in the vicinity of Marble Arch was created in 1996. A quartet of adjacent 17th-century Georgian town houses have been combined into a coherent whole. Today, the hotel presents a seamless, white-fronted façade to the rest of London, and offers residents a tasteful combination of genuine antiques and antique reproductions. Bedrooms have double-glazed windows to keep out street noises, a wallpapered décor that in every case is different from that of its neighbor, bathrooms trimmed with marble, and, in some cases, rooms with working fireplaces. Each unit has a VCR and hi-fi stereo system. Suites outnumber standard doubles here three to one. Those on the second floor are real gems, just waiting for Edward VII to check in. All mattresses are deluxe, and some beds are ornate with draped fabric copiously swagged over them. The bathrooms are tucked into the corner of the rooms and come complete with gleaming chrome fixtures, power showers, fluffy towels, luxurious toiletries, and basins countersunk into marble counters.

Dining: There's no restaurant, but a 24-hour cafe near the reception serves sandwiches and simple platters.

Amenities: Concierge; small-scale exercise room, surveying the rooftops of St. Marylebone from its top-floor aerie.

MODERATE

Bryanston Court Hotel. 56–60 Great Cumberland Place, London W1H 7FD. ☎ **0171/ 262-3141.** Fax 0171/262-7248. www.bryanstonhotel.com. E-mail: hotel@bryanstonhotel. com. 54 units. TV TEL. £110 ($181.50) double; £125 ($206.25) triple. Rates include continental breakfast. AE, DC, MC, V. Tube: Marble Arch.

This hotel is ideally located in a neighborhood with many lovely squares. Three individual houses were cleverly joined to form the hotel about two centuries ago. Today, it's one of the finest moderately priced hotels in the area, thanks to the refurbishing and maintenance efforts of the Theodore family. Family owned and operated, it offers bedrooms that, although small, are comfortably furnished and well maintained, with good mattresses. Bathrooms are small, but adequate for the job, with medium-size towels. *Warning:* Don't let them send you down to the basement room, or you'll feel like Cinderella before she met Prince Charming.

On chilly nights, we like to retreat to the bar, in the rear of a comfortable lounge, and relax with a pint in front of the roaring fireplace. Your hosts are happy to arrange theater and tour bookings for you.

Durrants Hotel. George St., London W1H 6BJ. ☎ **0171/935-8131.** Fax 0171/487-3510. 92 units. TV TEL. £135–£180 ($222.75–$297) double; £175 ($288.75) family room for 3; from £275 ($453.75) suite. AE, MC, V. Tube: Bond St.

This historic hotel off Manchester Square (established in 1789) with its Georgian-detailed facade is snug, cozy, and traditional—almost like a poor man's Brown's. We find it to be one of the most quintessentially English of all London hotels and a soothing retreat on a cold, rainy day. In the 100 years that the Miller family has owned the hotel, several neighboring houses have been incorporated into the original structure. A walk through the pine-and-mahogany-paneled public rooms is like stepping back into another time: You'll even find an 18th-century letter-writing room. The rooms are rather bland except for elaborate cove moldings and very comfortable furnishings, including good beds. They exude an aura of solidity; some are air-conditioned. Alas, all of them are small. Bathrooms are also tiny, but nearly all of them have both tubs and showers, but not much room to maneuver around. Each has a set of medium-size towels, but few other amenities except a bidet.

The in-house restaurant serves full afternoon tea and satisfying French or traditional English cuisine in one of the most beautiful Georgian rooms in the neighborhood. The less formal breakfast room is ringed with 19th-century political cartoons by a noted Victorian artist. The pub, a neighborhood favorite, has Windsor chairs, an open fireplace, and decor that hasn't changed much in two centuries. Services include 24-hour room service, laundry service, and baby-sitting.

Hotel La Place. 17 Nottingham Place, London W1M 3FF. ☎ **0171/486-2323.** Fax 0171/486-4335. www.hotellaplace.com. E-mail: reservations@hotellaplace.com. 21 units. MINIBAR TV TEL. £95–£115 ($156.75–$189.75) double; from £125 ($206.25) suite. Rates include English breakfast. AE, CB, DC, MC, V. Parking £8.50 ($14). Tube: Baker St.

This elegantly furnished West End town house gets lots of write-ups as a safe haven for women. Actually, it's a safe haven—and a good bet—for anyone. One of the most desirable hotels north of Oxford Street, in the vicinity of Madame Tussaud's and Baker Street (of Sherlock Holmes fame), this Victorian-era building is similar to many others, on a decent street of no particular charm. What makes it exceptional is that it's been completely refurbished inside and is now one of London's better B&Bs for the price. "Discreet and lovely," is how one guest described it, and we agree. Bedrooms are done in Laura Ashley style, with traditional furnishings. Tall windows are opulently swagged and draped. Rooms are moderate in size—not cramped—and each contains such amenities as coffeemakers, orthopedic mattresses, with hair dryers and medium-size towels in the tiled bathrooms. For such a small hotel, there are a surprising number of services, including concierge, room service, dry cleaning and laundry service, and baby-sitting. Instead of a dreary little cafe, you get **Jardin,** a chic, intimate wine bar and restaurant with an indoor/outdoor atmosphere and good food and drink.

INEXPENSIVE

Boston Court Hotel. 26 Upper Berkeley St., Marble Arch, London W1H 7PF. ☎ **0171/ 723-1445.** Fax 0171/262-8823. 13 units. TV TEL. £55 ($90.75) double with shower only, £69–£75 ($113.85–$123.75) double with bath; £79–£85 ($130.35–$140.25) triple with bath. Rates include continental breakfast. MC, V. Tube: Marble Arch.

Upper Berkeley is a classic street of B&Bs; in days of yore, it was a prestigious address, home to Elizabeth Montagu (1720–1800), "queen of the bluestockings," who defended Shakespeare against attacks by Voltaire. Today, it's a good, safe, respectable retreat at an affordable price. This unfrilly hotel offers accommodations in a centrally located Victorian-era building within walking distance of Oxford Street shopping and Hyde Park. The small, basic rooms have been refurbished and redecorated with a no-nonsense décor, but with good mattresses; now all have private showers and tubs combined, central heating, medium-size towels, hair dryers, coffeemakers, and small refrigerators.

Edward Lear Hotel. 28–30 Seymour St., London W1H 5WD. ☎ **0171/402-5401.** Fax 0171/706-3766. www.edlear.com. E-mail: edwardlear@aol.com. 31 units (12 with bathroom). TV TEL. £60 ($99) double without bathroom, £79.50–£89.50 ($131.15–$147.65) double with bathroom; from £105 ($173.25) suite. Rates include English breakfast. MC, V. Tube: Marble Arch.

This popular hotel 1 block from Marble Arch is made all the more desirable by the bouquets of fresh flowers in the public rooms. It occupies a pair of brick town houses, both of which date from 1780. The western house was the London home of the 19th-century artist and poet Edward Lear, famous for his nonsense verse; his illus-trated limericks adorn the walls of one of the sitting rooms. Steep stairs lead up to the cozy rooms, which are fairly small but comfortable, with firm mattresses. One major drawback: This is an extremely noisy part of London. Rooms in the rear are quieter. Bathrooms are tidily arranged and well maintained, complete with hair dryers and medium-size towels.

Hallam Hotel. 12 Hallam St., Portland Place, London W1N 5LF. ☎ **0171/580-1166.** Fax 0171/323-4527. 25 units. MINIBAR TV TEL. £92–£97 ($151.80–$160.05) double. Rates include English breakfast. AE, DC, MC, V. Tube: Oxford Circus.

This heavily ornamented stone-and-brick Victorian—one of the few on the street to escape the blitz—is just a 10-minute stroll from Oxford Circus. It's the property of the Baker family, brothers Grant and David, who maintain it well. The guest rooms, which were redone in 1991, are comfortably furnished with good beds. Some of the singles are so small they're called *cabinettes*. Guest services include concierge, dry cleaning and laundry service, express checkout, and tour desk. Several of the twin-bedded rooms are quite spacious with adequate closet space. Bathrooms are a bit cramped but have hair dryers and adequate towels. There is also a bar where residents gather to swap stories, and a bright breakfast room overlooking the pleasant patio.

Hart House Hotel. 51 Gloucester Place, Portman Sq., London W1H 3PE. ☎ **0171/ 935-2288.** Fax 0171/935-8516. 16 units. TV TEL. £95 ($156.75) double; £115 ($189.75) triple; £130 ($214.50) quad. Rates include English breakfast. AE, MC, V. Tube: Marble Arch or Baker Street.

Hart House has been a long-enduring favorite with Frommer's readers. In the heart of the West End, this well-preserved historic building (one of a group of Georgian mansions occupied by exiled French nobles during the French Revolution) lies within easy walking distance of many theaters, as well as some of the most sought-after shopping areas and parks in London. Cozy and convenient, it's run by Andrew Bowden, one of Marylebone's best B&B hosts. The rooms—done in a combination of furnishings, ranging from Portobello antique to modern—are spic-and-span, each one with a different character. Favorites include no. 7, a triple with a big bath and shower. Ask for no. 11, on the top floor, if you'd like a brightly lit aerie. Housekeeping rates high marks here, and the bedrooms are comfortably appointed with chairs, an armoire, a desk, a chest of drawers, and a good bed with a firm mattress. Bathrooms, though small, are efficiently organized with a hair dryer and a set of medium-size towels. Guest services include baby-sitting, dry cleaning and laundry service, and massage service. Literary buffs, take note: Poet Elizabeth Barrett resided at no. 99 with her family for many years.

Kenwood House Hotel. 114 Gloucester Place, London W1H 3DB. ☎ **0171/935-3473.** Fax 0171/224-0582. E-mail: woutersz@msn.com. 16 units (11 with bathroom). TV. £46 ($75.90) double without bathroom, £65 ($107.25) double with bathroom; £78 ($128.70) triple with bathroom; £85 ($140.25) family room for 4 with bathroom. Rates include English breakfast. AE, DC, MC, V. Parking £10 ($16.50). Tube: Baker St.

This 1812 Adam-style town house converted into a small hotel (run by English-born Arline Woutersz and her Dutch husband, Bryan) is a historical landmark; the front balcony is said to be original. Guests gather in the mirrored lounge with its antimacassars in place, just as they were in Victoria's day. Most of the basically furnished bedrooms were upgraded and restored in 1993. Some rooms have en suite bathrooms; spic-and-span modern bathrooms with showers and medium-size towels are on every floor. Units that have a private bath are also furnished with hair dryers. No need to bring your Lysol bottle. Baby-sitting can be arranged.

Regency Hotel. 19 Nottingham Place, London W1M 3FF. ☎ **0171/486-5347.** Fax 0171/224-6057. 20 units. MINIBAR TV TEL. £85 ($140.25) double; £125 ($206.25) family room. Rates include English breakfast. AE, DC, MC, V. Parking £18 ($28.80) nearby. Tube: Baker St. or Regent's Park.

This centrally located hotel was built, along with most of its neighbors, in the late 1800s. Although it has functioned as some kind of hotel since the 1940s, in 1991 it was gutted and tastefully renovated into its upgraded present format. One of the better hotels on the street, it offers simple, conservatively decorated modern bedrooms scattered over four floors, and a breakfast room set in what used to be the cellar. Each room has a radio, hair dryer, coffeemaker, trouser press, and ironing board. Baths, although small, are well kept and come with a set of adequate-size towels and a hair dryer. Room service is available. The neighborhood is protected as a historic district, and Marble Arch, Regent's Park, and Baker Street all lie within a 12-minute walk. Hotel services include daily maid service and room service.

ST. JAMES'S
VERY EXPENSIVE

The Ritz. 150 Piccadilly, London W1V 9DG. ☎ **800/525-4800** or 0171/493-8181. Fax 0171/493-2687. www.ritzhotel.co.uk. E-mail: enquire@ritzhotel.co.uk. 130 units. A/C MINIBAR TV TEL. £245–£355 ($404.25–$585.75) double; from £385 ($635.25) suite. Children under 12 stay free in parents' room. AE, DC, MC, V. Parking £45 ($74.25). Tube: Green Park.

ⓕ Family-Friendly Hotels

Although the bulk of their clients are business travelers staying for short hauls, each of the major international hotel chains does its best to create the impression that its fully geared for family fun. Look for special summer packages at most hotel chains between June and August. Some of the most consistently generous offers come from **Travelodge** (☎ **800/435-4542**) and **Hilton International** (☎ **800/445-8667**) chains, but it all depends on the specific branch. For best results, call the 800 number and ask about special family packages.

London also has some less expensive options that are happy to accommodate traveling families. Also refer to section 1 of this chapter under "Best for Families Who Don't Want to Break the Bank."

• **Hart House Hotel** (Marylebone; *see p. 79*) This small, family-run B&B is right in the center of the West End, near Hyde Park. Many of its rooms are triples; if you need even more room, special family suites, with connecting rooms, can be arranged.

Built in the French-Renaissance style and opened by César Ritz in 1906, this hotel overlooking Green Park is synonymous with luxury: Gold-leafed molding, marble columns, and potted palms abound; and a gold-leafed statue, *La Source,* adorns the fountain of the oval-shaped Palm Court. After a major restoration, the hotel is better than ever: New carpeting and air-conditioning have been installed in the guest rooms, and an overall polishing has recaptured much of the Ritz's original splendor. Still, this Ritz lags far behind the much grander one in Paris (to which it is not affiliated). The belle époque guest rooms, each with its own character, are spacious and comfortable. Many have marble fireplaces, elaborate gilded plasterwork, and a decor of soft pastel hues. A few rooms have their original brass beds and marble fireplaces. Beds are deluxe with luxury mattresses, and the bathrooms are elegantly appointed in either tile or marble and filled with fluffy towels, robes, phones, deluxe toiletries, and a hair dryer.

Dining: The Ritz is still the most fashionable place in London to meet for afternoon tea at the **Ritz Palm Court** (see "Teatime," in chapter 5). The **Ritz Restaurant,** one of the loveliest dining rooms in the world, has already been faithfully restored to its original splendor. Service is efficient yet unobtrusive, and the tables are spaced to allow the most private of conversations (perhaps the reason Edward and Mrs. Simpson dined here so frequently before they married). The Palm Court also serves coffee and breakfast. Remember, both venues are very formal and require jacket and tie for gentlemen.

Amenities: 24-hour room service, valet, laundry service, baby-sitting, concierge, turndown, in-room massage, twice-daily maid service, express checkout, salon fitness center, business center.

The Stafford. 16–18 St. James's Place, London SW1A 1NJ. ☎ **800/525-4800** or 0171/ 493-0111. Fax 0171/493-7121. E-mail: info@thestaffordhotel.co.uk. 81 units. A/C TV TEL. £230–£260 ($379.50–$429) double; from £330 ($544.50) suite. AE, DC, MC, V. Tube: Green Park.

Famous for its American Bar, its clubby St. James's address, its discretion, and the warmth of its Edwardian décor, the Stafford is in a cul-de-sac off one of London's most centrally located and busiest neighborhoods. It's reached via St. James's Place or by a cobble-covered courtyard designed as a mews and known today as the Blue Ball Yard. The recently refurbished late-19th-century hotel has retained a country-house atmosphere, with touches of antique charm and modern amenities. It's not the Ritz, but the Stafford competes well with Dukes and 22 Jermyn Street (both highly recommendable as well) for a tasteful, discerning clientele. All the guest rooms are individually decorated, reflecting the hotel's origins as a private home. Many singles contain queen-size beds. Most of the units have king-size or twin beds, however, and all contain quality mattresses for a good night's sleep. Some of the deluxe units also offer four-posters, making you feel like Henry VIII. Nearly all the baths are clad in marble with tubs and stall showers, a hair dryer, a private bath, fluffy towels, toiletries, and quality chrome fixtures. A few of the hotel's newest and plushest accommodations in the historically restored stable mews require a walk across the yard. These rooms in some ways are even superior to those in the main building, and much has been saved to preserve their original style, including A-beams on the upper floors. But no horse in the 18th century ever slept like this. Units come with electronic safes, disc and stereo systems, and quality furnishings, mostly antique reproductions.

Dining: Classic international dishes are prepared from select fresh ingredients at the elegant **Stafford Restaurant,** lit with handsome chandeliers and accented with flowers, candles, and white linen. The famous **American Bar,** which brings to mind the memento-packed library of an English country house, is an especially cozy place serving light meals and cocktails.

Amenities: 24-hour room service, baby-sitting, concierge, secretarial services, laundry service, maid service, privileges at a nearby health club.

EXPENSIVE

۞ Dukes Hotel. 35 St. James's Place, London SW1A 1NY. ☎ **800/381-4702** or 0171/491-4840. Fax 0171/493-1264. www.dukeshotel.co.uk. E-mail: dukeshotel@csi.com. 81 units. A/C TV TEL. £245 ($392) double; from £265 ($437.25) suite. AE, DC, MC, V. Parking £32 ($52.80). Tube: Green Park.

Dukes provides elegance without ostentation in what was presumably someone's *Upstairs-Downstairs* town house. Along with its nearest competitors, the Stafford and 22 Jermyn Street, it caters to those looking for charm, style, and tradition in a hotel. A hotel since 1908 (last renovated in 1994), it stands in a quiet courtyard off St. James's Street with turn-of-the-century gas lamps that create the appropriate mood for what's coming once you walk through the front door. Each well-furnished guest room is decorated in the style of a particular English period, ranging from Regency to Edwardian. All rooms are equipped with marble baths, satellite TV, air-conditioning, and private bars, plus luxurious mattresses. Bathrooms are small but clad in marble, with robes, soft fluffy towels, and hair dryers. A short walk away are Buckingham Palace, St. James's Palace, and the Houses of Parliament; shoppers will be near Bond Street and Piccadilly; and literature buffs will be interested to note that Oscar Wilde lived and wrote in St. James's Place for a time.

Dining: **Dukes' Restaurant** is small, tasteful, and elegant, combining classic British and continental cuisine. The hotel also has a clublike bar, which is known for its rare collection of vintage ports, Armagnacs, and cognacs.

Amenities: Even though it's claustrophobically small—it was once described as England's smallest castle—Dukes offers full hotel services, including 24-hour room service, car-rental and ticket services, and photocopying and typing services, baby-sitting, dry cleaning and laundry service, a small health spa, conference rooms.

۞ 22 Jermyn Street. 22 Jermyn St., London SW1Y 6HL. ☎ **800/682-7808** or 0171/734-2353. Fax 0171/734-0750. www.22jermyn.com. E-mail: togna@22jermyn.com. 18 units. MINIBAR TV TEL. £205 ($338.25) double; from £280 ($462) suite. AE, DC, MC, V. Valet parking £30 ($48). Tube: Piccadilly Circus.

This is London's premier town-house hotel, a gem of elegance and discretion. Set behind a facade of gray stone with neoclassical details, this structure, only 50 yards from Piccadilly, was built in 1870 as an apartment house for English gentlemen doing business in London. Since 1915, it has been administrated by three generations of the Togna family, whose most recent scion closed it for a radical restoration in 1990. Now reveling in its new role as a chic and upscale boutique hotel, 22 Jermyn offers an interior filled with greenery, the kind of art you might find in an elegant private home, and the best "information superhighway services" of any hotel in London. This hotel doesn't have the bar or restaurant facilities of The Stafford or Dukes, but its rooms are even more richly appointed, done in traditional English style with masses of fresh flowers and chintz. Beds are exceedingly luxurious with deluxe mattresses, and the bathrooms are clad in granite and equipped with fluffy robes and towels, luxurious toiletries, phones, and hair dryers.

Amenities: 24-hour room service, concierge, baby-sitting, dry cleaning and laundry service, secretarial services, fax, videophones, video library, CD-ROM library, Internet access, and a weekly newsletter that keeps guests up to date with restaurants, theater, and exhibitions. Access to a nearby health club.

PICCADILLY CIRCUS
INEXPENSIVE

Regent Palace Hotel. 12 Sherwood St., London W1A 4BZ. ☎ **0171/734-7000.** Fax 0171/734-6435. www.forte-hotels.com. 842 units (none with bathroom). TV TEL. Sun–Thurs £54 ($89.10) double, Fri–Sat £94 ($155.10) double. Rates include English breakfast. AE, DC, MC, V. Parking £35 ($56). Tube: Piccadilly Circus.

The Regent Palace, a major focal point since it was built in 1915 at the edge of Piccadilly Circus, is one of the largest hotels in Europe, a beacon for those who want to be near the bright lights of London's theaterland. It's certainly a comedown from the deluxe Mayfair palaces recommended above, but you can't expect the same kinds of service, ambience, and amenities at these prices. This hotel is known for staunch loyalty to its original design: None of the simply furnished rooms have private bathrooms. The shared facilities in the hallways are adequate, though, and each room has a sink with hot and cold running water and coffee- and tea-making facilities. Here's your chance to live as your great, great-grandfather did when he visited London and headed down the corridor to the shared bath, towel in hand.

Calahan's, the Irish pub on-site, is the most central in London, in the very heart of the city actually, drawing a mixed crowd of friendly locals and visitors from all parts of the globe. Marco Pierre White, the leading chef of London, has also chosen this site to launch his first venture in the medium-priced dining field: **Titanic,** and it's not sinking.

SOHO
MODERATE

✪ **Hazlitt's 1718.** 6 Frith St., London W1V 5TZ. ☎ **0171/434-1771.** Fax 0171/439-1524. E-mail: reservation@hazlitts.co.uk. 23 units. TV TEL. £180 ($297) double; £260 ($429) suite. AE, DC, MC, V. Tube: Leicester Sq. or Tottenham Court Rd.

This gem, housed in three historic homes on Soho Square—the most fashionable address in London two centuries ago—is one of London's best small hotels. Built in 1718, the hotel is named for William Hazlitt, who founded the Unitarian church in Boston and wrote four volumes on the life of his hero, Napoléon; the essayist died here in 1830.

Hazlitt's is a favorite with artists, actors, media people, and models. It's eclectic, filled with odds and ends picked up around the country at estate auctions. Some find the Georgian decor a bit spartan, but the 2,000 original prints hanging on the walls brighten it considerably. Many bedrooms have four-poster beds, and some bathrooms have their original claw-footed tubs (only one unit has a shower). If you can afford it, opt for the elegant Baron Willoughby suite, with its giant four-poster bed and wood-burning fireplace. Some of the floors dip and sway and there's no elevator, but it's all part of the charm. Some rooms are a bit small, but most of them are spacious, and all contain state-of-the-art mattresses. Most of the bathrooms have 19th-century styling but up-to-date plumbing with oversize tubs and old brass fittings; the showers, how-ever, are mostly handheld. A rack of medium-size towels greets you. Amenities include a concierge, room service, baby-sitting, dry cleaning and laundry service, and a dis-counted rate on a car or limousine. Swinging Soho is at your doorstep; the young, hip staff will be happy to direct you to the local hot spots.

BLOOMSBURY
MODERATE

Academy Hotel. 17–21 Gower St., London WC1E 6HG. ☎ **800/678-3096** or 0171/ 631-4115. Fax 0171/636-3442. E-mail: academy@aol.com. 48 units. A/C TV TEL. £125–£145 ($206.25–$239.25) double; £185 ($305.25) suite. AE, DC, MC, V. Tube: Tottenham Court Rd., Goodge St., or Russell Sq.

Right in the heart of London's publishing district, the Academy attracts budding British John Grishams who haven't hit the big time yet. If you look out your window, you'll see where Virginia Woolf and other literary members of the Bloomsbury Group used to pass by every day. Many were headed for the British Museum, and you can follow in their footsteps. Many of the original architectural details were preserved when these three 1776 Georgian row houses were joined. The hotel was substantially upgraded in the 1990s, with a bathroom added to every bedroom (whether there was space or not). Fourteen have a tub-shower combination; the rest have showers only, but all contain a rack of medium-size towels. The beds, so they say, were built to "American specifica-tions." True or not, they assure you of a restful night's sleep. Grace notes include the glass panels, colonnades, and intricate plasterwork on the facade. Rooms with their overstuffed armchairs and half-canopied beds sometimes evoke English country-house living, but that of the poorer relations. The theater district and Covent Garden are within walking distance. The in-house, award-winning restaurant, **Alchemy,** has been recently refurbished to a much more modern design and offers a reasonably priced menu of modern European food. Other facilities include an elegant bar, a library room, a secluded patio garden, concierge, room service, and dry cleaning and laundry service.

Blooms Hotel. 7 Montague St., London WC1B 5BP. ☎ **0171/323-1717.** Fax 0171/ 636-6498. E-mail: blooms@mermaid.co.uk. 27 units. TV TEL. £155–£195 ($255.75–$321.75) double. Extra person £40 ($66). Rates include English breakfast. AE, DC, MC, V. Tube: Russell Sq.

This exquisitely restored town house has a pedigree: It stands in what were formerly the grounds of Montague House (now the British Museum). It's had a distinguished, if eccentric, list of former occupants: everybody from Richard Penn, the Whig member of Parliament from Liverpool, to Dr. John Cumming, who firmly believed he'd witness the end of the world (on long winter nights, his ghostly presence—still looking for the world to end, we suppose—has been spotted). Even though it's in the heart of London, the house evokes a country-home atmosphere, complete with cozy fireplace, period art, and copies of *Country Life* waiting in the magazine rack. Guests take morning coffee in a walled garden overlooking the British Museum. In summer, light meals are served. The small to medium-size bedrooms are individually designed with traditional elegance, in beautifully muted tones, each with a firm mattress. The bathrooms here are excellent, very well maintained with a hair dryer and a set of medium-size towels. Services include 24-hour room service, dry cleaning and laundry service, and concierge.

INEXPENSIVE

Avalon Private Hotel. 46–47 Cartwright Gardens, London WC1H 9EL. ☎ **0171/ 387-2366.** Fax 0171/387-5810. www.scoot.co.uk/avalon-hotel. E-mail: avalonhotellondon@ compuserve.com. 28 units (5 with shower). TV. £62 ($102.30) double without shower, £78 ($128.70) double with shower; £84 ($138.60) triple without shower, £96 ($158.40) triple with shower; £96 ($158.40) quad without shower, £108 ($178.20) quad with shower. Rates include English breakfast. AE, DC, MC, V. Tube: Russell Sq., King's Cross, or Euston.

One guidebook from Victoria's day claimed Bloomsbury attracted "Medical and other students of both sexes and several nationalities, American folk passing through London, literary persons 'up' for a week or two's reading in the British Museum, and Bohemians pure and simple." The same might be said for today's patrons of this hotel, built in 1807 as two Georgian houses in residential Cartwright Gardens. Guests feel privileged because they have use of a semiprivate garden across the street with tennis courts. Top-floor rooms, often filled with students, are reached via impossibly steep stairs, but bedrooms on the lower levels have easier access. The place obviously didn't hire a decorator; everything is wildly mismatched in the bedrooms and the droopy lounge—but the price is right. The bedrooms were recently renewed with new mattresses and fresh curtains were added. Private baths with shower are extremely small. Most guests in bathless rooms have to use the corridor baths, which are generally adequate and maintained well. Towels are a bit thin. Services include concierge, dry cleaning and laundry service, and a tour desk.

Crescent Hotel. 49–50 Cartwright Gardens, London WC1H 9EL. ☎ **0171/387-1515.** Fax 0171/383-2054. 24 units, 18 with bathroom (some with shower only; some with tub only). TV TEL. £80 ($132) double with bathroom. Rates include English breakfast. MC, V. Tube: Russell Sq., King's Cross, or Euston.

Although John Ruskin, Percy Bysshe Shelley, Leonard Woolf, and Dorothy Sayers no longer pass by the door, the Crescent still stands in the heart of academic London. The private square is owned by the City Guild of Skinners and guarded by the University of London, whose student residential halls are just across the street. You have access to the gardens with their private tennis courts. Mrs. Bessolo and Mrs. Cockle, the managers, are the kindest hosts along the street; they view Crescent as an extension of their private home and welcome you to its comfortably elegant Georgian surroundings, which date from 1810. Some guests have been returning for four decades. Bedrooms range from small singles with shared bathrooms to more spacious twin and double rooms with private plumbing. All rooms have good mattresses, plus TV and beverage makers; other thoughtful extras include alarm clocks and hair dryers. Twins and doubles have private plumbing, admittedly with very tiny baths. Many rooms are singles, however, ranging in price from £40 to £60 ($66 to $99), depending on the plumbing. You're given a set of medium-size towels. The good ladies will even let you do your ironing so that you'll look sharp when you go out on the town.

Harlingford Hotel. 61–63 Cartwright Gardens, London WC1H 9EL. ☎ **0171/387-1551.** Fax 0171/387-4616. 44 units. TV TEL. £80 ($132) double; £90 ($148.50) triple; £100 ($165) quad. Rates include English breakfast. AE, DC, MC, V. Tube: Russell Sq., King's Cross, or Euston.

This hotel is composed of three town houses built in the 1820s that were joined together around 1900 via a bewildering array of staircases and meandering hallways. Set in the heart of Bloomsbury, it's run by a management that seems genuinely concerned about the welfare of their guests, unlike many of their neighboring rivals. (In a scene straight from Dickens, they distribute little mincemeat pies to their guests during the Christmas holidays.) Double-glazed windows cut down on the street noise, and all the bedrooms are generally comfortable and inviting, especially their firm mattresses. Bathrooms are small, however, since the house wasn't originally designed for them. The most comfortable rooms are on the second and third levels; but expect to climb some steep English stairs (there's no elevator). Still, say no to the rooms on ground level, as they are darker and have less security. The tiny bathrooms have medium-size towels and hair dryers. You'll have use of the tennis courts in Cartwright Gardens.

Jenkins Hotel. 45 Cartwright Gardens, London WC1H 9EH. ☎ **0171/387-2067.** Fax 0171/383-3139. E-mail: reservations@jenkinshotel.demon.co.uk. 15 units (6 with bathroom). MINIBAR TV TEL. £62 ($102.30) double without bathroom, £72 ($118.80) double with bathroom; £83 ($136.95) triple with bathroom. MC, V. Rates include English breakfast. Tube: Russell Sq., King's Cross, or Euston.

Followers of the Agatha Christie TV series *Poirot* might recognize this Cartwright Gardens residence—it was featured in the series. The antiques are gone and the rooms are small, but some of the original charm of the Georgian house remain—enough so that the London *Mail on Sunday* recently proclaimed it one of the "ten best hotel values" in the city. All the rooms have been redecorated and many completely refurbished, with firm mattresses added to all the beds. Only a few rooms have private baths, and they're quite small, but the corridor baths are adequate and well maintained. Towels are medium size, and each guest room has a hair dryer. The location is great, near the British Museum, London University, theaters, and antiquarian bookshops. There are some drawbacks—no lift and no reception or sitting room, but it's a place where you can settle in and feel at home.

Ruskin Hotel. 23–24 Montague St., London WC1B 5BH. ☎ **0171/636-7388.** Fax 0171/323-1662. 32 units (6 with bathroom). £60 ($99) double without bathroom, £75 ($123.75) double with bathroom; £75 ($123.75) triple without bathroom, £85 ($140.25) triple with bathroom. Rates include English breakfast. AE, DC, MC, V. Tube: Russell Sq. or Holborn.

Although the hotel is named for author John Ruskin, the ghosts of other literary legends who lived nearby may haunt you: Mary Shelley plotting her novel, *Frankenstein;* James Barrie fantasizing about *Peter Pan;* and even the provocative Olive Schreiner (1855–1920), an early feminist who advocated that women should be independent in sexual matters. This hotel has been managed for two decades by a hard-working family who enjoy a repeat clientele. They keep the place spic-and-span, but don't expect a decorator's flair; and the furnishings, though well polished, are worn. But the mattresses are good. Double glazing in the front blots out the noise, but we prefer the cozy old-fashioned chambers in the rear, as they open onto a park. Sorry, no elevator. The greenery in the cellar-level breakfast room provides a grace note, and the breakfast is big enough to fortify you for a full day at the British Museum next door. *Insider tip:* Although the private bathrooms are ridiculously small, the shared bathrooms in the hall are generous and well maintained—and you'll save money by opting for one of the rooms without bathroom. Each guest is given a set of medium-size towels.

St. Margaret's Hotel. 26 Bedford Place, London WC1B 5JH. ☎ **0171/636-4277.** Fax 0171/323-3066. 64 units (6 with shower). TV TEL. £56.50–£68 ($93.25–$112.20) double without shower, £78.50–£82.50 ($129.55–$136.15) double with shower. Rates include English breakfast. No credit cards. Tube: Holborn or Russell Sq.

As you trudge along Bedford Place in the footsteps of Hogarth, Yeats, and Dickens, you'll come across this hotel, composed of four interconnected Georgian town houses. Furnishings are a badly mismatched medley, a bit tattered here and there, but endurable and fine nevertheless, including the mattresses. All is forgiven on a spring day when you look out back onto the Duke of Bedford's private gardens in full bloom. Rooms are fairly large, except for a cramped single here or there. Many still retain their original fireplaces, which is how the rooms were once heated. Families should ask for no. 53, with a glassed-in garden along the back. A single who doesn't mind sharing a bathroom will find ample space in no. 24. Only a few rooms have private showers, although several well-maintained bathrooms and showers are located throughout the building. Towels are a bit thin, however. Guests have use of two lounges, one with a TV. The staff here is so loyal that they often work until they retire.

Thanet Hotel. 8 Bedford Place, London WC1B 5JA. ☎ **0171/636-2869.** Fax 0171/323-6676. www.freepages.co.uk/thanet_hotel. 16 units. TV TEL. £80 ($132) double; £96 ($158.40) triple; £105 ($173.25) quad. Rates include English breakfast. AE, MC, V. Tube: Russell Sq.

The myriad hotels around Russell Square become peas in a pod at some point, but the Thanet stands out. It no longer charges the same rates it did when it first appeared in *England on $5 a Day,* but it's still a winning choice nonetheless, a fine address and an affordable option for those who want to be close to the British Museum, Theaterland, and Covent Garden. It's a landmark-status building on a quiet Georgian terrace between Russell and Bloomsbury Squares; although it was restored many times over the years, many original features remain. Third-generation hoteliers, the Orchard family offers small, comfortably furnished and well-decorated rooms—no glaring contrasts in decor here. Amenities include beverage makers and TV. The beds have firm mattresses, and many units were recently redecorated. Bathrooms are very small, but neatly maintained and equipped with a rack of medium-size towels and a hair dryer.

COVENT GARDEN
VERY EXPENSIVE

One Aldwych. 1 Aldwych, London WC2B 4BZ. ☎ **800/447-7462** in the U.S., or 0171/300-1000. www.onealdwych.co.uk. E-mail: sales@onealdwych.co.uk. 105 units. A/C MINIBAR TV TEL. £265–£320 ($437.25–$528) double; from £395 ($651.75) suite. AE, DC, MC, V. Parking £25 ($41.25). Tube: Temple.

Of the many hotels that compete for five-star ratings within London, this is the newest, and the one infused with a décor affected by the calm and simplicity of the Zen aesthetic. Just east of Covent Garden, it occupies the classic-looking Edwardian building that was erected in 1907 as the headquarters for the (now-defunct) *Morning Post,* and was designed, ironically enough, by the same architect who created the Ritz Hotels in London, Paris, and Madrid. Prior to its re-inauguration as a hotel in 1998, all but a fraction of its interior was stripped and gutted, and replaced with an artful simplicity. Bedrooms are outfitted with simple lines and rich color schemes of sage, purple, burnt orange, and deep reds, and accessorized with raw silk curtains, computer modems, and electrical outlets that can handle both North American and European electrical currents. The bedrooms are sumptuous with quality mattresses; bathrooms are deluxe, with hair dryers, robes, phones, fluffy towels, and luxurious toiletries.

Dining/Diversions: There's an all-day cafe and bistro, **Indigo,** that serves California-inspired platters daily, plus the more formal **Axis,** featuring a modern British and Pacific Rim cuisine.

Amenities: On-site is a state-of-the-art health club and a pool almost 60 feet long, 24-hour room service, laundry and dry cleaning, concierge, baby-sitting.

EXPENSIVE

Covent Garden Hotel. 12 Monmouth St., London WC2H 9HB. ☎ **0171/806-1000.** Fax 0171/806-1100. www.firmdale.com. E-mail: covent@firmdale.com. 50 units. A/C MINIBAR TV TEL. £200–£255 ($330–$420.75) double; £395–£550 ($651.75–$907.50) suite. AE, MC, V. Tube: Covent Garden or Leicester Sq.

Constructed as a French-directed hospital around 1850, this building lay derelict for years until it was reconfigured in 1996 by hot hoteliers Tim and Kit Kemp—whose flair for interior design is now legendary—into one of London's most charming boutique hotels, situated in one of the West End's hippest shopping neighborhoods. *Travel and Leisure* called it one of 1997's 25 hottest places to stay in the *world.* It remains so today.

Across from Neal's Yard and behind a bottle-green facade reminiscent of a 19th-century storefront, the hotel has a welcoming lobby outfitted with elaborate marquetry furniture and sweeping draperies, plus two charming restaurants. Upstairs, above a dramatic stone staircase, soundproof bedrooms are lushly furnished in English style with Asian fabrics, many elaborately adorned with hand-embroidered designs, some with crewel work. Their decorative trademark? Each room has a clothier's mannequin—a lithe female form draped in the fabric that's the predominant theme of that particular room. Each comes with VCR, CD player, a luxurious mattress, two phone lines with voice mail, and marble bathrooms with double vanities, deep soaking tubs, thick towels, and a hair dryer. The young, well-mannered staff works hard to please, and succeeds—the friendly concierge walked blocks in a downpour to hail us a cab.

Dining: Permeated with a sense of 19th-century nostalgia, **Max's Brasserie** serves up very good French-English bistro fare. With high stools at the bar and crisp table linens, it's a chic place for lunch.

Amenities: 24-hour room service, concierge, secretarial services, office facilities, small gym, small video library.

MODERATE

✪ **Fielding Hotel.** 4 Broad Ct., Bow St., London WC2B 5QZ. ☎ **0171/836-8305.** Fax 0171/497-0064. 24 units. TV TEL. £95–£120 ($156.75–$198) double. AE, DC, MC, V. Tube: Covent Garden.

One of London's more eccentric hotels, the Fielding is cramped, quirky, and quaint, but an enduring favorite nonetheless. The hotel is named after novelist Henry Fielding of *Tom Jones* fame, who lived in Broad Court. It lies on a pedestrian street still lined with 19th-century gas lamps; the Royal Opera House is across the street; and the pubs, shops, and restaurants of lively Covent Garden are just beyond the front door. Rooms are a little less than small, but they're charmingly old-fashioned and traditional. Some of the units are redecorated or at least "touched up" every year, and the mattresses are renewed as frequently as needed. Bathrooms are minuscule, and very few rooms have anything approaching a view; floors dip and sway, and the furnishings and fabrics have known better times—so be duly warned. The bathrooms have a set of good-size towels, but if you want a hair dryer you'll have to request one from the front desk. But with a location like this, in the very heart of London, the Fielding keeps guests coming back; many love the hotel's rickety charm. There's no room service or restaurant, but breakfast is served. Be sure to introduce yourself to Smokey the African Grey parrot in the bar; he's the hotel's oldest resident.

Royal Adelphi Hotel. 21 Villiers St., London WC2N 6ND. ☎ **0171/930-8764.** Fax 0171/930-8735. 49 units (35 with bathroom). TV TEL. £65 ($107.25) double without bathroom, £85 ($140.25) double with bathroom; £115 ($189.75) triple with bathroom. Extra bed

£15 ($24.75). Rates include continental breakfast. AE, DC, MC, V. Tube: Charing Cross or Embankment.

If you care most about location, consider the Royal Adelphi. Close to Convent Garden, theaterland, and Trafalgar Square, it's an unorthodox choice but it's away from the typical B&B stamping grounds. The hotel is upstairs above an Italian restaurant. Though the bedrooms quickly call to mind London's swinging 1960s heyday, accommodations are decently maintained and comfortable, with a good bed. Plumbing, however, is a bit creaky, and each unit is equipped with medium-size towels and a hair dryer. The higher up you go, the better the view. London has far better B&Bs, but not in this part of town, where you can walk to the Victoria Embankment Garden.

ALONG THE STRAND
VERY EXPENSIVE

✪ **The Savoy.** The Strand, London WC2R 0EU. ☎ **800/63-SAVOY** or 0171/836-4343. Fax 0171/240-6040. www.savoy-group.co.uk. E-mail: info@the-savoy.co.uk. 207 units. A/C MINIBAR TV TEL. £310–£325 ($511.50–$536.25) double; from £395 ($651.75) suite. AE, DC, MC, V. Parking £24 ($39.60). Tube: Charing Cross or Covent Garden.

Although not as swank as the Dorchester, this London landmark is the premier address if you want to be in the Strand and Covent Garden area. Impresario Richard D'Oyly Carte built the hotel in 1889 as an annex to his nearby Savoy Theatre, where many Gilbert and Sullivan operettas were originally staged. Eight stories of glazed tiles rising in ponderous dignity between the Strand and the Thames, it dwarfs all of its nearby competition, including the Waldorf at Aldwych and the Howard on Temple Place. Each guest room is individually decorated with color-coordinated accessories, solid and comfortable furniture, large closets, and an eclectic blend of antiques, such as gilt mirrors, Queen Anne chairs, and Victorian sofas; 48 have their own sitting rooms. The handmade beds, real luxury models, have top-of-the-line crisp linen clothing and luxury mattresses. Some baths have shower stalls, but most have a combination shower and tub. Bathrooms are spacious with hair dryers, deluxe toiletries, and a set of gargantuan towels. The expensive river-view suites are the most sought after, and for good reason—the views are the best in London.

Dining: The world-famous **Savoy Grill** has long been popular with the theater crowd; Sarah Bernhardt was a regular. The even more elegant **River Restaurant** has tables overlooking the Thames; there's dancing to live band music in the evening. The room known as **Upstairs** specializes in champagne, Chablis, and seafood.

Amenities: 24-hour room service, nightly turndown, same-day dry cleaning and laundry service, secretarial service, hairdresser, news kiosk, the city's best health club—the pool has fabulous views.

WESTMINSTER/VICTORIA
EXPENSIVE

Goring Hotel. 15 Beeston Place, Grosvenor Gardens, London SW1W 0JW. ☎ **0171/396-9000.** Fax 0171/834-4393. www.goringhotel.co.uk. E-mail: reception@goringhotel.co.uk. 75 units. A/C TV TEL. £195–£235 ($321.75–$387.75) double; from £230–£290 ($379.50–$478.50) suite. AE, DC, MC, V. Parking £25 ($41.25). Tube: Victoria.

For tradition and location, the Goring is our premier choice in the Westminster area—even better than the nearby Stakis London St. Ermins, its closest competitor. Located just behind Buckingham Palace, it lies within easy reach of the royal parks, Victoria Station, Westminster Abbey, and the Houses of Parliament. It also happens to offer the finest personal service of all its nearby competitors.

Built in 1910 by O. R. Goring, this was the first hotel in the world to have central heating and a private bathroom in every room. Today's well-furnished guest rooms still offer all the comforts, including refurbished bathrooms—which are most luxurious, with extra-long tubs, red marble walls, dual pedestal basins, bidets, deluxe toiletries, fluffy towels, hair dryers, and power showerheads. There is an ongoing refurbishment of all the bedrooms, including replacement of mattresses whenever needed. The beds, in fact, are among the most comfortable in London. The best rooms are those overlooking the garden. Queen Anne and Chippendale are usually the decor style. Maintenance is so high here that some discerning English clients call it "bang up to date." The charm of a traditional English country hotel is evoked in the paneled drawing room, where fires crackle in the ornate fireplaces on nippy evenings. The adjoining bar overlooks the rear gardens.

Dining: At the restaurant, the chef uses only the freshest ingredients in his classic English recipes; specialties include venison with a brussels sprout compote, roast breast of pheasant, rump of English lamb with bubble and squeak (cabbage and potatoes) and rosemary jus, and grilled Dover sole. The restaurant also offers one of the most extensive wine lists in London. Afternoon tea is served in the lounge.

Amenities: 24-hour room service, valet service, concierge, dry cleaning and laundry service, baby-sitting, secretarial services, free use of local health club.

The London Marriott Hotel. County Hall, Belvedere Rd., London, SE1 7PB. ☎ **800/ 228-9290** in the U.S., or 0171/928-5200. Fax 0171/928-5300. 200 units. A/C MINIBAR TV TEL. £153–£205 ($252.45–$338.25) double; from £250 ($412.50) suite. AE, DC, MC, V. Parking £25 ($41.25). Tube: Waterloo or Westminster.

The former seat of the government of London, and one of the city's most imposing Victorian buildings, has become the flagship of Britain's Marriott outposts. Just south of the Thames, it opens onto panoramic views of the Houses of Parliament and is close to the South Banks Arts Centre. In its restoration, the aura of its days as a seat of world political power is still evoked by its oak paneling and the Library Lounge with its marble busts and display cases of old books. Although chain owned, the hotel doesn't lack for individuality because of its unique setting. Former offices have been turned into sumptuous chambers, some grander and more spacious than others. Rooms are large, bright, and cheerful. Each has Marriott quality, with deluxe mattresses and ultimately comfortable furnishings, plus bathrooms that have state-of-the-art plumbing, a hair dryer, and plenty of fluffy towels. The staff is friendly and unassuming.

Dining: The restaurant isn't worth crossing the city for, but it's a fine place to dine if you're a hotel guest, offering a first-rate modern British cuisine from its à la carte menu.

Amenities: Swimming pool, concierge, dry cleaning and laundry, room service, baby-sitting.

MODERATE

Lime Tree Hotel. 135–137 Ebury St., London SW1W 9RA. ☎ **0171/730-8191.** Fax 0171/730-7865. 26 units. TV TEL. £100–£110 ($165–$181.50) double. Rates include English breakfast. AE, DC, MC, V. Tube: Victoria.

Long-time denizens of London's B&B business, the Wales-born Davies family has transformed what had been a run-down guest house into a cost-conscious but cozy hotel that appeals to budget travelers. The simply furnished bedrooms are scattered over four floors of a brick-fronted town house; each has been recently refitted with new curtains, cupboards, firm mattresses, and upholstery. The front rooms have small balconies overlooking Ebury Street; units in the back don't have balconies, but are quieter and sport views over the hotel's small rear garden. The rooms tend to be larger

Westminster & Victoria Hotels

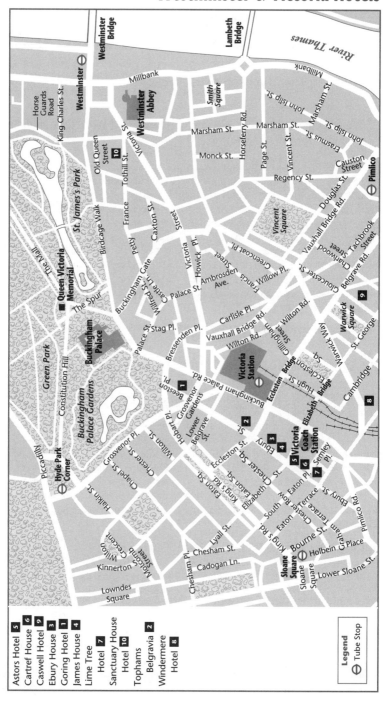

Astors Hotel **5**
Cartref House **6**
Caswell Hotel **9**
Ebury House **3**
Goring Hotel **1**
James House **4**
Lime Tree
  Hotel **7**
Sanctuary House
  Hotel **10**
Tophams
  Belgravia **2**
Windermere
  Hotel **8**

Legend
⊖ Tube Stop

than many at similar prices, and breakfasts are generous. Bathrooms are rather small but tidily maintained with a set of medium-size towels. Buckingham Palace, Westminster Abbey, and the Houses of Parliament are within easy reach, as is Harrods; nearby is the popular Ebury Wine Bar.

The Sanctuary House Hotel. 33 Tothill St., London, SW1H 9LA. ☎ **0171/799-4044.** Fax 0171/799-3657. 33 units. A/C TV TEL. £72.50–£99.50 ($119.65–$164.15) double. AE, DC, MC, V. Parking £20 ($33). Tube: St. James's Park.

The hotel is in a historic building close to Westminster Abbey. Only in the new London where hotels are bursting into bloom like spring daffodils would you expect to find a hotel so close to Westminster Abbey—a pub hotel, no less! It has been converted into traditional English-inn-style, with a pub downstairs and the rooms above. Rooms reflect this style and have a rustic feel, but they have first-rate beds and mattresses along with newly restored bathrooms with state-of-the-art plumbing, plus fluffy towels. The building was converted by Fuller Smith and Turner, a traditional brewery group in Britain. Downstairs a pub/restaurant, part of The Sanctuary, offers hearty old-style British meals that have ignored changing culinary fashions of the past quarter of a century. "We like tradition," one of the perky staff members told us. Why must everything be trendy? Some people come to England nostalgic for the old. Let others be trendy." Actually the food is excellent if you like the roast beef, Welsh lamb, and Dover sole known to Churchill's palate. Naturally, there's always plenty of brew on tap. The reception is open 24 hours a day.

Tophams Belgravia. 28 Ebury St., London SW1W 0LU. ☎ **0171/730-8147.** Fax 0171/823-5966. www.tophams.com. E-mail: tophams_belgravia@compuserve.com. 40 units (34 with bathroom). TV TEL. £120 ($198) double without bathroom, £130–£140 ($214.50–$231) double with bathroom; £170 ($280.50) triple. AE, DC, MC, V. Tube: Victoria.

Tophams came into being in 1937, when five small row houses were interconnected; with its flower-filled window boxes, the place still has a country-house flavor. It was completely renovated in 1997. The petite informal reception rooms are done in flowery chintzes and antiques. All rooms have coffeemakers, firm mattresses, hair dryers, and satellite TV; the best of the bunch are comfortably appointed with private bathrooms containing medium-size towels and four-poster beds. Not all the rooms have private bathrooms—ask for one when making reservations. The restaurant offers both traditional and modern English cooking for lunch and dinner. And the location is great, especially if you're planning to cover a lot of ground by Tube or train: It's only a 3-minute walk to Victoria Station. Services include concierge, room service, dry cleaning and laundry service, and baby-sitting.

INEXPENSIVE

Astors Hotel. 110–112 Ebury St., London SW1W 9QD. ☎ **0171/730-3811.** Fax 0171/823-6728. 22 units (12 with bathroom). TV. £58 ($95.70) double without bathroom, £70 ($115.50) double with bathroom; from £140 ($231) family unit with bathroom. Rates include English breakfast. MC, V. Parking £15 ($24.75) nearby. Tube: Victoria.

This well-located choice is a stone's throw from Buckingham Palace and just a 5-minute walk from Victoria's main line and Tube stations. The brick-fronted Victorian was once home to Margaret Oliphant (1828–97), a popular Victorian novelist; Noël Coward was a neighbor for 20 years, and H. G. Wells, Yeats, Bennett, and Shaw called down the street at no. 153 when poet, novelist, and racy autobiographer George Moore (1852–1933) was in residence. The guests today don't have such pedigrees, but are frugal travelers looking for a decent, affordable address in pricey London. Although more functional than glamorous, the rooms are satisfactory in every way. By the end of 1998, much of the hotel had been completely renovated. Each unit is fitted with a comfortable mattress, and the bathrooms have been renewed, each well maintained and containing a rack of medium-size towels. Since space and furnishings vary greatly, ask to take a little peek before committing yourself to a room. (As the hotel is often full, that won't always be possible.)

Caswell Hotel. 25 Gloucester St., London SW1V 2DB. ☎ **0171/834-6345.** 18 units (7 with bathroom). MINIBAR TV. £56 ($92.40) double without bathroom, £76 ($125.40) double with bathroom. Rates include English breakfast. MC, V. Tube: Victoria.

Run with consideration and thoughtfulness by Mr. and Mrs. Hare, Caswell lies on a cul-de-sac, a calm oasis in an otherwise busy area. Mozart lived nearby while he completed his first symphony, and that "notorious couple," Harold Nicholson and Victoria Sackville-West, are long departed, but this is still a choice address. Beyond the chintz-filled lobby, the decor is understated: There are four floors of well-furnished but not spectacular bedrooms, each with such amenities as hair dryers and beverage makers. Mattresses are worn but still have much comfort left in them. Private baths are very small units with a shower stall and few amenities except a hair dryer; however, corridor baths are adequate and well maintained. Guests receive a set of medium-size towels. How do they explain the success of the place? One staff member said, "This year's guest is next year's business."

Ebury House. 102 Ebury St., London SW1W 9QD. ☎ **0171/730-1350.** Fax 0171/259-0400. www.infotel.co.uk. 13 units (6 with bath). TV. £60–£75 ($99–$123.75) double; £75 ($123.75) triple; £95 ($156.75) family room for 4. Rates include English breakfast. MC, V. Tube: Victoria.

In 1920, Ruth Draper wrote: "I was very lucky in finding a sunny top floor room . . . a lovely big double room in front and I am so comfortably fixed . . . for one guinea a week." The first part of her statement could still be true—only the price has gone up a bit. On this highly competitive street, this comfortable guest house stands out, mainly thanks to the welcome you get from its owner-manager, Peter Evans. The bedrooms, while no pacesetters for style, are well maintained. Most of them have recently been redecorated, with new mattresses added where needed. The B&B has also recently upgraded its plumbing, installing new bathrooms, although they're quite tiny. Guests in rooms without a private bath will find a bath on each floor, plus a pay phone on one of the stairwells in case you want to call home for more money. Each client is given a set of medium-size towels. "We get just as many Canadians and Aussies as Yanks," one of the staff confided. "They seem to like us." Reserve well in advance in summer. The pine-paneled breakfast room is the morning rendezvous point.

✪ James House/Cartref House. 108 and 129 Ebury St., London SW1W 9QD. James House ☎ **0171/730-7338;** Cartref House ☎ **0171/730-6176.** Fax 0171/730-7338. E-mail: jamescartref@compuserve.com. 21 units (11 with bath). TV. £62 ($102.30) double without bathroom, £73 ($120.45) double with bathroom; £104 ($171.60) quad with bathroom. Rates include English breakfast. AE, MC, V. Tube: Victoria.

Hailed by many publications, including the *Los Angeles Times,* as one of the top 10 B&B choices in London, James House and Cartref House (across the street) deserve their accolades. Derek and Sharon James have real dedication in their work, and have the ability to make everyone feel right at home, even the first-time visitor to London. They're the finest hosts in the area, and they're constantly refurbishing, so everything looks up-to-date. Each room is individually designed; some of the large ones have bunk beds that make them suitable for families, although these mattresses are a bit thin; mattresses on the other beds are firm. Maintenance is exceedingly high. Clients in rooms with a private bath will find somewhat cramped quarters, but each room is tidily arranged. Corridor baths are adequate and frequently refurbished, and each guest is given a set of medium-size towels. The English breakfast is so generous that you might end up skipping lunch. There's no elevator, but the happy guests don't seem to mind. Don't worry about which house you're assigned; each one's a winner. Smokers be warned, both houses are no-smoking environments. You're just a stone's throw from Buckingham Palace should the Queen invite you over for tea.

Windermere Hotel. 142–144 Warwick Way, London SW1V 4JE. ☎ **0171/834-5163.** Fax 0171/630-8831. www.windermere_hotel.co.uk. E-mail: windermere@compuserve.com. 23 units (20 with bathroom). TV TEL. £75 ($123.75) double without bathroom, £93–£100 ($153.45–$165) double with bathroom; £120 ($198) triple with bathroom; £130 ($214.50) quad with bathroom. AE, CB, MC, V. Tube: Victoria.

This award-winning small hotel is an excellent choice for those who want to be near Victoria Station, less than a 10-minute walk away. The Windermere was built in 1857 as a pair of private dwellings on the site of the old Abbot's Lane. The lane linked Westminster Abbey to its abbot's residence—all the kings of medieval England trod here. A fine example of early-Victorian classical design, the hotel has lots of English character. All the refurbished rooms are comfortably furnished and have satellite TV, coffeemakers, and comfortable mattresses. Most rooms have a small private bath equipped with a hair dryer and a set of medium-size towels; public corridor baths are also adequate and well maintained. Rooms come in a wide range of sizes, some accommodating three or four—but the cheaper ones are somewhat cramped. The ground-floor rooms facing the street tend to be noisy at night. Hotel services include concierge, limited room service, dry cleaning, and a very popular restaurant, **The Pimlico Room.**

2 In & Around Knightsbridge

VERY EXPENSIVE

The Capital. 22–24 Basil St., London SW3 1AT. ☎ **800/926-3199** in the U.S., or 0171 /589-5171. Fax 0171/225-0011. www.capitalhotel.co.uk. E-mail: capitalhotel.co.uk. 48 units. A/C MINIBAR TV TEL. £235–£305 ($387.75–$503.25) double; from £350 ($577.50) suite. AE, DC, MC, V. Parking £20 ($33). Tube: Knightsbridge.

One of the most personalized hotels in the West End, this small, modern place is a stone's throw from Harrods. It doesn't have the five-star quality of the nearby Hyatt, but the cuisine is far better than at many of London's more highly rated hotels. With extensive refurbishment, the owner, David Levin, has created a warm town-house ambience with an elegant fin-de-siècle décor, matched by the courtesy and professionalism of the staff. Lined with original oils, the corridors and staircase literally function as an art gallery. The guest rooms are tastefully decorated, often with Ralph Lauren furnishings. The objets d'art and original paintings adorning the rooms were selected by the owners. Beds are comfortable with luxurious mattresses, and the bathrooms are equipped with powerful showers, a hair dryer, bathrobes, and a range of deluxe toiletries.

Dining: The Capital Restaurant was refurbished in the early 1990s in a vaguely French style, with David Linley panels for the windows (Linley is Princess Margaret's son). Under the direction of chef Phillip Britton, it's among the finest restaurants in London, specializing in seafood and offering exquisitely prepared French cuisine.

Amenities: 24-hour room service, concierge, dry cleaning and laundry service, baby-sitting, secretarial service, valet.

Hyatt Carlton Tower. 2 Cadogan Place, London SW1 X9PY. ☎ **800/233-1234** or 0171/235-1234. Fax 0171/235-9129. www.hyatt.com. 220 units. A/C MINIBAR TV TEL. £290 ($478.50) double; from £355 ($568) suite. AE, DC, MC, V. Parking £25 ($41.25). Tube: Knightsbridge.

Its location and towering height made this luxurious hotel a landmark even before Hyatt's decorators, painters, and antiques dealers transformed it into the chain's European flagship. It's one of the London's plushest and best-maintained hotels, with more style and grace than Knightsbridge's Sheraton Park Tower. And the setting is lovely—it overlooks one of the city's most civilized gardens and is surrounded by Regency-era town houses. Accommodations are mainly medium in size and tastefully appointed with French provincial pine, marble-topped tables, data ports, fax machines (upon request only), wingback chairs, and luxurious beds and mattresses. Bathrooms are marble swathed and fitted with chrome fixtures, hair dryers, scales, scissors-hinged vanity mirrors, and a set of fluffy towels. There are four no-smoking floors.

Dining: After the publicity it received from *Time Out* as "Britain's Tea Place of the Year," the hotel has remained one of the most fashionable spots to enjoy a mid-afternoon pick-me-up. The hotel has a new Northern Italian restaurant, **Grissini London,** a sibling restaurant to the Grissini at the Grand Hyatt Hong Kong. The newer Grissini serves specialties such as ravioli stuffed with lobster, and fried lemon-breaded monkfish medallions. Also worth trying is the **Rib Room,** where you can experience some of the finest ribs of Aberdeen Angus beef, as well as a wide range of fresh fish caught in Scottish waters.

Amenities: 24-hour room service, valet, laundry service, salon, baby-sitting, concierge, twice-daily maid service, turndown, express checkout, secretarial service, swimming pool, business center, health club with exercise equipment, aerobics studio, beauty experts, masseurs, sauna, solariums, tennis courts, Jacuzzi, shopping arcade.

EXPENSIVE

Basil Street Hotel. 8 Basil St., London SW3 1AH. ☎ **0171/581-3311.** Fax 0171/581-3693. E-mail: thebasil@aol.com. 92 units. TV TEL. £210 ($346.50) double; £280 ($462) family room. AE, DC, MC, V. Parking £28–£30 ($46.20–$49.50) at 24-hour lot nearby. Tube: Knightsbridge.

The Basil, an Edwardian charmer, has long been a favorite for those who make an annual pilgrimage to Harrods—"just 191 steps away"—and the Chelsea Flower Show. (Harvey Nichols is also nearby.) Several spacious, comfortable lounges are furnished in a fitting style and accented with 18th- and 19th-century accessories; off the many rambling corridors are smaller sitting rooms. No room is standardized: They come in varying shapes and dimensions, evocative of the Edwardian era when hotels housed everyone from grand dukes to their valets in the upper floors. Nearly all units are traditional (they even have TVs that broadcast the original *I Love Lucy* series). Persons with disabilities should check in elsewhere because the steps and stairs in all directions make this hotel an Olympic feat to traverse. Even so, older clients particularly like this hotel, which calls itself a "Hotel for Those Who Hate Hotels." We love its old-fashioned and fading Edwardian gentility, even the antiquated bathrooms that still function perfectly, and hold a rack of thick towels.

Dining: In the restaurant, candlelight and piano music re-create the atmosphere of a bygone era. **The Parrot Club,** a rendezvous reserved only for women, is ideal for afternoon tea.

Amenities: 24-hour room service, evening maid service, conference facilities, baby-sitting, dry cleaning and laundry service, shoe cleaning.

The Beaufort. 33 Beaufort Gardens, London SW3 1PP. ☎ **800/888-1199** or 0171/584-5252. Fax 0171/589-2834. www.thebeaufort.co.uk/index.htm. E-mail: thebeaufort@nol.co.uk. 28 units. TV TEL. £200–£290 ($330–$478.50) double; £325 ($536.25) junior suite. Rates include breakfast and afternoon tea. AE, DC, MC, V. Tube: Knightsbridge.

Hotels from Knightsbridge to Earl's Court

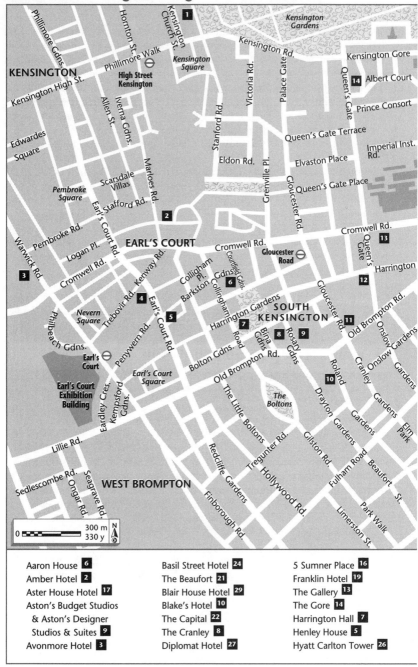

Aaron House **6**	Basil Street Hotel **24**	5 Sumner Place **16**
Amber Hotel **2**	The Beaufort **21**	Franklin Hotel **19**
Aster House Hotel **17**	Blair House Hotel **29**	The Gallery **13**
Aston's Budget Studios	Blake's Hotel **10**	The Gore **14**
& Aston's Designer	The Capital **22**	Harrington Hall **7**
Studios & Suites **9**	The Cranley **8**	Henley House **5**
Avonmore Hotel **3**	Diplomat Hotel **27**	Hyatt Carlton Tower **26**

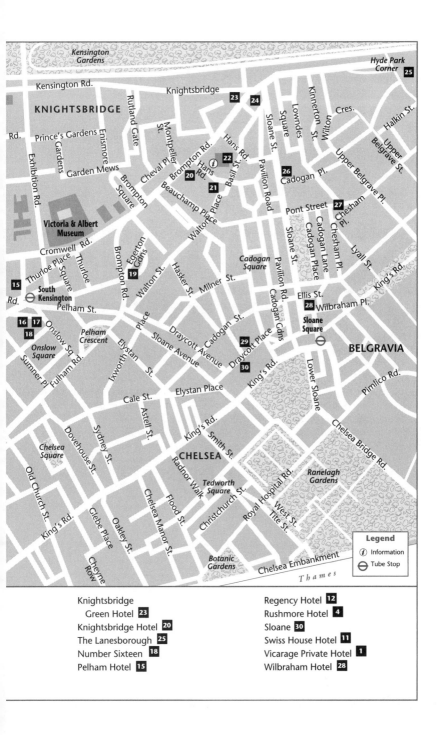

Kensington
Gardens

Hyde Park
Corner **25**

Kensington Rd.

Knightsbridge **23** **24**

KNIGHTSBRIDGE

Kinnerton St.

Lowndes
Square

Wilton St.

Cres.

Halkin St.

Rd.

Prince's Gardens

Enismore

Gardens

Rutland Gate

Montpelier St.

Cheval Pl.

Brompton Rd.

Hans Rd.

Sloane St.

Upper Belgrave St.

Upper Belgrave Pl.

Garden Mews

Brompton Square

Beauchamp Place

Hans Rd.

i **22**

20

Basil St.

21

Pavilion Road

Cadogan Pl.

26 Cadogan Pl.

Chesham Pl.

Lyall St.

Exhibition Rd.

Gardens

**Victoria & Albert
Museum**

Walton Place

Pont Street **27** Chesham Pl.

Cadogan Lane

Cromwell Rd.

Egerton Gdns.

Walton St.

Hasker St.

Milner St.

Sloane St.

Cadogan
Square

Cadogan Place

Pavilion Rd.

Chesham Pl.

King's Rd.

Thurloe Place

Thurloe

Brompton Rd.

Thurloe Square

19

Cadogan St.

Cadogan Gdns

Ellis St.

28 Wilbraham Pl.

15

**South
Kensington** ⊖

Rd.

Pelham St.

Place

Sloane Avenue

Draycott Avenue

**Sloane
Square** ⊖

BELGRAVIA

16 **17**

18

Onslow Sq.

**Pelham
Crescent**

Elystan St.

Ixworth Place

Draycott Place

29

30

King's Rd.

Lower Sloane

**Onslow
Square**

Sumner Pl.

Fulham Rd.

Cale St.

Elystan Place

Pimlico Rd.

King's Rd.

Smith St.

Chelsea Bridge Rd.

**Chelsea
Square**

Dovehouse St.

Sydney St.

Astell St.

Radnor Walk

CHELSEA

Chelsea Manor St.

Flood St.

Tedworth
Square

Christchurch St.

Royal Hospital Rd.

West St.

Tite St.

**Ranelagh
Gardens**

Old Church St.

King's Rd.

Glebe Place

Oakley St.

Cheyne
Row

**Botanic
Gardens**

Chelsea Embankment

T h a m e s

Legend

i Information

⊖ Tube Stop

Knightsbridge
 Green Hotel **23**
Knightsbridge Hotel **20**
The Lanesborough **25**
Number Sixteen **18**
Pelham Hotel **15**

Regency Hotel **12**
Rushmore Hotel **4**
Sloane **30**
Swiss House Hotel **11**
Vicarage Private Hotel **1**
Wilbraham Hotel **28**

If you'd like to stay at one of London's finest boutique hotels, offering personal service in an elegant, tranquil town-house atmosphere, head to the Beaufort or the Franklin (see below)—they're the market leaders. The Beaufort, only 200 yards from Harrods, sits on a cul-de-sac behind two Victorian porticoes and an iron fence. Owner Diana Wallis, a television producer, combined a pair of adjacent houses from the 1870s, ripped out the old decor, and created a stylish hotel of merit and grace that has the feeling of a private house in the heart of London. You register at a small desk extending off a bay-windowed parlor, and then climb the stairway used by the queen of Sweden during her stay. Each guest room is bright and individually decorated in a modern color scheme and adorned with several well-chosen paintings by London artists; each also comes with earphone radios, flowers, and a selection of books. Bedrooms are exceedingly small, but tasteful and efficiently organized with luxurious mattresses. The most deluxe and spacious rooms are in the front. Units contain such thoughtful extras as fax machines and trouser presses. Baths are adequate, not special in any way, but contain a set of medium-size towels and have tidy maintenance, plus a hair dryer. The all-female staff is exceedingly helpful—a definite plus.

Dining: Light meals are available from room service. There's a 24-hour honor bar.

Amenities: Concierge, theater-ticket service, car rental, secretarial services, fax machines, sightseeing, baby-sitting, massage, room service. Access to nearby health club for a small fee; Laundromat nearby.

✪ **Franklin Hotel.** 28 Egerton Gardens, London SW3 2DB. ☎ **0171/584-5533.** Fax 0171/584-5449. E-mail: bookings@thefranklin.force9.co.uk. 47 units. A/C MINIBAR TV TEL. £175–£295 ($288.75–$486.75) double; from £230 ($379.50) suite. AE, DC, MC, V. Tube: Knightsbridge/South Kensington.

This gem immediately attracted an audience when it opened in 1992, even drawing discerning patrons away from Claridge's and the Dorchester. It's the creation of David Naylor-Leyland, who first attracted attention with another little charmer, the Egerton House, down the street; he also owns Dukes Hotel. (See "St. James's" earlier in this chapter.) The Franklin doesn't offer the services and facilities of those giants, but it's intimate and charming. "Private but not so snobbish" is the motto here.

The hotel lies on a quiet Knightsbridge street halfway between Harrods and the center of South Kensington. A dark-red honor bar and a series of parlors constitute the lobby. We prefer the Garden Rooms, which open onto a row of redbrick Victorian town houses across the lawn. The medium-size bedrooms have canopied beds with firm mattresses, antiques, paintings, and floral prints from Colefax and Fowler. The marble bathrooms include such thoughtful extras as power showers, hair dryers, fluffy towels, and Floris toiletries; several also have bidets. All are air-conditioned, and many have four-poster beds.

Dining: Breakfast is served in the dining room; the surprisingly varied room-service menu ranges from green Thai curry with coconut and mangos to lamb cutlets with rosemary jus, and is served in the dining room all day as well.

Amenities: Room service from 11pm to 7am, dry cleaning and laundry service, turndown and twice-daily maid service, valet parking. Access to a nearby health club with pool.

MODERATE

Knightsbridge Green Hotel. 159 Knightsbridge, London SW1X 7PD. ☎ **0171/584-6274.** Fax 0171/225-1635. E-mail: theKGHotel@aol.com. 28 units. A/C MINIBAR TV TEL. £135 ($222.75) double; £160 ($264) suite. AE, DC, MC, V. Tube: Knightsbridge.

Many return guests from around the world view this dignified 1890s structure as their home away from home. In 1966, when it was converted into a hotel, the developers were careful to retain its wide baseboards, cove moldings, high ceilings, and spacious proportions. Even without kitchens, the well-furnished suites come close to apartment-style living; all have trouser presses and hair dryers in the well-appointed marble bathrooms with fluffy towels, a hair dryer, and power showers. Most of the rooms are quite spacious, with decorator colors and adequate storage space. Bedrooms are often individualized—one has a romantic sleigh bed, for example—and each comes with a deluxe mattress. This is still a solid choice, and it's just around the corner from Harrods. Coffee, tea, and pastries are available throughout the day; baby-sitting, dry cleaning, and laundry service are other perks.

Knightsbridge Hotel. 12 Beaufort Gardens, London SW3 1PT. ☎ **0171/589-9271.** Fax 0171/823-9692. www.knightsbridge.co.uk. E-mail: reception@knightsbridgehotel.co.uk. 40 units. MINIBAR TV TEL. £135 ($222.75) double. Rates include English or continental breakfast. AE, DC MC, V. Free parking on street from 6pm to 8am. Tube: Knightsbridge.

The Knightsbridge Hotel attracts visitors from all over the world seeking a small hotel in a high-rent district. It's fabulously located, sandwiched between fashionable Beauchamp Place and Harrods, and with many of the city's top theaters and museums close at hand, including the Royal Albert Hall and Madame Tussaud's. Built in the early 1800s as a private town house, this family-run place sits on a tranquil, tree-lined square, free from traffic. Small and unpretentious, with a subdued Victorian ambience, it's been recently renovated to a high standard: All the well-furnished rooms have private bathrooms, coffeemakers, trouser presses, and safety-deposit boxes. Most bedrooms are spacious and furnished with traditional English fabrics. The best are numbers 311 and 312 at the rear, each with a pitched ceiling and a small sitting area. Bathrooms are clad in marble or tile and contain medium-size towels and hair dryers. Amenities include room service, laundry service, and a concierge. There's also a small health club with a steam room and a spa for guests' use.

The Sloane. 29 Draycott Place, London SW3 2SH. ☎ **0171/581-5757.** Fax 0171/584-1348. 12 units. A/C TV TEL. £140 ($231) double; £225 ($371.25) suite. AE, DC, MC, V. Tube: Sloane Square.

This toff address, a redbrick Victorian-era town house that has been richly and tastefully renovated during recent years, is desirably located in Chelsea near Sloane Square. It combines worthy 19th-century antiques with modern comforts—if you happen to admire a piece of furniture, the staff at the front desk will probably quote you a price that could be attractive enough for you to actually buy it. Our favorite spot here is the rooftop terrace with its views opening onto Chelsea, ideal for breakfast or a drink. Bedrooms come in varying sizes, ranging from small to spacious, but are opulently furnished with flouncy draperies, tasteful fabrics, and sumptuous beds. Many rooms have draped four-posters or canopied beds, and, of course, those antiques. The deluxe bathrooms have combination tub and shower, chrome power showers, mostly wall-width mirrors, luxurious toiletries, and fluffy towels. Light meals can be ordered 24 hours a day, and the staff is accommodating, pan-European, and oh, so discreet if you'd fancy an off-the-record weekend.

IN NEARBY BELGRAVIA
VERY EXPENSIVE

✪ **The Lanesborough.** Hyde Park Corner, London SW1X 7TA. ☎ **800/999-1828** or 0171/259-5599. Fax 0171/259-5606. www.lanesborough.co.uk. 95 units. A/C MINIBAR TV TEL. £310–£410 ($511.50–$676.50) double; from £470 ($775.50) suite. AE, CB, DC, MC, V. Parking £2.50 ($4.15) hour. Tube: Hyde Park Corner.

One of London's grandest hotels was created from the dreary hospital wards that Florence Nightingale made famous. This Regency-style, four-story hotel vies with the Dorchester for sophistication (although it falls short of the Dorch's time-honored experience). When Rosewood Hotels and Resorts (known for managing top hotels like the Bel-Air in Los Angeles and Dallas's Mansion on Turtle Creek) upgraded the building into a luxury hotel, most of the Georgian details were retained. The guest rooms are as opulent and antique-stuffed as the public spaces; each has electronic sensors to alert the staff as to when a resident is in or out, a CD player, VCR, personal safe, fax machine, 24-channel satellite TV, triple glazing on the windows, and the services of a personal butler. Most accommodations are spacious suites with high ceilings. The beds are luxurious, and the bathrooms are opulently clad in milk marble with deluxe toiletries, hair dryers, robes, fluffy towels, and generous shelf space. Security is tight—there are at least 35 surveillance cameras.

Dining: The Conservatory is an elegant restaurant with decor inspired by the Chinese, Indian, and Gothic motifs of the Brighton Pavilion. **The Library Bar**—which opens into a Regency-era hideaway, charmingly named "The Withdrawing Room"— re-creates the atmosphere of an elegant private club.

Amenities: Personal butlers, concierges, room service, dry cleaning and laundry service, massage, baby-sitting, secretarial services, car rental, business center, small fitness studio. Exercise equipment (Stairmasters, stationary bicycles) can be delivered directly to your room.

MODERATE

Diplomat Hotel. 2 Chesham St., London SW1X 3DT. ☎ **0171/235-1544.** Fax 0171/ 259-6153. www.btinternet.com/-diplomat.hotel. E-mail: diplomat.hotel@btinternet.com. 27 units. TV TEL. £125–£155 ($206.25–$255.75) double. Rates include English buffet breakfast. AE, CB, DC, MC, V. Tube: Sloane Sq. or Knightsbridge.

Part of the Diplomat's charm is that it is small and reasonably priced in an otherwise prohibitively expensive neighborhood of privately owned Victorian homes and first-class, high-rise hotels. Only minutes from Harrods, it was built in 1882 as a private residence by the noted architect Thomas Cubbitt. It's very well appointed: The registration desk is framed by the sweep of a partially gilded circular staircase; above, cherubs gaze down from a Regency-era chandelier. The staff is helpful, well mannered, and discreet. The high-ceilinged guest rooms are tastefully done in Victorian style; many were renovated in 1996. You get good—not grand—comfort here. Rooms are a bit small and usually furnished with twin beds with exceedingly good mattresses. Bathrooms are also small but well maintained with medium-size towels and hair dryers. Amenities include a concierge, massage service, business center, afternoon tea, and a snack menu available daily from 1 to 8:30pm. A health club is located nearby. As a special feature, the hotel offers a complimentary 15-minute back and neck Shiatsu massage to its arriving guests.

3 Chelsea

MODERATE

Blair House Hotel. 34 Draycott Place, London SW3 2SA. ☎ **0171/581-2323.** Fax 0171/823-7752. 11 units. TV TEL. £105–£115 ($173.25–$189.75) double. Extra bed £18 ($29.70). AE, DC, MC, V. Tube: Sloane Sq.

If you can't afford a luxury hotel, this comfortable B&B-style hotel in the heart of Chelsea near Sloane Square is a good alternative. It's hard finding reasonably priced lodgings in this fashionable neighborhood, stamping ground of everybody from Oscar Wilde to Baroness Margaret Thatcher. A boutique hostel nearby charges rates six times the tariff here, so you get good value. Its ideal for shoppers—trendy King's Road and Peter Jones Department Store are a short walk away. It's been completely refurbished inside. The small rooms are individually decorated, but may have too many flowery prints for most tastes. They all come with coffeemakers and trouser presses, plus a tiny bath with medium-size towels and a hair dryer. Although most singles are small, some rooms are spacious enough to accommodate four. Baby-sitting and laundry service can be arranged. Only breakfast is served. If you're bothered by noise, ask for a quieter room in the back.

INEXPENSIVE

Wilbraham Hotel. 1–5 Wilbraham Place (off Sloane St.), London SW1X 9AE. ☎ **0171/ 730-8296.** Fax 0171/730-6815. 46 units. TV TEL. £100–£112 ($165–$184.80) double. No credit cards. Parking £17.50 ($28.90). Tube: Sloane Sq.

This dyed-in-the-wool British hotel is set on a quiet residential street, just a few hundred yards from Sloane Square. Occupying three Victorian town houses, it's a bit faded; but the traditionally furnished, wood-paneled bedrooms are well maintained and have fireplaces and leaded-glass windows. There are even heated towel racks in the bathroom— a lovely comfort on a cold gray London morning. Expect sagging beds, somewhat on the order of a London town house at the turn of the century. Accommodations vary widely in size from small to spacious. The plumbing is antiquated in the charmingly old-fashioned baths, but still works smoothly. The best double—certainly the most spacious—is no. 1. There's an attractive old-fashioned lounge where you can order drinks, simple lunches, and traditional English dinners. Despite its small size, guest services include room service, baby-sitting, and dry cleaning and laundry service.

4 Kensington & South Kensington

KENSINGTON
INEXPENSIVE

✪ **Vicarage Private Hotel.** 10 Vicarage Gate, London W8 4AG. ☎ **0171/229-4030.** Fax 0171/792-5989. www.londonvicaragehotel.com. E-mail: reception@londonvicaragehotel. com. 18 units (none with bathroom). £68 ($112.20) double; £89 ($146.85) triple; £100 ($165) family room for 4. Rates include English breakfast. No credit cards. Tube: Kensington High St. or Notting Hill Gate.

Eileen and Martin Diviney have a host of admirers on all continents. Their hotel is tops for old-fashioned English charm, affordable prices, and hospitality. Situated on a residential garden square close to Kensington High Street, not far from Portobello Road Market, this Victorian town house retains many original features. Individually furnished in a country-house style, the bedrooms can accommodate up to four. If you want a little nest to hide away in, opt for the top floor aerie (no. 19), a private retreat such as Noël Coward used to occupy before "I got rich enough to move downstairs." By the time you arrive, some small private baths may be added. For the moment, guests find the corridor baths adequate, and they are well maintained. Each year a few rooms are refurbished, and beds have decent mattresses. Guests meet in a cozy sitting room for conversation and to watch the telly. As a thoughtful extra, hot drinks are available 24 hours a day. In the morning, a hearty English breakfast awaits.

SOUTH KENSINGTON
VERY EXPENSIVE

✪ **Blake's Hotel.** 33 Roland Gardens, London SW7 3PF. ☎ **800/926-3173** or 0171/ 370-6701. Fax 0171/373-0442. E-mail: blakes@easynet.co.uk. 51 units. MINIBAR TV TEL.

£210–£310 ($346.50–$511.50) double; from £485 ($800.25) suite. AE, DC, MC, V. Parking £15–£30 ($24.75–$49.50). Tube: South Kensington or Gloucester Rd.

This opulent and highly individual creation of actress Anouska Hempel-Weinberg is one of London's best small hotels. No expense was spared in converting this former row of Victorian town houses into one of the city's most original hotels. It's now Oriental nights down in old Kensington: The richly appointed lobby boasts British Raj–era furniture from India; individually decorated, elaborately appointed rooms contain such treasures and touches as Venetian glassware, cloth-covered walls, swagged draperies, even Empress Josephine's daybed. Live out your fantasy: Choose an ancient Egyptian funeral barge or a 16th-century Venetian boudoir. Rooms in the older section have the least space and aren't air-conditioned, but are chic nevertheless. Beds are deluxe, and the marble baths are richly appointed with fluffy towels, toiletries, robes, and hair dryers; rooms have data ports and private safes. Although a formidable rival, the Pelham (see below) doesn't match Blake's in sophistication and style. Go for a deluxe room if you can manage it; the standard singles and doubles are tiny.

Dining: The stylish restaurant is one of the best in town. Neville Campbell's cuisine blends the finest of East and West, ranging from baked sea bass with a crispy fennel skin to chicken and crab shaped like a large delectable Fabergé egg. With cuisine this fabulous, it's no wonder that reservations are strictly observed.

Amenities: 24-hour room service, laundry service, baby-sitting, secretarial services, and an arrange-anything concierge. Access to a nearby health club for a fee.

EXPENSIVE

The Cranley. 10–12 Bina Gardens, London SW5 0LA. ☎ **800/553-2582** or 0171/373-0123. Fax 0171/373-9497. www.thecranley.co.uk. E-mail: thecranley@compuserve.com. 37 units. A/C TV TEL. £140–£170 ($231–$280.50) double; £180–£220 ($297–$363) suite. AE, DC, MC, V. Tube: Gloucester Rd.

A trio of adjacent 1875 town houses became the Cranley Hotel when its Michigan-based owners upgraded the buildings in South Kensington. All the high-ceilinged guest rooms have enormous windows, much of their original plasterwork, scattered antiques, and plush upholstery, and the public rooms are like a stage set for an English country house. It all adds up to a vivid 19th-century ambience that makes this feel more like a private residence than a hotel. All but one of the guest rooms have tiny kitchenettes; most units are spacious, although a few are small. Beds are first rate, and extras include trouser presses. Baths are small, tiled, and feature power showers, medium-size towels, and a hair dryer; some bathrooms even contain big mirrors bordered with Dutch tile. Ground-floor suites open onto a private terrace and have Jacuzzis.

Dining: There's no restaurant, but light meals are served in a small cafe.

Amenities: Room service daily from 7am to 11pm, dry cleaning and laundry service, secretarial services available during office hours. Access to a nearby health club.

✪ **The Gore.** 189 Queen's Gate, London SW7 5EX. ☎ **800/637-7200** or 0171/584-6601. Fax 0171/589-8127. www.gorehotel.co.uk. E-mail: reservations@gorehotel.co.uk. 54 units. MINIBAR TV TEL. £171–£236 ($282.15–$389.40) double; £257 ($424.05) the Tudor Room. AE, DC, MC, V. Tube: Gloucester Rd.

Once owned by the Marquess of Queensberry's family, the Gore has been a hotel since 1892—and it's always been one of our favorites. Victorians would still feel at home here among all the walnut and mahogany, Oriental carpets, and walls covered in antique photos and the hotel's collection of some 4,000 English prints. The Gore has always been known for eccentricity. Each room is different, so try to find one that suits your personality. The Venus Room has a bed once owned by Judy Garland. The dark-paneled Tudor Room is the most fascinating, with its gallery and fireplace. Rooms no longer go for the 1892 price of 50p, but they're still a good value. Although most are a bit small, there is still room for a sitting area. Well-maintained baths have thick towels, hair dryers, and custom brass taps. Some units contain a shower stall but no full tub, although most have a tub and shower combination. Some of the plumbing wares would be familiar to Queen Victoria, but everything works smoothly. Many rooms have four-poster beds or half testers, each with a good, firm mattress. Amenities include private safes.

Dining: It's worth a trip across town to dine at renowned chef Antony Worrall Thompson's **Bistro 190,** especially for the crispy squid, the chargrilled corn-fed chicken, and the seared tuna sashimi with spicy lentil relish.

Amenities: Concierge, room service daily from 7am to 12:20am, dry cleaning and laundry service. Newspaper delivery, baby-sitting, secretarial services, and express checkout may be arranged. Access to health club next door.

Pelham Hotel. 15 Cromwell Place, London SW7 2LA. ☎ **0171/589-8288.** Fax 0171/ 584-8444. www.firmdale.com. E-mail: pelham@firmdale.com. 50 units. A/C MINIBAR TV TEL. £175–£225 ($288.75–$371.25) double; from £285 ($470.25) suite. AE, MC, V. Parking £23.10 ($38.10) nearby. Tube: South Kensington.

This small hotel is sure to please discerning travelers. Hoteliers extraordinaire Kit and Tim Kemp preside over one of the most stunningly decorated establishments in London, formed from a row of early-19th-century terrace houses with a white portico facade. In the drawing room, 18th-century paneling, high ceilings, and fine moldings create a suitable backdrop for a collection of antiques and Victorian art; needlepoint rugs and cushions evoke a homelike warmth, and an honor bar completes the club-like atmosphere. The sumptuously decorated rooms are outfitted with Oriental carpets and unique oils; even the smallest room has a handsome desk. Most of the units have high ceilings, with tasteful fabrics such as silks. Many of the beds are either canopied or four-posters; each has a luxurious mattress and an eiderdown duvet. Bathrooms are trimmed in mahogany and clad with polished granite, along with robes, deluxe toiletries, hair dryers, and fluffy towels. Some of the better accommodations have sitting areas as well. The location is ideal, close to the Victoria and Albert Museum, Hyde Park, and Harrods, and returning guests are welcomed here like part of an extended family.

Dining: Kemps is one of the finest restaurants in South Kensington.

Amenities: 24-hour room service, concierge, baby-sitting, dry cleaning and laundry service, maid service, business services. A health club is nearby.

MODERATE

5 Sumner Place. 5 Sumner Place, London SW7 3EE. ☎ **0171/584-7586.** Fax 0171/ 823-9962. www.dspace.dial.pipex.com/no.5. E-mail: no.5@dial.pipex.com. 14 units. TV TEL. £130–£140 ($214.50–$231) double. Rates include English breakfast. AE, MC, V. Parking £20 ($33). Tube: South Kensington.

This little charmer is frequently cited as one of the best B&Bs in the greater Kensington area, and we agree. Completely restored in an elegant, classically English style that captures the flavor of its bygone era, this Victorian terrace house (ca. 1848) now enjoys landmark status. You'll feel the ambience as soon as you enter the reception hall and are welcomed by the graceful staff. After you register, you're given your own front-door key—and London is yours. An elevator will take you up to the guest floors, where the well-maintained rooms are tastefully done in traditional period furnishings; a few have refrigerators. Bedrooms are medium in size with extremely comfortable, soft beds where you may want to linger. Bathrooms are small but tidily kept and supplied with plenty of fluffy towels and a hair dryer. Hotel services include room service, massage, dry cleaning and laundry service, and concierge. Breakfast is served in a Victorian-style conservatory.

The Gallery. 8–10 Queensberry Place, London SW7 2EA. ☎ **0171/915-0000.** Fax 0171/915-4400. www.eeh.co.uk. E-mail: reservations@eeh.co.uk. 36 units. TV TEL. £115 ($189.75) double; £200 ($330) junior suite. Extra bed £35 ($57.75). Rates include buffet English breakfast. AE, DC, MC, V. Tube: South Kensington.

This is the place for you if you want to stay in an exclusive little town-house hotel, but don't want to pay £300 a night for the privilege. Two splendid Georgian residences have been completely restored and converted into this remarkable hotel (which remains relatively unknown). The location is ideal, near the Victoria and Albert Museum, Royal Albert Hall, Harrods, Knightsbridge, and King's Road. Bedrooms are individually designed and elegantly decorated in Laura Ashley style, with half-canopied beds with firm mattresses, plus luxurious marble-tiled bathrooms with brass fittings, thick towels, and hair dryers. The junior suites have private roof terraces, minibars, Jacuzzis, and air-conditioning. A team of butlers takes care of everything. The lounge, with its rich mahogany paneling and moldings and deep colors, has the ambience of a private club. The drawing room beckons you to a quiet corner. The Gallery Room displays works for sale by known and unknown artists. There's 24-hour room service, plus concierge, dry cleaning and laundry service, and baby-sitting.

Harrington Hall. 5–25 Harrington Gardens, London SW7 4JW. ☎ **800/44-UTELL** or 0171/396-9696. Fax 0171/396-9090. www.harringtonhall.co.uk. E-mail: harringtonres@compuserve.com. 200 units. A/C MINIBAR TV TEL. £160 ($264) double; £199 ($328.35) suite. AE, DC, MC, V. Tube: Gloucester Rd.

What a comeback! This six-story terrace house of once-battered apartments has been completely gutted and restored, and it's now an inviting address. One of London's few remaining large, privately owned hotels, it conceals its charm behind an original 1870 facade constructed at the peak of Victoria's reign. Rates are about half of those across the street at the stellar Gloucester—and this hotel is every bit as good. The beautifully designed classical lobby sets the tone for tasteful and stylish bedrooms (some are much more spacious than others); flowery fabrics and patterned carpets create a real English ambience. Rooms have such extras as coffeemakers and trouser presses, plus medium-size combination baths (tub and shower) as well as good-size towels and hair dryers. Each bed is outfitted with a comfortably firm mattress. Perks include 24-hour room service, same-day dry cleaning and laundry service, business center, concierge, and baby-sitting. There's also a fitness center with gym, saunas, and showers.

The lounge bar, furnished in exotic Burr Vavona and with a marble fireplace, is a good rendezvous point. A classically decorated restaurant serves up better-than-average food and a good-value buffet.

Number Sixteen. 16 Sumner Place, London SW7 3EG. ☎ **800/592-5387** or 0171/589-5232. Fax 0171/584-8615. E-mail: reservations@numbersixteenhotel.co.uk. 36 units (34 with bathroom). MINIBAR TV TEL. £125 ($206.25) double without bathroom, £160–£195 ($256–$312) double with bathroom; £205 ($338.25) suite. Rates include continental breakfast. AE, DC, MC–V. Parking £25 ($41.25). Tube: South Kensington.

This luxurious pension is composed of four early-Victorian town houses linked to form a dramatically organized whole. The hotel won four garden awards in 1994 and was named the best B&B in London in 1992. The scrupulously maintained front and rear gardens make this one of the most idyllic spots on the street. The rooms are done in an eclectic mix of English antiques and modern paintings, although some look a little faded. The rooms range in size from small to spacious, and have various themes such as tartan or maritime. The beds are most comfortable with quality mattresses.

Baths are tiled and outfitted with vanity mirrors, heated towel racks (medium-size towels), handheld showers over small tubs, and hair dryers. There's an honor-system bar in the library. On chilly days, a fire roars in the fireplace in the flowery drawing room, although some prefer the more macho library. Breakfast is served in your bedroom, and tea and coffee service is available from 7am to 10:30pm. You can also take breakfast in the conservatory or, if the weather's good, in the garden, with its bubbling fountain and fishpond. Guests have access to a nearby health club with pool.

The Regency Hotel. 100 Queen's Gate, London SW7 5AG. ☎ **800/223-5652** or 0171/ 370-4595. Fax 0171/370-5555. E-mail: regency.london@dial.pipex.com. 209 units. A/C MINIBAR TV TEL. £147 ($242.55) double; from £215–£255 ($354.75–$420.75) suite. AE, DC, MC, V. Tube: South Kensington.

On a street lined with Doric porticoes, close to museums, Kensington, and Knightsbridge, six Victorian terrace houses were converted into one stylish, seamless whole. A Chippendale fireplace, flanked by wing chairs, greets you in the polished reception area. One of the building's main stairwells has what could be London's most unusual lighting fixture: five Empire chandeliers suspended vertically, one on top of the other. Most bedrooms are small and furnished in a standard modern idiom with trouser presses, bedside controls, and firm mattresses; maintenance is top-notch. Bathrooms are excellent with hair dryers, robes, and phones, and they're clad either in marble or tile. Suites also have a Jacuzzi bath, plus an iron and ironing board.

The **Pavilion** is a glamorous but reasonably priced restaurant specializing in international cuisine (see chapter 5 for a review). Amenities include 24-hour room service; laundry service; baby-sitting; a health club with steam rooms, saunas, and sensory-deprivation tank; a mini gym; and a business center.

INEXPENSIVE

✪ Aston's Budget Studios & Aston's Designer Studios and Suites. 31 Rosary Gardens, London SW7 4NQ. ☎ **800/525-2810** in the U.S., or 0171/590-6000. Fax 0171/ 590-6060. www.astons_apartments.com. E-mail: sales@astons_apartments.com. 76 units. A/C TV TEL. Budget Studios £74 ($122.10) double; £105 ($173.25) triple; £135 ($222.75) quad. Designer Studios £110 ($181.50) double. 10% weekly discount. AE, MC, V. Tube: Gloucester Rd.

This carefully restored row of Victorian town houses offers comfortably furnished studios and suites that are among London's best values. Heavy oak doors and 18th-century hunting pictures give the foyer a rich traditional atmosphere. Accommodations range in size and style from budget to designer; every one has a compact but complete kitchenette concealed behind doors. The air-conditioned designer studios and two-room designer suites are decorated with rich fabrics and furnishings and each has its own marble bathroom with a hair dryer and medium-size towels. Mattresses are good. Amenities include laundry service, secretarial services, guests' message line, fax machines, private catering on request, car and limousine service, and daily maid service in the designer studios and suites.

Swiss House Hotel. 171 Old Brompton Rd., London SW5 OAN. ☎ **0171/373-2769.** Fax 0171/373-4983. www.webscape.co.uk/swiss_house/index.html-ssi. E-mail: recep@ swiss-hh.demon.co.uk. 16 units (15 with bathroom). TV TEL. £77 ($127.05) double with bathroom; £98 ($161.70) triple with bathroom; £110 ($181.50) quad with bathroom. Rates include continental breakfast. AE, CB, DC, MC, V. Tube: Gloucester Rd.

This appealing B&B, in a Victorian row house with a portico festooned with flowers and vines in the heart of South Kensington, is close to the South Kensington museums, Kensington Gardens, and the main exhibition centers of Earl's Court and Olympia. Some of its individually designed country-style guest rooms have fireplaces, and there's enough chintz to please the most avid Anglophile. Try to avoid the rooms along the street—traffic is heavy, and even with double glazing, they get noisy. Instead, book one of the rear bedrooms, which overlook a communal garden and have a view of the London skyline. Most of the rooms are small, but beds are fitted with good mattresses. Sometimes there's a private safe in the room. Baths are also small but contain medium-size towels and a hair dryer. And there's a luxury that you won't get in most B&Bs: Room service—nothing elaborate, just soups and sandwiches—is available from noon to 9pm. Additional services include baby-sitting, massage, tour desk, and laundry service.

IN NEARBY WEST KENSINGTON
INEXPENSIVE

Avonmore Hotel. 66 Avonmore Rd., London W14 8RS. ☎ **0171/603-4296.** Fax 0171/603-4035. www.dspace.dial.pipex.com/avonmore.hotel. E-mail: avonmore.hotel@dial.pipex.com. 9 units. MINIBAR TV TEL. £85 ($140.25) double; £95 ($156.75) triple. Rates include English breakfast. AE, CB, DC, MC, V. Tube: West Kensington.

Avonmore is easily accessible to West End theaters and shops, yet it's located in a quiet neighborhood, only 2 minutes from the West Kensington stop on the District Line. This privately owned place—a former National Award winner as the best private hotel in London—boasts wall-to-wall carpeting, radio alarms, and central heating in each tastefully decorated room. All rooms have excellent mattresses along with small bathrooms containing a set of medium-size towels and a hair dryer. The owner, Margaret McKenzie, provides lots of personal service, including room service (until midnight). An English breakfast is served in a cheerful breakfast room, and a wide range of drinks is available in the cozy bar.

5 Earl's Court

MODERATE

Amber Hotel. 101 Lexham Gardens, London W8 6JN. ☎ **0171/373-8666.** Fax 0171/835-1194. 38 units. TV TEL. £80–£125 ($132–$206.25) double. Rates include buffet breakfast. AE, DC, MC, V. Tube: Earl's Court.

This charming, graceful hotel is an inviting oasis in a sea of bad B&Bs. The welcoming staff makes you feel at home at this 1860 house on a terraced street, close to Kensington Gardens, the South Kensington museums, and Holland Park. The majority of the rooms are singles, but there are also twins and double-bedded rooms, along with two very attractive executive rooms. Each unit is fitted with a good mattress. The conservatively decorated rooms have such extras as a refreshment tray, radio, satellite TV, and trouser press, but they're all on the small side; the private bathrooms are cramped but well maintained, each with a hair dryer and a set of medium-size towels. The private garden out back is almost reason enough alone to stay here. Breakfast is served buffet style in the lounge. Basic services include dry cleaning and laundry service, and concierge.

INEXPENSIVE

Aaron House. 17 Courtfield Gardens, London SW5 OPD. ☎ **0171/370-3991.** Fax 0171/373-2303. 23 units (15 with bathroom). £44 ($72.60) double without bathroom, £53 ($87.45) double with bathroom; £58 ($95.70) triple without bathroom, £71 ($117.15) triple with bathroom; £83 ($136.95) quad with bathroom. Rates include continental breakfast. MC, V. Tube: Earl's Court.

In the budget district of London known as "Kangaroo Court" because so many Australians stay here, Aaron House stands out. You'll be welcomed with courtesy to this former family home on a Victorian square. Even though it's been considerably modernized and upgraded, many of its original features are intact. Look for the original tile entry and the lacy scrolled staircase leading to the pleasant bedrooms, which are small but beautifully kept. In January 1999, two floors of bedrooms were redecorated and refurbished. All units are fitted with comfortable beds, and most of them contain a small but well-maintained private bath offering a hair dryer and a set of medium-size towels. Corridor baths are adequate and well maintained for those who must share. Some rooms even have their original fireplaces (no longer in use). The largest accommodations overlook the street, which can be noisy at times. If you don't expect miracles, you'll find this an affordable and tasteful place to lay your head.

Henley House. 30 Barkston Gardens, London SW5 0EN. ☎ **0171/370-4111.** Fax 0171/370-0026. E-mail: henleyhse@aol.com. 20 units. TV TEL. £89 ($146.85) double. Rates include continental breakfast. AE, CB, DC, MC, V. Tube: Earl's Court.

This newly refurbished B&B stands out from the dreary pack around Earl's Court—and it's a better value than most. The redbrick Victorian row house is in a communal fenced-in garden that you can enter by borrowing a key from the reception desk. The helpful staff takes a keen interest in the welfare of their guests and is very happy to take bewildered newcomers under their wing. A ground-floor sitting room overlooks a rear courtyard. The decor is bright and contemporary; a typical room has warmly patterned Anna French wallpaper, chintz fabrics, and solid-brass lighting fixtures. Each room is fitted with a good mattress, plus a small and well-maintained private bath with a rack of medium-size towels. Breakfast is a cheerful event around here, served in a room decorated with terra-cotta accents and pots of dried flowers where guests meet and compare notes. For those who prefer to stay in after dark rather than hitting the area's hot spots (mostly gay bars), there's a shelf of books you're welcome to borrow. Baby-sitting is available for parents wanting to go to places children can't visit.

Rushmore Hotel. 11 Trebovir Rd., London SW5 9LS. ☎ **0171/370-3839.** Fax 0171/370-0274. 22 units. TV TEL. £79 ($130.35) double; £89 ($146.85) triple; £99 ($163.35) family room for 4 or 5. Rates include continental breakfast. AE, CB, MC, V. Tube: Earl's Court.

Although it became quite run-down in the early 1970s, this Victorian row house (behind a brick-faced Italianate facade) received a complete overhaul in 1987; today, it's one of the most pleasing hotels in a low-budget neighborhood. The hotel stands on the former site of the Manor House of Earl's Court Farm, where manorial courts were held until the mid-1850s. As long as you don't require atriums and minibars, the Rushmore proves that it's still possible to get good service and a fine room in London at an affordable price. The multilingual staff works hard to make your visit rewarding. The rooms are individually decorated in a variety of period schemes, and each has a good mattress. Those with private bathrooms have such touches as marble tiling and brass fittings, plus a rack of medium-size towels. The breakfast room is beautifully outfitted with French limestone floors, unique Murano glass wall- and floor-lighting created by Missoni, wrought-iron furniture from Tuscany, and antique terra-cotta urns holding exotic cacti. Amenities include laundry service, theater bookings, fax service, and security boxes for safeguarding valuables.

6 Notting Hill

MODERATE

The Abbey Court. 20 Pembridge Gardens, London W2 4DU. ☎ **0171/221-7518.** Fax 0171/792-0858. www.telinco.co.uk/abbeycourt/.   E-mail: abbey@telinco.co.uk. 22 units. TV TEL. £130–£145 ($214.50–$239.25) double; £175 ($288.75) suite with 4-poster bed. AE, CB, DC, MC, V. Tube: Notting Hill Gate.

Marylebone, Paddington, Bayswater & Notting Hill Gate Hotels

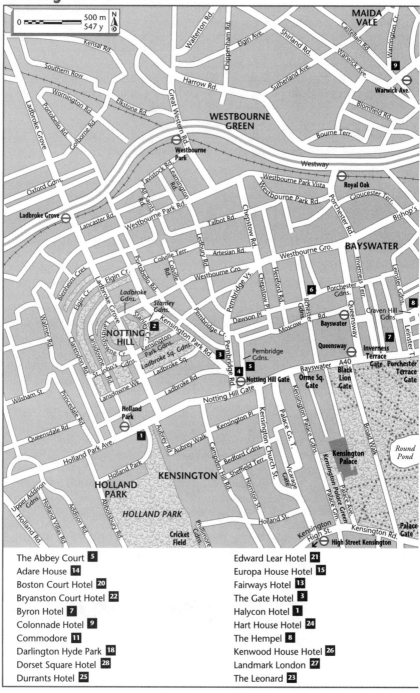

The Abbey Court **5**

Adare House **14**

Boston Court Hotel **20**

Bryanston Court Hotel **22**

Byron Hotel **7**

Colonnade Hotel **9**

Commodore **11**

Darlington Hyde Park **18**

Dorset Square Hotel **28**

Durrants Hotel **25**

Edward Lear Hotel **21**

Europa House Hotel **15**

Fairways Hotel **13**

The Gate Hotel **3**

Halycon Hotel **1**

Hart House Hotel **24**

The Hempel **8**

Kenwood House Hotel **26**

Landmark London **27**

The Leonard **23**

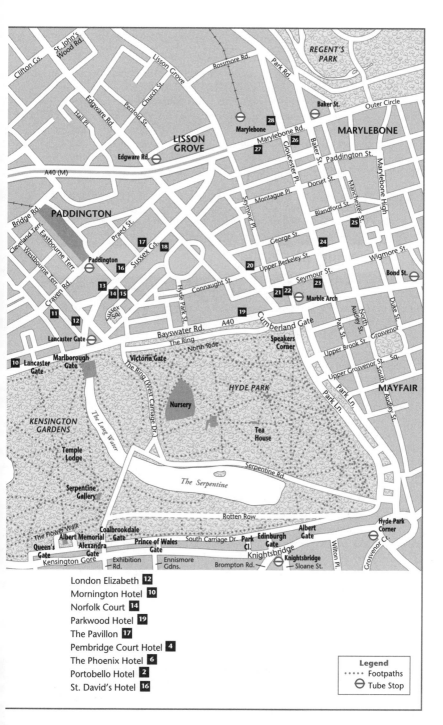

London Elizabeth 12
Mornington Hotel 10
Norfolk Court 14
Parkwood Hotel 19
The Pavillon 17
Pembridge Court Hotel 4
The Phoenix Hotel 6
Portobello Hotel 2
St. David's Hotel 16

Legend
•••• Footpaths
⊖ Tube Stop

This first-rate hotel is a small white-fronted mid-Victorian town house with a flower-filled patio in front and a conservatory in back. Its recently renovated lobby has a sunny bay window, floral draperies, and a comfortable sofa and chairs. You'll always find fresh flowers in the reception area and the hallways. Each room, although small, has carefully coordinated fabrics and fine furnishings, mostly 18th- and 19th-century country antiques, plus excellent mattresses. Done in Italian marble, bathrooms are equipped with a Jacuzzi bath, shower, and heated racks of medium-size towels. Light snacks and drinks are available from room service 24 hours a day, and breakfast is served in the newly renovated conservatory. Kensington Gardens is a short walk away, as are the antiques stores along Portobello Road and Kensington Church Street. Other amenities include a tour desk, dry cleaning and laundry service, and concierge.

Pembridge Court Hotel. 34 Pembridge Gardens, London W2 4DX. ☎ **0171/229-9977.** Fax 0171/727-4982. www.pemct.co.uk. E-mail: reservations@pemct.co.uk. 20 units. A/C TV TEL. £145–£180 ($239.25–$297) double. Rates include English breakfast. AE, DC, MC, V. Tube: Notting Hill Gate.

This hotel presents an elegant cream-colored neoclassical facade in an increasingly fashionable Notting Hill Gate residential neighborhood. Avid antiques hunters like its proximity to Portobello Road. Most guest rooms contain at least one antique, as well as 19th-century engravings and plenty of warm-toned floral fabrics, plus first-rate mattresses. Some of the largest and most stylish rooms are on the top floor. Bathrooms are tiled in Italian marble, with hair dryers and medium-size towels. Three air-conditioned deluxe rooms, all with VCRs, overlook Portobello Road: The Spencer and Churchill rooms are decorated in blues and yellows, and the Windsor Room has a contrasting array of tartans. Also called Spencer and Churchill are a pair of ginger cats, two of the most adorable in London. Churchill likes the pop stars who stay at the hotel; Spencer tries to avoid them.

Good international food is served at **Caps,** the hotel restaurant, which also boasts a well-chosen wine list; it's open to guests only from 4 to 11pm. Services include 24-hour room service, same-day dry cleaning and laundry service. A car-rental agency is on the premises, and day membership in a nearby health club is available.

The Portobello Hotel. 22 Stanley Gardens, London W11 2NG. ☎ **0171/727-2777.** Fax 0171/792-9641. 24 units. TV TEL. £150–£155 ($240–$248)double; £185–£240 ($296–$384). Rates include continental breakfast. Tube: Notting Hill Gate.

Mixing an eclectic medley of styles, two six-floor town houses dating from 1850 on an elegant Victorian terrace near the Portobello antiques market were combined to form a quirky property that doesn't please everybody, but has its devotees. We remember these rooms when they looked better, but although they're tattered here and there, they still have plenty of character—whimsy and a fair measure of flamboyance went into their design. Who knows what will show up in what nook? Perhaps a Chippendale, a multi-nozzle claw-foot tub, or a round bed tucked under a gauze canopy. Try for no. 16, with a full-tester bed facing the garden. Some of the cheaper rooms are so tiny they're cabinlike garrets (some consider them romantic). But some of these have been combined into large doubles. The comfortable beds are standard throughout with decent mattresses, and most of the small bathrooms lack tubs (shower stalls instead) but have a rack of medium-size towels. An elevator will take you as far as the third floor; after that, it's the stairs. Some rooms are air-conditioned. Don't expect top-notch service; it's erratic at best. A 24-hour bar and restaurant in the basement is a local favorite, and provides hotel room service.

INEXPENSIVE

The Gate Hotel. 6 Portobello Rd., London W11 3DG. ☎ **0171/221-2403.** Fax 0171/
221-9128. www.go_london.co.uk/hp/gatehotel.html. E-mail: gatehotel@aol.com. 6 units.
TV TEL. £75–£78 ($123.75–$128.70) double. Rates include continental breakfast. MC, V.
Tube: Notting Hill Gate.

This antiques-hunters' favorite is the only hotel along the entire length of Portobello
Road—and because of rigid zoning restrictions, it will probably remain the only one
for many years to come. It was built in the 1820s as housing for farmhands working
the orchards and vegetable plots at the now-defunct Portobello Farms and has functioned as a hotel since 1932. It has two cramped but cozy bedrooms on each of its
three floors, plus a renovated breakfast room in the cellar. Be prepared for some *very*
steep English stairs. Rooms are color-coordinated, with a bit of style, and have such
amenities as full-length mirrors, built-in wardrobes, and excellent mattresses. Bathrooms are small but adequate with a set of good-size towels; housekeeping is excellent.
Especially intriguing are the wall paintings that show what the Portobello Market was
in its early days: Every character looks straight from a Dickens novel. The on-site manager can direct you to the antiques markets and the attractions of Notting Hill Gate
and nearby Kensington Gardens, both of which lie within a 5-minute walk.

IN NEARBY HOLLAND PARK
VERY EXPENSIVE

✪ **Halcyon Hotel.** 81 Holland Park Ave., London W11 3RZ. ☎ **800/592-5416,** or
0171/727-7288. Fax 0171/229-8516. www.halcyon-hotel.co.uk. E-mail: halcyon_hotel@
compuserve.com. 63 units. A/C MINIBAR TV TEL. £260 ($429) double; from £295 ($486.75)
suite. AE, DC, MC, V. Tube: Holland Park.

Only a small brass plaque distinguishes the aptly named Halcyon from other buildings on its street. The grandest of London's small hotels, it was formed in 1985 by
uniting a pair of Victorian mansions; today, they constitute a hotel of charm, comfort,
and urban sophistication. The clientele includes international film and recording stars
who like the privacy and anonymity it offers. This is where Brad Pitt stays when he's
in London. Nearly half the accommodations are suites, lavishly outfitted like an
Edwardian country house with a modern twist. Several boast such whimsical touches
as tented ceilings; all have been refurbished and have all the modern conveniences,
including deluxe mattresses. The Italian marble baths are complete with robes, deluxe
toiletries, hair dryers, and fluffy towels. The public rooms are inviting oases, with
trompe l'oeil paintings against backgrounds of turquoise.

   Dining: The hotel's superb French restaurant, **The Room at the Halcyon,** is recommended in chapter 5.

   Amenities: 24-hour room service, 1-hour pressing service, message-paging system
(for which beepers are provided) extending 20 miles from the hotel, baby-sitting,
night safes, and a theater desk, business center. Access to tennis club and health club.

7 Paddington & Bayswater

VERY EXPENSIVE

The Hempel. 31–35 Craven Hill Garden Square, London W2 3EA. ☎ **0171/298-9000.**
Fax 0171/402-4666. www.hempelhotel.com. E-mail: the-hempel@easynet.co.uk. 47 units.
A/C MINIBAR TV TEL. £220–£255 ($363–$420.75) double; from £370 ($610.50) suite.
AE, CB, DC, DISC, MC, V. Tube: Lancaster Gate.

Set in a trio of nearly identical 19th-century row houses, this hotel is the newest statement of flamboyant interior designer Anouska Hempel-Weinberg. Don't expect the

swags, tassels, and labyrinthine elegance of her better-established hotel, Blake's (see above)—the feeling here is radically different. The Hempel manages to combine a grand Italian sense of proportion with Asian simplicity, all meant for capitalists rich enough to afford it. Its artful simplicity is like that of a Zen temple. Soothing monochromatic tones prevail. The deliberately underfurnished lobby is flanked by symmetrical fireplaces; throughout the hotel are carefully positioned mementos from Asia, including Thai bullock carts that double as coffee tables. Bedrooms continue the minimalist theme, except for their carefully concealed battery of electronic accessories, which includes a VCR, satellite TV control, CD player, twin phone lines, and a modem hookup. Baths have cut-stone walls, with both the countertops and bathtubs crafted from the same material. Extras include a hair dryer, deluxe toiletries, robes, slippers, and a rack of fluffy towels. The hotel mostly caters to business travelers from around the world, most of whom appreciate its tactful service and undeniably snobbish overtones.

Dining: In the cellar is an innovative restaurant and bar, **I-Thai** (see review in chapter 5).

Amenities: 24-hour room service, concierge, dry cleaning and laundry service, turndown and twice-daily maid service, massage, express checkout, limited business services; baby-sitting can be arranged. Conference rooms, access to nearby health club.

EXPENSIVE

London Elizabeth Hotel. Lancaster Terrace, Hyde Park, London W2. ☎ **0171/402-6641.** Fax 0171/224-8900. www.londonelizabethhotel.co.uk. E-mail: reservations@london-elizabethhotel.co.uk. 55 units. TV TEL. A/C TV TEL. £115–£150 ($189.75–$247.50) double; £135–£250 ($222.75–$412.50) suite. AE, DC, MC, V. Parking £9 ($14.85). Tube: Lancaster Gate or Paddington.

This elegant and refined early Victorian town house is ideally situated overlooking Hyde Park. Despite being in the midst of all the buzz and excitement of central London, the gentle, graceful atmosphere offers a haven of charm and refinement. The hotel has just completed a restoration costing three million pounds. The place has plenty of charm and character. Individually decorated rooms range from executive to deluxe, and are more akin to English country-house living than a hotel room in a large city. Deluxe rooms might be galleried split level, and are fully air-conditioned; some contain four poster beds. Executive units usually contain one double bed. Some rooms have special features such as Victorian antique fireplaces, and all contain beds with first-rate mattresses and well-shined bathrooms with hair dryers and a rack of fluffy towels. Suites have grand comfort and luxury—the Conservatory Suite, for example, houses its own veranda, part of the original conservatory of 1850.

Dining/Diversions: The hotel offers two restaurants: the intimate and elegant gourmet restaurant, **The Rose,** and the less formal yet chic **Theatre Bar.**

Amenities: 24-hour room service, concierge, private car park.

MODERATE

Commodore. 50 Lancaster Gate, London W2 3NA. ☎ **0171/402-5291.** Fax 0171/262-1088. www.commodore/hotel.com. E-mail: mhendry@commodore_hotel.com. 90 units. MINIBAR TV TEL. £105–£115 ($173.25–$189.75) double; £140 ($231) triple; £150 ($247.50) family room. Rates include buffet breakfast. AE, DC, MC, V. Tube: Lancaster Gate.

Although it's been here for nearly three decades, this hotel is newly fashionable since the traveling public has rediscovered the charm of its eclectically shaped rooms with their eccentric layout. The hotel was composed from the union of three side-by-side town houses set within the verdant, tree-lined neighborhood of Lancaster Gate. About a quarter of the rooms are split-level, with a sleeping gallery at the top of a short flight of stairs; many of the others seem to have some quirky touch—stained glass, an unexpectedly large closet, or a layout that only the Edwardians could have devised. Overall, the décor is comfortable and cozy, representing relatively good value. All bedrooms have been newly refurbished and are of medium size, with excellent mattresses; and renewed bathrooms contain hair dryers and a set of fluffy towels, the kind that the late Frank Sinatra always demanded when he checked into a hotel. An on-site restaurant offers a wide choice of international cuisine, a late breakfast, and even a quick lunch. But on the Commodore's doorsteps are hundreds of specialty eateries as well.

Darlington Hyde Park. 111–117 Sussex Gardens, London W2 2RU. ☎ **0171/460-8800.** Fax 0171/460-8828. www.members.aol.com/darlinghp. E-mail: darlinghp@aol.com. 40 units. TV TEL. £100 ($165) double; £110–£120 ($181.50–$198) suite. Rates include continental breakfast. AE, DC, MC, V. Tube: Paddington or Lancaster Gate.

Although not flashy and lacking a full range of services, the Darlington Hyde Park is a winning choice and good value for central London. Rooms, which have been newly renovated, are in an updated Victorian style, tasteful and neat, albeit a bit short of flair. Rooms range from small to medium, but each is fitted with a good mattress, plus a tiny but adequate bath. The maintenance is good, however, and a happy blend of business people and vacationers check in here. Five bedrooms are no-smoking. The hotel restaurant serves breakfast only (continental or English). There is no bar, but guests are invited to BYOB (bring your own bottle) and drink in the lounge. A number of neighboring restaurants cater room service for the hotel; they are listed in a restaurant book found in each room. Dry cleaning and laundry service are available, and there's a health club nearby.

Mornington Hotel. 12 Lancaster Gate, London W2 3LG. ☎ **800/528-1234** or 0171/ 262-7361. Fax 0171/706-1028. www.mornington.se. E-mail: mornington.hotel@mornington. co.uk. 66 units. TV TEL. £105–£140 ($173.25–$231) double. Rates include Scandinavian and English cooked breakfast. AE, CB, DC, MC, V. Tube: Lancaster Gate.

Affiliated with Best Western, the Mornington brings a touch of northern European hospitality to the center of London. Just north of Hyde Park and Kensington Gardens, the hotel has a Victorian exterior and a Scandinavian-inspired decor. The area isn't London's most fashionable, but the location is close to Hyde Park and convenient to Marble Arch, Oxford Street shopping, and the ethnic restaurants of Queensway. The recently renovated guest rooms are tasteful and comfortable; all include coffee/tea facilities, pay movies, and fine mattresses. Baths are small but tidy, with medium-size towels and a hair dryer. You can wind down in the library and order snacks or afternoon tea from the well-stocked bar. Every year we get our annual Christmas card from "the gang"—the hotel staff, and what a helpful crew they are. Guest services include concierge, and dry cleaning and laundry service.

INEXPENSIVE

Adare House. 153 Sussex Gardens, London W2 2RY. ☎ **0171/262-0633.** Fax 0171/ 706-1859. www.freespace.virgin.net/adare.hotel. E-mail: adare.hotel@virgin.net. 20 units. TV TEL. £69 ($113.85) double with shower (slightly less in winter). Rates include full English breakfast. MC, V. Tube: Paddington.

This longstanding bed-and-breakfast remains one of the best choices for the budget traveler along B&B-crazed Sussex Gardens; the place still has a little soul, even though so many of its neighbors have lost theirs. The property is well maintained and has been gradually improved over the years, with the addition of private bathrooms in admittedly cramped space. Each room has a hair dryer. The public areas are relatively modest, but smart Regency-era wallpaper and red carpeting give them a touch of class. Many of the homey rooms are quite small, but they're spic-and-span and comfortably furnished, each with a good mattress. All have beverage makers.

The Byron Hotel. 36–38 Queensborough Terrace, London W2 3SH. ☎ **0171/243-0987.** Fax 0171/792-1957. www.capricornhotels.co.uk. E-mail: byron@capricornhotels.co.uk. 45 units. A/C TV TEL. £96–£105 ($158.40–$173.25) double; £120 ($198) triple; from £135 ($222.75) suite. Rates include English/continental breakfast. AE, DC, MC, V. Tube: Bayswater or Queensway.

A mostly American clientele appreciates this family-run hotel just north of Kensington Gardens for its country-house atmosphere, its helpful staff (who spend extra time with guests hoping to make their stay in London special), and the good value it offers. This is one of the best examples of a Victorian house conversion that we've seen; it was modernized without ruining its traditional appeal. The interior was recently redesigned and refurbished, and the rooms are better than ever, with ample closets, fine mattresses, tile bathrooms with good-size towels and a hair dryer, good lighting, and extra amenities like trouser presses, coffeemakers, and safes. An elevator services all floors, and breakfast is served in a bright and cheery room. Services include concierge, room service (limited hours), and dry cleaning.

Europa House Hotel. 151 Sussex Gardens, London W2 2RY. ☎ **0171/402-1923** or 0171/723-7343. Fax 0171/224-9331. www.visitus.co.uk/london/europa.html. E-mail: europahouse@enterprise.net. 18 units. TV TEL. £50–£65 ($82.50–$107.25) double; £18–£23 ($29.70–$37.95) per person family room. Rates include English breakfast. AE, DC, MC, V. Parking £10 ($16.50). Tube: Paddington.

Another budget find along Sussex Gardens, this family-run hotel attracts those who want a private shower with their room but don't want to pay too much extra for the luxury. Like most along Sussex Gardens, the bedrooms are a bit cramped, but they're well maintained and often color coordinated; each has private plumbing, plus good towels and a coffeemaker. Most of the rooms have been recently refurbished. Some rooms are custom built for groups, with three, four, or five beds per unit. Some of the multiple rooms have rather thin mattresses, but most are firm and comfortable. A hearty English breakfast awaits you in the bright dining room every morning.

Fairways Hotel. 186 Sussex Gardens, London W2 1TU. ☎ **0171/723-4871.** Fax 0171/ 723-4871. www.scoot.co.uk/fairways_hotel. E-mail: fairwayshotel@compuserve.com. 17 units (10 with bathroom). TV. £62 ($102.30) double without bathroom, £68 ($112.20) double with bathroom. Rates include English breakfast. MC, V. Tube: Paddington.

Jenny and Steve Adams welcome you into one of the finest B&Bs along Sussex Gardens. Even though it doesn't enjoy the pedigree it used to, this little place near Hyde Park is still a favorite address of bargain hunters. The black-and-white town house is easily recognizable: Just look for its colonnaded front entrance with a wrought-iron balustrade stretching across the second floor. Scorning the modern, the Adams family opts for traditional charm and character whenever possible. They call their breakfast room "homely" (Americans might say "homelike"); it's decorated with photographs of the family and a collection of china. Bedrooms are attractive and comfortably furnished, each with hot and cold running water, intercom, and beverage makers. Beds are fitted with firm mattresses, and units with private baths are small but tidy. Those who must share the corridor baths will find them clean and well maintained. The breakfast is hearty and home cooked, fit fortification for a day of sightseeing.

Norfolk Court & St. David's Hotel. 16–20 Norfolk Sq., London W2 1RS. ☎ **0171/ 723-4963.** Fax 0171/402-9061. 70 units (35 with shower). TV TEL. £50 ($82.50) double without bath, £60 ($99) double with bath or shower; £60 ($99) triple without bath, £75

($123.75) triple with shower; £70 ($115.50) quad without bath, £90 ($148.50) quad with shower. Rates include full English breakfast. AE, DC, MC, V. Tube: Paddington.

George and Foula Neokledos, two of the more welcoming hosts in this B&B area, manage to run both these properties with a certain style. Lying only a 2-minute walk from Paddington station, these small and friendly hotels were built when Norfolk Square knew a grander age, attracting such Victorian luminaries as John Addington Symonds (1840–93), the eccentric scholar and literary critic and author of the seven-volume *The Renaissance in Italy.* The bluebloods are long gone, but the area is still safe and recommendable. An interior designer might turn up his nose at the mismatched decor, but each room is well maintained and comfortably, if not elegantly, furnished. There's a homespun quality here. You get good beds with firm mattresses, an affordable price, and, in a few rooms, your own cubicle shower that's not made for lingering, but does the job. Towels are a bit thin.

Parkwood Hotel. 4 Stanhope Place, London W2 2HB. ☎ **0171/402-2241.** Fax 0171/402-1574. 18 units (12 with bathroom). TV TEL. £64.50 ($106.45) double without bathroom, £87.50 ($144.40) double with bathroom; £77 ($127.05), triple without bathroom, £97 ($160.05) triple with bathroom. Children under 13 sharing parents' room £7.50 ($12.40) Mon–Fri, free Sat and Sun. Rates include English breakfast. MC, V. Tube: Marble Arch.

Parkwood occupies one of the best locations for a good-value hotel in London: near Oxford Street and Marble Arch and just 50 yards from Hyde Park, in a section known as Connaught Village. The well-maintained, simple bedrooms have coffeemakers and radios, plus a firm mattress. The private baths are small with a set of medium-size towels, but corridor baths are adequate and well maintained. The hotel prides itself on an excellent breakfast; in fact, the menu states that if you're still hungry, you can have another meal—for free.

✪ The Pavilion. 34–36 Sussex Gardens, London W2 1UL. ☎ **0171/262-0905.** Fax 0171/262-1324. www.msi.com.mt/pavilion. 27 units. TV TEL. £90 ($148.50) double. Rates include breakfast. AE, DC, MC, V. Parking £5 ($8.25). Tube: Edgwater Road.

Until the early 1990s, this was a rather dull, ordinary-looking B&B. Then, a team of entrepreneurs with inroads to the fashion industry took over and radically redecorated the rooms with sometimes wacky themes, turning it into an idiosyncratic little hotel. The result is a theatrical and often outrageous décor that's much appreciated by the many fashion models and music-industry buffs who regularly make this their temporary home in London. Behind a blackened 1830s Victorian façade of stock bricks and stucco, the hotel offers rooms without any particular frills, but each has a distinctive decorative style. Examples include a kitsch 1970s room ("Honky-Tonk Afro"), an Oriental bordello theme ("Enter the Dragon"), and even some with 19th-century ancestral themes. One Edwardian-style room, a gem of emerald brocade and velvet, is called "Green with Envy." Each contains tea-making facilities, a firm mattress; and they are, regrettably, rather small. Bathrooms are also small, but efficiently organized, with excellent plumbing fixtures and a set of good-size towels. No meals are served other than breakfast.

The Phoenix Hotel. 1–8 Kensington Garden Sq., London W2 4BH. ☎ **800/528-1234** or 0171/229-2494. Fax 0171/727-1419. www.phoenixhotel.co.uk. E-mail: phoenixhotel@dial. pipex.com. 128 units. TV TEL. £92 ($151.80) double; £120 ($198) family room; £145 ($239.25) suite. Price includes buffet breakfast. AE, DC, MC, V. Tube: Bayswater.

This hotel occupies the entire south side of one of the most famous garden squares in Europe. Well situated in what is now an ethnically mixed neighborhood, the Phoenix was created from a series of 1854 town houses. The atmosphere is welcoming and gracious, and the well-furnished bedrooms keep to a smart international standard, with a decor done in muted tones and fabrics and beds with firm mattresses. Everything is designed for comfort and ease, including the luggage racks. Baths are a bit small but are well kept with a rack of medium-size towels. The bar is a good place to unwind; moderately priced meals are served in the downstairs café. Our biggest complaint? The public areas are too small for a hotel of this size. Services include room service (11am to 1am), dry cleaning, and a tour desk.

IN NEARBY MAIDA VALE
MODERATE

Colonnade Hotel. 2 Warrington Crescent, London W9 1ER. ☎ **0171/289-2167.** Fax 0171/286-1057. www.colonnade.demon.co.uk. E-mail: louise@colonnade.demon.co.uk. 43 units. A/C MINIBAR TV TEL. £160–£195 ($264–$321.75) double; £230 ($379.50) suite. Rates include English breakfast. AE, DC, MC, V. Parking £10 ($16.50). Tube: Warwick Ave.

The Colonnade, former home of Sigmund Freud, has been a landmark in the neighborhood since 1938, and during the life of this edition it may be considerably upgraded and refurbished. It lies in the fashionable section of Little Venice, about 10 minutes by Tube from London's West End. It's been run by the Richards family for about a half-century, and they continue to maintain its charm and special atmosphere. What we like about the place is the variety of rooms—they range from standard singles to suites with four-poster beds. All have private bathrooms and plenty of amenities, including radios, hair dryers, medium-size towels, and trouser presses (some suites even have Jacuzzis). Foam pillows, featherless duvets, cots, and bed boards are also available upon request. Each unit is fitted with a firm mattress. Every room and corridor is centrally heated around the clock from the first chilly breeze of autumn until the last retreating wind of winter—a rarity in London—and about half of the rooms are air-conditioned. Additional services include a concierge desk, dry cleaning and laundry service, and room service; baby-sitting can be arranged.

SMITHFIELD
EXPENSIVE

✪ **The Rookery.** 12 Peters Lane, Cowross Street, London EC1M 6DS. ☎ **0171/336-0931.** Fax 0171/336-0932. 33 units. A/C MINIBAR TV TEL. £170 ($280.50) double; £230 ($379.50) suite. AE, DC, MC, V. Tube: Farrington.

Newly fashionable Smithfield now has a quirky hotel worth considering as the center of your London sojourn. The only remaining Georgian houses in Peter's Lane have been united to form a delightful small hotel only a short walk from the Square Mile. The brainchild of Peter McKay and Douglas Blain, who gave the world the trendy Hazlitt's in Soho, the Rookery has been patiently restored with its period features relatively intact—even the coal-fired bread ovens still survive in the basement, which was a former bakery. They spent thousands of hours combing auction rooms, antiques shops, and flea markets for pictures, furniture, beds, and carpets to create maximum atmosphere. Regardless of where the bed came from, it is fitted with an absolutely superb mattress and fine bed linen. Each room is different and full of character. The Rook's Nest, for example, is on two levels with a 40-foot ceiling, boasting a panoramic view across London's rooftops from St. Paul's to the Old Bailey. The bathrooms are a special treat, all with Victorian cast-iron fittings, polished-copper pipe work, and an array of fluffy towels.

Dining: The owners say they're surrounded by wonderful places to eat (and they are)—"So why start another restaurant?" But there is an interesting menu served around the clock, and the fluffy breakfast croissants are baked on the premises.

Amenities: 24-hour room service, concierge, a tiny garden (unusual for a City location), dry cleaning, and laundry.

8 Near the Airports

NEAR HEATHROW
EXPENSIVE

London Heathrow Hilton. Terminal 4, Hounslow TW6 3AF. ☎ **0181/759-7755.** Fax 0181/759-7579. E-mail: gm_heathrow@comhilton.com. 395 units. A/C MINIBAR TV TEL. Sun–Thurs £160–£295 ($264–$486.75) double, Fri–Sat £110–£150 ($181.50–$247.50) double; all week suite from £430 ($709.50). AE, DC, MC, V. Parking £6.50 ($10.75).

This eye-catching, first-class hotel with its five-story atrium evoking the feel of a hangar is linked to Heathrow's Terminal 4 by a covered walkway. A glass wall faces the runways, so you can see planes land and take off. You can take buses to Terminals 1, 2, or 3. Bedrooms are fairly standardized and medium in size, but comfortably decorated with built-in wood furniture, upholstered sofas, and first-class mattresses on the beds. Bathrooms are tiled and trimmed in marble, containing a phone, a hair dryer, and a set of fluffy towels. The best accommodations are on the fifth floor with private robes and better amenities such as a private lounge with airport vistas.

Dining/Diversions: An open brasserie lies in the main lobby, and is "shaded" by umbrellas and canopies. There's also a rather good Chinese and Thai restaurant on-site, plus a stand-up bar with a grill section, decorated with a movie theme.

Amenities: Room service, concierge, TV with flight information, automated checkout.

Radisson Edwardian Heathrow. 140 Bath Rd., Hayes UB3 5AW. ☎ **0181/759-6311.** Fax 0181/759-4559. www.radisson.com. E-mail: resreh@radisson.com. 459 units. A/C MINIBAR TV TEL. £180–£210 ($297–$346.50) double; from £383 ($631.95) suite. AE, DC, MC, V. Parking £7 ($11.55). Heathrow Hopper bus service.

The poshest digs at Heathrow, this deluxe hotel lies just south of the M4 and about five minutes east of the long tunnel that leads to Terminals 1, 2, and 3. Since 1991, it has housed tired air travelers from all over the world. Its grand spa has a swimming pool and two bubbling whirlpools. You enter in a courtyard with potted trees and a koi pond. Persian rugs, a brass-railed staircase, and chandeliers live up to the Edwardian in the hotel's name. Rooms are medium in size but richly adorned with hand-painted hardwood furnishings, including deluxe mattress, and such extras as trouser presses and ironing boards, plus flight information broadcast on the TV. The baths are in tile and marble with robes, a hair dryer, and a set of fluffy towels.

Dining/Diversions: On-site are both a formal restaurant and a cheaper garden-style brasserie, each serving from an international and British menu. The sportsy bar has a polo theme, with saddles instead of stools.

Amenities: Steam room, spa, sauna, plunge pool, room service, concierge.

MODERATE

Renaissance London Heathrow Hotel. Bath Rd., Houndslow, London TW6 2AQ. ☎ **0181/987-6363.** Fax 0181/897-1113. E-mail: 106047.3556@compuserve.com. 650 units. A/C MINIBAR TV TEL. Sun–Thurs £139 ($229.35) double, Fri–Sat £82 ($135.30) double; all-week suite from £315 ($519.75). AE, DC, MC, V. Heathrow Hopper bus service to air terminals.

This is no airport sleeping dormitory. A bustling hotel factory, it lies just inside the perimeter of the airport and is spotted just before you reach the long airport entrance tunnel. Three cantilevered concrete floors attract a bevy of international travelers. Rooms have recently been renovated and are fairly standardized and a bit small, with coffeemakers, bedside controls, inlaid wood and laminate furnishings, and first-class mattresses, along with tiled combination baths (tub and shower), plus hair dryers, marble sinks, medium-size towels, and toilet articles. We prefer the units facing the airport itself (double glazing keeps down the noise). A brasserie serving international food overlooks the runaways, and there's also an international bar decorated with vintage aeronautical wall prints. Amenities include a solarium, sauna, gym, and restored health club.

Stanwell Hall. Town Lane, Stanwell, Staines, Middlesex TW19 7PW. ☎ **01784/252292.** Fax 01784/245250. 19 units (18 with bathroom). TV TEL. £100 ($165) double; £130 ($214.50) suite. Rates include breakfast. AE, DC, MC, V. Free parking.

This sunny Victorian house was purchased in 1951 by the Parke family, who converted it into a comfortable hotel. The cheery house with its side garden is located in a small village just minutes from Heathrow; it's perfect for business people who are tired of staying in standard airport hotels. About half the rooms have been fully renovated. The renovated rooms are comfortably furnished, papered in warm shades, and have chintz curtains covering the windows—a dramatic improvement over the washed-out, prerenovation rooms. All have coffeemakers and good mattresses. Bathrooms are efficiently organized and tidy, each with a hair dryer and a rack of medium-size towels. **St. Anne's Restaurant,** located on the ground floor, is small but inviting and serves modern British cuisine. The bar, which is popular with locals, serves drinks and snacks at lunchtime. Basic services include dry cleaning and laundry.

NEAR GATWICK
EXPENSIVE

Hilton London Gatwick Airport. South Terminal, Gatwick Airport, Gatwick, West Sussex RH6 0LL. ☎ **800/HILTONS** or 01293/518080. Fax 01293/528980. www.hilton.com. E-mail: gathitwrm@hilton.com. 550 units. A/C TV TEL. £187–£240 ($308.55–$396) double; from £260 ($429) suite. AE, DC, MC, V. Parking £10.40 ($17.15).

This deluxe five-floor hotel—Gatwick's most convenient resting place—is linked to the airport terminal with a covered walkway; an electric buggy service transports people between the hotel and airport. The most impressive part of the hotel is the first-floor lobby; its glass-covered portico rises four floors and contains a scale replica of the de Havilland Gypsy Moth airplane *Jason,* used by Amy Johnson on her solo flight from England to Australia in 1930. The reception area has a lobby bar and lots of greenery. The well-furnished, soundproofed rooms have triple-glazed windows, firm mattresses, and coffeemakers. Baths are tidily kept and equipped with a hair dryer and a rack of medium-size towels. Recently, 123 of the rooms were refurbished, in addition to the executive floor and all the junior suites. Now 300 of the rooms have minibars, stocked upon request.

Dining/Diversions: The American-themed restaurant **Amy's** serves buffet breakfasts, lunches, and dinners. **The Garden Restaurant,** outfitted in a formal English garden theme, serves drinks and full meals. There's also the 24-hour **Lobby Bar,** plus a polo-themed watering hole aptly named the **Jockey Bar.**

Amenities: Same-day dry cleaning and laundry service, up-to-date flight information channel, 24-hour room service, salon, bank, gift shop. Concierge, newspapers, baby-sitting, health club (sauna, steam room, massage room, swimming pool, gymnasium, Jacuzzi). Conference rooms, business center, shopping arcade.

Dining 5

George Mikes, Britain's famous Hungarian-born humorist, once wrote about the culinary prowess of his adopted country: "The Continentals have good food. The English have good table manners."

Quite a lot has happened since.

London has emerged as one of the great food capitals of the world, more so at the millennium than ever before. In the last few years, both its veteran and upstart chefs have fanned out around the globe for culinary inspiration, and have returned with innovative dishes, flavors, and ideas that London diners have never seen before. These chefs are pioneering a new style of cooking called "Modern British," which is forever changing, forever innovative, and yet comfortingly familiar in many ways. They've committed to centering their dishes around local ingredients, and have become daringly innovative with traditional recipes—too much so in the view of some critics, who don't like fresh mango over their blood pudding.

Traditional British cooking has made a comeback, too. The dishes that British mums nationwide have been forever feeding their reluctant families are fashionable again. Yes, we're talking British soul food: bangers and mash, Norfolk dumplings, nursery puddings, cottage pie—the works. This may be a rebellion against the excessive minimalism of the nouvelle cuisine that ran rampant over London in the 1980s, but who knows? Maybe it's just plain old nostalgia. Pig's nose with parsley-and-onion sauce may not be your idea of cutting-edge cuisine, but Simpson's-in-the-Strand is serving it for breakfast.

These days, many of the personality chefs spend a lot more time writing cookbooks and performing on TV than they do cooking in their own kitchens. As is so often the case, that chef you've read about in *Condé Nast Traveler* or *Travel & Leisure* may not be in the kitchen when you get here. But never fear: The cuisine isn't suffering. Many an up-and-comer, who's even better, has taken over. And with many London restaurants becoming so mammoth—with 200+ seats—the identity of the chef presiding over the kitchen is irrelevant as long as he or she can cook.

If you want a lavish meal, London is the place: gourmet havens such as Le Gavroche or Chez Nico at Ninety Park Lane, and a half-dozen others you'll find reviewed in the following pages. For those of you who don't want to break the bank, we've included many more affordable restaurants where you can dine really well. You'll find that London's food revolution has infiltrated every level of the dining

---

Area Code Change

After June 2000, London's area code will become **020.** The present seven-digit numbers will not change, but all 0171 numbers will add a "7" and all 0181 will add an "8." See the box in chapter 3 for more details.

---

scene—even the lowly pub has entered the culinary sweepstakes. Believe the unthinkable: At certain pubs, you can now dine better than in many restaurants. In some, standard pub grub has given way to Modern British and Mediterranean-style fare; in others, oyster bars have taken hold. See "Haute Cuisine Comes to the Lowly Boozer," below, for the best of the bunch.

SOME DINING NOTES

HOURS   Restaurants in London keep varied hours, but in general, lunch is offered from noon to 2pm and dinner is served from 7:30 to 9:30pm—but more and more restaurants are staying open later these days. Sunday is the typical closing day for London restaurants, but there are many exceptions. (Many restaurants also close for a few days or a week around Christmas, so call ahead if you're dining during the holiday season.) We've listed serving hours in the descriptions below.

RESERVATIONS   Nearly all places, except pubs, cafeterias, and fast-food joints prefer or require reservations. Almost invariably, you get a better table if you book in advance. For a few of the really famous places, you might need to reserve weeks in advance, even before leaving home. (Such reservations should always be confirmed when you land in London.)

TAXES & TIPPING   All restaurants and cafes are required to display prices of their food and drink in a place visible from outside the establishment. Charges for service as well as any minimum charge or cover charge must also be made clear. The prices shown must include $17^1/_2$% VAT. Most of the restaurants add a 10% to 15% service charge to your bill, but you'll have to check to make sure of that. If nothing has been added to your bill, leave a 12% to 15% tip.

1 Restaurants by Cuisine

AFTERNOON TEA

The Blue Room (Leicester Square)
Brown's Hotel (Mayfair)
Claridge's (Mayfair)
The Garden Café (Notting Hill)
The Georgian Restaurant
    (Knightsbridge)
The Lanesborough (Belgravia)
MJ Bradley's (Covent Garden)
The Orangery (Kensington)
Palm Court at the Waldorf Meridien
    (Covent Garden)
Palm Court Lounge (Mayfair)
Richoux (Knightsbridge)
Ritz Palm Court (St. James's)

St. James Restaurant & The Fountain
    Restaurant (St. James's)
The Tearoom at Chelsea Physic
    Garden (Chelsea)

AMERICAN

Chicago Rib Shack (Knightsbridge, *I*)
Christopher's (Covent Garden, *M*)
Deal's Restaurant and Diner
    (Chelsea Harbour, *I*)
Hard Rock Café (Mayfair, *I*)
Joe Allen (Covent Garden, *I*)
Pizzeria Condotti (Mayfair, *I*)

ASIAN

Oxo Tower (South Bank, *E*)

Key to Abbreviations: *VE* = Very Expensive; *E* = Expensive; *M* = Moderate; *I* = Inexpensive

BELGIAN

Belgo Centraal (Covent Garden, *M*)

BRITISH-TRADITIONAL

Butler's Wharf Chop House
(Docklands, *M*)
Dickens Inn by the Tower
(Docklands, *I*)
English Garden (Chelsea, *M*)
English House (Chelsea, *M*)
Fox & Anchor (The City, *I*)
The George (The Strand, *I*)
The George & Vulture (The City, *I*)
The Georgian Restaurant
(Knightsbridge, *E*)
The Granary (Piccadilly, *I*)
Langan's Bistro (Marylebone, *I*)
Langan's Brasserie (Mayfair, *M*)
Maggie Jones (Kensington, *I*)
Porter's English Restaurant
(Covent Garden, *I*)
Quo Vadis (Soho, *E*)
Rules (Covent Garden, *E*)
Scotts (Mayfair, *M*)
Shepherd's (Westminster, *M*)
Simpson's-in-the-Strand
(The Strand, *E*)
The Stockpot (Leicester Square, *I*)
Veronica's (Bayswater, *M*)
Wiltons (Piccadilly Circus, *E*)

BRITISH-MODERN

Alastair Little (Soho, *E*)
Atlantic Bar & Grill
(Piccadilly Circus, *M*)
Butler's Wharf Chop House
(Docklands, *M*)
Canteen (Chelsea Harbour, *M*)
Circus (Piccadilly Circus, *M*)
Clarke's (Notting Hill Gate, *M*)
The Criterion Brasserie-Marco Pierre
White (Piccadilly Circus, *M*)
English House (Chelsea, *M*)
Fifth Floor at Harvey Nichols
(Knightsbridge, *M*)
The Georgian Restaurant
(Knightsbridge, *E*)
Greenhouse (Mayfair, *M*)
Ivy (Soho, *M*)
Joe's (Kensington, *M*)
Launceston Place (Kensington, *M*)

Mirabelle (Mayfair, *E*)
Nico Central (Fitzrovia, *M*)
Oak Room/Marco Pierre White
(Mayfair, *VE*)
Quo Vadis (Soho, *E*)
Rhodes in the Square (Pimlico, *E*)
St. John (Clerkenwell, *M*)
Teatro Club & Restaurant
(Piccadilly Circus, *M*)
Titanic (Piccadilly Circus, *M*)

CANTONESE

Ming (Soho, *I*)

CHINESE

Chuen Cheng Ku (Soho, *I*)
Dumpling Inn (Soho, *I*)
Kai Mayfair (Mayfair, *M*)
Ken Lo's Memories of China
(Victoria, *E*)
Poons in the City (The City, *M*)

CONTINENTAL

Achy Ramp (Notting Hill Gate, *M*)
Alstair Little (Soho, *E*)
Blue Bird (Chelsea, *E*)
Hilaire (South Kensington, *E*)
L'Oranger (Mayfair, *M*)
Maison Novelli (Clerkenwell, *E*)
Mash (Soho, *M*)
Mezzo (Soho, *E*)
Oxo Tower (South Bank, *E*)
Quaglino's (Mayfair, *M*)
The Stockpot (Leicester Square, *I*)
Villandry (Soho, *M*)

FRENCH

Au Jardin des Gourmets (Soho, *M*)
Aubergine (Chelsea, *E*)
Bibendum/The Oyster Bar
(South Kensington, *E*)
Brasserie St. Quentin
(South
Kensington, *M*)
Canteen (Chelsea Harbour, *M*)
Chez Nico at Ninety Park Lane
(Mayfair, *VE*)
Connaught (French, *VE*)
Gordon Ramsay (Chelsea, *E*)
Langan's Bistro (Marylebone, *I*)
Langan's Brasserie (Mayfair, *M*)
Le Gavroche (Mayfair, *VE*)

L'Odéon (Piccadilly Circus, *E*)
Maison Novelli (Clerkenwell, *E*)
Magno's (Covent Garden, *M*)
Nico Central (Fitzrovia, *M*)
Pied-à-Terre (Fitzrovia, *E*)
The Room at the Halcyon
    (Holland Park, *E*)
Ship Hispaniola (Embankment, *M*)
Simply Nico (Victoria, *M*)
Vong (Knightsbridge, *E*)

HUNGARIAN

Gay Hussar (Soho, *E*)

INDIAN

The Bengal Clipper (Butler's
    Wharf, *M*)
Bombay Brasserie (South
    Kensington, *M*)
Café Spice Namaste (The City, *M*)
Soho Spice (Soho, *M*)
Tamarind (Mayfair, *I*)

INTERNATIONAL

Brinkley's Garden Restaurant &
    Chapter 11 Bar (West
    Brompton, *I*)
Chelsea Kitchen (Chelsea, *I*)
Circus (Piccadilly Circus, *M*)
Coast (Piccadilly Circus, *E*)
Collection (South Kensington, *M*)
Great Eastern Dining Room
    (Shoreditch, *I*)
Le Pont de la Tour (Docklands, *E*)
Odin's (Marylebone, *M*)
Pavilion Restaurant (South
    Kensington, *M*)
Turner's (South Kensington, *E*)
Villandry (Soho, *M*)

ITALIAN

Great Eastern Dining Room
    (Shoreditch, *I*)
I-Thai (Bayswater, *VE*)
Neal Street Restaurant
    (Covent Garden, *E*)
Pizzeria Condotti (Mayfair, *I*)
The River Café
    (Hammersmith, *E*)
San Lorenzo (Knightsbridge, *E*)
Zafferano (Knightsbridge, *E*)

JAPANESE

Nobu (Mayfair, *E*)
Suntory (St. James's, *VE*)

LEBANESE

Phoenicia (Kensington, *M*)

MEDITERRANEAN

Bibendum/The Oyster Bar
    (South Kensington, *E*)
Bistro 190 (South Kensington, *M*)
dell'Ugo (Soho, *I*)
Mezzo (Soho, *E*)

MOROCCAN/NORTH AFRICAN

Momo (Piccadilly Circus, *M*)
Moro (Clerkenwell, *M*)
Oxo Tower (South Bank, *E*)
Pasha (South Kensington, *M*)

PACIFIC RIM

Axis (Covent Garden, *E*)
Sugar Club (Soho, *M*)

PAKISTANI/MUGHLAI

Salloos (Belgravia, *M*)

PUBS

Antelope (Belgravia)
Bill Bentley's (Knightsbridge)
The Cow (Westbourne Park)
The Engineer (Camden Town)
The Enterprise (South Kensington)
Front Page (Chelsea)
Grenadier (Belgravia)
King's Head & Eight Bells (Chelsea)
Museum Tavern (Bloomsbury)
Nag's Head (Belgravia)
Nag's Head (Covent Garden)
Old Coffee House (Soho)
Prince Bonaparte (Westbourne Park)
Red Lion (St. James's)
Salisbury (Leicester Square)
Shepherd's Tavern (Mayfair)
Sherlock Holmes (Westminster)
Ye Olde Cheshire Cheese (The City)
Ye Olde Cock Tavern (The City)
Ye Olde Watling (The City)

SEAFOOD

Greens Restaurant & Oyster Bar
    (Piccadilly Circus, *M*)

In case you want to see the world.

At American Express, we're here to make your journey a smooth one. So we have over 1,700 travel service locations in over 130 countries ready to help. What else would you expect from the world's largest travel agency?

do more

Travel

In case you want to be welcomed there.

We're here to see that you're always welcomed at establishments everywhere. That's why millions of people carry the American Express® Card – for peace of mind, confidence, and security, around the world or just around the corner.

do more **AMERICAN EXPRESS**

Cards

And in case you'd rather be safe than sorry.

We're here with American Express® Travelers Cheques. They're the safe way to carry money on your vacation, because if they're ever lost or stolen you can get a refund, practically anywhere or anytime. To find the nearest place to buy Travelers Cheques, call 1 800 495-1153. Another way we help you do more.

do more

Travelers Cheques

North Sea Fish Restaurant
(Holborn, *I*)
Scotts (Mayfair, *M*)

SPANISH
Moro (Clerkenwell, *M*)

SUDANESE
Mondola (Notting Hill, *I*)

SZECHUAN
Zen Central (Mayfair, *M*)

THAI
Blue Elephant (West Brompton, *M*)
Chiang Mai (Soho, *I*)
Deal's Restaurant and Diner
(Chelsea Harbour, *I*)

I-Thai (Bayswater, *VE*)
Vong (Knightsbridge, *E*)

VEGETARIAN
Crank's in London (Mayfair, *I*)

WINE BARS
Boaters Wine Bar (Chelsea Harbour)
Bow Wine Vaults (The City)
Bubbles (St. James's)
Cork & Bottle Wine Bar
(Leicester Square)
Daniel's Bar/Cafe Royal Grill
(Piccadilly Circus)
Ebury Wine Bar (Victoria)
Jamaica Wine House (The City)
Le Metro (Knightsbridge)
Shampers (St. James's)

2 West End Restaurants

MAYFAIR
VERY EXPENSIVE

✪ **Chez Nico at Ninety Park Lane.** In Grosvenor House, 90 Park Lane, W1. ☎ **0171/ 409-1290.** Reservations required (at least 2 days in advance for lunch, 7 days for dinner). Fixed-price 3-course lunch £25–£40 ($41.25–$66); à la carte 2-course dinner £54 ($89.10), 3-course dinner £66 ($108.90). AE, DC, MC, V. Mon–Fri noon–2pm; Mon–Sat 7–11pm. Closed 10 days around Christmas/New Year's. Tube: Marble Arch. FRENCH.

Although the setting is as opulent as the cuisine, nothing takes precedence over food here. It's the work of one of London's supreme culinary artists, the temperamental but always amusing Nico Ladenis, assisted today by Paul Rhodes, who interprets the master's culinary ideas with flair and zest. Landenis, a former oil-company executive, self-taught cook, and economist, remains one of Britain's most talked-about chefs; his food is always impressive, always stylish, and he's constantly reinventing dishes we thought he had already perfected. As starters go, who can top his quail salad with sweetbreads, flavored with an almond vinaigrette? The main courses are a tour de force in the best post-nouvelle tradition, in which the tenets of classical cuisine are creatively and flexibly adapted to local fresh ingredients. With masterful technique, Nico's chefs dazzle with ever-changing fare, including a ravioli of langoustine that's a virtual signature dish. The chargrilled sea bass with basil purée or the Bresse pigeon are rivaled only by the work of Le Gavroche (see below). The only complaint we've ever heard about Chez Nico is that it attracts too many Michelin three-star groupies.

The Connaught Restaurant. In the Connaught Hotel, Carlos Place, W1. ☎ **0171/ 499-7070.** Reservations required. Main courses £18–£35 ($29.70–$57.75); fixed-price 3-course menu £60 ($99). AE, DC, MC, V. Daily 12:30–2:30pm and 6:30–10:45pm. Tube: Green Park. FRENCH/BRITISH.

Any restaurant that changes the tablecloths before serving dessert has to be special. You get service here with a smile, though you may tire of hearing "thank-you very much" repeated endlessly in the course of the evening. Hailed as "the last bastion of civilization," the Connaught would be the only safe place in London to invite the late Onassis, were he to miraculously return and emerge as your dining companion. This

West End Restaurants

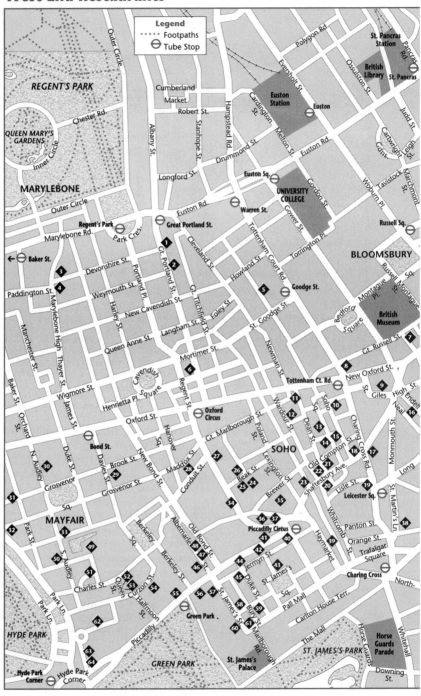

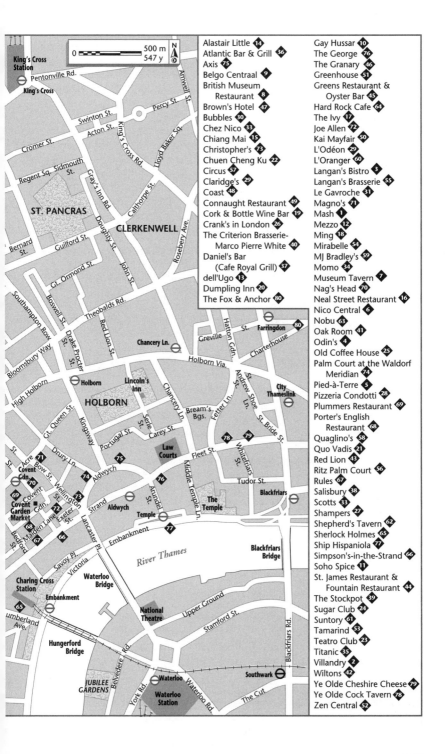

King's Cross Station
King's Cross
Pentonville Rd.
Swinton St.
Acton St.
Cromer St.
Regent Sq. Sidmouth St.
ST. PANCRAS
Bernard St.
Guilford St.
CLERKENWELL
Gt. Ormond St.
Theobalds Rd.
Chancery Ln.
Holborn Via.
Greville St. Farringdon
Charterhouse St.
City Thameslink
HOLBORN
Holborn
Lincoln's Inn
Bloomsbury Way
High Holborn
Southampton Row
Bream's Bgs.
Fetter Ln.
St. Bride St.
Carey St.
Fleet St.
Law Courts
Aldwych
Tudor St.
Blackfriars
Covent Gdn.
Covent Garden Market
Drury Ln.
Kingsway
Strand
Aldwych
Temple
The Temple
Embankment
Blackfriars Bridge
Charing Cross Station
Embankment
Waterloo Bridge
River Thames
Blackfriars Rd.
umberland Ave.
Hungerford Bridge
National Theatre
Upper Ground
Stamford St.
JUBILEE GARDENS
Waterloo
Waterloo Station
The Cut
Southwark
York Rd.
Belvedere Rd.
Waterloo Rd.

0 ——— 500 m
547 y

King's Cross Rd.
Gray's Inn Rd.
Doughty St.
John St.
Red Lion St.
Drake St.
Procter St.
Gt. Queen St.
Bow St.
Wellington St.
Bedford St.
Maiden Lane
Exeter St.
Savoy Pl.
Victoria
Lancaster Pl.
Arundel St.
Middle Temple Ln.
Whitefriars St.
Andrew St.
Hatton Gdn.
Shoe Ln.
Chancery Ln.
Amwell St.
Percy St.
Lloyd Baker St.
Rosebery Ave.
Calthorpe St.
Boswell St.
Southampton Bldgs.

heavily paneled dining room, with its patrol of tail-coated waiters with impeccable manners, serves food that may have gone out of fashion decades ago but which remains delectable. Those old standbys are still offered—Irish stew, and kidney and bacon—and their soufflé potatoes are so palate satisfying we hope that this long forgotten classic will make a comeback. In season, game—some 8 to 10 varieties—is incomparable and perfectly prepared. Their lamb sweetened on Welsh grass remains reason enough to visit, and the fish tastes almost startlingly fresh—The turbot and lobster are incomparable. Of course, all those truffles and foie gras would have pleased Escoffier. The untranslated French dishes, in the words of one Parisian food critic, are in "Paleolithic terminology," but are they ever good! An example would be the classic veal dish, mignon de veau Prince Orloff, which has virtually disappeared from Paris restaurants. One final conclusion: The Connaught kitchen has the biggest cream bill in Europe. The dessert trolley continues the stroll down Memory Lane: sherry triffle, treacle tart, or an apple tart in custard that surely would have delighted Queen Victoria.

✪ **Le Gavroche.** 43 Upper Brook St., W1. ☎ **0171/408-0881.** Reservations required as far in advance as possible. Main courses £29.10–£36.80 ($48–$60.70); fixed-price lunch £37 ($61.05); menu exceptionnel, for entire table, £78 ($128.70) per person. AE, DC, MC, V. Mon–Fri noon–2pm and 7–11pm. Tube: Marble Arch. FRENCH.

Le Gavroche has long stood for quality French cuisine, perhaps England's finest, although Michelin gives it only two stars. Though it may have fallen off briefly in the early 1990s, it's fighting its way back to the stellar ranks. There's always something special coming out of the kitchen of Burgundy-born Michel Roux; the service is faultless and the ambience formally chic without being stuffy. The menu changes constantly, depending on the fresh produce that's available and the current inspiration of the chef. But it always remains classically French, although not of the "essentially old-fashioned bourgeois repertoire" that some critics suggest. There are signature dishes that have been honed over years of unswerving practice: Try the soufflé Suissesse, *papillote* of smoked salmon, or whole Bresse chicken with truffles and a Madeira cream sauce. Game is often served, depending on availability. New menu options include cassoulet of snails with frog thighs seasoned with herbs, mousseline of lobster in champagne sauce, pavé of braised turbot with red Provençal wine and smoked bacon, and fillet of red snapper with caviar and oyster-stuffed tortellini. Desserts, including the sablé of pears and chocolate, are sublime. The wine cellar is among the most interesting in London, with many quality Burgundies and Bordeaux. The *menu exceptionnel* is, in essence, a tasting menu for the entire table. It usually consists of four to five smaller courses, followed by one or two desserts and coffee. At £78 ($128.70) per person, this may prove to be a smarter choice as opposed to the à la carte items.

✪ **Oak Room/Marco Pierre White.** in Le Méridien Piccadilly, 21 Piccadilly, W1. ☎ **0171/734-8000.** Reservations required as far in advance as possible. Fixed-price lunch £29.50 ($48.70); fixed-price dinner £80–£90 ($132–$148.50). AE, MC, V. Mon–Fri noon–2:15pm; Mon–Sat 7–11pm. Closed Christmas. Tube: Piccadilly Circus. MODERN BRITISH.

Put simply, "MPW" is the best chef in London. Picture Liam Neeson in a chef's jacket. The man's talent is prodigious, and by 1995 he had become one of the few three-star Michelin chefs in Britain. Not bad for a lad born in working-class Leeds, and a high-school dropout at that. He serves London's finest cuisine in the city's most beautiful dining room, which has been restored to its original oak-and-gilt splendor and filled with art, including works by Cocteau and Chagall.

Creative, sophisticated, and bold, this daring chef claims he never apprenticed in France other than a couple of weeks of eating in Paris restaurants. Lavish in his choice of ingredients, White explores the depths of flavor in food. As you peruse the dozen or so appetizers, you'll note that most feature foie gras, caviar, and truffles. Afterward, you can proceed to such main courses as Bressole of Bresse pigeon (with foie gras again), or braised pig's trotter. Platters sometimes appear with brilliant colors, including a gratinée of brill with a soft herb crust, young spinach, and a sabayon of chives. Among all this fancy fare, Marco Pierre White makes the world's greatest mashed potatoes, which one diner claims were "sieved, puréed, and squeezed through silk stockings." White vies with Nico Ladenis as the most temperamental chef in London. In White's view, "I'd rather be arrogant than insecure." He's clearly a magician. If you can afford it, try to catch the "show" of London's chef du jour.

EXPENSIVE

✪ **Mirabelle.** 56 Cruzon St., W1. ☎ **0171/499-4636.** Reservations required. Main courses £14.50–£26 ($23.90–$42.90); set lunch £15.95–£18.95 ($26.30–$31.25). AE, MC, V. Daily noon–2:30pm and 6pm–midnight. Tube: Green Park. MODERN BRITISH.

Marlene Dietrich and Noël Coward have long faded, of course, but you are likely to encounter today's media tabloid fodder, including Johnny Depp, battling paparazzi outside. Inside Marco Pierre White, the high-school dropout from Leeds, now an acclaimed chef, has brought new life to this long-standing legend. The chef has become so famous in London he's often simply "MPW." He calls Mirabelle, former stamping ground of the likes of Princess Margaret or Aristole Onassis, "my little love affair." The fading vestige of the seventies is all gone now, with a smart new art deco glimmer, a sexy red leather floor, and a little English garden in the heart of Mayfair. He's known for throwing some of the biggest names in the world out of his restaurants, but claims they deserve it when he tosses them out. This master chef has long abandoned his well-publicized bouts with drugs and alcohol, and tired old Mirabelle has become a shining new star.

On his menu, he remains a French classicist who refuses to Anglicize or even diversify his complex cuisine. For starters, foie gras terrine appears with amber jelly, a delectable opening. For more daring selections, opt for the pork cheeks flavored with ginger and spices. His squid ink risotto with calamari is now a familiar feature at his restaurants, and his sea bass with fennel and béarnaise is worth traveling through the Chunnel from France. His boneless oxtail, topped by a filigree potato galette, is the finest we've ever sampled. Save room for dessert, especially the bitter-chocolate tart with ice cream.

✪ **Nobu.** In the Metropolitan Hotel, 19 Old Park Lane, W1. ☎ **0171/447-4747.** Reservations required. Main courses £13–£27.50 ($21.45–$45.40); sushi and sashimi £2.50–£4.75 ($4.15–$7.85) per piece; fixed-price menu £60 ($99). AE, DC, MC, V. Mon–Fri noon–2:15pm; Mon–Fri 6–10:15pm, Sat 6–11:15pm, Sun 6–9:45pm. Tube: Hyde Park Corner. JAPANESE.

Robert de Niro and his restaurant gang of Nobu Matsuhisa and Como Holdings have taken their New York hot spot to London, where they offer an intensely innovative and experimental Japanese cuisine. With a beauty like Isabella Rossellini claiming that eating at Nobu keeps her lean and mean, how can you go wrong here?

The kitchen staff is brilliant and as finely tuned as their New York cousins. Sushi chefs don't just create sushi, but gastronomic pyrotechnics. Those on the see-and-be-seen circuit don't seem to mind the high prices that go with these incredibly fresh dishes. Elaborate preparations lead to perfectly balanced flavors. Where can you find a good sea urchin tempura these days but at Nobu? Salmon tartare with caviar is a brilliant appetizer, and Madonna agrees. Follow with a perfectly done fillet of sea bass in a sour bean paste or soft-shell crab rolls. The squid pasta is sublime, as is the black cod with miso, this latter dish incredibly popular and with good reason. Cold sake arrives in a green bamboo pitcher. If it's featured, finish with the savory ginger crème brûlée.

MODERATE

Greenhouse. 27A Hays Mews, W1. ☎ **0771/499-3331.** Reservations essential. Main courses £9.50–£18.50 ($15.65–$30.55). AE, DC, MC, V. Mon–Fri noon–2:45pm and 7–10:45pm; Sat 7–11pm; Sun 12:30–3pm and 7–10:30pm. Closed Christmas, bank holidays. Tube: Green Park. MODERN BRITISH.

Head chef Graham Grafton is quite inspired by modern British food. Grafton has a winning way with fish, if his poached skate is any example—and his deep-fried cod-and-chips is galaxies beyond what you'd get at the local chippie. But you may prefer the lip-smacking fare from the heart of England, which includes a roast breast of pheasant that Henry VIII would have loved, and grilled farmhouse pork—we're also fond of the wilted greens wrapped in bacon. The menu is backed up by a well-chosen wine list of some 20 selections. Some of the delightfully sticky desserts, including a moist bread-and-butter pudding and a ginger pudding with orange marmalade, would have pleased your Midlands grannie. It does look a bit like a greenhouse with plants scattered about. There are even prints of vegetables and flowers on the wall. Simply conceived dishes with a resolutely British slant draw a never-ending line of satisfied customers. The ingredients are first class and beautifully prepared, without ever destroying the natural flavor of a dish.

✪ Kai Mayfair. 65 S. Audley St., W1. ☎ **0171/493-8988.** Reservations recommended. Main courses £7.50–£30 ($12.40–$49.50). AE, DC, MC, V. Daily noon–2:30pm and 6:30–11pm. Tube: Marble Arch or Hyde Park Corner. CHINESE.

London is filled with sterile Chinese eateries using recipes that didn't transport well from the Far East. An exception is this winning earth-toned dining room, one of the glitziest Chinese restaurants in town, near the American Embassy. The owners wisely import specialty chefs from all parts of Asia, even one from Szechuan; and once in London, they prepare the dishes for which they became known. The menu promises dishes in such fanciful categories as "The Whims and Fancies of the Empress" or "Buddha Jumps Over the Wall." Tried-and-true Chinese dishes are here, everything from roast duckling with pineapple to sweet-and-sour pork. But many other dishes show imagination and flair, particularly shark's fin and abalone. Bang-bang chicken in a nut sauce packs a powerful taste punch. The Peking duck is worth the trek across town. Children are especially catered to, with dishes prepared just for them.

Langan's Brasserie. Stratton St., W1. ☎ **0171/491-8822.** Reservations recommended. Main courses £12.75–£14.95 ($21.05–$24.65). AE, DC, MC, V. Mon–Fri 12:15–11:45pm; Sat 7–11:45pm. Tube: Green Park. TRADITIONAL BRITISH/FRENCH.

Since its heyday in the early 1980s, when it was one of the hippest restaurants in London, this upscale brasserie has welcomed an average of 700 diners a day. The 1976 brainchild of actor Michael Caine and chef Richard Shepherd, the brasserie sprawls over two noisy, see-and-be-seen floors, each filled with potted plants and spinning ceiling fans that create a 1930s kind of feel. The menu is defined as "mostly English with a French influence" and includes a spinach soufflé with anchovy sauce, croustade of quail eggs in a pastry case served with a duxelle of mushrooms and hollandaise sauce, and roast crispy duck with apple sauce and sage-lemon stuffing. There's always a selection of English fare, including bangers and mash and fish-and-chips. Their dessert menu (and they call them desserts here instead of the English "puddings") reads like a journey into nostalgia: bread-and-butter pudding, treacle tart with custard, and apple pie with clotted cream. But how did mango sorbet slip in here?

L'Oranger. 5 St. James's St. SW1A. ☎ **0171/839-3774.** Reservations recommended. Set-price lunch £19.50–£23.50 ($32.15–$38.80); set-price dinner £33.50 ($55.30). AE, DC, MC, V. Mon–Fri noon–3pm; Mon–Sat 6–11:15pm. Tube: Green Park. CONTINENTAL.

This bistro-cum-brasserie occupies a large, rectangular, high-ceilinged space in an affluent neighborhood near the bottom of St. James's Street, and as such, manages to elevate a Gallic brasserie into an artfully upscale dining experience. Amid touches of paneling and burnt-orange paint, patterned carpeting, immaculate napery, masses of flowers, and uniformed waiters, you'll appreciate the artfully choreographed set menus of executive chef Kamel Benamar. His arrangement of flavors has been praised by a clientele that London pundits call "people who have made it." All menus are set-price—depending on the inspiration of the chef, they may include foie gras poached in a red Pessac wine sauce, and panfried fillet of sea bass with zucchini, tomatoes, basil, and a black-olive vinaigrette. Other staples might include crispy fillets of cod with bouillabaisse sauce and new potatoes, and braised leg of rabbit in Madeira sauce with whole cloves of yellow garlic *en confit* and braised cabbage. Particularly artful starters include a terrine of ham and tongue served with gherkins and parsley, bound together with a layer of spinach and served on a bed of choron sauce.

✪ **Quaglino's.** 16 Bury St., SW1. ☎ **0171/930-6767.** Reservations recommended. Main courses £11–£17 ($18.15–$28.05); fixed-price menu (available only for lunch and pre-dinner theater between 5:30 and 6:30pm) 2-courses £12.50 ($20.65), 3 courses £15 ($24.75). AE, DC, MC, V. Daily noon–3pm; Mon–Thurs 5:30–11:30pm, Fri–Sat 5:30pm–12:30am, Sun 5:30–10:30pm. Tube: Green Park. CONTINENTAL.

It's vast, it's convivial, it's fun. A restaurant on these premises was established in 1929 by Giovanni Quaglino, from Italy's Piedmont. Personalities who paraded through here in ermine and pearls could fill a between-the-wars roster of Who's Who for virtually every country of Europe. In 1993, noted restaurateur and designer Sir Terence Conran brought the place into the postmodern age with a vital new décor—eight artists were commissioned to decorate the octet of massive columns supporting the soaring ceiling. A mezzanine with a bar features live jazz every Friday and Saturday night and live piano music the rest of the week, and an "altar" in the back is devoted to the most impressive display of crustaceans and shellfish in Britain.

Everything seems to be served in bowls. Menu items have been criticized for their quick preparation and standardized format. But considering that on some nights up to 800 people might show up here for food, laughter, and gossip, the marvel is that the place functions as well as it does. That's not to say there isn't an occasional delay. Come for fun, not culinary subtlety and finesse. The menu changes often, but your choices might include goat cheese and caramelized onion tart, seared salmon with potato pancakes, crab tartlet with saffron, and roasted cod and ox cheek with char-grilled vegetables. The prawns and oysters—so delectable, so fresh—are the most ordered items.

Scotts. 20 Mount St., W1Y 6HE. ☎ **0171/629-5248.** Reservations required. Main courses £14.50–£32 ($23.90–$52.80); fixed-price 2-course lunch £19.50 ($32.15); fixed-price 3-course lunch or dinner from £24.50 ($40.40). AE, DC, MC, V. Daily noon–3pm; Mon–Sat 6–11pm, Sun 6–10pm. Oyster Terrace Mon–Fri noon–11pm; Sat 5–11pm. Tube: Green Park or Bond St. TRADITIONAL BRITISH/SEAFOOD.

In addition to a spacious dining room (refurbished in 1996) and cocktail bar, Scotts has a widely noted raw bar. Its origins were humble, dating back to a fishmonger on Coventry Street in 1851. However, its fame rests on its heyday, when the proprietors often entertained Edward VII and his guests in private dining rooms. Today the place has the style of a 1930s luxury liner.

The chef, who believes in British produce, handles the kitchen with consummate skill and authority. You get top-notch quality and ingredients. Lobster, crab, and oysters are featured along with meat dishes such as cumberland sausage and black pudding or corn-fed chicken with grain mustard. Dover sole is prepared a variety of ways, although the English prefer it "on the bone," considering fillet fish for sissies. The starter menu is so tempting you may never make it to the main dishes. There's even deep-fried whitebait so beloved by Victorians. Try the herb-flavored goat-cheese salad with baby spinach or the duck liver pâté with onion chutney, and most definitely the Loch Fyne oak-smoked Scottish salmon on rye bread. More down-to-earth dishes, such as fish cakes, appear regularly on the lunch menu served in the Oyster Terrace.

Zen Central. 20-22 Queen St., W1. ☎ **0171/629-8103.** Reservations recommended. Main courses £10–£35 ($16.50–$57.75). DC, MC, V. Mon–Sat 12:15–2:30pm and 6:15–11:15pm; Sun 12:15–2:30pm and 6:30–11:15pm. Tube: Green Park. SZECHUAN.

Movie stars always seem to have an advance scouting party informing them of the best places to dine when they visit a foreign city. When we heard that Eddie Murphy and Tom Cruise were heading for the Szechuan cuisine here, we followed in their foot-steps. Whoever directed them here was right. We didn't spot any stars, but found a designer chic Mayfair restaurant with a cool, dignified decor in minimalist black and white. Mirrors cover much of the place (maybe that's why movie stars like it). Served by a competent staff, the cuisine is first rate. Start with the coriander and crabmeat croquettes, or the soft-shelled crabs tenderly cooked in a crust of salt. The steamed sea bass is perfectly cooked and, for extra flavor, served with a black-bean sauce. Pork chops with lemon grass have a Thai flavor, and the baked lobster with crushed roast garlic and livers of tangerine peel is worth the walk across Mayfair. Habitués with some justification praise the cold pig's trotter, although this is an acquired taste for some. Vegetarian meals are also available. What do we really like about this place? The chef's braised fish cheek, shark's fin, and bird's nest soup evokes flavors enjoyed in China, and there is little catering to conventional Western palates. We find the wine list pricey, but the jasmine tea is lovely.

INEXPENSIVE

✪ Crank's In London. 8 Marshall St., W1 ☎ **0171/437-9431.** Main courses £2.00–£3.65 ($3.30–$6). No credit cards. Mon–Tues 8am–8pm; Wed–Fri 8am–9pm. Tube: Oxford Circus. VEGETARIAN.

Located just off Carnaby Street, this is the headquarters of a chain of vegetarian restau-rants with seven other branches in London. Outfitted in natural wood, wicker-basket lamps, pinewood tables, and handmade ceramic bowls and plates, Crank's is a com-pletely self-service restaurant: You carry your own tray to one of the tables. Organic-white and stone-ground flour is used for breads and rolls. The uncooked vegetable salad is especially good, and there's always a hot stew of savory vegetables (with "secret" seasoning) served in a hand-thrown stoneware pot with a salad. Their couscous with asparagus is an original concoction, and their stir-fry vegetable dishes continue to draw a funky crowd of 25- to 35-year-olds. Homemade honey cake, cheesecake, tarts, and crumbles are featured. Bakery goods, nuts, and general health-food supplies are sold in an adjoining shop.

Hard Rock Cafe. 150 Old Park Lane, W1. ☎ **0171/629-0382.** Main courses £8.50–£15 ($14–$24.75). AE, DC, MC, V. Sun–Thurs 11:30am–12:30am; Fri–Sat 11:30am–1am. Closed Dec. 25–26. Tube: Green Park or Hyde Park Corner. AMERICAN.

This is the original Hard Rock, now a world-wide chain of rock-and-roll-themed southern-cum-midwestern American roadside diners serving up good food and service with a smile. Since it was established on June 14, 1971, more than 12 million people have eaten here. Almost every night there's a line waiting to get in. The portions on the beef-laden menu are generous, and the price of a main dish includes not only a salad but also fries or baked potatoes. The fajitas are always a good choice. The tempting dessert menu offers homemade apple pie and thick, cold shakes. There's also a good selection of beers. The collection of rock memorabilia is worth seeking out if you're a fan.

Pizzeria Condotti. 4 Mill St., W1. ☎ **0171/499-1308.** Reservations not required. Pizzas £6.50–£7.95 ($10.75–$13.10); pastas £7.25 ($11.95); salads £2.95–£9.10 ($4.85–$15). AE, DC, MC, V. Mon–Sat 11:30am–midnight. Tube: Oxford Circus. ITALIAN/AMERICAN.

On pizza there can never be any agreement, but many aficionados claim this is London's best (frankly, we think dozens of New York spots have it beat). Nevertheless, when you're in London, you can hardly find a better choice for your pizza fix. Tastefully decorated with fresh flowers and local art from the 1970s, this place just off Regent Street looks more costly than it is.

Pizzas are light and crisp, and arrive at your table bubbling hot from the oven. They range from a simple margherita to the sublime King Edward with potato, four cheeses, and tomato. Dare to try the "American Hot," with mozzarella, pepperoni, sausages, and hot peppers. There are also huge salads, freshly made. Only two pastas are featured, savory versions of lasagna and cannelloni. Even the wine list is impressive and reasonable in price. Finish off perhaps with a scoop of creamy tartufo ice cream made with chocolate liqueur, a grace note that will evoke a memory of a visit to Rome's Piazza Navona.

Tamarind. 20 Queen St., W1. ☎ **0171/629-3561.** Reservations required. Main courses £10.50–£17.75 ($17.35–$29.30). AE, DC, MC, V. Sun–Fri noon–3pm; Mon–Sat 6–11:30pm, Sun 6–10:30pm. Tube: Green Park. INDIAN.

Currently in favor with food critics as well as the local lunchtime business crowd, Tamarind is the hottest Indian restaurant in Mayfair. A small basement dining room, it has gold pillars and a "tandoor window" for watching the chefs pull their flavorful, spicy dishes from the ovens. Chef Atul Kochhar leads a culinary brigade direct from Delhi that tries to maintain the style of cooking they knew back home, depending on the availability of spices and produce; only the best and freshest ingredients are selected daily in the markets. The kitchen prides itself on its "nouvelle" dishes, but they also excel at traditional Indian fare—including fabulous breads. The monkfish marinated in saffron and yogurt is especially delectable, as is the mixed kebab platter, cooked in a charcoal-fired tandoor—these chefs are king of the kebabs. Your best bet for a curry? Opt for the prawns cooked in a five-spice mixture. Vegetarians will find a safe refuge here, especially if they go for the Dal Bukhari, a black-lentil specialty of northwest India.

MARYLEBONE
MODERATE

Odin's. 27 Devonshire St., W1. ☎ **0171/935-7296.** Reservations required. Fixed-price 2-course lunch or dinner £24.95 ($41.15), fixed-price 3-course lunch or dinner £26.45 ($43.65). AE, DC, MC, V. Mon–Fri 12:30–2:30pm and 6:30–11pm. Tube: Regent's Park. INTERNATIONAL.

This elegant restaurant is one of at least four in London owned by chef Richard Shepherd and actor Michael Caine (whose stable includes Langan's Brasserie). Set adjacent to its slightly less expensive twin, Langan's Bistro (see below), it features ample space between tables and an eclectic decor that includes evocative paintings and deco accessories. As other restaurants nearby have come and gone, the cookery here remains solid and reliable; the standard of fresh ingredients and well-prepared dishes is always maintained. The menu changes with the seasons: Typical fare might include forest mushrooms in brioche, braised leeks glazed with mustard and tomato sauce, roast duck with apple sauce and sage and onion stuffing, or roast fillet of sea bass with a juniper cream sauce.

INEXPENSIVE

Langan's Bistro. 26 Devonshire St., W1. ☎ **0171/935-4531.** Reservations recommended. Fixed-price 2-course lunch or dinner £18.50 ($30.55), fixed-price 3-course lunch or dinner £20.50 ($33.80). AE, DC, MC, V. Mon–Fri 12:30–2:30pm; Mon–Sat 6:30–11:30pm. Tube: Regent's Park. TRADITIONAL BRITISH/FRENCH.

This unpretentious restaurant has been a busy fixture on the London scene since the mid-1960s, when it was established by the late restaurateur Peter Langan with chef Richard Shepherd and actor Michael Caine. Of the several restaurants in this chain (see Langan's Brasserie and Odin's, above), it's the least expensive, but the most visually appealing. Set behind a brightly colored storefront on a residential street, the dining room is decorated with fanciful clusters of Japanese parasols, rococo mirrors, surrealistic paintings, and old photographs. The menu is "mostly English with a French influence"; it changes with the seasons, but might include as a starter red-pepper and Brie tarlets or grilled goat cheese with rocket salad. Long-time brasserie favorites here are reassuringly familiar, and just as good as they ever were. Always check out the dish of the day or opt for the chargrilled tuna Niçoise or the cod with an herb crust (served in a butter sauce). Chocaholics should finish off with the dessert extravaganza known as "Mrs. Langan's Chocolate Pudding."

ST. JAMES'S
VERY EXPENSIVE

✪ **Suntory.** 72-73 St. James's St., SW1. ☎ **0171/409-0201.** Reservations required. Main courses £10–£48 ($16.50–$79.20); fixed-price lunch £15–£30 ($24.75–$49.50); fixed-price dinner £53–£90 ($87.45–$148.50). AE, DC, MC, V. Mon–Sat noon–2pm and 6–10pm; Sun 6–10pm. Tube: Green Park. JAPANESE.

London's longest established and one of its best-known Japanese restaurants, Suntory is still holding its own against increased competition from Nobu. Unlike Nobu, it doesn't cater to Western palates, continuing instead to concentrate on the artistic presentation of the highest-quality produce. Prices are as lofty as ever. Owned and operated by Japanese distillers and brewers, Suntory offers a choice of dining rooms in a setting evocative of a Japanese manor house. First-time visitors seem to prefer the tappanyaki dining room downstairs, where, through iron grills on your table you can watch the mastery of the high-hatted, knife-wielding chef up close. In other rooms you can dine on sukiyaki, tempura, and sushi (especially good is the delicately sliced raw tuna). Waitresses in traditional dress serve you with all the highly refined ritual of Japan. Appetizers are artful and delicate; even the tea is superior.

PICCADILLY CIRCUS & LEICESTER SQUARE
EXPENSIVE

Coast. 26B Albemarle St., W1X 3FA. ☎ **0171/495-5999.** Reservations required. Main courses £13.50–£22.50 ($22.30–$37.15). AE, MC, V. Mon–Sat noon–3pm and 6pm–midnight; Sun noon–3:30pm and 6–11pm. Tube: Piccadilly Circus. MODERN INTERNATIONAL.

Coast is so cutting edge, so 21st century, that you might get the feeling that it strains a bit to maintain its hip image. Set in a former auto showroom with lots of parquet woodwork, it's painted in colors that resemble, according to your tastes, either spring green or the color of aged bilge water, and accented with lighting fixtures that protrude like alien bug eyes. There's only one piece of art (by the terribly fashionable artist Angela Bulloch), but it's a doozy: a drawing machine that uses a robotic arm to scribble a graph simulating the movement on an electronic screen—like a giant Etch-a-Sketch, it's wiped clean when it becomes unreadable.

With all this forced hipness, we didn't really want to like this place, but it won us over with its surprisingly good food. Innovative chef Bruno Loubet is an original (some say too innovative), but we liked his willingness to go where others fear to tread. He handles textures well and brings out the best of the flavors in the light cuisine, particularly the fish dishes. This is no beans-on-toast place. Loubet tempts with his seared salmon spring roll in fermented black-bean aïoli, monkfish and pickled vegetable terrine, rabbit ravioli, or peppered Hereford duck with honey and Asian greens. Of course, none of these exact items will be on the menu presented to you because Loubet will have long changed them, but expect a surprise and a delight to your palate regardless of what he's dishing out.

L'Odéon. 65 Regent St., W1. ☎ **0171/287-1400.** Reservations required. Main courses £14.50–£25 ($23.90–$41.25); fixed-price 2-course lunch £15.50 ($25.60), fixed-price 3-course lunch £19.50 ($32.15). AE, DC, MC, V. Mon–Sat and Sun noon–2:30pm; Mon–Sat 5:30–11:30pm. Tube: Piccadilly Circus. FRENCH.

When the Michelin-starred chef Bruno Loubet opened this chic 1930s-style brasserie, headlines read "Loubet Cooks for the Masses." His sous-chef, Erwan Louaisil, carries on since Loubet's departure, but the menu remains rooted in the Loubet repertoire. You can opt for a table looking out on Regent Street and its bright-red double-deckers. In all, some 250 diners can pack this place (and often do).

The culinary style isn't as daring and provocative as before, and has switched to a more classic French cuisine. Opt for the panfried seam bream with a peppery butter sauce or else the roast farmhouse chicken with Parmesan, served with Basmatic rise. Louaisil learned a lot when he worked at Daniel's in New York and was a protégé of the great Pierre Garnier in Paris. Each dish reflects his own special taste, as evoked by his starters, a light mussel saffron mousse or a risotto of flap mushrooms with Parmesan shavings. For dessert, he dazzles, especially his poached apple in saffron with dried-fig ice cream or his roast papaya with whiskey-and-caramel ice cream.

✪ **Wiltons.** 55 Jermyn St., SW1. ☎ **0171/629-9955.** Reservations required. Jacket and tie required for men. Main courses £15–£25 ($24.75–$41.25). AE, DC, MC, V. Mon–Fri 12:30–2:30pm and 6–10:30pm; Sun 12:30–2:30pm and 6:30–10pm. Closed Sat. Tube: Green Park or Piccadilly Circus. TRADITIONAL BRITISH.

This is one of the top purveyors of traditional British cuisine and our favorite of the current bunch. Opened in 1742, this thoroughly British restaurant—it's been called "as British as a nanny"—is known for its fine fish and game. Gourmets flock here for the best oysters and lobsters in London, and they know it's the place to go to find unusual seafood. You might begin with an oyster cocktail and follow with Dover sole, plaice, salmon, or lobster, prepared in any number of ways. In season (from mid-August), there are such delights as roast partridge, pheasant, or grouse; you might even be able to order widgeon, a wild, fish-eating river duck (the chef might ask you if you want it "blue" or "black," a reference to roasting times). Game is often accompanied by bread sauce (milk thickened with bread crumbs). To finish, consider a savory such as Welsh rarebit, soft roes, or anchovies; if that's too much, try the sherry trifle or syllabub.

We consistently find the service, by a bevy of bosomy matrons, to be the most helpful in the West End. Since this is a bastion of traditionalism, however, don't show up wearing the latest Covent Garden fashion—you might not get in. Instead, don your oldest suit and look like you believe the Empire still exists.

MODERATE

Atlantic Bar & Grill. 20 Glasshouse St., W1. ☎ **0171/734-4888.** Reservations required. Main courses £10.50–£18 ($17.35–$29.70); fixed-price 3-course lunch £14.90 ($24.60). AE, DC, MC, V. Mon–Fri noon–3pm; Mon–Sat 6pm-3am, Sun 6–10:30pm. Tube: Piccadilly Circus. MODERN BRITISH.

A titanic restaurant installed in a former art deco ballroom off Piccadilly Circus, this 160-seat locale draws a trendy crowd to London's tawdry heartland. The restaurant remains cosmopolitan, and it's one of the best choices for an after-theater crowd because it closes at 3am on most nights. It doesn't attract the celebrities like Goldie Hawn as it did back in its 1994 heyday, but it's still going strong nonetheless. The original chef, Richard Sawyer, is back, serving his second tour of duty and doing much to recapture the restaurant's mid-1990s chic. He is turning out a new menu that places more emphasis on organic and homegrown produce. Some dishes are quite compli- cated and taste as good as they sound—swordfish dumplings with a salsa of plum tomatoes, fresh cilantro, seated shiitake, soy-infused ginger, and fresh wilted spinach. The menu changes every two months, but is always strong on seafood and meats. For a starter, we recommend the Caesar club salad (the chicken is smoked on the premises). Memorable also is the loin of yellow-fin tuna served with a wild parsley and eggplant relish with a roasted red bell pepper pesto. The desserts, however, are pur- posefully (and inexplicably) unsophisticated: rice pudding, poire Belle Hélène (poached pear). If you're rushed, you can drop into Dick's Bar, where they serve up everything from lamb burgers sparked with yogurt and fresh mint to Cashel blue cheese and pumpkin seeds on ciabatta bread, for a quick bite.

Circus. 1 Upper James St. W1. ☎ **0171/534-4000.** Reservations required. Main courses £12.50–£17.50 ($20.65–$28.90); fixed-price menus before 7:30pm and 10:15pm–midnight £15.75–£17.75 ($26–$29.30). AE, DC, MC, V. Daily noon–3pm and Mon–Sat 6pm–midnight. Bar menu daily noon–1:30am. Tube: Piccadilly Circus. BRITISH/INTERNATIONAL.

A minimalist haven for power design and eating in the very heart of London, this new restaurant took over the ground floor and basement of what used to be the Granada Television building at the corner of Golden Square and Beak Street. It buzzes during pre- and post-theater times, and chef Richard Lee has already acquired a fashionable following of London foodies. The place evokes a London version of a Left Bank Parisian brasserie. For some country cousins from the north of England who missed out on the food revolution of the past decades, Lee offers braised faggot with bubble and squeak (bubble and squeak is cabbage and potatoes, and faggots aren't what you thought, but are highly seasoned squares of pig's liver, pork, onion, herbs, and nutmeg—bound with an egg and baked wrapped in a pig's caul). You might want to go on instead to taste the divine skate wing with "crushed" new potatoes accompanied by a thick pestolike medley of rocket blended with black olives. Or else try the tasty sautéed chili-flavored squid with bak choi, made even more heavenly with the tamarind dressing. The sorbets are a nice finish to a meal, especially the delectable mango and pink grapefruit version. Of course, if you're ravenous, there's always the velvety smooth Amaretto cheesecake with a coffee sauce. Service is a delight.

The Criterion Brasserie-Marco Pierre White. 224 Piccadilly, W1. ☎ **0171/930-0488.** Main courses £11–£15 ($18.15–$24.75); fixed-price 2-course lunch £16.95 ($27.95), fixed-price 3-course lunch £19.95 ($32.90). AE, MC, V. Daily noon–2:30pm and 6pm– midnight. Tube: Piccadilly Circus. MODERN BRITISH.

Known as the bad boy of British cookery, Michelin-starred Marco Pierre White runs what he calls his "junior" restaurant here. Designed by Thomas Verity in the 1870s, this palatial neo-Byzantine mirrored marble hall is a glamorous backdrop for the master chef's cuisine, served under a golden ceiling, with theatrical peacock-blue draperies. The menu is wide ranging, from Paris brasserie food to "nouvelle-classical," and served by a mainly French staff. The food is excellent, but falls short of sublime. Still, the roast skate wing with deep-fried snails is delectable, as is the roast saddle of lamb stuffed with mushrooms and spinach.

Greens Restaurant & Oyster Bar. 36 Duke St., St. James's SW1. ☎ **0171/930-4566.** Reservations recommended. Main courses £10.50–£37 ($17.35–$61.05). AE, DC, MC, V. Restaurant daily 12:15–3pm; Mon–Sat 5:30–11pm. Oyster Bar Mon–Sat 11:30am–3pm and 5:30–11pm; Sun 12:30–3pm and 5:30–9pm. Tube: Piccadilly Circus or Green Park. SEAFOOD.

Critics say it's a triumph of tradition over taste but, as far as seafood goes in London, this is a tried-and-true favorite, thanks to an excellent menu, a central location, and a charming staff. This busy place has a cluttered entrance leading to a crowded bar where you can stand to sip fine wines and, from September to April, enjoy oysters. In the faux-Dickensian dining room, you can select from a long menu of fresh seafood dishes, which changes monthly depending what is in season. The standard menu ranges from fish cakes with roast pepper and tomato sauce to whole Scottish lobster. For zesty starters, try either the smoked eel fillets (Cockney) or the avocado-and-bacon salad with baby-leaf spinach. Desserts include bread-and-butter pudding. The menu changes monthly, but it's always based on the freshest of ingredients deftly prepared by the kitchen staff. Be alert that London has two different Duke streets. Greens is in St. James's.

Momo. 25 Heddon St., W1. ☎ **0171/434-4040.** Reservations required 2 weeks in advance. Main courses £9.50–£16.50 ($15.65–$27.20); fixed-price 2-course lunch £12.50 ($20.65), fixed-price 3-course lunch £15.50 ($25.60). AE, DC, MC, V. Mon–Fri noon–2:30pm; Mon–Sat 7–11:30pm. Tube: Piccadilly Circus. MOROCCAN/NORTH AFRICAN.

You'll be greeted by a friendly and casual staff member clad in a black-and-white T-shirt and fatigue pants. The setting is like Marrakesh, with stucco walls, a wood-and-stone floor, patterned wood window shades, burning candles, and cozy banquettes. You can fill up on the freshly baked bread, along with appetizers such as garlicky marinated olives and pickled carrots spiced with pepper and cumin. These starters are a "gift" from the chef. Other appetizers, which you'll pay for, are also tantalizing, especially the *briouat,* paper thin and very crisp triangular packets of puffed pastry that are filled with saffron-flavored chicken and other treats. One of the chef's finest specialties is *pastilla au pigeon,* a traditional poultry pie with almonds. Many diners visit for the couscous maison, among the best in London. Served in a decorative pot, this aromatic dish of raisins, meats (including merguez sausage), chicken, lamb, and chickpeas is given added flavor with that powerful hot sauce of the Middle East, marissa. After all this, the refreshing cinnamon-flavored orange slices are a tempting treat for dessert.

Teatro Club & Restaurant. 93-107 Shaftesbury Ave., W1. ☎ **0171/494-3040.** Reservations required. Main courses £15.50–£19.50 ($25.60–$32.15); fixed-price menus (lunch or dinner) £16–£18 ($26.40–$29.70). AE, DC, MC, V. Mon–Fri noon–3pm and Mon–Sat 6–11:45pm. Tube: Piccadilly Circus. MODERN BRITISH.

Opening to instant glory and a lot of press hype, this restaurant burst onto the scene in 1998. It became highly acclaimed for its contemporary British fare. Having Gordon Ramsay, one of London's most acclaimed chefs, as its consultant also helped. Ramsay must have given good advice because the cuisine is quite delectable. The restaurant with its minimalist chic decor is the creation of Lee Chapman, a footballer, and his wife, actress Leslie Ash. The actual chef is Stuart Gillies, an artist who cooks with flavor, precision, and great skill.

The cuisine is a lot richer than the interior, beginning with such starters as sweet corn ravioli with truffle oil and chanterelles, or panfried crispy pig's trotter. The crab bisque is velvety smooth, as is the foie gras du jour. Salmon appears with a lemony couscous or else you can venture into the roast fillet of cod with "crushed" potatoes, or perhaps the breast of guinea fowl with braised lettuce. The grilled halibut would put a "chippie" to shame, and it's given added zest by horseradish butter. Desserts are a journey into nostalgia—treacle tart, banana sticky toffee, and the like.

The Titanic. In the Regent Palace Hotel, 12 Sherwood St., near Piccadilly Circus, W1A. ☎ **0171/437-1912.** Reservations required. Main courses £9–£11.50 ($14.85–$18.95); breakfast platters £7–£12.50 ($11.55–$20.65). AE, DC, MC, V. Daily noon–2:30 and 5:30–11:30pm. Breakfast daily 11:30pm–2:30am. Tube: Piccadilly. MODERN BRITISH.

Just before Christmas 1998, the most celebrated and gilt-edged of chefs (Marco Pierre White or "MPW") took a plebian plunge into the waters of middle-bracket dining with the establishment of this sought-after bistro. Despite its phone number ("1912" is the year the famous ship went down) and its name, the staff is eager to point out that the nautical art deco decor is modeled after the *Queen Mary,* not *The Titanic,* partly because they feared that there might be a public loss of appetite "because of the name's association with dead people." Expect a large, crowded venue where tables turn over several times during the course of a night, and where food items are designed for the young at heart and for palates a lot less sophisticated than those that dine in Marco Pierre's other upscale gastronomic temples. Menu items include bresaola (Scottish beef cured in the Mediterranean style with olive oil and herbs), snails in garlic butter, oysters, mussels in white wine, Caesar salads, fish-and-chips with mushy peas, brochettes of lamb in the Provençal style, and caramelized skate. After 11:30pm, the focus moves to breakfast, presumably for night owls who have worked up an appetite at the disco, in bed, or whatever, or for any transatlantic flyer suffering from jet lag and a hankering for eggs benedict, an omelet, kippers, or shirred eggs with calves liver.

INEXPENSIVE

The Granary. 39 Albemarle St., W1. ☎ **0171/493-2978.** Main courses £7–£8.60 ($11.55–$14.20). MC, V. Mon–Fri 11:30am–8pm; Sat–Sun noon–2:30pm. Tube: Green Park. TRADITIONAL BRITISH.

This family-operated country-style restaurant has served a simple but flavorful array of home-cooked dishes, listed daily on a blackboard, since 1974. The daily specials might include lamb casserole with mint and lemon; panfried cod; or avocado stuffed with prawns, spinach, and cheese. Vegetarian meals include mushrooms stuffed with mixed vegetables, stuffed eggplant with curry sauce, and vegetarian lasagna. Tempting desserts are bread-and-butter pudding and brown Betty (both served hot). The large portions guarantee that you won't go hungry. Cookery is standard, rather routine, but still quite good for the price.

The Stockpot. 38 Panton St. (off Haymarket, opposite the Comedy Theatre), SW1. ☎ **0171/839-5142.** Reservations accepted for dinner. Main courses £2.35–£5.65 ($3.90–$9.30); fixed-price 2-course lunch £3.50 ($5.75); fixed-price 3-course dinner £5.90 ($9.75). No credit cards. Mon–Sat 7am–11:30pm; Sun 7am–10pm. Tube: Piccadilly Circus or Leicester Square. TRADITIONAL BRITISH/CONTINENTAL.

Penny for penny, we'd hazard a guess that this cozy little restaurant offers one of the best dining bargains in London. Meals include a bowl of minestrone, spaghetti bolognese (the eternal favorite), a plate of braised lamb, and the apple crumble (or another dessert). At these prices, the food is hardly refined, but filling and satisfying nonetheless. With two levels of dining in a modern room, The Stockpot has a share-the-table policy during peak dining hours.

SOHO
EXPENSIVE

Alastair Little. 49 Frith St., W1. ☎ **0171/734-5183.** Reservations recommended. Fixed-price dinner £33 ($54.45); fixed-price 3-course lunch £25 ($41.25). AE, MC, V. Mon–Fri noon–3pm; Mon–Sat 6–11pm. Tube: Leicester Sq. or Tottenham Court Rd. MODERN BRITISH/CONTINENTAL.

In a brick-fronted town house (ca. 1830)—which for a brief period supposedly housed John Constable's art studio—this informal, cozy restaurant is a pleasant place to enjoy a well-prepared lunch or dinner. Some loyal critics still claim that Alastair Little is the best chef in London, but lately he's been buried under the avalanche of new talent. Actually, Little himself is not often here; he spends a good deal of time at other enterprises and at a cooking school in Umbria. The talented James Rix is in charge. Style is now modern European with a heavy slant toward Italian. The menu still changes daily. Starters might include a salad of winter leaves with crispy pork or chicken livers in Vin Santo flavored with fresh tomatoes and basil. The terrine of wild duck and foie gras is a surefire pleaser, followed by such main-course delights as risotto with both flap and field mushrooms or home-salted cod with spicy chickpeas and greens. For dessert, you can select an array of British cheeses or else order such classics as a pear-and-red-wine tart. Ever have olive oil cake? It's served here with a winter-fruit compote.

✪ **Quo Vadis.** 26–29 Dean St., W1. ☎ **0171/437-9585.** Reservations required. Main courses £13–£27.50 ($21.45–$45.40); fixed-price lunches and pre- and post-theater £14.75–£17.95 ($24.35–$29.60). AE, MC, V. Mon–Fri noon–3pm; Mon–Sat 6–11pm, Sun 6–10:30pm. Tube: Leicester Sq. or Tottenham Court Rd. MODERN BRITISH.

This hyper-trendy restaurant occupies the former apartment house of Communist patriarch Karl Marx, who would never recognize it. It was a stodgy Italian restaurant from 1926 until the mid-1990s, when its interior was ripped apart and changed into the stylish postmodern place you'll find today. The stark street-level dining room is a showcase for the hyper-modern paintings of the controversial Damien Hirst and other contemporary artists. Many bypass the restaurant altogether for the upstairs bar, where Hirst has put a severed cow's head and a severed bull's head on display in separate aquariums. Why? They're catalysts to conversation, satirical odes to the destructive effects of Mad Cow Disease, and perhaps tongue-in-cheek commentaries on the flirtatious games that patrons conduct here.

Quo Vadis is associated with Marco Pierre White, but don't expect to see the temperamental culinary superstar here; as executive chef, he only functions as a consultant. Also, don't expect that the harassed and overburdened staff will have the time to pamper you; they're too preoccupied dealing with the glare of frenetic publicity. And the food? It's appealingly presented and very good, but not nearly as artful or innovative as the setting might lead you to believe. We suggest beginning with the tomato and red mullet broth perfumed with basil or the terrine of foie gras and duck confit before moving on to the escallop of tuna with tapenade and eggplant caviar (actually eggplant and black olives puréed and seasoned, which gives it the look of caviar) or the roast chicken à la souvaroff, truffle oil, herb dumplings, and vegetable broth.

MODERATE

The Gay Hussar. 2 Greek St., W1. ☎ **0171/437-0973.** Reservations recommended. Main courses £11.50–£16 ($18.95–$26.40); fixed-price lunch £17.50 ($28.90). AE, DC, MC, V. Mon–Sat 11:45–2:30pm and 5:30–10:45pm. Tube: Tottenham Court Rd. HUNGARIAN.

The Gay Hussar has been called the best Hungarian restaurant in the world. Since 1953, it's been an intimate place with undeniably authentic cuisine, drawing upon a loyal clientele of politicians, but also enjoying a large international following, especially among visiting Hungarians. You can begin with a chilled wild-cherry soup or mixed Hungarian salami. Gutsy main courses might include cabbage stuffed with minced veal and rice, half a perfectly done chicken served in mild paprika sauce with cucumber salad and noodles, excellent roast duck with red cabbage and Hungarian-style caraway potatoes, and, of course, veal goulash with egg dumplings. Expect gigantic portions. For dessert, go with either the poppy-seed strudel or walnut pancakes.

Mezzo. 100 Wardour St., W1. ☎ **0171/314-4000.** Reservations required for Mezzonine. Mezzo 3-course dinner £35–£40 ($57.75–$66). £5 ($8.25) cover at Mezzo Wed–Sat after 10pm. Mezzonine 3-course dinner £25–£30 ($41.25–$49.50). AE, DC, MC, V. Mezzo: Mon–Fri noon–3pm; Sun noon–4pm; Mon–Thurs 6pm–1am; Fri–Sat 6pm–3am; Sun 6–11pm. Mezzonine: Mon–Fri noon–3pm; Sat noon–4pm; Mon–Thurs 5:30pm–1am; Fri–Sat 5:30pm–3am. Tube: Tottenham Court Rd. CONTINENTAL/MEDITERRANEAN.

This blockbuster 750-seat Soho restaurant—the latest creation of entrepreneur Sir Terence Conran—may be the biggest in Europe. The mammoth space, on the former site of rock's legendary Marquee club, has been split into several separate restaurants: Mezzonine upstairs, serving a Thai/Asian cuisine with European flair (deep-fried salt-and-pepper squid, garlic, and coriander; roast marinated lamb with yogurt and cumin on flat bread); the swankier Mezzo downstairs offering a modern European cuisine, in an atmosphere of 1930s Hollywood (at any minute you expect Marian Davies—drunk or sober—to descend the grand staircase); and Mezzo Café, where you can stop in for a sandwich.

The food is at its most ambitious downstairs, where 100 chefs work behind glass to feed up to 400 diners at a time. This is dinner-as-theater. Not surprisingly, the cuisine tends to be uneven. We suggest the rotissere rib of beef with red wine and creamed horseradish, or the roast cod, which was crisp skinned and cooked to perfection. For dessert, you can't beat the butterscotch ice cream with a pitcher of hot fudge. A live jazz band entertains after 10pm from Wednesday to Saturday, and the world of Marlene Dietrich and Noël Coward comes alive again.

✪ The Ivy. 1-5 West St., WC2. ☎ **0171/836-4751.** Reservations required. Main courses £8–£21.75 ($13.20–$35.90); Sat–Sun fixed-price 3-course lunch £15.50 ($25.60) plus £1.50 ($2.45) cover charge. AE, DC, MC, V. Daily noon–3pm and 5:30pm–midnight (last order). Tube: Leicester Sq. MODERN BRITISH/INTERNATIONAL.

Effervescent and sophisticated, The Ivy has been intimately associated with the West End theater district since it opened in 1911. With its ersatz 1930s look and tiny bar near the entrance, this place is fun—and it hums with the energy of London's glamour scene. The menu may seem simple, but the kitchen has a solid appreciation for fresh ingredients and a talent for skillful preparation. Favorite dishes include white asparagus with sea kale and truffle butter; seared scallops with spinach, sorrel, and bacon; and salmon fish cakes. There's also Mediterranean fish soup, a great mixed grill, and such English desserts as sticky toffee and caramelized bread-and-butter pudding. Meals are served quite late to accommodate the post-theater crowd.

Mash. 19-21 Great Portland St. W1. ☎ **0171/637-5555.** Reservations required. Main courses £7.50–£13.50 ($12.40–$22.30); set lunch Sat £16.50 ($27.20). AE, DC, MC, V. Daily Mon–Sat noon–3pm and 6–11:30pm, Sun noon–3pm and 6–10:30pm. Tube: Great Portland Street. MODERN CONTINENTAL.

What is it? you ask. A bar? A deli? A microbrewery? All of the above, and, oh, yes, a restaurant. Breakfast and weekend brunch are the highlights, but don't ignore dinner either. The novelty decor includes the likes of curvy "sci-fi" lines and "lizard-eye" lighting fixtures, but ultimately the food is the attraction. The owners of the hot Atlantic Bar & Grill and the Coast Restaurant have opened this place that invites

ⓕ Family-Friendly Restaurants

Pizzeria Condotti (Mayfair; *see p. 131*) Your kid's pizza fix can be satisfied here better than anywhere else in London. Pies with succulent toppings emerge bubbling hot from the oven. The "American Hot" comes with mozzarella, pepperoni, sausages, and hot peppers—and the menu isn't just confined to pizzas.

Deal's Restaurant and Diner (Chelsea; *see p. 162*) After enjoying the boat ride down to Chelsea Harbour, kids will love the burgers and other American fare served here. Reduced-price children's portions are available.

Dickens Inn by the Tower (Docklands; *see p. 152*) Even fussy kids will find something they like at this former spice warehouse, now a three-story restaurant with sweeping Thames and Tower Bridge views. The fare ranges from parent-pleasing modern British to yummy lasagna and pizza.

Ye Olde Cheshire Cheese (The City; *see p. 179*) Fleet Street's most famous chophouse, established in 1667, is an eternal family favorite. If "ye famous pudding" turns your kids off, the sandwiches and roasts will tempt them into digging in instead.

Hard Rock Cafe (Mayfair; *see p. 130*) This is a great place for older children. Teenagers like the rock 'n' roll memorabilia as well as the juicy burgers with a heap of fries and a salad doused with Thousand Island dressing.

Porter's English Restaurant (Covent Garden; *see p. 147*) This restaurant serves traditional English meals that most kids love—especially the pies, stews, and steamed "puds." They'll get a real kick out of ordering wonderfully named food like bubble and squeak and mushy peas.

diners to a "sunken chill out zone" created by leading designer John Currin. "The food is good," one local patron informed us, "but I really come here for the mirrored loos." He left after that enigmatic statement, allowing us to launch into suckling pig with spring cannellini stew, our companion opting for one of the terrific pizzas emerging from the wood-fired oven. On another occasion, we returned for the fish freshly grilled over wood. It was sea bass and presented enticingly with grilled artichokes. Try also the marinated quail with thin slices of crisp deep-fried taro root. Desserts are often startling, but be brave. An example is the rhubarb compote with a crisp polenta shortcake and a custardlike ice cream flavored with fresh basil.

✪ **The Sugar Club.** 21 Warwick St. W1. ☎ **0171/437-7776.** Main courses £12–£18 ($19.80–$29.70). AE, DC, MC, V. Daily noon–3pm and 6–11pm. Tube: Piccadilly Circus or Oxford Circus. PACIFIC RIM.

Ashley Sumner and Vivienne Hayman originally launched their restaurant in Wellington, New Zealand in the mid-1980s. Now they have moved deep into Soho with their original chef, the talented Peter Gordon, who is known for attracting homesick Aussies with the best loin of grilled kangaroo in London (very tender with a rich piquant sauce). The setting is inviting with soft textures and colors of pale creams, bone and olive green, everything enhanced by wooden floors. The restaurant is both elegant and spacious, offering a bar waiting area for diners, a separate non-smoking floor, and a kitchen open to view. The flavors are often stunning, as evoked by the sashimi of Iki Jimi yellowtail with a black-bean-and-ginger salsa. The fish tastes amazingly fresh here, and flavors are surprising at times to the palate, but only in the most exciting way. You might also dig into the duck leg braised in tamarind and star anise with coconut rice or else try the panfried turbot with spinach, sweet potato, a red-curry sauce, and onion raiata. Many of the starters are vegetarian and can be upgraded to a main course. For dessert, the blood-orange curd tart with crème fraîche is drop-dead delicious.

Villandry. 170 Great Portland St., W1. ☎ **0171/631-3131.** Reservations recommended. Main courses £11–£14 ($18.15–$23.10). AE, MC, V. Mon–Sat noon–3pm and 7–10pm. Food store Mon–Sat 8am–8pm. Tube: Great Portland Street. INTERNATIONAL/CONTINENTAL.

Food lovers and gourmands flock to this combination food store, delicatessen, and restaurant, where racks of the finest meats, cheese, and produce in the world are displayed and changed virtually every hour. Some of the best of the merchandise is quickly and almost whimsically transformed into the restaurant's menu choices. The setting—dating in this particular form only since 1997—is an oversized Edwardian-style storefront north of Oxford Circus. The inside is an artfully minimalist kind of pared-down temple to the glories of fresh produce and esoteric foodstuffs. Ingredients change here so frequently that the menu is revamped and rewritten twice a day—during our latest visit, it proposed such perfectly crafted dishes as breast of duck with fresh spinach and a gratin of baby onions; boiled haunch of pork with blood sausages, mashed potatoes, kale, and mustard sauce; and panfried turbot with deep-fried celery, artichoke hearts, and hollandaise sauce.

INEXPENSIVE

Chiang Mai. 48 Frith St., W1. ☎ **0171/437-7444.** Main courses £5–£8 ($8.25–$13.20). AE, MC, V. Mon–Sat noon–3pm and 6–11pm; Sun 6–10:30pm. Tube: Leicester Sq. or Tottenham Court Rd. THAI.

This restaurant in the center of Soho is named after the ancient northern capital of Thailand, a region known for its rich, spicy foods. Try their hot-and-sour dishes or vegetarian meals. It's located next door to Ronnie Scott's, the most famous jazz club in England, so it's a good stop for an early dinner before a night on the town. Children's specials are available.

Chuen Cheng Ku. 17 Wardour St., W1. ☎ **0171/437-1398.** Reservations recommended on weekend afternoons. Main courses £7–£18 ($11.55–$29.70); fixed-price menus £9.50–£32 ($15.65–$52.80) per person. AE, DC, MC, V. Daily 11am–11:45pm. Closed Dec 24–25. Tube: Piccadilly Circus or Leicester Square. CHINESE.

This is one of the finest places in Soho's "New China." A large restaurant on several floors, Chuen Cheng Ku has the longest and most interesting Cantonese menu in London. Specialties of the house are paper-wrapped prawns, rice in lotus leaves, steamed spareribs in black-bean sauce, and shredded pork with cashew nuts—all served in generous portions. Other featured dishes include lobster with ginger and spring onion, sliced duck in chili and black-bean sauce, and Singapore noodles (thin, rich noodles, sometimes mixed with curry and pork or shrimp with red and green pepper). Dim sum is served from 11am to 5:30pm. We must note, however, that we think the standard of service has slipped over the years.

dell'Ugo. 56 Frith St., W1. ☎ **0171/734-8300.** Reservations required. Main courses £6.50–£13.50 ($10.75–$22.30). AE, DC, MC, V. Mon–Fri noon–3pm; Mon–Sat 7pm–midnight. Tube: Tottenham Court Rd. MEDITERRANEAN.

This immensely popular multistory restaurant serves very good food at affordable prices. Critics claim there's too long a wait between courses, and dishes are overly contrived. But we have to agree with its legions of (mostly young) devotees: We've found the robust Mediterranean dishes to be prepared with the finest ingredients and packed with flavor. Most everything tastes fresh and appealing. Both the restaurant and bistro change their menus frequently, but generally feature an array of pasta, meat, fish, and vegetarian dishes. If you can, start with the goat cheese in a spicy tomato vinaigrette, and follow it with the linguini with langoustines or the rosemary-skewered lamb with a charred eggplant. Fish dishes, delectably seasoned and not allowed to dry out on the grill, range from monkfish to sea bass. Not everything works out—some dishes are tough (especially the duck) and lack spice. The crème brûlée (when it *finally* arrived) was excellent. All in all, not the spot for a romantic tête-à-tête, but immensely appealing. The ground-floor "caff" offers snacks all day, from tapas to meze.

Dumpling Inn. 15a Gerrard St., W1. ☎ **0171/437-2567.** Reservations recommended. Main courses £7–£15 ($11.55–$24.75); fixed-price lunch or dinner £14–£25 ($23.10–$41.25). MC, V. Sun–Thurs 11:30am–11:30pm; Fri–Sat 11:30am–12:45pm. Tube: Piccadilly Circus. CHINESE.

Despite its incongruous name, this is a cool and rather elegant restaurant serving a delectable brand of Peking Mandarin cuisine that dates back almost 3,000 years and owes some of its special piquancy to various Mongolian ingredients, best represented by its savory stew called "hot pot." Regulars come here for the shark's-fin soup, the beef in oyster sauce, the seaweed and sesame-seed prawns on toast, duck with chili and black-bean sauce, and the fried sliced fish with sauce. Naturally, the specialty is dumplings; you can make a meal from the dim sum list. Portions aren't large, so you can order a good variety without fear of leftovers. Chinese tea is extra. Service is leisurely, so don't dine here before a theater date.

Ming. 35–36 Greek St., W1. ☎ **0171/734-2721.** Main courses £7.50–£18 ($12.40–$29.70); fixed-price 2-course dinner £15 ($24.75), fixed-price 3-course dinner £20 ($33). AE, MC, V. Mon–Sat noon–11:45pm. Tube: Tottenham Court Rd. CANTONESE/ PEKINESE.

In bustling Soho, this winning Chinese restaurant lies on Shaftesbury Avenue behind the Palace Theatre. The chefs in the kitchen, Mr. Bib and Mr. Bun (we're not making this up), welcome you to their Far East outpost, gaily decorated in green and pink. This is no chop suey–and–chow mein menu joint. Many of the recipes have real flair. One is fancifully described as an 18th-century recipe from the Emperor Qian Long's head chef. What dazzled the emperor? Lean pieces of tender lamb with a slightly sweetened soy sauce. Fish, especially prawns and squid, are prepared in delectable ways, as are a number of tofu combinations. Cauliflower, sautéed in butter and flavored with bits of chili and slivers of spring onions, is an unusual appetizer. You might follow with spiced and peppered duck breast, or simmered chicken with ginger and orange. White fish rolls are an intriguing choice, wrapped in a bean "skin." Mussels in black-bean sauce are worth a return visit, as is a whole sea bass cooked Thai style. However, better skip the "Chiu Yim sliced eel–and–sea spice shredded pork." We weren't sure what it was!

Soho Spice. 124–126 Wardour St., W1. ☎ **0171/434-0808.** Reservations recommended. Main courses £8.50–£14.50 ($14–$23.90); set lunch £8.50 ($14); set dinner £15.95–£22.95 ($26.30–$37.85). AE, DC, MC, V. Sun–Thurs noon–midnight; Fri–Sat noon–3am; Sun 12:30–10:30pm. Tube: Tottenham Court Road. SOUTH INDIAN.

One of central London's most stylish Indian restaurants combines a sense of media and fashion hip with the flavors and scents of southern India. You might opt for a drink at the cellar-level bar before heading to the large street-level dining room decorated in the saffron, cardamom, bay, and pepper hues evocative of the place's piquant cuisine. A staff member dressed in a similarly vivid uniform will propose choices from a wide array of dishes, including a range of slow-cooked Indian tikkas that feature combinations of spices with lamb, chicken, fish, or all-vegetarian. The cuisine will satisfy traditionalists, but has a modern, nouveau-Soho flair. The presentation takes it a step above typical Indian restaurants, here or elsewhere.

IN NEARBY FITZROVIA
EXPENSIVE

Pied-à-Terre. 34 Charlotte St., W1. ☎ **0171/636-1178.** Reservations recommended. Fixed-price 3-course lunch £23 ($37.95); fixed-price 3-course dinner £35–£46 ($57.75–$75.90); 8-course tasting menu £60 ($99). AE, DC, MC, V. Mon–Fri 12:15–2:15pm (last order); Mon–Sat 7–10:45pm. Closed last week of Dec and first week of Jan and last 2 weeks of Aug. Tube: Goodge St. MODERN FRENCH.

This foodie heaven has deliberately understated its decor in favor of a more intense focus on its subtle and very sophisticated cuisine. You'll dine in a strictly (some say rigidly) minimalist room, where gray and pale-pink walls alternate with metal furniture and focused lighting that highlights a prize collection of modern art. France is the inspiration for the impressive wine list and some, but not all, of the cuisine. The menu changes with the seasons, but might include braised snails with celeriac, garlic, and morille-creamed sauce; roasted scallops with apple and puréed ginger; halibut fillets with queen scallops and caramelized endive; roasted partridge with pear; and the house specialty, ballotine of duck confit. If you're not dining with a vegetarian who would be appalled, braised pig's head is another specialty. The smoothest item on the menu? Sea bass with vichyssoise and caviar sauce. The food is beautifully presented on hand-painted plates with lush patterns that offset the stylish starkness of the setting.

MODERATE

✪ **Nico Central.** 35 Great Portland St., W1. ☎ **0171/436-8846.** Reservations required. Fixed-price 2-course lunch £20.50 ($33.80), fixed-price 3-course lunch £23.50 ($38.80); fixed-price 3-course dinner £25.50 ($42.05). AE, DC, MC, V. Mon–Fri noon–2pm; Mon-Sat 7–11pm. Tube: Oxford Circus. FRENCH/MODERN BRITISH.

This brasserie—founded and inspired by London's legendary chef, Nico Ladenis (who spends most of his time at Chez Nico at Ninety Park Lane)—delivers earthy French cuisine that's been called "haute but not haughty" and consistently praised for its "absurdly good value." Of course, everything is handled with considerable culinary urbanity. Guests sit on bentwood chairs at linen-covered tables. Nearly a dozen starters—the pride of the chef—will tempt you. The menu changes seasonally and according to the chef's inspiration, but might include grilled duck served with risotto with cèpes (flap mushrooms) and Parmesan, panfried foie gras with brioche and a caramelized orange, braised knuckle of veal, and baked fillet of brill with assorted vegetables. Save room for one of the desserts—they are, in the words of one devotee, "divine."

CLERKENWELL
EXPENSIVE

✪ **Maison Novelli.** 29–31A Clerkenwell Green, EC1. ☎ **0171/251-6606.** Reservations required. Main courses in restaurant £15–£25 ($24.75–$41.25); main courses in brasserie £11–£16 ($18.15–$26.40). AE, MC, V. Mon–Fri 12:30–2:30pm; Mon–Sat 6:30–10:30pm. Closed 2 weeks July–Aug. Tube: Farringdon. CONTINENTAL/MODERN FRENCH.

You often have to abandon the heart of London these days to experience the city's finest and most imaginative cookery. High rents have driven such stellar chefs as Jean-Christophe Novelli to this up-and-coming area of the city. The cuisine is worth the trouble to get here. Novelli, who oversees the entire operation, is aided by the capable Richard Guest, a devotee of bold flavors, the freshest of ingredients, and imaginative culinary twists.

The ground floor is a brasserie with seats outside in fair weather. More formal service and a more expensive menu are found upstairs. The brasserie and restaurant share a blue-violet decor lined with modern art. The brasserie serves such hearty fare as mackerel and lemongrass kebab or braised onion filled with cubed lamb. But it is in the restaurant that Guest and Novelli truly shine. The signature dish is a perfumed halibut that we could dine on every day of the week. But that's only the beginning. Opt for the baby squid and scallop nage, followed by the sublime grilled John Dory (St-Pierre to the French diners) or the ever-popular corn-fed chicken. It comes with sliver of foie gras and a green pea-pod emulsion. Stuffed pig's trotters are stunningly rich and appear with mashed almonds for an exquisite flavor.

MODERATE

Moro. 34–36 Exmouth Market, EC1. ☎ **0171/833-8336.** Reservations essential. Main courses £12–£15 ($19.80–$24.75). MC, V. Mon–Fri 12:30–2:30pm and 7–10:30pm. Tube: Farringdon. SPANISH/NORTH AFRICAN.

If you've been hearing about all those trendy restaurants sprouting up in fashionable Clerkenwell, and want to try one, make it Moro. With its streamlined interior, it invites the chic and fashionable from posh spots in Belgravia. In the streamlined interior, there's nothing to hide as the kitchen is in open view. The wafting aromas of delicious meats emerging from the charcoal grill will attract carnivores, although vegetarian meals are also sold here. At the long zinc bar, you can fill up on some of the city's best tapas, or stick around for a Maghreb-inspired dinner of impeccable quality. The recipes were inspired by the time the Arab culture met Europe during an occupation of southern Spain that lasted from the 8th to the 15th century. From the chargrill emerges a delectable veal chop with spicy chorizo and cabbage, and the leg of lamb is tantalizingly prepared with okra and coriander. The quail on flatbread is to make the angels weep with joy. Begin with the lusty white-bean soup and the night is yours. Extra-fresh products go into the creation of these dishes such as squid emerging from the grill and served with harissa. But no seasoning or flavor overpowers.

✪ **St. John.** 26 St. John St., EC1. ☎ **0171/251-0848.** Reservations required. Main courses £8–£20 ($13.20–$33). AE, DC, MC, V. Mon–Fri noon-11:30pm; Sat 6–11:30pm. Tube: Farringdon. MODERN BRITISH.

Located in a former smokehouse just north of Smithfield Market, this canteenlike dining room is the restaurant of choice for carnivores. This dining oddity is a showcase for the talents of owner-chef Fergus Henderson, a leader in the resurgent offal movement. In true British tradition, he doesn't use just part of the animal, he uses it all—we're talking neck, trotter, tail, liver, heart, the works.

Don't think you'll be served warmed-over haggis: The food is excellent and flavorpacked. In fact, there's a straightforward earthiness and simplicity to this cuisine that's unequaled anywhere in London. Both the grilled lamb chops and the pigs tongue, bacon salsify, and dandelion are matchless. Roast bone marrow appears with a parsley salad, and pork chops are called pig chops. It's getting hard these days to find an eel, bacon, and clam stew, but you'll find one here. French wines help to wash it all down. Desserts run to puddings such as vanilla rice, or dates and walnuts with butterscotch. Dessert oddity? Where can you get a good goat curd, marc, and rhubarb concoction these days? You've heard of goat curd and rhubarb, but what is this marc? It's the refuse of grapes, seeds, and fruits after pressing, of course. The breads served here can be purchased in an on-site bakery.

SHOREDITCH
INEXPENSIVE

✪ **The Great Eastern Dining Room.** 54 Great Eastern Street, EC2. Reservations required. Main courses £7.50–£10 ($12.40–$16.50). AE, DC, MC, V. Mon–Fri noon–3:30pm and Mon–Sat 6:30–11pm. Tube: Liverpool Street. ITALIAN/INTERNATIONAL.

Johnny Depp hasn't (as of yet) battled the paparazzi outside this restaurant, but it is still hipper than hip, the new hangout for London's fashionable elite. Rub shoulders with the likes of celebrated fashion designer Alexander McQueen, or take Joan Collins here for dinner. It's that kind of place in spite of its modest prices. On the cutting edge, this is the domain of a young Aussie about town, Will Ricke, who decided to make it big in the English capital, and has succeeded admirably. The 1880s building housing the restaurant was a former fabric warehouse until its remarkable transformation in the late autumn of 1998 by the renowned Australian designer, Chris Connell. Overall it has a modernist 1950s aura to it: You expect Marilyn Monroe and James Dean to walk in the door at any minute. There are ceiling-high murals and spectacular Italian chandeliers lighting the beautiful (or would be) people below.

"The food is divine, dear heart," claimed London's leading drag queen (actually a member of the House of Lords). And so it is, beginning with the heavenly antipasti, which features the likes of bruschetta with Jerusalem artichokes and pomegranate dressing, or the chargrilled garlic squid with mixed greens. The spaghetti vongole (clams) is as good as you get in a Roman trattoria, and you can proceed to the fish of the day, often served with pickled eggplant. To evoke merrie old English, the chefs always prepare something for the traditional English palate—perhaps braised lamb shank with garlic and white-bean mash (it's given a dosage of mint pesto to keep the food modern). Desserts appear as "dolci" here, ranging from a red-plum tart in polenta pastry to a velvety chocolate and almond mousse with brandy oranges. Naturally, you finish this debauch with an espresso.

HOLBORN
INEXPENSIVE

○ **North Sea Fish Restaurant.** 7–8 Leigh St., WC1. ☎ **0171/387-5892.** Reservations recommended. Fish platters £6–£12 ($9.90–$19.80). AE, DC, MC, V. Mon–Sat noon–2:30pm and 5:30–10:30pm. Tube: King's Cross, or Russell Sq. SEAFOOD.

The fish served in this bright and clean restaurant is purchased fresh every day; the quality is high, and the prices low. In the view of London's diehard chippie devotees, it's the best in town. The fish is most often served battered and deep-fried, but you can also order it grilled. The menu is wisely limited. Students from the Bloomsbury area flock to the place.

COVENT GARDEN & THE STRAND
EXPENSIVE

Axis. In the Hotel One Aldwych, 1 Aldwych. ☎ **0171/300-1000.** Reservations recommended. Set-price menus £14.95–£17.95 ($24.65–$29.60); main courses £14–£25 ($23.10–$41.25). AE, DC, MC, V. Mon–Fri noon–3pm; Mon–Sat 6–11:30pm. Tube: Covent Garden or Charing Cross. MODERN BRITISH/PACIFIC RIM.

One of the newest very stylish restaurants in London occupies what was once the printing room for a now-defunct newspaper. In 1998, a team of architects and designers took advantage of its soaring, cathedral-like ceilings and installed a serpentine-shaped travertine staircase leading down from the dramatic bar upstairs. They brought in a culinary team, and opened their doors to discriminating palates across London. The result has an old-clubby feel with a dramatic mural of an "ambiguous and timeless metropolis executed in the vorticist style."

The menu manages to fuse old-fashioned English truffles and jam puddings with sushi and Pacific Rim novelties into the same, well-conceived, and almost obsessively eclectic menu. Menu items include a poached haddock-and–cheese soufflé tart; crispy duck noodle salad with watercress, spring onion, and coriander; chilled and curried apple-and-cardamon soup; grilled Scottish lobster with chicory, lemon verbena, and grapefruit salad; braised or seared breast of Norfolk duck with orange sauce, spiced red cabbage and chestnuts; and an artfully old-fashioned recipe from 1922 that features jugged hare served boneless with creamed celeriac, and a turnip and potato bake. Desserts include trifle from a recipe that originated in 1889, elderflower jelly with champagne sorbet, and roasted pineapple with cracked-pepper ice cream.

Neal Street Restaurant. 26 Neal St., WC2. ☎ **0171/836-8368.** Reservations recommended. Main courses £16.50–£22 ($27.20–$36.30). AE, DC, MC, V. Mon–Sat 12:30–2:30pm and 6–11pm. Tube: Covent Garden. ITALIAN.

This is another stylish restaurant that has an extravagant variety of mushrooms, truffles, and other fungi. It's operated by Turin-born Antonio Carluccio, a noted author on the use of culinary mushrooms from around the world. The brick walls of what was a turn-of-the-century warehouse are hung with the works of such modern masters as Frank Stella and David Hockney, as well as many lesser luminaries. The restaurant operates an aperitif bar in the cellar, where prospective diners sometimes wait until a table becomes available. Between 10 and 20 of the world's most exotic mushrooms are available at any time, including a highly desirable assortment of truffles. Imported according to season from China, Tibet, Japan, France, and California, they pop up in such recipes as foie gras with balsamic sauce, wild mushroom soup, pheasant consommé with morels and port, and tagliolini with truffle sauce. Equally appealing—but less expensive because they don't contain the exotics—might be venison ravioli with butter and sage, pappardelle with mixed funghi, truffled egg tagliolini, or homemade black angel-hair pasta with seafood and bottarga. Service is attentive and polite and the ambience agreeable. Their tiramisu is justifiably popular.

Simpson's-in-the-Strand. 100 The Strand (next to the Savoy Hotel), WC2. ☎ **0171/836-9112.** Reservations required. Main courses £15–£22 ($24.75–$36.30); fixed-price 2-course lunch and pre-theater dinner £14 ($23.10); fixed-price breakfast from £13.95 ($23). AE, DC, MC, V. Mon–Fri 7–11am; Mon–Sat noon–2:30pm and 5:30–11pm; Sun noon–2pm and 6–9pm. Tube: Charing Cross or Embankment. TRADITIONAL BRITISH.

Simpson's is more of an institution than a restaurant—it's been in business since 1828. This very Victorian place boasts Adam paneling, crystal, and an army of grandly formal waiters to whom nouvelle cuisine means anything after Henry VIII. But most diners agree that Simpson's serves the best roasts in London, an array that includes roast sirloin of beef; roast saddle of mutton with red-currant jelly; roast Aylesbury duckling; and steak, kidney, and mushroom pie. (Remember to tip the tailcoated carver.) For a pudding, you might order the treacle roll and custard or Stilton with vintage port.

Taking advantage of the recent upsurge in popularity of traditional British cooking, Simpson's now serves traditional breakfasts. The most popular one, curiously enough, is called "The Ten Deadly Sins" for £15.95 ($26.30): a plate of sausage, fried egg, streaky and back bacon, black pudding, lamb's kidneys, bubble and squeak, baked beans, lamb's liver, and fried bread, mushrooms, and tomatoes. That will certainly fortify you for the day.

Jacket and tie is no longer essential; however, we do recommend smart casual attire.

Rules. 35 Maiden Lane, WC2. ☎ **0171/836-5314.** Reservations recommended. Main courses £13.95–£17.95 ($23–$29.60). AE, DC, MC, V. Daily noon–11:30pm. Tube: Covent Garden. TRADITIONAL BRITISH.

If you're looking for London's most quintessentially British restaurant, eat here or at Wiltons (see p. 133). London's oldest restaurant was established in 1798 as an oyster bar; today, on the site of the original premises, it rambles through a series of antler-encrusted Edwardian dining rooms exuding patriotic nostalgia. You can order such classic dishes as Irish or Scottish oysters, jugged hare, and mussels. Game dishes are offered from mid-August to February or March: wild Scottish salmon or wild sea trout; wild Highland red deer; and game birds like grouse, snipe, partridge, pheasant, and woodcock. As a finale, the "great puddings" continue to impress decade after decade.

MODERATE

Belgo Centraal. 50 Earlham St., WC2. ☎ **0171/813-2233.** Reservations required for the restaurant. Main courses £8.95–£18.95 ($14.75–$31.25); fixed-price menus £6–£13 ($9.90–$21.45). AE, DC, MC, V. Mon–Sat noon–11:30pm; Sun noon–10:30pm. Closed Christmas. Tube: Covent Garden. BELGIAN.

Chaos reigns supreme in this audacious and cavernous basement, where mussels marinière with frites and 100 Belgian beers are the *raison d'être*. You'll take a freight elevator down past the busy kitchen and into a converted cellar, which has been divided into two large eating areas. One is a beer hall seating about 250; the menu here is the same as in the restaurant, but reservations aren't needed. The restaurant side has three nightly seatings: 5:30, 7:30, and 10pm. Between 5:30 and 8pm you can choose one of three fixed-price menus, and you pay based on the time of your order: The earlier you order, the less you pay. Although heaps of fresh mussels are the big attraction here, you can also opt for fresh Scottish salmon, roast chicken, a perfectly done steak, or one of the vegetarian specialties. Gargantuan plates of wild boar sausages arrive with *stoemp*, Belgian mashed spuds and cabbage. Belgian stews called *waterzooi* are also served. With waiters dressed in maroon monk's habits with black aprons, barking orders into headset microphones, it's all a bit bizarre.

Christopher's. 18 Wellington St., WC2. ☎ **0171/240-4222.** Reservations recommended. Main courses £15–£24 ($24.75–$39.60); pre-theater 2-course dinner £14.50 ($23.90) from 5:30-7:30pm; Sat–Sun brunch £6–£13 ($9.90–$21.45). AE, DC, MC, V. Restaurant Mon–Fri noon–3pm and 6pm–midnight; Sat noon–midnight; Sun noon–4pm. Tube: Covent Garden or Charing Cross. AMERICAN.

Many visitors to Christopher's are tempted to remain at street level, where oysters, fresh salads, and other dishes are served in a bistro-style setting. Serious drinkers descend into the basement, where a bar awaits. The real showcase, however, is the restaurant, one floor above street level. Beneath a lavishly frescoed ceiling, an elaborate corkscrew-shaped stone staircase ascends to a pair of Italianate dining rooms. Here, flavorful and modern American dishes are served, including smoked tomato soup, roasted red peppers with buffalo mozzarella and basil, roast breast of duck with Kentucky bourbon peaches, and blackened salmon with spinach salad. Pasta is featured daily. A London food critic, when asked what he thought of the American cuisine served here, said he thinks, "Yanks cook with punch. And that Texas steak sauce. Amazing if a bit cheeky." Homesick expats come here for the Caesar salad, the crabcakes evoking Maryland, and that New York cheesecake. Naturally the wine list is strong on California. Christopher's also serves our favorite Sunday brunch in London.

Magno's. 65a Long Acre, WC2. ☎ **0171/836-6077.** Reservations required. Main courses £10.95–£15.95 ($18.05–$26.30); fixed-price 2-course menu £13.95 ($23), fixed-price 3-course menu £16.95 ($27.95); fixed-price pre-theater supper (5:30–7:30pm) £10.95 ($18.05). AE, DC, MC, V. Mon–Fri noon–2:30pm; Mon–Sat 5:30–11:30pm. Tube: Covent Garden. FRENCH.

This well-recommended French restaurant operates in a brasserie-inspired room of green-and-cream-colored walls, closely spaced tables, and efficient service. The menu is inspired by traditional French bistro cuisine, and might include such stalwarts as a *feuilleté au Rocquefort* (blue cheese in puff pastry); duckling with celeriac confit; rack of lamb with ratatouille sauce and couscous; or panfried pork with cracked wheat, apple, and cider sauce. The place is especially popular for before- and after-theater meals; make sure you reserve ahead. The cookery is very reliable and tasty, the classics often given lighter treatments than traditional grandmère recipes suggest.

INEXPENSIVE

The George. 213 The Strand, WC2. ☎ **0171/427-0941.** Main courses £5.25–£9.60 ($8.65–$15.85). AE, DC, MC, V. Mon–Fri 11am–11pm; Sat noon–3pm (food served Mon–Fri noon–3pm and 5:30–8:30pm; Sat noon–2:30pm). Tube: Temple. TRADITIONAL BRITISH.

Although its half-timbered facade would have you believe that it's older than it is, this pub was built as a coffeehouse in 1723. Set on the Strand, at the lower end of Fleet Street opposite the Royal Courts of Justice, the George is a favorite of barristers, their clients, and the handful of journalists who haven't yet moved to other parts of London. The pub's illustrious history saw Samuel Johnson having his mail delivered here during his heyday, and Oliver Goldsmith enjoying many tankards of what eventually became draught Bass. Today, the setting seems only slightly changed from those days; much of the original architecture is still intact. Hot and cold platters, including bangers and mash, fish-and-chips, steak-and-kidney pie, and lasagna, are served from a food counter at the back of the pub. Additional seating is available in the basement, where a headless cavalier is said to haunt the same premises where he enjoyed his liquor in an earlier day.

✪ **Joe Allen.** 13 Exeter St., WC2. ☎ **0171/836-0651.** Reservations required. Main courses £10.50–£13.50 ($17.35–$22.30); pre-theater dinner £12–£14 ($19.80–$23.10); Sat–Sun brunch £13–£15 ($21.45–$24.75). AE, MC, V. Mon–Sat noon–12:45am; Sun noon–midnight. Tube: Covent Garden or Charing Cross. AMERICAN.

This fashionable American restaurant near the Savoy attracts primarily theater crowds. Like the New York branch, it's decorated with theater posters. The menu has grown increasingly sophisticated and might include dishes such as grilled corn-fed chicken with sunflower-seed pesto, marinated sweet peppers, and garlic roast new potatoes, as well as specialties like black-bean soup and pecan pie. The Sunday brunch is one of the best in London. You get such main dishes as a mixed grill with lamb chop, calf's liver, and Cumberland sausage, and a choice of a Bloody Mary, Bucks Fizz, or a glass of champagne. The food here has been called "unimaginative." Loyal patrons say, "Who cares? We love it!"

✪ **Porter's English Restaurant.** 17 Henrietta St., WC2. ☎ **0171/836-6466.** Reservations recommended. Main courses £8 ($13.20); fixed-price menu £15 ($24.75). AE, DC, MC, V. Mon–Sat noon–11:30pm; Sun noon–10:30pm. Tube: Covent Garden or Charing Cross. TRADITIONAL BRITISH.

In 1979, the 7th Earl of Bradford opened this restaurant, stating "it would serve real English food at affordable prices," and he has succeeded notably—and not just because Lady Bradford turned over her carefully guarded recipe for banana and ginger steamed pudding. A comfortable, two-storied restaurant with a friendly, informal, and lively atmosphere, Porter's specializes in classic English pies, including Old English fish pie; lamb and apricot; ham, leek, and cheese; and, of course, bangers and mash. Main courses are so generous—and accompanied by vegetables and side dishes—that you hardly need appetizers. They have also added grilled English fare to the menu, with sirloin and lamb steaks and pork chops. The puddings, including bread-and-butter pudding or steamed syrup sponge, are the real puddings (in the American sense); they're served hot or cold, with whipped cream or custard. The bar does quite a few exotic cocktails, as well as beers, wine, or English mead. A traditional English tea is also served from 2:30 to 5:30pm for £3.50 ($5.75) per person. Who knows? You may even bump into his Lordship.

ON THE EMBANKMENT
MODERATE

✪ **Ship Hispaniola.** River Thames, Victoria Embankment, Charing Cross, WC2. ☎ **0171/ 839-3011.** Reservations recommended. Main courses £12.75–£19.75 ($21.05–$32.60); fixed-price 2-course menu £12.50 ($20.65), fixed-price 3-course menu £15 ($24.75); £15 ($24.75) minimum per person. AE, DC, MC, V. Mon–Fri noon–2pm and 6–11pm (last order); Sat 6–11:30pm. Closed Dec 24–Jan 4. Tube: Embankment. FRENCH.

This large, comfortably outfitted ship was built in 1953 to haul passengers around the islands of Scotland. Stripped of its engine in 1976, the ship is permanently moored to a quay beside the Thames, a few steps from the Embankment Underground station. Good food and spectacular views of the passing river traffic are part of the waterborne experience. The menu changes frequently, but might include such dishes as flambéed Mediterranean prawns with garlic, fried fish cakes with tartar sauce, supreme of Guinea fowl stuffed with spinach, fine champagne sauce, grilled Scotch sirloin of beef, rack of lamb flavored with rosemary and shallots, and several vegetarian dishes. Alternatively, try the set menu known as "sharing the captain's table." There's live music on most nights.

WESTMINSTER/VICTORIA
EXPENSIVE

Ken Lo's Memories of China. 67–69 Ebury St., SW1. ☎ **0171/730-7734.** Reservations recommended. Main courses £10–£30 ($16.50–$49.50); fixed-price lunch £19.50–£22 ($32.15–$36.30); fixed-price 3-course dinner from £25 ($41.25). AE, DC, MC, V. Mon–Sat noon–2:30pm; daily 7–11:15pm. Tube: Victoria Station. CHINESE.

Many food critics consider this the finest Chinese restaurant in London, although in the past few years the competition has considerably heated up. It was founded by the late Ken Lo, whose grandfather was the Chinese ambassador to the Court of St. James (he was knighted by Queen Victoria in 1880). Mr. Lo wrote more than 30 cookbooks and a well-known autobiography, and once hosted his own TV cooking show. The restaurant, which is impeccably staffed and outfitted in an appealing minimalist decor, has been called "a gastronomic bridge between London and China." The menu spans broadly divergent regions of China, and might include Cantonese quick-fried beef in oyster sauce, lobster with handmade noodles, pomegranate prawn balls, and "bang-bang chicken" (a Szechuan dish), among many others.

✪ **Rhodes in the Square.** Dolphin Square, Chichester St., SW1. ☎ **0171/798-6767.** Reservations required. Main courses £15.50–£23.50 ($25.60–$38.80); set lunch £19.50 or £21.50 Sun ($32.15 or $35.50 Sun). AE, DC, MC, V. Sun–Fri noon–2:30pm, Mon–Sat 7–10pm, Sun 7–9pm. Tube: Pimlico. MODERN BRITISH.

In this discreet residential district, super-chef and media darling, Gary Rhodes has done it again. Rhodes has long been known for taking the most traditional of British cookery and giving it daring twists and adding new flavors. Count on some delightful surprises—always—from this major culinary talent. The glitterati can be seen nightly in the apartment-block-cum-hotel, sampling his offerings in an elegant high-ceilinged room done in midnight blue—it's been likened to the grand ballroom of an ocean liner. You never know what's available, perhaps his whole red mullet stuffed with a delectable medley of eggplant, anchovies, fresh garlic, and peppers, appearing with a cream-laced sauce flavored with fennel. Start, perhaps with his chicken liver parfait with foie gras, and go on to an open omelet with chunky bits of lobster topping it along with a Thermidor sauce and cheese crust. His glazed duck served with bitter orange jus is how this dish is supposed to taste and so often doesn't. For dessert, make your selection from the British "pudding plate" that ranges from lemon meringue tart to a simple seared "carpaccio" of pineapple oozing with good flavor.

MODERATE

Shepherd's. Marsham Court, Marsham St., at the corner of Page St., SW1. ☎ **0171/ 834-9552.** Reservations recommended. Fixed-price 2-course meal £22.95 ($37.85), fixed-price 3-course meal £24.95 ($41.15). AE, DC, MC, V. Mon–Fri noon–2:30pm and 6:30–11:30pm (last order at 11pm). Tube: St. James's. TRADITIONAL BRITISH.

Some political observers claim that many of the inner workings of the British government operate from the precincts of this conservative, likable restaurant. Set in the shadow of Big Ben, 2 blocks north of the Tate Gallery, it enjoys a regular clientele of barristers, members of Parliament, and many of their constituents from far-flung districts of Britain. Don't imagine that the intrigue here occurs only at lunchtime; evenings seem just as ripe an hour for negotiations, particularly over the restaurant's roast rib of Scottish beef served with (what else?) Yorkshire pudding. So synchronized is this place to the goings-on at Parliament that a Division Bell rings in the dining room, calling MPs back to the House of Commons when it's time to vote. Even the decor is designed to make them feel at home, with leather banquettes, sober 19th-century accessories, and a worthy collection of English portraits and landscapes.

The menu reflects many years of British culinary tradition, and dishes are prepared intelligently and with fresh ingredients. In addition to the classic roast, they include a cream-based mussel stew, hot salmon and potato salad with dill dressing, fillet of lemon sole, roast leg of lamb with mint sauce, wild rabbit, salmon fillet with tarragon and chive butter sauce, and the English version of crème brûlée, known as "burnt Cambridge cream."

✪ **Simply Nico.** 48A Rochester Row, SW1. ☎ **0171/630-8061.** Reservations required. Fixed-price 2-course lunch £20.50 ($33.80), fixed-price 3-course lunch £23.50 ($38.80); fixed-price 3-course dinner £25.50 ($42.05). AE, DC, MC, V. Mon–Fri 12:30–2pm; Mon–Sat 7–11pm. Tube: Victoria or St. James's Park. FRENCH.

The brainchild of Nico Ladenis, of the much grander and more expensive Chez Nico at Ninety Park Lane, Simply Nico is run by his sous-chef. In Nico's own words, it's "cheap and cheerful." We think it's the best value in town. The wood floors reverberate the din of contented diners, who pack in daily at snug tables to enjoy the simply prepared—and invariably French-inspired—food. The fixed-price menu changes frequently, but options might include starters such as panfried foie gras followed by shank of lamb with parsnips, or the ever-popular monkfish.

SOUTH BANK
EXPENSIVE

Oxo Tower Restaurant. Barge House St., South Bank, SE1. ☎ **0171/803-3888.** Main courses £15–£30 ($24.75–$49.50); set lunch £26.50 ($43.70). AE, DC, MC, V. Mon–Fri noon–3pm, Mon–Sat 6–11:30pm, Sun 6:30–10:30pm. Tube: Blackfriars or Waterloo. MEDITERRANEAN/CONTINENTAL/ASIAN.

In the South Bank shopping complex, on the eighth floor of the art deco Ozo Tower Wharf, this is a London dining sensation. It's called "the other tower" and is operated by the Knightsbridge department store, Harvey Nichols. Just down the street from the newly rebuilt Globe Theater, this 140-seat restaurant might be visited for its view alone; fortunately the cuisine is also stellar. As you dine, you'll enjoy a sweeping view of St. Paul's Cathedral and the City, all the way to the House of Parliament. This is a stunning building with structural waves and curves designed to suggest the ebb and flow of the mighty Thames itself. The decor is in a stylish 1930s style, and, after a shaky start, the cuisine under Chef Simon Arkless offers a finesse and richness that makes dining here a rewarding experience. Menu items change based on the season and the market. Count on a modern interpretation of British cookery. The fish is incredibly fresh, and you can also order the English classics. The whole sea bass for two is delectable, as is the cannon of lamb with creamed garlic. The grilled escalopes of salmon with smoked chili and mango salsa adds an exotic touch, and the panfried fillet of John Dory and scallops is delicately flavored with a *fines herbes* risotto and a champagne sauce.

3 The City

MODERATE

✪ **Café Spice Namaste.** 16 Prescot St., E1. ☎ **0171/488-9242.** Reservations required. Main courses £8.95–£14.95 ($14.75–$24.65). AE, DC, MC, V. Mon–Fri noon–3pm and 6:15–10:30pm; Sat 6:30–10pm. Tube: Tower Hill. INDIAN.

This is our favorite Indian restaurant in London, where the competition is stiff, with Tamarind, and Bombay Brasserie also vying for top honors. It's cheerfully housed in a landmark Victorian hall near Tower Bridge, just east of the Tower of London. The chef, Cyrus Todiwala, is a Parsi and former resident of Goa, where he learned many of his culinary secrets. He concentrates on southern and northern Indian dishes with a strong Portuguese influence. Chicken and lamb are prepared a number of ways, from mild to spicy hot. As a novelty, Todiwala occasionally even offers a menu of emu dishes; when marinated, the meat is rich and spicy and evocative of lamb. Emu is not the only dining oddity here. Ever have ostrich gizzard kebab; alligator tikka; or minced moose, bison, and blue boar? Many patrons journey here just for the complex chicken curry known as *xacutti*. Lambs' livers and kidneys are also cooked in the tandoor. A weekly specialty menu complements the long list of regional dishes. The homemade chutneys alone are worth the trip; our favorite is made with kiwi. All dishes come with fresh vegetables and Indian bread. With the exotic ingredients, the often time-consuming preparation, the impeccable service, the warm hospitality, and the spicy but subtle flavors, this is hardly a curry hash house.

✪ **Poons in the City.** 2 Minster Lane, Minster Court, Mincing Lane, EC3. ☎ **0171/626-0126.** Reservations recommended for lunch. Fixed-price lunch and dinner £22.50–£30.80 ($37.15–$50.80); main courses £6.50–£8.50 ($10.75–$14). AE, DC, MC, V. Mon–Fri noon–10:30pm. Tube: Tower Hill or Meriment. CHINESE.

In 1992, Poons opened this branch in the City, less than a 5-minute walk from the Tower of London and close to other City attractions. It's modeled on the Luk Yew Tree House in Hong Kong. Main courses feature crispy aromatic duck, prawns with cashew nuts, and barbecued pork. Poons's famous *lap yuk soom* (like Cantonese tacos) has finely chopped wind-dried bacon. Special dishes can be ordered on 24-hour notice. At the end of the L-shaped restaurant is an 80-seat fast-food area and take-out counter that's accessible from Mark Lane. The menu changes every 2 weeks.

INEXPENSIVE

The George & Vulture. 3 Castle Court, Cornhill, EC3. ☎ **0171/626-9710.** Reservations accepted if you agree to arrive by 12:45pm. Main courses £6.45–£12.45 ($10.65–$20.55). AE, DC, MC, V. Mon–Fri noon–2:30pm. Tube: Bank. TRADITIONAL BRITISH.

Westminster & Victoria Restaurants

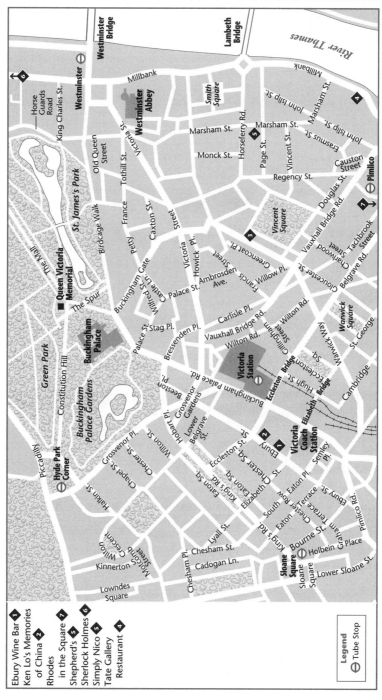

Ebury Wine Bar 1
Ken Lo's Memories of China 2
Rhodes in the Square 7
Shepherd's 5
Sherlock Holmes 6
Simply Nico 5
Tate Gallery Restaurant 4

Legend
Ⓤ Tube Stop

River Thames

Westminster Bridge
Lambeth Bridge

Ⓤ Westminster
Millbank
Westminster Abbey
Smith Square
Horse Guards Road
King Charles St.
Old Queen Street
Victoria St.
Marsham St.
Monck St.
Horseferry Rd.
Page St.
Vincent St.
John Islip St.
Erasmus St.
Marsham St.
Millbank
Ⓤ Pimlico
Causton Street
Regency St.
Douglas St.
Vauxhall Bridge Rd.
Charlwood Street
Tachbrook Street
Belgrave Rd.
Vincent Square
France
Tothill St.
Caxton St.
Street
Victoria St.
Howick Pl.
Greencoat Pl.
Gloucester St.
Petty
Birdcage Walk
The Spur
St. James's Park
Queen Victoria Memorial
The Mall
Buckingham Gate
Wilfred St.
Castle Ln.
Palace St.
Francis Street
Ambrosden Ave.
Willow Pl.
Carlisle Pl.
Wilton Rd.
Warwick Way
Warwick Square
St. George
Green Park
Constitution Hill
Buckingham Palace
Buckingham Palace Gardens
Stag Pl.
Palace St.
Bressenden Pl.
Vauxhall Bridge Rd.
Wilton Rd.
Gillingham Street
Victoria Station
Ⓤ
Eccleston Bridge
Elizabeth Bridge
Hugh St.
Eccleston Sq.
Cambridge
Piccadilly
Hyde Park Corner Ⓤ
Halkin St.
Chapel St.
Grosvenor Pl.
Chester St.
Wilton St.
Hobart Pl.
Lower Belgrave St.
Grosvenor Gardens
Beeston Pl.
Buckingham Palace Rd.
Eaton Sq.
Eccleston St.
Chester Sq.
Ebury St.
Semley Pl.
Victoria Coach Station
Eaton Pl.
King's Rd.
Elizabeth St.
Eaton Terrace
South Eaton Pl.
Chester Row
Chester Terrace
Graham Terrace
Ebury Rd.
Pimlico Rd.
Wilton Crescent
Motcombe Street
Kinnerton Street
Lyall St.
Chesham Pl.
Chesham St.
Cadogan Ln.
Lowndes Square
Sloane Square
Sloane Square
Holbein Pl.
Bourne St.
Lower Sloane St.
King's Rd.

Dickens enthusiasts should seek out this old Pickwickian place. Founded in 1660, it claims that it's "probably" the world's oldest tavern, and refers to an inn on this spot in 1175. While they no longer put up overnight guests here, English lunches are still served on the tavern's three floors. Besides the daily specials, the menu includes a mixed grill, a loin chop, and fried Dover sole fillets with tartar sauce. Potatoes and buttered cabbage are the standard vegetables, and the apple tart is always reliable. The system is to arrive and give your name, then retire to the Jamaican pub opposite for a drink; you're "fetched" when your table is ready. After, be sure to explore the mazes of pubs, shops, wine houses, and other old buildings near the tavern.

By the way, the Pickwick Club meets in this pub about six times a year for reunion dinners. This literary club is headed by Cedric Dickens, a great-great-grandson of Charles Dickens.

✪ **Fox & Anchor.** 115 Charterhouse St., EC1. ☎ **0171/253-4838.** Reservations recommended. "Full house" breakfast £7 ($11.55); steak breakfast £7–£9 ($11.55–$14.85). AE, DC, MC, V. Mon–Fri 7am–3pm. Tube: Barbican or Farringdon. TRADITIONAL BRITISH.

For British breakfast at its best, try this place, which has been serving traders from the nearby famous Smithfield meat market since the pub was built in 1898. Breakfasts are gargantuan, especially if you order the "Full House"—a plate with at least eight items, including sausage, bacon, kidneys, eggs, beans, black pudding, and a fried slice of bread, along with unlimited tea or coffee, toast, and jam. Add a Black Velvet (champagne with Guinness) and the day is yours. More fashionable is a Bucks Fizz, with orange juice and champagne (we usually call it a Mimosa). The Fox and Anchor is noted for its range of fine English ales, all available at breakfast. Butchers from the meat market, spotted with blood, still appear, as do nurses getting off their shifts and clerks and tycoons from the City who've been working at bookkeeping chores (or making millions) all night.

4 On the Thames: Docklands & South Bank

For more Thames-side dining in the West End, see Ship Hispaniola, p. 000.

ST. KATHARINE'S DOCK
INEXPENSIVE

✪ **Dickens Inn by the Tower.** St. Katharine's Way, E1. ☎ **0171/488-2208.** Reservations recommended. In Pickwick Grill, main courses £17.50–£35 ($28.90–$57.75); in Tavern Room, snacks and platters £3.75–£6 ($6.20–$9.90); in pizza restaurant, pizzas £9–£15 ($14.85–$24.75). AE, DC, MC, V. Restaurant daily noon–3pm and 6:30–10pm; pizza restaurant daily noon–10pm; bar daily 11am–11pm. Tube: Tower Hill. TRADITIONAL BRITISH.

This three-floor restaurant is in an 1830 brick warehouse, deliberately devoid of carpets, curtains, or anything that might conceal its unusual antique trusses, including a set of massive redwood timbers that were part of the original construction. Large windows afford a sweeping view of the nearby Thames and Tower Bridge. On the ground level, you'll find a bar and the Tavern Room, serving sandwiches, platters of lasagna, steaming bowls of soup and chili, bar snacks, and other foods kids love. On the floor above is Pizza on the Dock, offering four sizes of pizzas that should also make the kids happy when they have a craving for the familiar. Above that, you'll find a relatively formal dining room, Wheelers Restaurant, serving more elegant modern British meals; specials include steaks, chargrilled brochette of wild mushrooms, panfried calf's ~ with tangy lime and ginger sauce, and baked fillet of cod.

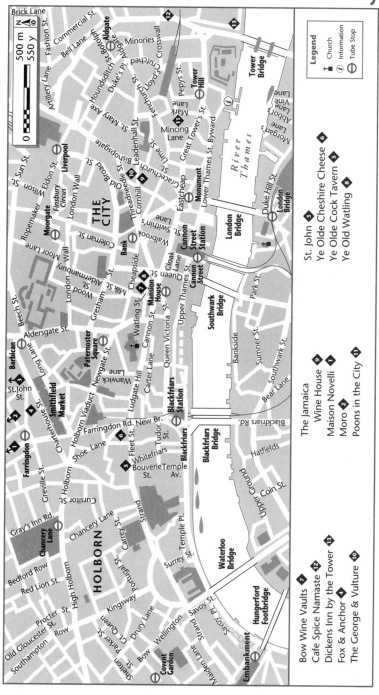

Restaurants in & Around the City

Brick Lane

500 m
550 y

Legend
✠ Church
ⓘ Information
Ⓤ Tube Stop

St. John 3
Ye Olde Cheshire Cheese 6
Ye Olde Cock Tavern 5
Ye Old Watling 8

The Jamaica
Wine House 9
Maison Novelli 1
Moro 2
Poons in the City 11

Bow Wine Vaults 7
Cafe Spice Namaste 12
Dickens Inn by the Tower 13
Fox & Anchor 4
The George & Vulture 10

BUTLER'S WHARF
EXPENSIVE

Le Pont de la Tour. 36D Shad Thames, Butler's Wharf, SE1. ☎ **0171/403-8403.** Reservations not accepted in the Bar and Grill; recommended in the restaurant. Bar and Grill main courses £9–£18 ($14.85–$29.70); restaurant main courses £17.50–£23.50 ($28.90–$38.80); fixed-price 3-course lunch £28.50 ($47.05). Mon–Sat special pre- and post-theater menu £19.50 ($32.15) (from 6–6:45pm/from 10:30–11:30pm). AE, DC, MC, V. Restaurant Mon–Fri noon–3pm; Mon–Sat 6–11:30pm; Sun 12:30–3pm and 6–11pm. Bar and Grill daily 11:30am–midnight. Tube: Tower Hill or London Bridge. INTERNATIONAL.

At the edge of the Thames near Tower Bridge, the Butler's Wharf complex holds condos, rental apartments, offices, and an assortment of food and wine shops collectively known as the Gastrodome. Built in the mid–19th century as a warehouse, it's now another Terence Conran playland. From its windows, diners and shoppers enjoy sweeping views of some of the densest river traffic in Europe.

The **Bar and Grill**'s live piano music (on evenings and weekends) together with a wide choice of wines and cocktails creates one of the most lively, convivial ambiences in the area. Although such dishes as ham and foie gras terrine; a half lobster with roast peppers, olives, and fennel, and langoustines mayonnaise are featured, the culinary star is a heaping platter of fresh shellfish—perfect when shared with a friend, accompanied by a bottle of wine.

In bold contrast is the large, more formal room known simply as **The Restaurant.** Filled with burr oak furniture and decorated with framed lithographs of early-20th-century Parisian cafe society, it offers excellent food and a polite but undeniable English reserve. The menu might list such temptations as roast rabbit wrapped in herbs with pancetta and a mustard vinaigrette or whole roast-buttered lobster with herbs. One especially winning selection is best end of lamb, with a black olive and herb crust in a red-pepper sauce. All the fish is excellent, but none better than the Dover sole, which can be ordered grilled or meunière.

MODERATE

Butler's Wharf Chop House. 36E Shad Thames, SE1. ☎ **0171/403-3403.** Reservations recommended. Fixed-price 2-course lunch £18.75 ($30.95), fixed-price 3-course lunch £22.75 ($37.55); dinner main courses £12–£29.50 ($19.80–$48.70). AE, DC, MC, V. Sun–Fri noon–3pm (last order); Mon–Sat 6–11pm. Tube: Tower Hill. TRADITIONAL BRITISH.

Of the four restaurants housed in Butler's Wharf, this one is the closest to Tower Bridge. It maintains its commitment to moderate prices, and though there's an even cheaper restaurant, La Cantina del Ponte, most diners consider that merely a place for pastas. (See above for the complex's more upscale set of restaurants.) The Chop House was modeled after a large boathouse, with russet-colored banquettes, lots of exposed wood, flowers, candles, and big windows overlooking Tower Bridge and the Thames. Lunchtime crowds include workers from the City's nearby financial district; evening crowds are largely made up of friends dining together under less pressing circumstances.

Dishes are largely adaptations of British recipes: fish-and-chips with mushy peas; steak and kidney pudding with oysters; stewed rabbit leg with bitter leaves and mustard; roast rump of lamb, garlic mash and rosemary; and grilled pork fillet, apples, chestnuts, and cider sauce. To follow, there might be a dark-chocolate tart with whiskey cream or sticky toffee pudding. The bar offers such stiff-upper-lip choices as Theakston's best bitter, sev-

English wines, and a half-dozen French clarets served by the jug.

VE

.lipper. Shad Thames, Butler's Wharf, SE1. ☎ **0171/357-9001.** Reservations .d. Main courses £8–£15 ($13.20–$24.75); set menu from £10 ($16.50); Sunday

It's a big world.

And we've got the network to cover it.

Global connection with the AT&T Network

AT&T direct service

Enjoy going to the corners of the earth? We're with you. With the world's most powerful network, **AT&T Direct**® Service gives you fast, clear connections from more countries than anyone,* and the option of an English-speaking operator. All it takes is your AT&T Calling Card or credit card† And the planet is yours.

FOR A LIST OF **AT&T ACCESS NUMBERS**, TAKE THE ATTACHED WALLET GUIDE.

For
Travelers
who want more than
the Official Line

For Travelers Who Want More Than the Official Line

the Unofficial Guide® to Florida with Kids

For Travelers Who Want More Than the Official Line

the Unofficial Guide® to Walt Disney World®

♦ Tips for Saving Time
Family-Friendly Hotels & R...
Attractions Rated for Each ...

The Series with More Than **3 Million** Copies Sold!

♦ Tips & Warnings
♦ Save Money & Time
♦ All Attractions Candidly Rated & Ranked, Including Disney's New Animal Kingdom

Bob Sehlinger

For Travelers Who Want More Than the Official Line

the Unofficial Guide® to Las Vegas

The Series with More Than **3 Million** Copies Sold!

♦ Save Time & Money
♦ Insider Gambling Tips
♦ Casinos & Hotels
Candidly Rated & Ranked

Bob Sehlinger

Macmillan Publishing USA

Also Available:

- The Unofficial Guide to Branson
- The Unofficial Guide to California with Kids
- The Unofficial Guide to Chicago
- The Unofficial Guide to Cruises
- The Unofficial Disney Companion
- The Unofficial Guide to Disneyland
- The Unofficial Guide to the Great Smoky & Blue Ridge Region
- The Unofficial Guide to Miami & the Keys
- Mini-Mickey: The Pocket-Sized Unofficial Guide to Walt Disney World
- The Unofficial Guide to New Orleans
- The Unofficial Guide to New York City
- The Unofficial Guide to San Francisco
- The Unofficial Guide to Skiing in the West
- The Unofficial Guide to Washington, D.C.

buffet £7.35 ($12.15). AE, DC, MC, V. Daily 11am–3pm and 6–11:30pm. Tube: Tower Hill. INDIAN.

A former spice warehouse by the Thames serves—with much justification—what it calls "India's most remarkable dishes." This likable and often animated restaurant is outfitted with cream-colored walls, tall columns, and modern artwork inspired by the Moghul Dynasty's replicas of royal figures, soaring trees, and well-trained elephants. Seven windows afford sweeping views over the industrialized Thames-side neighborhood. As music from a live pianist emanates from the convivial bar, you can enjoy a cuisine that includes many vegetarian choices derived from the formerly Portuguese colony of Goa and the once-English colony of Bengal. There is a zestiness and spice to the cuisine, but it is never overpowering. The chefs keep the menu fairly short so that all ingredients can be purchased fresh every day. A tantalizing and tasty specialty is stuffed murgh masala, a tender breast of chicken with potato, onion, apricots, and almonds cooked with yogurt and served with a delectable curry sauce. The perfectly cooked duckling (off the bone) comes in a tangy sauce with a citrus bite. One of the finest dishes we've ever tasted in North India is also served here, and has lost nothing in the transfer: marinated lamb simmered in cream with cashew nuts and seasoned with fresh ginger. One of the best offerings from the Goan repertoire is the karkra chop, a spicy patty of minced crab blended with mashed potatoes and peppered with Goan spices. The poppadums and homemade chutneys add to the savory experience.

5 In & Around Knightsbridge

VERY EXPENSIVE

La Tante Claire. Wilton Place, Knightsbridge, SW1. ☎ **0171/823-2003.** Reservations essential. Main courses £24–£35 ($39.60–$57.75). AE, DC, MC, V. Mon–Fri 12:30–2pm, Mon–Sat 7–11pm. Tube: Hyde Park Corner, Knightsbridge.

In swanky new digs, "Aunt Claire" has once again emerged as one of the stellar restaurants of London. Pierre Koffmann remains the chef behind this fabled place, a man more interested in turning out culinary fireworks than in creating a media feeding frenzy. The restaurant was designed by leading interior designer David Collins of Ireland. The lilac walls and the soothing green floors are a mere backdrop to the cuisine which uses only the freshest and best of produce to be found in London. The standards of Chef Koffmann are the benchmark other chefs aspire to. To sample perfection, dishes bringing out mouthwatering flavors and precise textures, try his now legendary ravioli langoustine or pig's trotters. Who would have thought that the lowly pig trotter, long a staple of the menu in Paris's Les Halles district, could be transformed into such a sublime concoction? His soup made with truffles is to make gourmands shed tears of joy. His nage de homard (lobster) with Sauterne and fresh ginger is a culinary work of skill, as is his steamed lamb with a vegetable couscous. For dessert, his hot pistachio soufflé served with its own ice cream will linger long in your memory. The service proceeds like a perfectly trained and talented orchestra.

EXPENSIVE

Georgian Restaurant. On the fourth floor of Harrods, 87-135 Brompton Rd., SW1. ☎ **0171/225-5930** or 0171/225-6800. Reservations recommended for lunch and tea. Main courses £21–£25.50 ($34.65–$42.05); fixed-price 3-course lunch £28.50 ($47.05); sandwiches and pastries at teatime £17 ($28.05) per person. AE, DC, MC, V. Mon–Sat noon–3pm; tea Mon–Sat 3:45–5:15pm. Tube: Knightsbridge. TRADITIONAL BRITISH.

The Georgian Restaurant, set under elaborate ceilings and belle-époque skylights atop London's fabled emporium, is one of the neighborhood's most appealing places for lunch and afternoon tea. At lunchtime one of the rooms, big enough for a ball, features a pianist whose music trills among the crystal of the chandeliers. A buffet features cold meats and an array of fresh salads; for a hot meal, head for the carvery, where a uniformed crew of chefs dishes out poultry, fish, and pork. During afternoon tea be charmed by the tones of a string quartet while you sip tea and snack on an elaborate array of sandwiches, scones, and pastries.

San Lorenzo. 22 Beauchamp Place, SW3. ☎ **0171/584-1074.** Reservations required. Main courses £14.50–£25.50 ($23.90–$42.05). No credit cards. Mon–Sat 12:30–3pm and 7:30–11:30pm. Tube: Knightsbridge. ITALIAN.

This fashionable restaurant, once a favorite of Princess Di, specializes in regional cuisines from Tuscany and the Piedmont. Frequently mentioned in the London tabloids thanks to its high-profile clients, San Lorenzo is the domain of effervescent owners Lorenzo and Mara Berni. Reliability is the keynote of their seasonal cuisine, which often includes homemade fettuccine with salmon, risotto with fresh asparagus, veal piccata, and partridge in white-wine sauce. Regional offerings might include salt cod with polenta. Though some critics have dismissed this as a once-great place that had its heyday in the 1970s, its continuing popularity is illustrated by how difficult it is to get a table. And while the food is really good, the attitudes and service need improvement. But it's still a great choice, especially if you're doing some upscale shopping along Beauchamp Place.

✪ Vong. In the Berkeley Hotel, Wilton Place, SW1. ☎ **0171/235-1010.** Reservations recommended. Main courses £12.75–£26.75 ($21.05–$44.15); vegetarian main courses £10.25–£13.50 ($16.90–$22.30); tasting menu £45 ($74.25); fixed-price 3-course lunch £20 ($33); fixed-price 3-course dinner £29–£39 ($47.85–$64.35); pre- and post-theater dinner £17.50 ($28.90). AE, DC, MC, V. Mon–Sat noon–2:30pm and 6–11pm; Sun 11:30am–2:30pm and 6–9:30pm. Dim Sum available Sat–Sun 11:30am–2:30pm from £2.50 ($4.15) per plate. Pre- and post-theater dinner available 6–7pm and 10:30–11:30pm. Tube: Knightsbridge. FRENCH/THAI.

Just 600 yards from Harrods, this strikingly modern restaurant on three levels is one of the chic rendezvous of London. Jean-Georges Vongerichten, the darling of New York culinary circles, has brought his award-winning French/Thai menu to London and boldly states that the superior Thai ingredients available in London will make the offspring better than the parent. The results here are subtle, innovative, and inspired.

In a minimalist setting, you can partake of the "Black Plate," featuring samples of six starters, if you'd like a taste of everything. Other options are a perfectly roasted halibut or a lobster and daikon roll, the latter with rosemary and ginger sauce. You can virtually eat everything on the menu and be filled with wonder and admiration, especially by the crab spring roll with a vinegary tamarind dipping sauce. The sautéed foie gras with ginger and mango literally melts in the mouth. Spiced cod with curried artichokes is well worth a try. Desserts are equally exotic, especially the salad of banana and passion fruit with white-pepper ice cream (yes, you heard right).

Zafferano. 15 Lowndes St., SW1. ☎ **0171/235-5800.** Reservations required. Set menus £26.50–£36.50 ($43.70–$60.20). AE, MC, V. Mon–Sat noon–2:30pm and 7–11pm. Tube: Knightsbridge. ITALIAN.

There's something honest and satisfying about this restaurant, where decor consists of little more than ochre-colored walls, immaculate napery, and a bevy of diligent, uniformed staff members. A quick review of past clients might convince you of its desirability: They include Margaret Thatcher, Michael Hesseltine, Richard Gere, Princess Margaret, and Eric Clapton. An elegantly modernized interpretation of Italian cuisine incorporates such dishes as ravioli of pheasant with black truffles, rabbit with Parma ham and polenta, sea bream with spinach and balsamic vinegar, and monkfish with almonds. Joan Collins claimed the chefs produce "culinary fireworks," but found the bright lighting far too harsh. The owners pride themselves on one of the most esoteric and well-rounded collections of Italian wine in London: You'll find as many as 20 different vintages each of Brunello and Barolos, and about a dozen vintages of Sassecaia.

MODERATE

Fifth Floor at Harvey Nichols. 109-125 Knightsbridge, at Sloane St., SW1. ☎ **0171/235-5250.** Reservations recommended. Fixed-price 3 course lunch £23.50 ($38.80); main courses £12–£30 ($19.80–$49.50); à la carte dishes available at dinner only. AE, DC, MC, V. Mon–Fri noon–3pm, Sat and Sun noon–3:30pm; Mon–Sat 6:30–11:30pm (last order). Tube: Knightsbridge. MODERN BRITISH.

This restaurant in the Harvey Nichols flagship store is the most carefully orchestrated of London's large department-store eateries. There's a simple cafe near the entrance, which tends to be the domain of package-laden shoppers looking for a quick cup of tea and a salad. Serious diners head directly to the high-ceilinged blue-and-white restaurant, where big windows overlook the redbrick Edwardian walls of the Hyde Park Hotel across the street. The menu is appropriately fashionable, and waiters imbue any meal with a polite kind of formality. Starters include goat-cheese-and-lemon risotto with deep-fried baby artichokes, and potted foie gras with orange-and-onion confit and toasted brioche. Main courses include panfried scallops in a bordelaise sauce; shredded duck confit; smoked haddock fish cakes; and a spinach, bacon, and avocado salad.

Although the department store closes at 6pm, a pair of elevators continues to haul patrons to the restaurant. There's a glamorous food emporium (open during store hours) set just outside the restaurant's entrance.

INEXPENSIVE

Chicago Rib Shack. 1 Raphael St., SW7. ☎ **0171/581-5595.** Reservations accepted, except Sat. Main courses £8–£12 ($13.20–$19.80). AE, CB, MC, V. Daily 11:45am–11:45pm. Tube: Knightsbridge. AMERICAN.

Just 100 yards from Harrods, this place specializes in real American barbecue, cooked in imported smoking ovens and marinated in a sauce made with 15 ingredients. Their decadent onion loaf is a famous treat. Visitors are encouraged to eat with their fingers, and bibs and hot towels are provided. A TV screen suspended in the bar shows American sports. The British touch is evident in an overwhelming number of Victorian architectural antiques, which have been salvaged from demolished buildings all over the country. The 45-foot-long ornate mahogany-and-mirrored bar was once part of a Glasgow pub, and eight massive stained-glass windows came from a chapel in Lancashire.

IN NEARBY BELGRAVIA
MODERATE

Salloos. 62–64 Kinnerton St., SW1. ☎ **0171/235-4444.** Reservations recommended. Main courses £10–£17 ($16.50–$28.05); fixed-price 3-course lunch £16 ($26.40); fixed-price 4-course dinner £25 ($41.25). AE, DC, MC, V. Mon–Sat noon–2:30pm and 7–11:15pm. Tube: Hyde Park Corner. PAKISTANI/MUGHLAI.

One of London's most elegant Pakistani restaurants is located in one of the city's most fashionable and expensive neighborhoods. This small hideaway has only about 60 seats; the elegant corniced interior is done in pale creamy white with burgundy accents. The lighting is dim and soothing; spotlights focus on Pakistani embroideries. The cosmopolitan clientele comes for such dishes as lamb chops grilled in a tandoori oven,

Restaurants from Knightsbridge to Kensington

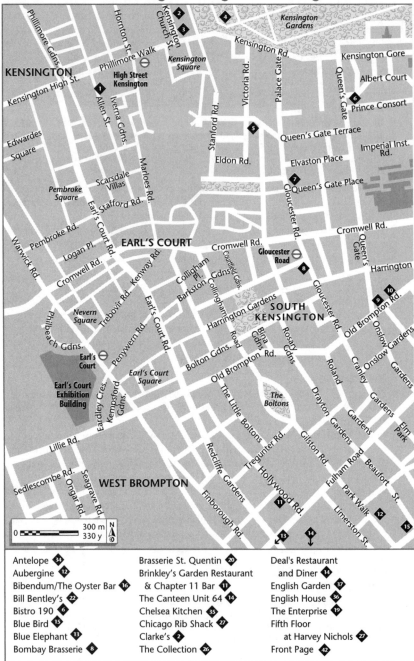

Antelope **34**

Aubergine **12**

Bibendum/The Oyster Bar **16**

Bill Bentley's **22**

Bistro 190 **6**

Blue Bird **15**

Blue Elephant **13**

Bombay Brasserie **8**

Brasserie St. Quentin **20**

Brinkley's Garden Restaurant & Chapter 11 Bar **11**

The Canteen Unit 64 **14**

Chelsea Kitchen **35**

Chicago Rib Shack **27**

Clarke's **2**

The Collection **26**

Deal's Restaurant and Diner **14**

English Garden **37**

English House **36**

The Enterprise **19**

Fifth Floor at Harvey Nichols **27**

Front Page **42**

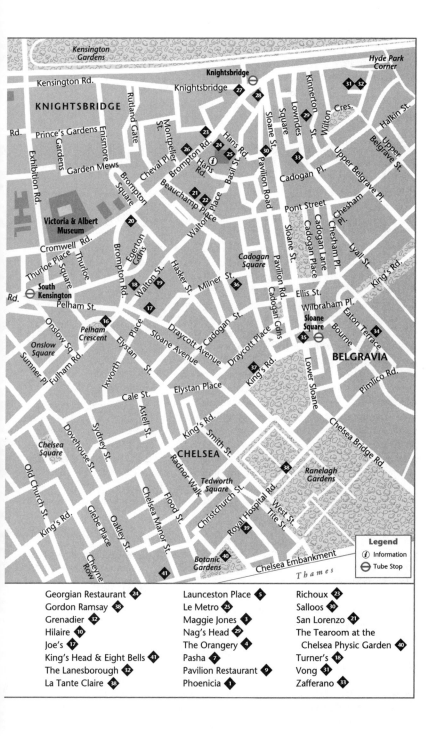

Georgian Restaurant 24	Launceston Place 5	Richoux 23
Gordon Ramsay 38	Le Metro 25	Salloos 30
Grenadier 32	Maggie Jones 3	San Lorenzo 21
Hilaire 10	Nag's Head 29	The Tearoom at the
Joe's 17	The Orangery 4	Chelsea Physic Garden 40
King's Head & Eight Bells 41	Pasha 7	Turner's 18
The Lanesborough 32	Pavilion Restaurant 9	Vong 31
La Tante Claire 38	Phoenicia 1	Zafferano 33

chicken shish kebabs, chicken cooked and served in a karahi (spicy, with curry), chicken korma (moderately spicy and served with yogurt sauce), and a house specialty of *haleem akbari* (shredded lamb cooked in wheat germ with lentils and spices). Most of these specialties were developed during the reign of North India's Moghul emperors. The owner, Muhammad Salahuddin (whose nickname is Salloos), is assisted by his charming and articulate daughters, Farizeh and Nafiseh, who greet customers at the door.

6 Chelsea

VERY EXPENSIVE

✪ **Gordon Ramsay.** 68 Royal Hospital Rd., SW3. ☎ **0171/352-4441.** Reservations essential (1 month in advance). Set 2-course lunch £28 ($46.20), set 3-course lunch £50 ($82.50); set 3-course dinner £50 ($82.50), set 7-course dinner £65 ($107.25). Mon–Fri noon–2:30pm and 6:45–11pm. Tube: Sloane Square. FRENCH.

If there's a "hot flash" in restaurant news around London, the buzz spins around one of the city's most innovative and talented chefs, Gordon Ramsay. He's taken over the premises of La Tante Claire (see p. 155), and this genius of a chef is serving a cuisine even more innovative and exciting than the long-established "La Tante" herself. *Tout* London is rushing to sample Mr. Ramsay's viands, and he's had to turn away some big names. The Queen hasn't been denied a table yet, but that's only because she hasn't called. Already gourmand Andrew Lloyd Weber has visited, and acclaimed Ramsay as one of Europe's grandest chefs. The producer said you "can get better food here than anywhere else in London." Food critic Dominic Bradbury called Ramsay a "Captain Ahab, a dedicated monomaniac, hell-bent on cruising his kitchen until he finds his second Michelin star." Every dish from his kitchen is gratifying, reflecting subtlety and delicacy without any sacrifice to the food's natural essence. Try, for example, his celebrated cappuccino of white beans with grated truffles. His appetizers are likely to dazzle: salad of crispy pig's trotters with calf's sweetbreads, fried quail eggs, and a cream vinaigrette, or else foie gras three ways—sautéed with quince, *mi-cuit* with an Earl Grey consomme, or pressed with truffle peelings. From here, you can grandly proceed to fillet of brill poached in red wine, grilled fillet of red mullet on a bed of caramelized endives, or else caramelized Challandaise duck cooked with dates. Desserts are equally stunning, especially the pistachio soufflé with chocolate sorbet or the passion fruit and chocolate parfait.

EXPENSIVE

✪ **Aubergine.** 11 Park Walk, SW10. ☎ **0171/352-3449.** Reservations essential and accepted up to 4 weeks in advance. Fixed-price 2-course lunch £23.50 ($38.80); fixed-price 3-course dinner £39.50 ($65.20); menu gourmand £45 ($74.25). AE, DC, MC, V. Mon–Fri noon–2:30pm; Mon–Sat 6:45–11pm. Tube: South Kensington. FRENCH.

"Eggplant" is luring savvy diners down to the lower reaches of Chelsea where new chef Williams Drabble takes over from where the renowned Gordon Ramsay left off. Drabble, who earned his first Michelin star in 1998 has remained true to the style and ambience of this famous establishment. Although popular with celebrities, the restaurant remains unpretentious and refuses to pander to the special whims of the rich and famous. (When Princess Margaret complained that the air-conditioning was too cold, she was lent a cardigan; and Madonna was refused a late-night booking!)

Every dish is satisfyingly flavorsome, from the warm salad of truffled vegetables with asparagus purée to the roasted monkfish served with crushed new potatoes, roasted leeks, and a red-wine sauce. Starters continue to charm and delight palates, ranging from the ravioli of crab with mussels, chili, ginger, and coriander nage, to the terrine of foie gras with confit of duck with pears poached in port. Also resting on your Villeroy or Boch aubergine plate might be mallard with a celeriac fondant or assiette of lamb with a thyme-scented jus. Another stunning (in the good sense) main course is a tranche of sea bass with bouillabaisse potatoes. A new dish likely to catch your eye is roasted veal sweetbreads with caramelized onion purée and a casserole of flap mushrooms. There are only 14 tables, so bookings are imperative.

Blue Bird. 350 King's Rd., SW3. ☎ **0171/559-1000.** Reservations recommended. Set lunch Mon–Fri £12.75–£15.75 ($21.05–$26); main courses £9.25–£28.50 ($15.25–$47.05). AE, DC, MC, V. Mon–Fri noon–3pm and 6–11:30pm; Sat 11am–4pm and 6–11:30pm; Sun 11am–4pm and 6–10:30pm. Tube: Sloane Sq. MODERN CONTINENTAL.

Loyal Rangers from the surrounding neighborhood, as well as members of its French and Australian staff, refer to this 21st-century twist on Bibendum as a *restaurant de gare*—a railway station restaurant. It's an enormous echoing space that resounds every night with clinking silverware and peals of laughter. Although there's a cafe and an upscale delicatessen and housewares store on the street level, the heart and soul of this place is one floor above in the restaurant. It holds up to 275 diners at a time, and you'll find a color scheme of red-and-blue-canvas cutouts that replicate birds in flight. Tables are close together, but the sheer scale of the place makes dining strangely private and intimate. The massive upscale menu emphasizes savory, cooked-to-the-minute cuisine, some of it emerging from a wood-burning stove used to roast everything from lobster to game. An immense shellfish bar stocks on ice every crustacean you can think of, and a bar off to one side does a thriving business with the Sloane Square subculture. Perennial favorites include the marinated lamb with baked beans and aïoli, as well as versions of pasta and fresh fish. Prior to its role as a restaurant, the site functioned as a garage that repaired the legendary Bluebird, a very fast English sports car that, alas, is no longer produced.

MODERATE

English Garden. 10 Lincoln St., SW3. ☎ **0171/584-7272.** Reservations required. Main courses £9.50–£19.25 ($15.65–$31.75); fixed-price lunch £16.75 ($27.65). AE, CB, DC, MC, V. Mon–Sat 12:30–2:30pm, Sun 12:30–2pm; Mon–Sat 7:30–11:30pm, Sun 7–10:30pm. Tube: Sloane Sq. TRADITIONAL BRITISH.

This is a metropolitan restaurant par excellence. The decor is pretty and lighthearted in the historic town house: The Garden Room is whitewashed brick with a domed conservatory roof; vivid florals, rattan chairs, banks of plants, and candy-pink napery complete the scene. Every component of a meal here is chopped or cooked to the right degree and well proportioned. Launch into a fine repast with a caramelized red-onion-and-cheddar cheesecake or mussel-and-watercress soup. For a main course, opt for such delights as roast baron of rabbit with oven-dried tomato, prunes, and olive oil mash, or saddle of venison with potted cabbage. Some of these dishes sound as if they were cloned from an English cookbook of the Middle Ages—and are they ever good. Desserts, especially the rhubarb-and-cinnamon ice cream or the candied orange tart with orange syrup, would've pleased Miss Marple.

English House. 3 Milner St., SW3. ☎ **0171/584-3002.** Reservations required. Main courses £8–£17 ($13.20–$28.05); fixed-price lunch £15.75 ($26). AE, DC, MC, V. Mon–Sat 12:30–2:30pm and 7:30–11:15pm; Sun 12:30–2pm and 7:30–9:45pm. Tube: Sloane Sq. TRADITIONAL BRITISH.

Another design creation of Roger Wren (who did the English Garden, above), this tiny restaurant will make you feel like you're a guest in an elegant but cozy Victorian house. The food is British, the menu seasonal, and each dish is given a subtle, modern treatment. Some foodies find the cuisine outdated, but year after year—based on the mail we get—readers find it immensely satisfying. Begin with the butter bean and bacon soup (which sounds almost medieval), or deviled crabcakes with green herb salsa. For a main dish, try either the calf's liver and bacon with bubble and squeak (cabbage and potatoes), or roast filet of beef with a horseradish crust and Yorkshire pudding. Game is available in season, as is a fresh fish of the day. Summer berries in season predominate on the pudding menu, including fresh berries laced with elderflower syrup. Other offerings include a "Phrase of Apples," the chef's adaptation of a 17th-century recipe for a delectable apple pancake. London is filled with trendy places these days; every time we visit, we're newly pleased that there's still a retreat that focuses on rescuing long-forgotten recipes and bringing them to a new audience.

INEXPENSIVE

Chelsea Kitchen. 98 King's Rd., SW3. ☎ **0171/589-1330.** Reservations recommended. Main courses £3–£5.50 ($4.95–$9.05); fixed-price menu £6 ($9.90). No credit cards. Daily 8am–11:30pm. Tube: Sloane Sq. INTERNATIONAL.

This simple restaurant feeds large numbers of Chelsea residents in a setting that's changed very little since 1961. The food and the clientele move fast, almost guaranteeing that the entire inventory of ingredients is sold out at the end of each day. Menu items usually include leek-and-potato soup, chicken Kiev, chicken parmigiana, steaks, sandwiches, and burgers. The clientele includes a broad cross section of patrons—all having a good and cost-conscious time.

IN NEARBY CHELSEA HARBOUR

The Chelsea Harbour Complex is a multimillion-dollar development of formerly abandoned piers and wharves southwest of central London.

MODERATE

✪ **The Canteen.** Unit G4, Harbour Yard, Chelsea Harbour, SW10. ☎ **0171/351-7330.** Reservations recommended. Cover charge £1 ($1.65) per person. Main courses £6–£10.40 ($9.90–$17.15). AE, MC, V. Mon–Sat noon–3pm; Mon–Fri 6:30–10:30pm; Sat 6:30–11:15pm. Tube: Earl's Court, then Chelsea Harbour Hoppa Bus C3; on Sun, take a taxi. MODERN BRITISH/FRENCH.

The most viable and popular of the several restaurants in the Chelsea Harbour Complex, its whimsical setting, influenced by *Alice in Wonderland,* is very fantastical and the kind of thing that children as well as adults love. The cuisine is exceptional, too. The menu changes every 2 months, but may include risotto of plum tomatoes and champagne; pappardelle with field mushrooms and truffle oil; a warm salad of sea scallops, apples, and cashew nuts; sliced breast of corn-fed chicken with apple, potato-and-sage casserole, along with Spätzli and beans; or, a real treat, seared peppered tuna with herb potatoes, a sweet shallot pickle, and crème fraîche. The chocolate soufflé is the smoothest item on the menu, and are those crêpe suzette soufflés ever tempting. Or else you can settle for a selection of farmhouse cheeses so delectable it isn't a compromise at all to pass up all those rich desserts.

INEXPENSIVE

Deal's Restaurant and Diner. Harbour Yard, Chelsea Harbour, SW10. ☎ **0171/795-1001.** Reservations recommended. Main courses £6.75–£17 ($11.15–$28.05). AE, DC, MC, V. Mon–Thurs noon–3:30pm and 5:30–11pm; Fri–Sat noon–11:30pm; Sun noon–10pm. Tube: Earl's Court, then Chelsea Harbour Hoppa Bus C3; on Sun, take a taxi. AMERICAN/THAI.

Deal's is co-owned by Princess Margaret's son, Viscount Linley, and Lord Lichfield. As soon as the Queen Mother arrived here on a barge to order a Deal's burger, the success of this place was assured. The early-1900s atmosphere includes ceiling fans and bentwood banquettes. The food is American diner–style, with a strong Thai influence: Try a teriyaki burger, the prawn curry, spareribs, or a vegetarian dish, and finish with New England–style apple pie. We can't promise that the viscount himself is in the kitchen supervising the menu, but he is said to have tasted everything, and given it his aristocratic approval.

7 Kensington & South Kensington

KENSINGTON
MODERATE

Launceston Place. 1A Launceston Place, W8. ☎ **0171/937-6912.** Reservations required. Main courses £14.50–£16.50 ($23.90–$27.20); fixed-price 2-course menu for lunch and early dinner till 8pm, £14.50 ($23.90), fixed-price 3-course menu £17.50 ($28.90). AE, MC, V. Mon–Fri 12:30–2:30pm, Sun 12:30–3pm; Mon–Sat 7–11:30pm. Tube: Gloucester Rd. or High St. Kensington. MODERN BRITISH.

Launceston Place—sporting a new look as of 1996—is situated in an affluent, almost villagelike neighborhood where many Londoners would like to live, if only they could afford it. The stylish restaurant is a series of uncluttered Victorian parlors illuminated by a rear skylight and decorated with Victorian oils and watercolors, plus contemporary paintings. Since its opening in spring 1986, it has been known for its new British cuisine. The menu changes every 6 weeks, but you're likely to be served such appetizers as smoked salmon with horseradish crème fraîche, or seared foie gras with lentils and vanilla dressing. For a main dish, perhaps it'll be roast partridge with bacon, onions, and parsnip mash; or grilled sea bass with tomato and basil cream.

✪ **Phoenicia.** 11–13 Abingdon Rd., W8. ☎ **0171/937-0120.** Reservations required. Main courses £9.90–£15 ($16.35–$24.75); buffet lunch £10.95–£12.95 ($18.05–$21.35); fixed-price dinner £16.80–£30.95 ($27.70–$51.05). AE, DC, MC, V. Daily 12:15pm–midnight; buffet lunch Mon–Sat 12:15–2:30pm, Sun 12:15–3:30pm. Tube: High St. Kensington. LEBANESE.

Phoenicia is highly regarded for the quality of its Lebanese cuisine—outstanding in presentation and freshness—and for its moderate prices. For the best value, go for lunch, when you can enjoy a buffet of more than two dozen *meze* (appetizers), presented in little pottery dishes. Each day at lunch, the chef prepares two or three home-cooked dishes to tempt your taste buds, including chicken in garlic sauce or stuffed lamb with vegetables. Many Lebanese patrons begin their meal with the *apéritif arak*, a liqueur some have compared to ouzo. To start, you can select from such classic Middle Eastern dishes as hummus or stuffed vine leaves. The chefs bake fresh bread and two types of pizza daily in a clay oven. Minced lamb, spicy and well flavored, is an eternal favorite. Various charcoal-grilled dishes are also offered.

INEXPENSIVE

Maggie Jones. 6 Old Court Place (off Kensington Church St.), W8. ☎ **0171/937-6462.** Reservations required. Main courses £9.95–£15.95 ($16.40–$26.30). AE, DC, MC, V. Daily 12:30–2:30pm and 6:30–11pm. Tube: High St. Kensington. TRADITIONAL BRITISH.

This whimsical, staunchly English restaurant is a longtime favorite, thanks to its good food and its associations with Princess Margaret (a long-ago frequent client after whom the restaurant was named). There's dining on three floors, but the basement is the most intimate. The furniture is plain pine with candles stuck into bottles, and the allure is that of an old-fashioned English farmhouse. Menu items include grilled English rack of lamb with rosemary or garlic, baked mackerel and gooseberries, and

Maggie's famous fish pie. Desserts include treacle tart. Everything is reliably cooked and good, but never thrilling.

SOUTH KENSINGTON
EXPENSIVE

Bibendum/The Oyster Bar. 81 Fulham Rd., SW3. ☎ **0171/581-5817.** Reservations required in Bibendum; not accepted in Oyster Bar. Main courses £15–£25 ($24.75–$41.25); fixed-price 3-course lunch £28 ($46.20); cold seafood platter in Oyster Bar £45 ($74.25) for 2. AE, DC, MC, V. Bibendum Mon–Fri noon–2:30pm and 7–11:15pm; Sat 12:30–3pm and 7–11:15pm; Sun 12:30–3pm and 7–10:15pm. Oyster Bar Mon–Sat noon–11:30pm; Sun noon–3pm and 7–10:30pm. Tube: South Kensington. FRENCH/MEDITERRANEAN.

In trendy Brompton Cross, this still-fashionable restaurant occupies two floors of a garage—the former home of the Michelin tire company—that's an art deco master-piece. Although it's still going strong, Bibendum's heyday was in the early 1990s; it no longer enjoys top berth on the lists of London's food critics. The white-tiled room, with stained-glass windows, streaming sunlight, and a chic clientele, is an extremely pleasant place to dine. The fabulously eclectic cuisine, known for its freshness and sim-plicity, is based on what's available seasonally. Dishes might include roast pigeon with celeriac purée and apple sauté; rabbit with anchovies, garlic, and rosemary; or grilled lamb cutlets with a delicate sauce. Some of the best dishes are for dining *à deux:* Bresse chicken flavored with fresh tarragon, or grilled veal chops with truffle butter.

Simpler meals and cocktails are available in the **Oyster Bar** on the building's street level. The bar-style menu stresses fresh shellfish presented in the traditional French style, on ice-covered platters occasionally adorned with strands of seaweed. It's a crustacean-lover's lair.

Hilaire. 68 Old Brompton Rd., SW7. ☎ **0171/584-8993.** Reservations recommended. Fixed-price 2-course lunch £19.50 ($32.15), fixed-price 3-course lunch £23.50 ($38.80); fixed-price 3-course dinner £34 ($56.10), fixed-price 4-course dinner £37 ($61.05); dinner main courses £13.50–£21.50 ($22.30–$35.50). AE, DC, MC, V. Mon–Fri 12:15–2:30pm; Mon–Sat 6:30–11:30pm. Closed bank holidays. Tube: South Kensington. CONTINENTAL.

After this former Victorian storefront was refurbished following a fire, it became one classy joint, like an elegant restaurant you might find in a town in the heart of France. With its large vases of flowers and shiny mirrors, it has a fitting ambience for enjoying some of South Ken's finest food. Chef Bryan Weber prepares a mixture of classical French and *cuisine moderne,* always following his own creative impulses and good culi-nary sense and style. The menu reflects the best of the season's offerings. A typical lunch might begin with a red-wine risotto with radicchio and sun-dried tomato pesto, followed with sautéed scallops with creamed chicory, and ending with rhubarb sorbet. At dinner, main courses might include rack of lamb with tapenade and wild garlic, saddle of rabbit, or grilled tuna with Provençal vegetables. An aperitif bar, extra tables, and a pair of semi-private alcoves are in the lower dining room.

Turner's. 87–89 Walton St., SW3. ☎ **0171/584-6711.** Reservations required. Mon–Fri fixed-price lunch £12.50–£15 ($20.65–$24.75), Sun £21.50 ($35.50); fixed-price dinner £26.50–£29.50 ($43.70–$48.70). AE, DC, MC, V. Mon–Fri and Sun 12:30–2:30pm; Mon–Sat 7:30–11:15pm, Sun 6–8:30pm. Tube: South Kensington. INTERNATIONAL.

This is the domain of Brian J. Turner, a Yorkshire native turned accomplished London chef who gained fame at a number of establishments, including the Capital Hotel, before acquiring his own place in the culinary sun. As one critic aptly put it, his food comes not only fresh from the market each day but also "from the heart." He doesn't imitate anyone, but sets his own goals and standards. The fixed-price menus change every day, and the à la carte listings at least every season. You might find chicken liver pâté with foie gras, terrine of fresh salmon with a dill sauce, roast rack of lamb with herb crust, smoked and roasted breast of duck in a port and green peppercorn sauce, or sea bass on a bed of stewed leeks with a bacon dressing. Is the place dated? Well, yes. It seems caught in a time capsule of the eighties, or as one critic put it, the "era of yuppies and Thatcherism." But the cuisine is so excellent and prepared with such fresh ingredients, that it's still hard to get a table here.

MODERATE

Bistro 190. In the Gore Hotel, 190 Queen's Gate, SW7. ☎ **0171/581-5666.** Reservations not accepted. Main courses £10–£15 ($16.50–$24.75). AE, DC, MC, V. Mon–Sat 7am–midnight; Sun 7:30am–11:30pm. Tube: Gloucester Rd. MEDITERRANEAN.

In the airy front room of the Gore Hotel (see chapter 4), this restaurant features a light Mediterranean cuisine much appreciated by the music and media crowd that keeps the place hopping. In an artfully simple setting of wood floors, potted plants, and framed art accented by a convivial but gossipy roar, you can dine on such dishes as lamb grilled over charcoal and served with deep-fried basil, a cassoulet of fish with chili toast, Mediterranean chowder with pesto toast, and, if available, a rhubarb crumble based loosely on an old-fashioned British dessert. Service isn't particularly fast, and the policy on reservations is confusing: Although membership is required for reservations, nonmembers may leave their name at the door and have a drink at the bar while they wait for a table. In the crush of peak dining hours, your waiter may or may not remember the nuances you expressed while placing your order, but the restaurant is nonetheless memorable. Go down to Downstairs 190 for a seafood or vegetarian meal.

✪ **Bombay Brasserie.** Courtfield Close, adjoining Bailey's Hotel, SW7. ☎ **0171/370-4040.** Reservations required. Main courses £14.50 ($23.90); buffet lunch £15.95 ($26.30). AE, DC, MC, V. Buffet daily 12:30–3pm; daily 7:30–11:30pm. Tube: Gloucester Rd. INDIAN.

This was London's best, most popular, and most talked-about Indian restaurant in the early 1990s, although lately its fame—not its culinary standards—seems to have fallen off a bit. It's still an impressive place, if a bit frayed, and most visitors still find the cuisine fabulous. It remains one of the best places in London for late-night dining. Before heading into dinner, you might enjoy a drink amid the wicker of the pink-and-white bar, where the bartender's specialty is a mango Bellini.

The waitstaff is professional and accommodating, willing to advise you on the spice-laden delicacies. One look at the menu and you're launched on a grand culinary tour of the subcontinent: tandoori trout, fish with mint chutney, chicken tikka, and vegetarian meals. One corner of the menu is reserved for Goan cookery, representing that part of India seized from Portugal in 1961. The cookery of North India is represented by Mughlai specialties, including chicken biryani, the famous Muslim pilaf dish. Under the category "Some Like It Hot," you'll find such main courses as lamb korma, prepared Kashmiri style.

Brasserie St. Quentin. 243 Brompton Rd., SW3. ☎ **0171/581-5131.** Reservations required. Main courses £10–£17 ($16.50–$28.05); fixed-price 2-course lunch £13.50 ($22.30); fixed-price 2-course dinner £10 ($16.50) from 6:30–7:30pm only. AE, DC, MC, V. Mon–Sat noon–3pm and 6:30–11pm; Sun noon–3pm and 6:30–11pm. Tube: Knightsbridge or South Kensington. FRENCH.

St. Quentin is the most authentic-looking French brasserie in London. Modeled after—but much more intimate than—the famous La Coupole in Paris, it attracts many members of London's French community, all of whom seem to talk at once (which tends to raise the level of noise and conviviality here to a subdued roar). The decor of mirrors and crystal chandeliers reflects a fashion- and trend-conscious clientele who enjoy the social hubbub. The waiters take it all in stride, usually with seemingly effortless Gallic tact. Try the baked sea bass with thyme, the scallops and Bayonne ham, or the duck confit with lentils. Look also for a salad of crab and baby spinach or the artichoke heart with poached egg and mushrooms.

The Collection. 264 Brompton Rd., SW3. ☎ **0171/225-1212.** Reservations recommended. Main courses £11–£16 ($18.15–$26.40); set-price menu £35 ($57.75). AE, DC, MC, V. Daily noon–3pm and 6:30–11pm. Tube: South Kensington. INTERNATIONAL.

This is a temple to voyeurism and the vanities, catering to the aesthetics and preoccupations of the fashion industry. It occupies an echoing warehouse; the only access is by a 30-foot underlit catwalk that emulates what you'd expect to find at a showing of next season's *couture*. Don't worry about a snobbish chill: Manager Julian Shaw is one of the most adept and humorous in London, becoming something of a celebrity in his own right because of his skill at dealing with big-ticket, big-ego fashion moguls. Yummy menu items include crispy duck with *yaki soba* noodles, sesame-crusted tuna steak with sweet potatoes and *bok choi,* seam bream with cilantro, and panfried calves liver with sage and onions. Incidentally, don't overlook this site as a venue for your after-dark barhopping.

Joe's. 126 Draycott Ave., SW3. ☎ **0171/225-2217.** Reservations required. Main courses £10–£17.50 ($16.50–$28.90). AE, DC, MC, V. Mon–Sat noon–3pm and 7–11pm; Sun 10:30am–4pm. Tube: South Kensington. MODERN BRITISH.

This is one of three London restaurants established by fashion designer Joseph Ettedgui. Thanks to its sense of glamour and fun, it's often filled with well-known names from the British fashion, music, and entertainment industries. You can enjoy such dishes as spiced venison strips and vegetables, roast cod in a champagne crab sauce, chargrilled swordfish with cracked wheat and salsa verde (green sauce), or fresh lobster lasagna. It's all safe, but a bit unexciting. No one will mind if your meal is composed exclusively of appetizers. There's a bar near the entrance, a cluster of tables for quick meals near the door, and more leisurely (and gossipy) dining available in an area a few steps up. Brunch is served on Sunday, which is the cheapest way to enjoy this place. The atmosphere remains laid-back and unstuffy, just like trendsetters in South Ken prefer it. With a name like Joe's, what else could it be?

Pasha. 1 Gloucester Rd., SW7. ☎ **171/589-7969.** Reservations recommended. Main courses £10–£17 ($16.50–$28.05). AE, DC, MC, V. Daily noon–3pm and 7–11:30pm. Tube: Gloucester Road. MOROCCAN.

You'll find virtually every kind of ethnic restaurant within London, but few equal the zest and stylishness of this re-creation of a palace within the medina at Marrakesh. Within a duet of dining rooms outfitted with Bedouin colors, rich upholsteries, flickering candles, and belly-dancing music, you'll enjoy regional and time-honored specialties that once were the domain only of cherished family guests. Examples include a crispy lamb salad with pomegranate and mint, grilled sea bass with warm hummus and parsley salad, chicken merguez (spicy sausage) with a coriander tagine, and chargrilled skewered chicken with green chili salsa. And if you have a fondness for the semolina specialty of North Africa (couscous), you'll have at least three different kinds from which to choose.

Pavilion Restaurant. In the Regency Hotel, 100 Queen's Gate, SW7. ☎ **0171/370-4595.** Reservations recommended. À la carte menu £10–£25 ($16.50–$41.25); lunch buffet £19 ($31.35). AE, DC, MC, V. Mon–Fri noon–2:30pm; daily 5:30–10:15pm. Tube: Gloucester Rd. or South Kensington. INTERNATIONAL.

This is a glamorous but reasonably priced choice if you're staying at one of the many hotels in South Kensington. From the minute you walk in the door and are greeted with the warmth of the maître d', his staff, and the traditional surroundings, you'll know you're in a setting of refined splendor. The chef offers an extensive à la carte menu; there's also a table d'hôte menu that changes weekly. Selections are modern dishes based on prime seasonal produce; they include English lamb cutlets served with tomatoes, mushrooms, and watercress; a cod steak that's lightly grilled and served with anchovy butter; Dover sole that can be grilled or panfried at your request; and vegetarian dishes. Care and attention also go into such appetizers as salmon and sole roulade or goat-cheese crostini.

IN NEARBY WEST BROMPTON
MODERATE

Blue Elephant. 4-6 Fulham Broadway, SW6. ☎ **0171/385-6595.** Reservations required. Main courses £7.50–£16.50 ($12.40–$27.20); Royal Thai banquet £29–£34 ($47.85–$56.10); Sun buffet £16.75 ($27.65). AE, DC, MC, V. Mon–Fri noon–2:30pm; Mon–Sat 7pm–12:30am, Sun noon–3pm and 7–10:30pm. Tube: Fulham Broadway. THAI.

This is the counterpart of the famous L'Éléphant Bleu in Brussels. Located in a converted factory building, the Blue Elephant has been all the rage since it opened in 1986. It's remains the leading Thai restaurant in London, where the competition seems to grow daily. In an almost magical garden setting of lush tropical foliage, diners are treated to an array of MSG–free Thai dishes. You can begin with a "Floating Market" (shellfish in clear broth flavored with chili paste and lemongrass), then go on to a splendid and varied selection of main courses, for which many of the ingredients have been flown in from Thailand. We recommend the roasted duck curry served in a clay cooking pot.

INEXPENSIVE

Brinkley's Garden Restaurant & Chapter 11 Bar. 47 Hollywood Rd., SW10. ☎ **0171/351-1683.** Reservations required. Main courses £7.50–£14 ($12.40–$23.10); bar snacks £3.50–£14 ($5.75–$23.10). MC, V. Mon–Sat 7–11:30pm; Sun noon–4pm. Closed Dec 23–27. Tube: Earl's Court. INTERNATIONAL.

At one time, the best cuisine you could hope to find in this neighborhood was bangers and mash. But today, shops selling some of the most exclusive and costly goods in town have drawn fashionable young Londoners here. There's a small heated, covered garden terrace out back and lower-level dining room inside. At the bar (with a happy hour from 6 to 8:30pm), you can get a grilled burger and other bar snacks. The menu in the restaurant is wisely limited to well-prepared dishes based on fresh ingredients. You might begin with spring rolls with a sweet chili sauce, deep-fried brie with cranberry sauce, or chargrilled satay-spiced king prawns, then follow with Thai prawn curry or a roasted duck breast.

8 Notting Hill
MODERATE

Achy Ramp. 150 Notting Hill Gate, W11. ☎ **0171/221-2442.** Reservations required Fri–Sat; otherwise strongly recommended. Main courses £13.50–£16.50 ($22.30–$27.20). AE, DC, MC, V. Daily noon–2:45pm and 6:45–10pm. Tube: Notting Hill Gate. MODERN CONTINENTAL.

The theme of this medical-chic restaurant will remind you either of a harmless small-town pharmacy or a drug lord's secret stash of mind-altering pills. That ambiguity is richly appreciated by the arts-conscious crowd that flocks here, partly because they're interested in what Damien Hirst (*enfant terrible* of London's contemporary art world) has created, and partly because the place can be a lot of fun. You'll enter the street-level bar, where a drink menu lists lots of highly palatable martinis as well as a somewhat icky concoction known as a Cough Syrup (cherry liqueur, honey, and vodka that's shaked, not stirred, over ice). Bottles of pills; bar stools whose seats are shaped like aspirins; and painted representations of Fire, Water, Air, and Earth decorate a scene favored by minor celebs and party people. Upstairs in the restaurant, the hospital theme is a lot less pronounced, but nonetheless subtly omnipresent. Menu items include such trendy but comforting food items as carpaccio of sea bass; lamb cooked with celery, spinach, and herb juices; fisherman's pie; home-salted cod and eggplant pie; and roasted duck with white peaches and French fries.

✪ **Bali Sugar Club.** 33A All Saints Rd., W11. ☎ **0171/221-4477.** Main courses £12–£17 ($19.80–$28.05); set lunch menu £17.50 ($28.90). AE, DC, MC, V. Daily 12:30–2:30pm and 6:30–11pm. Tube: Westbourne Park. FUSION.

The owners originally opened The Sugar Club here and achieved fame across London. But they have now moved and turned the original site into Bali Sugar, which is every bit as good as the original. They have acquired the talents of Claudio Aprile, one of Canada's most exciting and innovative young chefs, regarded as a rising star on the culinary scene. Originally from Uruguay, he trained in New York. He brings an exotic, bold, and extraordinary new look to fusion cuisine which has been labeled here "Southern Hemisphere Pacific Rim Modern Mediterranean Cosmopolitan British cookery"—whatever. Claudio has created a menu using Japanese and South American ingredients to great effect. For starters, dig into his lobster ceviche with coconut, lime, and mango, followed by rare tuna. The taste is magical. His cured salmon is perfect and wonderfully accompanied by a side order of wasabi mash. The overall effect, in the words of one diner, is the meeting of the Pacific Rim with Neuvo Latino. Try also the duck salad integrated distinctively with an irresistibly rich fufu. The two-floor eatery is a delight with a sunken garden. Chic London goes here, and there's a separate non-smoking floor.

✪ **Clarke's.** 124 Kensington Church St., W8. ☎ **0171/221-9225.** Reservations recommended. Fixed-price lunch £8–£14 ($13.20–$23.10); fixed-price 4-course dinner £42 ($69.30). AE, DC, MC, V. Mon–Fri 12:30–2pm and 7–10pm. Tube: Notting Hill Gate or High St. Kensington. MODERN BRITISH.

Sally Clarke is one of the finest chefs in London, and this is one of the hottest restaurants around. *Still.* She opened it back in the Thatcher era and it's still going strong, winning new converts every year. Clarke honed her skills at Michael's in Santa Monica and the West Beach Café in Venice (California) before heading back to her native land. In this excellent restaurant, everything is bright and modern, with wood floors, discreet lighting, and additional space in the basement, where tables are more spacious and private. Some people are put off by the fixed-price menu, which offers no choices, but the food is so well prepared that diners rarely object to what ends up in front of them. The menu, which changes daily, emphasizes chargrilled foods with herbs and seasonal veggies. You might begin with an appetizer of blood orange salad with red onion, watercress, and black olive–anchovy toast, then follow with grilled breast of chicken with black truffle, crisp polenta, and arugula. Desserts are likely to include a warm pear and raisin puff pastry with maple-syrup ice cream. Just put yourself in Clarke's hands—you'll be glad you did.

INEXPENSIVE

Mondola. 139 Westbourne Grove, W11. ☎ **0171/229-4734.** Reservations recommended. Fixed-price meals £7.50–£8.95 ($12.40–$14.75); vegetarian fixed-price meals £5–£7.50 ($8.25–$12.40). No credit cards. Daily 1–11pm. Tube: Notting Hill Gate. SUDANESE.

Of all the African restaurants of London, this presumably is the only one that special-izes in the spicy cuisine of the Sudan. It may be the only Sudanese restaurant in Europe, although we can't prove that. Very small and intimate, on the fringe of trendy Notting Hill, this bohemian hangout is far from trendy itself. It doesn't have a liquor license, but you're free to brown-bag it. A Moorish archway and various photos and artifacts evoke the African milieu.

The food is a blend of various cuisines. The chefs borrow their eclectic and inex-pensive fare from various kitchens of North Africa, Ethiopia, and even the Middle East. Begin with the classic soup of the region, made with meat and peanuts. Although the menu is limited, the dishes are well prepared from fresh ingredients. Opt for lamb, especially the tasty chops marinated in African spices. Ground red chilies add zest to any dish. Lentils with caramelized garlic is another treat, and there's a generous salad bar costing £7.95 ($13.10) for two persons. Skip the desserts and ask for a traditional African coffee. The place is a dining oddity for London and a bit of a culinary adventure.

IN NEARBY HOLLAND PARK
EXPENSIVE

The Room at the Halcyon. In the Halcyon Hotel, 81 Holland Park Ave., W11. ☎ **0171/ 727-7288.** Reservations recommended. Fixed-price 2-course lunch £18–£35 ($29.70–$57.75); fixed-price 2-course dinner £35 ($57.75), fixed-price 3-course dinner £43 ($70.95). AE, DC, MC, V. Mon–Fri and Sun noon–2:30pm; Mon–Thurs 7–10:30pm, Fri–Sat 7–11pm, Sun 7–10pm. Tube: Holland Park. FRENCH.

Dining at this restaurant is a great way to experience the posh life at the Halcyon Hotel (see chapter 4). Located on the hotel's lower level, the restaurant attracts the rich and famous, including royalty. You might enjoy an aperitif in the cream-colored bar before heading to the tastefully uncluttered dining room. Rich tapestried curtains of blue-green and gold enhance a subdued candlelit dining atmosphere.

Of the sophisticated and highly individualized menu, one food critic wrote that it "reads like a United Nations of cuisine." The daily bill of fare is based on the inspira-tion of the chef and the freshest ingredients available. You might begin with tomato consommé with goat-cheese ravioli or pressed foie gras terrine with sauterne jelly. Main dishes are likely to feature escalope of sea bass with an oyster beignet and roisettes of calves sweetbreads with carrots and morels. There's also a special vegetarian menu. The warm banana pancakes are a luscious way to finish off your meal.

9 Bayswater
VERY EXPENSIVE

I-Thai. In the Hempel Hotel, Hempel Square, 31-35 Craven Hill Gardens, W2. ☎ **0171/ 298-9000.** Reservations required. Main courses £19–£26.50 ($31.35–$43.70). AE, DC, MC, V. Daily 12:30–2:30pm and 7–10:30pm. Tube: Lancaster Gate. ITALIAN/THAI.

Part of the aggressively minimalist The Hempel (see chapter 4), this newcomer spe-cializes in upscale clients, upscale Thai and Italian food, and upscale prices. The antithesis of the kind of showy, lushly decorated restaurants of the 1980s it was designed to compete with, I-Thai prides itself on a Zenlike calm that permeates the whole place. The sparse but innovative menu is quite expensive—dining here is more fun if you're on an expense account. We suggest beginning with one of the soups, either the spicy squid-ink version with lemongrass and coconut cream or the chicken, coconut, and foie gras soup flavored with Thai basil. Main dishes are prepared exquis-itely; we loved the truffle and mascarpone risotto and the stir-fried cellophane noodles

Marylebone, Paddington, Bayswater & Notting Hill Gate Restaurants

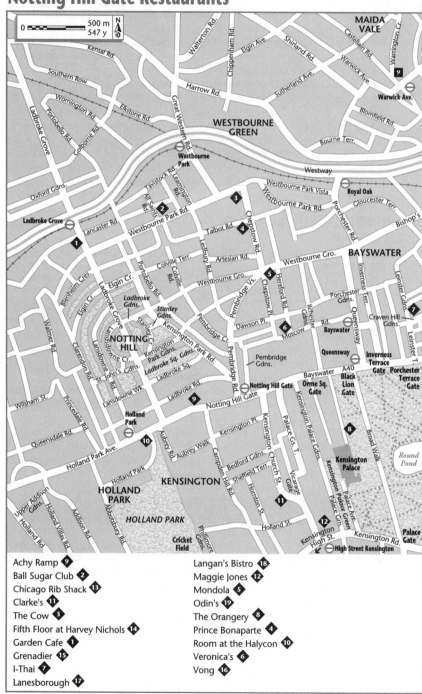

Achy Ramp **9**

Ball Sugar Club **2**

Chicago Rib Shack **13**

Clarke's **11**

The Cow **3**

Fifth Floor at Harvey Nichols **14**

Garden Cafe **1**

Grenadier **15**

I-Thai **7**

Lanesborough **17**

Langan's Bistro **18**

Maggie Jones **12**

Mondola **5**

Odin's **19**

The Orangery **8**

Prince Bonaparte **4**

Room at the Halcyon **10**

Veronica's **6**

Vong **16**

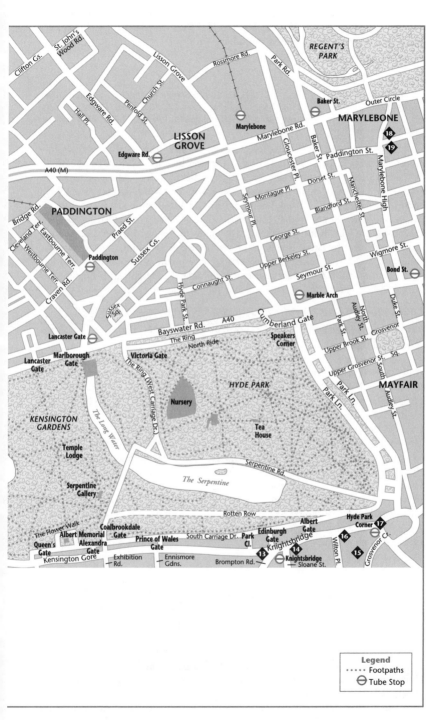

with tiger prawns in a black-ink parcel. On our most recent trip, we tried the red chicken gingko-nut curry served with sweet Thai basil. For dessert, try almost anything, especially the steamed Pandan pudding garnished with a warm coconut-and-blueberry sauce.

MODERATE

✪ **Veronica's.** 3 Hereford Rd., W2. ☎ **0171/229-5079.** Reservations required. Main courses £10.50–£18.50 ($17.35–$30.55); fixed-price meals £12.50–£16.50 ($20.65–$27.20). AE, DC, MC, V. Mon–Fri noon–3pm; Mon–Sat 6pm–midnight. Tube: Bayswater or Queensway. TRADITIONAL BRITISH.

Called the "market leader in cafe salons," Veronica's offers traditional and, in fact, historical fare at tabs you won't mind paying. It's a celebration of British cuisine over a 2,000 year period, with some dishes based on medieval, Tudor, and even Roman-age recipes, but all given an imaginative modern twist by owner Veronica Shaw. One month she'll focus on Scotland, another month on Victorian foods, yet another on Wales, and the next on Ireland. Your appetizer might be a salad called *salmagundy*, made with crunchy pickled vegetables, that Elizabeth I enjoyed in her day. Another concoction might be Tweed Kettle, a 19th-century recipe to improve the monotonous taste of salmon. Many dishes are vegetarian, and everything tastes better when followed with a British farmhouse cheese or a pudding. The restaurant is brightly and attractively decorated, and the service warm and ingratiating.

10 A Bit Farther Afield: Hammersmith

EXPENSIVE

✪ **The River Café.** Thames Wharf, Rainville Rd., W6. ☎ **0171/381-8824.** Reservations required. Main courses £17.50–£26 ($28.90–$42.90). AE, DC, MC, V. Mon–Sat noon–3pm and 7–11pm; Sun noon–3pm. Tube: Hammersmith. ITALIAN.

For the best Italian viands in London today, head to this Thames-side bistro operated by Ruth Rogers and Rose Gray. The charmingly contemporary venue with a highly polished steel bar was designed by Ruth's husband, Richard, who also designed the Pompidou Centre in Paris. The cafe attracts a trendy crowd that comes to see and be seen, and to eat fabulous food. The owners' goal was to re-create the kind of cuisine they'd enjoyed in private homes in the Italian countryside, and they've succeeded beautifully. Some chefs can be seen shopping in London's markets—but not these chefs. The market comes to them: first-spring asparagus harvested in Andalusia and arriving in London within the day, live scallops and langoustines taken by divers in the icy North Sea, and, of course, a daily shipment of the finest harvest of Italy, ranging from radicchio to artichokes. Even tiny bulbs of fennel are zipped across the Channel from France. Britain's own rich bounty appears in pheasant and wild salmon. The best dishes are either slowly roasted or quickly seared.

11 Teatime

Everyone should indulge in a formal afternoon tea at least once while in London. It's a relaxing, drawn-out, civilized affair that usually consists of three courses, all elegantly served on delicate china: first, dainty finger sandwiches (with the crusts cut off, of course), then fresh-baked scones served with jam and deliciously decadent clotted cream (also known as Devonshire cream), and, lastly, an array of bite-sized sweets. All the while, an indulgent server keeps the pot of tea of your choice fresh at hand. Sometimes, ports and aperitifs are on offer to accompany your final course. It's a quintessential British experience; we've listed our favorites below. We've also included a handful of less formal alternatives, in case high tea just isn't your style.

MAYFAIR

J Brown's Hotel. 29–34 Albemarle St., W1. ☎ **0171/493-6020.** Reservations not accepted. Afternoon tea £17.95 ($29.60). AE, DC, MC, V. Daily 3–5:45pm. Tube: Green Park.

Along with the Ritz, Brown's ranks as one of the most chic venues for tea in London. Tea is served in the drawing room; done in English antiques, oil paintings, and floral chintz—much like the drawing room of a country estate—it's an appropriate venue for such an affair. Give your name to the concierge upon arrival; he'll seat you at one of the clusters of sofas and settees or at low tables. There's a choice of 10 teas, plus sandwiches, scones, and pastries (all made right in the hotel kitchens) that are rolled around on a trolley for your selection.

Claridge's. Brook St., W1. ☎ **0171/629-8860.** Reservations recommended. Jacket and tie required for men. High tea £18 ($29.70). AE, DC, MC, V. Daily 3–5pm. Tube: Bond St.

Claridge's teatime rituals have managed to persevere through the years with as much pomp and circumstance as the British Empire itself. It's never stuffy, though; you'll feel very welcomed. Tea is served in The Reading Room. A portrait of Lady Claridge gazes benevolently from above as a choice of 17 kinds of tea is served ever so politely. The various courses are served consecutively, including finger sandwiches with cheese savories, apple and raisin scones, and yummy pastries.

Palm Court Lounge. In the Park Lane Hotel, Piccadilly, W1. ☎ **0171/290-7328.** Reservations recommended. Afternoon tea £16 ($26.40), with a glass of Park Lane champagne £22 ($36.30). AE, DC, MC, V. Daily 3–6pm. Tube: Hyde Park Corner or Green Park.

This is one of the great London favorites for tea. Restored to its former charm, the lounge has an atmosphere straight from 1927, with a domed yellow-and-white-glass ceiling, torchères, and palms in Compton stoneware *jardinières*. A delightful afternoon tea that includes a long list of different teas is served daily. Many guests come here after the theater for a sandwich and drink. A pianist plays every weekday afternoon.

Ritz Palm Court. In The Ritz Hotel, Piccadilly, W1. ☎ **0171/493-8181.** Reservations required at least 8 weeks in advance. Jeans and sneakers not acceptable. Jacket and tie required for men. Afternoon tea £24.50 ($40.40). AE, DC, MC, V. 2 seatings daily at 3:30 and 5pm. Tube: Green Park.

This is the most fashionable place in London to order afternoon tea—and the hardest to get into without reserving way in advance. Its spectacular setting is straight out of *The Great Gatsby,* complete with marble steps and columns and a baroque fountain. You have your choice of a long list of teas, served with delectable sandwiches and luscious pastries.

✪ St. James Restaurant & The Fountain Restaurant. In Fortnum & Mason, 181 Piccadilly, W1. ☎ **0171/734-8040.** In the St. James, full tea £16.50 ($27.20). In The Fountain, full teas £12.95 ($21.35). AE, DC, MC, V. St. James, Mon–Sat 3–5pm; The Fountain, Mon–Sat 3–6pm. Tube: Piccadilly Circus.

This pair of tea salons functions as a culinary showplace for London's most prestigious grocery store, Fortnum & Mason. As such, the tea-drinking ritual is spiffier than at establishments less dependent on maintaining an impeccable public image. The more formal of the two venues, the St. James, on the venerable store's fourth floor, is a pale green-and-beige homage to formal Edwardian taste. More rapid, less formal, and better tuned to the hectic pace of London shoppers and London commuters is The Fountain Restaurant, on the street level, where a sense of tradition and manners is very

The Art of Taking Tea

Tea is serious business in Britain. In a nation where per-capita consumption of tea has risen to five cups a day, the tea-taking ritual is as intricate and powerful in the national psyche as football, rugby, and dishing the Royal Family. Arguments rage regularly (but usually ever-so-politely) about the proper way to prepare a pot of tea, accompanied by debate about how to warm, stir, and flavor it, and what blend of leaves is either the most flavorful, most prestigious, or both. (More reputations were ruined by the tea-drinking ceremony than virtually anything else in the Edwardian social roster.) Lest you be led astray by the wide choice of teas, remember that delicate China blends tend to be favored by dowagers and socialites and the robust Indian ones are what construction workers consume on chilly worksites a few hours before breaking off for a round of bitter in a local pub.

The emphasis on mid-afternoon tea has some illustrious antecedents. The ceremony developed during an era when the diets of even the richest of Britons were sorely lacking in basic vitamins, so teatime—with its emphasis on caffeine and some kind of sustenance—provided the bursts of energy that helped fuel the British Empire. Entire flotillas of clipper ships embarked for India and China to gather leaves, and navies left for to the West Indies to acquire sugar to sweeten the brewed tea and the delectable pastries that sometimes accompanied it.

Who are the quintessential arbiters of taste when it comes to tea-taking etiquette? The Queen Mother and Noël Coward, who were once spotted sipping Earl Grey together in the lobby of London's Ritz. On that long-ago day, we and our fellow tea-drinkers became suspicious that something was up when the hotel's director (a figurehead not usually preoccupied with fine-tuning service) appeared to check the patina on the appallingly valuable antique porcelain and silver (probably the best the Ritz owned) that was laid out at a table adjoining ours. Our suspicions were more than confirmed when in walked the Queen Mother, sine qua non figurehead for millions of English-speaking tea-drinkers during the darkest days of World War II, accompanied by Noël ("a talent to

much a part of the teatime experience, but in a less opulent setting. The quantities of food served in both venues are usually ample enough to be defined as full-fledged early suppers for most theatergoers.

PICCADILLY CIRCUS & LEICESTER SQUARE

The Blue Room. 3 Bateman St., W1. ☎ **0171/437-4827.** Reservations not accepted. Cup of tea £1 ($1.65), cakes and pastries 60p–£2.40 ($1–$3.95), sandwiches £3–£3.70 ($4.95–$6.10). No credit cards. Mon–Sat 9am–midnight; Sun 10am–11pm. Tube: Leicester Sq.

Nothing about this place has been patterned on the grand dame tearooms mentioned above, where tea-drinking is presented as an intricate and elaborate social ritual. What you'll find here instead is a cozy, somewhat eccentric enclave lined with the artworks of some of the regular patrons, battered sofas that might have come out of somebody's college dormitory, and a gathering of likable urban hipsters to whom very little is sacred. You can enjoy dozens of varieties of tea, including herbals, served in steaming mugfuls. Lots of arty and eccentric types gather here during the late afternoon, emulating some of the rituals of the old-fashioned tea service but with absolutely none of the hauteur.

amuse") Coward. Elizabeth mère had invited the playwright to tea in order to thank him for the hospitality he had extended to her in Jamaica, where he'd recently served her lunch.

We later learned—through a perfectly acceptable teatime ritual, polite eavesdropping—that the lobster mousse intended for her lunch had melted in the Jamaican heat and that he'd been forced to open a can of split-pea soup instead. That's what one talks about at tea: What you had for lunch. Frilly things like that. Keep it light. Keep it pleasant.

The tea-drinking ritual is not without its literary precedents. Samuel Pepys, after his first "cuppa" in 1660, found the experience so exhilarating that he devoted an entire diary entry to it. The reputation of the Duchess of Bedford was assured forever when, in 1840, she devised a medley of cakes intended for consumption with her brews. And everybody's favorite aesthete, Oscar Wilde, elevated the scathing *bon mot* to an art form over a cup of tea.

"Would you mind pouring the tea, my dear, as I seem to have sprained my wrist," is considered a standard but lethal trap that brides-to-be should avoid whenever meeting their prospective mothers-in-law for the first time. No one could pour tea like a dowager empress of a large country estate, and only the most brazen of social-climbing neophytes ever dared to try.

If you should experience cultural vertigo before the yawning abyss of insecurity induced by such formidable precedents, forego the tea-drinking ritual completely and do instead what the masses do: Elbow up next to a stranger in a local cafe, order a frothy cappuccino, then segue gradually into a bout of lagers-with-lime in a local pub (where, contrary to whatever you might be told, many Brits actually feel more comfortable anyway). At least there, you won't feel compelled to wear a floppy hat, watch your manners, or emulate the Queen Mother—at least in any of the ways required by sit-down tea, of which actress Gladys Cooper once asked, "Is there any other kind?"

COVENT GARDEN & THE STRAND

MJ Bradley's. 9 King St., WC2. ☎ **0171/240-5178.** Cup of tea 95p ($1.55), sandwiches £1.85–£4.50 ($3.05–$7.45) each. No credit cards. Mon–Fri 8am–8:30pm; Sat–Sun 10am–8:30pm. Tube: Covent Garden or Charing Cross.

Although it defines itself as a coffeehouse, many of MJ Bradley's fans resolutely drop in for a cup of as many as 20 different kinds of tea, everything from Earl Grey and Assam to such herbal brews as peppermint. Outfitted like a brasserie, it manages to mingle nostalgia with modern wall sculptures. If you're hungry, consider one of the imaginative sandwiches with fillings of herb-flavored cream cheese with sun-dried tomatoes.

✪ **Palm Court at the Waldorf Meridien.** In the Waldorf Hotel, Aldwych, WC2. ☎ **0171/836-2400.** Reservations required for tea dance. Jacket and tie required for men at tea dance. Afternoon tea £18–£21 ($29.70–$34.65); tea dance £25–£28 ($41.25–$46.20). AE, DC, MC, V. Afternoon tea Mon–Fri 3–5:30pm; tea dance Sat 2:30–5pm; Sun 4–6:30pm. Tube: Covent Garden.

The Waldorf's Palm Court combines afternoon tea with afternoon dancing (the foxtrot, quickstep, and the waltz). The Palm Court is aptly compared to a 1920s movie set (which it has been several times in its long life). You can order tea on a terrace or in a pavilion the size of a ballroom lit by skylights. On tea-dancing days, the orchestra leader will conduct such favorites as "Ain't She Sweet" and "Yes, Sir, That's My Baby," as a butler in a cutaway asks if you want a cucumber sandwich.

KNIGHTSBRIDGE

✪ The Georgian Restaurant. On the 4th floor of Harrods, 87-135 Brompton Rd., SW1. **☎ 0171/225-6800.** High tea £17 ($28.05) or £23 ($37.95) per person with Harrods champagne. AE, DC, MC, V. Teatime Mon–Sat 3:30–5:15pm (last order). Tube: Knightsbridge.

As long as anyone can remember, teatime at Harrods has been one of the most distinctive features of Europe's most famous department store. A flood of visitors is somehow gracefully herded into a high-volume but nevertheless elegant room. Many come here expressly for the tea ritual, where the staff hauls silver pots and trolleys laden with pastries and sandwiches through the cavernous dining hall. Most exotic is Betigala tea, a rare blend from China, similar to Lapsang Souchong.

Richoux. 86 Brompton Rd. (opposite Harrods), Knightsbridge, SW3. **☎ 0171/584-8300.** Full tea £12.75 ($21.05); English tea £7.50 ($12.40). AE, DC, MC, V. Jan to mid-May, Mon–Sat 8am–8pm, Sun 10am–9:30pm; mid-May to Dec, Mon–Sat 8am–9:30pm, Sun 10am–9:30pm. Tube: Knightsbridge.

Try the old-fashioned atmosphere of Richoux, established in the 1920s. You can order four hot scones with strawberry jam and whipped cream or choose from a selection of pastries behind a display case. Of course, tea is obligatory; always specify lemon or cream, one lump or two. A full menu, with fresh salads, sandwiches, burgers, and more is served all day. There are three other locations, all open Monday to Saturday 8:30am to 11pm, Sunday 10am to 11:30pm. There's a branch at the bottom of Bond Street, 172 Piccadilly (**☎ 0171/493-2204,** Tube: Piccadilly Circus or Green Park); one at 41A S. Audley St. (**☎ 0171/629-5228,** Tube: Green Park or Hyde Park Corner); and one at 3 Circus Rd. (**☎ 0171/483-4001,** Tube: St. John's Wood).

BELGRAVIA

The Lanesborough. Hyde Park Corner, SW1. **☎ 0171/259-5599.** Reservations required. High tea £19.50 ($32.15), high tea with strawberries and champagne £24.50 ($40.40); pot of tea £3.70 ($6.10). AE, DC, MC, V. Daily 3:30–6pm (last order). AE, DC, MC, V. Tube: Hyde Park Corner.

You'll suspect that many of the folks sipping exotic teas here have dropped in to inspect the public areas of one of London's most expensive hotels. The staff rises to the challenge with aplomb, offering a selection of seven teas that include the Lanesborough special blend, and such herbal esoteria as Rose Cayou. The focal point for this ritual is the Conservatory, a glass-roofed Edwardian fantasy filled with potted plants and a sense of the long-gone majesty of empire. The finger sandwiches, scones, and sweets are all appropriately lavish and endlessly correct.

CHELSEA

The Tearoom at the Chelsea Physic Garden. 66 Royal Hospital Rd., SW3. **☎ 0171/352-5646.** Tea with cake £3.50 ($5.75). MC, V (in shop only). Wed 2:30–4:45pm; Sun 2:30–5:45pm. Closed Nov–Mar. Tube: Sloane Sq.

It encompasses only 3½ acres, crisscrossed with gravel paths and ringed with a high brick wall that shuts out the roaring traffic of Royal Hospital Road. These few spectacular acres, however, revere the memory of entire industries that were spawned from seeds developed and tested within its walls. Founded in 1673 as a botanical education center, the Chelsea Physic Garden's list of successes includes the exportation of rubber from South America to Malaysia and tea from China to India.

On the two days a week it's open, the tearoom is likely to be filled with botanical enthusiasts merrily sipping cups of tea as fortification for their garden treks. The setting is a rather banal-looking Edwardian building. Since the tearoom is only an adjunct to the glories of the garden itself, don't expect the lavish rituals of teatime venues. But you can carry your cakes and cups of tea outside into a garden that, despite meticulous care, always looks a bit unkempt. (Herbaceous plants within its hallowed precincts are left untrimmed to encourage bird life and seed production.) Botanists and flower lovers in general find the place fascinating.

KENSINGTON

✪ **The Orangery.** In the gardens of Kensington Palace, W8. ☎ **0171/376-0239.** Reservations not accepted. Pot of tea £2 ($3.30), summer cakes and puddings £1.95–£4.25 ($3.20–$7), sandwiches £6 ($9.90). MC, V. Daily 10am–6pm; closing time half an hour before gates close (usually between 4 and 5pm) in winter. Mar–Oct 10am–6pm; Nov–Mar 10am–4pm. Tube: High St. Kensington or Queensway.

In its way, the Orangery is the most amazing place for midafternoon tea in the world. Set about 50 yards north of Kensington Palace, it occupies a long and narrow garden pavilion built in 1704 by Queen Anne as a site for her tea parties. In homage to that monarch's original intentions, rows of potted orange trees bask in sunlight from soaring windows, and tea is still served amid Corinthian columns, ruddy-colored bricks, and a pair of Grinling Gibbons wood carvings. There are even some urns and statuary that the Royal Family imported to the site from Windsor Castle. The menu includes lunchtime soups and sandwiches, which come with a salad and a portion of upscale potato chips known as "kettle chips." There's also an array of different teas, served with high style, usually accompanied by freshly baked scones with clotted cream and jam, and Belgian chocolate cake.

NOTTING HILL

The Garden Café. London Lighthouse, 111-117 Lancaster Rd., W11. ☎ **0171/792-1200.** Cup of tea 40p (65¢), platter of food £2–£2.50 ($3.30–$4.15). No credit cards. Mon–Sat noon-2:30pm. Tube: Ladbroke Grove.

This is the most unusual of the places we recommend, and it also may be one of the most worthwhile. The Garden Café is in The Lighthouse, the largest center in Europe for people affected with HIV and AIDS. The late Princess Diana made the organization one of her projects, and slugged down a cuppa here. The cafeteria is open to the public and is less institutional looking than you might expect; French doors open onto a spectacular garden with fountains and summertime tables. Tea is available throughout the day, although midafternoon, between 3:30 and 5:30pm, seems to be the most convivial time. Its Notting Hill location is only a short walk from Portobello Road.

12 Pubs

IN THE WEST END
MAYFAIR

Shepherd's Tavern. 50 Hertford St., W1. ☎ **0171/499-3017.** Reservations recommended. Main courses £7–£11 ($11.55–$18.15). AE, DC, MC, V. Restaurant daily noon–3pm; Sun–Fri 6:30–9:30pm; Sat 6:30–10:30pm. Bar Mon–Sat 11am–11pm; Sun noon–10:30pm. Tube: Green Park. BRITISH.

This pub is one of the focal points of the all-pedestrian shopping zone of Shepherd's Market. It's set amid a warren of narrow, cobble-covered streets behind Park Lane, in an 18th-century town house very similar to many of its neighbors. The street-level bar is cramped but congenial. Many of the regulars recall this tavern's popularity with the pilots of the Battle of Britain. Bar snacks include simple platters of shepherd's pie and fish-and-chips. More formal dining is available upstairs in the cozy, cedar-lined Georgian-style restaurant; the classic British menu probably hasn't changed much since the 1950s. If you're a little leery of the roast beef with Yorkshire pudding, go with the Oxford ham instead.

ST. JAMES'S

Red Lion. 2 Duke of York St. (off Jermyn St.), SW1. ☎ **0171/930-2030.** Sandwiches £2.50 ($4.15); fish-and-chips £8 ($13.20). No credit cards. Mon–Fri 11:30am–11pm; Sat noon–11pm. Tube: Piccadilly Circus. BRITISH.

This little Victorian pub, with its early-1900s decorations and mirrors 150 years old, has been compared in spirit to Édouard Manet's painting *A Bar at the Folies-Bergère* (on display at the Courtauld Institute Galleries). You can order premade sandwiches, but once they're gone you're out of luck. On Saturday, homemade fish-and-chips are also served. Wash down your meal with Ind Coope's fine ales or the house's special beer, Burton's, an unusual brew made of spring water from the Midlands town of Bourton-on-Trent.

LEICESTER SQUARE

Salisbury. 90 St. Martin's Lane, WC2. ☎ **0171/836-5863.** Reservations not necessary. AE, DC, MC, V. Mon–Sat 11am–11pm; Sun noon–10:30pm. Tube: Leicester Sq. BRITISH.

Salisbury's glittering cut-glass mirrors reflect the faces of English stage stars (and hopefuls) sitting around the curved buffet-style bar. A less prominent place to dine is the old-fashioned wall banquette with its copper-topped tables and art nouveau decor. The pub's specialty—home-cooked pies set out in a buffet cabinet with salads—is really quite good and inexpensive. Both a hot and a cold food buffet is available at all times.

SOHO

Old Coffee House. 49 Beak St., W1. ☎ **0171/437-2197.** Main courses £2.50–£4.20 ($4.15–$6.95). No credit cards. Restaurant Mon–Sat noon–3pm; pub Mon–Sat 11am–11pm; Sun noon–3pm and 7–10:30pm. Tube: Oxford Circus or Piccadilly Circus. BRITISH.

Once honored as "Soho Pub of the Year" by the *Good Pub Guide*, the Old Coffee House takes its name from the coffeehouse heyday of 18th-century London, when coffee was called "the devil's brew." The pub still serves pots of filtered coffee. The place is heavily decorated with bric-a-brac, including archaic musical instruments and World War I recruiting posters. Have a drink at the long, narrow bar; or retreat to the upstairs restaurant, where you can enjoy good pub food at lunch, including steak-and-kidney pie, one of three vegetarian dishes, scampi-and-chips, or a burger and fries.

BLOOMSBURY

Museum Tavern. 49 Great Russell St., WC1. ☎ **0171/242-8987.** Bar snacks £2–£6 ($3.30–$9.90). AE, MC, V. Mon–Sat 11am–11pm; Sun noon–10:30pm. Tube: Holborn or Tottenham Court Rd. BRITISH.

Across the street from the British Museum, this pub (ca. 1703) retains most of its antique trappings: velvet, oak paneling, and cut glass. It lies right in the center of the University of London area and is popular with writers, publishers, and researchers from the museum. (Supposedly, Karl Marx wrote over meals in the pub.) Traditional English food is served, with shepherd's pie, sausages cooked in English cider, and chef's specials on the hot-food menu. Cold fare includes turkey-and-ham pie, ploughman's lunch, and salads. Several English ales, cold lagers, cider, Guinness, wines, and spirits are available. Food and coffee are served all day; the pub gets crowded at lunchtime.

COVENT GARDEN

Nag's Head. 10 James St., WC2. ☎ **0171/836-4678.** Reservations not accepted. Sandwich platters with salad £3.75–£6.50 ($6.20–$10.75); full meal salads £6.50 ($10.75). AE, DC, MC, V. Mon–Fri 11am–11pm; Sat noon–11pm; Sun noon–10:30pm. Tube: Covent Garden. BRITISH.

The Nag's Head is one of London's most famous Edwardian pubs. In days of yore, patrons had to make their way through lorries of fruit and flowers to drink here. But when the market moved, 300 years of British tradition faded away. Today, the pub is patronized mainly by young people. The draft Guinness is very good. Lunch is typical pub grub: sandwiches, salads, pork cooked in cider, and garlic prawns. The sandwich platters mentioned above are served only during the lunch hour (noon to 4pm); however, snacks are available in the afternoon.

WESTMINSTER (NEAR TRAFALGAR SQUARE)

Sherlock Holmes. 10 Northumberland St., WC1. ☎ **0171/930-2644.** Reservations recommended for restaurant. Main courses £7.95–£12.95 ($13.10–$21.35); ground-floor snacks £2.25–£6.95 ($3.70–$11.45). AE, DC, MC, V. Restaurant Mon–Thurs noon–3pm and 5–10:45pm, Fri–Sun noon–11:45pm; pub Mon–Sat 11am–11pm, Sun noon–10:30pm. Tube: Charing Cross or Embankment. BRITISH.

It would be rather strange if the Sherlock Holmes was not the old gathering spot for the Baker Street Irregulars, a once-mighty clan of mystery lovers who met here to honor the genius of Sir Arthur Conan Doyle's most famous fictional character. Upstairs, you'll find a re-creation of the living room at 221B Baker Street and such "Holmesiana" as the serpent of *The Speckled Band* and the head of *The Hound of the Baskervilles*. In the upstairs dining room, you can order complete meals with wine. Try "Copper Beeches" (grilled butterfly chicken breasts with lemon and herbs). You select dessert from the trolley. Downstairs is mainly for drinking, but there's a good snack bar with cold meats, salads, cheeses, and wine and ales sold by the glass.

THE CITY

⭘ **Ye Olde Cheshire Cheese.** Wine Office Court, 145 Fleet St., EC4. ☎ **0171/353-6170.** Main courses £8.95–£13.95 ($14.75–$23). AE, DC, MC, V. Mon–Fri 11:30am–11pm; Sat 11:30am–2:30pm and 5:30–11pm; Sun noon–3pm. Drinks and bar snacks daily 11:30am–11pm. Tube: St. Paul's or Blackfriars. BRITISH.

The foundation of this carefully preserved building was laid in the 13th century, and it holds the most famous of the old City chophouses and pubs. Established in 1667, it claims to be the spot where Dr. Samuel Johnson (who lived nearby) entertained admirers with his acerbic wit. Charles Dickens and other literary lions also patronized the place. Later, many of the ink-stained journalists and scandalmongers of 19th- and early-20th-century Fleet Street made it their locale. You'll find six bars and two dining rooms here. The house specialties include "Ye Famous Pudding" (steak, kidney, mushrooms, and game) and Scottish roast beef with Yorkshire pudding and horseradish sauce. Sandwiches, salads, and standby favorites such as steak-and-kidney pie are also available, as are dishes such as Dover sole.

Ye Olde Cock Tavern. 22 Fleet St., EC4. ☎ **0171/353-8570.** Reservations not required. Main courses £4.50–£6 ($7.45–$9.90). AE, DC, MC, V. Carvery Mon–Fri noon–2:30pm; pub Mon–Fri 11am–11pm. Tube: Temple or Chancery Lane. BRITISH.

Dating back to 1549, this tavern boasts a long line of literary patrons: Samuel Pepys mentioned the pub in his diaries; Dickens frequented it; and Tennyson referred to it in one of his poems, a copy of which is framed and proudly displayed near the front entrance. It's one of the few buildings in London to have survived the Great Fire of

1666. At street level, you can order a pint as well as snackbar food, steak-and-kidney pie, or a cold chicken-and-beef plate with salad. At the Carvery upstairs, a meal includes a choice of appetizers, followed by lamb, pork, beef, or turkey.

Ye Olde Watling. 29 Watling St., EC4. ☎ **0171/653-9971.** Reservations are accepted. Main courses £5.75–£6.50 ($9.50–$10.75); bar snacks from £2 ($3.30). AE, MC, V. Mon–Fri 10am–10pm. Tube: Mansion House. BRITISH.

Ye Olde Watling was rebuilt after the Great Fire of 1666. On the ground level is a mellow pub; upstairs is an intimate restaurant where, under oak beams and at trestle tables, you can dine on simple English main dishes for lunch. The menu varies daily, with such choices and reliable standbys as fish-and-chips, lamb satay, lasagna, fish cakes, and usually a vegetarian dish. All are served with two vegetables or salad, plus rice or potatoes.

KNIGHTSBRIDGE

Bill Bentley's. 31 Beauchamp Place, SW3. ☎ **0171/589-5080.** Reservations recommended. Main courses £9–£18.95 ($14.85–$31.25). MC, V. Mon–Sat noon–3pm and 7–11pm; Sun brunch 11am–3pm. Tube: Knightsbridge. MODERN EUROPEAN.

Bill Bentley's, on fashionable Beauchamp Place, has a varied and reasonable wine list with a good selection of Bordeaux. Many visitors come here just to sample the wines, including some New World choices along with popular French selections. In summer, a garden patio opens to patrons. If you don't prefer the formality of the restaurant, you can order from the wine-bar menu that begins with a half-dozen oysters, or you can enjoy the chef's fish soup with croutons and *rouille*. Main dishes include the famous salmon cakes, served with tomato sauce, and daily specialties. In keeping with contemporary trends, the restaurant menu has been simplified and is rather less expensive than before. It changes frequently, but typical dishes might include avocado, crab, and prawn salad as an appetizer, followed by suprême of chicken with oyster mushrooms and a madeira jus, or else grilled rainbow trout with a petit garni and lemon sauce. A large selection of bottled beers and spirits is also available.

IN NEARBY BELGRAVIA

Antelope. 22 Eaton Terrace, SW1. ☎ **0171/730-7781.** Reservations recommended for upstairs dining room. Main courses £5.95–£6.50 ($9.80–$10.75). AE, MC, V. Mon–Sat 11:30am–11pm; Sun noon–3pm and 7–10:30pm. Tube: Sloane Sq. BRITISH.

Located on the fringe of Belgravia, at the gateway to Chelsea, the Antelope caters to a hodgepodge of clients from all classes and creeds (including English rugby aficionados). At lunchtime, the ground-floor bar provides hot and cold pub food, but in the evening, only drinks are served there. Upstairs, the lunch menu includes principally English dishes: fish-and-chips, English roasts, and the like.

✪ **Grenadier.** 18 Wilton Row, SW1. ☎ 0171/235-3074. Reservations recommended. Main courses £11.95–£18.95 ($19.70–$31.25). AE, DC, MC, V. Mon–Sat noon–3pm and 6–10pm, Sun noon–3:30pm and 7–10:30pm. Tube: Hyde Park Corner. BRITISH.

Tucked away in a mews, the Grenadier is one of London's reputedly haunted pubs. Aside from the poltergeist, the basement houses the original bar and skittles alley used by the Duke of Wellington's officers on leave from fighting Napoléon. The scarlet front door of the one-time officers' mess is guarded by a scarlet sentry box and shaded by a vine. The bar is nearly always crowded. Lunch and dinner are offered daily—even on Sunday, when it's a tradition to drink Bloody Marys here. In the stalls along the side, you can order good-tasting fare based on seasonal ingredients. Well-prepared dishes include pork Grenadier, chicken, and Stilton roulade. Snacks like fish-and-chips are available at the bar.

Nag's Head. 53 Kinnerton St., SW1. ☎ **0171/235-1135.** Main courses £3.50–£5.80 ($5.75–$9.55). No credit cards. Daily 11am–11pm. Tube: Hyde Park. BRITISH.

The Nag's Head, snuggled on a back street, is a short walk from the Berkeley Hotel. Previously a jail dating from 1780, it's said to be the smallest pub in London, although others claim that distinction. In 1921, it was sold for £12 and 6p. Have a drink up front or wander to the tiny little bar in the rear. For food, you might enjoy "real ale sausage" (made with pork and ale), shepherd's pie, or even the quiche of the day. This warm and cozy pub, with a welcoming staff, is patronized by a cosmopolitan clientele—newspaper people, musicians, and curious tourists. This pub touts itself as an "independent," or able to serve any "real ale" they choose because of their lack of affiliation.

CHELSEA

Front Page. 35 Old Church St., SW3. ☎ **0171/352-0648.** Main courses £5.95–£9.95 ($9.80–$16.40). AE, MC, V. Restaurant Mon–Fri noon–2:30pm; Sat–Sun 12:30–3pm; daily 7–10pm, Sun 7–9:30pm; pub Mon–Sat 11am–11pm; Sun noon–10:30pm. Tube: Sloane Sq. MODERN EUROPEAN.

Front Page is favored by young professionals who like the mellow atmosphere provided by its wood paneling, wooden tables, and pews and benches. In one section, an open fire burns on cold nights. The pub stands in an expensive residential section of Chelsea and is a good place to go for a drink. You can also order bottled Budweiser. Check the chalkboard for the daily specials, which might include hot chicken salad, fish cakes, and smoked salmon and cream cheese on a bagel.

King's Head & Eight Bells. 50 Cheyne Walk, SW3. ☎ **0171/352-1820.** Main courses £5.25–£7.75 ($8.65–$12.80). MC, V. Mon–Sat 11am–11pm; Sun noon–10:30pm. Tube: Sloane Sq. BRITISH.

Many distinguished personalities once lived near this historic Thames-side pub; a short stroll will take you to the former homes of Carlyle, Swinburne, and George Eliot. In other days, press gangs used to roam these parts of Chelsea seeking lone travelers to abduct for a life at sea. Today, it's popular with stage and TV celebrities as well as writers. The best English beers are served here, as well as a good selection of reasonably priced wine. The menu features homemade specials of the day, such as fish-and-chips or sausage and chips, and includes at least one vegetable main dish. On Sunday, a roast of the day is served.

13 Wine Bars

IN THE WEST END
ST. JAMES'S

Bubbles. 41 N. Audley St., W1. ☎ **0171/491-3237.** Reservations recommended. Main courses £5.50–£11.80 ($9.05–$19.45); vegetarian main courses £6–£6.25 ($9.90–$10.30). AE, DC, MC, V. Daily 11am–11pm. Tube: Bond St. BRITISH/INTERNATIONAL VEGETARIAN.

This interesting wine bar lies between Upper Brook Street and Oxford Street (in the vicinity of Selfridges). The owners attach equal importance to their food and to their impressive wine list (some wines are sold by the glass). On the ground floor, you can enjoy not only fine wines but also draft beer and liquor, along with a limited but well-chosen selection of bar food, such as smoked salmon on brown bread, or homemade steak burger with fries and salad and cheese. Downstairs, the restaurant serves both

Haute Cuisine Comes to the Lowly Boozer

After decades—nay, centuries—of enduring some of the worst food in England, pubbers still can't believe what has happened to their neighborhood boozers (as the locals like to call their favorite pubs): They've become foodie havens. More and more pubs are offering food you can actually eat—not just canned beans on stale toast. Believe it or not, some of the chefs cooking in pubs today could even hold court in top restaurants.

What's brought about such a sea of change in the lowly pub? Many up-and-coming chefs simply can't afford the price tag of opening a restaurant, so they've turned to the pub as an alternative venue. They clean up the decades-old beer and nicotine stains and throw out the smoke-scented draperies hung when Edward VII had his portly butt on the throne—and lo!, the place becomes light and airy. A modern kitchen and a new menu follows, and suddenly your locale is a hot new dining destination.

You don't have to be a young fashion victim to enjoy the superb viands served at **The Cow,** 89 Westbourne Park Rd., W2 (☎ **0171/221-0021;** Tube: Westbourne Grove). Tom Conran (son of entrepreneur Sir Terence Conran) holds forth nightly in this increasingly hip Notting Hill watering hole. It looks like an Irish pub, but the accents you'll hear are trustafarian rather than street-smart Dublin. With a pint of Fuller's or London Pride firmly in hand, you can linger over the modern European menu, which changes daily but is likely to include ox tongue poached in milk; mussels in curry and cream; or a mixed grill of lamb chops, calf's liver, and sweetbreads. The seafood selections are especially delectable. "The Cow Special"—a half-dozen Irish rock oysters with a pint of Guinness or a glass of wine for £8 ($13)—is the star of the show. A raw bar downstairs serves other fresh seafood choices. To finish, skip the filtered coffee served upstairs (it's wretched), and opt for an espresso downstairs. Main courses run £12.20 to £15.50 ($20.15 to $25.60); a fixed-price 2-course dinner Sunday to Tuesday costs £15.50 ($25.60) or £17.95 ($29.60) for 3 courses. Open Monday to Saturday 7 to 11pm and Sunday 12:30 to 3:30pm for brunch and 7:30 to 10:30pm; bar open daily from noon to 11pm. MC, V accepted.

Another of our favorites is **The Engineer,** 65 Gloucester Ave., NW1 (☎ **0171/722-0950;** Tube: Chalk Farm or Camden Town), a stylishly converted pub owned by Abigail Osborne and Tamsin Olivier, daughter of Lord Olivier (or "Larry's daughter," as she's called locally). This citadel of North London chic is named for Victorian bridge, tunnel, and railway builder Isambard Kingdom Brunel; it sits beside Regent's Canal, one of Brunel's creations. The pub is divided into a bar, a dining room, and a garden area for warm days. The decor is light and modern; the cuisine is accurately billed as modern European with Thai influence and relies on seasonal produce and organic meat and eggs. Choices include Thai fish cakes, crispy duck confit with roasted sweet potatoes, and a warm salad

English and continental dishes, including an appealing vegetarian selection. You might begin with French onion soup, followed by bangers and mash with onion gravy, Dover sole, or grilled chicken breast with apple rice and creamed leeks.

Shampers. 4 Kingly St. (between Carnaby and Regent sts.), W1. ☎ **0171/437-1692.** Reservations recommended. Main courses £6.50–£10.95 ($10.75–$18.05). AE, DC, MC, V. Mon–Sat 11am–11pm. Closed Easter and Christmas. Tube: Oxford Circus. CONTINENTAL.

of shiitake mushrooms with celeriac-and-red-onion confit. A tantalizing appetizer is the deep-fried Camembert with kiwi-fruit relish. Desserts change nightly and might include an orange and cardamom pudding. From the tap, go with the Caffrey's or a Guinness. Main courses run £8.50 to £14.95 ($14 to $24.65). Open daily 8am to 10:30pm, with the bar closing at 11pm. Reservations are recommended. MC, V accepted.

The poshest pub conversion in town is **The Enterprise,** 35 Walton St., SW3 (☎ **0171/584-3148;** Tube: South Kensington). Its proximity to Harrods attracts both regulars and out-of-towners loaded down with packages. Although the joint is cruisy at night (whatever your preference), during the day it attracts the ladies-who-lunch crowd. With banquettes, white linen, and fresh flowers on the tables, you won't mistake it for a lowly boozer. The kitchen serves very respectable traditional English fare as well as European favorites, all prepared with fresh ingredients. Featured dishes include fried salmon cakes with perfectly done fries and grilled steak with fries and salad. They're not so grand that they won't prepare an entrecôte with frites if that's what pleases you—actually, the juicy, properly aged, and flavorful thin French-style slice of beef is about the best you can have in London. Main courses cost £9.65 to £13.95 ($15.90 to $23). Open daily 12:30 to 2:30pm, Saturday and Sunday 12:30 to 3:30pm, Monday to Saturday 7 to 10:45pm, and Sunday 7 to 10:30pm (the bar is open all day). Reservations are accepted for lunch but not for dinner. MC, V accepted.

The offbeat **Prince Bonaparte,** 80 Chepstow Rd., W2 (☎ **0171/313-9491;** Tube: Notting Hill Gate or Westbourne Park), serves great pub grub in what was a grungy boozer in the days before Notting Hill Gate became fashionable. Now pretty young things show up, spilling out onto the sidewalk when the evenings are warm; one patron called it "an ad-man's dream beer shot." The pub is filled with mismatched furniture from schools and churches; jazz and lazy blues fill the air, competing with the babble. It may seem at first that the staff doesn't have its act together, but once the food arrives, you won't care one way or the other: It's very good. The menu roams the world for inspiration: Moroccan chicken with couscous is as good or better than any you'll find in Marrakesh; seafood risotto is delicious, as is the salad of beet root, new potatoes, walnuts, and eggplant. Roast lamb, tender and juicy, appears on the traditional Sunday menu. We recommend the London Pride or Grolsch to wash it all down with. Main courses run £6.75 to £9.50 ($11.15 to $15.65). Open Monday, Wednesday, Thursday, and Friday from noon to 11pm; Tuesday 6:30 to 10:30pm; and Sunday 12:30 to 3:30pm and 6:30 to 10pm. MC, V accepted.

If this nouvelle trend's got you down, don't worry: You still can dig into traditional pub grub in dozens of genuinely lowly boozers that slept through the revolution.

For a number of years now, this has been a favorite of West End wine-bar aficionados. In addition to the street-level wine bar where platters of food are served, there's a more formal basement-level restaurant. In either section, you can order such main dishes as grilled calf's liver with bacon, chips, and salad; panfried large prawns with ginger, garlic, and chili; and platters of assorted cheese. Salads are especially popular, including grilled eggplant salad with tomato, avocado, buffalo mozzarella, and pesto;

and spicy chicken salad. A platter of Irish mussels cooked in a cream-and-tarragon sauce seems to be everybody's favorite. The restaurant is closed in the evening, but the bar serves an extended menu, incorporating not only the luncheon menu but also such dishes as fresh squid, tuna steak, panfried tiger prawns, free-range chicken, and a variety of other dishes.

PICCADILLY CIRCUS

Daniel's Bar (Café Royal Grill). 68 Regent St., W1. ☎ **0171/437-9090,** ext. 277. Reservations not required. Main courses £4–£14 ($6.60–$23.10); fixed-price 2-course lunch menu £12.50 ($20.65). AE, DC, MC, V. Mon–Sat noon–3pm and 5–11pm (open only for drinks and snacks during evening hours). Tube: Piccadilly Circus. BRITISH.

An unpretentious annex to the chillingly expensive Café Royal Grill, Daniel's dates from 1865. It's accessible from the grand cafe s marble-floored lobby, where all the literary greats of 19th-century England have trod, including Oscar Wilde. Despite its opulent decor—art nouveau moldings, oaken half-paneling, abundant framed cartoons and illustrations—the bar is very informal. At lunchtime, order from a long list of platters, sandwiches, and appetizers, or the *menu du jour,* which might include a main course like bangers and mash and bread pudding for dessert. The evening menu is limited to a short list of snacks, including chicken satay, pizza bread, and nachos with guacamole and salsa, as most of the clientele come just to drink. They have also recently introduced high tea for £12.50 ($20.65), which includes the traditional array of sandwiches (of which cucumber is definitely included), pastries, and scones, all served with your choice of teas. For £5 ($8.25) more you can heighten the experience with a glass of chilled champagne.

LEICESTER SQUARE

✪ **Cork & Bottle Wine Bar.** 44–46 Cranbourn St., WC2. ☎ **0171/734-7807.** Reservations not accepted after 6pm. Main courses £3.95–£11.95 ($6.50–$19.70); glass of wine from £3.30 ($5.45). AE, DC, MC, V. Mon–Sat 11am–11:30pm; Sun noon–10:30pm. Tube: Leicester Sq. INTERNATIONAL.

Don Hewitson, a connoisseur of fine wines for more than 30 years, presides over this trove of blissful fermentation. The ever-changing wine list features an excellent selection of Beaujolais from Alsace, 30 selections from Australia, 30 champagnes, and a good selection of California labels. If you want something to wash down, the most successful dish is a raised cheese-and-ham pie, with a cream cheese–like filling and crisp well-buttered pastry—not your typical quiche. There's also chicken and apple salad, Lancashire hot pot, Mediterranean prawns with garlic and asparagus, lamb in ale, and tandoori chicken.

VICTORIA

Ebury Wine Bar. 139 Ebury St., SW1. ☎ **0171/730-5447.** Reservations recommended. Main courses £9.50–£16 ($15.65–$26.40). AE, DC, MC, V. Mon–Sat 11am–10:30pm; Sun 6–10pm. Tube: Victoria or Sloane Square. INTERNATIONAL.

Older professional people who don't mind smoke and the smell of sizzling steaks close to their tables gravitate here. It's one of the most popular and long-enduring wine bars in the area—all dark and woodsy. In addition to those steaks, the wine-bar menu is surprisingly varied. Some dishes have a Pacific Rim influence, including spicy fish cakes. Others are more typically English, as exemplified by roast pork with a crackling-and-apple sauce.

THE CITY

Bow Wine Vaults. 10 Bow Churchyard, EC4. ☎ **0171/248-1121.** Reservations recommended. Cover £1.40 ($2.30). Main courses £7.20–£13 ($11.90–$21.45). AE, DC, MC, V.

Mon–Fri 11am–11pm. Tube: Mansion House, Bank or St. Paul's. BRITISH/MODERN EUROPEAN.

Bow Wine Vaults has existed since long before the wine-bar craze began in the 1970s. One of the most famous wine bars of London, it attracts cost-conscious diners and drinkers to its vaulted cellars for such traditional fare as deep-fried Camembert, lobster ravioli, and a mixed grill, along with fish. More elegant meals, served in the street-level dining room, include mussels in cider sauce, English wild mushrooms in puff pastry, beef Wellington, and steak with brown-butter sauce. Adjacent to the restaurant is a cocktail bar that's popular with City employees after work (open weekdays from 11:30am to 8pm).

Jamaica Wine House. St. Michael's Alley off Cornhill, EC3. ☎ **0171/626-9496.** Reservations not necessary. Bar snacks £3.50–£4.50 ($5.75–$7.45). AE, DC, MC, V. Mon–Fri 11am–11pm. Tube: Bank. BRITISH.

Jamaica Wine House was one of the first coffeehouses in England and, reputedly, the Western world. For years, merchants and daring sea captains came here to transact deals over rum and coffee. Nowadays, the two-level house dispenses beer, ale, lager, and fine wines, among them a variety of ports. The oak-paneled bar is on the street level, attracting a jacket-and-tie crowd of investment bankers. You can order standard but filling dishes such as a ploughman's lunch and toasted sandwiches.

KNIGHTSBRIDGE

Le Metro. 28 Basil St., SW3. ☎ **0171/589-6286.** Reservations required. Main courses £6–£8 ($9.90–$13.20). AE, DC, MC, V. Mon–Sat 7:30am–10:30pm. Tube: Knightsbridge. INTERNATIONAL.

Located just around the corner from Harrods, Le Metro draws a fashionable crowd to its basement precincts. The place serves good, solid, and reliable food prepared with flair. The menu changes frequently, but try the mushroom risotto or confit of duck with lentils, garlic, and shallots if you can. You can order special wines by the glass.

CHELSEA HARBOR

Boaters Wine Bar. Harbour Yard, Chelsea Harbour, SW10. ☎ **0171/352-3687.** MC, V. Mon–Fri noon–7pm. Tube: Earl's Court, then Chelsea Harbour Hoppa Bus C3. BRITISH.

This restaurant occupies the premises of one of London's new "villages," Chelsea Harbour. Well-heeled locals who own the soaringly expensive apartments nearby often come here to drink champagne by the bottle at the long wooden bar; visitors from all over the world pour in here as well. Most of the emphasis at the bar is on an impressive array of bottled beer and beer on tap; an impressive list also offers wine by the glass.

6 Exploring London

Dr. Samuel Johnson said, "When a man is tired of London, he is tired of life, for there is in London all that life can afford." Indeed, it would take a lifetime to explore every alley, court, street, and square in this vast city (and volumes to discuss them). Since you don't have a lifetime to spend here, we've discussed the best of what London has to offer in this chapter. Still, what's included is more than enough to keep you busy on a dozen trips to the "city by the Thames."

For the first-time visitor, the question is never what to do, but what to do *first*. The "Suggested Itineraries" and "The Top Attractions" should help.

A Note about Admission and Open Hours: In the listings below, children's prices generally apply to those 16 and under. To qualify for a senior discount, you must be 60 or older. Students must present a student ID to get discounts, where available. In addition to shutting down on bank holidays, many attractions close around Christmas and New Year's (and, in some cases, early in May), so be sure to call ahead if you're visiting in those seasons.

Suggested Itineraries

If You Have 1 Day

No first-time visitor should leave London without a visit to Westminster Abbey, with Poet's Corner and its royal tombs. Afterward, walk over to see Big Ben and the Houses of Parliament. Also see the Changing of the Guard at Buckingham Palace if it's on, and walk over to 10 Downing Street, home of the prime minister. Dine at one of the little restaurants in Covent Garden such as Porter's, owned by the earl of Bradford. Try one of their classic English pies (maybe lamb and apricot). For a nightcap, head over to the ultimate Victorian pub, the Red Lion in Mayfair; it's the kind of place Oscar Wilde might have chosen for a brandy.

If You Have 2 Days

Day 1 Spend day 1 as above.
Day 2 Devote a good part of the second day exploring the British Museum, one of the best museums in the world. Spend the afternoon visiting the Tower of London and seeing the Crown Jewels (expect slow-moving lines). Later, go to a really local place for dinner, such as

Shepherd's in Westminster, where you'll be able to dine alongside MPs from the House of Commons.

If You Have 3 Days

Days 1–2   Spend days 1 and 2 as above.
Day 3   In the morning visit the masterworks in the National Gallery. For a change of pace in the afternoon, head to Madame Tussaud's waxworks. Take a walking tour of St. James's (see chapter 7, "London Walks"). In the evening, take in a West End play or a performance at the National Theatre or Queen Elizabeth Hall at South Bank Centre.

If You Have 4 or 5 Days

Days 1–3   Spend days 1, 2, and 3 as above.
Day 4   In the morning, head for the City, London's financial district. Your major sightseeing goal here will be St. Paul's Cathedral, designed by Sir Christopher Wren. Take our walking tour of the City (see chapter 7) and visit such attractions as the Guildhall. In the afternoon, head for King's Road in Chelsea for some boutique hopping and to dine at one of Chelsea's many restaurants. Later that evening, take in a show at a Soho nightclub, such as Ronnie Scott's, which hosts some of the city's best jazz.
Day 5   Explore the Victoria and Albert Museum in the morning, then go to the Tate Gallery for a look at some of its many masterpieces; have lunch at its restaurant, which offers some of the best values on wine in Britain. For a historic glimpse of the dark days of World War II, visit the Cabinet War Rooms at Clive Steps, where Churchill directed British operations in the war against the Nazis. Spend the evening at the theater.

Take in as many West End shows as you can manage in your evenings in London.

1 Sights & Attractions by Neighborhood

BELGRAVIA
Apsley House, the Wellington Museum (p. 213)

BLOOMSBURY
British Library (p. 213)
British Museum (p. 189)
Dickens House (p. 212)
Percival David Foundation of Chinese Art (p. 220)
St. Pancras Station (p. 210)

CAMDEN TOWN
Jewish Museum (p. 217)

CHELSEA
Carlyle's House (p. 212)
Chelsea Physic Garden (p. 223)
Chelsea Royal Hospital (p. 209)
National Army Museum (p. 218)

THE CITY
All Hallows Barking-by-the-Tower (and Brass Rubbing Centre) (p. 203)
Guildhall (p. 244)
London Bridge (p. 225)
Middle Temple Hall (p. 211)
Museum of London (p. 218)
Old Bailey (p. 211)
St. Bride's (p. 204)
St. Giles Cripplegate (p. 205)
St. Mary-le-Bow (p. 206)
St. Paul's Cathedral (p. 197)
Samuel Johnson's House (p. 213)
Temple Church (p. 206)
Temple of Mithras (p. 224)
Tower Bridge (p. 225)
Tower of London (p. 198)

2 The Top Attractions

✪ **British Museum.** Great Russell St., WC1. ☎ **0171/323-8299** or 0171/636-1555 for recorded information. Free admission. Mon–Sat 10am–5pm, Sun noon–6pm. Tube: Holborn or Tottenham Court Rd.

Set in scholarly Bloomsbury, this immense museum grew out of a private collection of manuscripts purchased in 1753 with the proceeds of a lottery. It grew and grew, fed by legacies, discoveries, and purchases, until it became one of the most comprehensive collections of art and artifacts in the world. It's utterly impossible to take in this museum in a day.

The overall storehouse splits basically into the national collections of antiquities; prints and drawings; coins, medals, and banknotes; and ethnography. Even on a cursory first visit, be sure to see the Asian collections (the finest assembly of Islamic pottery outside the Islamic world), the Chinese porcelain, the Indian sculpture, and the Prehistoric and Romano-British collections. Special treasures you might want to seek out on your first visit include the **Rosetta Stone,** whose discovery led to the deciphering of hieroglyphs, in the Egyptian Room; the **Elgin Marbles,** a priceless series of pediments, metopes, and friezes from the Parthenon in Athens, in the Duveen Gallery; and the legendary **Black Obelisk,** dating from around 860 B.C., in the Nimrud Gallery. Other treasures include the contents of Egyptian royal tombs (including mummies); fabulous arrays of 2,000-year-old jewelry, cosmetics, weapons, furniture, and tools; Babylonian astronomical instruments; and winged lions (in the Assyrian Transept) that once guarded Ashurnasirpal's palace at Numrud. The latest additions include a Mexican gallery, a Hellenistic gallery, and a "History of Money"

Time-Saver

With 2¹/₂ miles of galleries, the British Museum is overwhelming. To get a handle on it, we recommend taking a 1¹/₂-hour overview tour for £6 ($9.90) Monday to Saturday at 10:45am, 11:15am, 1:45pm, and 2:15pm, or Sunday at 3pm, 3:20pm, and 3:45pm. After, you can return to the galleries that most interested you. If you have only minutes to spare for the museum, concentrate on the Greek and Roman rooms (1 to 15), which hold the golden hoard of booty both bought and stolen from the Empire's once far-flung colonies.

Central London Sights

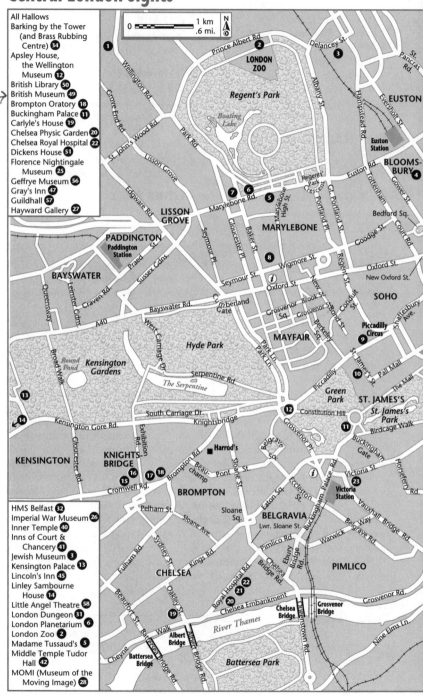

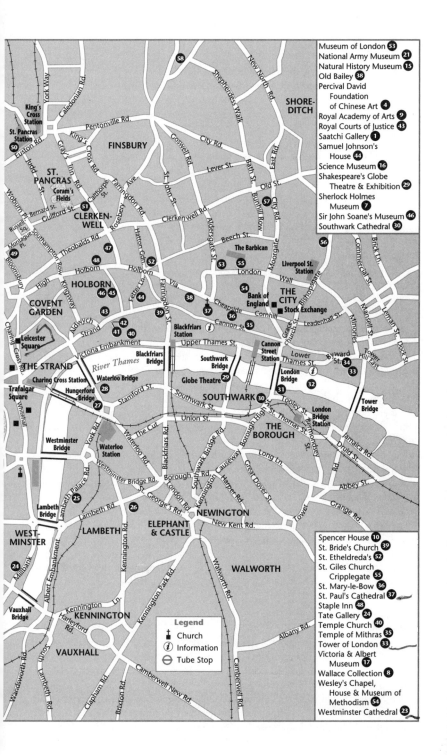

Museum of London 53
National Army Museum 21
Natural History Museum 15
Old Bailey 38
Percival David
    Foundation
    of Chinese Art 4
Royal Academy of Arts 9
Royal Courts of Justice 43
Saatchi Gallery 1
Samuel Johnson's
    House 44
Science Museum 16
Shakespeare's Globe
    Theatre & Exhibition 29
Sherlock Holmes
    Museum 7
Sir John Soane's Museum 46
Southwark Cathedral 30

Spencer House 10
St. Bride's Church 39
St. Etheldreda's 52
St. Giles Church
    Cripplegate 55
St. Mary-le-Bow 36
St. Paul's Cathedral 37
Staple Inn 48
Tate Gallery 24
Temple Church 40
Temple of Mithras 35
Tower of London 33
Victoria & Albert
    Museum 17
Wallace Collection 8
Wesley's Chapel,
    House & Museum of
    Methodism 54
Westminster Cathedral 23

Legend
✝ Church
ⓘ Information
⊖ Tube Stop

191

You can avoid the long queues at Buckingham Palace by purchasing tickets before you go through **Edwards & Edwards,** 1270 Avenue of the Americas, Suite 2414, New York, NY 10020 (☎ **800/223-6108** or 212/332-2435). Visitors with disabilities can reserve tickets directly through the palace by calling **0171/930-5526.**

exhibit. The exhibits change throughout the months, so if your heart is set on seeing a specific treasure, call ahead to make sure it's on display.

The year 2000 will see changes to the historic museum. Dubbed the "Great Court" project, the inner courtyard will be canopied by a lightweight, transparent roof transforming the area into a covered square, housing a Centre for Education, exhibition space, bookshops, and restaurants. The center of the Great Court will feature the Round Reading Room restored to its original decorative scheme.

For information on the British Library, see p. 213.

✪ **Buckingham Palace.** At end of The Mall (on the road running from Trafalgar Sq.). ☎ **0171/839-1377.** Palace tours (usually offered in Aug and Sept) £10 ($16.50) adults, £7.50 ($12.40) seniors, £5 ($8.25) children under 17. Changing of the Guard free. Tube: St. James's Park, Green Park, or Victoria.

This massive, graceful building is the official residence of the queen. The redbrick palace was built as a country house for the notoriously rakish duke of Buckingham. In 1762, it was bought by King George III, who needed room for his 15 children. It didn't become the official royal residence, though, until Queen Victoria took the throne; she preferred it to St. James's Palace. From George III's time, the building was continuously expanded and remodeled, faced with Portland stone, and twice bombed (during the Blitz). Located in a 40-acre garden, it's 360 feet long and contains 600 rooms. You can tell whether the Queen is at home by the Royal Standard flying at the masthead.

For most of the year, you can't visit the palace unless you're officially invited. Since 1993, though, much of it has been open for tours during an 8-week period in August and September, when the royal family is usually vacationing outside London. Elizabeth II agreed to allow visitors to tour the State Room, the Grand Staircase, Throne Room, and other areas designed by John Nash for George IV, as well as **The Queen's Gallery,** which displays masterpieces by Van Dyck, Rembrandt, Rubens, and others. The admission charges help pay for repairing Windsor Castle, badly damaged by fire in 1992.

Buckingham Palace's most famous spectacle is the **Changing of the Guard.** This ceremony begins (when it begins) after 11am and lasts for a half hour. It's been called

Any schedule of the ceremony announced at Buckingham Palace is not written in stone, and plans are never revealed a year in advance, which poses a dilemma for guidebook writers. In theory at least, the guard is changed daily from some time in April to mid-July, at which time it goes on its "winter" schedule—that is, every other day. Always check locally with the tourist office to see if it's likely to be staged at the time of your visit. The ceremony has been cut at the last minute, leaving thousands of tourists feeling they have missed out on a London must-see.

the finest example of military pageantry extant. The new guard, marching behind a band, comes from either the Wellington or Chelsea Barracks and takes over from the old guard in the forecourt of the palace. The changing of the guard is not always daily and varies depending on the time of year. Call **0839/123-411** to check times.

✪ **Houses of Parliament.** Westminster Palace, Old Palace Yard, SW1. House of Commons ☎ **0171/219-4272;** House of Lords ☎ **0171/219-3107.** Free admission. House of Lords open to public Mon–Wed from 2:30pm, Thurs from 3pm, and some Fridays (check by phone). House of Commons open Mon–Tues 2:30–10:30pm, Wed 9:30am–10:30pm, Thurs 11:30am–7:30pm, Fri call ahead—not always open. Join line at St. Stephen's entrance. Tube: Westminster.

The Houses of Parliament, along with their trademark clock tower, are the ultimate symbol of London. They're the stronghold of Britain's democracy, the assemblies that effectively trimmed the sails of royal power. Both the House of Commons and the House of Lords are in the former royal Palace of Westminster, the king's residence until Henry VIII moved to Whitehall. The current Gothic Revival buildings date from 1840 and were designed by Charles Barry. (The earlier buildings were destroyed by fire in 1834.) Assisting Barry was Augustus Welby Pugin, who designed the paneled ceilings, tiled floors, stained glass, clocks, fireplaces, umbrella stands, and even the inkwells. There are more than 1,000 rooms and 2 miles of corridors.

The clock tower at the eastern end houses the world's most famous timepiece. **"Big Ben"** refers not to the clock tower itself, but to the largest bell in the chime, which weighs close to 14 tons and is named for the first commissioner of works. At night a light shines in the tower whenever Parliament is in session.

You may observe parliamentary debates from the **Stranger's Galleries** in both houses. Sessions usually begin in mid-October and run to the end of July, with recesses at Christmas and Easter. Although we can't promise you the oratory of a Charles James Fox or a William Pitt the Elder, the debates in the House of Commons are often lively and controversial (seats are at a premium during crises). The chances of getting into the House of Lords when it's in session are generally better than for the more popular House of Commons, where even the queen isn't allowed. Many political observers maintain that the peerage speak their minds more freely and are less likely to adhere to the party line than their counterparts in the Commons; they do behave, however, in a much more civilized fashion, without the yelling that sometimes accompanies Commons debates.

The general public is admitted to the Strangers' Galleries on "sitting days." You have to join a public line outside the St. Stephen's entrance on the day in question, and there's often considerable delay before the public is admitted. The line forms on the left for the House of Commons, on the right for the Lords. You can speed matters up somewhat by applying at the American Embassy or the Canadian High Commission for a special pass, which should be issued well in advance of your trip, but this is too cumbersome for many people. Besides, the embassy has only four tickets for daily distribution, so you might as well stand in line. It's usually easier to get in after about 5:30pm; debates often continue until about 11pm. To arrange a tour before you leave home, you can write **House of Commons Information Office,** 1 Derby Gate, Westminster, London SW1A 2TT. Tours are usually conducted on Friday.

Stay tuned for developments surrounding the House of Lords, which London's tabloid newspapers portray as a bunch of "Monty Pythonesque upper-class twits." For years this house has given Britain its wit and wisdom, including a 1992 remark by the earl of Longford, "A girl is not ruined for life by being seduced—a young fellow is." Today, under Tony Blair's Labour government, the Houses of Parliament are facing radical reforms. In 1999, more than 600 of the 752 hereditary peers, often descendants of royal mistresses and ancient landowners, have been fired from the upper chamber. By 2000 a parliamentary commission will report who will replace them. Britain's foreign secretary has already called the House of Lords "medieval lumber."

The right of the dukes, the marquesses, the earls, the viscounts, and the barons to sit in the House of Lords has been granted to them for centuries. But as long as it's still there, the House of Lords is busy, often voting down measures passed by the House of Commons. For example, it defeated a measure that would have lowered the age of consent for homosexual sex from 18 to 16. The measure had passed in Commons with a wide majority. The House of Lords, obviously, is overwhelmingly conservative. Recent debates have ranged from outlawing spitting by sports figures to banning chewing gum altogether. Lord Dean, a life peer, defended his colleagues. "Life peers aren't overburdened with geniuses any more than any other group."

Kensington Palace. The Broad Walk, Kensington Gardens, W8. ☎ **0171/937-9561.** Admission £8.50 ($14) adults, £6.70 ($11.05) seniors/students, £6.10 ($10.05) children, £26.10 ($43.05) family. June–Sept daily 10am–5pm; off-season Wed–Sun 10am–3pm. Tube: Queensway or Bayswater on north side of gardens; High St. Kensington on south side.

Once the residence of British monarchs, Kensington Palace hasn't been the official home of reigning kings since George II. It was acquired in 1689 by joint monarchs William III and Mary II as an escape from the damp royal rooms along the Thames. Since the end of the 18th century, the palace has been home to various members of the royal family, and the State Apartments are open for tours.

It was here in 1837 that a young Victoria was roused from her sleep with the news that her uncle, William IV, had died and that she was now queen of England. You can view a nostalgic collection of Victoriana, including some of her memorabilia. In the apartments of Queen Mary II, is a striking 17th-century writing cabinet inlaid with tortoiseshell. Paintings from the Royal Collection line the walls of the apartments. A rare 1750 lady's court dress and splendid examples of male court dress from the 18th century are on display in rooms adjacent to the State Apartments.

Kensington Palace is now the London home of Princess Margaret as well as the duke and duchess of Kent. Of course, it was once the home of Diana, Princess of Wales, and her two sons. (Harry and William now live with their father at St. James's Palace, where Diana's body lay in the Chapel Royal during the week prior to her funeral.) Kensington Palace is probably best known for the millions of flowers that were placed in front of it during the days following Diana's death.

Kensington Gardens are open daily to the public for leisurely strolls through the manicured grounds and around the Round Pond. One of the most famous sights here is the controversial Albert Memorial, a lasting tribute not only to Victoria's consort but also to the questionable artistic taste of the Victorian era. There's a wonderful afternoon tea offered in The Orangery; see "Teatime" in chapter 5.

Madame Tussaud's. Marylebone Rd., NW1. ☎ **0171/935-6861.** Admission £10 ($16.50) adults, £7.50 ($12.40) seniors, £6.50 ($10.75) children under 16, free for children under 5. Combination tickets including the new planetarium £12.25 ($20.20) adults, £9.30 ($15.35) seniors, £8 ($13.20) children under 16. Mon–Fri 10am–5:30pm, Sat–Sun 9:30am–5:30pm. Tube: Baker St.

Madame Tussaud's is not so much a wax museum as an enclosed amusement park. A weird, moving, sometimes terrifying collage of exhibitions, panoramas, and stage settings, it manages to be most things to most people, most of the time.

Madame Tussaud attended the court of Versailles and learned her craft in France. She personally took the death masks from the guillotined heads of Louis XVI and

Trafalgar, London's Most Famous Square

London is a city full of landmark squares. Without a doubt, the best-known is Trafalgar Square (Tube: Charing Cross), which honors one of England's great military heroes, Viscount Horatio Nelson (1758–1805). Although he suffered from seasickness all his life, he went to sea at the age of 12 and was an admiral by the age of 39. Lord Nelson was a hero of the Battle of Calvi in 1794, where he lost an eye; the Battle of Santa Cruz in 1797, where he lost an arm; and the Battle of Trafalgar in 1805, where he lost his life. He is also famous for his affair with Lady Hamilton, subject of many books and films. (For a highly romanticized version of this love affair, seek out the Laurence Olivier/Vivien Leigh film, *That Hamilton Woman;* it runs fairly regularly on American Movie Classics.)

The square today is dominated by the 145-foot granite Nelson's Column, the work of E. H. Baily in 1843. The column looks down Whitehall toward the Old Admiralty, where Lord Nelson's body lay in state. The figure of the naval hero towers 17 feet high—not bad for a man who stood 5'4" in real life. The capital is made of bronze cast from cannons recovered from the wreck of the *Royal George.* Queen Victoria's favorite animal painter, Sir Edward Landseer, added the four lions at the base of the column in 1868. The pools and fountains weren't added until 1939, the last work of Sir Edwin Lutyens.

Political demonstrations still take place in the square and around the column, which has the most aggressive pigeons in London. These birds will even land on your head (or perform less desirable stunts). The birds are part of a long feathery tradition—this site was once used by Edward I to keep birds of prey, called "Longshanks" (1239–1307). (You'll remember him as the villain king in *Braveheart.*) Richard II, who ruled from 1377 to 1399, also kept goshawks and falcons here. By the time of Henry VII, who ruled from 1485 to 1509, the square had become the site of the royal stables. Sir Charles Barry, who designed the Houses of Parliament, created the present square in the 1830s.

Much of the world focuses on the square via TV cameras on New Year's Eve, as they certainly will do for the millennium countdown on December 31, 1999. New Year's here is a wild and raucous time, with crazy revelers jumping into the chilly waters of the fountains. The giant Christmas tree that's installed here every December is an annual gift from Norway to the British people in appreciation for sheltering their royal family during World War II; it's surrounded by carolers most December evenings. Year-round, street performers (now officially licensed) will entertain you in hopes of receiving a token of appreciation for their efforts. To the southeast of the square, at 36 Craven Street, stands a house occupied by Benjamin Franklin from 1757 to 1774. On the north side of the square rises the National Gallery, constructed in the 1830s. In front of the building is a copy of a statue of George Washington by J. A. Houdon.

To the left of St. Martin's Place is the National Portrait Gallery, a collection of portraits of famous Brits—everyone from Chaucer and Shakespeare to Nell Gwynne, Margaret Thatcher, and The Who's Pete Townshend. Also on the square is the towering steeple of St. Martin-in-the-Fields, the final resting place of Sir Joshua Reynolds, William Hogarth, and Thomas Chippendale.

Marie Antoinette (which you'll find among the exhibits). She moved her original museum from Paris to England in 1802. Her exhibition has been imitated in every part of the world, but never with the realism and imagination on hand here. Madame herself molded the features of Benjamin Franklin, whom she met in Paris. All the rest—from George Washington to John F. Kennedy, Mary Queen of Scots to Sylvester Stallone—have been subjects for the same painstaking (and breathtaking) replication.

In the well-known Chamber of Horrors—a kind of underground dungeon—there are all kinds of instruments of death, along with figures of their victims. The shadowy presence of Jack the Ripper lurks in the gloom as you walk through a Victorian London street. Present-day criminals are portrayed within the confines of prison. The latest attraction to open here is "The Spirit of London," a musical ride that depicts 400 years of London's history, using special effects that include audio-animatronic figures that move and speak. Visitors take "time-taxis" that allow them to see and hear "Shakespeare" as he writes and speaks lines, to be received by Queen Elizabeth I, and to feel and smell the Great Fire of 1666 that destroyed London.

✪ **National Gallery.** Northwest side of Trafalgar Sq., WC2. ☎ **0171/747-2885.** Free admission. Thurs–Tues 10am–6pm; Wed 10am–9pm. Tube: Charing Cross, Embankment, or Leicester Square.

This stately neoclassical building contains an unrivaled collection of Western art that spans seven centuries—from the late 13th to the early 20th—and covers every great European school. For sheer skill of display and arrangement, it surpasses its counterparts in Paris, New York, Madrid, and Amsterdam.

The largest part of the collection is devoted to the Italians, including the Sienese, Venetian, and Florentine masters. They're now housed in the Sainsbury Wing, which was designed by noted Philadelphia architects Robert Venturi and Denise Scott Brown and opened by Elizabeth II in 1991. On display are such works as Leonardo's *Virgin of the Rocks;* Titian's *Bacchus and Ariadne;* Giorgione's *Adoration of the Magi;* and unforgettable canvases by Bellini, Veronese, Botticelli, and Tintoretto. Botticelli's *Venus and Mars* is eternally enchanting. (The Sainsbury Wing is also used for large temporary exhibits.)

Of the early-Gothic works, the *Wilton Diptych* (French or English school, late 14th century) is the rarest treasure; it depicts Richard II being introduced to the Madonna and Child by John the Baptist and the Saxon kings, Edmund and Edward the Confessor.

Then there are the Spanish giants: El Greco's *Agony in the Garden,* and portraits by Goya and Velázquez. The Flemish-Dutch school is represented by Brueghel, Jan van Eyck, Vermeer, Rubens, and de Hooch; the Rembrandts include two of his immortal self-portraits. There's also an immense French impressionist and postimpressionist collection that includes works by Manet, Monet, Degas, Renoir, and Cézanne. Particularly charming is the peep-show cabinet by Hoogstraten in one of the Dutch rooms: It's like spying through a keyhole.

British and modern art are the specialties of the Tate Gallery (see below), but the National Gallery does have some fine 18th-century British masterpieces, including works by Hogarth, Gainsborough, Reynolds, Constable, and Turner.

Insider Tip: The National Gallery has a computer information center where you can design your own personal tour map. The computer room, located in the Micro Gallery, includes a dozen hands-on workstations. The online system lists 2,200 paintings and has background notes for each artwork. The program includes four indexes that are cross-referenced for your convenience. Using a touch-screen computer, you design your own personalized tour by selecting a maximum of 10 paintings that you would like to view. Once you have made your choices, you print a personal tour map with your selections; this mapping service is free.

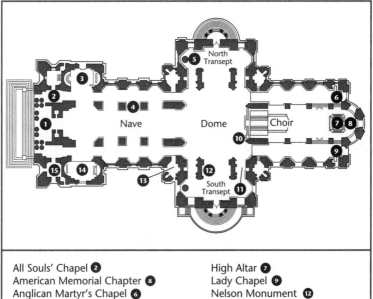

All Souls' Chapel **2**
American Memorial Chapter **8**
Anglican Martyr's Chapel **6**
Chapel of St. Michael
  & St. George **14**
Dean's Staircase **15**
Entrance to Crypt
  (Wren's grave) **11**
Font **5**

High Altar **7**
Lady Chapel **9**
Nelson Monument **12**
Pulpit **10**
St. Dunstan's Chapel **3**
Staircase to Library,
  Whispering Gallery & Dome **13**
Wellington Monument **4**
West Doorway **1**

✪ St. Paul's Cathedral. St. Paul's Churchyard, EC4. **☎ 0171/236-4128.** Cathedral £4 ($6.60) adults, £2 ($3.30) children 6–16. Galleries £3.50 ($5.75) adults, £1.50 ($2.45) children. Free for children 5 and under. Guided tours £2 ($3.30); recorded tours £3 ($4.95). Sightseeing Mon–Sat 8:30am–4pm; galleries Mon–Sat 9:30am–4pm. No sightseeing Sun (services only). Tube: St. Paul's.

During World War II, newsreel footage reaching America showed St. Paul's Cathedral standing virtually alone among the rubble of the City, its dome lit by fires caused by bombings all around it. That it survived at all is a miracle, since it was badly hit twice during the early years of the bombardment of London in World War II. But St. Paul's is accustomed to calamity, having been burned down three times and destroyed once by invading Norsemen. It was during the Great Fire of 1666 that the old St. Paul's was razed, making way for a new structure designed by Sir Christopher Wren and built between 1675 and 1710. It's the architectural genius's ultimate masterpiece.

The classical dome of St. Paul's dominates the City's square mile. The golden cross surmounting it is 365 feet above the ground; the golden ball on which the cross rests measures 6 feet in diameter yet looks like a marble from below. Surrounding the interior of the dome is the Whispering Gallery, an acoustic marvel in which the faintest whisper can be heard clearly on the opposite side—so be careful of what you say. You can climb to the top of the dome for a spectacular 360° view of London.

Although the interior looks almost bare, it houses a vast number of monuments. The duke of Wellington (of Waterloo fame) is entombed here, as are Lord Nelson and Sir Christopher Wren himself. At the east end of the cathedral is the American Memorial

---

Insider Tip _____

One of the most enjoyable aspects of a spring visit to London is sauntering through the free gardens of St. Paul's when the roses are in bloom.

Chapel, honoring the 28,000 U.S. service personnel who lost their lives while stationed in Britain in World War II.

Guided tours last 1¹/₂ hours and include parts of the cathedral not open to the general public. They take place Monday to Saturday at 11am, 11:30am, 1:30pm, and 2pm. Recorded tours lasting 45 minutes are available throughout the day.

St. Paul's is an Anglican cathedral with daily services at the following times: matins at 7:30am Monday to Friday, 8:30am on Saturday; Holy Communion Monday to Saturday at 8am and 12:30pm; and evensong Monday to Saturday at 5pm. On Sunday, there's Holy Communion at 8am and again at 11:30am, matins at 10:15am, and evensong at 3:15pm. Admission charges don't apply if you're attending a service.

Tate Gallery. Millbank, SW1. ☎ **0171/887-8000.** Free admission; special exhibitions sometimes incur a charge. Daily 10am–5:50pm. Tube: Pimlico. Bus: 77A, 88, or C10.

Fronting the Thames near Vauxhall Bridge in Pimlico, the Tate looks like a smaller and more graceful relation of the British Museum. The most prestigious gallery in Britain, it houses the national collections covering British art from the 16th century on, as well as an international array of moderns. The Tate's holdings are split between the traditional and the contemporary. Since only a portion of the collections can be displayed at any one time, the works on view change from time to time. Because it's difficult to take in all the exhibits, we suggest that you try to schedule two visits—the first to see the classic British works, the second to take in the modern collection—or concentrate on whichever section interests you more, if your time is limited.

The older works include some of the best of Gainsborough, Reynolds, Stubbs, Blake, and Constable. William Hogarth is well represented, particularly by his satirical _O the Roast Beef of Old England_ (known as _The Gate of Calais_). The illustrations of William Blake, the incomparable mystical poet for such works as _The Book of Job_, _The Divine Comedy_, and _Paradise Lost_ are here. The collection of works by J. M. W. Turner is its largest collection of works by a single artist; Turner himself willed most of the paintings and watercolors here to the nation.

Also on display are the works of many major 19th- and 20th-century painters, including Paul Nash. In the modern collections are works by Matisse, Dalí, Modigliani, Munch, Bonnard, and Picasso. Truly remarkable are the several enormous abstract canvases by Mark Rothko, the group of paintings and sculptures by Giacometti, and the paintings of one of England's best-known modern artists, the late Francis Bacon. Sculptures by Henry Moore and Barbara Hepworth are also occasionally displayed.

Plans call for the Tate Gallery to split into two separate galleries, the original to be known as the Tate Gallery of British Art. The modern international collection will move across the Thames and will become the new Tate Gallery of Modern Art. The galleries will be linked by a pedestrian bridge across the river. Dates of this transfer and split have not been announced. Stay tuned.

Downstairs is the internationally renowned **Tate Gallery Restaurant** (see chapter 5), with murals by Whistler, as well as a coffee shop.

✪ **Tower of London.** Tower Hill, EC3. ☎ **0171/709-0765.** Admission £10.50 ($17.35) adults, £7.90 ($13.05) students and seniors, £6.90 ($11.40) children, free for children under

5; £31 ($51.15) family ticket for 5 (but no more than 2 adults). Mar–Oct Mon–Sat 9am–5pm, Sun 10am–5pm; off-season Tues–Sat 9am–4pm, Mon and Sun 10am–4pm. Tube: Tower Hill.

This ancient fortress continues to pack in the crowds, largely because of its macabre associations with all the legendary figures who were imprisoned and/or executed here. James Street once wrote, "There are more spooks to the square foot than in any other building in the whole of haunted Britain. Headless bodies, bodiless heads, phantom soldiers, icy blasts, clanking chains—you name them, the Tower's got them." Even today, centuries after the last head rolled on Tower Hill, a shivery atmosphere of impending doom lingers over the mighty walls. Plan on spending a lot of time here.

The Tower is actually an intricately patterned compound of structures built throughout the ages for varying purposes, mostly as expressions of royal power. The oldest is the **White Tower,** begun by William the Conqueror in 1078 to keep London's native Saxon population in check. Later rulers added other towers, more walls, and fortified gates, until the building became something like a small town within a city. Until the reign of James I, the Tower was also one of the royal residences. But above all, it was a prison for distinguished captives.

Every stone of the Tower tells a story—usually a gory one. In the **Bloody Tower,** according to Shakespeare, the two little princes (the sons of Edward IV) were murdered by henchmen of Richard III. (Modern historians, however, tend to think that Richard may not have been the guilty party.) Here, too, Sir Walter Raleigh spent 13 years before his date with the executioner. On the walls of the **Beauchamp Tower,** you can actually read the last messages scratched by despairing prisoners. Through **Traitors' Gate** passed such ill-fated, romantic figures as Robert Devereux, the second earl of Essex, a favorite of Elizabeth I. A plaque marks the eerie place at **Tower Green** where two wives of Henry VIII, Anne Boleyn and Catherine Howard; Sir Thomas More; and the 4-day queen, Lady Jane Grey, all lost their lives. Lady Jane's husband, Lord Guildford Dudley, was executed across the way at Tower Hill.

The Tower, besides being a royal palace, a fortress, and a prison, was also an armory, a treasury, a menagerie, and in 1675 an astronomical observatory. Reopened in 1999, the White Tower holds the **Armouries,** which date from the reign of Henry VIII, as well as a display of instruments of torture and execution that recall some of the most ghastly moments in the Tower's history. In the Jewel House, you'll find the tower's greatest attraction, the **Crown Jewels.** Here, some of the world's most precious stones are set into the robes, swords, scepters, and crowns. The Imperial State Crown is the most famous crown on earth; made for Victoria in 1837, it's worn today by Queen Elizabeth when she opens Parliament. Studded with some 3,000 jewels (principally diamonds), it includes the Black Prince's Ruby, worn by Henry V at Agincourt. The 530-carat Star of Africa, a cut diamond on the Royal Sceptre with Cross, would make Harry Winston turn over in his grave. You'll have to stand in long lines to catch just a glimpse of the jewels as you and hundreds of others scroll by on moving sidewalks, but the wait is worth it.

Insider Tip

Spare a little time for the Art Now Gallery, which houses recent works of both new and established artists, some highly controversial. There's always something on the art world's cutting edge here. For hard-to-get tickets to popular exhibits, we suggest calling **First Call** (☎ **0171/420-0002;** fax 01293/433-702; Ocean House, Hazelwide Ave., Three Bridges, Crawley, West Sussex RHT 1NP), the agency responsible for distributing tickets to these events.

Tower of London

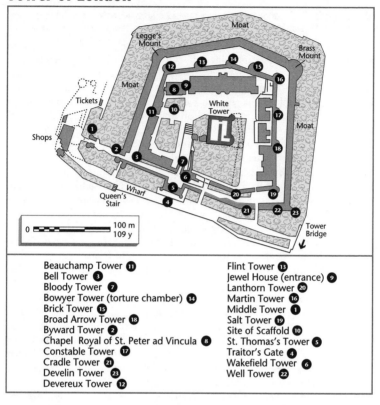

Beauchamp Tower **11**
Bell Tower **3**
Bloody Tower **7**
Bowyer Tower (torture chamber) **14**
Brick Tower **15**
Broad Arrow Tower **18**
Byward Tower **2**
Chapel Royal of St. Peter ad Vincula **8**
Constable Tower **17**
Cradle Tower **21**
Develin Tower **23**
Devereux Tower **12**

Flint Tower **13**
Jewel House (entrance) **9**
Lanthorn Tower **20**
Martin Tower **16**
Middle Tower **1**
Salt Tower **19**
Site of Scaffold **10**
St. Thomas's Tower **5**
Traitor's Gate **4**
Wakefield Tower **6**
Well Tower **22**

A **palace** once inhabited by King Edward I in the late 1200s stands above Traitors' Gate. It's the only surviving medieval palace in Britain. Guides are dressed in period costumes. Reproductions of furniture and fittings, including Edward's throne, evoke the era, along with burning incense and candles.

Oh, yes—and don't forget to look for the ravens. Six of them (plus two spares) are all registered as official Tower residents. According to a legend, the Tower of London will stand as long as those black, ominous birds remain; so, to be on the safe side, one of the wings of each raven is clipped.

One-hour guided tours of the entire compound are given by the Yeoman Warders (also known as "Beefeaters") every half hour, starting at 9:25am from the Middle Tower near the main entrance. The last guided walk starts about 3:25pm in summer, 2:25pm in winter, weather permitting, of course.

You can attend the nightly **Ceremony of the Keys,** the ceremonial locking up of the Tower by the Yeoman Warders. For free tickets, write to the Ceremony of the Keys, Waterloo Block, Tower of London, London EC3N 4AB, and request a specific date, but also list alternative dates. At least 6 weeks' notice is required. All requests must be accompanied by a stamped, self-addressed envelope (British stamps only) or two International Reply Coupons. With ticket in hand, you'll be admitted by a Yeoman Warder at 9:35pm.

Victoria and Albert Museum. Cromwell Rd., SW7. ☎ **0171/938-8500.** Admission £5 ($8.25) adults, £3 ($4.95) seniors, free for children under 18 and persons with disabilities. Daily 10am–5:45pm. Tube: South Kensington. Bus: C1, 14, or 74.

Insider Tip

The secret of avoiding the Tower's notoriously long lines is to arrive the moment the gates open, before the hordes descend in the afternoon. Choose a day other than Sunday if you can—crowds are at their worst then.

The Victoria and Albert is the greatest museum in the world devoted to the decorative arts. It's also one of the liveliest and most imaginative museums in London—where else would you find the quintessential "little black dress" in the permanent collection?

The medieval holdings include such treasures as the early-English Gloucester Candlestick; the Byzantine Veroli Casket, with its ivory panels based on Greek plays; and the Syon Cope, a highly valued embroidery made in England in the early 14th century. An area devoted to Islamic art houses the Ardabil Carpet from 16th-century Persia.

The V&A houses the largest collection of Renaissance sculpture outside Italy. A highlight of the 16th-century collection is the marble group *Neptune with Triton* by Bernini. The cartoons by Raphael, which were conceived as designs for tapestries for the Sistine Chapel, are owned by the queen and on display here. A most unusual, huge, and impressive exhibit is the Cast Courts, life-size plaster models of ancient and medieval statuary and architecture.

The museum has the greatest collection of Indian art outside India, plus Chinese and Japanese galleries as well. In complete contrast are suites of English furniture, metalwork, and ceramics, and a superb collection of portrait miniatures, including the one Hans Holbein the Younger made of Anne of Cleves for the benefit of Henry VIII, who was again casting around for a suitable wife. The Dress Collection includes a collection of corsetry through the ages that's sure to make you wince. There's also a remarkable collection of musical instruments.

Because of redevelopment, the entire run of British Galleries won't be fully open until 2001. But the museum has a lively program of changing exhibitions and displays, so there's always something new to see.

Insider Tip: As incongruous as it sounds, the museum hosts a jazz brunch on Sunday from 11am to 3pm. You can hear some of the hottest jazz in the city, accompanied by a full English brunch for only £8.50 ($14). And don't miss the V&A's most bizarre gallery, "Fakes and Forgeries." The impostors here are amazingly authentic—in fact, we'd judge some of them as better than the old masters themselves.

✪ **Westminster Abbey.** Broad Sanctuary, SW1. ☎ **0171/222-7110** or 0171/222-5897. Admission £5 ($8.25) adults, £3 ($4.95) for students and seniors, £2 ($3.30) children 11–18, free for children under 11, family ticket £16 ($26.40). Mon–Fri 9:15am–3:45pm, Sat 9:15am–1:45pm. Tube: Westminster or St. James's Park.

With its square twin towers and superb archways, this early-English Gothic abbey is one of the greatest examples of ecclesiastical architecture on earth. But it's far more than that: It's the shrine of a nation, the symbol of everything Britain has stood for and stands for, the place in which most of its rulers were crowned and where many lie buried.

Nearly every figure in English history has left his or her mark on Westminster Abbey. Edward the Confessor founded the Benedictine abbey in 1065 on this spot, overlooking Parliament Square. The first English king crowned in the abbey was Harold in 1066. The man who defeated him at the Battle of Hastings the next year,

William the Conqueror, was also crowned here. The coronation tradition has continued to the present day, broken only twice (Edward V and Edward VIII). The essentially early–English Gothic structure existing today owes more to Henry III's plans than to those of any other sovereign, although many architects, including Wren, have contributed to the abbey.

Built on the site of the Ancient Lady Chapel in the early 16th century, the **Henry VII Chapel** is one of the loveliest in Europe, with its fan vaulting, Knights of Bath banners, and Torrigiani-designed tomb of the king himself, over which hangs a 15th-century Vivarini painting, *Madonna and Child.* Also here, ironically buried in the same tomb, are Catholic Mary I and Protestant Elizabeth I (whose archrival, Mary Queen of Scots, is entombed on the other side of the Henry VII Chapel). In one end of the chapel, you can stand on Cromwell's memorial stone and view the **Royal Air Force Chapel** and its Battle of Britain memorial window, unveiled in 1947 to honor the RAF.

You can also visit the most hallowed spot in the abbey, the **shrine of Edward the Confessor** (canonized in the 12th century). In the chapel is the Coronation Chair, made at the command of Edward I in 1300 to display the Stone of Scone. Scottish kings were once crowned on it (it has since been returned to Scotland).

When you enter the transept on the south side of the nave and see a statue of the Bard with one arm resting on a stack of books, you've arrived at **Poets' Corner.** Shakespeare himself is buried at Stratford-upon-Avon, but resting here are Chaucer, Ben Jonson, Milton, Shelley, and many others; there's even an American, Henry Wadsworth Longfellow, as well as monuments to just about everybody: Chaucer, Shakespeare, "O Rare Ben Johnson" (his name misspelled), Samuel Johnson, George Eliot, Dickens, and others. The most stylized monument is Sir Jacob Epstein's sculptured bust of William Blake. More recent tablets commemorate poet Dylan Thomas and Lord Olivier.

Statesmen and men of science—such as Disraeli, Newton, Charles Darwin—are also interred in the abbey or honored by monuments. Near the west door is the 1965 memorial to Sir Winston Churchill. In the vicinity of this memorial is the tomb of the **Unknown Soldier,** commemorating the British dead in World War I.

Off the Cloisters, the **College Garden** is the oldest garden in England, under cultivation for more than 900 years. Surrounded by high walls, flowering trees dot the lawns and park benches provide comfort where you can hardly hear the roar of passing traffic. It's open only on Tuesday and Thursday. In the Cloisters, you can make a rubbing at the **Brass Rubbing Centre (☎ 0171/222-2085).**

Insider Tip: Far removed from the pomp and glory is the **Abbey Treasure Museum,** with a bag of oddities. They're displayed in the undercroft or crypt, part of the monastic buildings erected between 1066 and 1100. Here are royal effigies that were used instead of the real corpses for lying-in-state ceremonies because they smelled better. You'll see the almost lifelike effigy of Admiral Nelson (his mistress arranged his hair) and even that of Edward III, his lip warped by the stroke that felled him. Other oddities include a Middle English lease to Chaucer, the much-used sword of Henry VI, and the Essex Ring Elizabeth I gave to her favorite when she was feeling good about him.

The only time photography is allowed in the abbey is Wednesday evening from 6 to 7:45pm. On Sunday, the Royal Chapels are closed, but the rest of the church is open unless a service is being conducted. For times of services, phone the **Chapter Office (☎ 0171/222-5152).** Up to six supertours of the abbey are conducted by the vergers Monday to Saturday, beginning at 10am and costing £3 ($4.95) per person.

Westminster Abbey

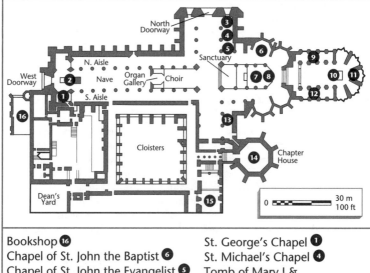

Bookshop ⑯
Chapel of St. John the Baptist ⑥
Chapel of St. John the Evangelist ⑤
Chapter House ⑭
Henry V's Chantry ⑧
Poets' Corner ⑬
Royal Air Force Chapel ⑪
St. Andrew's Chapel ③
St. Edward's Chapel
  (Coronation Chair) ⑦

St. George's Chapel ①
St. Michael's Chapel ④
Tomb of Mary I &
  Elizabeth I ⑨
Tomb of Henry VII ⑩
Tomb of Mary,
  Queen of Scots ⑫
Tomb of the Unknown Warrior/
  Memorial to Churchill ②
Undercroft Museum ⑮

3 More Central London Attractions

CHURCHES & CATHEDRALS

Many of London's churches offer free lunchtime concerts; a full list of these concerts is available from the London Tourist Board. It's customary to leave a small donation.

All Hallows Barking-by-the-Tower. Byward St., EC3. ☎ **0171/481-2928.** Free admission; crypt museum tour £2 ($3.30). Museum Mon–Fri 11am–4:30pm, Sat 10am–4:30pm, Sun 1–4:30pm. Church Mon–Fri 9am–6pm, Sat–Sun 10am–5pm. Tube: Tower Hill.

The brass-rubbing center at this fascinating church, next door to the Tower, has a crypt museum, Roman remains, and traces of early London, including a Saxon arch predating the Tower. Samuel Pepys, the famed diarist, climbed to the spire of this church to watch the raging fire of London in 1666. In 1644, William Penn was baptized here, and in 1797, John Quincy Adams was married here. Bombs destroyed the church in 1940, leaving only the tower and walls standing. The church was rebuilt from 1949 to 1958.

✪ **Brompton Oratory.** Brompton Rd., SW7. ☎ **0171/589-4811.** Free admission. Daily 6:30am–8pm. Tube: South Kensington.

A group of Victorian intellectuals turned Catholic, the Oxford Movement certainly didn't go halfway when they created this church in 1884. Done in the Italian Renaissance style, this dramatic Roman Catholic church is famous for its musical services, and its organ with nearly 4,000 pipes. After Westminster Cathedral and York Minster, it has the widest nave in England.

American Connection

The parents of Virginia Dare, the first English child born in America at Roanoke in 1587, were married in St Bride's. An effigy of Virginia can be seen over the baptismal font.

St. Bride's. Fleet St., EC4. ☎ **0171/353-1301.** Free admission. Mon–Fri 8am–4:45pm, Sat–Sun 11am–7:30pm. Concerts at 1:15pm. Tube: Blackfriars.

Known as the "the church of the press" thanks to its location at the end of Fleet Street, St. Bride's is a remarkable landmark. The current church is the eighth one that's stood here. After it was bombed in 1940, an archaeologist excavated the crypts and was able to confirm much of the site's legendary history: A Roman house was discovered preserved in the crypt, and it was established that St. Brigit of Ireland had founded the first Christian church here. Among the famous parishioners have been writers John Dryden, John Milton, Richard Lovelace, and John Evelyn; the diarist Samuel Pepys was baptized here, and novelist Samuel Richardson and his family are buried here. After the Great Fire destroyed it, the church was rebuilt by Christopher Wren, with a spire that's been described as a "madrigal in stone." This soaring confection (234 feet tall) inspired the wedding cakes of a pastry cook who lived in Fleet Street in the late 17th century, it's said. The crypt was a burial chamber and charnel house for centuries; today, it's a museum. Concerts are given on Tuesday and Friday, and there's an organ recital on Wednesday. Concerts are often suspended during Lent and Christmas.

St. Clement Danes. Strand, WC2. ☎ **0171/242-8282.** Free admission. Mon–Sat 10am–4pm. Closed Sun. Tube: Temple or Embankment.

It's not known for certain why Danes is part of the church's name, but we do know that there was a wooden Saxon church on this site, which was rebuilt in stone in the late 10th century. Although the church survived the Great Fire, it was declared unsafe, and Christopher Wren was commissioned to rebuild it. The spire was designed by James Gibbs. The interior is decorated with ornate plasterwork. Samuel Johnson attended services regularly, and the wife of poet John Donne is buried here. The Blitz totally gutted the church, and it was reconstructed yet again in the late 1950s. Today, this is the central church of the Royal Air Force, with memorials to the British, Commonwealth, and American airmen who flew in World War II. Among its more famous rectors is William Webb Ellis who, as a schoolboy playing soccer at Rugby School, infringed soccer rules when he picked up the ball and ran with it—thereby inventing the game of rugby. Worship is held each Sunday at 11am.

St. Etheldreda's. Ely Place, Holborn Circus, EC1. ☎ **0171/405-1061.** Free admission. Daily 8am–6pm, Sun masses. Tube: Farringdon or Chancery Lane.

The oldest Roman Catholic church in London, St. Etheldreda's stands on Ely Place, off Charterhouse Street at Holborn Circus. Built in 1251, it was mentioned by the Bard in both *Richard II* and *Richard III*. A survivor of the Great Fire of 1666, the church and place were the property of the diocese of Ely, in the days when many bishops had episcopal houses in London as well as in the cathedral cities in which they held their sees. The place is still a private road, with impressive iron gates and a lodge for the gatekeeper, all administered by six elected commissioners.

St. Etheldreda, whose name is sometimes shortened to St. Audrey, was a 7th-century king's daughter who left her husband and established an abbey on the Isle of Ely. St. Etheldreda's has a distinguished musical tradition, with the 11am mass on Sunday sung in Latin. Other masses are on Sunday at 9am, Monday to Friday at 8am and 1pm, and on Saturday at 9:30am. Lunch, with a varied choice of hot and cold dishes, is served Monday to Friday from 11:30am to 2pm in the Pantry.

St. Giles Cripplegate. At Fore and Wood sts., London Wall, EC2. ☎ **0171/638-1997.** Free admission. Mon–Fri 9am–5pm, Sat 9am–noon for services. Tube: Moorgate or St. Paul's.

Named for the patron saint of cripples, St. Giles was founded in the 11th century. The church survived the Great Fire, but the Blitz left only the tower and walls standing. Oliver Cromwell was betrothed to Elizabeth Bourchier here in 1620, and John Milton, author of *Paradise Lost,* was buried here in 1674. More than a century later, someone opened the poet's grave, knocked out his teeth, stole a rib bone, and tore hair from his skull. Guided tours are available on most Tuesday afternoons. Call to confirm.

St. James's Church. 197 Piccadilly, W1. ☎ **0171/734-4511.** Free admission. Recitals Wed–Fri at 1:10pm. Tube: Piccadilly Circus or Green Park.

When the aristocratic area known as St. James's was developed in the late 17th century, Sir Christopher Wren was commissioned to build its parish church. Diarist John Evelyn wrote of the interior, "There is no altar anywhere in England, nor has there been any abroad, more handsomely adorned." The reredos, organ case, and font were all carved by Wren's master carver Grinling Gibbons. As might be expected, this church has rich historical associations: The poet William Blake and William Pitt, the first earl of Chatham, who became England's youngest prime minister at age 24, were both baptized here; caricaturist James Gillray, auctioneer James Christie, and coffeehouse founder Francis White are all buried here. One of the more colorful marriages celebrated here was that of explorer Sir Samuel Baker and the woman he had bought at a slave auction in a Turkish bazaar. St. James's Church is a radical, inclusive Anglican church. It's also the Centre for Health and Healing, and holds seminars on New Age and Creation Spirituality. There's a Bible Garden and a craft market in the courtyard. The Wren Café is open 7 days a week, and lunchtime and evening concerts are held.

Insider's Tip: There is also an antiques market on Tuesday from 10am to 7pm and a craft market from Wednesday to Saturday 10am to 7pm.

St. Martin-in-the-Fields. Trafalgar Sq., WC2. ☎ **0171/930-0089.** Mon–Sat 10am–8pm, Sun noon–8pm as long as there is no service taking place. Tube: Charing Cross.

Designed by James Gibbs, a disciple of Christopher Wren, and completed in 1726, this classical temple stands at the northeast corner of Trafalgar Square, opposite the National Gallery. Its spire, added in 1824, towers 185 feet (taller than Nelson's Column, which also rises on the square). The steeple became the paradigm for many churches in colonial America. Since the first year of World War I (1914), the homeless have sought "soup and shelter" at St. Martin, a tradition that continues.

At one time the crypt held the remains of Charles II (he's in Westminster Abbey now), who was christened here, giving St. Martin a claim as a royal parish church. His mistress, Nell Gwynne, was also interred here, as was the notorious highwayman Jack Sheppard (they're both still here). The floors of the crypt are actually gravestones, and the walls date from the 1500s. The little restaurant, **Café in the Crypt,** is still called "Field's" by its devotees. Also in the crypt is The London Brass Rubbing Centre (☎ **0171/930-9306**) with 88 exact copies of bronze portraits ready for use. Paper, rubbing materials, and instructions on how to begin are furnished, and there's classical music for you to enjoy as you proceed. The charges range from £2.50 to £15 ($4.15 to $24.75), the latter price for the largest, a life-size Crusader knight. There's also a gift shop with brass-rubbing kits for children, budget-priced ready-made rubbings, Celtic jewelry, miniature brasses, and model knights. The center is open Monday to Saturday 11am to 4pm and Sunday 1 to 4pm.

Insider's Tip: In back of the church is a crafts market. Lunchtime and evening concerts are staged Monday, Tuesday, and Friday at 1:05pm, and Thursday to Saturday at 7:30pm. Tickets cost £6 to £15 ($9.90 to $24.75).

St. Mary-le-Bow. Cheapside, EC2. ☎ **0171/248-5139.** Free admission. Mon–Wed 6:30am–6pm, Thurs 6:30am–6:30pm, Fri 6:30am–4pm. Tube: St. Paul's or Bank or Mansion House.

A true Cockney is said to be born within hearing distance of this church's famous Bow bells. The church certainly hasn't been blessed by the series of disasters that mark its sometimes gruesome history: In 1091, its roof was ripped off in a storm; the church tower collapsed in 1271 and 20 people were killed; in 1331, Queen Philippa and her ladies-in-waiting fell to the ground when a balcony collapsed during a joust celebrating the birth of the Black Prince; it was rebuilt by Wren after being engulfed by the Great Fire; and the original "Cockney" Bow bells were destroyed in the Blitz, but have been replaced. The church was rededicated in 1964 after extensive restoration work.

St. Paul's, the Actors Church. Covent Garden, WC2. ☎ **0171/836-5221.** Free admission. Tue–Fri 9:30am–4:30pm, Mon 9:30am–2pm, Sun service 11am. Tube: Covent Garden.

With the Drury Lane Theatre, the Royal Opera House, and many other theaters within its parish, St. Paul's has long been associated with the theatrical arts. Inside you'll find scores of memorial plaques dedicated to such luminaries as Vivien Leigh, Boris Karloff, Margaret Rutherford, and Noel Coward, to name only a few. Designed by Inigo Jones in 1631, this church has been substantially altered over the years, but it retains a quiet garden-piazza in the rear. Among the famous who are buried here are wood-carver Grinling Gibbons, writer Samuel Butler, and actress Ellen Terry. Landscape painter J. M. W. Turner and librettist W. S. Gilbert were both baptized here.

Southwark Cathedral. Montague Close, London Bridge, SE1. ☎ **0171/407-3708.** Free admission; suggested donation £2 ($3.30). Daily 8:30am–6pm. Tube: London Bridge.

There's been a church on this site, in the heart of London's first theater district, for more than a thousand years. The present one dates from the 15th century; it was partly rebuilt in 1890. The previous one was the first Gothic church (1106) to be constructed in London. Shakespeare and Chaucer worshiped at services here; a Shakespeare birthday service is held annually, and inside is a memorial to the playwright. A wooden effigy of a knight dates from 1275. In 1424, James I of Scotland married Mary Beaufort here. During the reign of Mary Tudor, Stephen Gardiner, the Bishop of Winchester, held a consistory court in the retro choir that condemned seven Protestants, the Marian martyrs, to death. Later, the same retro choir was rented to a baker and even used to house pigs. Lunchtime concerts are regularly given on Monday and Tuesday; call for exact times and schedules.

Temple Church. The Temple (within the Inner Temple), EC4. ☎ **0171/353-1736.** Free admission. Wed–Sat 10am–4pm, Sun 1–3pm. Tube: Temple.

One of three Norman "round churches" left in England, this one was first completed in the 12th century; not surprisingly, it has been restored. Look for the knightly effigies and the Norman door, and take note of the circle of grotesque portrait heads, including a goat in a mortarboard.

On Inner Temple Lane, about where the Strand becomes Fleet Street going east, you'll see the memorial pillar called **Temple Bar,** which marks the boundary of the City of London.

Wesley's Chapel, House & Museum of Methodism. 49 City Rd., EC1. ☎ **0171/253-2262.** Chapel free. House and museum £4 ($6.60) adults, £2 ($3.30) seniors, students, and children 5–17. House and museum Mon–Sat 10am–4pm. Both free on Sun after service, between noon and 2pm. Tube: Old St. or Moorgate.

John Wesley, the founder of Methodism, established this church in 1778 as his London base. The man who rode on horseback throughout the English countryside and preached in the open air lived at no. 47 next door, and he's buried in a grave behind the chapel. Surviving the Blitz, the church later fell into serious disrepair; major restoration was completed in the 1970s. In the crypt, a museum traces the history of Methodism to today.

Across the road in Bunhill Fields is the **Dissenters Graveyard,** where Daniel Defoe, William Blake, and John Bunyan are buried.

Westminster Cathedral. Ashley Place, SW1. ☎ **0171/798-9055.** Cathedral free, audio tours £2.50 ($4.15). Tower, £2 ($3.30). Cathedral, daily 7am–7pm. Tower, Apr–Nov daily 9am–1pm and 2–5pm; otherwise Thurs–Sun only. Tube: Victoria.

This spectacular brick-and-stone church (1903) is the headquarters of the Roman Catholic Church in Britain. Adorned in early-Byzantine style, it's massive: 360 feet long and 156 feet wide. One hundred different marbles compose the richly decorated interior, and eight marble columns support the nave. The huge baldachino over the high altar is lifted by eight yellow marble columns. Mosaics emblazon the chapels and the vaulting of the sanctuary. If you take the elevator to the top of the 273-foot-tall campanile, you're rewarded with sweeping views that take in Buckingham Palace, Westminster Abbey, and St. Paul's Cathedral. There is a cafe serving light snacks and soft drinks from 9am to 5pm and a gift shop open from 9:30am to 5:15pm.

HISTORIC BUILDINGS

Banqueting House. Whitehall Palace, Horse Guards Ave., SW1. ☎ **0171/930-4179.** Admission £3.50 ($5.75) adults, £2.70 ($4.45) seniors and students, £2.30 ($3.80) children. Mon–Sat 10am–5pm (last admission 4:30pm). Tube: Westminster, Charing Cross, or Embankment.

The feasting chamber in Whitehall Palace is probably the most sumptuous dining hall on earth. (Unfortunately, you can't dine here unless you happen to be a visiting head of state.) Designed by Inigo Jones and decorated with, among other things, original ceiling paintings by Rubens, the hall is dazzling enough to make you forget food altogether. Among the historic events that took place here were the beheading of King Charles I, who stepped through a window onto the scaffold outside, and the restoration ceremony of Charles II, marking the return of the monarchy after Cromwell's brief Puritan Commonwealth.

Cabinet War Rooms. Clive Steps, at end of King Charles St. (off Whitehall near Big Ben), SW1. ☎ **0171/930-6961.** Admission £4.80 ($7.90) adults, £3.50 ($5.75) seniors and students, £2.40 ($3.95) children. Apr–Sept daily 9:30am–6pm (last admission at 5:15pm); Oct–Mar daily 10am–5:30pm. Tube: Westminster or St. James's.

This is the bombproof bunker from which Sir Winston Churchill and his government ran the nation during World War II. Many of the rooms are exactly as they were in September 1945: Imperial War Museum curators studied photographs to put notepads, files, typewriters, even pencils, pins, and clips, in their correct places.

Along the tour, you'll have a step-by-step personal sound guide that provides a detailed account of the function and history of each room of this World War II nerve center. They include the Map Room, with its huge wall maps. Next door is Churchill's bedroom-cum-office; it has a very basic bed and a desk with two BBC microphones

Covent Garden, the Strand & St. James

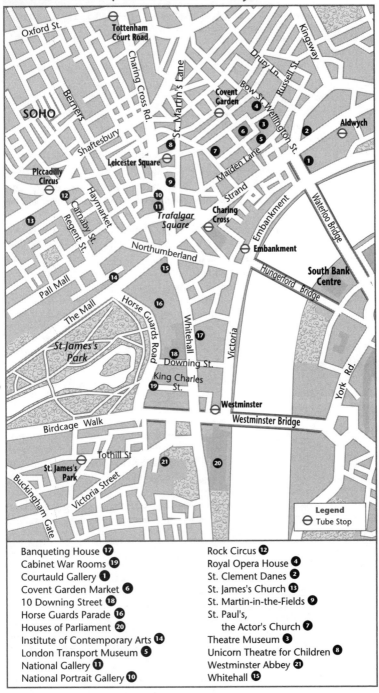

Banqueting House **17**
Cabinet War Rooms **19**
Courtauld Gallery **1**
Covent Garden Market **6**
10 Downing Street **18**
Horse Guards Parade **16**
Houses of Parliament **20**
Institute of Contemporary Arts **14**
London Transport Museum **5**
National Gallery **11**
National Portrait Gallery **10**

Rock Circus **12**
Royal Opera House **4**
St. Clement Danes **2**
St. James's Church **13**
St. Martin-in-the-Fields **9**
St. Paul's,
   the Actor's Church **7**
Theatre Museum **3**
Unicorn Theatre for Children **8**
Westminster Abbey **21**
Whitehall **15**

for those famous broadcasts that stirred the nation. The Transatlantic Telephone Room is little more than a broom closet, but it held the extension linked to the special scrambler phone (called "Sig-Saly"), that allowed Churchill to confer with Roosevelt. (The scrambler equipment itself was actually too large to house in the bunker, so it was placed in the basement of Selfridges department store on Oxford Street.)

Chelsea Royal Hospital. Royal Hospital Rd., SW3. ☎ **0171/730-0161.** If you want a tour, you must apply in writing to Adjutant, Royal Hospital Chelsea, London, SW3 4SR. Guided tours are free, but donations are gratefully accepted. Otherwise, you're welcome to explore on your own. Free admission. Mon–Sat 10am–noon and 2–4pm, Sun 2–4pm. Tube: Sloane Sq.

This dignified institution, founded by Charles II in 1682 as a home for veteran soldiers, was designed and completed by Sir Christopher Wren in 1692. There's been little change to Wren's design, except for minor work done by Robert Adam in the 18th century, and the addition of the stables, designed by Sir John Soane in 1814. The main block containing the hall and chapel is flanked by east and west wings. The duke of Wellington lay in state in the hall from November 10 to 17, 1852. So many people thronged here to see him that two were crushed to death.

✪ Horse Guards. Whitehall, SW1. ☎ **0171/414-2396.**

North of Downing Street, on the west side of Whitehall, is the building of the Horse Guards, designed by William Kent, chief architect to George II, as the headquarters of the British Army. The real draw here is the Horse Guards themselves: Their unit is the Household Cavalry Mounted Regiment, which is a union of the two oldest and most senior regiments in the British Army: The Life Guards and the Blues and Royals. In theory, their duty is to protect the sovereign. "Life Guards" wear red tunics and white plumes and the "Blues and Royals" are attired in blue tunics with red plumes. Two much-photographed mounted members of the Household Cavalry keep watch daily from 10am to 5pm. The mounted sentries change duty every hour as a benefit to the horses. Foot sentries change every two hours. The chief guard rather grandly inspects the troops here daily at 4pm. The guard, with flair and fanfare, dismounts at 5pm.

Some visitors prefer the **changing of the guards** here to the more famous ceremony at Buckingham Palace. Beginning around 11am Monday to Saturday and 10:30am on Sunday, a new guard leaves the Hyde Park Barracks, rides down Pall Mall, and arrives at the Horse Guards building, all in about 30 minutes. The old guard then returns to the barracks.

If you pass through the arch at Horse Guards, you'll find yourself at the **Horse Guards Parade,** which opens onto St. James's Park. This spacious court provides the best view of the various architectural styles that make up Whitehall. Regrettably, the parade ground itself is now a parking lot.

The military pageant—the most famous in Britain—known as **Trooping the Colour,** which celebrates the queen's birthday, takes place in June at the Horse Guards Parade (see the "London Calendar of Events" in chapter 2). The "Colour" refers to the flag of the regiment. For devotees of pomp and circumstance, "Beating the Retreat" is staged here 3 or 4 evenings a week during the first 2 weeks of June. It's only a dress rehearsal, though, for Trooping the Colour.

Spencer House. 27 St. James's Place, SW1. ☎ **0171/499-8620.** £6 ($9.90) adults, £5 ($8.25) children under 16, children under 10 not allowed. Sun 10:30am–5:30pm. Closed Jan and Aug. Tube: Green Park.

This is one of the city's most beautiful buildings. It was constructed in 1766 for the first Earl Spencer, who intended it as an exuberant shrine to Georgiana Poyntz, his childhood sweetheart whom he had secretly married the year before. It hasn't been a private residence since 1927, and had something of a checkered history until it was restored and opened as a museum in 1990. Rooms are filled with period furniture and art loans, some even from Queen Elizabeth herself. The most spectacular salon is the Palm Room, all in white, gold, and green.

St. Pancras Station. Euston Rd., NW1. Tube: King's Cross/St. Pancras.

The London terminus for the Midland Railway, St. Pancras Station (1863–67) is a masterpiece of Victorian engineering. Designed by W. H. Barlow, the 689-foot-long glass-and-iron train shed spans 240 feet in width and rises to a peak of 100 feet above the rails. The platforms were raised 20 feet above the ground because the tracks ran over the Regent's Canal before entering the station. The pièce de résistance, though, is Sir George Gilbert Scott's fanciful Midland Grand Hotel. Done in high Gothic style, it's graced with pinnacles, towers, and gables; it now functions as office space. The facade runs 565 feet and is flanked by a clock tower and a west tower.

LEGAL LONDON

The smallest borough in London, bustling **Holborn** (*ho*-burn) is often referred to as "Legal London"; it's home to the majority of the city's barristers, solicitors, and law clerks as well as the ancient **Inns of Court** (Tube: Holborn, Chancery Lane). All barristers (litigators) must belong to one of these institutions, and many work from their dignified ancient buildings: **Gray's Inn, Lincoln's Inn** (the best preserved of the three), and the **Middle and Inner Temple** (just over the line inside the City). They were severely damaged during World War II, and the razed buildings were replaced with modern offices, but the borough still retains pockets of its former days.

Gray's Inn. Gray's Inn Rd. (north of High Holborn; entrance on Theobald's Rd.), WC1. ☎ **0171/458-7800.** Free admission to squares and gardens. Daily 6am–midnight. Tube: Chancery Lane.

To enter the hall, guests must make a written application. Gray's Inn is the fourth of the ancient Inns of Court still in operation. As you enter, you'll see a late-Georgian terrace lined with buildings that, like many of the other houses in the inns, serve as both residences and offices. Gray's was restored after suffering heavy damage in World War II. It contains a rebuilt Tudor Hall, but its greatest attraction is the tree-shaded lawn and handsome gardens. The 17th-century atmosphere exists today only in the square. Scientist-philosopher Francis Bacon (1561–1626) was the inn's most eminent tenant.

Law Courts. Strand, WC2. Free admission. No cameras, tape recorders, video cameras, or cellular phones allowed during sessions. Mon–Fri 10am–4:30pm. Tube: Holborn or Temple.

At these 60 or more courts presently in use, all civil and some criminal cases are heard. Designed by G. E. Street, the neo-Gothic buildings (1874–1882) contain more than 1,000 rooms and 3½ miles of corridors. Sculptures of Jesus, King Solomon, and King Alfred grace the front door; Moses is depicted at the back entrance. On the second Saturday in November, the annually elected lord mayor is sworn in by the lord chief justice.

Lincoln's Inn. Carey St., WC1. ☎ **0171/405-1393.** Free admission. Mon–Fri 7am–7pm. Tube: Holborn or Chancery Lane.

Lincoln's Inn is the oldest of the four Inns of Court. Between the City and the West End, Lincoln's Inn comprises 11 acres, including lawns, squares, gardens, a 17th-century chapel (open Monday to Friday 12:30 to 2pm), a library, and two halls. One of these,

Old Hall, dates from 1490 and has remained almost unaltered with its linenfold paneling, stained glass, and wooden screen by Inigo Jones. It was once the home of Sir Thomas More, and it was where barristers met, ate, and debated 150 years before the *Mayflower* sailed on its epic voyage. Old Hall set the scene for the opening chapter of Charles Dickens's *Bleak House.* The other hall, Great Hall, remains one of the finest Tudor Revival buildings in London, and was opened by Queen Victoria in 1843. It's now the center of the inn and is used for the formal ceremony of calling students to the bar.

Middle Temple Hall. Middle Temple Lane, EC4. ☎ **0171/427-4800.** Free admission. Mon–Fri 10–11:30am and 3–4pm. Tube: Temple.

From the Victoria Embankment, Middle Temple Lane runs between Middle and Inner Temple Gardens to the area known as The Temple, named after the medieval order of the Knights Templar (originally formed by the Crusaders in Jerusalem in the 12th century). It was in the Middle Temple Garden that Henry VI's barons are supposed to have picked the blooms of red and white roses and started the War of the Roses in 1430; today only members of the Temple and their guests are allowed to enter the gardens. But the Middle Temple contains a Tudor hall, completed in 1570, that's open to the public. It's believed that Shakespeare's troupe played *Twelfth Night* here for the first time in 1602. A table on view is said to have been built from timber from Sir Francis Drake's *The Golden Hind.*

Old Bailey. Newgate St., EC4. ☎ **0171/248-3277.** Free admission. Court in session Mon–Fri 10:30am–1pm and 2–4:30pm. Children under 14 not admitted; those 14–16 must be accompanied by a responsible adult. No cameras, tape recorders, or cell phones (and there are no checking facilities). Tube: St. Paul's. To get here from the Temple, travel east on Fleet St., which becomes Ludgate Hill; cross Ludgate Circus and turn left at the Old Bailey, a domed structure with the figure of *Justice* atop it.

This courthouse replaced the infamous Newgate Prison, once the scene of hangings and other forms of "public entertainment." It's affectionately known as the "Old Bailey" after a street that runs nearby. It's fascinating to watch the bewigged barristers presenting their cases to the high-court judges. Entry is strictly on a first-arrival basis, and guests line up outside; security will then direct you to one of the rooms where cases are being tried. You enter courts 1 to 4, 17, and 18 from Newgate Street, and the balance from Old Bailey (the street).

Royal Courts of Justice. The Strand, WC2. ☎ **0171/936-6751.** Free admission. No cameras, video cameras, tape recorders, or cell phones. Mon–Fri 10am–4:30pm. Tube: Temple.

Completed in 1882 but designed in 13th-century style, this is the home of such courts as admiralty, divorce, probate, chancery, appeals, and Queen's Bench. There's a new exhibition of judicial robes at the Carey Street entrance. Leave the Royal Courts building by the rear door, and you'll be on Carey Street, not far from New Square.

Staple Inn. High Holborn, WC1. ☎ **0171/242-5240.** Free admission. Tube: Chancery Lane.

This half-timbered old inn, near the Chancery Lane Tube stop, and eight other former Inns of Chancery are no longer in use in the legal world. Now lined with shops, it was built between 1545 and 1589 and has been reconstructed many times. Dr. Johnson moved here in 1759, the year *Rasselas* was published.

LITERARY LANDMARKS

For more literary sightseeing, see "Hampstead" in "Attractions on the Outskirts," below.

A Neighborhood of One's Own:
The Homes of Virginia Woolf

Born in London in 1882, author and essayist Virginia Woolf used the city as the setting of many of her novels, including *Jacob's Room* (1922). The daughter of Sir Leslie Stephen and his wife Julia Duckworth, Virginia spent her formative years at **22 Hyde Park Gate,** off Kensington Road, west of Royal Albert Hall. Her mother died in 1895 and her father in 1904.

After the death of their father, Virginia and her sister Vanessa left Kensington for Bloomsbury, settling near the British Museum. It was an interesting move, as Bloomsbury was a neighborhood that upper-class Victorians didn't view as "respectable." But Virginia was to make it her own, and in the process, make the district world famous as the hub of literary London. From 1905, the Stephens lived at **46 Gordon Square,** east of Gower Street and University College. It was here that the celebrated circle known as the "Bloomsbury Group" came into being. In time it would embrace Clive Bell and Leonard Woolf, future husbands of Vanessa and Virginia. Later, Virginia went to live at **29 Fitzroy Square,** west of Tottenham Court Road, in a house once occupied by Bernard Shaw.

During the next two decades, Virginia resided at several more Bloomsbury addresses, including **Brunswick Square, Tavistock Square,** and **Mecklenburg Square.** These places have either disappeared or been altered beyond recognition. During this time, the Bloomsbury Group reached out to include the artists Roger Fry and Duncan Grant, and Virginia became a friend of economist John Maynard Keynes and author E. M. Forster (*A Passage to India*). At Tavistock Square (1924–39) and at Mecklenburg Square (1939–40), she operated the Hogarth Press with Leonard. She published her own early work here, as well as T. S. Eliot's *The Waste Land.*

To escape urban life, Leonard and Virginia purchased Monk's House, in the village of Rodmell, between Lewes and Newhaven in Sussex. They lived there until 1941, when Virginia, deeply disturbed by the horrors of war, drowned herself in the nearby Ouse. Her ashes are buried in the garden at Monk's House.

Carlyle's House. 24 Cheyne Row, SW3. ☎ **0171/352-7087** or 01494/755-559. Admission £3.30 ($5.45) adults, £1.65 ($2.70) children. Wed–Fri 2–5pm, Sat–Sun 11am–5pm. Tube: Sloane Sq. Bus: 11, 19, 22, 49, or 239.

From 1834 to 1881, Thomas Carlyle, author of *The French Revolution,* and Jane Baillie Welsh Carlyle, his noted letter-writing wife, resided in this modest 1708 terraced house. Furnished essentially as it was in Carlyle's day, the house is located about three-quarters of a block from the Thames, near the Chelsea Embankment, along King's Road. It was described by his wife as being "of most antique physiognomy, quite to our humour; all wainscotted, carved, and queer-looking, roomy, substantial, commodious, with closets to satisfy any Bluebeard." The second floor contains Mrs. Carlyle's drawing room, but the most interesting chamber is the not-so-soundproof "soundproof" study in the skylit attic. Filled with Carlyle memorabilia—his books, a letter from Disraeli, personal effects, a writing chair, even his death mask—this is where the author did his work.

Dickens House. 48 Doughty St., WC1. ☎ **0171/405-2127.** Admission £3.50 ($5.75) adults, £2.50 ($4.15) students, £1.50 ($2.45) children, £7 ($11.55) families. Mon–Fri 9:45am–5:30pm, Sat 10am–5pm. Tube: Russell Sq.

Here in Bloomsbury stands the simple abode in which Charles Dickens wrote *Oliver Twist* and finished *The Pickwick Papers* (his American readers actually waited at the dock for the ship that brought in each new installment). The place is almost a shrine: It contains his study, manuscripts, and personal relics, as well as reconstructed interiors.

Samuel Johnson's House. 17 Gough Sq., EC4. ☎ **0171/353-3745.** Admission £3 ($4.95) adults, £2 ($3.30) students and seniors, £1 ($1.65) children, free for children 10 and under. Apr–Sept Mon–Sat 11am–5:30pm; Oct–Mar Mon–Sat 11am–5pm. Tube: Blackfriars or Temple. Bus from Trafalgar: 11, 15, or 23. Walk up New Bridge St. and turn left onto Fleet; Gough Sq. is tiny and hidden, north of Fleet St.

Dr. Johnson and his copyists compiled his famous dictionary in this Queen Anne house, where the lexicographer, poet, essayist, and fiction writer lived from 1748 to 1759. Although Johnson also lived at Staple Inn in Holborn and at a number of other places, the Gough Square house is the only one of his residences remaining in London. The 17th-century building has been painstakingly restored, and it's well worth a visit.

After you're done touring the house, you might want to stop in at **Ye Olde Cheshire Cheese,** Wine Court Office Court, 145 Fleet St. (☎ **0171/353-6170**), Johnson's favorite locale. He must have had some lean nights at the pub, because by the time he had compiled his dictionary, he'd already spent his advance of 1,500 guineas. G. K. Chesterton, author of *What's Wrong with the World* (1910) and *The Superstition of Divorce* (1920), was also a familiar patron at the pub.

MUSEUMS & GALLERIES

Apsley House, The Wellington Museum. 149 Piccadilly, Hyde Park Corner, SW1. ☎ **0171/499-5676.** Admission £4.50 ($7.45) adults, £3 ($4.95) seniors and children 12–17, free for children under 12. Tues–Sun 11am–5pm. Tube: Hyde Park Corner.

This was the mansion of the duke of Wellington, one of Britain's greatest generals. The "Iron Duke" defeated Napoléon at Waterloo, but later, for a short period while prime minister, he had to have iron shutters fitted to his windows to protect him from the mob outraged by his autocratic opposition to reform. (His unpopularity soon passed, however.)

The house is crammed with art treasures, including three original Velázquez paintings, and military mementos that include the duke's medals and battlefield orders. Apsley House also holds some of the finest silver and porcelain pieces in Europe in the Plate and China Room. Grateful to Wellington for saving their thrones, European monarchs endowed him with treasures. The collection includes a Sèvres Egyptian service that was intended as a divorce present from Napoléon to Josephine (but she refused it); Louis XVIII eventually presented it to Wellington. The Portuguese Silver Service, created between 1812 and 1816, has been hailed as the single greatest artifact of Portuguese neoclassical silver.

✪ **British Library.** 96 Euston Rd., NW1. ☎ **0171/412-7000.** Free admission. Mon, Wed–Fri 9:30am–6pm, Tues 9:30am–8pm, Sat 9:30am–5pm, Sun 11am–5pm. Tube: King's Cross/St. Pancras.

One of the world's greatest libraries is no longer at the British Museum but has moved to St. Pancras. The move began in December 1996, as the library shifted some 12 million books, manuscripts, and other items. In the new library, you get modernistic beauty rather than the fading glamour and the ghosts of Karl Marx, Thackery, and Virginia Woolf of the famous old library at the British Museum. You are also likely to get the book you want within an hour instead of three days. Academics, students, writers, and bookworms from all over the world come here. On our left was a student researching the history of pubs.

The bright, roomy interior is far more inviting than the rather dull redbrick exterior suggests (it earned the condemnation of Prince Charles). The writer, Alain de Botton, likened the exterior to a Tesco, a reference to one of Britain's supermarket chains. The architect, Colin St. John Wilson, has been delighted by the positive response to his building. Even Prince Charles, taking a private tour, was very encouraging, although he failed to publicly air his comments after his earlier dismissal. The most spectacular room is the Humanities Reading Room, constructed on three levels and with daylight filtered through the ceiling.

The fascinating collection includes such items of historical and literary interest as two of the four surviving copies of King John's Magna Carta (1215), a Gutenberg Bible, Nelson's last letter to Lady Hamilton, and the journals of Captain Cook. Almost every major author—Dickens, Jane Austen, Charlotte Brontë, Keats, hundreds of others—is represented in the section devoted to English literature. Beneath Roubiliac's 1758 statue of Shakespeare stands a case of documents relating to the Bard, including a mortgage bearing his signature and a copy of the First Folio of 1623. There's also an unrivaled collection of philatelic items.

Visitors can also view the Diamond Sutra, dating from 868, said to be the oldest surviving printed book. Using headphones set up around the room, you can also hear thrilling audio snippets, even James Joyce reading a passage from *Finnegans Wake*. Curiosities include the earliest known tape of a birdcall, dating from 1889. Particularly intriguing is an exhibition called "Turning the Pages." You can, for example, electronically read a complete Leonardo da Vinci notebook, putting your hands on a special computer screen that flips from one page to another. There is a copy of the *Canterbury Tales* from 1410, even manuscripts from *Beowulf* (ca. 1000). Illuminated texts from some of the oldest known Biblical displays include the *Codex Sinaitticus* and *Codex Alexandrius*, 3rd-century Greek gospels. In the Historical Documents section are epistles by everybody from Henry VIII to Napoléon, from Elizabeth I to Churchill. In the music displays, you can seek out works by Beethoven, Handel, and Stravinsky, even lyric drafts by Paul McCartney and John Lennon. An entire day spent here will only scratch the surface.

Walking tours of the library cost £4 ($6.60) for adults or £3 ($4.95) for seniors, students and children. They are conducted Wednesday to Monday at 3pm, Tuesday at 6:30pm, with an extra tour on Saturday at 10:30am. Reservations are advised three weeks in advance.

An Open Sesame to Viewing

If you're coming to London to pub crawl, forget it, but if you want to become a serious museumgoer, you can save a lot of money by purchasing the London White Card. Available to individuals or families, it is a real saver pass if you plan to visit a lot of museums, including some of the major attractions of London: the Museum of Moving Image, the Victoria and Albert Museum, the Science Museum, and the Design Museum, plus a lot more. Validity ranges from 3 to 7 days. An adult 3-day costs £16 ($26.40), a 7-day card going for £26 ($42.90). Families of two adults and up to four children can purchase a 3-day card for £32 ($52.80) or a 7-day card for £50 ($82.50). Cards are sold at British tourist information centers, London Transport centers, airports, and various attractions. For more details, call ☎ **0171/923-0807.**

✪ **Courtauld Gallery.** Somerset House, The Strand, WC2. ☎ **0171/873-2526.** Admission £4 ($6.60) adults, £2 ($3.30) students, free for children under 18. Mon–Sat 10am–6pm, Sun noon–6pm; last admission 5:15pm. Tube: Temple or Covent Garden.

Although surprisingly little-known, the Courtauld contains a fabulous wealth of paintings. It has one of the world's greatest collections of Impressionist works outside of Paris. There are French Impressionists and post-Impressionists, with masterpieces by Monet, Manet, Degas, Renoir, Cézanne, van Gogh, and Gauguin. The gallery also has a superb collection of Old-Master paintings and drawings, including works by Rubens, Michelangelo, and Tiepolo; early-Italian paintings, ivories, and majolica; the Lee collection of old masters; early-20th-century English and French paintings, as well as 20th-century British paintings.

Like the Frick Collection in New York, it's a superb display, a visual feast in a jewel-like setting. We come here at least once every season to revisit one painting in particular: Manet's *A Bar at the Folies-Bergère*—exquisite. Many of the paintings are displayed without glass, giving the gallery a more intimate feeling than most.

Design Museum. Butler's Wharf, Shad Thamas, SE1. ☎ **0171/378-6055.** Admission £5.50 ($9.05) adults, £4 ($6.60) children, £12 ($19.80) family ticket. Daily 11:30am–6pm. Tube: Tower Hill or London Bridge.

The Design Museum is a showcase of modern design—kind of like Conran's without the price tags. It's the only museum in Europe that explains why and how mass-produced objects work and look the way they do and how design contributes to the quality of our lives. The collection of objects includes cars, furniture, domestic appliances, graphics, and ceramics, as well as changing displays of new products and prototypes from around the world. The cafe offers panoramic views of Tower Bridge and the Thames.

Florence Nightingale Museum. St. Thomas' Hospital, 2 Mabeth Palace Rd., SE1. ☎ **0171/620-0374.** Admission £3.50 ($5.75) adults, £2.50 ($4.15) seniors and children. Tues–Sun 10am–5pm. Tube: Waterloo Station.

The life and work of one of England's most influential women of the 1800s is highlighted in this museum dedicated to her. You learn that her most famous accomplishment—nursing soldiers at Scutari Hospital in Turkey during the Crimean War—was only a small part of a career spanning half a century. Recapturing her life are such artifacts as an original letter written from the hospital and by the light of her famous lamp. Nightingale did everything from raise the image of the British soldier from a brawling lowlife to a heroic working man to making nursing a respectable profession. Believe it or not, before the "Lady with Her Lamp," nursing was seen as fit only for prostitutes.

In 1896 Nightingale "retired to her bed," but didn't slow down. She continued to write on public health. Much of her advice is still valid today. When she died in 1910 at the age of 90, she had become so reclusive that the general public assumed she was already dead.

Geffrye Museum. Kingsland Rd., E2. ☎ **0171/739-9893.** Free admission. Tues–Sat 10am–5pm, Sun 2–5pm. Gardens open Apr–Oct. Tube: Liverpool. Bus: 149 from Bishopsgate or 242.

Those who'd like a preview of British interiors and lifestyles over the past four centuries, head here to the East End for a series of restored 18th-century almshouses that escaped Hitler's blitz. Period rooms are arranged chronologically allowing you to follow changing tastes in the days of the Empire. You'll see the development of furnishings and objets d'art in English middle-class homes. Originally, in 1715, these almshouses belonged to the Ironmongers' Company. The architecture alone is worth a visit. Gardens in front attract much attention, especially the herb garden. The collection inside is particularly rich in Jacobean and Georgian interiors, and strongest in the Victorian period. In the 20th century, you'll see the richness of art deco and the bleakness of the utilitarian designs that followed in the aftermath of World War II. Newer galleries showcase the decor of the latter 20th century, and there is also a design center and a cafe/restaurant.

Hayward Gallery. On the South Bank, SE1, ☎ **0171/960-4242,** or 0171/261-0127 for recorded information. Admission £6 ($9.90) adults, £4 ($6.60) students, seniors, and children, free for children under 12, £14 ($23.10) family ticket. Fee varies according to exhibitions; children are often half price. Thurs–Mon 10am–6pm, Tues–Wed 10am–8pm. Tube: Waterloo or Embankment.

Opened by Elizabeth II in 1968, this gallery presents a changing program of major contemporary and historical exhibits. It's managed by the South Bank Board, which also includes the Royal Festival Hall, the Queen Elizabeth Hall, and the Purcell Room. The gallery closes between exhibitions, so call before crossing the Thames.

Imperial War Museum. Lambeth Rd., SE1. ☎ **0171/416-5321.** Admission £5.20 ($8.60) adults, £4.20 ($6.95) seniors and students, £2.70 ($4.45) children; free daily 4:30–6pm. Daily 10am–6pm. Tube: Lambeth North or Elephant and Castle.

One of the few major sights south of the Thames, this museum occupies one city block the size of an army barracks, greeting you with 15-inch guns from the battleships *Resolution* and *Ramillies.* The large domed building, constructed in 1815, was the former Bethlehem Royal Hospital for the insane, known as "Bedlam."

A wide range of weapons and equipment is on display, along with models, decorations, uniforms, posters, photographs, and paintings. You can see a Mark V tank, a Battle of Britain Spitfire, and a German one-man submarine, as well as a rifle carried by Lawrence of Arabia. In the Documents Room, you can view the self-styled "political testament" that Hitler dictated in the chancellery bunker in the closing days of World War II, witnessed by henchmen Joseph Goebbels and Martin Bormann, as well as the famous "peace in our time" agreement that Neville Chamberlain brought back from Munich in 1938. (Of his signing the agreement, Hitler later said, "[Chamberlain] was a nice old man, so I decided to give him my autograph.") It's a world of espionage and clandestine warfare in the major new permanent exhibit known as the "Secret War Exhibition," where you can discover the truth behind the image of James Bond—and find out why the real secret war is even stranger and more fascinating than fiction. Displays include many items never before seen in public: coded messages, forged documents, secret wirelesses, and equipment used by spies from World War I to the present day.

Public film shows take place on weekends at 3pm and on certain weekdays during school holidays and on public holidays.

Institute of Contemporary Arts. The Mall, SW1. ☎ **0171/930-3647.** Admission £1.50 ($2.45) Mon–Fri, £2.50 ($4.15) Sat–Sun adults; £1 ($1.65) Mon–Fri, £1.50 ($2.45) Sat–Sun students. Galleries daily noon–7:30pm. Bookstore daily noon–9pm. Three film screenings daily. Tube: Piccadilly Circus or Charing Cross.

London's liveliest cultural program takes place in this temple to the avant-garde, launched in 1947. It keeps Londoners and others up-to-date on the latest in the worlds of cinema, theater, photography, painting, sculpture, and other performing and visual arts media. Technically you have to be a member to visit, but membership is immediately granted. Foreign or experimental movies are shown, and special tributes—perhaps a retrospective of the films of Rainer Werner Fassbinder—are often the order of the day.

The Great Millennium Wheel

The world's largest observation wheel is now rising on the South Bank and should be luring thousands of visitors to London at the millennium. Called the **British Airways London Eye,** it is run by the Tussauds Group of the famous waxworks.

Built by a European consortium with steel by British Steel, this "eye" was conceived and designed by London architects Julia Barfield and David Marks. Sweeping one of the world's most famous skylines at 450 feet, the British Airways London Eye will become the capital's fourth tallest structure when it opens in 2000 on the South Bank of the Thames.

From 32 fully enclosed, high-tech capsules, each accommodating 25 people, its gradual 30-minute, 360-degree rotation will give passengers new perspective of some of London's most famous landmarks, providing a bird's-eye view usually accessible only by aircraft or helicopter.

Barfield and Marks claim inspiration from both the Statue of Liberty in New York and the Eiffel Tower in Paris. They set out to create a millennium monument that people could actively enjoy and take part in—not just look at. More than two million visitors are expected to ride the eye in the first year alone.

It lies close to Westminster Bridge (you can hardly miss it). Tickets for the attraction cost £6.95 ($11.45) for adults and £4.80 ($7.90) for children. When the Eye opens, tickets will be sold on-site, and there will be a telephone box-office number to call. Before heading here check with one of the local British tourist information centers for full details.

The classics are frequently dusted off, along with cult favorites. On Saturday and Sunday at 3pm, the cinémathèque offers screenings for the kids. Sometimes well-known writers and artists speak here, which makes the low cost of membership even more enticing. Experimental plays are also presented. The American computer company that wrote the computer language that helped spawn the Internet, Sun Microsystems, donated £2 million to build a state-of-the-art New Media Centre in 1998. The photo galleries, showing the latest from British and foreign photographers, wouldn't necessarily win the approval of right-wing senator Jesse Helms.

Jewish Museum. 129–131 Albert St., Camden Town, NW1. ☎ 0171/284-1997. £3 ($4.95) adults, £2 ($3.30) seniors, £1.50 ($2.45) children. Sun–Thurs 10am–4pm. Closed Fri, Sat, bank holidays, and Jewish festivals. Tube: Camden Town.

This museum tells the story of Jewish life in Britain. Arriving at the time of the Norman Conquest, Jews survived in England until King Edward I forced them out in 1290. From that time, no Jews (or at least no known Jews) lived in Britain until a small community returned in 1656 during the reign of Elizabeth I. The museum has recently been awarded designated status by the Museums and Galleries Commission for its outstanding collections of Jewish ceremonial art. On display are silver Torah bells made in London and two loving cups presented by the Spanish and Portuguese Synagogue to the lord mayor in the 18th century. The museum also sponsors walking tours of Jewish London; call for details.

Linley Sambourne House. 18 Stafford Terrace, W8. ☎ **0171/937-0663**. Admission £3 ($4.95) adults, £1.50 ($2.45) children 15 and under. Mar–Oct Wed 10am–4pm, Sun 2–5pm. Closed Nov–Feb. Tube: High St. Kensington. Bus: 9, 9a, 10, 27, 33, 49.

You'll step back into the days of Queen Victoria when you visit this house, which has remained unchanged for more than a century. Part of a terrace built in the late 1860s, this five-story, Suffolk brick structure was the home of Linley Sambourne, a legendary cartoonist for *Punch*. In the entrance hall, you see a mixture of styles and clutter that typified Victorian decor, with a plush portière, a fireplace valance, stained glass, and a large set of antlers vying for attention. The drawing room alone contains an incredible number of items of Victoriana.

London Transport Museum. The Piazza, Covent Garden, WC2. ☎ **0171/379-6344.** Admission £4.45 ($7.35) adults, £2.50 ($4.15) children, £12.85 ($21.20) family ticket, free for children under 5. Sat–Thurs 10am–6pm, Fri 11am–6pm (last entrance at 5:15pm). Tube: Covent Garden.

A collection of nearly 2 centuries of historic vehicles is displayed in a splendid Victorian building that formerly housed the Flower Market at Covent Garden. The museum shows how London's transport system evolved, and a representative collection of road vehicles includes a reconstruction of George Shillibeer's Omnibus of 1829. A steam locomotive that ran on the world's first underground railway, a knifeboard horse bus, London's first trolleybus, and the Feltham tram are also of particular interest. One of the unique and popular features of the museum is the number of participatory exhibits, which allow you to operate the controls of a Tube train, a tram, a bus, and full-size signaling equipment. The shop sells those fabulous "London by Tube" posters you see throughout the Underground. They've recently added "Kidzones"—interactive programs for children so parents can enjoy the museum without having to entertain the kids.

✪ **Museum of London.** 150 London Wall, EC2. ☎ **0171/600-3699.** Admission £5 ($8.25) adults, £3 ($4.95) children, students, and seniors, £12 ($19.80) family ticket. Tues–Sat 10am–5:50pm, Sun noon–5:50pm. Tube: St. Paul's or Barbican.

In London's Barbican district near St. Paul's Cathedral, overlooking the city's Roman and medieval walls, the museum traces the history of London from prehistoric times to the 20th century through archaeological finds; paintings and prints; social, industrial, and historical artifacts; and costumes, maps, and models. Exhibits are arranged so that you can begin and end your chronological stroll through 250,000 years at the main entrance to the museum. The museum's pièce de résistance is the Lord Mayor's Coach, a gilt-and-scarlet fairy-tale coach built in 1757 and weighing in at 3 tons, but you can also see the Great Fire of London in living color and sound; the death mask of Oliver Cromwell; cell doors from Newgate Prison, made famous by Charles Dickens; and most amazing of all, a shop counter showing pre–World War II prices.

Museum of the Moving Image (MOMI). South Bank (underneath Waterloo Bridge), SE1. ☎ **0171/401-2636.** Admission £6.25 ($10.30) adults, £5.25 ($8.65) students, £4.50 ($7.45) children and seniors, £17 ($28.05) family ticket (up to 2 adults and 2 children). Daily 10am–6pm (last admission 5pm). Tube: Waterloo or Embankment.

MOMI, part of the South Bank complex, traces the history of cinema and TV, taking you on an incredible journey from cinema's earliest experiments to modern animation, from Charlie Chaplin to the operation of a TV studio. There are artifacts to handle, buttons to push, and a cast of actors to tell visitors more. Three to four changing exhibitions are presented yearly; it's wise to allow 2 hours for a visit.

National Army Museum. Royal Hospital Rd., SW3. ☎ **0171/730-0717.** Free admission. Daily 10am–5:30pm. Closed Good Friday, first Mon in May, and for some days around Christmas. Tube: Sloane Sq.

The National Army Museum occupies a building adjoining the Royal Hospital, a home for retired soldiers. Whereas the Imperial War Museum is concerned only with wars in the 20th century, the National Army Museum tells the colorful story of British armies from 1485 on. Here you'll find uniforms worn by British soldiers in every corner of the world, plus weapons and other gear, flags, and medals. Even the skeleton of Napoléon's favorite charger is here. Also on display are Florence Nightingale's jewelry, Hitler's telephone exchange (captured in 1945), and Orders and Medals of HRH the Duke of Windsor. A more recent gallery, "The Rise of the Redcoats," contains exhibitions detailing the life of the British soldier from 1485 to 1793. Included in the exhibit are displays on the English Civil War and the American War of Independence.

✪ National Portrait Gallery. St. Martin's Place, WC2. ☎ **0171/306-0055.** Free admission; fee charged for certain temporary exhibitions. Mon–Sat 10am–6pm, Sun noon–6pm. Tube: Charing Cross.

In a gallery of remarkable and unremarkable pictures (they're collected here for their notable subjects rather than their artistic quality), a few paintings tower over the rest, including Sir Joshua Reynolds's first portrait of Samuel Johnson ("a man of most dreadful appearance"). Among the best are Nicholas Hilliard's miniature of a handsome Sir Walter Raleigh and a full-length Elizabeth I, along with the Holbein cartoon of Henry VIII. There's also a portrait of William Shakespeare (with a gold earring, no less) by an unknown artist that bears the claim of being the "most authentic contemporary likeness" of its subject. One of the most famous pictures in the gallery is the group portrait of the Brontë sisters (Charlotte, Emily, and Anne) painted by their brother, Bramwell. An idealized portrait of Lord Byron by Thomas Phillips is also on display.

The galleries of Victorian and early-20th-century portraits were radically redesigned recently. Occupying the whole of the first floor, they display portraits from 1837 (when Victoria took the throne) to present day; later 20th-century portraiture includes major works by such artists as Warhol and Hambling. Portraits of some of the more flamboyant personalities of the last two centuries are on show: T. S. Eliot, Disraeli, Macmillan, Sir Richard Burton, Elizabeth Taylor, Baroness Thatcher, and our two favorites: G. F. Watts' famous portrait of his great actress wife, Ellen Terry, and Vanessa Bell's portrait of her sister, Virginia Woolf. The late Princess Diana is on the Royal Landing, and this portrait seems to attract the most viewers. The Gallery has recently opened a new cafe and art bookshop.

Natural History Museum. Cromwell Rd., SW7. ☎ **0171/938-9123.** Admission £6 ($9.90) adults, £3.20 ($5.30) seniors and students, £3 ($4.95) children 5–17, free for children 4 and under, £16 ($26.40) family ticket; free to everyone Mon–Fri after 4:30pm and Sat–Sun after 5pm. Mon–Sat 10am–5:50pm, Sun 11am–5:50pm. Tube: South Kensington.

This is the home of the national collections of living and fossil plants, animals, and minerals, with many magnificent specimens on display. Exciting exhibits designed to encourage people of all ages to learn about natural history include "Human Biology—An Exhibition of Ourselves," "Our Place in Evolution," "Origin of the Species," "Creepy Crawlies," and "Discovering Mammals." The Mineral Gallery displays marvelous examples of crystals and gemstones. Also in the museum is the Meteorite Pavilion, which exhibits fragments of rock that have crashed into the earth, some from the farthest reaches of the galaxy. What attracts the most attention is the huge dinosaur exhibit, displaying 14 complete skeletons. The center of the show depicts a trio of full-size robotic Deinonychus enjoying a freshly killed Tenontosaurus for lunch. The latest addition is "Earth Galleries," an exhibition outlining humankind's relationship with planet Earth. Here in the exhibition "Earth Today and Tomorrow," visitors are invited to explore the planet's dramatic history from the big bang to its inevitable death.

Percival David Foundation of Chinese Art. 53 Gordon Sq., WC1. ☎ **0171/387-3909.**
Free admission. Donations encouraged; £4 ($6.60) for a guided tour of 10–20 people. Admission to the library must be arranged with the curator ahead of time. Mon–Fri 10:30am–5pm.
Tube: Russell Sq. or Euston Sq. Bus: 7, 8, 10, 14, 18, 19, 24, 25, or 27.

This foundation displays the greatest collection of Chinese ceramics outside of China. Approximately 1,700 ceramic objects reflect Chinese court taste from the 10th to 18th centuries, and include many pieces of exceptional beauty. An extraordinary collection of stoneware from the Song (960–1279) and Yuan (1279–1368) dynasties includes examples of rare Ru and Guan wares. Among the justifiably famous blue-and-white porcelains are two unique temple vases, dated by inscription to A.D. 1351. A wide variety of polychrome wares is also represented; these include examples of the delicate doucai wares from the Chenghua period (1465–87) as well as a remarkable group of 18th-century porcelains.

Royal Academy of Arts. Burlington House, Piccadilly, W1. ☎ **0171/300-8000.** Admission varies, depending on the exhibition. Daily 10am–6pm (last admission 5:30pm). Tube: Piccadilly Circus or Green Park.

Established in 1768, this organization included Sir Joshua Reynolds, Thomas Gainsborough, and Benjamin West among its founding members. Since its beginning, each member had to donate a work of art, and so over the years the academy has built up a sizable collection. The outstanding treasure is Michelangelo's beautiful relief of *Madonna and Child.* The annual Summer Exhibition has been held for more than 200 years; see the "London Calendar of Events," in chapter 2 for details.

Royal Mews. Buckingham Palace. Buckingham Palace Rd., SW1. ☎ **0171/839-1377.**
Admission £4.20 ($6.95) adults, £3.20 ($5.30) seniors, £2.10 ($3.45) children under 17.
Tues–Thurs noon–4pm. Tube: Green Park or Victoria.

This is where you can get a close look at Her Majesty's State Coach, built in 1761 to the designs of Sir William Chambers and decorated with paintings by Cipriani. Traditionally drawn by eight gray horses, it was formerly used by sovereigns when they traveled to open Parliament and on other state occasions; Queen Elizabeth traveled in it to her 1953 coronation and in 1977 for her Silver Jubilee Procession. The queen's carriage horses are also housed here, as well as other state coaches.

✪ The Saatchi Gallery. 98A Boundary Rd., NW8. ☎ **0171/624-8299.** Admission £4 ($6.60), children under 12 free. Thurs–Sun 12–6pm. Tube: St. John's Wood or Swiss Cottage.

In the world of contemporary art, this collection is unparalleled. Charles Saatchi is one of Britain's greatest private collectors, and this personal museum features rotating displays from his vast holdings. Enter through the unmarked metal gateway of a former paint warehouse. The aim, as set forth by Saatchi, is to introduce new and unfamiliar art to a wider audience. The collection comprises more than 1,000 paintings and sculptures. Works that are not on display at the gallery are frequently on loan to museums around the world.

The main focus is works by young British artists, including such controversial ones as Damien Hirst's 14-foot tiger shark preserved in a formaldehyde-filled tank. Also on occasional exhibit is Marc Quinn's frozen "head" cast from nine pints of plasma taken from the artist over several months. Art critics were shocked at Richard Wilson's art when it was introduced: 2,500 gallons of used sump oil that flooded through an entire gallery. Young American and European artists are also represented, their work often controversial as well. Regardless of the exhibition on display at the time of your visit, it's almost guaranteed to be fascinating. And if you've ever wondered what many British people think American tourists look like, catch Duane Hanson's *Tourists II* (1988). It's devastating!

Science Museum. Exhibition Rd., SW7. ☎ **0171/938-8000.** Admission £6.50 ($10.75) adults, £3.50 ($5.75) children 5–17, free for children under 5. Free to all after 4:30pm. Daily 10am–6pm. Tube: South Kensington.

This museum traces the development of science and industry and their influence on everyday life. These are among the largest, most comprehensive, and most significant scientific collections anywhere. On display is Stephenson's original rocket, the tiny prototype railroad engine; you can also see Whittle's original jet engine and the Apollo 10 space module. The King George III Collection of scientific instruments is the highlight of a gallery on science in the 18th century. Health Matters is a permanent gallery on modern medicine. The museum has two hands-on galleries, as well as working models and video displays.

Shakespeare's Globe Theatre & Exhibition. New Globe Walk, Southwork, SE1. ☎ **0171/902-1500.** Exhibition and tour admission £6 ($9.90) adults, £4 ($6.60) children 15 and under, £5 ($8.25) seniors and students. Guided tours £5 ($8.25) adults, £4 ($6.60) students and seniors, £3 ($4.95) children 15 and under. May–Sept daily 9:30am–2pm, Oct–Apr daily 10am–5pm (guided tours every 30 minutes or so). Tube: Mansion House or London Bridge.

This is a recent re-creation of what was probably the most important public theater ever built—on the exact site where many of Shakespeare's plays opened. The late American filmmaker, Sam Wanamaker, worked for some 20 years to raise funds to re-create the theater as it existed in Elizabethan times, thatched roof and all. A fascinating exhibit tells the story of the Globe's construction, using the material (including goat hair in the plaster), techniques, and craftsmanship of 400 years ago. The new Globe isn't an exact replica: It seats 1,500 patrons, not the 3,000 that regularly squeezed in during the early 1600s; and *this* thatched roof has been specially treated with a fire retardant. Guided tours of the facility are offered throughout the day.

In May 1997, the Globe's company staged its first slate of plays. See "The Play's the Thing: The London Theater Scene" in chapter 9 for details on attending a play here.

Sherlock Holmes Museum. 221B Baker St., NW1. ☎ **0171/935-8866.** Admission £5 ($8.25) adults, £3 ($4.95) children, under 7 free. Daily 9:30am–6pm. Tube: Baker St.

Where but on Baker Street would there be a museum displaying mementos of this famed fictional detective? Museum officials call it "the world's most famous address" (although 10 Downing St. is a rival for the title); it was here that mystery writer Sir Arthur Conan Doyle created a residence for Sherlock Holmes and his faithful Dr. Watson. These sleuths "lived" here from 1881 to 1904. In Victorian rooms, you can examine a range of exhibits, including published Holmes adventures, and letters written to Holmes. This is a very commercial and artificial museum, but Holmes buffs don't seem to mind.

۞ Sir John Soane's Museum. 13 Lincoln's Inn Fields, WC2. ☎ **0171/430-0175.** Free admission (donations invited). Tues–Sat 10am–5pm; first Tues of each month 6–9pm. Tours given Sat at 2:30pm; £3 ($4.95) tickets distributed at 2pm on a first-come, first-served basis (group tours by appointment only; call 0171/405-2107). Tube: Holborn.

This is the former home of Sir John Soane (1753–1837), an architect who rebuilt the Bank of England (not the present structure). With his multiple levels, fool-the-eye mirrors, flying arches, and domes, Soane was a master of perspective and a genius of interior space (his picture gallery, for example, is filled with three times the number of paintings that a room of similar dimensions would be likely to hold). One prize of the collection is William Hogarth's satirical series *The Rake's Progress,* which includes his much-reproduced *Orgy* and *The Election,* a satire on mid-18th-century politics. Soane also filled his house with classical sculpture including the sarcophagus of Pharaoh

Seti I, which was found in a burial chamber in the Valley of the Kings. Also on display are architectural drawings from Soane's collection of 30,000.

Theatre Museum. Russell St., WC2. ☎ **0171/836-7891.** £4.50 ($7.45) adults, £2.50 ($4.15) seniors and children 5–17. Tues–Sun 11am–7pm. Tube: Covent Garden.

This branch of the Victoria and Albert Museum contains the national collections of the performing arts, encompassing theater, ballet, opera, music hall, pantomime, puppets, circus, and rock and pop music. Daily makeup demonstrations and costume workshops are run using costumes from the Royal Shakespeare Company and the Royal National Theatre. The museum also has a major Diaghilev archive.

Insider Tip: The box office inside offers tickets to West End plays—including the hot ones—as well as to concerts, dramas, and musicals, with almost no markup in most cases.

Wallace Collection. Manchester Sq., W1. ☎ **0171/935-0687.** Free admission. Mon–Sat 10am–5pm, Sun 2–5pm. Tube: Bond St. or Baker St.

Located in a palatial setting (the modestly described "town house" of the late Lady Wallace), this collection is a contrasting array of art and armaments. The art collection (mostly French) includes works by Watteau, Boucher, Fragonard, and Greuze, as well as such classics as Frans Hals's *Laughing Cavalier* and Rembrandt's portrait of his son Titus. The paintings of the Dutch, English, Spanish, and Italian schools are outstanding. The collection also contains important 18th-century French decorative art, including furniture from a number of royal palaces, Sèvres porcelain, and gold boxes. The European and Asian armaments, shown on the ground floor, are works of art in their own right: superb inlaid suits of armor, some obviously for parade rather than battle, together with more businesslike swords, halberds, and magnificent Persian scimitars. The Heritage Lottery Fund and Christie's in London have awarded a £7$^1/_2$ million grant to the gallery's Centenary Project for the addition of museum facilities by the summer of 2000.

A BIT FARTHER AFIELD

Royal Air Force Museum. Grahame Park Way, Hendon, NW9. ☎ **0181/205-2266,** or 0891/600-5633 for 24-hour information. Admission £6.50 ($10.75) adults, £4.90 ($8.10) seniors, £3.25 ($5.35) children 5–16. Daily 10am–6pm. Tube: Colindale. BritRail: Mill Hill Broadway, then bus no. 303. By car, take A41, A1, and M1 (junction 4).

Britain's national museum of aviation tells the story of flight through the display of more than 60 aircraft, one of the world's finest collections of historic aircraft. The museum stands on 15 acres of the former airfield at Hendon in North London, and its main aircraft hall occupies two large hangars from World War I. Custom-built halls house *The Battle of Britain Experience,* including "The Friendly Invasion," commemorating the contribution of the U.S. Army and U.S. Army Air Corps to the Allied war effort in World War II, plus a collection of famous bomber aircraft. Special features include a flight simulator offering a selection of different flying experiences, film shows, a "sit-in" jet trainer, and guided tours.

PARKS & GARDENS

London's parks are the most advanced system of "green lungs" of any large city on the globe. Although not as rigidly maintained as those of Paris (Britons traditionally prefer a more natural look), they're cared for with a loving and lavishly artistic hand that puts their American equivalents to shame.

The largest of the central London parks is **Hyde Park** (Tube: Marble Arch, Hyde Park Corner, or Lancaster Gate), once a favorite deer-hunting ground of Henry VIII.

With the adjoining Kensington Gardens (see below), it covers 615 acres of central London with velvety lawns interspersed with ponds, flower beds, and trees. Running through its width is a 41-acre lake known as the Serpentine, where you can row, sail model boats, or swim (provided you don't mind sub-Florida water temperatures). Rotten Row, a 1¹/₂-mile sand horseback riding track, attracts some skilled equestrians on Sunday. At the northeastern tip, near Marble Arch, is Speakers' Corner.

Blending with Hyde Park and bordering on the grounds of Kensington Palace, well-manicured **Kensington Gardens** (Tube: High Street Kensington or Queensway) contains the famous statue of Peter Pan, with the bronze rabbits that toddlers are always trying to kidnap. It's also home to that Victorian extravaganza, the Albert Memorial. The Orangery is an ideal place to take afternoon tea (see "Teatime" in chapter 5).

East of Hyde Park, across Piccadilly, stretch **Green Park** (Tube: Green Park) and **St. James's Park** (Tube: St. James's Park), forming an almost unbroken chain of landscaped beauty. This is an ideal area for picnics; you'll find it hard to believe that this was once a festering swamp near a leper hospital. There's a romantic lake stocked with a variety of ducks and some surprising pelicans, descendants of the pair that the Russian ambassador presented to Charles II back in 1662.

Regent's Park (Tube: Regent's Park or Baker Street), covers most of the district of that name, north of Baker Street and Marylebone Road. Designed by the 18th-century genius John Nash to surround a palace for the prince regent that never materialized, this is the most classically beautiful of London's parks. Its core is a rose garden planted around a small lake alive with waterfowl and spanned by Japanese bridges; in early summer, the rose perfume in the air is as heady as wine. The park is home to the Open-Air Theatre (see chapter 9) and the London Zoo (see "Especially for Kids," below). As at all the local parks, hundreds of deck chairs are scattered around the lawns, just waiting for sunbathers. The deck-chair attendants, who collect a small fee, are mostly college students on break.

Chelsea Physic Garden, 66 Royal Hospital Rd., SW3 (☎ **0171/352-5646;** Tube: Sloane Square), founded in 1673 by the Worshipful Society of Apothecaries, is the second-oldest surviving botanical garden in England. Sir Hans Sloane, doctor to George II, required the apothecaries of the empire to develop 50 plant species a year for presentation to the Royal Society. The objective was to grow plants for medicinal study; plant specimens and even trees arrived at the gardens by barge, many to grow in English soil for the first time. Cottonseed from this garden launched an industry in the new colony of Georgia. Some 7,000 plants still grow here, everything from the pomegranate to the willow Pattern tree; there's even exotic cork oak, as well as England's earliest rock garden. The garden is open April to November, Wednesday from noon to 5pm and Sunday from 2 to 6pm. Admission is £4 ($6.60) for adults, £2 ($3.30) for children 5 to 15 and students. The garden is also the setting for a well-recommended afternoon tea, where you can carry your cuppas on promenades through the garden (see "Teatime," in chapter 5).

Battersea Park, SW11 (☎ **0181/871-7530;** Tube: Sloane Square), is a vast patch of woodland, lakes, and lawns on the south bank of the Thames, opposite Chelsea Embankment between Albert Bridge and Chelsea Bridge. Formerly known as Battersea Fields, the present park was laid out between 1852 and 1858 on an old dueling ground. (The most famous duel here was between Lord Winchelsea and the duke of Wellington in 1829.) There's a lake for boating, a deer field with fenced-in deer and wild birds, and areas for tennis and soccer. There's even a children's zoo, open from Easter to late September, daily from 10am to 5pm. Open weekends only in winter 1 to 3pm. The park's architectural highlight is the Peace Pagoda, built by Japanese craftspeople in cooperation with British architects; the stone and wood pagoda was dedicated in 1986 to the now-defunct Council of Greater London by an order of Japanese monks. The park is open daily from dawn to dusk. From the Sloane Square Tube stop, it's a brisk 15-minute walk to the park, or you can pick up bus no. 137 (get off at the first stop after the bus crosses the Thames).

The hub of England's—and perhaps the world's—horticulture are the **Royal Botanic Gardens** (also known as Kew Gardens), at **Kew** in Surrey (see "Attractions on the Outskirts," below).

ROMAN LONDON

Rising out of the ground on Victoria Street is London's finest fragment of ancient Rome, the **Temple of Mithras** (Tube: Bank or Mansion House). Discovered in 1954 during construction, the remains were transferred from their original location and assembled to form the foundation and lower walls of a Roman temple. Built in A.D. 240, the temple belonged to an obscure religion, the Cult of Mithras, devoted to the Persian god of heavenly light. The Mithraic religion shared many elements with the fledging Christian religion, including the common idea of a savior who shed his blood for all mankind, and the symbolic ceremonial repast. Many historians claim that early Christians may have borrowed these tenets from the Mithraists. Because of the rivalry between these two religions, many sacred relics and shrines to Mithras were destroyed by the Christians. However, some sacred objects were found buried near the temple site, including several idols made of Italian marble and various silver trinkets; they're all on display at the Museum of London (see "Museums & Galleries," above).

4 Sightseeing & Boat Tours Along the Thames

All of London's history and development is linked with the River Thames: This winding ribbon of water connects the city with the sea, from which it drew its wealth and power, and it was London's chief commercial thoroughfare and royal highway. Every royal procession was undertaken on gorgeously painted and gilded barges (which you can still see at the National Maritime Museum in Greenwich). All important state prisoners were delivered to the Tower of London by water, eliminating the chance of an ambush by their friends in one of those narrow, crooked alleys surrounding the fortress. Much of the commercial traffic disappeared when London's streets were widened enough for horse-drawn coaches to maintain a decent pace.

RIVER CRUISES

A trip up or down the river will give you an entirely different view of London from the one you get from dry land. You'll see exactly how the city grew along and around the Thames and how many of its landmarks turn their faces toward the water. Several companies operate motor launches from the Westminster piers (Tube: Westminster), offering panoramic views of one of Europe's most historic waterways en route.

Westminster-Greenwich Thames Passenger Boat Service, Westminster Pier, Victoria Embankment, SW1 (☎ **0171/930-4097**), concerns itself only with downriver traffic from Westminster Pier to such destinations as Greenwich (see "Attractions on the Outskirts," below). The most popular excursion departs for Greenwich (a 50-minute ride) at half-hour intervals between 10am and 4pm April to October, and between 10:30am and 5pm from June to August; from November to March, boats depart from Westminster Pier at 40-minute intervals daily from 10:40am to 3:20pm. One-way fares are £6 ($9.90) for adults, £3.20 ($5.30) for children under 16. Round-trip fares are £7.30 ($12.05) for adults, £3.70 ($6.10) for children. A family ticket for two adults and up to three children under 15 costs £16.20 ($26.75) one-way, £19.20 ($31.70) round-trip.

Westminster Passenger Association (Upriver) Ltd., Westminster Pier, Victoria Embankment, SW1 (☎ **0171/930-2062** or 0171/930-4721), offers the only river-boat service upstream from Westminster Bridge to Kew, Richmond, and Hampton Court. There are regular daily sailings from the Monday before Easter until the end of October, on traditional riverboats, all with licensed bars. Trip time, one-way, can be as little as 1¹/₂ hours to Kew and between 2¹/₂ to 4 hours to Hampton Court, depending on the tide. Cruises from Westminster Pier to Hampton Court via Kew Gardens leave daily at 10:30am, 11:15am, and noon. Round-trip tickets are £9 to £13.50 ($14.85 to $22.30) adults, £6.50 to £11 ($10.75 to $18.15) seniors, and £4.50 to £8 ($7.45 to $13.20) children 4 to 14; one child under 4 accompanied by an adult goes free. Evening cruises from May to September are also available departing Westminster Pier at 7:30pm and 8:30pm (9:30pm on demand) for £5.50 ($9.05) adults and £4 ($6.60) children.

Pool of London, inaugurated in 1997, allows travelers to visit sites along the Thames River between London Bridge and St. Katharine's Dock by taking a hop-on, hop-off ferry. For only £2 ($3.30) adults, £1 ($1.65) for children, you can use the ferry as often as you like within a day. The ferry stops at five piers, including Tower Pier, London Bridge Pier, H.M.S. Belfast, Butlers Wharf, and St. Katharine's Dock. The ferry runs between 11am and 5pm until the end of October. From then until the end of March, it operates only on Saturday and Sunday, running every half hour. Beginning in April again, daily service resumes. Tickets are sold on board. For more information, call ☎ **0171/488-0344.**

THAMES-SIDE SIGHTS
THE BRIDGES

Some of the Thames bridges are household names. **London Bridge,** contrary to the nursery rhyme, never fell down, but it has been replaced a number of times, and is vastly different from the original London Bridge, which was lined with houses and shops. The one that you see now is the ugliest of the bunch; the previous incarnation was dismantled and shipped to Lake Havasu, Arizona, in the 1960s.

Its neighbor to the east is the more interesting **Tower Bridge** (SE1; ☎ **0171/403-3761;** Tube: Tower Hill), one of the city's most celebrated landmarks and possibly the most photographed and painted bridge on earth. Its outward appearance is familiar to Londoners and visitors alike. (This is the one that a certain American thought he'd purchased instead of the one farther up the river that really ended up in the middle of the desert.) In spite of its medieval appearance, Tower Bridge was actually built in 1894.

In 1993, an exhibition opened inside the bridge to commemorate its century-old history; it takes you up the north tower to high-level walkways between the two towers with spectacular views of St. Paul's, the Tower of London, and the Houses of Parliament—a photographer's dream. You're then led down the south tower and onto the bridge's original engine room, with its Victorian boilers and steam-pumping engines that used to raise and lower the bridge for ships to pass. Exhibits housed in the bridge's towers use advanced technology, including animatronic characters, video, and computers to illustrate the history of the bridge. Admission to the **Tower Bridge Experience** (☎ **0171/403-3761**) is £6.15 ($10.15) for adults and £4.15 ($6.85) for children 5 to 15, students, and seniors; it's free for children 4 and under. Open April to October daily 10am to 6:30pm, November to March daily 9:30am to 6pm; last entry is 1¹/₄ hours before closing. Closed Good Friday and January 1 to 28 as well as a few days around Christmas.

HMS BELFAST

An 11,500-ton cruiser, the **HMS** *Belfast* (Morgan's Lane, Tooley Street, SE1; ☎ **0171/940-6328;** Tube: Monument, Tower Hill, or London Bridge) is a World War II ship now preserved as a floating naval museum. It's moored opposite the Tower of London, between Tower Bridge and London Bridge. During the Russian convoy period and on D day, the *Belfast* saw distinguished service, and in the Korean War it was known as "that straight shootin' ship." You can explore all the decks of the ship, right down to the engine room; exhibits above and below deck show how sailors have lived and fought over the past 50 years. It's open daily from 10am, with last boarding at 6pm in summer, 5pm in winter. Admission is £4.70 ($7.75) adults and £2.40 ($3.95) children, seniors and students pay £3.60 ($5.95), and family admission (two adults and two children) is £11.80 ($19.45). A ferry runs from Tower Pier (closed in winter). The cost of the ferry is £1 ($1.65) for adults and 80p ($1.30) for children.

DOCKLANDS

What was a dilapidated wasteland in 8 square miles of property surrounded by water—some 55 miles of waterfront acreage within a sailor's cry of London's major attractions—has been reclaimed, restored, and rejuvenated. **London Docklands** is coming into its own as a leisure, residential, and commercial lure.

Next to the Tower of London, **St. Katharine's Dock** was the first of the docks to be given an entirely new role. Originally built in 1827–28, this was for many years a leading dock, with the advantage of being closest to the City. Today, as a residential center and yacht marina, St. Katharine's again profits from its proximity to the City. The modern World Trade Centre looks down on the brick-brown sails of sailing barges and gleaming hulls of moored luxury yachts. Blocks of fashionable Manhattan-style loft apartments sit between docks and river.

Canary Wharf, on the Isle of Dogs, is the heart of Docklands; this huge 71-acre site is dominated by a 800-foot-high tower, the tallest building in the United Kingdom, designed by Cesar Pelli. The **Piazza** is lined with shops and restaurants. A visit to the **Exhibition Centre** on the Isle of Dogs gives you an overview of the Docklands—past, present, and future. Already, the area has given space to the overflow from the City of London's square mile, and its development is more than promising.

On the south side of the river at Surrey Docks, the Victorian warehouses of **Butler's Wharf** have been converted by Sir Terence Conran into offices, workshops, houses, shops, and restaurants; it's also home to the **Design Museum** (see "Museums & Galleries," above).

Docklands can be reached via the **Dockland Light Railway,** which links the Isle of Dogs to London Underground's Tower Hill station. To see the whole complex, take the railway at Tower Gateway near Tower Bridge for a short journey through Wapping and the Isle of Dogs. You can get off at Island Gardens and then cross through the 100-year-old Greenwich Tunnel under the Thames to see the attractions at Greenwich (see "Attractions on the Outskirts," below).

A FAMOUS SHIP AT GREENWICH

Four miles east of London, at Greenwich Pier, now in permanent dry dock, lies the last and ultimate word in sail power: the *Cutty Sark,* King William Walk, Greenwich, SE10 (☎ **0181/858-3445;** bus: 177, 180, 188, 199, 286, or 386). Named after the witch in Robert Burns's poem "Tam O'Shanter," it was the greatest of the breed of clipper ships that carried tea from China and wool from Australia in the most exciting ocean races ever sailed. The *Cutty Sark's* record stood at a then-unsurpassed 363 miles in 24 hours. Launched in Scotland in 1869, the sleek black three-master represented the final fighting run of canvas against steam. Although the age of the clippers was brief, they did outpace the steamers as long as there was wind to fill their billowing mountain of sails. On board the *Cutty Sark* you'll find a museum devoted to clipper lore. Admission is £3.50 ($5.75) for adults and £2.50 ($4.15) for children over 5, students, and seniors. A family ticket costs £8.50 ($14). It's open daily from 10am to 5pm.

5 Attractions on the Outskirts

These sights are perfect for a morning or afternoon jaunt, and are easily accessible by Tube, train, boat, or bus.

HAMPSTEAD

About 4 miles north of the center of London is the lovely village of Hampstead (Tube: Hampstead), and scenic Hampstead Heath.

The 800-acre expanse of high heath known as **Hampstead Heath** is a continuous chain of formal parkland, woodland, heath, meadowland, and ponds. On a clear day you can see St. Paul's Cathedral and even the hills of Kent. Londoners would certainly mount the barricades if Hampstead Heath were imperiled; for years, they've come here to sun worship, fly kites, fish the ponds, swim, picnic, and jog. In good weather, it's also the site of big one-day fairs. At the shore of Kenwood Lake, in the northern section, is a concert platform devoted to symphony performances on summer evenings. In the northeast corner, in Waterlow Park, ballets, operas, and comedies are staged at the Grass Theatre in June and July.

Once the Underground came to **Hampstead Village** in 1907, writers, artists, architects, musicians, and scientists were among those who decamped for the leafy village. Keats, D. H. Lawrence, Rabindranath Tagore, Shelley, and Robert Louis Stevenson all once lived here, and Kingsley Amis and John Le Carré still do.

The Regency and Georgian houses of the village and the rolling greens of the heath are just 20 minutes by Tube from Piccadilly Circus. The village has a quirky mix of historic pubs, toy shops, and chic boutiques along **Flask Walk**, a pedestrian mall. The original village, on the side of a hill, still has old alleys, steps, courts, and groves that are ideal for strolling.

Burgh House. New End Sq., NW3. ☎ **0171/431-0144.** Free admission. House and museum, Wed–Sun noon–5pm. Buttery, Wed–Sun 11am–5:30pm. Tube: Hampstead.

This Queen Anne home (1703) in the center of the village was the residence of the daughter and son-in-law of Rudyard Kipling, who often visited here. It's now used for local art exhibits, concerts, recitals, talks, and public meetings on many subjects, and the house is the home of several local societies, including the Hampstead Music Club and the Hampstead Scientific Society. **Hampstead Museum,** in Burgh House, illustrates the local history of the area. It has a room devoted to reproductions of works by the great artist John Constable, who lived nearby for many years and is buried in the local parish church. There's also a licensed **buttery** (☎ **0171/431-7401**) that's popular for lunch or tea, with lunches for just £5 ($8.25). In pricey Hampstead, it's a real dining bargain.

Fenton House. Windmill Hill, NW3. ☎ **0171/435-3471.** Admission £4.10 ($6.75) adults, £2.05 ($3.40) children, £10 ($16.50) family ticket. Mar Sat–Sun 2–5pm; Apr–Oct Sat–Sun 11am–5pm, Wed–Fri 2–5pm. Closed Good Friday and Nov–Feb. Tube: Hampstead.

This National Trust property is in a village area on the west side of Hampstead Grove, just north of Hampstead Village. Built in 1693, its paneled rooms contain furniture and pictures; 18th-century English, German, and French porcelain; and an out-standing collection of early keyboard musical instruments.

Freud Museum. 20 Maresfield Gardens, NW3. ☎ **0171/435-2002.** Admission £4 ($6.60) adults, £2 ($3.30) full-time students, free for children under 12. Wed–Sun noon–5pm. Tube: Finchley Rd.

This is the spacious house in which the founder of psychoanalysis lived, worked, and died after escaping with his family and possessions from Nazi-occupied Vienna. The rooms hold his furniture (including the famous couch), letters, photographs, paint-ings, and personal effects, as well as those of his daughter, Anna Freud, also a noted psychoanalyst. Temporary exhibitions and an archive film program are also offered.

Keats House. Wentworth Place, Keats Grove, NW3. ☎ **0171/435-2062.** Free admission; donations welcome. Apr–Oct Mon–Fri 10am–1pm and 2–6pm, Sat 10am–1pm and 2–5pm, Sun and bank holidays 2–5pm; Nov–Mar Mon–Fri 1–5pm, Sat 10am–1pm and 2–5pm, Sun 2–5pm. Tube: Hampstead.

This was the home of the poet John Keats for only two years, but it was here in 1819 that he wrote two of his most famous poems, "Ode to a Nightingale" and "Ode on a Grecian Urn." This Regency house contains some of his manuscripts and letters. Call before coming here, as the house is experiencing ongoing renovation and will be closed at random periods until 2003.

Kenwood House. Hampstead Lane, NW3. ☎ **0181/348-1286.** Free admission. Apr–Oct daily 10am–6pm; Nov–Mar daily 10am–4pm. Tube: Golders Green, then bus 210.

This structure was built as a gentleman's country home and later enlarged and deco-rated by the famous Scottish architect Robert Adam, starting in 1764. The house con-tains period furniture and paintings by Rembrandt, Vermeer, Gainsborough, and Turner, among others. It's also a venue for special visiting exhibitions and evening con-certs (at which time, admission is charged).

IN NEARBY HIGHGATE

✪ **Highgate Cemetery.** Swain's Lane, N6. ☎ **0181/340-1834.** Western Cemetery guided tour £3 ($4.95). Eastern Cemetery £1 ($1.65) admission, £2 ($3.30) camera pass charge (no video, handheld cameras only). Western Cemetery, Mar–Dec guided tours only Mon–Fri at noon, 2, and 4pm, and Sat–Sun hourly 11am–4pm; Dec–Mar, tours Mon–Fri at noon, 2, and 4pm, and Sat–Sun hourly 11am–3pm; Eastern Cemetery, Apr–Oct daily 10am–5pm; Nov–Mar daily 10am–4pm. Both cemeteries closed at Christmas and during funerals. Tube: Archway, then walk through Waterlow Park. Bus: from Archway, 143, 271, or 210.

Described in the British press as everything from "walled romantic rubble" to "an anthology of horror," this 37-acre burial ground is the ideal setting for a fine collec-tion of Victorian sculpture, as well as the graves of Karl Marx and others, including George Eliot, Christina Rossetti, and Elizabeth Siddell, wife of Dante Gabriel Rossetti and the Pre-Raphaelites' favorite model. There are no guided tours of the Eastern Cemetery; guests wander about at will.

GREENWICH

Greenwich Mean Time is the basis of standard time throughout most of the world, and Greenwich has been the zero point used in the reckoning of terrestrial longitudes since 1884. But this lovely village—the center of British seafaring when Britain ruled the seas—is also home of the Royal Naval College, the National Maritime Museum, and the Old Royal Observatory. In dry dock at Greenwich Pier is the clipper ship *Cutty Sark* (see "Sightseeing & Boat Tours Along the Thames," above). Greenwich also has some wonderful shopping, including a famous weekend market (see chapter 8).

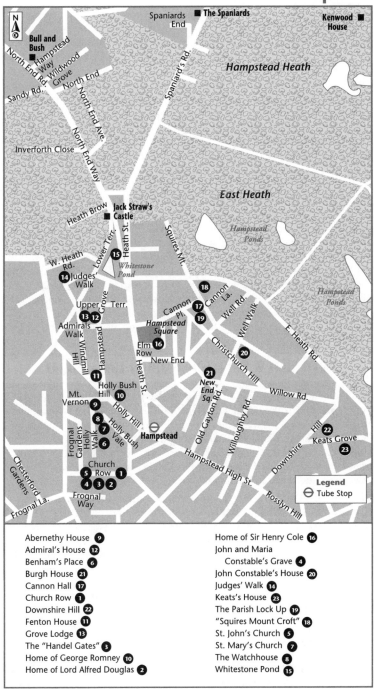

Hampstead

Legend
⊖ Tube Stop

Abernethy House ⑨
Admiral's House ⑫
Benham's Place ⑥
Burgh House ㉑
Cannon Hall ⑰
Church Row ①
Downshire Hill ㉒
Fenton House ⑪
Grove Lodge ⑬
The "Handel Gates" ③
Home of George Romney ⑩
Home of Lord Alfred Douglas ②

Home of Sir Henry Cole ⑯
John and Maria
   Constable's Grave ④
John Constable's House ⑳
Judges' Walk ⑭
Keats's House ㉓
The Parish Lock Up ⑲
"Squires Mount Croft" ⑱
St. John's Church ⑤
St. Mary's Church ⑦
The Watchhouse ⑧
Whitestone Pond ⑮

Greenwich is the site of Britain's Millennium Dome, which has been billed as "the most spectacular event on earth." At least it's the largest on earth, a multimedia extravaganza that mixes education and entertainment. As of this writing, it's still not known what the dome will contain, only a vague theme called "Time." A live show of some sort will run in the dome's central arena, with a series of themed exhibitions around the edge. Most of the project's cost, estimated at more than $1.25 billion U.S. dollars, came from national lottery revenues. See the following box for more information.

GETTING THERE   Long anticipating millions of visitors, the London Underground has extended the Jubilee Line. This Tube follows a new line from Green Park via Westminster, Waterloo, London Bridge, the Docklands, and North Greenwich through to Stratford in East London. Greenwich North is the largest station on the London Underground not connected to the British Rail network.

The Tube is for speed, but if you'd like to go to Greenwich the way Henry VIII did, you still can. Part of the fun of going to Greenwich, about 4 miles from the City, is getting there—still. The most appealing way involves boarding any of the frequent ferryboats that cruise along the Thames at intervals that vary from every half hour (in summer) to every 45 minutes (in winter). Boats that depart from Westminster Pier (Tube: Westminster) are maintained by **Westminster Passenger Services, Ltd.** (☎ **0171/930-4097**). Boats that leave from Charing Cross Pier (Tube: Embankment) and Tower Pier (Tube: Tower Hill) are run by **Catamaran Cruises, Ltd.** (☎ **0171/987-1185**). Depending on the tides and the carrier you select, travel time varies from 50 to 75 minutes each way. Passage is £7.25 to £7.30 ($11.95 to $12.05) round-trip for adults, £3.70 to £3.95 ($6.10 to $6.50) round-trip for children 5 to 12; it's free for those under 5.

You can also take the train from Charing Cross Station. **Rail Europe** (☎ **0345/484950** in London or 800/848-7245 in the U.S.) trains take about 15 minutes to reach Greenwich from Charing Cross, costing between £1.90 to £2.90 ($3.15 to $4.80) round-trip, depending on the time of day you travel. A commuter train that can get you here is the **Docklands Light Railway** (☎ **0171/918-4000**), a tourist attraction in its own right: a narrow-gauge railway supported on stilts high above the Docklands. Passengers board the blue-and-white cars at Tower Gateway (Tube: Tower Hill) or Bank. The DLR has extended its line: The train passes above the Isle of Dogs before arriving at Island Gardens, in the Docklands, and goes on to the new stations—Lewisham, Greenwich, and Cutty Sark. The one-way fare is £1.70 ($2.80).

VISITOR INFORMATION   The **Greenwich Tourist Information Centre** is at 46 Greenwich Church St. (☎ **0181/858-6376**). From April to October, it's open daily 10am to 5pm; November to March, Monday to Thursday 11am to 1pm and 1:45 to 4pm, Friday to Sunday 10am to 5pm. The Tourist Information Centre conducts **walking tours** of Greenwich's major sights. The tours, which cost £4 ($6.60), depart daily at 12:15 and 2:15pm and last 1 1/2 to 2 hours. Advance reservations aren't required, but it's a good idea to phone in advance to find out if there have been any last-minute schedule changes. Those who take a walking tour get a 50% reduction in admission to the National Maritime Museum, Old Royal Observatory, and Queen's House.

SEEING THE SIGHTS   Most visitors will flock to Greenwich to visit the Millennium Dome, but the historic old town was a tourist attraction long before anyone ever heard of the Dome.

One ticket will admit you to Greenwich's three traditional attractions, the **National Maritime Museum,** the **Old Royal Observatory,** and **Queen's House.** The three attractions stand together in a beautiful royal park, high on a hill overlooking the Thames. Combination tickets cost £5 ($8.25) adults, £4 ($6.60) seniors and students,

The World's Biggest Dome at the Millennium

Mired in controversy, with four out of five Brits opposed to it, according to polls, the **Greenwich Millennium Dome** should be open to the world by the time you read this. As one local in favor of the Dome said, "The bloody Parisians opposed the Eiffel Tower. Now it's the symbol of Paris." Prime minister, Tony Blair called the Dome, "The most exciting thing to happen anywhere in the world in the year 2000."

Greenwich is the official "start-point" of the millennium, despite where the sun first rises. The millennium starts here because in 1884 an international conference in Washington, D.C., agreed to have a "Universal Day," that date to begin at the prime meridian of the world (that is, zero longitude). Hence, each and every day since begins in Greenwich, including, of course, January 1, 2000. (Of course, the millennium and the 21st century don't officially start until January 2, 2001.) But the party begins in 2000, and Britain is planning to put on quite a show for its visitors.

Some of the exhibits for the Millennium Dome have already been announced as we go to press: a state-of-the-art life-raft system for ships (no more *Titanics*), an artificial heart for training surgeons, a more environmentally friendly passenger jet engine, and a 150-foot androgynous human figure with working arteries and veins. From agriculture to automobiles, Britain is developing ground-breaking products, and the Millennium Dome showcases these breakthroughs.

The Dome's performance area is the setting for shows with live performers and stunning visual effects repeated throughout the day.

Blair has said the Dome will "make a statement for the whole nation at the dawn of the millennium. It will open a window to the future." What takes place inside the Dome is supposed to inspire, entertain, educate, and involve visitors as participants. It is estimated that some 12 million people will visit the Dome. The 181-acre site for the Dome lies on a north-Greenwich peninsula, bounded on three sides by the River Thames. Part of a 300-acre former gasworks, it had been derelict for more than two decades and was the largest undeveloped site on the river. The prime meridian cuts across the north of the site, which is about a mile from the historic core of Greenwich.

When plans are announced (long past our printing deadline), British tourist offices and visitors' centers will have complete details. Tickets will be on sale from travel agents (many will purchase tickets before winging their way to Britain)—and, of course, at various box offices on-site.

£2.50 ($4.15) children 5 to 16, free for those 5 and under; a family ticket, for two adults and up to three children, is £15 ($24.75). All three attractions are open daily from 10am to 5pm. For more information, call ☎ **0181/858-4422.**

From the days of early seafarers to 20th-century sea power, the **National Maritime Museum** illustrates the glory that was Britain at sea. The cannon, relics, ship models, and paintings tell the story of a thousand naval battles and a thousand victories, as well as the price of those battles. Look for some oddities here—everything from the dreaded cat-o'-nine-tails used to flog sailors until 1879 to Nelson's Trafalgar coat, with the fatal bullet hole in the left shoulder clearly visible. In time for the millennium, the museum spent 20 million pounds in a massive expansion that added 16 new galleries devoted to British maritime history and improved visitor facilities.

Old Royal Observatory is the original home of Greenwich Mean Time. It has the largest refracting telescope in the United Kingdom, and a collection of historic time-keepers and astronomical instruments. You can stand astride the meridian and set your watch precisely by the falling time ball. Wren designed the Octagon Room. Here, the first royal astronomer, Flamsteed, made his 30,000 observations that formed the basis of his *Historia Coelestis Britannica.* Edmond Halley, who discovered Halley's Comet, succeeded him. In 1833, the ball on the tower was hung to enable shipmasters to set their chronometers accurately.

Designed by Inigo Jones, **Queen's House** (1616) is a fine example of this architect's innovative style. It's most famous for the cantilevered tulip staircase, the first of its kind. Carefully restored, the house contains a collection of royal and marine paintings and other objets d'art.

Nearby is the **Royal Naval College,** King William Walk (off Romney Road; **0181/858-2154**). Designed by Sir Christopher Wren in 1696, it occupies 4 blocks named after King Charles, Queen Anne, King William, and Queen Mary. Formerly, Greenwich Palace stood here from 1422 to 1640. It's worth stopping in to see the magnificent Painted Hall by Thornhill, where the body of Nelson lay in state in 1805, and the Georgian chapel of St. Peter and St. Paul. Open daily 2:30 to 4:45pm; admission is free.

KEW

Nine miles southwest of central London near Richmond, Kew is home to the best-known botanic gardens in Europe. It's also the site of **Kew Palace,** former residence of George III and Queen Charlotte. The gardens are the big attraction, not the palace which is scheduled to reopen in 2001. The most convenient way to get to Kew is to take the **District Line** Tube to the Kew Gardens stop, on the south bank of the Thames.

✪ **Royal Botanic (Kew) Gardens.** Kew. ☎ **0181/940-1171.** Admission £5 ($8.25) adults, £3.50 ($5.75) students and seniors, £2.50 ($4.15) children, £13 ($21.45) family ticket. Daily 9:30am–5pm. Tube: Kew Gardens.

These world-famous gardens offer thousands of varieties of plants. But Kew is no mere pleasure garden—it's essentially a vast scientific research center that happens to be beautiful. The gardens, on a 300-acre site, encompass lakes, greenhouses, walks, pavilions, and museums, along with fine examples of the architecture of Sir William Chambers. Among the 50,000 plant species are notable collections of ferns, orchids, aquatic plants, cacti, mountain plants, palms, and tropical water lilies.

No matter what season you visit Kew, there's always something to see, from the first spring flowers through winter. Gigantic hothouses grow species of shrubs, blooms, and trees from every part of the globe, from the Arctic Circle to tropical rain forests. Attractions include a newly restored Japanese gateway in traditional landscaping, as well as exhibitions that vary with the season. The newest greenhouse, the Princess of Wales Conservatory (beyond the rock garden), encompasses 10 climatic zones, from arid to tropical; it has London's most thrilling collection of miniature orchids. The Marianne North Gallery (1882) is an absolute gem, paneled with 246 different types of wood that the intrepid Victorian artist collected on her world journeys; she also collected 832 paintings of exotic and tropical flora, all of which are displayed on the walls. Afternoon tea is offered at the Orangery; there's no better place in the gardens. The Visitor Centre at Victoria Gate houses an exhibit telling the story of Kew, as well as a bookshop.

AFTERNOON TEA   Across the street from the Royal Botanic Gardens is one of the finest tearooms in the area, the **Original Maids of Honour Tearooms,** 288 Kew Rd. (☎ **0181/940-2752**). Its oak paneling and old leaded-glass windows give the place a cozy warmth. The homemade cakes are delectable, as are the delightfully light scones. The Maids of Honour is their pastry specialty, originally baked for Henry VIII, who liked it so much that its secret recipe has been passed along through the centuries. Afternoon tea is £4.25 ($7). The tearoom is open Monday 9:30am to 2pm and Tuesday to Saturday 9:30am to 5pm, and tea is served from 2:30 to 5:30pm.

HAMPTON COURT

Hampton Court, on the north side of the Thames, 13 miles west of London in East Molesey, Surrey, is easily accessible. Frequent **trains** (☎ **0345/484950** in the U.K. only or 01603/764776) run from Waterloo Station (Network Southeast) to Hampton Court Station. **London Transport** (☎ **0171/730-3466** or 0990/808080) buses nos. 111, 131, 216, 267, and 461 make the trip from Victoria Coach Station on Buckingham Palace Road (just southwest of Victoria Station). Boat service is offered to and from Kingston, Richmond, and Westminster (see "Sightseeing & Boat Tours Along the Thames," above). If you're **driving** from London, take A308 to the junction with A309 on the north side of Kingston Bridge over the Thames.

✪ **Hampton Court Palace.** ☎ **0181/781-9500.** Admission £10 ($16.50) adults, £7.60 ($12.55) students and seniors, £6.60 ($10.90) children 5–15, free for children under 5. Gardens open year-round daily 7am–dusk (no later than 9pm); free admission to all except Privy Garden (admission £2.10 ($3.45) without palace ticket during summer months). Cloisters, courtyards, state apartments, great kitchen, cellars, and Hampton Court exhibition open mid-Mar to mid-Oct daily 9:30am–6pm; mid-Oct to mid-Mar daily 9am–4:30pm. Tudor tennis court open mid-Mar to mid-Oct.

Cardinal Wolsey's 16th-century Hampton Court Palace can teach us a lesson: Don't try to outdo your boss—particularly if he happens to be Henry VIII. The rich cardinal did just that, and he eventually lost his fortune, power, and prestige and ended up giving his lavish palace to the Tudor monarch.

Today, you can parade through the apartments, filled with porcelain, furniture, paintings, and tapestries. You see that Henry even outdid Wolsey when he took over the palace. Tudor additions included the **Anne Boleyn Gateway,** with its 16th-century astronomical clock that even tells the high-water mark at London Bridge. From **Clock Court,** you can see one of Henry's major contributions, the aptly named **Great Hall,** with its hammerbeam ceiling. Henry cavorted through the various apartments with his wife of the moment, from Anne Boleyn to Catherine Parr (the latter reversed things and lived to bury her erstwhile spouse). Later, Charles I was imprisoned here at one time, and temporarily managed to escape his jailers.

Although the palace enjoyed prestige and pomp in Elizabethan days, it owes much of its present look to William and Mary—or, rather, to Sir Christopher Wren, who designed and had built the northern or **Lion Gates,** intended to be the main entrance to the new parts of the palace. **The King's Dressing Room** is graced with some of the best art, mainly paintings by old masters on loan from Queen Elizabeth II. Be sure to inspect the **royal chapel**—Wolsey wouldn't recognize it. To confound yourself totally, you may want to get lost in the serpentine shrubbery **maze** in the garden, also the work of Sir Christopher Wren. The fine wrought-iron screen at the south end of the south gardens was made by Jean Tijou around 1694 for William and Mary. There's a cafe and restaurant in the Tiltyard Gardens.

6 Especially for Kids

London has fun places for kids of all ages. In addition to what's listed below, kids love Madame Tussaud's, the Science Museum, the London Transport Museum, the Natural

History Museum, the Tower of London, and the National Maritime Museum in Greenwich, all discussed above.

Kidsline (☎ **0171/222-8070**) offers computerized information about current events that might interest kids. The line is open from 4 to 6pm during school-term time, 9am to 4pm on holidays. The only problem is, when every parent in London is calling for information, it's almost impossible to get through.

Bethnal Green Museum of Childhood. Cambridge Heath Rd., E2. ☎ **0181/980-2415.** Free admission. Sat–Thurs 10am–5:50pm. Tube: Bethnal Green.

This branch of the Victoria and Albert specializes in toys. The variety of dolls alone is staggering; some have such elaborate period costumes that you don't even want to think of the price tags they would carry today. With the dolls go dollhouses, from simple cottages to miniature mansions, complete with fireplaces, grand pianos, kitchen utensils, household pets, and carriages. There are also optical toys, marionettes, puppets, a considerable exhibit of soldiers and war toys from both world war eras, trains and aircraft, and a display of clothing and furniture relating to the social history of childhood.

Little Angel Theatre. 14 Dagmar Passage, N1. ☎ **0171/226-1787.** Admission £5.50 ($9.05) adults, £4.50 ($7.45) children. Show times Sat–Sun 11am and 3pm; some weekdays. Tube: Angel or Highbury & Islington.

Puppetry in all its forms is presented at this charming small theater in Islington. There are homegrown shows that tour nationally and internationally as well as the work of a wide variety of visiting companies. The range of puppetry is wide, from marionettes (string puppets) to rod-and-glove puppets. Most of the work is targeted at children; age limits are stated for every show presented (for example, "no under-3s allowed"); grown-ups will enjoy them, too. There's a coffee bar and the theater is accessible to people with disabilities. There's also an adjacent workshop where the puppets, sets, and costumes are made. One show per season is adult oriented, call for information.

The London Dungeon. 28–34 Tooley St., SE1. ☎ **0171/403-0606** or 0171/403-7221. Admission £9.50 ($15.65) adults, £7.50 ($12.40) students and seniors, £6.50 ($10.75) children under 15. Admission includes Judgment Day boat ride. Daily 10:30am–5pm. Tube: London Bridge.

This ghoulish place was deliberately designed to chill the blood while reproducing the conditions of the Middle Ages. Set under the arches of London Bridge Station, the dungeon is a series of tableaux that are more grisly than the ones in Madame Tussaud's. The rumble of trains overhead adds to the atmosphere, and tolling bells bring a constant note of melancholy; dripping water and caged rats make for even more atmosphere. Naturally, there's a burning at the stake as well as a torture chamber with racking, branding, and fingernail extraction, and a spine-chilling "Jack the Ripper Experience." The special effects were originally conceived for major film and TV productions. They've recently added a new show called "Judgment Day." Performed by actors, you will be sentenced to death and taken on a boat ride to meet your fate. If you survive, there's a Pizza Hut on the premises, and a souvenir shop selling certificates that testify that you made it through the works.

London Planetarium. Marylebone Rd., NW1. ☎ **0171/935-6861.** £6 ($9.90) adults, £4.60 ($7.60) seniors, £4 ($6.60) children 5–17. Weekdays daily from 10am, Sat–Sun 9:30am with shows beginning at 12:20pm (10:20am on weekends) and last show at 5pm. Tube: Baker St.

Next door to Madame Tussaud's, the planetarium explores the mysteries of the stars and the night sky. The most recent star show starts with a spaceship of travelers forced to desert their planet when a neighboring star explodes; accompanying them on their journey, the audience travels through the solar system, visiting its major landmarks and witnessing spectacular cosmic activity. There are also several hands-on exhibits that relate to planets and space; for example, you can see what shape or weight you'd be on other planets. You can also hear Stephen Hawking talk about mysterious black holes.

✪ **London Zoo.** Regent's Park, NW1. ☎ **0171/722-3333.** Admission £8.50 ($14) adults, £6.50 ($10.75) children, free for children under 4. Mar–Oct daily 10am–5:30pm; Nov–Feb daily 10am–4pm. Tube: Regent's Park or Camden Town, then bus C2 or 274.

One of the greatest zoos in the world, the London Zoo is more than a century and a half old. This 36-acre garden houses about 8,000 animals, including some of the rarest species on earth. There's an insect house (incredible bird-eating spiders), a reptile house (huge dragonlike monitor lizards and a fantastic 15-foot python), and others, such as the Sobell Pavilion for Apes and Monkeys and the Lion Terraces. In the Moonlight World, special lighting effects simulate night for the nocturnal beasties, while rendering them clearly visible to onlookers, so you can see all the night rovers in action.

In 1999, a new building opened, the Millennium Conservation Centre, combining animals, visuals, and interactive displays to demonstrate the diverse nature of life on this planet. Many families budget almost an entire day here, watching the penguins being fed, enjoying an animal ride in summer, and meeting elephants on their walks around the zoo.

Rock Circus. London Pavilion, Piccadilly Circus, W1. ☎ **0171/734-7203.** £8.25 ($13.60) adults, £7.25 ($11.95) seniors and students, £6.25 ($10.30) children under 16. Sun–Mon and Wed–Thurs 10am–8pm, Tues 11am–8pm, Fri–Sat 10am–9pm. Off-season Sun–Mon and Wed–Thurs 10am–5:30pm, Tues 11am–5:30pm, Fri–Sat 10am–8pm. Tube: Piccadilly Circus.

This outpost of Madame Tussaud's presents the history of rock and pop music from Bill Haley and the Beatles to Sting and Madonna through wax and audio-animatronic figures, which move and perform golden oldies and more recent chart toppers in an eerily lifelike way. Authentic memorabilia, videos, and personal stereo sound surround you.

Unicorn Theatre for Children. The Arts Theatre, 6–7 Great Newport St., WC2. ☎ **0171/ 379-3280;** box office 0171/836-3334. Admission £10 ($16.50), £7.50 ($12.40), £5 ($8.25) depending on seat locations. Show times Sept–June daily 11am and/or 2:30pm (times may vary). Tube: Leicester Sq.

The Unicorn is the only children's theater in London's West End theater district. Founded in 1947 and going stronger than ever, it presents a season of plays for 4- to 12-year-olds from September to June. The schedule includes specially commissioned plays and adaptations of old favorites, all performed by adult actors. You can also become a temporary member while you're in London and join in an exciting program of weekend workshops.

7 Organized Tours

ORIENTATION TOURS
BUS TOURS

For the first-timer, the quickest and most economical way to bring the big city into focus is to take a bus tour. One of the most popular is **The Original London Sightseeing Tour,** which passes by all the major sights in just about 1¹/₂ hours. The tour, which uses a traditional double-decker bus with live commentary by a guide, costs £12

($19.80) for adults, £6 ($9.90) for children under 16, free for those under 5. The popular London Plus Hop On/Hop Off ticket has been discontinued and is now incorporated into the sightseeing tour, allowing you to hop off or hop on the bus at any point in the tour at no extra charge. The tour plus admission to Madame Tussaud's is £21 ($34.65) for adults, £12 ($19.80) for children.

Departures are from convenient points within the city; you can choose your departure point when you purchase your ticket. Tickets can be purchased on the bus or at a discount from any London Transport or London Tourist Board Information Centre. Most hotel concierges also sell tickets. For information or phone purchases, call **0181/877-1722.** It's also possible to write for tickets: **London Coaches,** Jews Row, London SW18 1TB.

A double-decker air-conditioned coach in the distinctive green-and-gold livery of **Harrods,** 87–135 Brompton Rd. (☎ **0171/581-3603;** Tube: Knightsbridge), offers sightseeing tours around London. The first departure from Door 8 of Harrods is at 10:30am; afternoon tours begin at 1:30 and 4pm. Tea, coffee, and orange juice are served on board. It's £20 ($33) for adults, £10 ($16.50) for children under 14, free for those under 5. All-day excursions to Blenheim Palace, Windsor, Stratford-upon-Avon, and outlying areas of London are available. You can purchase tickets at Harrods, Sightseeing Department, lower-ground floor.

Big Bus Company Ltd., Waterside Way, London SW17 (☎ **0181/944-7810**), operates a 2-hour tour in summer, departing from 8:30am to 6 or 7pm daily (depending on time of year; in winter, 9am to 4:30pm) from Marble Arch by Speakers Corner, Green Park by the Ritz Hotel, and Victoria Station (Buckingham Palace Road by the Royal Westminster Hotel). Tours cover the highlights—18 in all—ranging from the Houses of Parliament and Westminster Abbey to the Tower of London and Buckingham Palace (exterior looks only), accompanied by live commentary. The cost is £12 ($19.80) for adults, £6 ($9.90) for children. There's also a 1-hour tour that follows the same route, but covers only 13 sights. Tickets are valid all day; you can hop on and off the bus as you wish.

WALKING TOURS

The Original London Walks, 87 Messina Ave. (P.O. Box 1708), London NW6 4LW (☎ **0171/624-3978**), is the oldest established walking-tour company in London, run by an Anglo-American journalist/actor couple, David and Mary Tucker. Their hallmarks are variety, reliability, reasonably sized groups, and—above all—superb guides, including renowned crime historian Donald Rumbelow (the leading authority on Jack the Ripper) and the author of the classic guidebook *London Walks* as well as several prominent actors (including classical actor Edward Petherbridge). Walks are regularly scheduled daily, and cost £4.50 ($7.45) for adults, £3.50 ($5.75) for students and seniors, and children under 15 go free. Call for schedule; no reservations needed.

Discovery Walks, 67 Chancery Lane, London WC2 (☎ **0181/530-8443;** www.Jack-the-Ripper-Walk.co.uk), are themed walks, led by Richard Jones, author of *Frommer's Memorable Walks in London.* **Stepping Out** (☎ **0181/881-2933;** www.walklon.ndirect.co.uk), offers a series of offbeat walks led by qualified historians, as does **Guided Walks in London,** 20 Denman Dr. North, London NW11 (☎ **0171/243-1097;** www.guided-walks-in-london.net/). Tours generally cost £4 to £5 ($7 to $8).

John Wittich, 88 Woodlawn St., Whitstable, Kent, CT5 1HH (☎ **0122/ 777-2619**), started offering walks around London in 1960. A Freeman of the City of London and a member of two of London's ancient guilds, he is the author of several books on London walks. All the tours are conducted by John himself. He only does private tours, so call ahead to reserve. The cost is £25 ($41.25) for 2 adults for ¹/₂ day tour, plus £5 ($8.25) for each additional person.

CANAL TOURS

London's canals were once the city's major highways. Since the Festival of Britain in 1951, some of the traditional painted canal boats have been resurrected for Venetian-style trips through the waterways. One of them is *Jason,* which takes you on a 90-minute trip from Bloomfield Road in Little Venice through the long Maida Hill tunnel under Edgware Road, through Regent's Park, past the Mosque, the London Zoo, and Lord Snowdon's Aviary, and the Pirate's Castle to Camden Lock, and finally back to Little Venice. Passengers making the 45-minute one-way journey disembark at Camden Lock.

The season runs from March 27 to the end of October, with trips at 10:30am, 12:30, and 2:30pm. In June, July, and August, an additional trip on weekends and bank holidays leaves at 4:30pm. A canalside seafood specialty restaurant/cafe at Jason's moorings offers lunches, dinners, and teas, all freshly made. Advance notice must be made for lunch service on the boat. The round-trip fare is £5.95 ($9.80) for adults and £4.50 ($7.45) for children and seniors. One-way fares are £4.95 ($8.15) for adults and £3.75 ($6.20) for children and seniors. Family tickets cost £17.50 ($28.90). For reservations, contact **Jason's Trip,** Jason's Wharf, opposite 60 Blomfield Rd., Little Venice, London W9 (☎ **0171/286-3428;** Tube: Warwick Avenue).

8 Staying Active

Call **Sportsline** (☎ **0171/222-8000**) Monday to Friday from 10am to 6pm with any questions you may have about participatory sports in London.

BICYCLING   The asphalt pavements and dense traffic of London make biking a challenge. But that doesn't deter dozens of hardy souls from taking two wheels onto the streets. **On Your Bike** rents new bikes for £15 ($24.75) a day. You'll find them at 52–54 Toley St., SE1 (☎ **0171/378-6669;** Tube: London Bridge). **The Mountain Bike and Ski Co.,** 18 Gillingham St., SW1 (☎ **0171/834-8933;** Tube: Pimlico), rents 21-speed bikes starting at £7.99 ($13.20) per day. The **London Cycling Campaign,** 3 Stamford St., SE1 (☎ **0171/928-7220;** Tube: Waterloo), offers a *Cyclist's Route Map.*

BOATING   You can rent a paddleboat or a rowboat from the boathouse (open March to October) on the north side of **Hyde Park's Serpentine** (☎ 0171/ 262-1330). Rowboats and sailing dinghies are also available in **Regent's Park** (☎ **0171/486-4759**) and at the **Royal Victoria Dock Water Sport Centre** (Royal Victoria Dock, Tidal Basin Rd., E16 (☎ **0171/511-2326**). Sailing and canoeing cost £5 ($8.25) for 1¹/₂ hours.

HEALTH & FITNESS CENTERS   If your hotel doesn't have or provide access to a gym, try one of the following facilities:

Jubilee Hall Sports Centre, 30 The Piazza, Covent Garden, WC2 (☎ 0171/ **836-4835;** Tube: Covent Garden), is one of London's best and most centrally located sports centers, with the capital's largest weight room and an avid corps of body-building regulars. It also offers badminton, basketball, aerobics, gymnastics, martial arts, and soccer. Open Monday to Friday 7am to 10pm, Saturday and Sunday 10am to 5pm. Admission is £6.50 ($10.75) for use of the weight room, £5.50 ($9.05) for an aerobics class; both prices include use of sauna and showers.

If you're into a casual workout, try **Lambton Place Health Club,** Lambton Place,

Westbourne Grove, W11 (☎ **0171/229-2291;** Tube: Notting Hill Gate). For everything from a beauty studio to a sauna with a TV, go to **The Peak,** Hyatt Carlton Tower, 2 Cadogan Place, SW1 (☎ **0171/235-1234;** Tube: Knightsbridge). An exclusive, women-only club is **The Sanctuary,** 12 Floral St., WC2 (☎ **0171/420-5151;** Tube: Covent Garden). Another excellent facility is **The Savoy Fitness Gallery,** The Savoy, Strand, WC2 (☎ **0171/836-4343;** Tube: Charing Cross). If you just want the basics in a pleasant gym, try the **Aquilla Health Club,** which looks like a Roman bath, 11 Thurloe Place, SW7 (☎ **0171/225-0225;** Tube: South Kensington).

If you prefer to get fit through dancing, try **Danceworks,** 16 Balderton St., W1 (☎ **0171/629-6183;** Tube: Marble Arch), which offers a wide range of dance and fitness classes. **The Life Centre,** 15 Edge St., W8 (☎ **0171/221-4602;** Tube: Notting Hill Gate), conducts yoga classes at all levels. For a small membership fee, plus class fees, you can take dance classes daily at the **Pineapple Dance Studio,** 7 Langley St., WC2 (☎ **0171/836-4004;** Tube: Covent Garden).

Swimmers can find a pool with a wave machine at the small but modern **Brittania Leisure Centre,** 40 Hyde Rd., N1 (☎ **0171/729-4485;** Tube: Old Street). It also has badminton and squash courts, and soccer and volleyball fields. Admission is £2.70 ($4.45) for adults, £1.35 ($2.25) for children. The complex is open Monday, Tuesday, Thursday, and Friday from 9am to 10pm and on Wednesday, Saturday, and Sunday from 9am to 5:45pm. Other indoor pools with facilities are at **Chelsea Sports Centre,** Chelsea Manor Street, SW3 (☎ **0171/352-6985;** Tube: Sloane Square); **Fulham Pools,** Normand Park, Lillie Road, SW6 (☎ **0171/385-7628;** Tube: West Kensington); and **Golden Lane Pool,** Golden Lane, EC1 (☎ **0171/250-1464;** Tube: Old Street).

HORSEBACK RIDING   The **Ross Nyde Riding School,** 8 Bathurst Mews, W2 (☎ **0171/262-3791;** Tube: Lancaster Gate), is a public stable in Hyde Park. The school has 16 horses that are reliable and not easily spooked by traffic. It's recommended that you go riding early in the morning to avoid crowds in the park. On weekdays (except Monday), the stable opens at 7am, with rides leaving each hour during the week until dark. On the weekend, scheduled rides are Saturday and Sunday at 10 and 11am, Saturday at 2 and 3pm, and Sunday at 1:30 and 2:30pm. Cost is £25 ($41.25) for 1 hour. The **Stag Lodge Stables,** Robin Hood Gate, Richmond Park, SW15 (☎ **0181/974-6066**), provides a more pastoral setting. They also have a pony club for children, the Red Riders, that meets on Saturday.

IN-LINE SKATING   London's parks are great places to skate. Rental skates are available at **The London Blade Skate Centre,** 229 Brompton Rd., SW3 (☎ **0171/ 581-2039;** Tube: Knightsbridge), and at **Road Runner,** Lancaster Rd. at Portobello Rd., W11 (☎ **0171/792-0584;** Tube: Ladbroke Grove).

RUNNING   Scenic routes for joggers and runners are in London's Royal Parks, including Green Park, Hyde Park, Regent's Park, and St. James's Park. Try Hampstead Heath, Hyde Park, and Regent's Park. Most of the routes are about 2 miles in length and can be extended to 4 miles by combining two routes. They're not only scenic, but also fairly free of traffic; some pass historic sites such as Buckingham Palace, as well as some less-noted but still splendid residences. One of the more scenic routes in all of London is the loop that borders the Grand Union Canal. This path, which is for the exclusive use of joggers, runs between Regent's Park and Little Venice and takes you through St. John's Wood.

Of course, as in most places today, it's best not to jog after dark. For information on where to jog, call **London Hash House Harriers** (☎ **0181/995-7879**). For a small fee, they'll arrange hour-long runs through interesting parts of town.

TENNIS   Six outdoor courts are available to the public in **Holland Park,** Holland Park, W8 (☎ **0171/602-2226;** Tube: Holland Park). You must book in person, as priority is given to local residents. **Regent's Park Tennis,** Outer Circle, Regent's Park, NW1 (☎ **0171/724-0643;** Tube: Regent's Park), has one floodlit court.

9 Spectator Sports

Sportsline (☎ **0171/222-8000**) can answer questions about spectator sports Monday to Friday from 10am to 6pm. Check the papers or call the venues listed below for schedules and ticket information.

CRICKET   In summer, attention turns to cricket, played either at **Lord's,** St. John's Wood Road, NW8 (☎ **0171/289-1611;** Tube: St. John's Wood), in north London; or at the somewhat less prestigious **Oval Cricket Ground,** The Oval, Kennington, London SE11 (☎ **0171/582-6660;** Tube: The Oval), in south London. During the international test matches between Britain and Australia, the West Indies, India, or New Zealand (as important as the World Series in the United States), Britons go into a collective trance, with everyone glued to the nearest radio or TV.

FOOTBALL (SOCCER)   The season runs from August to April and attracts fiercely loyal fans. Games usually start at 3pm and are great to watch, but the stands can get very rowdy, so think about reserving seats. Centrally located first-division football clubs include **Arsenal,** Arsenal Stadium, Avenell Road, N5 (☎ **0171/704-4000,** box office 0171/704-4040; Tube: Arsenal); **Tottenham Hotspur,** 748 High Rd., N17 (☎ **0181/365-5000,** box office 0870/840-2468; Tube: Seven Sisters); and **Chelsea,** Stamford Bridge, Fulham Road, SW6 (☎ **0171/385-5545,** box office (☎ 0891/ 121-011; Tube: Fulham Broadway). Tickets cost £21 to £34 ($34.65 to $56.10). The country's most visible site of world-class soccer matches is **Wembley Stadium,** Wembley, Middlesex (☎ **0181/902-8833;** Tube: Wembley Park), about 6 miles north of London's center.

HORSE RACING   Within easy reach of central London are horse-racing tracks at Kempton Park, Sandown Park, and the most famous of them all, Epsom, where the Derby is the main feature of the meeting in early June. Racing takes place both mid-week and on weekends, but not continuously. Contact **United Racecourses Ltd.** (☎ **01372/470047**) for information on the next races on one of these tracks.

TENNIS   Fans from around the world focus on **Wimbledon** (Tube: Southfields). At the All England Lawn Tennis & Croquet Club, you'll see some of the world's greatest tennis players in action. The famous annual championships span roughly the last week in June to the first week in July, with matches lasting from about 2pm until dark. (The gates open at 10:30am.) Tickets usually range in price from £15 to £60 ($24.75 to $99). Center-court seats are sold by lottery. A limited number of tickets for the out-side courts are available at the gate. For recorded ticket information, call ☎ 0181/ 946-2244, or send a self-addressed stamped envelope (only from August to December) to the **All England Lawn Tennis & Croquet Club,** P.O. Box 98, Church Road, Wimbledon, SW19 5AE.

7 London Walks

The best way to discover London is on foot. A jumble of ancient mews and antique-filled alleyways, it's a city that's easy and fun to get lost in. Since many of the major sights are concentrated in specific areas of the city—official London in Westminster and Whitehall, gentlemanly London in St. James's, and so on—walking is a good way to take in a number of London sights at one time.

For additional information on many of the sights mentioned below, see chapter 6.

Walking Tour 1
Where London Was Born: The City

Start: The southern terminus of London Bridge. Tube: London Bridge or Monument.

Finish: St. Paul's Cathedral. Tube: St. Paul's.

Time: About 3 hours, excluding interior visits.

Best Times: Weekday mornings, when the financial district is functioning, but churches aren't crowded.

Worst Times: Weekends, when the district is almost deserted.

The area known as the City—the original one-square mile that the Romans called "Londinium"—offers the densest concentration of historic and cultural monuments in Britain. It's also one of the financial capitals of the world—Britain's Wall Street, as it were.

Our tour begins on the southern edge of the Thames, directly to the west of London Bridge, one of the world's most famous bridges. Facing the Thames rises the bulk of:

1. **Southwark Cathedral.** When built in the 1200s, it was an outpost of the faraway diocese of Winchester. Deconsecrated after Henry VIII's Reformation, it later housed bakeries and pigpens. Much of what you see is a result of a sorely needed 19th-century rebuilding, but its Gothic interior, with its multiple commemorative plaques, gives an idea of the religious power of the medieval church.

    After your visit, walk across the famous:

2. **London Bridge.** Originally designed by Henry de Colechurch under the patronage of Henry II in 1176 but replaced several times since. Until 1729, it was the only bridge across the

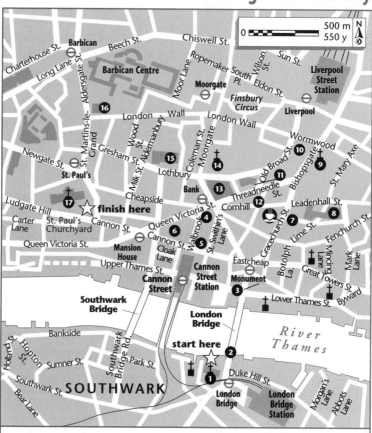

0 | 500 m
| 550 y

N

1. Southwark Cathedral
2. London Bridge
3. Monument
4. Mansion House
5. Church of
   St. Stephen Walbrook
6. The Temple of Mithras
7. Leadenhall Market
8. Lloyd's of London Building
9. St. Helen Bishopsgate
10. NatWest Tower
11. London Stock Exchange
12. Royal Exchange
13. Bank of England
14. St. Margaret, Lothbury
15. Guildhall
16. Museum of London
17. St. Paul's Cathedral

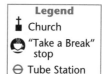

Legend

✝ Church

☕ "Take a Break" stop

⊖ Tube Station

Thames. During the Middle Ages, the bridge was lined with shops; houses crowded its edges. The bridge served as the showplace of severed heads—preserved in tar—of enemies of the British monarchs. (The most famous of these was the head of Sir Thomas More, the highly vocal lord chancellor, beheaded in 1535.) The 1825–31 bridge was moved to the United States and is now a tourist attraction in Lake Havasu, Arizona. The current bridge was completed in 1973.

After crossing the river, head east along Monument Street, the steep cobbled street that descends to the right. Detour down it a short distance to read the commemorative plaques attached to the:

3. Monument. Commemorating the Great Fire of 1666, this soaring Doric column is appropriately capped with a carved version of a flaming urn. The disaster it memorializes started in a bakery in nearby Pudding Lane; the fire raged for 4 days and nights, and destroyed 80% of the City. A cramped and foreboding set of stairs spirals up to the top. It's a tough climb, but the view of the cityscape, so heavily influenced after the fire by architect Sir Christopher Wren (who also designed the Monument itself), is worth it.

Retrace your steps toward London Bridge, but this time head northwest along King William Street until you reach the Bank Underground station, within a stone's throw of some of England's most powerful financial institutions. As you reach Mansion House Place, make a left, looking right to:

4. Mansion House, the official residence of the Lord Mayor, built between 1739 and 1752 and designed by George Dance the Elder. A rather optimistic pediment frieze depicts London defeating Envy and ushering in Plenty. The mansion's architectural showcase is the Egyptian Hall. Official banquets are staged here, but unless you get an invitation, you'll have to confine your viewing to the exterior.

From the mansion, proceed into a small passageway, St. Stephen's Row, and at the end make a left into Walbrook, the site of a polluted brook that was paved over in medieval times. On the left is the entrance to:

5. St. Stephen Walbrook. One of Sir Christopher Wren's finest works, the splendid dome of this church served as a model for St. Paul's Cathedral. The British sculptor Henry Moore carved the travertine altar under the dome in 1986.

Now walk across Walbrook and head into Bucklersbury, continuing until you reach Queen Victoria Street. Turn left, walk 1 block, make another left, and climb the steps outside the major entrance to Temple Court. Here on your left you can peer over the railings at:

6. The Temple of Mithras, London's archaeological jewel. Although shaped like a miniature Christian church, the temple was held sacred by the Mithraic cult, which had its origins in Iran and reached the Roman Empire prior to Christianity. For more details, see "Roman London" in "More Central London Attractions," in chapter 6.

After you've looked around, walk back to the Bank Underground. Here, head east along Cornhill, which becomes Leadenhall Street. Just after the intersection with Gracechurch Street, behind Lloyd's of London, you'll come upon:

7. Leadenhall Market, the City's central and conspicuously nonfinancial market. Horace Jones designed these curved arcades in 1881, which have been home ever since to a colorful collection of butchers, fishmongers, cheesemongers, and flowermongers, as well as pubs and restaurants.

Once you're finished buying or browsing, return to Gracechurch Street and walk north, and then right (east) on Leadenhall Street. Take the second right (south) on Lime Street, where you can admire the soaring and iconoclastically modern:

8. **Lloyd's of London Building.** Designed by Richard Rogers in 1986, this striking glass, steel, and concrete structure in the heart of ancient Roman London is the company's most recent home. Lloyd's was founded in the 1680s as a marine insurer; today it is perhaps the most famous—and financially troubled—insurer in the world. Immense underwriting losses in the early 1990s threatened the company's survival. The viewing gallery and exhibit on the role of Lloyd's past and present have been closed since a massive IRA bomb went off in Bishopsgate in 1992.

Nearby are the **London Metal Exchange,** the **London Futures and Options Exchange,** and other financial institutions whose clout is felt around the world.

Next follow Lime Street back to Leadenhall and turn left. Take the first right on Bishopsgate, and then the second right, and turn into an alleyway known as Great St. Helen's. Toward the end, you'll find the largest surviving medieval church in London:

9. **St. Helen Bishopsgate,** built in the 1400s and dedicated to St. Helen, the legendary British mother of the Roman emperor Constantine. Fashionable during the Elizabethan and Jacobean periods, its interior monuments, memorials, and grave markers are of special interest.

Exit back onto Bishopsgate and turn right (north). Two blocks later, turn left onto Wormwood Street. Then take the first left, Old Broad Street. Towering above you rises the modern bulk of the tallest building in Britain and the second-highest in Europe, the:

10. **NatWest Tower.** Richard Seifert designed these headquarters of National Westminster Bank in 1981. Its massive concrete foundations are built on top of mostly impervious clay, allowing the building to sway gently in the wind. Unfortunately, since it has no observation tower open to the public, you'll have to admire it from afar.

Continue south along Old Broad Street, noticing on your right the imposing headquarters of the:

11. **London Stock Exchange.** Built in the early 1960s to replace its outmoded original quarters, this institution has become much less boisterous since most of the City's financial operations went modern in 1986, from face-to-face agreements between brokers to computerized deal making, with the exchange functioning as an electronic clearinghouse.

🕮 **TAKE A BREAK**   Continue southwest along Old Broad Street until it merges with Threadneedle Street. Cross Threadneedle Street, walk a few paces to your left, and head south along the narrow confines of Finch Lane. Cross busy Cornhill to the south side of the street. Follow it east to St. Michael's Alley to **Jamaica Wine House,** St. Michael's Alley, EC3 (☎ **0171/626-9496**), one of Europe's oldest coffeehouses. Once a favorite hangout of London merchants and the sea captains who imported their goods, today it also dispenses ale, lager, wine, and bar snacks.

After tippling, take time to explore the medieval maze of narrow alleyways that provides shelter from roaring weekday traffic. Then head back to the major boulevard, Cornhill, just north of your refueling stop. Here, near the junction of five major streets, rises the:

12. **Royal Exchange.** Designed by William Tite in the early 1840s, its imposing neoclassical pediment is inset with Richard Westmacott's sculpture of *Commerce.*

Launched by a partnership of merchants and financiers during the Elizabethan Age, the Royal Exchange was a direct attempt to lure European banking and trading functions from Antwerp (then the financial capital of northern Europe) to London. Frenzied trading and auctioning of raw materials continued here until 1982, when the building became the headquarters of the London International Financial Futures Exchange (LIFFE).

On the opposite side of Threadneedle Street rises the massive bulk of the:

13. **Bank of England.** Originally established "for the Publick Good and Benefit of Our People" in a charter granted in 1694 by William and Mary, it's a treasure trove of gold bullion, British banknotes, and historical archives. The only part of this massive building open to the public is the **Bank of England Museum,** whose entrance is on a narrow side street, Bartholomew Lane (☎ 0171/ **601-5793;** open Monday through Friday from 10am to 5pm; free admission).

From the Bank of England, walk northwest along Prince's Street to Lothbury. On the northeast corner of the intersection rises yet another church by Sir Christopher Wren, this one completed in 1690:

14. **St. Margaret Lothbury.** Filled with statues of frolicking cupids, elaborately carved screens, and a soaring eagle near the altar, the interior is well worth a visit.

Now walk west on Lothbury, which will become Gresham Street. After passing a handful of alleyways, on your right you'll see the gardens and the grand historical facade of the:

15. **Guildhall.** The power base for the Lord Mayor of London since the 12th century (continually rebuilt and enlarged since), Guildhall was the site of endless power negotiations throughout the Middle Ages between the English kings (headquartered outside the City at Westminster) and the guilds, associations, and brotherhoods of the City's merchants and financiers. Today, the rituals associated with the Lord Mayor are almost as elaborate as those of the monarchy itself. The Guildhall's medieval crypt is the largest in London; its east facade was rebuilt by Sir Christopher Wren after the Great Fire of 1666.

Continue westward on Gresham and turn right onto Wood Street. Walk north to London Wall, and then left for about a block. On the right you'll see the modern:

16. **Museum of London.** Located in new quarters built in 1975, it contains London memorabilia gathered from several earlier museums, as well as one of the best collections of period costumes in the world. Built on top of the western gate of the ancient Roman colony of Londinium, the museum has a strong collection of archaeological remnants unearthed during centuries of City construction projects, as well as dioramas portraying the Great Fire and Victorian prison cells.

Now head south on Aldersgate, which quickly becomes St. Martins-le-Grand. After you merge with Newgate Street, the enormous stately dome of one of Europe's most important churches slowly appears in front of you:

17. **St. Paul's Cathedral.** Sir Christopher Wren's undisputed masterpiece is known to many as the site of the ill-fated wedding of Prince Charles and Princess Diana. St. Paul's also held the state funerals of Nelson, Wellington, and Churchill, and it served as an inspiration to a generation of Londoners who survived the bombings of World War II. The only cathedral in England to be constructed with a dome, and the country's only church built in the English baroque style, St. Paul's was also the first English cathedral designed and built by a single architect.

From St. Paul's, you can catch the Underground's Central Line to your next destination.

Walking Tour 2
Official London: Westminster & Whitehall

Start: Entrance of the Tate Gallery. Tube: Pimlico.
Finish: National Portrait Gallery, Trafalgar Square. Tube: Charing Cross or Leicester Square.
Time: About 3 hours, excluding interior visits.
Best Times: Monday through Thursday, when Parliament is in session.
Worst Times: Evenings and Sunday, when the district becomes almost deserted except for fast-moving traffic.

This tour will take you on a route parallel to the Thames, immersing you in some of the most visible symbols of England's historic democracy and monarchy.

After leaving the Pimlico Station, continue east along Bessborough Street, which becomes Bessborough Gardens as it leads toward the Thames and the Vauxhall Bridge. Once you reach Millbank, fronting the Thames, head north (left) along this major artery. On your left you can begin your tour in front of the grand Palladian entrance to one of the most interesting art museums in the world, the:

1. **Tate Gallery.** Built in 1897 and donated to London by the scion of a sugar baron, it holds the works of virtually every great painter in British history. You'll want to return to enjoy the collection at your leisure, but for the moment, walk north along the west bank of the Thames (known at this point as Millbank), with the Houses of Parliament looming ahead of you. Just past Lambeth Bridge, turn inland onto Dean Stanley Street and after 1 block you'll arrive at:

2. **Smith Square** and its centerpiece **St. John's Church.** Built in a highly personal neoclassical style by Thomas Archer in 1728, the church was heavily damaged by bombing in 1941. Since rebuilding, it serves as a concert venue.

   Retrace your steps to the Thames and turn left (north) in the direction of the Houses of Parliament. Enter the verdant triangular-shaped park at the southern entrance, a tranquil oasis rich with sculpture, the:

3. **Victoria Tower Gardens.** Here you'll find a 1915 replica of Auguste Rodin's 1895 masterpiece *The Burghers of Calais*, and A. G. Walker's monument to Emmeline Pankhurst, the early-20th-century leader of the British suffragette movement who was frequently imprisoned for her efforts.

   Near the northern perimeter of the garden, detour inland by turning left on Great College Street for about a block and on your right notice:

4. **Abbey Garden.** Associated with nearby Westminster Abbey and continuously cultivated over the past 900 years, it's one of the oldest gardens in England, rich with lavender and ecclesiastical ruins. Even if the gate is locked, parts of this charming historic oddity are visible from the street outside.

   Retrace your steps along Great College Street to Millbank (which on some maps might be referred to as Abingdon Street) and turn left (north), remaining on the side of Millbank opposite the Houses of Parliament. The tower on your left, completed in 1366 by Edward III for storing treasures, is the:

5. **Jewel Tower.** This is all that remains of the domestic portions of the once-mighty Palace of Westminster. A small museum details the construction of the Houses of Parliament.

   Now continue north along Millbank (or Abingdon Street) for 2 blocks, passing on your left the semicircular apse of the rear side of one of Britain's most densely packed artistic and cultural highlights:

6. Westminster Abbey, one of the most majestic and frequently visited sights in Europe. Completed in 1245, it's the spiritual heart of London, steeped in enough tradition, majesty, sorrow, and blood to merit a volume of its own. Turn left, skirting the building's northern flank, and enter through its western facade.

After your visit, leave the abbey through the Cloisters, emerging into Dean's Yard, site of Westminster School. Look for an arch straight ahead on the right, which leads to the west door of the abbey and the:

7. Sanctuary. Consisting of two streets, called Broad Sanctuary and Little Sanctuary, the Sanctuary in medieval days was a jumble of buildings and narrow winding lanes. Enclosed by the precinct wall of Westminster, the complex offered safe haven for the downtrodden, and, occasionally, for political refugees. Over time, the Sanctuary gained a reputation for sheltering a "mire of cutthroats, whores, pickpockets, and murderers." It became so disease ridden and crime infested that James I ordered it closed. Although slums existed here for centuries, urban renewal has successfully removed all remnants of its more notorious days.

After a walk around, look to your right, just beyond the abbey's north transept, to see the much-restored:

8. St. Margaret's Church. Built between 1504 and 1523, it is the parish church for the House of Commons. It contains a noteworthy collection of stained-glass windows as well as the body of Sir Walter Raleigh (who was beheaded just outside its front entrance). Both poet John Milton (1656) and Winston Churchill (1908) were married here.

Exiting from St. Margaret's, you'll see the neo-Gothic grandeur of the:

9. Houses of Parliament. The mother of all Parliaments was built between 1840 and 1860 by architects Sir Charles Barry and Augustus Pugin (both of whom are said to have suffered several nervous breakdowns and early deaths as a result of the overwork and stress involved in its building). The Houses cover 8 acres and proudly display perhaps the greatest volume of ornate stonework in the world. Your tour of the interior (which you might choose to reserve for another day) begins at the base of:

10. Big Ben. The tall clock tower of the Houses of Parliament is located near the building's northwest corner (not that you could miss it!). Just as the Eiffel Tower is the symbol of Paris, Big Ben is the international icon of London. Completed in 1858 to 59, the 316-foot clock tower takes its name from Sir Benjamin Hall, the first commissioner of public works and evidently a gentleman of considerable proportions. Perhaps not inappropriately, the clock mechanism in this tower alone weighs 5 tons. Big Ben kept time for 117 years before succumbing to "metal fatigue" in 1976, at which time major repairs were needed to keep it running. When the House of Commons is in session, the light above the clock is lit.

One of the best views of the Houses of Parliament can be enjoyed from:

11. Westminster Bridge, built in 1862 in cast iron and one of the most ornate bridges in London. To reach the bridge from Big Ben, turn right on Bridge Street. The western base of the bridge, aptly named Westminster Pier, is the departure point for many boat trips down the Thames; see "Sightseeing & Boat Tours Along the Thames" in chapter 6.

Now retrace your footsteps along Bridge Street, passing Big Ben, and take the second right along the busy thoroughfare of Parliament Street. Take the first left along King Charles Street where, at Clive Steps on the left, you'll reach the:

12. Cabinet War Rooms. This unpretentious handful of rooms served as the meeting place for Churchill's Cabinet during World War II, the site where many of the statesman's most stirring speeches were crafted. The rooms were built

Walking Tour—Westminster & Whitehall

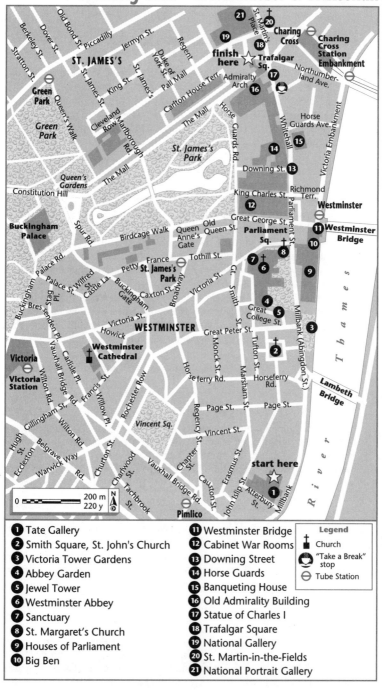

1. Tate Gallery
2. Smith Square, St. John's Church
3. Victoria Tower Gardens
4. Abbey Garden
5. Jewel Tower
6. Westminster Abbey
7. Sanctuary
8. St. Margaret's Church
9. Houses of Parliament
10. Big Ben
11. Westminster Bridge
12. Cabinet War Rooms
13. Downing Street
14. Horse Guards
15. Banqueting House
16. Old Admirality Building
17. Statue of Charles I
18. Trafalgar Square
19. National Gallery
20. St. Martin-in-the-Fields
21. National Portrait Gallery

Legend

✝ Church

☕ "Take a Break" stop

⊖ Tube Station

17 feet underground for protection from Nazi air raids; a half dozen of them are open to visitors.

Retrace your steps back to Parliament Street, turning left (north) and left again at:

13. Downing Street. Although security might prevent you from getting a close look, no. 10 is the famed official residence of the British prime minister; no. 11, the residence of the chancellor of the exchequer; and no. 12, the office of the chief government whip—the member of Parliament responsible for maintaining discipline and cooperation among party members in the House of Commons.

Continue north along Parliament Street, which becomes Whitehall near Downing Street. Here both sides of the street reflect the administrative soul of Britain; meetings and negotiations inside these majestic buildings influence politics around the world. One of the most noteworthy of these is the:

14. Horse Guards. Completed in 1760 and designed by William Kent, it's one of the most symmetrical and imposing of the many buildings along Whitehall. The ceremonial Mounting of the Guard is held here (the first step of an equestrian ceremony that ends with the Changing of the Guard in front of Buckingham Palace; see chapter 6 for details).

Across the avenue rise the pure proportions of one of London's most superlative examples of Palladian architecture, the:

15. Banqueting House. Commissioned by James I and designed by Inigo Jones in the early 1600s, it's one of the most aesthetically perfect buildings in England. Its facade was the backdrop for one of the seminal events in British history: the beheading of Charles I. The ceilings in the magnificent dining hall were painted by Peter Paul Rubens.

Continuing north 1 block along Whitehall, you'll come to a great place for a breather:

☕ TAKE A BREAK **The Clarence Pub,** 53 Whitehall, W1 (☎ **0171/ 930-4808**). One of London's most famous pubs, beloved by Parliamentarians throughout England. Opened in the 18th century, it has been quenching the thirsts of government administrators ever since. With oak ceiling beams and battered wooden tables ringed by churchlike pews, at least a half-dozen real ales are on tap, complemented by the usual pub grub. A restaurant serves hardier fare.

After drinks (perhaps with a few members of Parliament), notice the building almost directly across Whitehall, the:

16. Old Admiralty Building, Spring Gardens. Designed in 1725 by Sir Thomas Ripley (and strictly off-limits except for official business), it served for almost 2 centuries as the administrative headquarters of the British Navy until it was replaced by new quarters between the wars.

Continue north until you see what may be the finest and most emotive equestrian statue in London, the:

17. Statue of Charles I. On an island in the middle of speeding traffic, it commemorates the tragic fate of this British king and signals the beginning of:

18. Trafalgar Square. The grandest plaza in London, it is centered around a soaring monument to Lord Nelson, the hero of the Battle of Trafalgar who decisively defeated Napoléon's navy off the coast of Spain in 1805. Against the square's northern perimeter rises the grand neoclassical:

19. National Gallery. The collection—one of the finest in the world of Western art—definitely merits a detailed tour of its own.

The church that flanks the eastern edge of Trafalgar Square is one of London's most famous:

20. St. Martin-in-the-Fields. Designed in the style of Sir Christopher Wren in 1726 by James Gibbs, it has a Corinthian portico and a steeple whose form inspired the architects of many American churches. The christening place of Charles II and the burial place of his fun-loving mistress, Nell Gwynne, the church also boasts a noted orchestra.

Finally, for an overview of the faces instrumental in British and world history, walk to the right (eastern) side of the National Gallery, where the greatest repository of portraits in Europe awaits your inspection at the:

21. National Portrait Gallery, 2 St. Martin's Place. They're all here: kings, cardinals, mistresses, playwrights, poets, coquettes, dilettantes, and other names rich in historical connotations (and modern ones—look for the likes of Paul McCartney, Sir Richard Attenborough, and others on the first floor). The museum celebrates the portraits' subjects more than their authors. An hour or two here is a great way to wind up your tour.

Walking Tour 3
Aristocratic St. James's

Start: Admiralty Arch. Tube: Charing Cross.
Finish: Buckingham Palace. Tube: St. James's Park or Green Park.
Time: About 2 hours, not including stops.
Best Time: Before 3pm.
Worst Time: After dark.

Incorporating neighborhoods reserved almost since their development for the British aristocracy, this walking tour includes many of the grandest sights of 18th- and 19th-century imperial England.

After leaving Charing Cross Station, walk left (west) along the Strand toward the Mall, Trafalgar Square on your right, and look straight ahead for the monumental eastern entrance of the:

1. Admiralty Arch. Commissioned by Queen Victoria's son, King Edward VII (who died before it was completed), it was designed in 1911 by Sir Aston Webb. Piercing its center is a quintet of arches faced with Portland stone, marking the first (and widest) stage of a majestic processional route leading from Buckingham Palace eastward to St. Paul's Cathedral. The centermost of the five arches is opened only for ceremonial occasions; the two side arches are for vehicular traffic, and the two smallest arches for pedestrians.

Pass beneath the arch and enter the wide panoramic thoroughfare, which will eventually lead to Buckingham Palace. With your back to the Admiralty Arch, stretching out before you is:

2. The Mall. Lined with even rows of plane trees, The Mall was originally the garden of nearby St. James's Palace and host to aristocratic games of *paille maille* (a precursor of croquet) by the courtiers of Charles II. The present planned avenue was designed by Sir Aston Webb as a memorial to the recently departed Queen Victoria and was opened in 1911. The Mall is often closed to traffic on Sundays, when it becomes a pedestrian extension of adjacent St. James's Park. The Mall's expanse is a favorite exercise area for London's equestrians and their mounts.

Immediately to your left (with your back to the Admiralty Arch) are the inter-connected buildings of the:

3. New and Old Admiralties. Important nerve centers of the British military, they have seen their share of drama since the early 18th century.

As you stroll southwest down The Mall, on your right will be one of the most regal ensembles of town houses in London:

4. Carlton House Terrace. These buildings replaced the once-palatial home of the 18th-century prince regent, who later became George III. He built, and subse-quently demolished at staggering expense, the most beautiful private home in Britain. Only the columns were saved, which were later recycled into the portico of Trafalgar Square's National Gallery. The resulting row of ivory-colored neo-classical town houses was one of architect John Nash's last works before he died, much maligned from financial scandal in 1835. Today, in addition to art galleries and cultural institutions, Carlton House Terrace houses the headquarters of one of the most highly reputed scientific bodies in the world, the Royal Society.

Midway along the length of Carlton House Terrace, its pristine neoclassical expanse is pierced by:

5. The Duke of York Column and Steps. Built in honor of the second son of George III, this massive sculpture was funded by withholding 1 day's pay from every soldier in the British Empire. The resulting column was chiseled from pink granite, and the statue created by Sir Richard Westmacott in 1834. Contemporary wits, aware that the duke died massively in debt, joked that placing his effigy on a column was the only way to keep him out of his creditors' grasp. The soaring column and monument (the statue weighs 7 tons) dominates the square it prefaces:

6. Waterloo Place. One of the most prestigious examples of urban planning in London, it symbolizes both aristocratic elegance and nostalgia for England's great military victories over Napoléon. No. 107 (designed in 1830 and one of the finest examples of early-19th-century neoclassical architecture in London) is headquarters for one of the most distinguished gentlemen's clubs in Britain, the Athenaeum Club.

Notice, within Waterloo Place, the:

7. Statue of Edward VII, by Sir Bertram Mackennal. It honors the man who ush-ered in the Edwardian Age and who was responsible for much of the grand neighborhood northeast of Buckingham Palace. The son of long-lived Victoria, he ascended the throne at the age of 60, only 9 years before his death. As if to create a sense of historical perspective, a statue dedicated to the victims of the Crimean War, part of which honors Florence Nightingale, stands at the opposite end of Waterloo Place.

History buffs especially will appreciate Carlton House Gardens, running into Carlton House Terrace's western end. Devotees of French history in particular should read the plaques that identify:

8. No. 4 Carlton House Gardens, the World War II London headquarters of Charles de Gaulle's French government in exile and the site of many of his French-language radio broadcasts to the French underground. (A second façade of this same building faces The Mall, on the opposite side of the block.)

One of the streets intersecting Waterloo Place is an avenue replete with exclu-sive private clubs. Not to be confused with the longer and broader expanse of The Mall, this is:

Walking Tour—St. James's

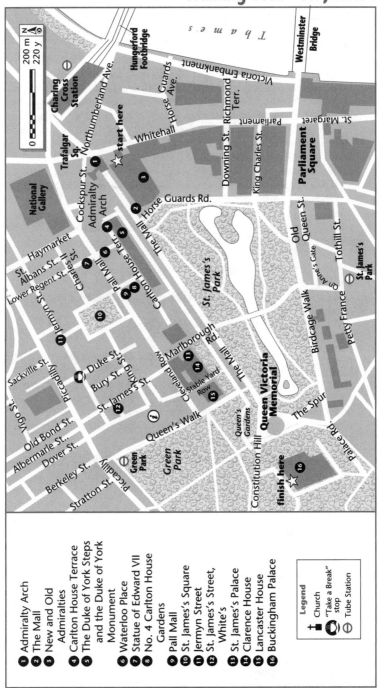

Legend

✝ Church
☕ "Take a Break" stop
Ⓣ Tube Station

1. Admiralty Arch
2. The Mall
3. New and Old Admiralties
4. Carlton House Terrace
5. The Duke of York Steps and the Duke of York Monument
6. Waterloo Place
7. Statue of Edward VII
8. No. 4 Carlton House Gardens
9. Pall Mall
10. St. James's Square
11. Jermyn Street
12. St. James's Street, White's
13. St. James's Palace
14. Clarence House
15. Lancaster House
16. Buckingham Palace

251

9. Pall Mall. (Note that Londoners say "pell mell" rather than "paul mawl"). Membership in many of the clubs here is very prestigious and sought after; wait lists of up to a decade for membership to the most exclusive of them are not uncommon (and many on these lists will never get in).

Walk west for a block along Pall Mall (beware of the dangerously fast one-way traffic) and take the first right (north) into the elegant 18th-century precincts of:

10. St. James's Square. Laid out in the 1660s, it was built on land donated by the first earl of St. Albans, Henry Jermyn, a friend of the widow of Charles I and the future king Charles II. Magnificent private houses, occupied by noble families wishing to live near the seat of royal power at nearby St. James's Palace, originally lined the square on all sides. Of special interest is no. 10 (Chatham House), the private residence of three British prime ministers, the last of whom was Queen Victoria's nemesis, William Gladstone. At no. 32, General Eisenhower and his subordinates planned the 1942 invasion of North Africa and the 1944 Allied invasion of Normandy. At no. 16, a bloodstained officer delivered the announcement of Wellington's climactic defeat of Napoléon's forces at Waterloo (along with the captured eagle-shaped symbols of Napoléon's army).

After you circumnavigate the square, exit at its northern edge via Duke of York Street. One block later, turn left onto the most prestigious shopping street in London:

11. Jermyn Street. Expensive, upscale, and politely attended shops here are the best of British tradition and luxury goods.

Follow Jermyn to Duke Street, where you can:

🔵 **TAKE A BREAK   Green's Champagne and Oyster Bar,** 36 Duke St., SW1 (☎ **0171/930-4566**). Its façade and paneled decor might call to mind gentlemen's clubs in the neighborhood. This one, however, welcomes non-members, and many clients are female. From the battered bar, you can order spirits and wine, as well as platters of oysters, caviar, shrimp, and crab (to take at the bar or a table) and a wide variety of English appetizers and main courses. The place is especially popular at lunchtime.

Exit from Duke Street onto Jermyn Street, turn right (west), and continue along the shops. Two blocks later, turn left onto:

12. St. James's Street. It too contains its share of private clubs, the most fashionable of which is arguably **White's,** at no. 37, designed in 1788 by James Wyatt. Prince Charles' friends held his stag party here the night before his marriage to Lady Diana. Past members have included Evelyn Waugh (who took refuge here from his literary "hounds of modernity"). Even should you be recommended for membership (which is unlikely), the wait list is eight years.

At the bottom (southern end) of St. James's Street is one of the most historic buildings in London:

13. St. James's Palace. Birthplace of many British monarchs, it served as the principal royal residence from 1698 (when Whitehall Palace burned down) until the ascent of Victoria—who preferred Buckingham Palace—in 1837. Originally enlarged from a Tudor core built by Henry VIII for one of his ill-fated queens, it was altered by Sir Christopher Wren in 1703. The palace, rich in history, gave its name to the entire neighborhood.

All the world seemingly viewed this palace on TV during the funeral of Princess Diana in 1997. The cortege began at her former residence, Kensington Palace, but stopped at St. James's Palace, the present residence of Prince Charles.

At St. James's, the cortege picked up not only Charles, but the young princes Harry and William, along with Prince Philip and Diana's brother, Earl Spencer.

After your visit, walk southwest along Cleveland Row, and then turn left (southeast) onto Stable Yard Row. On your left rises the side of:

14. Clarence House. Designed in 1829 by John Nash, it's the official London home of the Queen Mother. On the opposite side of Stable Yard Row rises the side of the decidedly formal:

15. Lancaster House. Designed in 1827 by Benjamin Wyatt, it has been known variously as York House and Stafford House. Chopin performed his ballads and nocturnes for Queen Victoria here. Edward VIII lived here during the renunciation of his throne (required as a precondition for his marriage to the notorious Mrs. Simpson). Heavily damaged by World War II bombings, it has since been gracefully restored and furnished in the French Louis XV style, and it serves as a setting for state receptions and dinners.

Within a few steps you arrive at the multiple plane trees of The Mall; here, turn right for a view of the front of fabled:

16. Buckingham Palace. Known the world over, the official London residence of every British monarch since Victoria is many things: regal, mysterious, magical and, yes, vital. Tours are offered in the summer months; For more information, see chapter 6.

Walking Tour 4
Chelsea, London's Quintessential Village

Start: Sloane Square. Tube: Sloane Square.
Finish: National Army Museum. Tube: Sloane Square.
Time: About 2 hours, not counting stops.
Best Times: Wednesday through Saturday from 10am to 4pm when most attractions are open. Saturday morning is best for shopping along King's Road.
Worst Times: After 5pm and on Sunday when shops and most interiors are closed (although on Sunday there is less traffic).

Historically, Chelsea has been home to artists and writers; today, it's home to the prosperous and one of the most complete and attractively scaled "villages" within the city. Its residents have included Henry VIII, Henry James, J. M. W. Turner, John Singer Sargent, Thomas Carlyle, Oscar Wilde, Mick Jagger, and Baroness Margaret Thatcher.

From Sloane Square station, you'll be facing:

1. Sloane Square. This northernmost gateway to Chelsea was laid out in 1780 on land belonging to Sir Hans Sloane (1660–1753), whose collection of minerals, fossils, and plant specimens formed the core of the British Museum. A few steps to the right of the Tube station is the **Royal Court Theatre,** which opened in 1888. The theater became famous staging plays by George Bernard Shaw, including the first performance of *Candida* (1904). Since the 1956 premier of John Osborne's *Look Back in Anger,* it has been known for producing new and often adventurous plays.

Walk back past the Tube station straight ahead (south) along:

2. Sloane Gardens. Honoring Sir Hans Sloane, former president of the Royal Society, are gardens flanked by splendid redbrick houses. Curiously enough, the developer, William Willett, invented daylight saving time, a concept that wasn't terribly popular with workers in 1889. Chelsea has counted a great many promi-nent names among its residents, including Sir Philip Gibbs (1877–1962), the novelist, journalist, historian, and political analyst who lived at 8 Sloane Gar-dens; and Egerton Castle (1858–1920), the novelist and dramatist who resided at 49 Sloane Gardens in his later years.

When you reach the end of Sloane Gardens, take a left onto Lower Sloane Street and proceed 2 blocks, crossing the street to:

3. The Old Burial Ground. Adjoining Chelsea Royal Hospital, it's estimated that some 10,000 soldiers were interred here, though few gravestones remain. One local newspaper reported that in the 1700s a 123-year-old man was buried here. Although you can't go inside to visit the burial grounds, you can get a good view through the railings.

Next take a right onto Royal Hospital Road (the burial ground will be on your left). After about 100 yards, go left through:

4. Ranelagh Gardens. Informal and undulating, this was once the 1690 house and gardens of Lord Ranelagh, paymaster general to the British Armed Forces. At one time, this was one of the most fashionable pleasure gardens of London, attracting the *beau monde*. Gibbon called it "the most convenient place for courtships of every kind," while Goldsmith loved the "fashionable frivolity" of the place. Only the Chelsea Royal Hospital remains in the park; all other build-ings were demolished.

Head right after leaving the gardens and backtrack through London Gate, taking another left into the driveway. From here, continue straight through the wooden doors leading into the foreground of:

5. Chelsea Royal Hospital. Designed in 1682 in the aftermath of the Great Fire of London, this is Sir Christopher Wren's second-greatest masterpiece (after St. Paul's Cathedral). The hospital was inspired by Louis XIV's Hôtel des Invalides in Paris; both were planned as homes for wounded or aging soldiers, and both are grandiose. The hospital is home to more than 400 war veteran pen-sioners who, in their blue or scarlet uniforms and three-cornered hats worn on special occasions, show visitors about.

Exit on Royal Hospital Road, take a pedestrian-only walkway to Franklin's Row, and continue in a northwesterly direction to:

6. The Duke of York's Headquarters. The Duke of York, second son of George III, founded this school, constructed in 1801 for the children of soldiers. The duke had been a military reformer, protesting against the selling of commissions until a scandal revealed that his own mistress was involved in hawking these commis-sions; the reformer resigned in disgrace. Today England's National Guard inhabits the grounds, and the headquarters are off-limits.

After viewing the well-kept grounds, take a left and head west along:

7. St. Leonard's Terrace, one of London's most delightful residential streets. No. 7 was the former residence of Sir Lawrence Olivier (1907–89) in the late 1970s. Bram Stoker (1847—1912), the creator of Count Dracula, lived here in 1896. The Irish author published his famous novel a year after moving here. The ter-race boasts some of London's most beautiful homes: see nos. 19, 21, 22, and especially no. 26, one of the oldest houses in the row.

Backtrack a bit to Olivier's former abode, turning left onto Royal Avenue, filled with stately redbrick Victorian homes. The street itself is much older, having been first laid out in 1682 by Sir Christopher Wren. At the end of the avenue, turn left onto dynamic:

Walking Tour—Chelsea

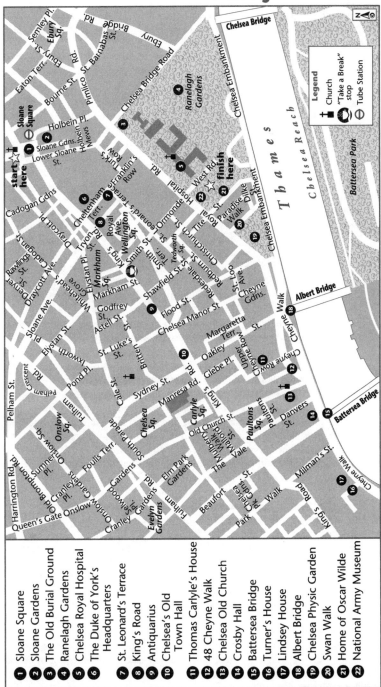

Legend
- ✠ Church
- 🚶 "Take a Break" stop
- Ⓞ Tube Station

1. Sloane Square
2. Sloane Gardens
3. The Old Burial Ground
4. Ranelagh Gardens
5. Chelsea Royal Hospital
6. The Duke of York's Headquarters
7. St. Leonard's Terrace
8. King's Road
9. Antiquarius
10. Chelsea's Old Town Hall
11. Thomas Carlyle's House
12. 48 Cheyne Walk
13. Chelsea Old Church
14. Crosby Hall
15. Battersea Bridge
16. Turner's House
17. Lindsey House
18. Albert Bridge
19. Chelsea Physic Garden
20. Swan Walk
21. Home of Oscar Wilde
22. National Army Museum

8. King's Road. Jammed with antiques stores, booksellers, restaurants, coffee-houses, tearooms, and designer boutiques, and peopled with hip "Sloane Rangers," or "Sloanies," it's a delightful area in which to observe the human comedy. Today it hardly recalls its origins; it was named King's Road because it was designed for Charles II as his route between his London palace and Hampton Court Palace.

TAKE A BREAK   Henry J. Bean's Bar & Grill, 195–197 King's Rd. (☎ **0171/352-9255**). This "Cheers"-style bar lures the homesick Yankees with big burgers, meaty hot dogs, and other Americana. In summer, you can eat and drink in the rose garden in the back. Happy hour with reduced drink prices is daily from 6 to 8pm (except Sunday).

After relaxing, continue walking southwest along King's Road. Midway between Shawfield Street and Flood Street is a warren of antiques sellers, clustered together into a complex known as:

9. Antiquarius, 135–141 King's Rd., SW3. Browse at will—maybe you'll find a near-heirloom you can't live without.

As you continue down King's Road, oval-shaped blue-and-white plaques identify buildings of particular interest. One that you should watch for is:

10. Chelsea's Old Town Hall. On the south side of King's Road, midway between Chelsea Manor and Oakley Street, it's the favorite hangout of everyone from punkers with nowhere else to go to soon-to-be-married couples applying for a marriage license. Many wedding parties stage photographs in front of its Georgian grandeur.

Continue to Oakley Street and head south until you come to Upper Cheyne Row. Follow it to Cheyne Row and the address at no. 24 that was:

11. Thomas Carlyle's House. One of the most interesting houses in London, particularly to literary enthusiasts, it's also one of the neighborhood's few houses open to the public. The former home of "the sage of Chelsea" and his wife Jane offers fascinating insight into Victorian life. Notice the small gravestone in the garden marking the burial place of the author's favorite dog.

After leaving the author's house, continue south to the Thames and Cheyne Walk, one of London's most famous streets, filled with expensive and chic town houses. Occupants of these elegantly proportioned buildings have included some very famous people. Pause a moment at:

12. No. 48 Cheyne Walk, where Mick Jagger lived for a while, alongside neighbors like bandmate Keith Richards, publishing magnate Lord Weidenfeld, and the grandson of oil industry giant J. Paul Getty. Artistic denizens of an earlier age included George Eliot, who spent part of her unconventional life (and later died) at no. 41. The star of the Pre-Raphaelite movement, Dante Gabriel Rossetti, lived in perhaps the street's finest building, no. 16.

If you head west toward Battersea Bridge, you'll come to Old Church Street, containing the parish church of St. Thomas More:

13. Chelsea Old Church (All Saints). Its graceful beauty survived the heavy damages inflicted on it and the surrounding neighborhood by Nazi bombing during World War II. Lovingly repaired, it contains a chapel partly designed by Hans Holbein; an urn holding the earthly remains of the man who owned most of Chelsea during the 1700s, Sir Hans Sloane; and a plaque commemorating the American novelist Henry James, a longtime Chelsea resident who died nearby in

1916. The building's Lawrence Chapel is reputed to have been the scene of Henry VIII's secret marriage to Jane Seymour several days before their official marriage in 1536.

Midway between heavily trafficked Beauford Street and quieter Danvers Street (both opening onto Cheyne Walk) is:

14. Crosby Hall. Unmarked by a street number, its chapel-like original brick-and-stone wing was built in the early 1400s and owned by both Richard III and Sir Thomas More. It was transported stone-by-stone from Bishopsgate in the early 1900s, partly under the financial incentive of American-born Lady Nancy Astor. With a modern wing of gray stone added in the 1950s, today it provides apartments and dining facilities for the British Federation of University Women. Sections of its interior (containing paintings by Holbein, a trussed roof, and some Jacobean furniture) are open free to the public (Monday through Saturday from 10am to noon and 2:15 to 5pm).

Back on Cheyne Walk, you can continue west, passing on your left:

15. Battersea Bridge. Although not the most famous bridge in London, it will help orient you and provide a clue to Chelsea's vital link to the Thames.

Next go westward to 119 Cheyne Walk, which is:

16. Turner's House. Its tall and narrow premises sheltered perhaps England's greatest painter, J. M. W. Turner (1775–1851), during the last years of his life. His canvases, although predating those of the French Impressionists, shimmer with color (you'll find a wonderful array at the Tate Gallery). When he died in this house, his very appropriate final words were, "God is Light."

Just to the east, at nos. 96–100, is one of Chelsea's most beautiful buildings, completed in the 1670s:

17. Lindsey House. Built around 1674 by the Swiss-born physician to two British kings (James I and Charles II), this house became the British headquarters of the Moravian Church around 1750. Later divided and sold as four separate residences, it housed the American-born painter James Whistler (at no. 96) between 1866 and 1879. Britain's most celebrated Edwardian architect, Sir Edwin Lutyens (1869–1944), designed the gardens of nos. 99 and 100.

At this point, retrace your steps eastward to Battersea Bridge. Here begins a beautiful walk eastward along Cheyne Walk through a historic neighborhood, marred only by the roar of the riverside traffic. Across the water is Battersea, a rapidly gentrifying neighborhood. Looming in the distance is:

18. Albert Bridge. Rivaled only by Tower Bridge and Westminster Bridge, this might be the most-photographed bridge in London. It was designed in 1873—at the height of the Victorian fascination with cast iron—by R. M. Ordish.

Continue past the Albert Bridge along Cheyne Walk until you reach Royal Hospital Road. The turf at this intersection (its entrance is at 66 Royal Hospital Road) belongs to the oldest surviving botanic garden in Britain, the:

19. Chelsea Physic Garden (also known as Chelsea Botanic Garden). In 1673, the Worshipful Society of Apothecaries founded these gardens for the collection, study, and dissemination of plants with medicinal value. Sir Hans Sloane, a botanist and physician to George II, provided permanent funding for them in 1722. Its 4 acres continue to serve as a research and educational facility. The exotic trees and shrubs, aromatic herbs, rock garden, tranquil pond, and greenhouses, make this a delightful place in which to stroll and take tea.

Now, continue your walk northeast along Royal Hospital Road, and turn right at the first cross street onto:

20. Swan Walk, a charming and obscure part of Chelsea worth a look for its wonderful 18th-century rowhouses. Walk down it, making the first left onto Dilke Street, and at the dead end turn left again onto Tite Street. At 34 Tite St., you'll see a plaque commemorating the:

21. Home of Oscar Wilde. Here, Wilde wrote many of his most charming plays, including *The Importance of Being Earnest* and *Lady Windermere's Fan*. After Wilde was arrested and imprisoned following the most famous trial for homosexuality in British history, the house was sold to pay his debts. The plaque was presented in 1954, a century after Wilde's birthday.

A few steps away on the same street are houses that once belonged to two famous American expatriate painters: No. 31 was the home of John Singer Sargent (and the studio where he painted many of his portraits); James McNeill Whistler lived at no. 35.

At the end of Tite Street, turn right onto Royal Hospital Road. Within a block are the fortresslike premises of the:

22. National Army Museum. Its premises contain galleries devoted to weapons, uniforms, and art, with dioramas of famous battles and such memorabilia as the skeleton of Napoléon's favorite horse.

Next door to the museum, a short distance to the northeast, is the building where the annual Chelsea Flower Show is held each May. For more information, see the "London Calendar of Events" in chapter 2.

To get back to the Sloane Square station, continue east along Royal Hospital Road until you come to Holbein Place, and then cut left (north) to Sloane Square.

Shopping | 8

When Prussian Field Marshal Blücher, Wellington's stout ally at Waterloo, first laid eyes on London, he allegedly slapped his thigh and exclaimed, "Herr Gott, what a city to plunder!" He was gazing at what, for the early 19th century, was a phenomenal mass of shops and stores—overwhelming to Herr Blücher's unsophisticated eyes. Since those days, other cities may have equaled London as a shopping mecca, but none have surpassed it.

1 Shopping London

Although London is one of the world's best shopping cities, it often seems made for visitors who sleep by a pot of gold at the end of the rainbow; locals are far more careful with their hard-earned pounds. To find real values, you'll have to do what most Londoners do: Wait for sales or search out specialty finds.

American-style shopping has taken Britain by storm, both in concept—warehouse stores and outlet malls—and in actual name: One block from Hamley's, you'll find the Disney Store. GAP is everywhere; Tiffany sells more wedding gifts than Asprey these days. Your best bet is to ignore anything American and to concentrate on British goods. You can also do well with French products; values are almost as good as those you'd find in Paris.

TAXES & SHIPPING Value-Added Tax (VAT) is the British version of sales tax. VAT is a whopping 17.5% on most goods, but it's already included in the price, so the number you see on the price tag is exactly what you'll pay at the register. Non-EU residents can get back much of the tax they pay by applying for a VAT refund.

In Britain, the minimum expenditure needed to qualify for a refund on Value-Added Tax is £50. Not every single store honors this minimum (it's £100 at Harrods; £75 at Selfridges; £62 at Hermès), but it's far easier to qualify for a tax refund in Britain than almost any other country in the European Union.

Vendors at flea markets might not be equipped to provide the paperwork for a refund, so if you're contemplating a major purchase and really want that refund, ask before you buy. Be suspicious of any dealer who tells you there's no VAT on antiques. Once this was true, but things have changed—the European Union has made the British add VAT to antiques. Since dealers still have mixed stock, pricing should reflect this fact. So ask if it's included—before you bargain on a price. Get to the price you're comfortable with first, then ask for the VAT refund.

How to Get Your VAT Refund

You *must* get your VAT refund form from the retailer. Several readers have reported that merchants have told them that they can get refund forms at the airport on their way out of the country. *This is not true.* Don't leave the store without a form—it must be completed by the retailer on the spot. After you have asked if the store does VAT refunds and determined their minimum, request the paperwork.

Fill out your portion of the form and then present it—along with the goods—at the Customs office in the airport. Allow a half hour to stand in line. Remember: You're required to show the goods at your time of departure, so put them in your carry-on.

Once the paperwork has been stamped by the officials, you have two choices: You can mail the papers (remember to bring a stamp) and receive your refund either as a British check (no!) or a credit card refund (yes!), or you can go directly to the Cash VAT Refund desk at the airport and get your refund in cash. The bad news: If you accept cash other than sterling, you will lose money on the conversion rate.

Be advised that many stores charge a flat fee for processing your refund, so £3 to £5 may be automatically deducted from the total that you receive. But since the VAT in Britain is 17.5%, if you get back 15%, you're doing fine.

Note: If you're traveling to other countries within the European Union, you go through this at your final destination in the EU, filing all your VAT refunds at one time.

VAT is not charged on goods shipped out of the country, whether you spend £50 or not. Many London shops will help you beat the VAT rap by shipping for you. But watch out: Shipping can double the cost of your purchase. Also expect to pay U.S. duties when the goods get to you at home.

You can ship on your flight home by paying for excess baggage (rates vary with the airline), or can have your packages shipped independently. Independent operators are generally less expensive than the airlines. Try **London Baggage,** London Air Terminal, Victoria Place, SW1 (☎ **0171/828-2400;** Tube: Victoria), or **Burns International Facilities,** at Heathrow Airport Terminal 1 (☎ **0181/745-5301**) and Terminal 4 (☎ **0181/745-7460**). But remember, you can only avoid the VAT up front if you have the store ship directly for you. If you ship via excess baggage or London Baggage, you'll still have to pay the VAT up front, and apply for a refund.

HOURS   London keeps fairly uniform store hours, mostly shorter than American equivalents. The norm is 10am opening and 5:30pm closing, with a late Wednesday or Thursday night until 7pm, maybe 8pm. Some stores in districts such as Chelsea and Covent Garden tend to keep slightly later hours.

Sunday shopping is now legal. Stores may be open for six hours; usually they choose 11am to 5pm. Stores in designated tourist areas and flea markets are exempt from this law and may stay open all day on Sunday. Therefore, Covent Garden, Greenwich, and Hampstead are big Sunday destinations for shoppers.

2 London's Best Buys

BUYING BRITISH   Bargain hunters should zero in on goods that are manufactured in England and are liable to cost much more when exported. These are—above all—anything from **The Body Shop, Filofax,** or **Dr. Martens;** many woolens and some cashmeres; most English brands of bone china; antiques; used silver; and rare books.

Antiques   Whether you're looking for museum-quality antiques or simply fun junk, London has the stores, the resources, the stalls, and the markets. While it might not be 1969 any more (you won't find priceless majolica for £20), there are still plenty of great finds along Portobello Road and the myriad other markets.

Aromatherapy   The British must have invented aromatherapy—just about every store sells gels, creams, lotions, and potions made with the right herbs and essential oils to cure whatever ails you, including jet lag. Whether it all works or not is secondary to the fact that most of the British brands are half the U.S. price. **The Body Shop** becomes the best store in the world at prices like these. Check out drugstore brands as well, especially The Body Shop knockoffs that **Boots The Chemist** makes, as well as their own line (sold in another part of the store) of healing foot gels.

Bone China   Savings actually depend on the brand, but can be as much as 50% off U.S. prices. Shipping and U.S. duties may wipe out any savings, so know what you're doing before you buy.

Cashmere   Some shoppers may be shocked at the price of cashmere, even on sale. While sale prices on Scottish cashmere are generally fair, most American shoppers are used to prices on Chinese cashmere, which is cheaper and of much lesser quality. It's rare to even find Chinese cashmere in the better stores in London, so before you throw down a piece in horror, check the quality. On an oranges-for-oranges basis, Scottish cashmere when on sale in London can be an excellent buy.

Cosmetics   Inexpensive brands of makeup cost less than they do in the United States. The French line **Bourjois** (made in the same factories that make Chanel makeup) sells for less in London than in Paris and isn't sold in the United States; **Boots** makes its own Chanel knockoff line, No. 7.

Designer Wear   Designer clothing from any of the international makers may be more expensive or cost less in London than in the United States or Paris—so know your prices. Often, the only differential is the VAT refund, which is substantial. This game is also highly dependent on the value of the dollar.

While you won't get a VAT refund on used designer clothing, London has the best prices on used Chanel (and similar) clothing of any major shopping city.

Royal Souvenirs   Forget about investing in Diana memorabilia; word is that it won't appreciate significantly because there is so much of it. Still, royal collectibles can be cheap kitsch bought in street markets or serious pieces from coronations long past found in specialty shops. If you're buying new for investment purposes, it must be kept in mint condition.

Teen Fashions   Street fashion, punk, grunge, whatever you want to call it is alive and well, with several areas in town, including Carnaby Street, Covent Garden, and Kensington High Street, catering to the young mod squad.

SALES   Traditionally, stores in Britain only held two sale periods: January and July. Now, whenever they need cash, they have a sale. July sales begin in June—or earlier—and promotions are commonplace. Still, the January sale is the big event of the year. Though a few stores hold their after-Christmas sale on December 27, the really famous sales usually start after the first week in January, when round-trip airfares are in the low range, and savings on sale items might earn your travel money back if you find enough bargains.

Discounts can range from 25% to 50% at leading department stores, such as Harrods and Selfridges. Harrods produces this event, with special buyers and bins of imports. The best buys are on Harrods logo souvenirs, English china (seconds are trucked in from factories in Stoke-on-Trent), and English designer brands like Jaeger. But while the Harrods sale is the most famous in London, it's not the only game in town. Just about every other store—save Boots—also has a big sale at that time. Beware, though: There's a huge difference in the quality of the finds bought in genuine sales, where the stores are actually clearing the shelves, and the goods bought at "produced" sales, where special merchandise has been hauled in just for the sale.

DUTY-FREE AIRPORT SHOPPING   Shopping at airports is big business, so big business has taken over the management of some of Britain's airports to ensure that those in transit are enticed to buy. Whereas Terminal 4 at Heathrow is a virtual shopping mall, each terminal has a good bit of shopping, with not a lot of crossover between brands.

Prices at the airport for items like souvenirs and candy bars are actually higher than on the streets of London, but duty-free prices on luxury goods are usually fair. There are often promotions and coupons that allow for pounds off at the time of the purchase. Don't save all your shopping until you get to the airport, but do know prices on hand so that you know when to pounce.

3 The Top Shopping Streets & Neighborhoods

Thankfully for those with too little time to shop, there are several key streets that offer some of London's best retail stores—or simply one of everything—compactly located in a niche or neighborhood so you can just stroll and shop.

THE WEST END   As a neighborhood, the West End includes the tony Mayfair district and is home to the core of London's big-name shopping. Most of the department stores, designer shops, and multiples (chain stores) have their flagships in this area.

The key streets are **Oxford Street** for affordable shopping (start at Marble Arch Tube station if you're ambitious, or Bond Street station if you just want to see some of it) and **Regent Street,** which intersects Oxford Street at Oxford Circus (Tube: Oxford Circus). The Oxford Street flagship (at Marble Arch) of the private-label department store **Marks & Spencer** is worth visiting for high-quality goods. Regent Street has fancier shops—more upscale department stores (including the famed **Liberty of London**), multiples (**Laura Ashley**), and specialty dealers—and leads all the way to Piccadilly.

Parallel to Regent Street, **Bond Street** (Tube: Bond Street) connects Piccadilly with Oxford Street and is synonymous with the luxury trade. Divided into New and Old, it has experienced a recent revival and is the hot address for all the international designers; **Donna Karan** has not one but two shops here. A slew of international hotshots from **Chanel** to **Ferragamo** to **Versace** have digs nearby.

Burlington Arcade (Tube: Piccadilly Circus), the famous glass-roofed, Regency-style passage leading off Piccadilly, looks like a period exhibition and is lined with intriguing shops and boutiques. Lit by wrought-iron lamps and decorated with clusters of ferns and flowers, its small, smart stores specialize in fashion, jewelry, Irish linen, cashmere, and more. If you linger there until 5:30pm, you can watch the beadles, those ever-present attendants in their black-and-yellow livery and top hats, ceremoniously put in place the iron grills that block off the arcade until 9am the next morning, at which time they just as ceremoniously remove them to mark the start of a new business day. (There are only three beadles remaining; they're the last London representatives of Britain's oldest police force.) Also at 5:30pm, a hand bell called the Burlington Bell is sounded, signaling the end of trading.

Tucked right behind Regent Street is **Carnaby Street** (Tube: Oxford Circus). While it no longer dominates the world of pacesetting fashion as it did in the 1960s, it's become a comeback street for cheap souvenirs, a purple wig, or a little something in leather. There's also a convenient branch of **Boots** here.

For a total contrast, check out **Jermyn Street** (Tube: Piccadilly Circus), on the far side of Piccadilly, a tiny 2-block-long street devoted to high-end men's haberdasher's and toiletries shops; many have been doing business for centuries. Several hold royal warrants, including **Turnbull & Asser,** where HRH Prince Charles has his pjs made.

The West End theater district borders two more shopping areas: the still-not-ready-for-prime-time **Soho** (Tube: Tottenham Court Road), where the sex shops are slowly converting into cutting-edge designer shops; and **Covent Garden** (Tube: Covent Garden), which is a masterpiece unto itself. The original marketplace has overflowed its boundaries and eaten up the surrounding neighborhood; it's fun to wander the narrow streets and shop. Covent Garden is mobbed on Sundays.

KNIGHTSBRIDGE & CHELSEA   The home of **Harrods, Knightsbridge** (Tube: Knightsbridge) is the second-most famous of London's retail districts. (Oxford Street edges it out.) Nearby **Sloane Street** is chock-a-block with designer shops; in the opposite direction, **Cheval Place** is lined with designer resale shops.

Walk toward Museum Row and you'll soon find **Beauchamp** (*Bee*-cham) **Place.** It's only 1 block long, but it's very "Sloane Ranger or Sloanie," (as the Brits would say) featuring the kinds of shops where young British aristos buy their clothing for "The Season."

King's Road (Tube: Sloane Square), the main street of Chelsea, will forever remain a symbol of the Swinging Sixties. Today, it's still popular with the young crowd, but there are fewer Mohawk haircuts, Bovver boots, and Edwardian ballgowns than before. More and more, King's Road is a lineup of markets and "multi-stores," large or small conglomerations of indoor stands, stalls, and booths within one building or enclosure. About a third of King's Road is devoted to these kinds of antiques markets, another third houses design-trade showrooms and stores of household wares for British yuppies, and the remaining third is faithful to the area's teeny-bopper roots.

If you walk west from Harrods along Brompton Road, you connect to **Brompton Cross,** another hip area for designer shops made popular when Michelin House was rehabbed by Sir Terence Conran for **The Conran Shop.**

Also seek out **Walton Street,** a tiny little snake of a street running from Brompton Cross back toward the museums. Most of the street is devoted to fairy-tale shops for m'lady where you can buy aromatherapy from **Jo Malone,** needlepoint, or costume jewelry.

Finally, don't forget all those museums in nearby South Kensington—they all have great gift shops.

KENSINGTON, NOTTING HILL & BAYSWATER   Kensington High Street (Tube: High Street Kensington) is the hangout of the classier breed of teen, one who has graduated from Carnaby Street and is ready for street chic. While there are a few staples of basic British fashion on this strip, most of the stores feature items that stretch; are very, very short; very, very tight; and very, very black.

From Kensington High Street, you can walk up **Kensington Church Street,** which, like Portobello Road, is one of the city's main shopping avenues for antiques, selling everything from antique furniture to Impressionist paintings.

London Shopping

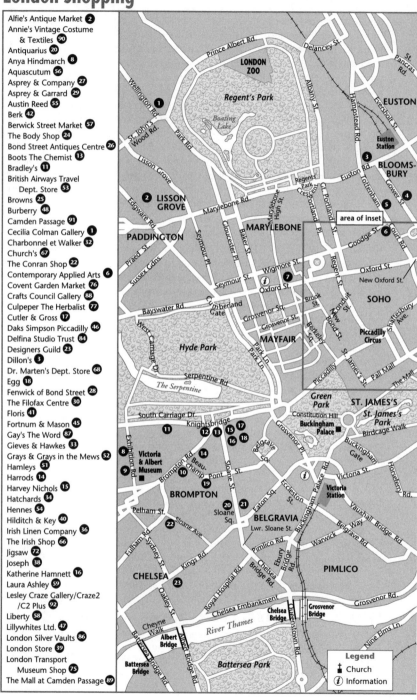

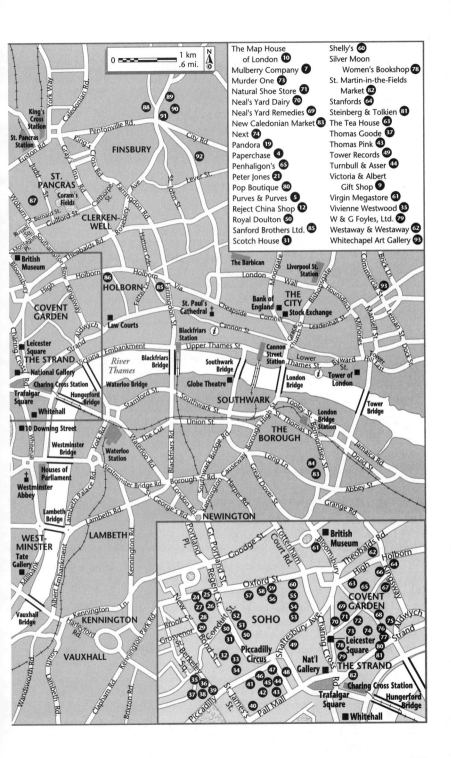

The Map House
of London **10**
Mulberry Company **7**
Murder One **73**
Natural Shoe Store **71**
Neal's Yard Dairy **70**
Neal's Yard Remedies **69**
New Caledonian Market **83**
Next **74**
Pandora **19**
Paperchase **4**
Penhaligon's **65**
Peter Jones **21**
Pop Boutique **80**
Purves & Purves **5**
Reject China Shop **12**
Royal Doulton **50**
Sanford Brothers Ltd. **85**
Scotch House **31**

Shelly's **60**
Silver Moon
Women's Bookshop **78**
St. Martin-in-the-Fields
Market **82**
Stanfords **64**
Steinberg & Tolkien **81**
The Tea House **63**
Thomas Goode **37**
Thomas Pink **43**
Tower Records **49**
Turnbull & Asser **44**
Victoria & Albert
Gift Shop **9**
Virgin Megastore **61**
Vivienne Westwood **35**
W & G Foyles, Ltd. **79**
Westaway & Westaway **62**
Whitechapel Art Gallery **93**

A Great Way to Spend a Sunday: Shopping Greenwich

Even though many shops throughout London are now open on Sundays, the best Sunday shopping is still in the stalls of the flea and craft markets in the royal city of Greenwich, now officially a London suburb.

The best way to enjoy the trip is to float downstream on a boat from Charing Cross or Westminster pier (service begins at 10:30am on Sundays; see "Sightseeing & Boat Tours Along the Thames" in chapter 6). The trip takes about a half hour, but you'll get a knowledgeable commentary on the Docklands development and the history of the river, and view The Tower and much of London from the water along the way.

The boat leaves you right in the heart of Greenwich, so you're minutes from the **craft market,** held on Saturday and Sunday. Follow the signs . . . or the crowd. After you're done here, head for (again, follow the crowd) Greenwich's several antiques markets. First is **Canopy Market,** which isn't under a canopy at all, but sprawls through several parking lots of junk and old books and then onto **High Street,** where the fancier flea market is held. It's possible that there's yet another antiques market at **Town Hall,** across the street, but these shows usually charge an admission fee.

You're only a half block from the Greenwich BritRail station now; there's a train back to London every half hour.

Kensington Church Street dead-ends at the Notting Hill Gate Tube station, jumping-off point for **Portobello Road;** the dealers and weekend market are 2 blocks beyond.

Not far from Notting Hill Gate is **Whiteleys of Bayswater,** Queensway, W2 (☎ **0171/229-8844;** Tube: Bayswater or Queensway), an Edwardian mall whose chief tenant is Marks & Spencer. There are also 75 to 85 shops (the number varies from year to year), mostly specialty outlets, and an array of restaurants, cafes, and bars as well as an eight-screen movie theater.

4 Street & Flea Markets

If Mayfair stores are not your cup of tea, don't worry; you'll have more fun, and find a better bargain, at any of the city's street and flea markets.

THE WEST END ✪ Covent Garden Market (☎ **0171/836-9136;** Tube: Covent Garden), the most famous market in all of England—possibly all of Europe—offers several different markets daily from 9am to 6:30pm (we think it's most fun to come on Sunday). It can be a little confusing until you dive in and explore it all. Apple Market is the fun, bustling market in the courtyard, where traders sell . . . well, everything. Many of the items are what the English call collectible nostalgia; they include a wide array of glassware and ceramics, leather goods, toys, clothes, hats, and jewelry. Some of the merchandise is truly unusual. Many items are handmade, with some of the craftspeople selling their own wares—except on Mondays, when antiques dealers take over. Out back is Jubilee Market (☎ **0171/836-2139**), also an antiques market on Mondays. Every other day, it's sort of a fancy hippie-ish market with cheap clothes and books. Out front there are a few tents of cheap stuff, except again on Monday.

The market itself (in the superbly restored hall) is one of the best shopping opportunities in London. Specialty shops sell fashions and herbs, gifts and toys, books and personalized dollhouses, hand-rolled cigars, automata, and much, much more. There are bookshops and branches of famous stores (**Hamley's, The Body Shop**), and prices are kept moderate.

St. Martin-in-the-Fields Market (Tube: Charing Cross) is good for teens and hipsters who don't want to trek all the way to Camden Market (see "North London," below) and can make due with imports from India and South America, crafts, and some local football souvenirs. Located near Trafalgar Square and Covent Garden; hours are Monday to Saturday 11am to 5pm, and Sundays noon to 5pm.

Berwick Street Market (Tube: Oxford Circus or Tottenham Court Road) may be the only street market in the world that's flanked by two rows of strip clubs, porno stores, and adult-movie dens. Don't let that put you off, however. Humming 6 days a week in the scarlet heart of Soho, this array of stalls and booths sells probably the best and cheapest fruit and vegetables in town. It also hawks ancient records, tapes, books, and old magazines, all of which may turn out to be collectors' items one day. It's open Monday to Saturday from 8am to 5pm.

On Sunday mornings along **Bayswater Road,** artists hang pictures, collages, and crafts on the railings along the edge of Hyde Park and Kensington Gardens for more than a mile. If the weather's right, start at Marble Arch and walk. You'll see much of the same thing by walking along the railings of **Green Park** along Piccadilly on Saturday afternoon.

NOTTING HILL   **Portobello Market** (Tube: Notting Hill Gate) is a magnet for collectors of virtually anything. It's mainly a Saturday happening, from 6am to 5pm. You needn't be here at the crack of dawn; 9am is fine. Once known mainly for fruit and vegetables (still sold here throughout the week), in the past 4 decades Portobello has become synonymous with antiques. But don't take the stallholder's word for it that the fiddle he's holding is a genuine Stradivarius left to him in the will of his Italian great-uncle; it might just as well have been "nicked" from an East End pawnshop.

The market is divided into three major sections. The most crowded is the antiques section, running between Colville Road and Chepstow Villas to the south. (*Warning:* There's a great concentration of pickpockets in this area.) The second section (and the oldest part) is the "fruit and veg" market, lying between Westway and Colville Road. In the third and final section, there's a flea market, where Londoners sell bric-a-brac and lots of secondhand goods they didn't really want in the first place. But looking around still makes for interesting fun.

The serious collector can pick up a copy of a helpful official guide, *Saturday Antique Market: Portobello Road & Westbourne Grove,* published by the Portobello Antique Dealers Association. It lists where to find what, ranging from music boxes to militaria, lace to 19th-century photographs.

Note: Some 90 antiques and art shops along Portobello Road are open during the week when the street market is closed. This is actually a better time for the serious collector to shop, because you'll get more attention from dealers and you won't be distracted by the organ grinder.

SOUTH BANK   Open on Fridays only, **New Caledonian Market** is commonly known as the Bermondsey Market, because of its location on the corner of Long Lane and Bermondsey Street (Tube: London Bridge, then bus 78 or walk down Bermondsey Street). The market is at the extreme east end, beginning at Tower Bridge Road. It's one of Europe's outstanding street markets for the number and quality of the antiques and other goods. The stalls are well known, and many dealers come into London from the country. Prices are generally lower here than at Portobello and the other markets. It gets under way at 5am—with the bargains gone by 9am—and closes at noon. Bring a "torch" (flashlight) if you go in the wee hours.

NORTH LONDON   If it's Wednesday, it's time for Camden Passage (☎ 0171/359-9969; Tube: Angel) in Islington, where each Wednesday and Saturday there's a very upscale antiques market. It starts in Camden Passage and then sprawls into the streets behind. It's on Wednesdays from 8am to 4pm, and Saturdays from 9am to 5pm.

Don't confuse Camden Passage with Camden Market (very, very downtown). **Camden Market** (Tube: Camden Town) is for teens and others into body piercing, blue hair (yes, still), and vintage clothing. Serious collectors of vintage may want to explore during the week, when the teen scene isn't quite so overwhelming. Market hours are 9:30am to 5:30pm daily, with some parts opening at 10am.

5 The Department Stores

Contrary to popular belief, Harrods is not the only department store in London. The British invented the department store, and they have lots of them—mostly in Mayfair, and each with its own customer profile.

Daks Simpson Piccadilly. 34 Jermyn St., W1. ☎ 0171/734-2002. Tube: Piccadilly Circus.

Opened in 1936 as the home of DAKS clothing, Simpson's has been going strong ever since. It's known for menswear—its basement-level men's shoe department is a model of the way quality shoes should be fitted—as well as women's fashions, perfume, jewelry, and lingerie. Many of the clothes are lighthearted, carefully made, and well suited to casual elegance. Its Simpson Collection rubs shoulders with international designer names such as Armani and Yves Saint Laurent.

Fenwick of Bond Street. 63 New Bond St., W1. ☎ 0171/629-9161. Tube: Bond St.

Fenwick (*Fen*-ick), dating from 1891, is a stylish fashion store that offers an excellent collection of designer womenswear, ranging from moderately priced ready-to-wear items to more expensive designer fashions. A wide range of lingerie in all price ranges is also sold.

✪ Fortnum & Mason. 181 Piccadilly, W1. ☎ 0171/734-8040. Tube: Piccadilly Circus.

The world's most elegant grocery store is a British tradition dating back to 1707. Down the street from the Ritz, it draws the carriage trade, those from Mayfair to Belgravia who come seeking such tinned treasures as pâté de foie gras or a boar's head. This store exemplifies the elegance and style you would expect from an establishment with three royal warrants. Enter and be transported to another world of deep-red carpets, crystal chandeliers, spiraling wooden staircases, and unobtrusive, tailcoated assistants.

The grocery department is renowned for its impressive selection of the finest foods from around the world—the best champagne, the most scrumptious Belgian chocolates, and succulent Scottish smoked salmon. You can wander through the four floors and inspect the bone china and crystal cut glass, find the perfect gift in the leather or stationery departments, or reflect on the changing history of furniture and ornaments in the antiques department. Dining choices include the **Patio,** the recently refurbished **St. James Restaurant, The Fountain Restaurant,** and the brand new **Salmon and Champagne Bar** (for details on taking afternoon tea here, see "Teatime" in chapter 5). After a £14 million development, Fortnum & Mason now offers exclusive and specialty ranges for the home, beauty, and fashions for both women and men.

✪ Harrods. 87–135 Brompton Rd., Knightsbridge, SW1. ☎ 0171/730-1234. Tube: Knightsbridge.

Harrods is an institution. As firmly entrenched in English life as Buckingham Palace and the Ascot Races, it's an elaborate emporium, at times as fascinating as a museum. Some of the goods displayed for sale are works of art, and so are the 300 departments displaying them. The sheer range, variety, and quality of merchandise are dazzling. The motto remains, "If you can eat or drink it, you'll find it at Harrods."

The whole fifth floor is devoted to sports and leisure, with a wide range of equipment and attire. Toy Kingdom is on the fourth floor, along with children's wear. The Egyptian Hall, on the ground floor, sells crystal from Lalique and Baccarat, plus porcelain. There's also a men's grooming room, an enormous jewelry department, and a fashion-forward department for younger customers. Along with the beauty of the bounty, check out the tiles and architectural touches. When you're ready for a break, you have a choice of 18 restaurants and bars. Best of all are the Food Halls, stocked with a huge variety of foods and several cafes. Harrods began as a grocer in 1849, and that's still the heart of the business.

In the basement you'll find a bank, a theater-booking service, and a travel bureau. Harrods Shop for logo gifts is on the ground floor.

Harvey Nichols. 109–125 Knightsbridge, SW1. ☎ **0171/235-5000.** Tube: Knightsbridge.

Locals call it Harvey Nicks. Once a favorite of the late Princess Di, the store is large, but doesn't compete with Harrods because it has a much more upmarket, fashionable image. Harvey Nicks has its own gourmet food hall and fancy restaurant, The Fifth Floor (see chapter 5), and a huge store crammed with the best designer home furnishings, gifts, and fashions for all, although women's clothing is the largest segment of its business. The store carries many American designer brands; avoid them, as they're more expensive in London.

Liberty. 214–220 Regent St., W1. ☎ **0171/734-1234.** Tube: Oxford Circus.

This major British department store is celebrated for its Liberty Prints, top-echelon, carriage-trade fabrics, often in floral patterns, that are prized by decorators for the way they add a sense of English tradition to a room. The front part of the store on Regent Street isn't particularly distinctive, but don't be fooled: Some parts of the place have been restored to Tudor-style splendor that includes half-timbering and lots of interior paneling. There are six floors of fashion, china, and home furnishings, as well as the famous Liberty Print fashion fabrics, upholstery fabrics, scarves, ties, luggage, and gifts.

Peter Jones. Sloane Sq., SW1. ☎ **0171/730-3434.** Tube: Sloane Sq.

Founded in 1877 and rebuilt in 1936, Peter Jones is known for household goods, household fabrics and trims, china, glass, soft furnishings, and linens. The linen department is one of the best in London.

6 Goods A to Z

ANTIQUES

Alfie's Antique Market. 13–25 Church St., NW8. ☎ **0171/723-6066.** Tube: Marylebone or Edgware Rd.

This is the biggest and one of the best-stocked conglomerates of antiques dealers in London, all crammed into the premises of what was built before 1880 as a department store. It has more than 370 stalls, showrooms, and workshops scattered over 35,000 square feet of floor space. You'll find the biggest Susie Cooper collection in Europe here (Susie Cooper was a well-known designer of tableware and ceramics for Wedgwood). A whole antiques district has grown up around Alfie's along Church Street.

Antiquarius. 131–141 King's Rd., SW3. ☎ **0171/351-5353.** Tube: Sloane Sq.

The recently redecorated Antiquarius echoes the artistic diversity of King's Road. More than 120 dealers offer specialized merchandise, usually of the small, domestic variety, such as antique and period jewelry, porcelain, silver, first-edition books, boxes, clocks, prints, and paintings, with an occasional piece of antique furniture. You'll also find a lot of items from the 1950s.

Bond Street Antiques Centre. 124 New Bond St., W1. ☎ **0171/351-5353.** Tube: Bond St. or Green Park.

This place, in the heart of London's finest shopping district, enjoys a reputation for being London's finest center for antique jewelry, silver, watches, porcelain, glass, and Asian antiques and paintings.

Grays & Grays in the Mews. 58 Davies St., and 1–7 Davies Mews, W1. ☎ **0171/ 629-7034.** Tube: Bond St.

These antiques markets have been converted into walk-in stands with independent dealers. The term "antique" here covers items from oil paintings to, say, the 1894 edition of the *Encyclopaedia Britannica.* Also sold here are exquisite antique jewelry; silver; gold; maps and prints; bronzes and ivories; arms and armor; Victorian and Edwardian toys; furniture; art nouveau and art deco items; antique lace; scientific instruments; craft tools; and Asian, Persian, and Islamic pottery, porcelain, miniatures, and antiquities. There's a cafe in each building. Check out the 1950s-style **Victory Café** on Davies Street for the delectable homemade cakes.

The Mall at Camden Passage. Islington, N1. ☎ **0171/351-5353.** Tube: Angel.

This mall contains one of Britain's greatest concentrations of antiques dealers. In individual shop units, you'll find some 35 dealers specializing in fine furniture, porcelain, and silver. This area expands into a street market on Wednesday and Saturday.

ART & CRAFTS

ACAVA (☎ **0171/603-3039**) represents about 250 artists located in West London. Call for individual open-studio schedules, as well as dates for the annual Open Studios weekend.

Cecilia Colman Gallery. 67 St. John's Wood High St., NW8. ☎ **0171/722-0686.** Tube: St. John's Wood.

One of London's most established crafts galleries features decorative ceramics, studio glass, jewelry, and metalwork. Among the offerings are glass sculptures by Lucien Simon, jewelry by Caroline Taylor, and pottery by Simon Rich. There's also a large selection of mirrors and original-design perfume bottles.

Contemporary Applied Arts. 2 Percy St., W1. ☎ **0171/436-2344.** Tube: Goodge St.

This association encourages both traditional and progressive contemporary artwork. Many of Britain's best-established craftspeople, as well as lesser-known but promising talents, are represented in galleries that house a diverse retail display of glass, ceramics, textiles, wood, furniture, jewelry, and metalwork—all by outstanding artisans currently producing in the country, ranging in price from £12 to £10,000 ($19.80 to $16,500). A program of special exhibitions, including solo and small-group shows, focuses on innovations in craftwork. There are new exhibitions every 6 weeks.

Crafts Council Gallery. 44A Pentonville Rd., Islington, N1. ☎ **0171/278-7700.** Tube: Angel.

The largest crafts gallery is run by the Crafts Council, the national body for promoting contemporary crafts. You'll discover some of today's most creative work here. There's also a shop specializing in craft objects and publications, a picture library, a reference library, and a cafe. The gallery is closed on Mondays.

Delfina Studio Trust. 50 Bermondsey St., SE1. ☎ **0171/357-6600.** Tube: London Bridge.

This registered charity provides studio space for 35 painters, photographers, and sculptors from Britain and abroad. The gallery doesn't have a fixed schedule; rather, exhibits are hung periodically, at which times the gallery keeps weekend hours. There's also a biannual open house. Call for a list of visiting artists, exhibition schedules, and sales information. All art is for sale, with prices generally starting at £250 ($412.50). The Trust takes no commission.

England & Co. 216 Westbourne Grove, W11. ☎ **0171/221-0417.** Tube: Notting Hill Gate.

Under the guidance of the energetic Jane England, this gallery specializes in Outsider Art (by untrained artists) and Art in Boxes, which incorporates a box structure into the composition or frame of a three-dimensional work, while focusing attention on neglected post-war British artists such as Tony Stubbings and Ralph Romney. One-person and group shows are mounted frequently, and many young artists get early exposure here.

✪ **Whitechapel Art Gallery.** 80–82 Whitechapel High St., E1. ☎ **0171/522-7888** or 7878 (recorded). Tube: Aldgate East.

Since it opened its art nouveau doors in 1901, savvy collectors have been heading to this East End gallery to find out what's hot and happening in the art world. It still maintains its cutting edge; to some, it's the incubation chamber for some of the most talented of East London's artists. The collections are fun, hip, often sexy, and definitely in your face.

BATH & BODY

✪ **The Body Shop.** 375 Oxford St., W1. ☎ **0171/409-7868.** Tube: Bond St. Other locations throughout London.

There's a branch of The Body Shop in every trading area and tourist zone in London. Some stores are bigger than others, but all are filled with politically and environmentally correct beauty, bath, and aromatherapy products. Prices are drastically lower in the United Kingdom than they are in the United States. There's an entire children's line, a men's line, and lots of travel sizes and travel products. You won't have as much fun in a candy store.

✪ **Boots The Chemist.** 72 Brompton Rd., SW3. ☎ **0171/589-6557.** Tube: Knightsbridge. Other locations throughout London.

This store has a million branches; we like the one across the street from Harrods for convenience and size. The house brands of beauty products are usually the best, be they Boots products (try the cucumber facial scrub), Boot's versions of The Body Shop (two lines, Global and Naturalistic), or Boot's versions of Chanel makeup (called No. 7). They also sell film, pantyhose (called tights), sandwiches, and all of life's little necessities.

Culpeper the Herbalist. 8 The Piazza, Covent Garden, WC2. ☎ **0171/379-6698.** Tube: Covent Garden.

This store has another shop in Mayfair (21 Bruton St., W1; ☎ 0171/629-4559) but the hours are better at Covent Garden, so you'll have to put up with the cramped space here to check out all the food, bath, and aromatherapy products. You can stock up on essential oils, or go for the dream pillows, candles, sachets, and many a shopper's fave: the aromatherapy fan, for home and the car.

✪ **Floris.** 89 Jermyn St., SW1. ☎ **0171/930-2885.** Tube: Piccadilly Circus.

A variety of toilet articles and fragrances fill Floris's floor-to-ceiling mahogany cabinets, which are architectural curiosities in their own right. They were installed relatively late in the establishment's history—that is, 1851—long after the shop had received its royal warrants as suppliers of toilet articles to the king and queen.

Neal's Yard Remedies. 15 Neal's Yard, WC2. ☎ **0171/379-7222.** Tube: Covent Garden.

Noted the world over for their cobalt-blue bottles, these chi-chi bath, beauty, and aromatherapy products are must-haves for those who pooh pooh The Body Shop as too common. Prices are much higher in the United States, so stock up here.

✪ **Penhaligon's.** 41 Wellington St., WC2. ☎ **0171/836-2150,** or 800/588-1992 in the U.S. for mail order. Tube: Covent Garden.

This Victorian perfumery, established in 1870, holds royal warrants to HRH Duke of Edinburgh and HRH Prince of Wales. All items sold are exclusive to Penhaligon's. It offers a large selection of perfume, aftershave, soap, and bath oils for women and men. Gifts include antique-silver scent bottles, grooming accessories, and leather traveling requisites. Penhaligon's is now in more than 20 Saks Fifth Avenue stores across the United States.

BOOKS, MAPS, & ENGRAVINGS

In addition to the specialty bookstores listed below, you'll also find well-stocked branches of the **Dillon's** chain around town, including one at 82 Gower St. (Tube: Euston Square).

Children's Book Centre. 237 Kensington High St., W8. ☎ **0171/937-7497.** Tube: High St. Kensington.

With thousands of titles, this is the best place to go for children's books. Fiction is arranged according to age, up to 16. There are also videos and toys for kids.

Gay's The Word. 66 Marchmont St., WC1. ☎ **0171/278-7654.** Tube: Russell Sq.

Britain's leading gay and lesbian bookstore offers a large collection of reading material as well as a selection of magazines, cards, and guides. There's also a used-books section.

Hatchards. 187 Piccadilly, W1. ☎ **0171/439-9921.** Tube: Piccadilly Circus or Green Park.

On the south side of Piccadilly, Hatchards offers a wide range of books on all subjects and is particularly renowned in the areas of fiction, biography, travel, cookery, gardening, and art, plus history and finance. In addition, Hatchards is second to none in its range of books on royalty.

The Map House of London. 54 Beauchamp Place, SW3. ☎ **0171/589-4325.** Tube: Knightsbridge.

This is an ideal place to find an offbeat souvenir. Map House sells antique maps and engravings and a vast selection of old prints of London and England, both original and reproduction. A century-old original engraving can cost as little as £6 ($9.90).

Murder One. 71–73 Charing Cross Rd., WC2. ☎ **0171/734-3483.** Tube: Leicester Sq.

Maxim Jakubowski's bookshop is dedicated to the genres of crime, romance, science fiction, and horror. Crime and science fiction magazines, some of them obscure, are also available.

Silver Moon Women's Bookshop. 64–68 Charing Cross Rd., WC2. ☎ **0171/836-7906.** Tube: Leicester Sq.

This place stocks thousands of titles by and about women, plus videos, jewelry, and a large selection of lesbian books.

Stanfords. 12–14 Long Acre, WC2. ☎ **0171/836-1321.** Tube: Leicester Sq. or Covent Garden.

Established in 1852, Stanfords is the world's largest map shop. Many of its maps, which include worldwide touring and survey maps, are unavailable elsewhere. It's also London's best travel bookstore (with a complete selection of Frommer's guides!).

W & G Foyle, Ltd. 113–119 Charing Cross Rd., WC2. ☎ **0171/439-8501.** Tube: Tottenham Court Rd.

Claiming to be the world's largest bookstore, W & G Foyle has an impressive array of hardcovers and paperbacks, as well as travel maps, records, videotapes, and sheet music.

CASHMERE & WOOLENS

London Store. Ritz Hotel, 150 Piccadilly, London W1. ☎ **0171/404-2606.** Tube: Green Park or Piccadilly Circus.

Here you'll find woolens from all over the British Islands, including the Scottish Shetlands. Some are handmade; many of the designers are well known. Some have a tweedy English look, while others are more high fashion.

Scotch House. 84–86 Regent St., W1. ☎ **0171/734-0203.** Tube: Piccadilly Circus.

For top-quality woolen fabrics and garments, go to Scotch House, renowned worldwide for its comprehensive selection of cashmere and wool knitwear for men, women, and children. Also available is a wide range of tartan garments and accessories, as well as Scottish tweed classics.

Westaway & Westaway. 64–65 and 92–93 Great Russell St. (opposite the British Museum), WC1. ☎ **0171/405-4479.** Tube: Tottenham Court Rd.

Stopping in here is a substitute for a shopping trip to Scotland. You'll find a large range of kilts, scarves, waistcoats, capes, dressing gowns, and rugs in authentic clan tartans. The staff is knowledgeable about the intricate clan symbols. They also sell cashmere, camel-hair, and Shetland knitwear, plus Harris tweed jackets, Burberry raincoats, and cashmere overcoats for men.

CHINA, GLASS & SILVER

✪ **Royal Doulton.** 154 Regent St., W1. ☎ **0171/734-3184.** Tube: Piccadilly Circus or Oxford Circus.

Founded in the 1930s, this store has one of the largest inventories of china in Britain. A wide range of English bone china, as well as crystal and giftware, is sold. The firm specializes, of course, in Royal Doulton, plus Minton, Royal Crown Derby, and Aynsley china; Lladró figures; David Winter Cottages; Border Fine Arts; and other famous names. Royal Doulton also sells cutlery. The January and July sales are excellent.

London Silver Vaults. Chancery House, 53–63 Chancery Lane, WC2. ☎ **0171/242-3844.** Tube: Chancery Lane.

Don't let the slightly out-of-the-way location, or the facade's lack of charm, slow you down. Downstairs, you go into real vaults—40 in all—that are filled with tons of silver and silverplate, plus a collection of jewelry. It's a staggering selection of old to new, with excellent prices and friendly dealers.

Reject China Shop. 183 Brompton Rd., SW3. ☎ **0171/581-0739.** Tube: Knightsbridge. Other locations throughout London.

Don't expect too many rejects or too many bargains, despite the name. This shop sells seconds (sometimes) along with first-quality pieces of china with such names as Royal Doulton, Spode, and Wedgwood. You also can find a variety of crystal, glassware, and flatware. If you'd like to have your purchases shipped home for you, the shop can do it for a fee.

Thomas Goode. 19 S. Audley St., W1. ☎ **0171/499-2823.** Tube: Bond St. or Green Park.

This is one of the most famous emporiums in Britain; it's worth visiting for its architectural interest and nostalgic allure alone. Originally built in 1876, Goode's has 14 rooms loaded with porcelain, gifts, candles, silver, tableware, and even a private museum. There's also a tearoom-cum-restaurant tucked into the corner (see "Teatime" in chapter 5).

THE CUTTING EDGE

Anya Hindmarch. 91 Walton St., SW3. ☎ **0171/584-7644.** Tube: South Kensington.

Although her fashionable bags are sold at Harvey Nichols, Liberty, Harrods, and in the United States and Europe, this is the only place to see the complete range of Anya Hindmarch's designs. Featuring handbags, wash bags, wallets, purses, and key holders, smaller items range in price from £42 ($69.30) whereas handbag prices stretch from £150 ($247.50) and up, with alligator being the most expensive. There's a limited bespoke service, and you may bring in your fabric to be matched.

۞ Browns. 23–27 S. Molton St., W1. ☎ **0171/491-7833.** Tube: Bond St.

This is the only place in London to find the designs of Alexander McQueen, now head of the House of Givenchy in Paris, and one of the fashion industry's major stars. Producing his own cottons, silks, and plastics, McQueen creates revealing and feminine women's couture and ready-to-wear, and has recently started marketing a well-received menswear line. McQueen made his reputation creating shock-value apparel more eagerly photographed than worn. But recently his outfits have been called more "consumer friendly" by fashion critics. Browns have recently introduced "Browns Living," which is an eclectic array of lifestyle products.

Egg. 36 Kinnerton St., SW1. ☎ **0171/235-9315.** Tube: Hyde Park Corner or Knightsbridge.

This shop is hot, hot, hot with fashionistas. It features imaginatively designed, contemporary clothing by Indian textile designer Asha Sarabhai and knitwear by Eskandar. Designs created from handmade textiles from a workshop in India range from everyday dresses and coats to hand-embroidered silk coats. Prices begin at £60 ($96). Crafts and ceramics are also available. Closed Sunday and Monday.

Hennes. 261–271 Regent St., W1. ☎ **0171/493-4004.** Tube: Oxford Circus.

Here are copies of hot-off-the-catwalk fashions at affordable prices. While the quality isn't much to brag about, the prices are. For disposable cutting-edge fashion, you can't beat it.

Hype DF. 48–52 Kensington High St., W8. ☎ **0171/937-3100.** Tube: High St. Kensington.

This retailer has been showcasing young designers since 1983, but in a different location that was known as Hyper-Hyper. Designs for men and women range from sports to evening wear, with plenty of accessories, including shoes. There's a wide range of prices; some of this stuff isn't cheap, but some styles are very affordable. Hype DF will definitely intrigue.

Joseph. 23 Old Bond St., W1. ☎ **0171/629-3713.** Tube: Green Park. Also at 16 Sloane St., SW1 (☎ 0171/235-1991; Tube: Sloane Sq.); 26 Sloane St., SW1 (☎ 0171/235-5470; Tube: Sloane Sq.); and 77 Fulham Rd., SW3 (☎ 0171/823-9500; Tube: South Kensington).

Joseph Ettedgui, a fashion retailer born in Casablanca, is a maverick in the fashion world—he's known for his daring designs and his ability to attract some of the most talented designers in the business to work with him. This is the flagship store among five London branches, and it carries the Ettedgui collection of suits, knitwear, suede, and leather clothing for men and women. The stretch jeans with flair ankles are the label's best-selling items.

The 16 Sloane St. branch carries only the label's womenswear; the 26 Sloane St. shop displays all Joseph products and stocks the complete menswear line. The Fulham Road store showcases mens- and womenswear collections by other designers, including Prada, Gucci, Marni, Misoni, and Anne Deimunister.

Katharine Hamnett. 20 Sloane St., SW1. ☎ **0171/823-1002.** Tube: Knightsbridge.

One of Britain's big-name designers—her so-called slut dresses earned her the title of the bad girl of Brit fashion—Katharine Hamnett is best known for her slogan T-shirts. Recent collections, although greeted with a media feeding frenzy, continue to receive mixed reviews. You can judge for yourself while browsing through her complete line of men's and women's day and evening wear. She's also a strong environmental activist and is known for using "nature friendly" fabrics.

Paul Smith's Westbourne House. 122 Kensington Park Rd. W11. ☎ **0171/727-3553.** Tube: Notting Hill Gate.

This shop was converted from a stately looking, three-story Edwardian town house into a showcase for the very stylish clothing of Paul Smith, whose well-made men's (and to a lesser extent, women's and children's) clothing seem to defy the preconceptions of Savile Row. Preferred colors, with occasional exceptions, include grays, browns, and blacks, except for a medley of velvet prints inspired by the Carnaby Street days of the 1960s. Look for women's clothes and accessories on the building's street level, and men's clothes and accessories on the two floors above street level. Men's suits begin at around £580 ($957) and go up to around £1,600 ($2,640), but be assured that whatever you opt for here will be very, very much the rage.

✪ Vivienne Westwood. 6 Davies St., W1. ☎ **0171/629-3757.** Tube: Bond St. Branches: World's End, 430 King's Rd., SW3 (☎ 0171/352-6551; Tube: Sloane Sq.); and Vivienne Westwood, 44 Conduit St., W1 (☎ 0171/439-1109; Tube: Oxford Circus).

No one in British fashion is hotter than the unstoppable Vivienne Westwood. While it's possible to purchase select Westwood pieces around the world, her U.K. shops are the best places to find her full range of fashion designs. The flagship location concentrates on her couture line, or The Gold Label, as it's known. Using a wide range of uniquely British resources, Westwood creates jackets, skirts, trousers, blouses, dresses, and evening dresses. Her latest line features taffeta ballgowns, made-to-measure tailored shirts, even some Highland plaids. If all this weren't enough, she came out with her own perfume in 1997 (who hasn't?).

The World's End branch carries casual designs, including T-shirts, jeans, and other sportswear. The sale shop on Conduit Street has a bit of everything: The Gold Label; her second women's line, The Red Label; and The Man Label, her menswear collection. Accessories available include women's and men's shoes, belts, and jewelry.

EYEGLASSES

Cutler & Gross. 16 Knightsbridge Green, SW1. ☎ **0171/581-2250.** Tube: Knightsbridge.

This is London's best optometry shop. Hand-crafted frames run £90 to £110 ($148.50 to $181.50); there's also a wide range of tints for prescription lenses. Orders usually require a 5-day waiting period. Eye exams and repair services are also available.

FASHION

While every internationally known designer worth his or her weight in shantung has a boutique in London, the best buys are on the sturdy English styles that last forever.

Aquascutum. 100 Regent St., W1. ☎ **0171/734-6090.** Tube: Piccadilly Circus.

It is about as quintessentially British as you'll get this side of Savile Row, and it's a popular stop-off for American tourists wanting to look more British than the Brits. On four floors, this classic shop offers only high-quality British and imported clothing (including leisurewear) for men and women.

Austin Reed. 103–113 Regent St., W1. ☎ **0171/734-6789.** Tube: Piccadilly Circus.

Austin Reed has long stood for superior-quality clothing and excellent tailoring. The suits of Chester Barrie, for example, are said to fit like *bespoke* (custom-made) clothing. The polite employees are unusually honest about telling you what looks good. The store always has a wide variety of top-notch jackets and suits, and men can outfit themselves from dressing gowns to overcoats. For women, there are carefully selected suits, separates, coats, shirts, knitwear, and accessories.

Berk. 46 Burlington Arcade, Piccadilly, W1. ☎ **0171/493-0028.** Tube: Piccadilly Circus or Green Park.

This store boasts one of the largest collections of cashmere sweaters in London—at least the top brands. The outlet also carries capes, stoles, scarves, and camel-hair sweaters.

✪ **Burberry.** 18–22 Haymarket, SW1. ☎ **0171/930-3343.** Tube: Piccadilly Circus.

The name has been synonymous with raincoats ever since Edward VII publicly ordered his valet to "bring my Burberry" when the skies threatened. An impeccably trained staff sells the famous raincoats, plus excellent men's shirts, sportswear, knitwear, and accessories. Raincoats are available in women's sizes and styles as well. Prices are high, but you get quality and prestige.

Dr. Marten's Department Store. 1–4 King St., WC2. ☎ **0171/497-1460.** Tube: Covent Garden.

Dr. Marten (called Doc Marten) makes a brand of shoe that has become so popular internationally that now there's an entire department store selling them in a huge variety of styles, plus accessories, gifts, and even an ever-expanding range of clothes. Teens come to worship here because ugly is beautiful, and because the prices are far better than they are in the United States or elsewhere in Europe.

Gieves & Hawkes. 1 Savile Row, W1. ☎ **0171/434-2001.** Tube: Piccadilly Circus or Green Park.

This place has a prestigious address and a list of clients that includes the Prince of Wales, yet its prices aren't as lethal as others on this street. They're high, but you get good quality. Cotton shirts, silk ties, Shetland sweaters, and exceptional ready-to-wear and bespoke (tailor-made) suits are sold.

Hilditch & Key. 37 and 73 Jermyn St., SW1. ☎ **0171/734-4707.** Tube: Piccadilly Circus or Green Park.

The finest name in men's shirts, Hilditch & Key has been in business since 1899. The two shops on this street offer men's clothing (including a bespoke shirt service) and women's ready-made shirts. There's also an outstanding tie collection. Shirts go for half price during the twice-yearly sales; men fly in from all over the world for them.

Jigsaw. 21 Long Acre, WC2. ☎ **0171/240-3855.** Tube: Covent Garden. Also at 9–10 Floral St., WC2 (☎ **0171/240/5651**) and other locations throughout London.

Branches of this fashion chain are too numerous to mention here, but the Long Acre shop features safely trendy, middle-market womenswear and children's clothing. Around the corner, the Floral Street shop carries menswear, including a wide range of colored moleskin items.

Laura Ashley. 256–258 Regent St., W1. ☎ **0171/437-9760.** Tube: Oxford Circus. Other locations around London.

This is the flagship store of the company whose design ethos embodies the English country look. The store carries a wide choice of women's clothing and home furnishings. Prices are lower than in the United States.

Next. 19–20 Long Acre, WC2. ☎ **0171/836-1516.** Tube: Covent Garden. Other locations throughout London.

This chain of "affordable fashion" stores knew its heyday when it became celebrated in the 1980s for its main-street fashion revolution. No longer at its peak, it still merits a stopover. The look is still very contemporary, with a continental flair worn not only by men and women but kids too.

✪ Thomas Pink. 85 Jermyn St., SW1. ☎ **0171/930-6364.** Tube: Green Park.

This Jermyn Street shirtmaker, named after an 18th-century Mayfair tailor, gave the world the phrases "hunting pink" and "in the pink." It has a prestigious reputation for well-made cotton shirts, for both men and women. The shirts are created from the finest two-fold Egyptian and Sea Island pure-cotton poplin. Some patterns are classic, others new and unusual. All are generously cut, with extra-long tails and finished with a choice of double cuffs or single-button cuffs. A small pink square in the tail tells all.

Turnbull & Asser. 71–72 Jermyn St., SW1. ☎ **0171/808-3000.** Tube: Piccadilly Circus.

Over the years, everyone from David Bowie to Ronald Reagan has been seen in a custom-made shirt from Turnbull & Asser. Excellent craftsmanship and simple lines—even bold colors—distinguish these shirts. The outlet also sells shirts and blouses to women, a clientele that has ranged from Jacqueline Bisset to Candice Bergen. Note that T&A shirts come in only one sleeve length and are then altered to fit. The sales department will inform you that its made-to-measure service takes 10 to 12 weeks, and you must order at least a half dozen. Of course, the monograms are included.

FILOFAX

All major department stores sell Filofax supplies, but the full range is carried in their own stores. They also have good sales; calendars for the next year go on sale very early the previous year (about 10 months in advance), so you can stock up and save.

The Filofax Centre. 21 Conduit St., W1. ☎ **0171/499-0457.** Tube: Oxford Circus. Also at 69 Neal St., WC2 (☎ 0171/836-1977; Tube: Covent Garden).

Get to the West End shop if you can; it's larger and fancier than the Covent Garden address, with the entire range of inserts and books, and prices that will floor you, at least half the U.S. going rate.

FOOD

English food has come a long way lately; it's worth enjoying and bringing home. Don't pass up the Food Halls in Harrods; consider the Fifth Floor at Harvey Nicks if Harrods is crammed with too many tourists—it isn't the same, but it'll do. Also, **Fortnum & Mason** is internationally famous as a food emporium. See "The Department Stores," above.

Charbonnel et Walker. 1 The Royal Arcade, 28 Old Bond St., W1. ☎ **0171/491-0939.** Tube: Green Park.

Charbonnel et Walker is famous for its hot chocolate in winter (buy it by the tin) and its strawberries-and-cream chocolates during "The Season." The firm will send messages of thanks or love spelled out on the chocolates themselves. Ready-made presentation boxes are also available.

Neal's Yard Dairy. 17 Shorts Gardens, WC2. ☎ **0171/379-7646.** Tube: Covent Garden.

The front is actually a photo-op; please take note. Then enjoy the cheeses as well as foodstuffs, snack items, and picnic supplies. It could be the highlight of a Sunday afternoon in Covent Garden.

GIFTS & SOUVENIRS

Asprey & Company. 167 New Bond St., W1. ☎ **0171/493-6767.** Tube: Green Park.

This is as well entrenched a name in luxury gift giving as anything you're likely to find in Britain, with a clientele that includes the likes of the Sultan of Brunei and Queen Elizabeth (some of her jewelry comes from here). Scattered over four floors of a dignified Victorian building, you'll find antiques, porcelain, leather goods, crystal, clocks, and enough unusual objects of dignified elegance to stock an English country house.

The Irish Shop. 14 King St., WC2. ☎ **0171/379-3625.** Tube: Covent Garden.

This family business has been selling a wide variety of articles shipped directly from Ireland since 1964. You'll find a wide selection of colorful knitwear, traditional Irish linens, hand-knitted Aran fisherman's sweaters, and Celtic jewelry. There's a little bit of everything here—even Guinness paraphernalia.

HANDBAGS

Bill Amberg's. 10 Chepstow Rd., W2. ☎ **0171/727-3560.** Tube: Notting Hill Gate.

Most famous for his logo-free handbags, Amberg has opened his own shop and expanded his line to include luggage, picture frames, and furniture. Supporters of Amberg's designs include Donna Karan, Romeo Gigli, Jerry Hall, and Christy Turlington. Given that, fashion-conscious shoppers may consider the £65 to £265 ($107.25 to $437.25) price range of most items a steal.

HOME DESIGN & HOUSEWARES

The Conran Shop. Michelin House, 81 Fulham Rd., SW3. ☎ **0171/589-7401.** Tube: South Kensington.

You'll find high style at reasonable prices from the man who invented it all for Britain: Sir Terance Conran. It's great for gifts, home furnishings, and table top—or just for gawking.

✪ **Designers Guild.** 267–271 and 275–277 King's Rd., SW3. ☎ **0171/351-5775.** Tube: Sloane Sq.

Often copied but never outdone—after more than 26 years in business, creative director Tricia Guild and her young designers still lead the pack in all that's bright and whimsical. There's an exclusive line of handmade furniture and accessories at the no. 267–271 location, and wallpaper and more than 2,000 fabrics at the neighboring no. 275–277 shop. The colors remain forever vivid, and the designs always irreverent. Also available are children's accessories, toys, crockery, and cutlery.

Purves & Purves. 80–81 and 83 Tottenham Court Rd., W1. ☎ **0171/580-8223.** Tube: Tottenham Court Rd. or Goodge St.

This store has a varied collection of modern furniture from Britain and the Continent. Many pieces are individually made by the designers themselves. The light and airy interior holds an eye-catching display of furniture, lighting, fabrics, rugs, and beds. Two doors up is an accessory shop with everything from clocks to cufflinks.

JEWELRY

Asprey & Garrard. 167 New Bond St., W1. ☎ **0171/493-6767.** Tube: Green Park.

Previously known as Garrard & Co., this recently merged jeweler specializes in both antique and modern jewelry and silverware. The in-house designers also produce pieces to order and do repairs. You can have a pair of pearl earrings or silver cufflinks for a mere £60 ($99)—but the prices go nowhere but up from there.

Lesley Craze Gallery/Craze 2/C2 Plus. 33–35 Clerkenwell Green, EC1. ☎ **0171/ 608-0393** (Gallery), 0171/251-0381 (Craze 2), 0171/251-9200 (C2 Plus). Tube: Farringdon.

This complex has developed a reputation as a showcase of the best contemporary British jewelry and textile design. The gallery shop focuses on precious metals, and includes pieces by such renowned designers as Wendy Ramshaw. Prices start at £50 ($82.50). Craze 2 features costume jewelry in materials ranging from bronze to paper, with prices starting at £12 ($19.80). C2 Plus features contemporary textile designs, including wall hangings, scarves, and ties by artists such as Jo Barker, Dawn DuPree, and Victoria Richards. C2 Plus has recently added a hanging gallery to display their textiles and wall hangings. The store is now billing itself as "London's only contemporary textile gallery."

Sanford Brothers Ltd. Old Elizabeth Houses, 3 Holborn Bars, EC1. ☎ **0171/405-2352.** Tube: Chancery Lane.

In business since 1923, this family firm sells all styles of jewelry, both modern and Victorian, silver of all kinds, and a fine selection of clocks and watches.

LINENS

Irish Linen Company. 35–36 Burlington Arcade, W1. ☎ **0171/493-8949.** Tube: Green Park or Piccadilly Circus.

This royal-warrant boutique carries items crafted of Irish linen, including hand-embroidered handkerchiefs and bed and table linens.

LINGERIE

Bradley's. 57 Knightsbridge, SW1. ☎ **0171/235-2902.** Tube: Knightsbridge or Hyde Park Corner.

Bradley's is the best-known lingerie specialty store in London; members of the royal family shop here. Established in the 1950s and very fashionable today, Bradley's fits "all sizes" in silk, cotton, lace, poly-cotton, or whatever.

LUGGAGE

Mulberry Company. 11–12 Gees Court, W1. ☎ **0171/493-2546.** Tube: Bond St.

This flagship store offers the complete line of the town's most cutting-edge designer luggage. The company's signature grosgrain and leather luggage begins at £150

($247.50). Mulberry is also earning a name in fashion for its English country-style ready-to-wear for both men and women; it also carries a fashionable display of furnishings and accessories for the home, including throws and cushions in chenille and damask.

MUSEUM SHOPS

London Transport Museum Shop. Covent Garden, WC2. ☎ **0171/379-6344.** Tube: Covent Garden.

This museum shop carries a wide range of reasonably priced repro and antique travel posters as well as tons of fun gifts and souvenirs. Those great London Underground maps that you see at every Tube station can be purchased here.

Victoria & Albert Gift Shop. Cromwell Rd., SW7. ☎ **0171/938-8500.** Tube: South Kensington.

Run by the Craft Council, this is the best museum shop in London—indeed, one of the best in the world. It sells cards, a fabulous selection of art books, and the usual items, along with reproductions from the museum archives.

MUSIC

Collectors should browse Notting Hill; there's a handful of good shops near the Notting Hill Gate Tube stop. Also browse Soho in the Wardour Street area, near the Tottenham Court Road Tube stop. Sometimes dealers show up at Covent Garden on the weekends.

In addition to the two listed below, also worth checking out is the ubiquitous **Our Price** chain, which offers only the current chart-toppers, but usually at great prices.

Tower Records. 1 Piccadilly Circus, W1. ☎ **0171/439-2500.** Tube: Piccadilly Circus. Other locations throughout London.

Attracting the throngs from a neighborhood whose pedestrian traffic is almost overwhelming, this is one of the largest record and CD stores in Europe. Sprawling over four floors, it's practically a tourist attraction in its own right. In addition to a huge selection of most of the musical styles ever recorded, there's everything on the cutting edge of technology, including interactive hardware and software, CD-ROMs, and laser discs.

Virgin Megastore. 14–16 Oxford St., W1. ☎ **0171/631-1234.** Tube: Tottenham Court Rd. Also at Kings Walk Shopping Centre, Kings Rd., Chelsea SW3 (☎ 0171/591-0957). Tube: Sloane Sq.

If a record has just been released—and if it's worth hearing in the first place—chances are this store carries it. It's like a giant musical grocery store, and you get to hear the release on headphones at listening stations before making a purchase. Even visiting rock stars come here to pick up new releases. A large selection of classical and jazz recordings is sold, as are computer software and video games. In between selecting your favorites, you can enjoy a coffee at the cafe, or purchase an airline ticket from the Virgin Atlantic office.

SHOES

Also see **Dr. Marten's Department Store** in "Fashion," above.

Church's. 1–4 King St., WC2. ☎ **0171/497-1460.** Tube: Covent Garden.

Well-made shoes, the status symbol of well-heeled executives in financial districts around the world, have been turned out by Church's since 1873. These are said to be recognizable to all the maîtres d'hôtel in London, who have always been suspected of appraising the wealth of their clients by their footwear.

Warning

Americans should beware of buying videotapes in the United Kingdom; the British standard is PAL, which is incompatible with the U.S. standard NTSC. Even if a tape says VHS, it won't play in your machine at home.

Natural Shoe Store. 21 Neal St., WC2. ☎ **0171/836-5254.** Tube: Covent Garden.

Shoes for both men and women are stocked in this shop, which also does repairs. The selection includes all comfort and quality footwear, from Birkenstock to the best of the British classics.

Shelly's. 266–270 Regent St., W1. ☎ **0171/287-0939.** Tube: Oxford Circus. Other locations throughout London.

This is the flagship of the mother of all London shoe shops, where they sell everything from tiny-tot hip shoes to grown-up hip shoes and boots at affordable prices. They're famous for their Dr. Martens, but there's much more—and none of it traditional.

SPORTING GOODS

○ **Lillywhites Ltd.** 24–36 Lower Regent St., Piccadilly Circus, SW1. ☎ **0171/915-4000.** Tube: Piccadilly Circus.

Europe's biggest and most famous sports store has floor after floor of sports clothing, equipment, and footwear. It also offers collections of fashionable leisurewear for men and women.

STATIONERY & PAPER GOODS

Paperchase. 213 Tottenham Court Rd., W1. ☎ **0171/580-8496.** Tube: Goodge St. or Tottenham Court Rd. Other locations throughout London.

This flagship store offers three floors of paper products including storage boxes, handmade paper, wrapping paper, ribbons, picture frames, and a huge selection of offbeat greeting cards. It's the best of its kind in London.

TEA

Of course, don't forget to visit Fortnum & Mason as well (see "The Department Stores," above).

The Tea House. 15 Neal St., WC2. ☎ **0171/240-7539.** Tube: Covent Garden.

This shop sells everything associated with tea, tea drinking, and teatime. It boasts more than 70 quality teas and tisanes, including whole-fruit blends, the best tea of China (Gunpowder, jasmine with flowers), India (Assam leaf, choice Darjeeling), Japan (Genmaicha green), and Sri Lanka (pure Ceylon), plus such longtime favorite English blended teas as Earl Grey. The shop also offers novelty teapots and mugs, among other items.

TOYS

○ **Hamleys.** 188–196 Regent St., W1. ☎ **0171/494-2000.** Tube: Oxford Circus. Also at Covent Garden and Heathrow Airport.

This flagship is the finest toy shop in the world—more than 35,000 toys and games on seven floors of fun and magic. The huge selection includes soft, cuddly stuffed animals as well as dolls, radio-controlled cars, train sets, model kits, board games, outdoor toys, and computer games.

TRAVEL SERVICES

British Airways Travel Department Store. 156 Regent St., W1. ☎ **0171/434-4700.** Tube: Piccadilly Circus or Oxford Circus.

The retail flagship of British Airways offers not only worldwide travel and ticketing, but also a wide range of services and shops, including a clinic for immunization, a pharmacy, a bureau de change, a passport and visa service, and a theater-booking desk. The ground floor sells luggage, guidebooks, maps, and other goods. Passengers with hand baggage only can check in here for a BA flight. Travel insurance, hotel reservations, and car rentals can also be arranged.

VINTAGE & SECONDHAND

Note that there's no VAT refund on used clothing.

Annie's Vintage Costume and Textiles. 10 Camden Passage, N1. ☎ **0171/359-0796.** Tube: Angel.

The shop concentrates on carefully preserved dresses from the 1920s and 1930s, but has a range of clothing and textiles from the 1880s through the 1960s. A 1920s fully beaded dress will run you about £400 ($640), but there are scarves for £10 ($16.50), camisoles for £20 ($33), and a range of exceptional pieces priced between £50 and £60 ($82.50 and $99). Clothing is located on the main floor; textiles, including old lace, bed linens, and tapestries, are upstairs.

Pandora. 16 Cheval Place, SW7. ☎ **0171/589-5289.** Tube: Knightsbridge.

A London institution since the 1940s, Pandora stands in fashionable Knightsbridge, a stone's throw from Harrods. Several times a week, chauffeurs will drive up with bundles packed anonymously by England's gentry. One woman voted best dressed at Ascot several years ago was wearing a secondhand dress acquired here. Prices are generally one-third to one-half the retail value. Chanel and Anne Klein are among the designers represented. Outfits are usually no more than two seasons old.

Pop Boutique. 6 Monmouth St., WC2. ☎ **0171/497-5262.** Tube: Covent Garden.

For the best in original streetwear from the 1950s, 1960s, and 1970s, this clothing store is tops. Right next to the chic Covent Garden Hotel, it has fabulous vintage wear at affordable prices: Leather jackets that would run $250 or $300 in the vintage shops of downtown New York go for as little as £45 ($74.25) here.

Steinberg & Tolkien. 193 King's Rd., SW3. ☎ **0171/376-3660.** Tube: Sloane Sq.

This place is London's leading dealer in vintage costume jewelry and clothing. There's also some used designer clothing that isn't old enough to be vintage but is prime for collectors; other pieces are merely secondhand designer thrills.

London After Dark

London's pulsating scene is the most vibrant in Europe. Although pubs still close at 11pm, the city is staying up later. More and more clubs extend partying into the wee hours.

London is on a real high right now, especially in terms of music and dance; much of the current techno and electronica (including the hip-hop, tribal, and drum-and-bass styles that aging rockers like Bowie and U2 have appropriated) originated in London clubs. Sounds made hip by Tricky and Aphex Twin reverberate not only throughout the city, but across the Continent and the Atlantic as well. Youth culture prevails; downtown denizens flock to the latest clubs where pop-culture superstars are routinely spotted.

London nightlife is always in a state of constant flux. What's hot today probably just opened, and many clubs have the lifespan of fruit flies. **Groucho,** at 44 Dean St., W1 (☎ **0171/439-4685**) is still the in club, though it is still a members-only club. The Marquee, the legendary live-music venue where the Rolling Stones played when they were still bad boys, has regrettably shut its doors. But a few perennials, like Ronnie Scott's, are still around.

London nightlife, however, is not just music and dance clubs. The city abounds with what's the world's best live theater scene, pubs oozing historic charm, and many more options for a night out.

HOW TO FIND OUT WHAT'S GOING ON

Weekly publications such as *Time Out* and *Where* provide the most complete up-to-the-minute entertainment listings. They contain information on live music and dance clubs as well as London's diverse theater scene, which includes everything from big-budget West End shows to fringe productions. Daily newspapers, notably the *Times* and the *Daily Telegraph*, also provide listings. The arts section of the weekend *Independent* is also a good reference.

If you really want to take full advantage of London's arts scene, your best bet is to do a bit of research before you leave home—even a few months in advance. To get a good idea of what's going on, check out *Time Out's* **World Wide Web page** at **www.timeout.co.uk**. If you're not online, *Time Out* is available at many international newsstands in the United States and Canada. In London, it can be picked up almost anywhere.

1 The Play's the Thing: The London Theater Scene

Even more than New York, London is the theater capital of the world; the number and variety of productions, as well as high standards of acting and directing, are unrivaled. The London stage accommodates both the traditional and the avant-garde and is uniquely accessible and affordable.

Few things in London are as entertaining and rewarding as the theater. A trip to London could be nothing more than a splendid orgy of drama and musicals.

GETTING TICKETS

Prices for London shows usually vary from £18 to £60 ($29.70 to $99), depending on the theater and the seat. Matinees, performed Tuesday to Saturday, are cheaper than evening performances, but London theater tickets are no longer the bargain they used to be.

Evening performances begin between 7:30 and 8:30pm, midweek matinees at 2:30 or 3pm, and Saturday matinees at 5:45pm. West End theaters are closed Sundays. Many theaters offer the bonus of licensed bars on the premises and coffee at intermissions (which Londoners call "intervals").

Many theaters accept telephone bookings at regular prices with a credit card. They'll hold your tickets for you at the box office, where you pick them up at show time with a credit card.

TICKET AGENCIES   If your heart is set on seeing a specific show, particularly one of the big hits, you'll have to reserve in advance through one of the many London ticket agencies. For tickets and information before you go, try **Edwards & Edwards,** 1270 Ave. of the Americas, Suite 2414, New York, NY 10020 (☎ **800/223-6108** or 914/328-2150; fax 914/328-2752). They also have offices in London at the **Palace Theatre,** Shaftesbury Avenue, W1 8AY (☎ **0171/734-4555**) or at the **Harrods** ticket desk, 87–135 Brompton Rd. (☎ **0171/589-9109**), located on the lower-ground floor opposite the British Airways desk. They'll mail tickets to your home, fax you a confirmation, or leave your tickets at the box office. Instant confirmations are available with special "overseas" rates for most shows. A booking and handling fee of up to 20% is added to the ticket price.

You might also try calling **Keith Prowse/First Call** (☎ **0129/343-3600**). This agency also has an office in the United States that allows you to reserve months in advance for hit shows: Suite 1000, 234 W. 44th St., New York, NY 10036 (☎ **800/669-8687** or 212/398-1430). Various locations exist in London. The fee for booking a ticket is 20% in London and 35% in the United States.

Another option is **Theatre Direct International (TDI)** (☎ **800/334-8457,** U.S. only). TDI specializes in providing London theater and fringe production tickets, but also has tickets to most London productions, including those of the Royal National Theatre and Barbican. The service allows you to arrive in London with your tickets or have them held for you at the box office.

GALLERY & DISCOUNT TICKETS   Sometimes gallery seats (the cheapest) are sold only on the day of the performance; you'll need to head to the box office early in the day and, since these are not reserved seats, return an hour before the performance to queue up. Many major theaters offer reduced-price tickets to students on a standby basis. When available, these tickets are sold 30 minutes prior to curtain. Line up early for popular shows, as standby tickets get snapped up. Of course, you'll need a valid student ID.

The **Society of London Theatre** (☎ **0171/557-6700**) operates a **discount ticket booth** in Leicester Square, where tickets for many shows are available at half price, plus a £2 ($3.30) service charge. Tickets (limited to four per person) are sold only on the day of performance. You cannot return tickets, and credit cards are not accepted. Hours are daily from noon to 6:30pm.

MAJOR THEATERS & COMPANIES

One of London's legendary theaters, the **Old Vic** in Waterloo Rd., SE1 (☎ **0171/ 928-7616**) has its future in doubt. At this fabled place, Sir John Gielgud made his debut in 1921, and Laurence Olivier spent much of his career here as actor and director of the National Theatre before it moved to its new home. The theater is up for sale, and what will happen is anybody's guess (it could even be turned into a disco).

In addition to the mostly repertory theaters listed below, consult *Time Out* for West End theaters and long-running shows.

Barbican Theatre–Royal Shakespeare Company. In the Barbican Centre, Silk St., Barbican, EC2. ☎ **0171/638-8891.** Barbican Theatre £5–£26 ($8.25–$42.90). The Pit matinees and evening performances £11–£18.50 ($18.15–$30.55). Box office daily 9am–8pm. Tube: Barbican or Moorgate.

The Barbican is the London home of the Royal Shakespeare Company, one of the world's finest theater companies. The core of its repertoire remains, of course, the plays of William Shakespeare. It also presents a wide-ranging program in its two theaters. There are three productions in repertory each week in the Barbican Theatre—a 2,000-seat main auditorium with excellent sight lines throughout, thanks to a raked orchestra. The Pit, a small studio space, is where the company's new writing is presented. The Royal Shakespeare Company performs both here and at Stratford-upon-Avon. It is in residence in London during the winter months; in the summer, it tours in England and abroad.

Open-Air Theatre. Inner Circle, Regent's Park, NW1. ☎ **0171/486-2431.** Tickets £8–£21 ($13.20–$34.65). Tube: Baker St.

This outdoor theater is in Regent's Park; the setting is idyllic, and both seating and acoustics are excellent. Presentations are mainly of Shakespeare, usually in period costume. Its theater bar, the longest in London, serves both drink and food. In the case of a rained-out performance, tickets are given for another date. The season runs from the end of May to mid-September, Monday to Saturday at 8pm, plus Wednesday, Thursday, and Saturday matinees at 2:30pm.

Royal Court Theatre. Sloane Sq., SW1. ☎ **0171/565-5000.** Tube: Sloane Sq.

This theater, always a leader in producing provocative, cutting-edge new drama, was still closed at press time, with opening slated for the autumn of 1999. In the 1950s, it staged the plays of the angry young men, notably John Osborne's then sensational *Look Back in Anger;* earlier it debuted the plays of George Bernard Shaw. A recent work was *The Beauty Queen of Leenane,* which won a Tony on Broadway. The theater is home to the English Stage Company, formed to promote serious stage writing. Tickets generally range in price from £5 to £19.50 ($8.25 to $32.20); call for the latest information.

✪ **Royal National Theatre.** South Bank, SE1. ☎ **0171/452-3400.** Tickets £9–£27 ($14.85–$44.55); midweek matinees, Sat matinees, and previews cost less. Tube: Waterloo, Embankment, or Charing Cross.

Home to one of the world's greatest stage companies, the Royal National Theatre is not one but three theaters—the Olivier, reminiscent of a Greek amphitheater with its open stage; the more traditional Lyttelton; and the Cottesloe, with its flexible stage and seating. The National presents the finest in world theater, from classic drama to award-winning new plays, including comedies, musicals, and shows for young people.

There is a choice of at least six plays at any one time. It's also a full-time theater center, with an amazing selection of bars, cafes, restaurants, free foyer music and exhibitions, short early-evening performances, bookshops, backstage tours, riverside walks, and terraces. You can have a three-course meal in Mezzanine, the National's restaurant; enjoy a light meal in the brasserie-style Terrace cafe; or have a snack in one of the coffee bars.

Shakespeare's Globe Theatre. New Globe Walk, Bankside, SE1. ☎ **0171/902-1500.** Box office: 0171/401-9919. Tickets £5 ($8.25) for groundlings, £5–£25 ($8.25–$41.25) for gallery seats. Tube: Mansion House.

In May 1997, the new Globe Theatre—a replica of the Elizabethan original, thatched roof and all—staged its first slate of plays (*Henry V* and *A Winter's Tale*) on the exact site of the 16th-century theater where the Bard originally staged his work.

Productions vary in style and setting; not all are performed in Elizabethan costume. In keeping with the historic setting, there's no lighting focused just on the stage, but floodlighting is used during evening performances to replicate daylight in the theater—Elizabethan performances took place in the afternoon. Theatergoers sit on wooden benches of yore—in thatch-roofed galleries, no less—but these days you can rent a cushion to make yourself more comfortable. About 500 "groundlings" can stand in the uncovered yard around the stage, just as they did when the Bard was here. Mark Rylane, the artistic director of the Globe, wanted the theater-going experience to be as authentic as possible—he told the press he'd be delighted if the audience threw fruit at the actors, as they did in Shakespeare's time.

From May to September, the company intends to hold performances Tuesday to Saturday at 3pm and 7pm, and Sunday at 4pm. There will be a limited winter schedule. In any season, the schedule may be affected by the weather, since this is an outdoor theater. Performances last $2^{1}/_{2}$ to 4 hours, depending on the play.

Also in the works is a second theater, the **Inigo Jones Theatre,** based on the architect's designs from the 1600s, where plays will be staged year-round. For details on the exhibition that tells the story of the painstaking re-creation of the Globe, as well as guided tours of the theatre, see "More Central London Attractions" in chapter 6.

Theatre Royal Drury Lane. Catherine St., Covent Garden, WC2. ☎ **0171/494-5060.** Tickets £8–£35 ($13.20–$57.75). Box office Mon–Sat 10am–8pm. Evening performances Mon–Sat 7:45pm; matinees Wed and Sat 3pm. Tube: Covent Garden.

Drury Lane is one of London's oldest and most prestigious theaters, crammed with tradition—not all of it respectable. This, the fourth theater on this site, dates from 1812; the first was built in 1663. Nell Gwynne, the rough-tongued cockney lass who

---

Warning

Beware of unlicensed ticket agencies in London. You could end up paying £28 ($46.20) for a ticket worth only £16 ($26.40). According to law, the face value of a ticket sold at a premium should be declared to the consumer at the time of sale. However, this code appears to be unenforceable. The **Society of London Theatre** (☎ 0171/557-6700) reports that it receives complaints of overcharging on a frequent basis. The society advises that you book your ticket at the theater box office by telephone or in person.

Beware also of scalpers who hang out in front of hit shows at London theaters. Even if the tickets they're selling are valid—there are many reports of forged tickets—scalpers charge very high prices.

Central London Theaters

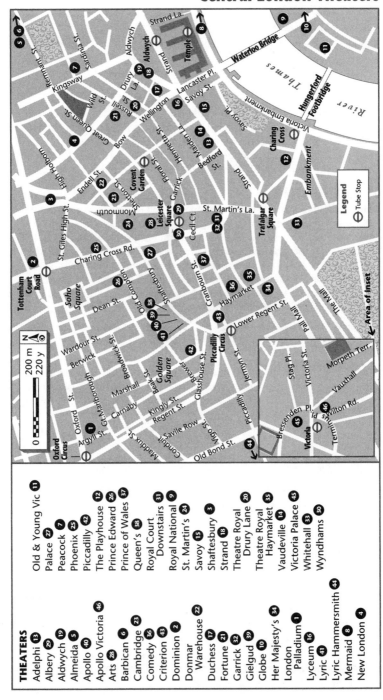

THEATERS

Adelphi	13
Albery	29
Aldwych	19
Almeida	5
Apollo	40
Apollo Victoria	46
Arts	28
Barbican	6
Cambridge	23
Comedy	36
Criterion	43
Dominion	2
Donmar Warehouse	22
Duchess	17
Fortune	21
Garrick	32
Gielgud	39
Globe	10
Her Majesty's	34
London Palladium	1
Lyceum	16
Lyric	41
Lyric Hammersmith	44
Mermaid	8
New London	4
Old & Young Vic	11
Palace	27
Peacock	7
Phoenix	25
Piccadilly	42
The Playhouse	12
Prince Edward	26
Prince of Wales	37
Queen's	38
Royal Court Downstairs	31
Royal National	9
St. Martin's	24
Savoy	15
Shaftesbury	3
Strand	18
Theatre Royal Drury Lane	20
Theatre Royal Haymarket	35
Vaudeville	14
Victoria Palace	45
Whitehall	33
Wyndhams	30

False Discounts ————————————————————————————

Many less-than-scrupulous agents near Leicester Square offer "discounted" tickets that are nothing of the kind. Out-of-towners could pay $30 to $35 for a "discount" ticket only to find them available at the box office for $25.

---

became Charles II's mistress, used to sell oranges under the long colonnade in front. Nearly every star of London theater has taken the stage here at some time. It has a wide-open repertoire but leans toward musicals, especially long-running hits. Guided tours of the backstage area and the front of the house are given most days at 10:30am and 12:30pm. Call ☎ **0171/494-5091** for more information.

FRINGE THEATER

Some of the best theater in London is performed on the "fringe"—at the dozens of so-called fringe theaters devoted to alternative plays, revivals, contemporary dramas, and musicals. These shows are usually more adventurous than established West End productions; they are also consistently lower in price. Expect to pay from £5–£22 ($8.25–$36.30). Most offer discounted seats to students and seniors.

Fringe theaters are scattered around London. Check the weekly listings in *Time Out* for schedules and show times. Some of the more popular and centrally located theaters are listed below; call for details on current productions.

✪ **Almeida Theatre.** Almeida St., N1. ☎ **0171/359-4404.** Tickets £6.50–£19.50 ($10.75–$32.15). Box office Mon–Sat 9:30am–7:30pm. Tube: Angel or Highbury & Islington.

Home to the annual Festival of Contemporary Music (also called the Almeida Opera) from mid-June to mid-July, the Almeida is also known for its adventurous staging of new and classic plays. The theater's legendary status is validated by consistently good productions at lower-than-average prices. Among the more recent celebrated productions have been *Hamlet* with Ralph Fiennes, and *Medea* with Dame Diana Rigg, both of which went to Broadway. Performances are usually held Monday to Saturday.

The Gate. In the Prince Albert Pub, 11 Pembridge Rd., Notting Hill, W11. ☎ **0171/229-0706.** Tickets £10 ($16.50) regular admission, £6 ($9.90) for students and senior citizens. MC, V. Box office Mon–Fri 10am–6pm. Tube: Notting Hill Gate.

This tiny room above a Notting Hill pub is one of the best alternative stages in London. Popular with local cognoscenti, the theater specializes in translated works by foreign playwrights. Performances are held Monday to Saturday at 7 or 7:30pm. Call for shows and times.

ICA Theatre. The Mall, SW1. ☎ **0171/930-3647.** Average tickets £7–£10 ($11.55–$16.50). Box office daily noon–9:30pm. Tube: Charing Cross or Piccadilly Circus.

In addition to a cinema, cafe, bar, bookshop, and two galleries, the Institute of Contemporary Arts (ICA) has one of London's top theaters for experimental work. ICA's government subsidies usually produce high-quality performances. Bar hours are Tuesday to Saturday from noon to 1am, Sunday noon to 9pm; galleries are open daily from noon to 7:30pm; and cinema showtimes are daily at 5, 7, and 9pm.

The King's Head. 115 Upper St., N1. ☎ **0171/226-1916.** Tickets £7–£12 ($11.55–$19.80). Box office Mon–Fri 10am–6pm, Sat 10am–8pm, Sun 10am–4pm. Tube: Angel.

Arguably London's most famous fringe locale, the King's Head is also the city's oldest pub-theater. Despite its tiny stage, the popular theater is heavy on musicals; several that opened here have gone on to become successful West End productions.

Matinee performances are held on Saturday and Sunday at 3:30pm. Evening performances are Tuesday to Saturday at 8pm.

Young Vic. 66 The Cut, Waterloo, SE1. ☎ **0171/928-6363.** Tickets £5–£20 ($8.25–$33) adults, £5–£10 ($8.25–$16.50) students and children. Performances Mon–Sat 7 or 7:30pm; matinee Sat 2pm. Tube: Waterloo.

Young Vic presents classical and modern plays in the round for theatergoers of all ages and backgrounds, but primarily focuses on young adults. Recent productions have included Shakespeare, Ibsen, Arthur Miller, and specially commissioned plays for children. Call for specific times, as they can fluctuate.

2 London's Classical Music & Dance Scene

Currently, London supports five major orchestras—the **London Symphony,** the **Royal Philharmonic,** the **Philharmonia Orchestra,** the **BBC Symphony,** and the **BBC Philharmonic**—several choirs, and many smaller chamber groups and historic-instrument ensembles. Look for the **London Sinfonietta,** the **English Chamber Orchestra,** and, of course, the **Academy of St. Martin in the Fields.** Performances are in the South Banks Arts Centre and the Barbican. For smaller recitals, there's Wigmore Hall and St. John's Smith Square.

British Music Information Centre, 10 Stratford Place, W1 (☎ **0171/499-8567**), is the city's clearinghouse and resource center for serious music. The center is open Monday to Friday noon to 5pm, and provides free telephone and walk-in information on current and upcoming events. Recitals featuring 20th-century British classical compositions cost up to £5 ($8.25) and are offered here weekly, usually on Tuesday and Thursday at 7:30pm; call ahead for day and time. Since capacity is limited to 40, you may want to check early. Take the tube to Bond Street.

✪ **Barbican Centre—London Symphony Orchestra (& more).** Silk St., the City, EC2. ☎ **0171/638-8891.** Tickets £6.50–£32 ($10.75–$52.80). Box office daily 9am–8pm. Tube: Barbican or Moorgate.

The largest art and exhibition center in Western Europe, the roomy and comfortable Barbican complex is a perfect setting for enjoying music and theater. Barbican Hall is the permanent home address of the **London Symphony Orchestra** as well as host to visiting orchestras and performers, from classical to jazz, folk, and world music.

In addition to the hall and the two theaters of the Royal Shakespeare Company, Barbican Centre includes: The Barbican Art Gallery, a showcase for visual arts; the Concourse Gallery and foyer exhibition spaces; Cinemas One and Two, which show recently released mainstream films and film series; the Barbican Library, a general lending library that places a strong emphasis on the arts; the Conservatory, one of London's largest plant houses; and restaurants, cafes, and bars.

Contemporary Dance. At The Place, 17 Duke's Rd., WC1. ☎ **0171/387-0031.** Tickets £10 ($16.50), £7 ($11.55) students and seniors. Box office Mon–Fri 10:30am–8pm, Sat noon–6pm, Sun noon–6pm (performance days). Tube: Euston.

This showplace usually offers good performances and cheap tickets. The space is small; the mirrors and bars you'll see give an indication of the theater's day job as a dance school.

English National Opera. London Coliseum, St. Martin's Lane, WC2. ☎ **0171/632-8300.** Tickets £5–£10 ($8.25–$16.50) balcony, £12.50–£55 ($20.65–$90.75) upper or dress circle or stalls; about 100 discount balcony tickets sold on the day of performance from 10am. Tube: Charing Cross or Leicester Sq.

Built in 1904 as a variety theater and converted into an opera house in 1968, the London Coliseum is the city's largest theater. One of two national opera companies, the English National Opera performs a wide range of works from classics to Gilbert and Sullivan to new and experimental works, staged with flair and imagination. All performances are in English. A repertory of 18 to 20 productions is presented 5 or 6 nights a week for 11 months of the year (dark in July). Although balcony seats are cheaper, many visitors seem to prefer the upper circle or dress circle.

Dance Umbrella. 20 Chancellor's St., W6. ☎ **0181/741-4040.** Tickets £10–£30 ($16.50–$49.50). Tube: Hammersmith.

This company's fall season showcase became *the* contemporary dance event in London. During its 6-week season, new works by up-and-coming choreographers are featured. Performances are held at a variety of theaters.

Royal Albert Hall. Kensington Gore, SW7. ☎ **0171/589-8212.** Tickets £3–£130 ($4.95–$214.50), depending on the event. Box office daily 9am–9pm. Tube: South Kensington.

Opened in 1871 and dedicated to the memory of Victoria's consort, Prince Albert, the circular building holds one of the world's most famous auditoriums. With a seating capacity of 5,200, it's a popular place to hear music by stars like Eric Clapton and Shirley Bassey. Occasional sporting events (especially boxing) figure strongly here, too.

Since 1941, the hall has been the setting for the BBC Henry Wood Promenade Concerts, known as **"The Proms,"** a concert series that lasts for 8 weeks between mid-July and mid-September. The Proms have been a British tradition since 1895. Although most of the audience occupies reserved seats, true aficionados usually opt for standing room in the orchestra pit, which affords close-up views of the musicians performing on stage. Newly commissioned works are often premiered here. The final evening of The Proms is the most traditional; the rousing favorites "Jerusalem" or "Land of Hope and Glory" echo through the hall. For tickets, call TicketMaster (☎ **0171/344-4444**) directly.

✪ **Royal Festival Hall.** On the South Bank, SE1. ☎ **0171/960-4242.** Tickets £5–£50 ($8.25–$82.50). Box office daily 9am–9pm. Tube: Waterloo or Embankment.

In the aftermath of World War II, the principal site of London's music scene shifted to the south bank of the Thames. Three of the most acoustically perfect concert halls in the world were erected between 1951 and 1964. They include Royal Festival Hall, the Queen Elizabeth Hall, and the Purcell Room. Together they hold more than 1,200 performances a year, including classical music, ballet, jazz, popular music, and contemporary dance. Also here is the internationally renowned **Hayward Gallery** (see chapter 6).

Royal Festival Hall, which opens daily at 10am, offers an extensive array of things to see and do, including free exhibitions in the foyers and free lunchtime music at 12:30pm. On Friday, Commuter Jazz in the foyer from 5:15 to 6:45pm is free. The Poetry Library is open from 11am to 8pm, and shops display a wide selection of books, records, and crafts. The Festival Buffet has a wide variety of food at reasonable prices, and bars dot the foyers. The People's Palace offers lunch and dinner with a panoramic view of the River Thames. Reservations by calling ☎ **0171/928-9999** are recommended.

✪ **The Royal Opera House—The Royal Ballet & the Royal Opera.** Bow St., Covent Garden, WC2. Closed for redevelopment. For information on Royal Opera and Royal Ballet performances, in other venues, call ☎ **0171/212-9123.**

The two world-famous companies, the Royal Opera and the great Royal Ballet have been temporarily dislodged from the Royal Opera House, their Covent Garden home, because of its ongoing renovation. They'll be back on their home stage in the autumn of 1999. In the meantime, they will be appearing at a number of venues around London and abroad, including the Barbican, Royal Albert Hall, and a West End theater. The Royal Ballet also has seasons at the Labatts Apollo in Hammersmith, the Royal Festival Hall, and the London Coliseum.

Performances of the Royal Opera are usually sung in the original language, but supertitles are projected, translating the libretto for the audience. The Royal Ballet, that ranks with top companies such as the Kirov and the Paris Opera Ballet, performs a repertory with a tilt toward the classics, including works by its earlier choreographer-directors Sir Frederick Ashton and Sir Kenneth MacMillan.

Sadler's Wells Theatre. Rosebery Ave., EC1. ☎ **0171/314-8800.** Tickets £7.50–£60 ($12.40–$99). Performances usually 8pm. Box office Mon–Sat noon–8pm. Tube: Angel.

This is a premier venue for dance and opera. It occupies the site of a theater that was built in 1683, on the location of a well prized for the healing powers of its waters. In the early 1990s, the old-fashioned, turn-of-the-century theater was demolished, and construction began on an innovative new design that was completed at the end of 1998. The original façade has been retained, however, but the interior has been completely revamped to create a stylish cutting-edge theater design.

The new theater will offer both traditional and experimental dance within two theaters, the new, state-of-the-art theater on the original site, and offshoot productions in the Peacock, which the Sadler's Wells Trust will continue to rent until sometime after the millennium.

Wigmore Hall. 36 Wigmore St., W1. ☎ **0171/935-2141.** Tickets £6–£20 ($9.90–$33). Performances nightly, plus Sun Morning Coffee Concerts and Sun concerts at 4 or 7pm. Tube: Bond St. or Oxford Circus.

An intimate auditorium, Wigmore Hall offers an excellent regular series of song recitals, piano and chamber music, early and baroque music, and jazz. A free list of the month's programs is available from Wigmore. A cafe-bar and restaurant are on the premises; a cold supper can be preordered if you are attending a concert.

OUTSIDE CENTRAL LONDON

Kenwood Lakeside Concerts. Kenwood, Hampstead Lane, Hampstead Heath, London NW3 7JR (☎ **0171/413-1443**). Tickets for adults £9 ($14.85) for seats on the grass lawn, £11–£16 ($18.15–$26.40) for reserved deck chairs. Reductions of 12.5% for students and persons over 60. Every summer Sat at 7:30pm from July to early Sept. Tube: Golders Green or Archway, then bus no. 210.

These band and orchestral concerts on the north side of Hampstead Heath have been a British tradition for some 50 years. In recent years, laser shows and fireworks have added to a repertoire that includes everything from rousing versions of the *1812 Overture* to jazz, and such operas as *Carmen*. The final concert of the season always features some of the Pomp and Circumstance marches of Sir Edward Elgar, everyone's favorite imperial composer. Music drifts across the lake to serenade wine-and-cheese parties on the grass.

3 The Club & Music Scene

It's the nature of live music and dance clubs to come and go with alarming speed, or shift violently from one trend to another. *Time Out* is the best way to keep current.

COMEDY & CABARET

Comedy Spot. The Spot, Maiden Lane, WC2. ☎ **0171/379-5900.** Cover Fri and Sat £5 ($8.25) after 10pm, cover Sun after 8pm; Mon cover £9 ($14.85) with a meal or £7 ($11.55) without. Mon–Thurs noon–midnight, Fri–Sat noon–1am, Sun 7–10:30pm.

This bar-restaurant has DJs Tuesday to Saturday; singers on Sunday; and "spotlight comedy" on Monday nights, with a host and three comedians, mixing beginners with old pros. If you're into stand-up comedy, English-style, this is one of the best places in town.

The Comedy Store. 1A Oxendon St., off Piccadilly Circus, SW1. ☎ **0171/344-0234.** Cover £11–£13 ($18.15–$21.45). Daily from 6:30pm. Tube: Leicester Sq. or Piccadilly Circus.

This is London's most visible showcase for established and rising comic talent. Inspired by comedy clubs in the United States, this London club has given many comics their start. Today a number of them are established TV personalities. Even if their names are unfamiliar, you'll enjoy the spontaneity of live comedy performed before a British audience. Visitors must be 18 and older; dress is casual. Reserve through TicketMaster (☎ **0171/344-4444**); the club opens 1¹/₂ hours before each show. *Insider's Tip:* Go on Tuesday when the humor is more cutting edge and topical.

BOUZOUKI

Elysée. 13 Percy St., W1. ☎ **0171/636-4804.** Cover Mon–Thurs £3 ($4.95), Fri–Sat £4 ($6.60). Meals Mon–Fri noon–3pm, Mon–Sat 7:30pm–4am. Tube: Goodge St. or Tottenham Court Rd.

Elysée is for *Never on Sunday* devotees who like the reverberations of bouzouki and the smashing of plates. The Karegeorgis brothers—Michael, Ulysses, and the incomparable George—offer hearty fun at moderate tabs. You can dance nightly to music by Greek musicians. Two different cabaret shows are presented (the last one at 1am). You can book a table on either the ground floor or the second floor, but the roof garden is the place to be in summer. The food is good, too, especially the house specialty, the classic moussaka, and kebabs from the charcoal grill.

LIVE MUSIC

Bagley's Studios. King's Cross Freigh Depot, off York Way, N1. ☎ **0171/278-2777.** Cover £10–£20 ($16.50–$33). Guaranteed openings Fri–Sun 10pm–7am. Otherwise, openings depend on whatever promoter wants to book the space. Tube: King's Cross.

The premises of this place are vast, echoing, a bit grimy, and warehouse-like. Set in the bleak industrial landscapes behind King's Cross Station, its interior is radically transformed three nights a week into an animated rave event. Its two floors, each the size of an American football field, are divided into trios of individual rooms, with their own ambience and sound system. You'll be happiest here if you wander from room to room, searching out the site that best corresponds to your energy level at the moment. Choices will probably include sites devoted to garage, club classics as promoted by AM/FM radio, "banging" (hard house) music, and "bubbly" upbeat dance music. If you happen to be in London on a weeknight, don't assume that the place will be dark, as various social groups, including lots of East Indian social clubs, rent the place for gatherings, some of which might be open to the public. Saturday night "Freedom" parties are more fun.

Barfly Club. At the Falcon Pub, 234 Royal College St., NW1. ☎ **0171/482-4884.** Cover £7–£11 ($11.55–$18.15). Nightly 7:30pm–2 or 3am, with most musical acts beginning at 8:15pm. Tube: Camden Town.

In a dingy residential neighborhood in north London, this traditional-looking pub is distinguished by the roster of rock-and-roll bands who come in from throughout the U.K. for bouts of beer and high-energy music. A recorded announcement tells fans what to expect on any given night, along with instructions on how to reach the place through a warren of narrow streets. You can get virtually anything here—which adds considerably to the sense of fun and adventure. The roster of world-class groups who were "discovered" here includes Oasis. You'll usually hear three different bands a night.

The Bull & Gate. 389 Kentish Town Rd., NW5. ☎ **0171/485-5358.** Cover £4 ($6.60). Tube: Kentish Town.

Outside central London, and smaller, cheaper, and often more animated and less touristed than many of its competitors, The Bull & Gate is the unofficial headquarters of London's pub rock scene. Indie and relatively unknown rock bands are often served up back to back by the half dozen in this somewhat-battered Victorian pub. If you like spilled beer, this is off-the-beaten-track London at its most authentic. Bands that played here and later ascended to Europe's clubby scene have included Madness, Blur, Pulp, and that 1980s music video oddity, Sigue-Sigue-Sputnik. The place operates pub hours, with music nightly from 9pm to midnight

The Rock Garden. 6–7 The Piazza, Covent Garden, WC2. ☎ **0171/836-4052.** Cover £5–£10 ($8.25–$16.50); diners enter free. Mon–Thurs 5pm–3am, Fri and Sat 5pm–4am, Sun 7pm–midnight. Tube: Covent Garden. Bus: Any of the night buses that depart from Trafalgar Square.

A long-established performance site, The Rock Garden maintains a bar and a stage in the cellar, and a restaurant on the street level. The cellar, known as The Venue, has hosted such acts as Dire Straits, Police, and U2 before their rise to stardom. Today bands vary widely, from promising up-and-comers to some who'll never be heard from again. Simple American-style fare is served in the restaurant.

Wag Club. 35 Wardour St., W1. ☎ **0171/437-5534.** Cover £5–£10 ($8.25–$16.50). Tues–Thurs 10pm–3am, Fri 10pm–4am, Sat 10pm–5am, Sun closed. No credit cards. Tube: Leicester Sq. or Piccadilly Circus.

The split-level Wag Club is one of the more stylish live-music places in town. The downstairs stage usually attracts newly signed, cutting-edge rock bands, while a DJ spins dance records upstairs. Door policy can be selective.

FOLK

Cecil Sharpe House. 2 Regent's Park Rd., NW1. ☎ **0171/485-2206.** No cover. Tube: Camden Town.

CSH was the focal point of the folk revival in the 1960s, and it continues to treasure and nurture the style. Here you'll find a whole range of traditional English music and dance. Call to see what's happening.

JAZZ & BLUES

Ain't Nothing But Blues Bar. 20 Kingly St., W1. ☎ **0171/287-0514.** Cover Fri £3–£5 ($4.95–$8.25), Sat £3–£5 ($5–$8), free before 9:30pm. Mon–Thurs 5:30–1am, Fri–Sat 6pm–3am, Sun 6pm–midnight. Tube: Oxford Circus or Piccadilly Circus.

The club, which bills itself as the only true blues venue in town, features local acts and occasional touring American bands. On weekends prepare to queue. From the Oxford Circus Tube stop, walk south on Regent Street, turn left on Great Marlborough Street, and then make a quick right on Kingly Street.

The World's Greatest Pub Crawl

Dropping into the local pub for a pint of real ale or bitter is the best way to soak up the character of the different villages that make up London. You'll hear local accents and slang and see firsthand how far removed upper-crust Kensington is from blue-collar Wapping. Catch the local gossip or football talk—and, of course, enjoy some of the finest ales, stouts, ciders, and malt whiskies in the world.

The Heart of the City   Central London is awash with wonderful historic pubs as rich and varied as the city itself.

Cittie of Yorke, 22 High Holborn, WC1 (☎ 0171/242-7670; Tube: Holborn Chancery Lane), boasts the longest bar in all of Britain, rafters ascending to the heavens, and a long row of immense wine vats, all of which give it the air of a great medieval hall—appropriate since a pub has existed at this location since 1430. Samuel Smiths is on tap, and the bar offers novelties such as chocolate-orange-flavored vodka.

Dickens once hung out in the **Lamb & Flag,** 33 Rose St., off Garrick Street, WC2 (☎ 0171/497-9504; Tube: Leicester Sq.), and the room itself is little changed from the days when he prowled this neighborhood. The pub has an amazing and somewhat scandalous history. Dryden was almost killed by a band of thugs outside its doors in December 1679; the pub gained the nickname the "Bucket of Blood" during the Regency era (1811–20) because of the routine bare-knuckled prizefights that broke out here. Tap beers include Courage Best and Directors, Old Speckled Hen, John Smiths, and Wadworths 6X.

Olde Mitre, Ely Place, EC1 (☎ 0171/405-4751; Tube: Chancery Lane), is the namesake of a working-class inn built here in 1547, when the Bishops of Ely controlled the district. It's a small pub with an odd assortment of customers. Friary Meux, Ind Coope Burton, and Tetleys are on tap.

Seven Stars, 53 Carey St., WC2 (☎ 0171/242-8521; Tube: Holborn), is tiny and modest except for its collection of toby mugs and law-related art, the latter a tribute to the pub's location at the back of the Law Courts and the large clientele of barristers who drink here. It's a great place to pick up some British legal jargon. Courage Best and Directors are on tap, as well as a selection of single malts.

Black Friar, 174 Queen Victoria St., EC4 (☎ 0171/236-5650; Tube: Blackfriars), will transport you to the Edwardian era. The wedge-shaped pub reeks of marble and bronze art nouveau, featuring bas-reliefs of mad monks, a low-vaulted mosaic ceiling, and seating carved out of gold marble recesses. It's especially popular with the City's after-work crowd, and it features Adams, Wadsworth 6X, Tetleys, and Brakspears on tap.

South London   In South London you can follow in the footsteps of Shakespeare and Dickens by quenching your thirst at the **Anchor,** 34 Park St., Bankside, SE1 (☎ 0171/407-1577; Tube: Barnes Bridge). If literary heroes are not your bag, then perhaps you'll enjoy knowing that Tom Cruise had a pint or two here during the filming of *Mission Impossible.* Rebuilt in the mid–18th century to replace a pub that withstood the Great Fire of 1666, the rooms are worn and comfortable, and you can choose from among Greenalls Best and Youngs Special on tap.

For even greater antiquarian ambience, retreat to the **Cutty Sark,** Ballast Quay, off Lassell Street, SE10 (☎ 0181/858-3146; train: Maze Hill), located inside a 16th-century dwelling with flagstones, barrel tables, open fires, and rough-hewn brick walls. The pub has such an old London feel that you may find yourself seeing Dickensian riffraff after a few pints of Bass or Worthington's Best.

Another historic option is the **George,** off 77 Borough High St., SE1 (☎ **0171/407-2056;** Tube: Borough, London Bridge). Preserved by the National Trust, the existing structure was built to replace the original pub, destroyed in the Great Fire. The pub's accolades date to 1598, when it was reviewed as a "faire inn for the receipt of travellers." No longer an inn, it's still a great place to enjoy Flowers Original, Boddingtons, and Whitbread Castle Eden on tap.

West London   Heading to the western part of town, you can relax by the Thames at the **Dove,** 19 Upper Mall, W6 (☎ **0181/748-5405;** Tube: Ravenscourt Park), the place where James Thomson composed "Rule Britannia" and part of his lesser-known "The Seasons." For toasting the old empire, you can hoist a Fullers London Pride or ESB, and then move on to the **Churchill Arms,** 119 Kensington Church St., W8 (☎ **0171/727-4242;** Tube: Notting Hill Gate or High St. Kensington), for a nod to the empire's end. Loaded with Churchill memorabilia, the pub hosts an entire week of celebration leading up to his birthday on November 30th. Show up then, and you may get recruited to help decorate the place; visitors are often welcomed like regulars here. Decorations and festivities are featured at Halloween, Christmas, and St. Paddy's Day as well, helping to create the most homey, village feel you're likely to find in London.

Ladbroke Arms, 54 Ladbroke Rd., W11 (☎ **0171/727-6648;** Tube: Holland Park), previously honored as London's *Dining Pub of the Year,* is that rare pub known for its food. A changing menu includes chicken breast stuffed with avocado and garlic steak in pink-peppercorn sauce. With background jazz and rotating art prints, the place strays a bit from a traditional pub environment, but it makes for a pleasant stop and a good meal. The excellent Eldridge Pope Royal is on tap, as well as John Smiths and Courage Directors, and several malt whiskies.

North London   Continuing clockwise around London, settle in for a touch of the Victorian and Edwardian eras, respectively, at the **Olde White Bear,** Well Rd., NW 31 (☎ **0171/435-3758;** Tube: Hampstead), and the **Holly Bush,** Holly Mount, NW3 (☎ **0171/435-2892;** Tube: Hampstead). The former is a friendly place for regulars decorated with Victorian prints, cartoons, and furnishings. Tap offerings include Greene King Abbott and Youngs Bitter. The Holly Bush is the real thing: authentic Edwardian gas lamps, open fires, private booths, and a tap selection of Benskins, Eldridge Pope, and Ind Coope Burton.

East London   Finally arriving in Cockney territory, head to **Grapes,** 76 Narrow St., E14 (☎ **0171/987-4396;** Tube: Shadwell), a rustic 16th-century pub that served as Dickens' inspiration for "Six Jolly Fellowship Porters" in *Our Mutual Friend.* Whistler came here, too, inspired by the view of the river. Taps include Friary Meux and Tetleys, with several malt whiskies to choose from as well.

The **Town of Ramsgate,** 62 Wapping High St., E1 (☎ **0171/264-0001;** Tube: Wapping), is another old-world pub, overlooking King Edward's Stairs and the Thames. Here you can enjoy Bass and Fullers London Pride on tap.

Bull's Head. 373 Lonsdale Rd., Barnes, SW13. ☎ **0181/876-5241.** Cover £3–£8 ($4.95–$13.20). Mon–Sat 11am–11pm, Sun noon–10:30pm. Tube: Hammersmith, then bus 9A to Barnes Bridge, then retrace the path of the bus for some 200 yds. on foot; or take Hounslow Look train from Waterloo Station and get off at Barnes Bridge Station, then walk 5 min. to the club.

This club has showcased live modern jazz every night of the week for more than 30 years. One of the oldest hostelries in the area, it was a mid-19th-century staging post where travelers on their way to Hampton Court could eat, drink, and rest while coach horses were changed. Today the bar features jazz by musicians from all over the world. Live jazz on Sunday from 2 to 4:30pm, 8 to 10:30pm; Monday to Saturday, from 8:30pm to 11pm. You can order lunch at the Carvery in the Saloon Bar or dinner in the 17th-century Stable Restaurant.

Jazz Café. 5 Parkway, NW1. ☎ **0171/916-6060.** Cover £5–£25 ($8.25–$41.25). No charge to book a table, but you will have to order a meal. Tube: Parkway.

Afro-Latin jazz fans are hip to this club hosting combos from around the globe. The weekends, described by one patron as "bumpy jazzy-funk nights," are the best time to decide for yourself what that means. Call ahead for listings, cover, and table reservations (when necessary); opening times can vary.

100 Club. 100 Oxford St., W1. ☎ **0171/636-0933.** Cover Fri £8 ($13.20) members and non-members; Sat £8 ($13.20) members, £9 ($14.85) non-members; Sun £6 ($9.90) members and non-members. Mon–Fri 8:30pm–3am, Sat 7:30pm–1am, Sun 7:30–11:30pm. Tube: Tottenham Court Rd. or Oxford Circus.

Although less plush and expensive than some jazz clubs, 100 Club is a serious contender. Its cavalcade of bands includes the best British jazz musicians and some of their Yankee brethren. Rock, R&B, and blues are also on tap.

✪ Pizza Express. 10 Dean St., W1. ☎ **0171/439-8722.** Cover £8.50–£20 ($14–$33). Daily 7:45pm–midnight. Tube: Tottenham Court Rd.

Don't let the name fool you: This restaurant-bar serves up some of the best jazz in London by mainstream artists. While enjoying a thin-crust Italian pizza, check out a local band or a visiting group, often from the United States. Although the club has been enlarged, it's important to reserve ahead of time.

✪ Ronnie Scott's Club. 47 Frith St., W1. ☎ **0171/439-0747.** Cover member £4–£8 ($6.60–$13.20), non-member £15–£20 ($24.75–$33). Mon–Sat 8:30pm–3am. Tube: Leicester Sq. or Piccadilly Circus.

Inquire about jazz in London and people immediately think of Ronnie Scott's, long the European vanguard for modern jazz. Only the best English and American combos, often fronted by a top-notch vocalist, are booked here. The programs inevitably make for an entire evening of cool jazz. In the heart of Soho, Ronnie Scott's is a 10-minute walk from Piccadilly Circus along Shaftesbury Avenue. In the Main Room, you can watch the show from the bar or sit at a table, from which you can order dinner. The Downstairs Bar is more intimate; among the regulars at your elbow may be some of the world's most talented musicians. On weekends, the separate Upstairs Room has a disco called Club Latino.

606 Club. 90 Lots Rd., SW10. ☎ **0171/352-5953.** Cover Sun–Thurs £4.75 ($7.85), Fri–Sat £5.45 ($9). Mon–Sat 8:30pm–2am, Sun 8:30pm–midnight. Bus: 11, 19, 22, 31, 39, or C3. Tube: Earl's Court.

Located in a discreet basement site in Chelsea, the 606 presents live music nightly. Predominantly a venue for modern jazz, style ranges from traditional to contemporary.

Local musicians and some very big names play here, whether planned gigs or informal jam sessions after their shows elsewhere in town. This is actually a jazz supper club in the boondocks of Fulham; because of license requirements, patrons can only order alcohol with food.

DANCE, DISCO & ECLECTIC

Bar Rumba. 26 Shaftesbury Ave., W1. ☎ **0171/287-2715.** Cover £3–£12 ($4.95–$19.80). Mon–Thurs 5pm–3:30am, Fri 5pm–4am, Sat 6pm–6am, Sun 8pm–1:30am. Tube: Piccadilly Circus.

Despite its location on Shaftesbury Avenue, this Latin bar and club could be featured in a book of "Underground London." A hush-hush address, it leans toward radical jazz fusion on some nights, phat funk on other occasions. Boasting two full bars and a different musical theme every night, Tuesday and Wednesday are the only nights you probably won't have to queue at the door. Monday's "That's How It Is" showcase features jazz, hip hop, and drum and bass; Friday's "KAT Klub" grooves with soul, R&B, and swing; and Saturday's "Garage City" buzzes with house and garage. On weeknights you have to be 18 and up; the age limit is 21 on Saturday and Sunday.

Camden Palace. 1A Camden High St., NW1. ☎ **0171/387-0428.** Cover Tues £5 ($8.25), Fri–Sat £7–£20 ($11.55–$33). Tues 10pm–2am, Fri 10pm–6am, and Sat 10pm–8am. Tube: Camden Town or Mornington Crescent.

Housed in a former theater built around 1910, Camden Palace draws an over-18 crowd that flocks here in trendy downtown costumes. Energy levels vary according to the night of the week, as does the music, so call in advance to see if that evening's musical program appeals to your taste. A live band performs only on Tuesday. There's a restaurant if you get the munchies.

The Cross. The Arches, Kings Cross Goods Yard, York Way, N1. ☎ **0171/837-0828.** Cover £10–£15 ($16.50–$24.75). Fri 10pm–4:30am, Sat 10:30pm–6am. Tube: Kings Cross.

In the backwaters of Kings Cross, this club has stayed hot since 1993. London hipsters come here for private parties thrown by Rough Trade Records or Red Or Dead, or just to dance in the space's cozy brick-lined vaults. It's always party time here. Call to find out who's performing.

Diva. 43 Thurloe St., SW7. ☎ **0171/584-2000.** Cover £1.50 ($2.45). Mon–Sat 6pm–3am, July–Sept also Sun noon–3pm. Tube: South Kensington.

Diva combines a first-class Italian restaurant with a dance club. So get down with your manicotti! Meals, from £25 to £30 ($41.25 to $49.50) per head, are mostly Neapolitan-inspired. Only restaurant patrons are allowed into the disco (where recorded music is played).

Equinox. Leicester Sq., WC2. ☎ **0171/437-1446.** Cover £5–£12 ($8.25–$19.80), depending on the night of the week. Mon–Thurs 9pm–3am, Fri–Sat 9pm–4am. Tube: Leicester Sq.

Built in 1992 on the site of the London Empire, a dance emporium that has witnessed the changing styles of social dancing since the 1700s, the Equinox has established itself as a perennial favorite. It contains nine bars, the largest dance floor in London, and a restaurant modeled after a 1950s American diner. With the exception of rave, virtually every kind of dance music is featured here, including dance hall, pop, rock, and Latin. The setting is lavishly illuminated with one of Europe's largest lighting rigs, and the crowd is as varied as London itself.

Equinox has been quite busy lately, hosting some of the U.K.'s hottest talents. Most recently, the Equinox featured those international sex symbols, the Spice Girls, Prince Harry's favorite group. Summer visitors can enjoy their theme nights, which are geared to entertaining a worldwide audience, including a once a month "Ibiza" foam party— you'll actually boogie the night away on a foam covered floor. Happy hour drinks are £1.50 ($2.45) from 5 to 7pm.

Hanover Grand. 6 Hanover St., W1. ☎ **0171/499-7977.** Cover £5–£15 ($8.25–$24.75). Wed–Sat 10:30pm–4am, Sat 10:30pm–6am. Tube: Oxford Circus.

Thursdays are funky and down and dirty. Fridays and Saturdays the crowd dresses up in their disco finery, clingy and form-fitting or politicized and punk. Dance floors are always crowded, and masses seem to surge back and forth between the two levels. Age and gender is sometimes hard to make out at this cutting-edge club.

Hippodrome. Corner of Cranbourn St. and Charing Cross Rd., WC2. ☎ **0171/437-4311.** Cover £4–£12 ($6.60–$19.80). Mon–Sat 9pm–3am. Tube: Leicester Sq.

Located near Leicester Square, the popular Hippodrome is London's grand old daddy of discos, a cavernous place with a great sound system and lights to match. It was Lady Di's favorite scene in her bar-hopping days. Tacky and touristy, the 'drome is packed on weekends.

Iceni. 11 White Horse St., W1. ☎ **0171/495-5333.** Cover Fri £12 ($19.80), Sat £10 ($16.50). Fri–Sat 10pm–3:30am. Tube: Queen's Park.

Attracting an older 20-something crowd on Fridays, and 18-to-25ers on Saturdays, this funky three-story nightclub features films, board games, tarot readings, and dancing to swing, soul, hip hop, and R&B. You can even get a manicure.

Limelight. 136 Shaftesbury Ave., WC2. ☎ **0171/434-0572.** Cover £6 ($9.90) before 10pm, £4–£12 ($6.60–$19.80) thereafter. Mon–Fri 10pm–3am (3:30am Fri), Sat 9pm–3:30am, Sun 6–11pm. Tube: Leicester Sq.

Although opened in 1985, this large dance club—located inside a former Welsh chapel that dates to 1754—has only recently come into its own. The dance floors and bars share space with plenty of cool Gothic nooks and crannies. DJs spin the latest house music.

✪ Ministry of Sound. 103 Gaunt St., SE1. ☎ **0171/378-6528.** Cover £12–£15 ($19.80–$24.75). Fri 10:30pm–6am, Sat midnight–9am. Tube: Elephant & Castle.

Removed from the city center, this club-of-the-hour is still going strong after all these years. It remains hot, hot, hot. With a large bar and an even bigger sound system, it blasts garage and house music to energetic crowds that pack the two dance floors. If the stimulants in the rest of the club have gone to your head, you can chill in the cinema room. Note: The club's cover charge is stiff, and bouncers decide who is cool enough to enter, so leave the sneakers and denim at home and slip into your grooviest and most glamorous club wear.

The Office. 3–5 Rathbone Place, W1. ☎ **0171/636-1598.** Cover £7–£9 ($11.55–$14.85). Mon–Tues noon–11:30pm, Wed–Fri noon–3am, Sat 9:30pm–3am. Tube: Tottenham Court Rd.

An eclectic club with a bureaucratic name, one of The Office's most popular nights is Wednesday's "Double Six Club," featuring easy listening and board games from 6pm to 2am. Other nights are more traditional recorded pop, rock, soul, and disco. Ambience wins out over decor.

Smollensky's on The Strand. 105 The Strand, WC2. ☎ **0171/497-2101.** Cover £4.50 ($7.45) on Sunday when they have a big jazz band. Thurs–Sat noon–12:30am, Sun 6:30–10:30pm, Mon–Wed noon–midnight. Tube: Charing Cross or Embankment.

This is an American eatery and drinking bar. At the Strand location, you can dance from Thursday to Saturday nights. Sunday night features a special live jazz session. Meals average £25 ($41.25).

Stringfellows. 16–19 Upper St. Martin's Lane, WC2. ☎ **0171/240-5534.** Cover £10–£15 ($16.50–$24.75). Mon–Thurs 7:30pm–3:30am, Fri and Sat 8pm–3:30am, Sun closed. Reservations recommended for restaurant. Tube: Leicester Sq. or Covent Garden.

This would-be glam club has a varied clientele and lots of velvet and gloss. In theory, it's members-only, but—at the discretion of management—non-members may be admitted. The disco has a glass dance floor and a dazzling sound-and-light system. A restaurant feeds late-night diners, and there's no charge for admission to the club if you dine in the restaurant.

Subterania. 12 Acklam Rd., W10. ☎ **0181/960-4590.** Cover £8–£10 ($13.20–$16.50). Fri–Sat 10:30pm–3am, other nights vary. Tube: Ladbroke Grove.

Affordable, unpretentious, and informal, the feel of this club changes according to the style of the live band performing at the time. Call ahead. The place has a busy street-level dance floor and a mezzanine-style bar upstairs. The decor is energetic orange, purple, and blue; if those colors work for you, there are also sofas covered in downtown *faux* leopard skin. More or less constant is the Friday music card of soul, funk, hip hop, and swing, and Saturday's house music. Other nights of the week, it's pot luck.

The Velvet Room (formerly The Velvet Underground). 143 Charing Cross Rd., WC2. ☎ **0171/734-4687.** Cover £6–£10 ($9.90–$16.50). Wed–Thurs 9pm–3am, Fri–Sat 9pm–4am. Tube: Tottenham Court Rd.

The Velvet Underground was a London staple for years. Times changed and the clientele grew up—hence The Velvet Room, a more mature setting that is luxurious but not stuffy. DJs Carl Cox and others spin favorite dance hits—more laid back to better represent the new theme. The Velvet Room hasn't sacrificed a shred of cool, and still sets a standard for the next generation of Soho bar life.

✪ **Zoo Bar.** 13–18 Bear St., WC2. ☎ **0171/839-4188.** Cover £3–£5 ($4.95–$8.25) after 11pm. Mon–Sat 4pm–3:30am, Sun 4–10:30pm. Tube: Leicester Sq.

The owners spent millions of pounds outfitting this club in the slickest, flashiest, and most psychedelic decor in London. If you're looking for a true Euro nightlife experience replete with gorgeous *au pairs* and trendy Europeans, this is it. Zoo Bar upstairs is a menagerie of mosaic animals beneath a glassed-in ceiling dome. Downstairs, the music is intrusive enough to make conversation futile. Clients range from 18 to 35; androgyny is the look of choice.

LATIN RHYTHMS
Cuba. 11 Kensington High St., W8. ☎ **0171/938-4137.** Cover £2–£7 ($3.30–$11.55). Mon–Sat noon–2am, Sun 2–11pm. Tube: High St. Kensington.

This Spanish/Cuban–style bar-restaurant, which has a music club downstairs, features live music acts from Cuba, Brazil, Spain, and the rest of Latin America. Odd as it may seem, the crowd is equal parts restaurant diners, after-work drinkers, Latinophiles, and dancers. Salsa dance classes are offered Monday, Tuesday, and Wednesday from 8:30 to 9:30pm. Classes cost £4 ($6.60) Monday or £5 ($8.25)Tuesday and Wednesday. Happy hour is Monday to Saturday, noon to 8:30pm.

Salsa. 96 Charing Cross Rd., WC2. ☎ **0171/379-3277.** Cover Fri–Sat £4 ($6.60) after 9pm. Mon–Sat 5:30pm–2am. Tube: Leicester Sq.

This lively bar-restaurant and music club for Latin music aficionados features mostly bands from Central and South America. Dance lessons are available nightly starting at

6:30pm; live music starts at 9pm. Some of the best dancers in London strut their stuff here.

GAMING CLUBS

Long before Monte Carlo, when Las Vegas was a glint in a slot machine's eye, London was a gambler's town. However, Queen Victoria's reign squelched games of chance to such an extent that no bartender dared to keep a dice cup on the counter. Only in 1960, with the institution of the Betting and Gaming Act, did gambling become permitted in bona fide gaming clubs.

In the West End alone are at least 25 gambling clubs, with many more scattered throughout the London periphery. But under British law, casinos may not advertise. Hence, if you wish to gamble away your beer money while in London, your best bet is to ask a knowledgeable concierge. You'll be required to become a member and wait 24 hours before you can play at the tables. Games are cash only and commonly include roulette, blackjack, Punto Banco, and Baccarat.

Men must wear jackets and ties in all the establishments below; hours for each club are from 2pm to 4am daily.

Some of the more popular clubs include **Crockford's,** a 150-year-old club with a large international clientele, located at 30 Curzon St., W1 (☎ **0171/493-7771;** Tube: Green Park). Offered here are American roulette, Punto Banco, and blackjack. Another favorite is the **Golden Nugget,** 22 Shaftesbury Ave., W1 (☎ **0171/ 439-0099;** Tube: Piccadilly Circus), where gamblers go to play blackjack, Punto Banco, and roulette. A final choice is **Sportsman Casino,** 3 Tottenham Court Rd., W1 (☎ **0171/414-0061;** Tube: Tottenham Court Rd.), featuring a dice table along with American roulette, blackjack, and Punto Banco.

4 Cocktail Bars

For a complete selection of pubs and wine bars, see chapter 5 and the "The World's Greatest Pub Crawl," above.

American Bar. In The Savoy, The Strand, WC2. ☎ **0171/836-4343.** Smart casual—no jeans, sneakers, T-shirts. Tube: Charing Cross, Covent Garden, or Embankment.

The bartender in this sophisticated gathering place is known for his special concoctions, "Savoy Affair" and "Prince of Wales," as well as what is reputedly the best martini in town. Monday to Saturday evenings, jazz piano is featured from 7 to 11pm. Near many West End theaters, the location is ideal for a pre- or post-theater drink.

Beach Blanket Babylon. 45 Ledbury Rd., W11. ☎ **0171/229-2907.** No cover. Tube: Notting Hill Gate.

Go here if you're looking for a hot singles bar that attracts a crowd in their 20s and 30s. This Portobello joint—named after a kitschy musical revue in San Francisco—is very cruisy. The decor is a bit wacky, no doubt designed by an aspiring Salvador Dalí, who decided to make it a fairy-tale grotto (or did he mean a medieval dungeon?). It's close to the Portobello Market. Saturday and Sunday nights are the hot, crowded times to show up for bacchanalian revelry.

The Dorchester Bar. In the Dorchester, Park Lane. ☎ **0171/629-8888.** Tube: Hyde Park Corner or Marble Arch.

This sophisticated and modern bar is on the lobby level, and you'll find an international clientele, confident of its good taste and privilege. The bartender knows his stuff. The bar serves Italian snacks, lunch, and dinner. A pianist performs every evening after 7pm.

The Library. In the Lanesborough Hotel, 1 Lanesborough Place, SW1. ☎ **0171/259-5599.**
Tube: Hyde Park Corner.

For one of London's poshest drinking retreats, head for this deluxe hotel with its high
ceilings, leather chesterfields, respectable oil paintings, and grand windows. Its collection of ancient cognacs is unparalleled in London.

Lillie Langtry Bar. In the Cadogan Hotel, Sloane St., SW1. ☎ **0171/235-7141.** Tube:
Sloane Sq. or Knightsbridge.

Next door to Langtry's Restaurant, this 1920s-style bar epitomizes the charm and elegance of the Edwardian era. Lillie Langtry, the turn-of-the-century actress and society
beauty (notorious as the mistress of Edward VII), once lived here. Oscar Wilde—
arrested in this very hotel bar—is honored on the drinks menu by his favorite libation,
the Hock and Seltzer. Sir John Betjeman's poem "The Arrest of Oscar Wilde at the
Cadogan Hotel" tells the story. The Cadogan Cooler seems to be the most popular
drink here. An international menu is served in the adjoining restaurant.

The Lobby Bar. In the Hotel One Aldwych, 1 Aldwych, WC2. ☎ **0171/300-1000.** Tube:
Temple.

This bar and the bar associated with the Axis restaurant are in London's newest five-
star hotel. We advise that you check out the dramatic visuals of both before selecting
your preferred nesting place for a drink or two. The Lobby Bar occupies what was
built in 1907 as the very grand, very high-ceilinged reception area for one of London's
premier newspapers. (It's the only part of the historically important hotel's interior
that wasn't demolished during a stylish renovation in 1998.) If that setting doesn't
appeal to you, check out the travertine, hardwood, and leather-sheathed bar in the
Axis restaurant. The Lobby Bar is open daily from 6am to 11pm; the Axis bar is open
at hours that correspond to those of the restaurant.

The Met. In the Metropolitan Hotel, 10 Old Park Lane, W1. ☎ **0171/447-1000**. Members-
only and hotel guests. Mon–Sat 9:30am–3am, Sun 9:30am–10:30pm. Tube: Hyde Park
Corner.

Very much the place to be seen, this has become the hottest bar in London. Mix with
the elite of the fashion, TV, and the music world. A lot of American celebrities have
been seen here, sipping on a martini, from Demi Moore to Courtney Cox. Despite
the caliber of the clientele, the bar has managed to maintain a relaxed and unpretentious atmosphere.

5 The Gay & Lesbian Scene

The most reliable source of information on gay clubs and activities is the **Lesbian and
Gay Switchboard** (☎ 0171/837-7324). The staff runs a 24-hour service for information on gay-friendly places and activities. *Time Out* also carries listings on such
clubs. Also a good place for finding out what's hot and hip is **Prowler Soho,** 3–7
Brewer St. Soho W1 (☎ 0171/734-4031; Tube: Piccadilly Circus), the largest gay
lifestyle store in London. (You can also buy anything from jewelry to CDs and books,
fashion and sex toys.) It's open till midnight on Friday and Saturday.

Bar Code. 3–4 Archer St. Soho, W1. ☎ **0171/734-3342**. No cover. Mon–Sat 1pm–1am,
Sun 1pm–10:30pm. Tube: Piccadilly Circus.

This is a very relaxed and friendly bar, the largest in what can often be terminally
trendy Soho. With everything from skinheads to "pint-of-lager" types, it has very
much a local atmosphere. "Code" is fairly male dominated, but does not object to
women entering.

The Box. 32–34 Monmouth St. (at Seven Dials), WC2. ☎ **0171/240-5828.** Daily 10am–11:30pm. Tube: Covent Garden.

Adjacent to one of Covent Garden's best-known junctions, Seven Dials, this sophisticated Mediterranean-style bar attracts more lesbians than many of its competitors. In the afternoon, it is primarily a restaurant, serving meal-size salads, club sandwiches, and soups. Food service ends abruptly at 5:30pm, after which the place reveals its core: a cheerful, popular place of rendezvous for London's gay and countercultural crowds. The Box considers itself a "summer bar," throwing open doors and windows to a cluster of outdoor tables that attracts a crowd at the slightest hint of sunshine.

Candy Bar. 4 Carlisle St., W1. ☎ **0171/494-4041.** Cover £2–£5 ($3.30–$8.25). Mon-Thurs 5pm–midnight, Fri 5pm–2am, Sat 2pm–2am, Sun 5pm–11pm. Tube: Tottenham Court Rd.

This is the most popular lesbian bar in London at the moment. It has an extremely mixed clientele from butch to fem and from young to old. There is a bar and a club downstairs. Design is simple with bright colors and lots of mirrors upstairs and darker and more flirtatious downstairs. Men are welcome as long as they are escorted by a woman.

The Complex. 1–5 Parkfield St., Islington, M1. ☎ **0171/738-2336**. Cover £8 ($13.20). Fri 10pm–4am. Tube: Angel.

On Fridays, this four-floor club is the site of Pop Starz, which has become one of the most popular nights in London. It offers a mix of indie, British pop, 1980s trash, and funk. Originally started as an alternative to the generic gay muscle boy dance parties, the once-weekly night has attracted a very mixed and loyal following.

Comptons of Soho. 53 Old Compton St., W1. ☎ **0171/479-7961.** Mon–Sat noon–11pm, Sun noon–10:30pm. Tube: Leicester Sq.

It's so firmly entrenched as a London institution that it's sometimes referred to as the official gay bar of Soho. It's also a network of information about what's new and hot on the London gay scene. Stop off here early in the evening just to find out what the latest gay event is around town. Shaved heads and leather bomber jackets aren't at all out of place here. All ages are attracted to this joint, and it's very cruisy—an evening testosterone fest, in fact.

The Edge. 11 Soho Sq., W1. ☎ **0171/439-1313.** No cover. Mon–Sat 11am–1am, Sun noon–10:30pm. Tube: Tottenham Court Rd.

Few bars in London can rival the tolerance, humor, and sexual sophistication found here. The first two floors are done up with accessories that, like an English garden, change with the seasons. Dance music can be found on the high-energy and crowded lower floors, while the upper floors are best if you're looking for intimate conversation. Three menus are featured: a funky daytime menu, a cafe menu, and a late-night menu. Dancers hit the floors starting around 7:30pm. Clientele ranges from the flamboyantly gay to hetero pub crawlers out for a night of slumming.

First Out. 52 St. Giles High St., W1 ☎ **0171/240-8042.** Mon–Sat 10am–11pm, Sun noon–10:30pm. Tube: Tottenham Court Rd.

First Out prides itself on being London's first (est. 1986) all-gay coffee shop. Set in a 19th-century building whose wood panels have been painted the colors of the gay liberation rainbow, the bar is intimate (that is, not particularly cruisy) and offers an exclusively vegetarian menu, with most items priced at £3.50 ($6). Cappuccino and whiskey are the preferred libations; curry dishes, potted pies in phyllo pastries, and salads are the foods of choice. Don't expect a raucous atmosphere—some clients come here with their grandmothers. Look for the bulletin board with leaflets and business cards of gay and gay-friendly entrepreneurs.

Heaven. The Arches, Villiers and Craven sts., WC2. ☎ **0171/930-2020.** Cover £3–£10 ($4.95–$16.50). Tube: Charing Cross or Embankment.

This club in the vaulted cellars of Charing Cross Railway Station is a London landmark. Owned by the same investors who brought the world Virgin Atlantic Airways, Heaven is one of the biggest and best-established gay venues in Britain. Painted black, and reminiscent of an air-raid shelter, the club is divided into at least four distinct areas connected by a labyrinth of catwalk stairs and hallways. Each area has a different activity going on. Heaven also has theme nights, which, depending on the night, are frequented by gays, lesbians, or a mostly heterosexual crowd. Thursday in particular seems open to anything, but on Saturday it's gay only. Call before you go.

Madame Jo Jo's. 8 Brewer St., W1. ☎ **0171/734-2473.** Cover £6–£22.50 ($9.90–$37.15). Daily 10pm–3am. Tube: Piccadilly Circus.

Tucked alongside Soho's most explicit girlie shows, Madame Jo Jo's also presents "girls." London's most popular transvestite showplace—an eye-popper with a decadent art nouveau interior—has attracted film directors such as Stanley Kubrick, who filmed scenes from *Eyes Wide Shut*, starring Tom Cruise, here. Other celebrities, including Hugh Grant and Mick Jagger, have dropped in to check out Jo Jo's drag cabaret. Drag shows are Thursday to Saturday nights, with outside promoters organizing entertainment on other nights.

Royal Vauxhall Tavern. 372 Kennington Lane, SE11. ☎ **0171/582-0833.** Cover Thurs–Sun £2–£4 ($3.30–$6.60). Mon–Sat 9pm–2am, Sun noon–midnight. Tube: Vauxhall.

Originally an 1880s vaudeville pub frequented by London's East End working class, this place has long been a bastion of campy humor and wit. It has been a gay pub since the end of World War II. The tavern received a jolt of fame when—as legend has it—Queen Elizabeth's ceremonial carriage broke down, and the monarch stopped in for a cup of tea. Since then, "Royal" has been gleefully affixed to the name, no doubt suiting the regular queens found here. Charington, one of the largest breweries in England, recently acquired this unabashedly gay pub.

Shaped like an amphitheater, the bar has a large stage area and gay themes on weekends. Friday nights are reserved for women only. Saturday is camp night, when the pub overflows with gay men fawning over their favorite cabaret acts.

Substation Soho. 1A Dean St., W1. ☎ **0171/287-9608.** Tues–Thurs 10:30pm–3:30am, Fri 10pm–5am, Sat 10pm–6am. Tube: Tottenham Court Rd.

This is a sprawling, and sometimes packed, enclave that features three bars, a dance floor with a rotating team of DJs, video screens, pool tables, and an environment where picking up a stranger is fully permissible. About 80% of the clients are gay men aged 18 to 50; the remainder are women, both gay and straight, who like the joint's tolerant sense of permissiveness. There's a cover charge that varies from £3 to £8 ($4.95 to $13.20), depending on the night of the week.

Turnmills on Clerkenwell. 63B Clerkenwell Rd., EC1. ☎ **0171/250-3409.** Cover: Trade £8–£12 ($13.20–$19.80); Melt £5–£10 ($8.25–$16.50). Trade Sun 4am–1pm; Melt Sun 10pm–6:30am. Tube: Faringdon.

For the serious gay partygoers, the two nights at this otherwise straight venue are a must. Trade, which begins when everyone else has long before gone home, has a big dance-party atmosphere complete with heavy techno dance music and a literal sea of Adonis-like men with their shirts off. Melt on Sunday nights is a slightly more relaxed version of Trade, with a funky house slant. The club is large with a 700-person capacity, and has two dance floors.

10 Side Trips from London

There's much more to England than London. But you could spend the best part of a year—or a lifetime—exploring *only* London, without risking either boredom or repetition. Still, we advise you to tear yourself away from Big Ben for at least a day or two, as the capital city is surrounded by some of the most memorable spots on earth.

1 Windsor & Eton

21 miles W of London

Windsor—the site of England's best-known and greatest castle and its most famous boys' school, Eton—would be a captivating Thames town to visit, even if it were not associated with the royal Windsors. In summer it's overrun by tourists, which tends to obscure its charm.

The good news is that, after the disastrous fire of 1992, things are on the mend at Windsor Castle. On Sundays in **Windsor Great Park** and at **Ham Common,** you may see Prince Charles playing polo and Prince Philip serving as umpire while the queen watches. The park is also the site of the queen's occasional equestrian jaunts. On Sunday she attends a little church near the Royal Lodge. Traditionally, she prefers to drive herself there, later returning to the castle for Sunday lunch. For more information, call the **Tourist Information Center (☎ 01753/743900).**

ESSENTIALS

GETTING THERE   The train from Waterloo or Paddington Station in London makes the trip in 30 minutes, involving a transfer at Slough to the Slough-Windsor shuttle train. There are more than a dozen trains per day, and fares start at £6.50 ($10.75) one-way or £6.70 ($11.05) for a day return ticket. For information call ☎ **0345/484950** (in the U.K. only) or 01603/764776.

Green Line coaches (☎ **0181/668-7261**) nos. 700 and 702 from Hyde Park Corner in London take about 1¹/₂ hours. A same-day round-trip costs £6.50 ($10.75). The bus will drop you near the Town Guildhall, to which Wren applied the finishing touches. It's only a short walk up Castle Hill to the top sights.

If you're traveling by car, take M4 west from London.

VISITOR INFORMATION   A **Tourist Information Centre** is located across from Windsor Castle on High Street (☎ **01753/743900**). There's also an information booth in the tourist center at

Windsor Coach Park. Both are open daily from 10am to 4pm, Saturday and Sunday 10am to 5pm.

CASTLE HILL SIGHTS

✪ **Windsor Castle.** Castle Hill. ☎ **01753/831118.** Admission £10 ($16.50) adults; £7.50 ($12.40) students and senior citizens; £5 ($8.25) children 16 and under; £22.50 ($37.15) family of 4, £18.50 ($30.55) on Sun, when St. George's Chapel is closed to sightseers. Mar–Oct daily 10am–5pm; Nov–Feb daily 10am–4pm. Last admissions are 1 hour before closing. Closed periods in Apr, June, and Dec when the royal family is in residence.

When William the Conqueror ordered Windsor Castle to be built, he established a base for English sovereignty that has known many vicissitudes: King John cooled his heels at Windsor while waiting to put his signature on the Magna Carta at nearby Runnymede; Charles I was imprisoned here before losing his head; Queen Bess renovated; Victoria mourned her beloved Albert, who died at the castle; the royal family rode out much of World War II behind its sheltering walls.

With 1,000 rooms, Windsor is the world's largest inhabited castle. Today, when Queen Elizabeth II is in residence, the royal standard flies. On display are many works of art, porcelain, armor, furniture, three Verrio ceilings, and several 17th-century Gibbons carvings. Several works by Rubens adorn the King's Drawing Room; in the relatively small King's Dressing Room is a Dürer, along with Rembrandt's portrait of his mother, and Van Dyck's triple portrait of Charles I. Of the apartments, the Grand Reception Room, with its Gobelin tapestries, is the most spectacular.

In November 1992, the fire that swept through part of Windsor Castle, severely damaged it. The castle has since reopened, and all the rooms that were once open to the public are available for viewing in 2000.

In our opinion, the Windsor **changing of the guard** is a much more exciting experience than the London exercises. The guard marches through the town whether the court is in residence or not, stopping the traffic as it wheels into the castle to the tune of a full regimental band; when the queen is not here, a drum-and-pipe band is mustered. From May to August, the ceremony takes place Monday to Saturday at 11am. In winter, the guard is changed every 48 hours Monday to Saturday. It's best to call ☎ **01753/868286** to find out which days the ceremony will take place.

Queen Mary's Doll's House. Windsor Castle. ☎ **01753/831118.** Castle tickets include admission here. Open same days and hours as Windsor Castle (see above).

A palace in perfect miniature, the Doll's House was given to Queen Mary in 1923 as a symbol of national goodwill. The house, designed by Sir Edwin Lutyens, was created on a scale of 1 to 12. It took 3 years to complete and involved the work of 1,500 tradesmen and artists. Every item is a miniature masterpiece, each room is exquisitely furnished, and every item is made exactly to scale. Working elevators stop on every floor, all five bathrooms have running water, and electric lighting brightens the house.

✪ **St. George's Chapel.** The Cloisters, Windsor Castle. ☎ **01753/865538.** Admission included in admission to Windsor Castle. Mon–Sat 10am–4pm. Sunday services open to public, but closed for sightseeing tours. Closed during services, Jan, and a few days in mid-June.

Along with Westminster Abbey, this Perpendicular-style chapel shares the distinction of being a pantheon of English monarchs. The present St. George's was founded in the late 15th century by Edward IV on the site of the original Chapel of the Order of the Garter. At the chapel's center is a flat tomb containing the vault of the beheaded Charles I, along with Henry VIII and his third wife, Jane Seymour. Other monarchs entombed here include George V, George VI, and Edward IV. History's path forked at

Princess Charlotte's memorial; had she survived childbirth in 1817, she—and not her cousin Victoria—would have ruled the British Empire.

NEARBY ETON

From Windsor, Eton is just an easy stroll across the Thames Bridge. Follow Eton High Street to the college.

Eton College (☎ 01753/671177) was founded by the adolescent Henry VI in 1440. Some of England's greatest men, notably the Duke of Wellington, have played on these fields. Twenty prime ministers were educated here, as well as such literary figures as George Orwell, Aldous Huxley, Ian Fleming, and Percy Bysshe Shelley—who, during his years at Eton (from 1804 to 1810), was called "Mad Shelley" by his fellow pupils.

The history of Eton College since its inception is depicted in the **Museum of Eton Life,** located in vaulted wine cellars under College Hall. The displays include a turn-of-the-century boy's room, schoolbooks, sports trophies, canes used by senior boys to apply punishment to their juniors, and birch sticks used by masters for the same purpose. Also on display are letters written home by students describing day-to-day life at the school, as well as samples of the numerous magazines produced by students over the centuries. Many of the items on display were provided by Old Etonians. If it's open, take a look at the **Perpendicular Chapel's** 15th-century paintings and reconstructed fan vaulting.

Admission to the school and museum costs £2.60 ($4.30) for adults. You can also take guided tours for £3.80 ($6.25). Eton College is open from March 19 to April 14 and June 27 to September 3, daily from 10:30am to 4:30pm; April 15 to June 26 and September 2 to October 4, daily from 2 to 4:30pm. Call in advance; Eton may close for special occasions. These dates vary every year depending on term and holiday dates. It's better to call.

ORGANIZED TOURS OF WINDSOR & ETON

HORSE-DRAWN CARRIAGE RIDES   You can also take a **horse-drawn carriage** for a half-hour promenade up the sycamore-lined length of Windsor Castle's Long Walk. Horses with carriages and drivers line up beside the castle waiting for fares, which run about £40 ($66) for up to four passengers.

BOAT TOURS   Tours depart from The Promenade, Barry Avenue, for a 35-minute ride to Boveney Lock. There's also a 35-minute tour from Runnymede on board the *Lucy Fisher,* a replica of a Victorian paddle steamer. The boat passes Magna Carta Island, among other places. Both tours cost £3.60 ($5.95) for adults, half price for children. A 2-hour tour through the Boveney Lock and up past stately private riverside homes, the Bray Film Studios, Queens Eyot, and Monkey Island, is £5.80 ($9.55) for adults, half price for children. In addition, longer tours between Maidenhead and Hampton Court are offered. The boats serve light refreshments and have a well-stocked bar, and the decks are covered in case of an unexpected shower. Contact **French Brothers, Ltd.,** Clewer Boathouse, Clewer Court Road, Windsor (☎ 01753/851900).

WHERE TO DINE
WINDSOR

✪ **Stroks Riverside Restaurant.** In Sir Christopher Wren's House Hotel, Thames St. ☎ **01753/861354.** Main courses £11–£18 ($18.15–$29.70). AE, DC, MC, V. Daily 12:30–2:30pm; Mon–Sat 6:30–10pm; Sun 6:30–9:30pm. MODERN BRITISH/FRENCH.

A 3-minute walk from the castle, this restaurant is the most elegant and charming restaurant in Windsor, with garden terraces and a conservatory. The dining room is designed a bit like a greenhouse, and a pianist entertains at dinner. Enjoy such dishes as roasted squab pigeon with goat cheese gnocchi; rosettes of spring lamb with green beans, roasted artichokes, and Yorkshire pudding; and traditional chateaubriand carved at your table with a medley of vegetables. The chef, Phillip Wild, studied at two- and three-star Michelin restaurants in Switzerland, and cooks with passion and intensity. Each dish is freshly prepared with the finest ingredients, which are obtained locally if possible. Lamb and beef are cooked "pink," and vegetables are served al dente.

ETON

Eton Wine Bar. 82–83 High St. ☎ **01753/854921.** Reservations recommended. Main courses £8.95–£13.50 ($14.75–$22.30). AE, DC, MC, V. Mon–Tues noon–2:30pm and 6–10pm; Wed–Thurs and Sun noon–10:30pm; Fri–Sat noon–11pm. MODERN BRITISH.

Just across the bridge from Windsor, this graceful dinner bar is set among the antiques shops on Eton's main street. Inside are pinewood tables and old church pews and chairs, and there's a glassed-in conservatory out back. A brigade of eight chefs turns out a fine array of modern British cookery. Appetizers usually include several well-prepared soups and a roasted sweet-pepper tart. Main dishes include pine-nut–and–spinach risotto topped with peccorino cheese, and roast lamb fillet served with boulangère potatoes and vegetables. For dessert, try the tarte tatin, a tasty and creative upside-down apple pie.

House on the Bridge. 71 High St. ☎ **01753/860914.** Reservations recommended. Main courses from £13.50 ($22.30); fixed-price meal £19.95 ($32.90) at lunch, £29.95 ($49.40) at dinner; Sun lunch £21.95 ($36.20). AE, DC, MC, V. Daily noon–3pm and 6–11pm. ENGLISH/INTERNATIONAL.

This charming restaurant is housed in a lovely redbrick and terra-cotta Victorian building, adjacent to the bridge at the edge of Eton. Near the handful of outdoor tables is a precipitous garden whose plants cascade into the Thames. Among the well-prepared main dishes are roasted Aylesburg duckling with poached apple and forcemeat stuffing and chicken Wellington topped with bacon, stilton, and creamy sherry sauce. Some specialties, such as roast rack of herb-flavored lamb, are served only for two. Although traditionally based, the preparations have many modern touches, and the chefs always use good fresh ingredients. Desserts include flambés and crêpes suzette.

2 Oxford, City of Dreaming Spires

54 miles NW of London

A walk down the long sweep of The High, one of the most striking streets in England; a mug of cider in one of the old student pubs; the sound of May Day dawn when choristers sing in Latin from Magdalen Tower; the Great Tom bell from Tom Tower, whose 101 peals traditionally signal the closing of the college gates; towers and spires piercing the clouds; the barges on the upper reaches of the Thames; nude swimming at Parson's Pleasure; the roar of a cannon launching the bumping races; a tiny, dusty bookstall where you can pick up a valuable first edition—all coincide in Oxford, home of one of the greatest universities in the world.

Romantic Oxford still exists, but to get to it, you'll have to navigate the bustling and crowded city that has grown about it. A never-ending stream of polluting buses and the fast-flowing pedestrian traffic can make the city core feel more like London than an ancient university town.

At any time of the year, you can enjoy a tour of the colleges, many of which are the loveliest England has to offer. The **Oxford Tourist Information Centre** (see below) conducts daily walking tours throughout the year.

ESSENTIALS

GETTING THERE   Trains from Paddington Station (☎ **0345/484950** or 01603/764776) reach Oxford in 1¼ hours. Service is every hour. A cheap, same-day round-trip ticket costs £14.20 ($23.45).

The **X90 London Express** departs from Victoria Station (☎ **0990/808080**) for the Oxford Bus Station daily. Coaches usually leave about every 20 minutes during the day, taking 1¾ hours. A same-day round-trip ticket costs £7 ($11.55).

Or take the **Oxford Tube,** an express coach that takes you from Oxford to London in 90 minutes. Coaches operate every 20 minutes, 24 hours a day. Single fares are £7 ($11.55) and £7.50 ($12.40) for a 24-hour round-trip return. For schedules, call ☎ **01865/772250.**

By car, take M40 west from London and follow the signs. Note, however, that parking is a nightmare in Oxford. There are four well-marked "Park and Ride" lots on the north, south, east, and west of the city's ring road. Parking is free, or 50p or 60p (85¢ or 99¢) depending on which parking lot, but from 9:30am on, and all day Saturday, you pay £1.50 ($2.45) for a bus ride into the city, which drops you off at St. Aldate's Cornmarket or Queen Street. The buses run every 8 to 10 minutes in each direction from Monday to Saturday. The parking lots are on the Woodstock Road near the Peartree traffic circle, on the Botley Road toward Farringdon, on the Abingdon Road in the southeast, and on A40 toward London.

VISITOR INFORMATION   **Oxford Tourist Information Centre** is at the Old School Gloucester Green, opposite the bus station (☎ **01865/726871**). The center sells a comprehensive range of maps and brochures, as well as the famous Oxford University T-shirt, and provides hotel booking services for £2.50 ($4.15). Open Monday to Saturday from 9:30am to 5pm and Sunday Easter to October and bank holidays from 10am to 3pm.

EXPLORING OXFORD UNIVERSITY

Many Americans arriving at Oxford ask: "Where's the campus?" If a local chortles when answering, it's because Oxford University is made up of 35 widely dispersed colleges. To tour all of these would be a formidable task. It's best to focus on just a handful of the better-known colleges.

The Oxford Story, 6 Broad St. (☎ **01865/790055**), has packaged Oxford's complexities into a concise and entertaining audiovisual ride through the campus. The exhibition reviews some of the architectural and historical features that hurried visitors might miss. The exhibition includes a trip through a three-level former warehouse and takes you through more than 800 years of history. You're also filled in on the backgrounds of the colleges and those who have passed through their portals. The audiovisual presentation runs Monday to Friday from 10am to 4:30pm, Saturday and Sunday 10am to 5pm. Tickets are £5.50 ($9.05) for adults and £4.50 ($7.45) for children. A family ticket for two adults and two children is £16.50 ($27.20).

GUIDED TOURS

The best way to get a running commentary on the important sights is to take a 2-hour walking tour through the city and the major colleges. The tours leave daily from the Oxford Tourist Information Centre at 11am and 2pm. Tours costs £4 ($6.60) for adults and £2.50 ($4.15) for children; they do not include New College or Christ Church.

For a good orientation, **Guide Friday** (office at the railway station, ☎ **01865/ 790522**) offers hour-long, open-top bus tours around Oxford. In the winter, buses leave every half hour beginning at 9:30am and increase in frequency as the summer

Oxford

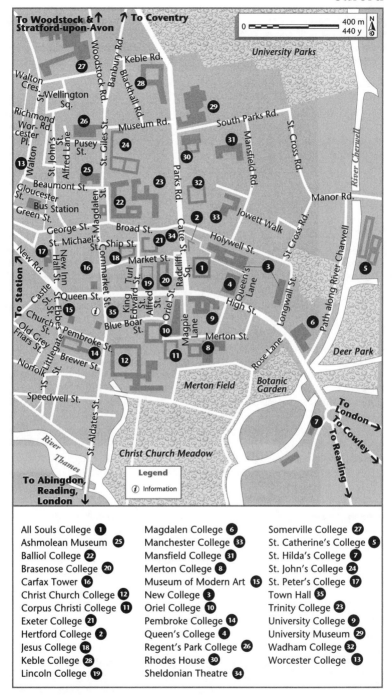

To Woodstock & ↑
Stratford-upon-Avon
↑ To Coventry

University Parks

0 ——————— 400 m
——————— 440 y

N

Walton Cres.
Wellington Sq.
Keble Rd.
Banbury Rd.
Blackhall Rd.
Woodstock Rd.
South Parks Rd.
St. Cross Rd.
River Cherwell

Richmond Rd.
Wor-cester Pl.
Walton St.
St. John's St.
Alfred Lane
St. Giles St.
Museum Rd.
Mansfield Rd.
Manor Rd.

Beaumont St.
Gloucester St.
Bus Station
Green St.
George St.
St. Michael's St.
Magdalen St.
Broad St.
Catte St.
Holywell St.
Jowett Walk

Pusey St.

New Rd.
New Inn Hall St.
Cornmarket St.
Ship St.
Market St.
Turl St.
King Edward St.
Alfred St.
Oriel St.
Radcliffe Sq.
Queen's Lane
Longwall St.
High St.

Castle St.
St. Ebbes St.
Church St.
Old Grey Friars St.
Littlegate St.
Pembroke St.
Brewer St.
Blue Boar St.
Magpie Lane
Merton St.
Rose Lane

Queen St.

Norfolk St.
Speedwell St.
St. Aldates St.

Deer Park

Botanic Garden

Merton Field

River Thames

Christ Church Meadow

To Abingdon, Reading, London ↓

To Station →

To London →
To Cowley →
To Reading →

Legend

ⓘ Information

All Souls College ❶	Magdalen College ❻	Somerville College ㉗
Ashmolean Museum ㉕	Manchester College ㉝	St. Catherine's College ❺
Balliol College ㉒	Mansfield College ㉛	St. Hilda's College ❼
Brasenose College ⓴	Merton College ❽	St. John's College ㉔
Carfax Tower ⓰	Museum of Modern Art ⓯	St. Peter's College ⓱
Christ Church College ⓬	New College ❸	Town Hall ㉟
Corpus Christi College ⓫	Oriel College ❿	Trinity College ㉓
Exeter College ㉑	Pembroke College ⓮	University College ❾
Hertford College ❷	Queen's College ❹	University Museum ㉙
Jesus College ⓲	Regent's Park College ㉖	Wadham College ㉜
Keble College ㉘	Rhodes House ㉚	Worcester College ⓭
Lincoln College ⓳	Sheldonian Theatre ㉞	

approaches. Tickets are good for the day and can be purchased from the driver. The cost is £8 ($13.20) adults, £6.50 ($10.75) students and seniors, and £2.50 ($4.15) children. A family ticket, costing £18.50 ($30.55) for 2 adults and 4 children, is also available.

A Bird's-Eye View From Carfax Tower

For a bird's-eye view of the colleges, climb Carfax Tower, located in the center of the city. Carfax Tower is all that remains from St. Martin's Church, where William Shakespeare once stood as godfather for the playwright William Davenant. The tower used to be higher, but after 1340 it was lowered following complaints that towns-people threw stones and fired arrows at students during town-and-gown disputes. Admission is £1.20 ($2) for adults, 60p ($1) for children. From November to March 31, hours are daily from 10am to 3:30pm. The rest of the year, hours are daily from 10am to 5:30pm. The tower is closed from Christmas Eve until January 2. For infor-mation, call ☎ 01865/792653.

The Colleges

○ **CHRIST CHURCH**   Begun by Cardinal Wolsey as Cardinal College in 1525, Christ Church (☎ **01865/276499**)—known as the House—was renamed by Henry VIII in 1546. Facing St. Aldate's Street, Christ Church has the largest quad-rangle of any college in Oxford.

Tom Tower houses Great Tom, the 18,000-pound bell that rings nightly at 9:05pm, signaling the closing of the college gates. Its 101 peals signify the number of students in residence at the time of the founding of Christ Church. Although the student body has grown significantly, Oxford traditions live on forever. In the 16th-century great hall hang several notable portraits, including works by Gainsborough and Reynolds. The walls are thick with prime ministers, since Christ Church was the training ground for 13 of them. The college also hosts a separate portrait gallery.

The **college chapel** was constructed over several hundred years, beginning in the 12th century. (Incidentally, it's also the cathedral of the diocese of Oxford.) The chapel's most impressive features are its 15th-century Norman pillars and the vaulting of the choir. Outside, in the center of the great quadrangle is a statue of Mercury mounted in the center of a fishpond. The college and chapel are open from 9am to 5:30pm. The entrance fee is £3 ($4.95) for adults and £2 ($3.30) for children. A family ticket costs £6 ($9.90).

MAGDALEN COLLEGE   Magdalen (*Maud*-lin) College, High Street (☎ **01865/ 276000**), was founded in 1458. Its alumni range from Wolsey to Wilde. Opposite the **botanic garden** (the oldest in England), is the **bell tower,** where the choristers sing in Latin at dawn on May Day. This 15th-century tower reflects mightily in the waters of the Cherwell below. Visit the equally old **chapel,** which feels ancient despite many of its latter-day trappings. Ask when the hall and other places of special interest are open. The grounds of Magdalen are the most extensive of any Oxford college; there's even a deer park. You can visit only from Easter to September, daily from 2 to 6pm. Admis-sion is £2 ($3.30) adults; £1 ($1.65) children.

MERTON COLLEGE   Founded in 1264, Merton College (☎ **01865/276310**) is among the three oldest colleges at the university. It stands near Corpus Christi College on Merton Street, the sole survivor of Oxford's medieval cobbled streets. Merton Col-lege is noted for its library, built between 1371 and 1379 and said to be the oldest col-lege library in England. One of the treasures is an astrolabe (an astronomical instrument used for measuring the altitude of the sun and stars) thought to have belonged to Chaucer. It costs £1 ($1.65) to visit the ancient library, including admission to the **Max**

A Word of Warning

To avoid distraction for students, Oxford has restricted visiting to certain hours and to groups of six or fewer. Furthermore, there are areas where visitors aren't allowed at all. The tourist office will be happy to advise you when and where you may take in the sights of this great institution.

Beerbohm Room, honoring the satirical English caricaturist who died in 1956. The library and college are open Monday to Friday from 2 to 4pm and Saturday and Sunday from 10am to 4pm. Merton College is closed for 1 week at Easter and at Christmas.

A favorite pastime is to take **Addison's Walk** through the water meadows. The stroll is so named after a former alumnus, Joseph Addison, the 18th-century essayist and playwright noted for his contributions to *The Spectator* and *The Tatler.*

UNIVERSITY COLLEGE   University College, High Street (☎ **01865/276602**), is the oldest college at Oxford and dates back to 1249, when an ecclesiastic, William of Durham, donated money for its foundation (the old claim that the real founder was Alfred the Great is fanciful). All the original structures have disappeared; the architecture of the 17th century predominates today, with subsequent additions in Victoria's day as well as in more recent times. The college's most famous alumnus, Shelley, was "sent down" for his part in collaborating on a pamphlet on atheism. But with poetical success, all was forgiven, as evidenced by a memorial to Shelley erected in 1894, a mere 72 years after his death. The hall and chapel of University College are open daily during vacations from 2 to 4pm for a charge of £1.50 ($2.45) for adults, 60p ($1) for children. Chapel services take place daily at 4 and 6pm.

NEW COLLEGE   New College, New College Lane, off Queen's Lane (☎ **01865/ 279555**), was founded in 1379. The **first quadrangle,** dating from before the end of the 14th century, was the initial quadrangle to be built in Oxford and formed the architectural boilerplate for many other colleges. In the **antechapel** is Sir Jacob Epstein's remarkable modern sculpture of Lazarus and a fine El Greco study of St. James. One of the treasures of the college is a crosier (pastoral staff of a bishop) belonging to the founding father. In the garden, you can stroll among the remains of the old city wall and the mound. The college (entered at New College Lane) can be visited Easter to September, daily from 11am to 5pm; off-season, daily from 2 to 4pm. Admission is free.

THE BODLEIN LIBRARY

This famed library on Catte Street (☎ **01865/277165**) was launched in 1602, initially funded by Sir Thomas Bodley. It is home to some 50,000 manuscripts and more than 5 million books. Over the years the library has expanded from the Old Library complex to other buildings, including the Radcliffe Camera next door. The easiest way to visit the library is by taking a guided tour, leaving from the Divinity School across the street from the main entrance. In summer there are four tours per day, Monday to Friday, and two on Saturday and Sunday; in winter, two tours leave per day. Call for specific times.

✪ PUNTING ON THE RIVER CHERWELL

Punting on the River Cherwell remains the favorite outdoor pastime in Oxford. At **Punt Station,** Cherwell Boathouse, Bardwell Road (☎ **01865/515978**), you can rent a punt (flat-bottom boat maneuvered by a long pole and a small oar) for £8 to £10 ($13.20 to $16.50) per hour, plus a £40 to £50 ($66 to $82.50) deposit. A punt can take up to six people. **Magdalen Bridge Boathouse** charges similar rates. Punts are available for rent from March to mid-June and late August to October, daily from 10am to dusk; a larger inventory of punts is available from mid-June to late August daily from 10am to 10pm. Hours of operation seem to be rather informal; you're not always guaranteed that someone will be here to rent you a boat, even if a punt is tied to the dock.

WHERE TO STAY

The **Oxford Tourist Information Centre,** Gloucester Green, opposite the bus station (☎ **01865/726871**), operates a year-round room-booking service for a fee of £2.50 ($4.15), plus a refundable deposit. If you'd like to seek lodgings on your own, the center has a list of accommodations, maps, and guidebooks.

EXPENSIVE

✪ **Old Parsonage Hotel.** 1 Banbury Rd., Oxford OX2 6NN. ☎ **01865/310210.** Fax 01865/311262. E-mail: oldparsonage@dial.pipex.com. 30 units. TV TEL. £145–£170 ($239.25–$280.50) double; £195 ($321.75) suite. Rates include English breakfast. AE, DC, MC, V.

This extensively renovated hotel near St. Giles Church and Keble College is so old (1660) that it looks like an extension of one of the ancient colleges. Once a 13th-century hospital, it was restored in the early 17th century. Oscar Wilde lived here for a time; this is where he said, "Either this wallpaper goes, or I do." In the 20th century, a modern wing was added, and in 1991, it was completely renovated and made into a first-rate hotel. The recently redecorated bedrooms are not large, but they're individually designed and have such amenities as satellite TV, hair dryers, and even phones in the bathrooms. All suites and some doubles have sofa beds with fine mattresses, and all open onto the private gardens. The Parsonage Bar serves everything from cappuccino to mixed drinks. You can order from a well-prepared menu of continental and English food from 7am until "late at night." There's also 24-hour room service.

MODERATE

Dial House. 25 London Rd., Headington, Oxford, Oxfordshire OX3 7RE. ☎ and fax **01865/769944.** www.oxfordcity.co.uk/accom/dialhouse. 8 units. TV. £50–£60 ($82.50–$99) double. MC, V. Bus: 7, 7A, 2, 2A, or 22.

This country house, built in the 1920s, rests beside the highway to London, 2 miles east of the heart of Oxford. Graced with mock-Tudor half-timbering and a prominent blue-faced sundial, it has roomy, recently renovated bedrooms, each equipped with tea-making facilities and firm mattresses. Bathrooms are small but have a set of good towels and a hair dryer. Most of them have a shower only, but a few offer a combination tub and shower. No smoking is permitted in the house. The owners, Julie and Tony Lamb, serve breakfast only in their bright dining room.

Eastgate Hotel. 23 Merton St., The High, Oxford, Oxfordshire OX1 4BE. ☎ **01865/ 248244.** Fax 01865/791681. 64 units. TV TEL. £130 ($214.50) double; £155 ($255.75) suite. AE, DC, MC, V.

Eastgate, built on the site of a 17th-century structure, stands opposite the ancient Examination Halls, next to Magdalen Bridge, and within walking distance of the city center. It offers recently refurbished facilities but retains the atmosphere of an English country house. The bedrooms are well worn but still cozy and comfortable, ranging in size from small to medium. All have radios and coffeemakers. Mattresses are replaced as needed, and the bathrooms have minimum space, medium-size towels, and a tidy maintenance. The **Shires Restaurant** serves continental food and the bar is popular with Oxford undergrads.

River Hotel. 17 Botley Rd., Oxford OX2 0AA. ☎ **01865/243475.** Fax 01865/724306. 21 units (19 with bathroom). £67.50 ($111.40) double with bathroom. Rates include breakfast. MC, V. Bus: 4C or 52.

This hotel lies a quarter-mile west of Oxford's commercial core, and charges less than many of its more central competitors. It was built around 1900 by a respected local craftsman whose casement windows and flower boxes are still in place. About a quarter of the accommodations are across the street in a comfortable stone-sided annex. There's a bar on the premises, a simple restaurant, and cozy furnishings within the bedrooms. Bedrooms are continually renewed, and you get comfortable beds here along with coffeemakers and clock radio alarms. Baths are small but equipped with medium-size towels and a hair dryer. Three singles without bathroom rent for £45 ($74.25).

Tilbury Lodge Private Hotel. 5 Tilbury Lane, Eynsham Rd., Botley, Oxford, Oxfordshire OX2 9NB. ☎ **01865/862138.** Fax 01865/863700. www.oxfordcity.co.uk/hotel/tilbury. 9 units. TV TEL. £60–£68 ($99–$112.20) double, £75 ($123.75) double with four-poster. Rates include English breakfast & VAT. MC, V. Bus: 42, 45, 45A, 45B, or 109.

This small hotel lies on a quiet country lane 2 miles west of the center of Oxford, less than a mile from the railway station. Eddie and Eileen Trafford house guests in well-furnished and comfortable bedrooms. (The most expensive room has a four-poster bed.) Rooms vary in size; most have adequate space and each comes with a firm mattress. Baths, although tiny, are well kept, usually with a shower stall. The hotel also has a Jacuzzi and welcomes children. If you don't arrive by car, Eddie can pick you up at the train station; a bus also stops nearby.

WHERE TO DINE
MODERATE

Bath Place Hotel. 4–5 Bath Place (at Holywell St.), Oxford OX1 3SU. ☎ **01865/791812.** Fax 01865/791834. www.oxlink.co.uk/oxford/hotels.bath.html. E-mail:bathplace@ compuserve.com. Reservations recommended. Main courses £18–£23 ($29.70–$37.95); fixed-price 6-course dinner £28 ($46.20). AE, MC, V. Wed–Sat noon–2pm, Sun 12:30–2:30pm; Sun–Thurs 7–10pm, Fri–Sat 7–10:30pm. Bus: 7. ANGLO/ITALIAN.

Composed of four interconnected 17th-century cottages, this place has been known since 1989 for sophisticated cuisine. Since it also houses 10 cozy bedrooms upstairs, it operates something like a French *restaurant avec chambres,* where diners can head directly upstairs after an evening meal. The menu, which usually changes every month, includes vegetarian selections and a pleasing mixture of English and Italian cuisine. Choices might include baked young English partridge, boned and encased in a puff pastry served with red wine jus and seasonal vegetables; a filet of Scottish beef, roasted and served in a chive-and-herb sauce with wild mushrooms and baby vegetables; or a risotto saffron with sweetbreads and tempura of seafood and vegetables.

Each of the no-smoking upstairs bedrooms features a TV and telephone. Including continental breakfast, doubles cost £95 to £135 ($156.75 to $222.75) per night.

Cherwell Boathouse Restaurant. Bardwell Rd. ☎ **01865/552746.** Reservations recommended. Main courses £9–£17 ($14.85–$28.05); fixed-price dinner from £19.50 ($32.15); fixed-price lunch £17.50 ($28.90). AE, DC, MC, V. Tues 6–11:30pm; Wed–Sat noon–2pm and 6–11:30pm; Sun noon–2pm. Closed Dec 24–30. Bus: Banbury Rd. Bus: 7. MODERN ENGLISH/FRENCH.

This landmark on the River Cherwell is owned by Anthony Verdin, who offers a fixed-price menu that changes every 2 weeks to take advantage of the availability of fresh vegetables, fish, and meat. On any given night, you might try starters such as game terrine with Cumberland sauce or a warm salad of black pudding and bacon with a damson dressing. For a main course, you might opt for breast of guinea fowl with tapenade or, for vegetarians, an eggplant gratin with saffron custard and a mixed-bean ragout. For dessert, few have resisted the "fallen" chocolate soufflé with "drunken" prunes and sour cream. The restaurant also has an exciting, reasonable wine list. In summer, dinner is served on the terrace. Before dinner, you can try punting; there's a rental agency on the other side of the boathouse (see "Punting on the River Cherwell," above).

Elizabeth. 82 St. Aldate's St. ☎ **01865/242230.** Reservations recommended. Main courses £13.25–£18.75 ($21.85–$30.95); lunch £17 ($28.05). AE, DC, MC, V. Tues–Sat 12:30–2:30pm and 6:30–11pm; Sun 7–10:30pm. Closed Easter weekend and Christmas week. Bus: 7. FRENCH/CONTINENTAL.

Despite the portraits of Elizabeth II that hang near the entrance in this stone-sided house opposite Christ Church College, this restaurant is named after the matriarch who founded the place in the 1930s. Today, you'll find a well-trained staff from Spain, who serve beautifully presented dishes in the French style. The larger of the two dining rooms exudes a restrained dignity; the smaller is devoted to *Alice in Wonderland* designs inspired by Lewis Carroll. Some of the kitchen's best dishes include a range of Scottish steaks; chicken royale, Dover sole, and sea bass in white-wine or lemon-butter sauce; and Basque *piperade*, the famous omelet dish of the Basque country.

INEXPENSIVE

Al-Shami. 25 Walton Crescent. ☎ **01865/310066.** Reservations recommended. Main courses £7.50–£12 ($12.40–$19.80); fixed-price menu £15 ($24.75). MC, V. Daily noon–midnight. Bus: 7. LEBANESE.

Ideal for meals all afternoon and late into the evening, this Lebanese restaurant has awakened Oxford's sleepy taste buds. Many diners don't go beyond the appetizers, more than 35 delectable hot-and-cold selections—everything from falafel to a lamb's-brain salad. Charcoal-grilled chopped lamb, chicken, or beef constitute most of the main-dish selections. In between, guests nibble on uncut raw vegetables; afterwards they choose desserts from the trolley. Al-Shami also serves vegetarian meals.

✪ **Munchy Munchy.** 6 Park End St. ☎ **01865/245710.** Reservations recommended. Main courses £4.85–£8.25 ($8–$13.60). MC, V. Tues–Sat noon–2pm and 5:30–10pm. Closed 2 weeks in Sept and 3 weeks in Dec. Bus: 52. SOUTHEAST ASIAN/INDONESIAN.

Some Oxford students think that this place offers the best food value in the city. The menu depends on what's available in the marketplace; Ethel Ow is adept at herbs and seasoning, and often uses fresh fruit creatively, as reflected in such dishes as king prawns sautéed with coriander and a five-spiced fresh pineapple purée, or a spicy lamb with ground pistachio nuts. At times, long lines form at the door, especially on Fridays and Saturdays. Children 5 and under are not permitted Friday and Saturday evenings.

PUBS

The Bear Inn. Alfred St. ☎ **01865/721783.** Snacks and bar meals £2–£6 ($3.30–$9.90). No credit cards. Mon–Sat noon–11pm; Sun noon–3pm and 7–10:30pm. Bus: 2A or 2B. ENGLISH.

A short block from The High, overlooking the north side of Christ Church College, this village pub is an Oxford tradition. Its swinging inn sign depicts the bear and ragged staff, the old insignia of the earls of Warwick, who were among its early patrons. Many famous Oxford students and residents have caroused within the pub's walls since the 13th century, earning it a well-worn place in English literature. The Bear has served a useful purpose in breaking down social barriers, bringing a wide variety of people together in a relaxed way. You might converse with a raja from India, a university don, a titled gentleman, or the latest in a line of owners that goes back more than 700 years. Some past owners developed a prankish and astonishing habit: clipping neckties. Around the lounge bar you'll see the remains of thousands of ties, all labeled with their owners' names. For those who seek to join this legacy of sartorial abuse, the bar patrons will cut a thin strip from the bottom of your tie (with your permission, of course). After this initiation, you may want to take part in some of the informal songfests of the undergraduates.

The Turf Tavern. 4 Bath Place (off Holywell St.). ☎ **01865/243235.** Main courses £3–£5 ($4.95–$8.25). MC, V. Mon–Sat 11am–11pm; Sun noon–10:30pm. Bus: 52. ENGLISH.

This 13th-century tavern, the oldest in Oxford, stands on a very narrow passageway near the Bodleian Library. Thomas Hardy used it as a setting in *Jude the Obscure,* and it was "the local" of Burton and Taylor when they were in Oxford many years ago making a film; today's patrons include a healthy sampling of the university's students and faculty. During his student days at Oxford, Bill Clinton was a frequent visitor here. During warm weather you can choose a table in one of the three separate gardens that radiate outward from the pub's core. For wintertime warmth, braziers are lighted in the courtyard and in the gardens.

A separate food counter, set behind a glass case, displays the day's fare. Present yourself to the employee behind the case, and carry your food back to your table. Menu choices include salads, soups, sandwiches, and platters of such traditional dishes as English beef pie, chili con carne, pork and cider, and chicken Kiev. Local ales (including a vicious brew named Headbanger) are served, as well as a range of wines. Food is served daily from noon to 8pm. The pub is reached via St. Helen's Passage, which stretches between Holywell Street and New College Lane. (You'll probably get lost, but any student worth his beer can direct you.)

3 The Pursuit of Science: Cambridge
55 miles N of London, 80 miles NE of Oxford

The university town of Cambridge is a collage of images: the Bridge of Sighs; spires and turrets; willows; dusty secondhand bookshops; the lilt of Elizabethan madrigals; lanes where Darwin, Newton, and Cromwell walked; the grassy "Backs" of the colleges, sweeping down to the banks of the Cam; punters; the tattered robes of hurried upperclassmen flying in the wind.

Along with Oxford, Cambridge is one of Britain's ancient seats of knowledge. In many ways their stories are similar. But beyond the campus, Cambridge has a thriving, high-tech industry. Yes, that was Bill Gates you spotted. And while Oxford recalls the arts, Cambridge has embraced the sciences. Both Isaac Newton and Stephen Hawking are graduates, joined by thousands of luminaries in every field.

There is much to explore in Cambridge, so give yourself time to wander.

ESSENTIALS
GETTING THERE   Trains depart frequently from London's Liverpool Street and King's Cross Stations, arriving an hour later. For inquiries, call **0345/484950** (in the U.K. only) or 01603/764776. An off-peak same-day round-trip is £13.50 ($22.30). A peak-time same-day round-trip is £16.10 ($26.55). An off-peak and a peak-time longer-stay round-trip (up to a 5-day period) is £18.40 ($30.35).

National Express buses run hourly between London's Victoria Coach Station for the 2-hour trip to Drummer Street Station in Cambridge. A one-way costs £6 ($9.90), a same-day round-trip £8 ($13.20). If you'd like to return in a day or 2 the cost is £11 ($18.15). Call **0990/808080** for information and schedules.

To drive from London, head north on the M11.

VISITOR INFORMATION   The **Cambridge Tourist Information Centre,** Wheeler Street (☎ **01223/322640**), in back of the Guildhall, offers a wide range of information. From April to October, hours are Monday to Friday 10am to 6pm, Saturday 10am to 5pm year-round, and Sunday 11:30am to 4:30pm (Easter to Dec only); July and August, open daily 10am to 7pm. From November to March hours are Monday to Friday 10am to 5:30pm; Saturday 10am to 5pm.

A tourist reception center for Cambridge and Cambridgeshire is operated by **Guide Friday Ltd.** on the concourse of Cambridge Railway Station (☎ **01223/362444**). The center sells brochures and maps, and books rooms. Open daily in summer from 9:30am to 7:30pm; the center closes at 4pm in winter.

GETTING AROUND   The center of Cambridge is made for pedestrians, so park your car at one of the many car parks (they increase in price as you approach the city center) and stroll among the widely dispersed colleges. Follow the courtyards through to the "Backs" (the college lawns) and walk through to Trinity College (where Prince Charles studied) and St. John's College, which contains the Bridge of Sighs.

Another popular way of getting around is bicycling. **Geoff's Bike Hire,** 65 Devonshire Rd. (☎ **01223/365629**), rents bicycles for £4 ($6.60) for 3 hours, £6 ($9.90) per day, or £12 ($19.80) per week. A deposit of £25 ($41.25) is required. Open daily in summer from 9am to 6pm; off-season Monday to Saturday from 9am to 5:30pm.

Stagecoach Cambus, 100 Cowley Rd. (☎ **01223/423554**), operates a network of buses, with fares ranging in price from 60p to £1.80 ($1 to $2.95). The local tourist office has schedules.

GUIDED TOURS

A good person to know if you're in the Cambridge area is Mrs. Isobel Bryant, who operates **Heritage Tours** from her 200-year-old home, Manor Cottage, Swaffham Prior CB5 0JZ (☎ **01638/741440**). An expert on the region, she will arrange tours starting from your hotel or Cambridge Railway Station to Lavenham with its thatched and timbered houses, to the fine medieval churches of the Suffolk villages, to Ely Cathedral, or to one of the nearby grand mansions with their many treasures. The charge of £110 ($181.50) is good for the day for up to four passengers, with all travel expenses, including the service of the driver/guide. Lunch in a village pub and admission fees add £3 to £6 ($4.95 to $9.90) per person. Mrs. Bryant also offers walking tours around the Cambridge colleges; they cost £40 ($66) for a family-size party and last about 2 hours.

Guide Friday, Ltd., on the concourse of Cambridge Railway Station (☎ **01223/362444**), has daily guided tours of Cambridge via open-top, double-decker buses. In summer, buses depart every 30 minutes from 9:45am to 2:45pm. Departures are curtailed off-season, depending on demand. The tour allows visitors to get off at any of the many stops and rejoin the tour whenever they wish. Tickets are valid all day. The fare is £8 ($13.20) for adults, £6.50 ($10.75) for senior citizens and students, and £2 ($3.30) for children 5 to 12, free for children 4 and under. A family ticket, costing £18.50 ($30.55) for 2 adults and 4 children, is also sold. Office hours are 9:30am to 4pm daily in winter and 9:30am to 7:30pm in summer.

EXPLORING THE UNIVERSITY

Oxford University predates Cambridge, but by the early 13th century scholars began gathering at Cambridge. Eventually, Cambridge won partial recognition from Henry

Cambridge

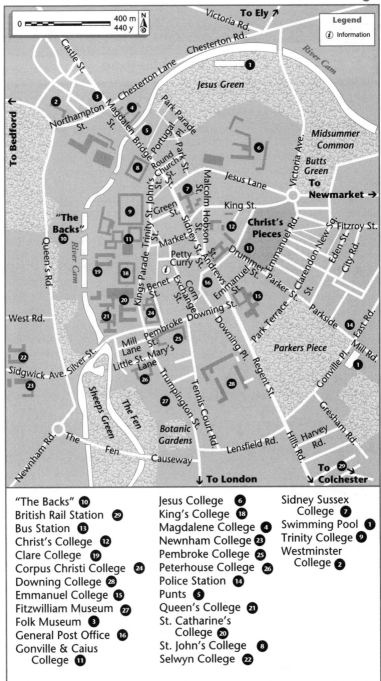

"The Backs" ❿	Jesus College ❻	Sidney Sussex College ❼
British Rail Station ㉙	King's College ⓲	Swimming Pool ❶
Bus Station ⓭	Magdalene College ❹	Trinity College ❾
Christ's College ⓬	Newnham College ㉓	Westminster College ❷
Clare College ⓳	Pembroke College ㉕	
Corpus Christi College ㉔	Peterhouse College ㉖	
Downing College ㉘	Police Station ⓮	
Emmanuel College ⓯	Punts ❺	
Fitzwilliam Museum ㉗	Queen's College ㉑	
Folk Museum ❸	St. Catharine's College ⓴	
General Post Office ⓰	St. John's College ❽	
Gonville & Caius College ⓫	Selwyn College ㉒	

III, rising or falling with the approval of subsequent English monarchs. Cambridge consists of 31 colleges for both men and women. Colleges are closed for exams from mid-April until the end of June.

The following listing is only a sample of some of the more interesting colleges. If you're planning to be in Cambridge awhile, you might also want to visit **Magdalene College,** on Magdalene Street, founded in 1542; **Pembroke College,** on Trumpington Street, founded in 1347; **Christ's College,** on St. Andrew's Street, founded in 1505; and **Corpus Christi College,** on Trumpington Street, which dates from 1352.

✪ **KING'S COLLEGE**   The adolescent Henry VI founded King's College on King's Parade (☎ **01223/331212**) in 1441. Most of its buildings today date from the 19th century, but its crowning glory, the perpendicular **King's College Chapel,** was built in the Middle Ages and is one of England's irreplaceable monuments. Owing to whims of royalty, the chapel wasn't completed until the early 16th century.

Henry James called King's College Chapel "the most beautiful in England." Its most striking features are the magnificent fan vaulting, all in stone, and the great windows, most of which were fashioned by Flemish artisans between 1517 and 1531 (the west window dates from the late-Victorian period). In hues of red, blue, and amber, the long range of windows around the back of the chapel depicts the Birth of the Virgin; the Annunciation; the Birth of Christ; the Life, Ministry, and Death of Christ; the Resurrection; the Ascension; the Acts of the Apostles; and the Assumption. The upper range contains Old Testament parallels to these New Testament stories. The chapel also boasts Rubens' *Adoration of the Magi* and a rood screen from the early 16th century. The chapel is famous for its choir and musical concerts.

The chapel is open during vacation time Monday to Saturday 9:30am to 4:30pm, and on Sunday 10am to 5pm. During term, the public is welcome to attend choral services Monday to Saturday at 5:30pm and on Sunday at 10:30am and 3:30pm, and the chapel is open to visitors Monday to Saturday 9:30am to 3:15pm and Sunday 1:15 to 2:15pm and 5 to 5:30pm; it's closed December 23 to January 1. It may be closed at other times for recording sessions, broadcasts, concerts, or other special events.

An exhibition in the seven northern side chapels recounts much of the history of the chapel. Admission to the college and chapel, including the exhibition, is £3 ($4.95) for adults, £2 ($3.30) for students and children 12 to 17, free for children under 12.

PETERHOUSE COLLEGE   On Trumpington Street, Peterhouse College (☎ **01223/338200**) attracts visitors largely because it's the oldest Cambridge college, founded in 1284 by Hugh de Balsham, the bishop of Ely. Of the original buildings, only the hall remains. It was restored in the 19th century and now has stained-glass windows by William Morris. Old Court, constructed in the 15th century, was renovated in 1754; the chapel dates from 1632. Ask permission to enter at the porter's lodge.

TRINITY COLLEGE   On Trinity Street, Trinity College (not to be confused with Trinity Hall) is the largest college in Cambridge. It was founded in 1546 by Henry VIII, who consolidated a number of smaller colleges that had existed on the site. The courtyard is the most spacious in Cambridge, built when Thomas Nevile was master. Sir Christopher Wren designed the library. For admission to the college, apply at the porter's lodge, or call ☎ **01223/338400** for information. There's a charge of £1.75 ($2.90) from March to November.

EMMANUEL COLLEGE   On St. Andrew's Street, Emmanuel (☎ **01223/ 334274**), was founded in 1584 by Sir Walter Mildmay, a chancellor of the exchequer

A Word of Warning

Because of disturbances caused by the influx of visitors to the university, Cambridge has had to limit, or exclude them altogether, from various parts of the university. In some cases, a small entry fee is charged. Small groups of up to six are generally admitted with no problem; you can inquire at the tourist office about visiting hours (see "Essentials").

to Elizabeth I. Harvardians take note: John Harvard, founder of Harvard University, studied here. You can take a scenic stroll around its attractive gardens and visit the chapel designed by Sir Christopher Wren and consecrated in 1677. Both the chapel and college are open daily during sunlight hours.

QUEENS' COLLEGE   On Queens' Lane, Queens' College (☎ **01223/335511**) is the loveliest of Cambridge's colleges. Dating back to 1448, it was founded by two English queens, Margaret of Anjou, the wife of Henry VI, and Elizabeth Woodville, the wife of Edward IV. Its second cloister is the most interesting, flanked by the early-16th-century half-timbered President's Lodge. Admission is £1 ($1.65), free for children under 12. A short printed guide is issued. From November until March 19, hours are daily 1:45 to 4:30pm; March 20 to May 15 Monday to Friday 1:45 to 4:30pm, Saturday and Sunday 10am to 4:45pm; closed May 17 to June 19. From June 20 to September 19 Monday to Friday 10am to 4:30pm, Saturday and Sunday 10am to 4:45pm; September 20 to October 31 Monday to Friday 1:45 to 4:30pm, Saturday and Sunday 10am to 4:45pm. Entry is by the old porter's lodge in Queens' Lane only. The old hall and chapel are usually open to the public when not in use.

ST. JOHN'S COLLEGE   On St. John's Street, this college (☎ **01223/338600**) was founded in 1511 by Lady Margaret Beaufort, mother of Henry VII, who had launched Christ's College a few years earlier. The impressive gateway bears the Tudor coat of arms, and Second Court is a fine example of late Tudor brickwork. Its best-known feature is the **Bridge of Sighs** crossing the Cam. Built in the 19th century, it was patterned after the covered bridge in Venice. It connects the older part of the college with New Court, a Gothic revival on the opposite bank from which there is an outstanding view of the famous "Backs." The Bridge of Sighs is closed to visitors, but can be seen from neighboring Kitchen Bridge. Wordsworth was an alumnus of the college, which is open March to October, daily 9:30am to 5pm. Admission is £1.75 ($2.90) for adults and £1 ($1.65) for children. During the winter months, there is no change and, subject to college activities, the public is welcome to wander through the grounds. Visitors are welcome to attend choral services in the chapel.

MORE CAMBRIDGE ATTRACTIONS

✪ **Fitzwilliam Museum.** Trumpington St., near Peterhouse. ☎ **01223/332900.** Free admission. Tues–Sat 10am–5pm, Sun 2:15–5pm. Guided tours, Sun 2:30pm. Closed Jan 1, Good Friday, May Day, and Dec 24–31.

This is one of Britain's finest museums. Founded by the bequest of the 7th viscount Fitzwilliam of Merrion to the University of Cambridge in 1816, this museum's permanent collections contain remarkable antiquities from ancient Egypt, Greece, and Rome. Newly created galleries display Roman and Romano-Egyptian art along with Western-Asiatic exhibits. The Fitzwilliam's Applied Arts section showcases English and European pottery and glass as well as furniture, clocks, armor, fans, rugs and samplers, Chinese jades, and ceramics from Japan and Korea. The museum also has married a

---

Insider's Tip

The Fitzwilliam stages occasional musical events, including evening concerts, in Gallery III. Throughout the year, it also plays host to some of the best lectures in England. For more details, call ☎ **01223/332900.**

---

rare ancient and medieval coin collection with a host of medals created from the Renaissance onward. But the Fitzwilliam is best loved for its paintings, which include masterpieces from the Renaissance to the 20th century.

Great St. Mary's. King's Parade. ☎ **01223/350914.** Admission to tower £1.50 ($2.45) adults, 50p (85¢) children. Tower Mon–Sat 10am–4:30pm, Sun 12:30–4:30pm. Church daily 9am–6pm.

Closely associated with events of the Reformation, this university church was built mostly in 1478 on the site of an 11th-century church. The cloth that covered the hearse of King Henry VII is on display in the church. A fine view of Cambridge may be seen from the top of the tower.

PUNTING THE CAM

Punting along the Cam in flat-bottomed wooden boats built somewhat like Venetian gondolas is a traditional pursuit here. Downstream, the Cam winds about the ivy-covered "Backs" of the colleges, their lush gardens sweeping riverward. Two miles upriver lies **Grantchester,** one of the shire's most beautiful villages, with an old church and gardens leading down to a series of peaceful meadows. Literary types flock to Grantchester's Green Man pub (see "Pubs," below), which can be reached by punting or by taking the path following the River Granta for less than an hour to Grantchester Meadows. The town lies about a mile from the meadows.

People sprawled along the banks of the Cam on a summer day wait to judge and ridicule you as you maneuver your punt with a 15-foot-long pole. The river's floor is muddy, and many a student has lost his pole in the riverbed shaded by the willows. If your pole gets stuck, it may be better to leave it sticking in the mud than to risk a plunge (and more ridicule) by trying to claim it too forcefully from the river.

Scudamore's Boatyards, Granta Place (☎ 01223/359750), by the Anchor Pub, has been in business since 1910. Punts, canoes, and rowboats rent for £10 ($16.50) per hour. A £50 ($82.50) cash or credit card deposit is required. There's a maximum of six persons per punt. They're open from March to late September or October daily from 9am until dusk, depending on the weather and number of clients. You may prefer a chauffeur, in which case there's a minimum charge of £25 ($41.25) for two people and £5 ($8.25) per person after that.

Cambridge Punt Company, working out of the Anchor Pub, Silver Street (☎ 01223/327280), conducts highly recommended 45-minute rowboat tours. A guide (usually a Cambridge student) appropriately dressed in a straw boater hat will simultaneously punt and deliver running commentary to groups of one to six persons. Tours cost £25 ($41.25) for two, and £5 ($8.25) per adult after that, £2.50 ($4.15) for children 5 to 12. Kids 4 and under ride free. The Anchor Pub's service staff can call a guide over to your table. For the independent, "unchauffeured" boats rent for £10 ($16.50) per hour plus a £50 ($82.50) deposit (cash or credit card). The company is open daily from 9am to dusk, though everyone packs up and goes home if it rains or if the winds get too high.

Impressions

Stands the Church clock at ten to three?
And is there honey still for tea?
—Rupert Brooke, "The Old Vicarage," Grantchester (1912)

WHERE TO STAY
MODERATE

Gonville Hotel. Gonville Place, Cambridge, Cambridgeshire CB1 1LY. ☎ **800/528-1234** or 01223/366611. Fax 01223/315470. www.hotelnet.co.uk. 64 units. TV TEL. £107–£150 ($176.55–$247.50) double. Rates include English breakfast. AE, CB, DC, MC, V.

This hotel and its grounds are opposite Parker's Piece, only a 5-minute walk from the center of town. The Gonville has been much improved in recent years, and is now better than ever, though not yet the equal of the University Arms (see below). It's not unlike an ivy-covered country house, with shade trees and a formal car entry. The recently refurbished rooms are comfortable and furnished in a modern style. Bedrooms are medium in size and have firm mattresses and such extras as coffeemakers. Bathrooms are small but contain an adequate supply of medium-size towels plus a hair dryer. There's central heating throughout and air-conditioning in the restaurant. For extra charges, laundry and dry cleaning, and secretarial services are made available.

University Arms Hotel. Regent St., Cambridge, Cambridgeshire CB2 1AD. ☎ **01223/ 351241.** Fax 01223/315256. www.devere.com. E-mail:devere-uniarms@airtime.co.uk. 116 units. TV TEL. £135 ($222.75) double; £270 ($445.50) suite. Rates include English breakfast. AE, DC, MC, V. Free parking. Bus: 1.

Built in 1834, this hotel maintains much of its Edwardian charm and many of its original architectural features despite modernization over the years. Near the city center and the university, it offers tastefully decorated bedrooms with central heating and radios, maintained in tip-top shape; 80 have recently been refurbished with new draperies and firm mattresses. Front rooms are smaller than those in the rear and double glazing cuts down on noise. Bathrooms are small but contain a set of good towels, a hair dryer, and a combination tub and shower. In addition to trouser presses, suite residents will find fresh flowers, fruits, and chocolates in their rooms. The Octagon Lounge, with its stained-glass domed ceiling and open log fire, is a popular place to meet for tea. The spacious oak-paneled restaurant features both table d'hôte and à la carte menus. The hotel porter arranges guided tours of the city. For a hotel of this price range, the expected amenities are delivered: room service, dry cleaning and laundry service, and baby-sitting.

INEXPENSIVE

Arundel Hotel. Chesterton Rd., Cambridge, Cambridgeshire CB4 3AN. ☎ **01223/ 367701.** Fax 01223/367721. 105 units. TV TEL. £65–£91 ($107.25–$150.15) double. Rates include continental breakfast. AE, DC, MC, V. Bus: 3 or 5.

Occupying one of the most desirable sites in Cambridge, until recently this hotel consisted of six identical Victorian row houses—all fronted with dark-yellow local bricks—that were interconnected many years ago. In 1994, after two additional row houses were purchased from the university, the hotel was enlarged, upgraded, and expanded into the well-maintained hostelry you'll see today. Although not as well appointed as the University Arms, it competes successfully with the Gonville. In fact, its cuisine is the best of the three hotels. Rooms overlooking the River Cam and Jesus Green cost more, and because there's no elevator, rooms on lower floors also cost more. Regardless of their location, all accommodations are clean, simple, and comfortable with firm mattresses, upholstered chairs, carpeting, and small but efficient and tidily kept bathrooms with a set of medium-size towels. There's a bar and restaurant (see "Where to Dine," below) on the premises and a garden with outdoor tables for warm-weather drinking. A coin-operated launderette is on the premises.

Regent Hotel. 41 Regent St., Cambridge, Cambridgeshire CB2 1AB. ☎ **01223/351470.** Fax 01223/566562. www.regentHotel.co.uk. E-mail:reservations@regenthotel.co.uk. 25 units. TV TEL. £82.50 ($136.15) double. Rates include continental breakfast. AE, DC, MC, V.

This is one of the most desirable of the reasonably priced small hotels in Cambridge. Right in the city center, overlooking Parker's Piece, the house was built in the 1840s as the original site of Newham College. It became a hotel when the college outgrew its quarters. The attractive, comfortable bedrooms have radios, coffeemakers, and trouser presses. Bedrooms are small to medium in size, and there is an ongoing series of redecorations. Bathroom are small but have adequate shelf space, a set of medium-size towels, and hair dryers. There's a cocktail bar on the street level, which is open until 11:45pm nightly.

WHERE TO DINE
MODERATE

Arundel House Restaurant. Chesterton Rd. ☎ **01223/367701.** Reservations recommended. Main courses £8.95–£14.95 ($14.75–$24.65); fixed-price 2-course lunch £10.75 ($17.75), fixed-price 3-course lunch £11.95 ($19.70), Sun lunch £11.95 ($19.70); fixed-price 2-course dinner £13.50 ($22.30), fixed-price 3-course dinner £15.95 ($26.30). AE, DC, MC, V. Daily 12:15–1:45pm and 6:30–9:30pm. Bus: 3 or 5. INTERNATIONAL.

One of the most acclaimed restaurants in Cambridge is in this hotel overlooking the River Cam and Jesus Green, a short walk from the city center. Winner of many awards, the cuisine is not only excellent and fresh, but is also good value. The warm decor features Louis XV–style chairs and spacious tables. The fare changes frequently, and you may dine à la carte or from the set menu. There's also a children's menu with a maximum price of £2.25 ($3.70). Appetizers may consist of a homemade golden pea and ham soup, or a white-rum and passion-fruit cocktail. Fish choices are likely to include plaice or salmon, which mightily compete against the roasted duckling or ostrich steak.

Midsummer House. Midsummer Common. ☎ **01223/69299.** Reservations required. Fixed-price 3-course lunch £19.50 ($32.15), Sun lunch £25 ($41.25); fixed-price 3-course dinner £39.50 ($65.20). AE, MC, V. Tues–Fri and Sun noon–1:45pm; Tues–Sat 7–9:45pm. CONTINENTAL.

Located near the River Cam in an Edwardian-era cottage, this is one of the dining discoveries of Cambridge. The preferred dining area is in an elegant conservatory, but you can also find a smartly laid table upstairs. The fixed-price menus are wisely limited, and quality control and high standards are much in evidence despite a frequent change of chefs. The waiters will be glad to assist you as you peruse the menu, which traditionally has offered some of the freshest and best food selections in Cambridge.

✪ **Twenty Two.** 22 Chesterton Rd. ☎ **01223/351880.** Reservations required. Fixed-price menu £23.50 ($38.80). AE, DC, MC, V. Tues–Sat 7:30–10pm. ENGLISH/CONTINENTAL.

Who would expect to find one of the best restaurants in Cambridge in this quiet residential and hotel district? In the vicinity of Jesus Green, it's an address jealously guarded by locals. This homelike but elegant Victorian dining room offers an ever-changing fixed-price menu based on fresh market produce. Owners David Carter and Louise Crompton meld time-tested recipes with their own inspirations. Typical dishes include grilled loin of tuna with pesto, spring onions, and chili; and supreme of chicken with pearl barley risotto and roast eggplant.

INEXPENSIVE

Browns. 23 Trumpington St. ☎ **01223/461655.** Main courses £7.55–£14.95 ($12.45–$24.65). AE, MC, V. Mon–Sat 11am–11:30pm; Sun noon–11:30pm. Bus: 2. ENGLISH/CONTINENTAL.

Long a favorite at Oxford, Browns became a sensation at Cambridge some time ago. It was built opposite the Fitzwilliam Museum in 1914 as the outpatient department of a hospital dedicated to Edward VII; that era's grandeur remains most vividly in the building's neoclassical colonnade. Today it's the most lighthearted place for dining in the city, with wicker chairs, high ceilings, pre–World War I woodwork, and a long bar covered with bottles of wine. The extensive bill of fare includes various pastas, scores of fresh salads, several selections of meat and fish (from charcoal-grilled leg of lamb with rosemary to fresh fish in season), hot sandwiches, and the chef's daily specials. If you drop by in the afternoon, you can also order thick milk shakes or natural fruit juices. In fair weather, outdoor seats are prized possessions.

PUBS

Cambridge Arms. 4 King St. ☎ **01223/505015.** Bar snacks £2–£6.25 ($3.30–$10.30). AE, DC, MC, V. Mon–Sat 11am–5pm; Sun noon–3pm. Pub Mon–Sat 11am–11pm; Sun noon–10:30pm. ENGLISH.

This no-nonsense pub in the center of town bustles with atmosphere and dispenses endless platters of food to clients over the bar's countertop. Favorites include the chef's daily specials, grilled steaks, vegetarian meals, and an array of both hot and cold dishes.

The pub was recently refurbished and now is a music-oriented theme pub. Guitars and various music paraphernalia adorn the walls.

✪ **The Green Man.** 59 High St., Grantchester. ☎ **01223/841178.** Main courses £3.50–£8 ($5.75–$13.20). MC, V. Daily noon–2:30pm and 6–9pm; Sun noon–10:30pm. Pub Mon–Sat 11am–3pm and 5–11pm; Sun noon–10:30pm. Bus: 118 from Cambridge. MEXICAN/INDIAN/ENGLISH.

Named in honor of Robin Hood, this 400-year-old inn is the most popular pub for outings from Cambridge. It's located on A604, 2 miles south of Cambridge in the hamlet of Grantchester, made famous by poet Rupert Brooke (see above). Even if you haven't heard of Brooke, you might enjoy spending a late afternoon wandering through the old church and then heading, as everybody does, to the Green Man. In winter a crackling fire welcomes the weary inside, but in summer it's more tempting to retreat to the beer garden, from which you can stroll to the edge of the River Cam. Place your order at the counter, after which an employee will bring your food to your table. The food is an eclectic mix of Indian, Mexican, and English. The fare ranges from Indian curries to burritos, fajitas, and on to traditional English pies and bangers and mash, as well as various vegetarian choices.

4 Canterbury

56 miles SE of London

Under the arch of the ancient West Gate went Chaucer's knight, pardoner, nun, squire, parson, merchant, miller, and others—all spinning tales. They were bound for the shrine of Thomas à Becket, archbishop of Canterbury, who was slain by four knights of Henry II on December 29, 1170 at the cathedral. (In penance, the king was later made to walk barefoot from Harbledown to the tomb of his former friend, and allow himself to be flogged.) The shrine was finally torn down in 1538 by Henry VIII, as part of his campaign to destroy monasteries and Catholic places of pilgrimage; but by then, Canterbury had become inexorably fixed in the pilgrims' imagination.

This Kentish city on the River Stour is the ecclesiastical capital of England. The city was once fully walled, and abundant traces of its old fortifications remain despite enormous damage caused by the Nazi Blitz of 1941. Pilgrims to Canterbury continue to arrive today, but are called "day-trippers," and have overrun the city and its monuments. The city has an active university life—mainly students from Kent—and an enormous number of pubs and shops. Canterbury is best seen in the early morning or the early evening, when day-trippers are scarce.

ESSENTIALS

GETTING THERE   There's frequent train service from Victoria, Charing Cross, Waterloo, and London Bridge Stations. The journey takes 1¹/₂ hours. For schedules and information, call ☎ **0345/484950** or 01603/764776.

The bus from Victoria Coach Station takes 2 to 3 hours and leaves twice daily. For schedules and information, call ☎ **0990/808080**.

To drive from London, take A2, then M2. Canterbury is signposted all the way. The city center is closed to cars, but it's only a short walk from several parking areas to the cathedral.

VISITOR INFORMATION   The **Visitors Information Centre** is at 34 St. Margaret's St. (☎ **01227/766567**), near St. Margaret's Church. Open April to October Monday to Saturday 9:30am to 5:30pm (closes at 5pm from November to March).

SEEING THE SIGHTS

✪ **Canterbury Cathedral.** 11 The Precincts. ☎ **01227/762862.** Admission £3 ($4.95) adults; £2 ($3.30) children, students and seniors. Guided tours (based on demand) £3 ($4.95) adults; £2 ($3.30) students, seniors, and children. Mon–Sat 9am–5pm; Sun 12:30–2:30pm and 4:30–5:30pm.

The foundation of this splendid cathedral dates back to when the first archbishop, Augustine, came from Rome in A.D. 597, but the earliest part of the present building is the great Romanesque crypt built around 1100. The monastic "quire" erected on top of this at the same time was destroyed by fire in 1174, only 4 years after Thomas à Becket was murdered on a gloomy December evening in the northwest transept. The quire was immediately replaced by a magnificent Gothic structure, the first major expression of its kind in England.

The cathedral is noteworthy for the medieval royal tombs of King Henry IV and Edward the Black Prince, as well as those of numerous archbishops. The cathedral stands amid the remains of the buildings of the monastery—cloisters, chapter house, and Norman water tower, which have survived intact from Henry VIII's Reformation to the present day.

Though Henry VIII destroyed Becket's shrine, its site is still honored in Trinity Chapel, near the high altar. The saint is said to have worked miracles, which were recounted in a number of panels of rare stained glass. Perhaps the greatest miracle is that, with some guile, the windows escaped both Henry VIII's rampage, Oliver Cromwell's idol smashers, and Hitler's Blitz. Though German bombs blew out windows in the cathedral, wise caretakers had stowed Becket's glass safely away. Behind

Canterbury

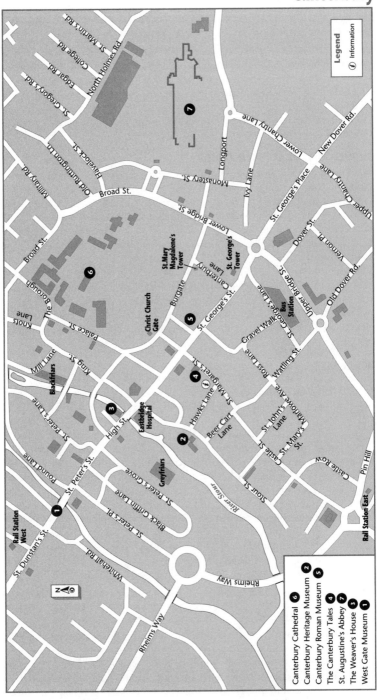

Legend
ⓘ Information

Canterbury Cathedral ❻
Canterbury Heritage Museum ❷
Canterbury Roman Museum ❹
The Canterbury Tales ❼
St. Augustine's Abbey ❸
The Weaver's House ❶
West Gate Museum ❺

the high altar stands St. Augustine's Chair, one of the symbols of the archbishop's authority, and of the history of Christianity in England.

The Canterbury Tales. 23 St. Margaret's St. (off High St., near the cathedral). ☎ **01227/ 454888.** Admission £5.25 ($8.65) adults, £4.50 ($7.45) seniors and students, £4 ($6.60) children 5–16, free for children 4 and under. Daily 9:30am–5:30pm.

One of the most visited museums in town re-creates the pilgrimages of Chaucer's England through a series of medieval tableaux. Visitors are handed headsets that replay five of Chaucer's *Canterbury Tales* and the story of the murder of St. Thomas à Becket in the nearby cathedral. A tour of all exhibits takes about 45 minutes.

GUIDED WALKS & RIVER TOURS

From Easter to early November, daily guided tours of Canterbury are organized by the **Guild of Guides,** Arnett House, Hawks Lane (☎ 01227/459779), costing £3.50 ($5.75) for adults and £3 ($4.95) for students and children over 14, and £8.50 ($14) for a family ticket. Leaving daily at 2pm from the end of March to the end of October, tours meet at the Visitors Information Centre, 34 St. Margaret's St., in the pedestrian zone near the cathedral. From July to August there's also a tour at 11:30am Monday to Saturday.

From just below the Weavers House, **Weavers River Trip,** Weavers House, 1 St. Peter's St. (☎ **01227/464660**), has boats that leave for half-hour trips along the river with a commentary on the history of the buildings you pass. Boats depart each half hour from 1pm to sunset from March to October. Tickets are £4 ($6.60) for adults and £3 ($4.95) for children. Umbrellas are available in case of inclement weather.

WHERE TO STAY
MODERATE

County Hotel. High St., Canterbury, Kent CT1 2RX. ☎ **01227/766266.** Fax 01227/451512. www.macdonaldhotels.co.uk/county/index. E-mail:info@county-macdonaldhotels.co.uk. 73 units. TV TEL. £106-£120 ($174.90–$198) double; £190 ($313.50) suite. AE, DC, MC, V. Parking £3 ($4.95).

This place has been a hotel since the closing years of Victoria's reign, with a recorded history going back to the end of the 12th century. The time-mellowed atmosphere is most evocative in the hewn timbers and carved antiques of the residents' lounge on the second floor. The hotel is fully refurbished, and is the finest lodging in central Canterbury. Each room has a fully tiled bathroom with a set of medium-size towels and a hair dryer. Some rooms contain Georgian or Tudor four-poster beds. Regardless of your room assignment, each contains a firm mattress. In 1999, 30 accommodations were refurbished. For fine dining, go to Sully's Restaurant, the hotel's fully air-conditioned dining room (see "Where to Dine," below). For snacks, vegetarian specialties, salads, and hot dishes, the coffee shop is your best bet. There's also the Tudor Bar, where you can have an aperitif or an after-dinner drink.

✪ **Howfield Manor.** Chartham Hatch, Canterbury, Kent CT4 7HQ. ☎ **01227/738294.** Fax 01227/731535. 16 units. TV TEL. £95 ($156.75) double; £105 ($173.25) suite. Rates include English breakfast. AE, MC, V. Take the A28 2¼ miles from Canterbury.

The Towns family is the latest innkeepers to operate on this spot, which has held an inn continuously since 1181. Once part of the estate of the Priory of St. Gregory, this is one of the most charming country manors in the vicinity of Canterbury. It's a good and reliable choice, full of beams and nooks, and with enough log fires blazing on a winter's evening to comfort any chilled stranger. Set on 5 acres of rolling meadows, the house offers tastefully furnished bedrooms, ranging from small to medium, with such amenities as alarm clocks, trouser presses, and firm mattresses. Each of the tidily kept but small bathrooms has a set of fluffy white towels and a hair dryer. Rooms in the original house have the most character, as reflected in their exposed beams. New-wing bedrooms are larger and furnished with solid oak pieces. The manor's restaurant, Old Well, is excellent (see "Where to Dine," below). Howfield Manor lies 2 miles from Canterbury along the A28 Ashford Road.

INEXPENSIVE

Cathedral Gate Hotel. 36 Burgate, Canterbury, Kent CT1 2HA. ☎ **01227/464381.** Fax 01227/462800. E-mail:cgate@cgate.demon.co.uk. 24 units (12 with bathroom). TV TEL. £51 ($84.15) double without bathroom, £76.50 ($126.25) double with bathroom. Rates include continental breakfast. AE, DC, MC, V.

Cathedral Gate is for modern-day pilgrims who want to rest their bones at an inn shouldering up to the cathedral's gateway. Built in 1438, the hotel adjoins Christchurch Gate and overlooks the Buttermarket. The small rooms are comfortable and modestly furnished, each with a good mattress, and betray medieval construction in their sloping floors, massive oak beams, and winding corridors. Thoughtful extras include a coffeemaker in each room, plus a small bath with a set of medium-size towels and a hair dryer. Its menu is like a time warp from the past—good items such as Lancashire hotpot, beef and ale stew, steak-and-kidney pie, and treacle sponge with custard and cream. An in-house bar is licensed to serve residents, and there's a courtyard garden with cathedral views. It's a 10-minute walk from the train station.

✪ **Ebury Hotel.** 65–67 New Dover Rd., Canterbury, Kent CT1 3DX. ☎ **01227/768433.** Fax 01227/459187. 15 units. TV TEL. £65–£75 ($107.25–$123.75) double; £85 ($140.25) triple; £95 ($156.75) quad. Rates include English breakfast. AE, DC, MC, V. Closed Dec 21–Jan 12. Follow the signs to A2, Dover Rd. on L.H.S. south of the city.

One of the finest B&B hotels in Canterbury, this gabled Victorian house stands at the edge of town set back from the New Dover Road in 2 acres of garden and within easy walking distance of the center. Built in 1850, it's composed of two separate houses that were joined several years ago. It's important to reserve here, since this well-furnished, roomy, family-run hotel is quite popular. The bedrooms range from small to medium in size, and are constantly refurbished as needed. Mattresses are firm and carpeting is a fine wool. Extras include a coffeemaker in each room; some units contain a four-poster. Baths are well maintained, although small, and have a rack of medium-size towels plus a hair dryer. The hotel has a heated indoor swimming pool and spa, as well as a spacious lounge and a licensed restaurant serving English meals prepared with fresh vegetables. Chargrills and dishes based on family recipes are especially good, including lamb chops with watercress. They also rent flats on a weekly basis.

Three Tuns Inn. 24 Watling St. (just off Castle St.), Canterbury, Kent CT1 2UD. ☎ **01227/767371.** Fax 01227/785962. 5 units. TV TEL. £42.50–£50 ($70.15–$82.50) double. AE, DC, MC, V.

In the center of town, this old-fashioned inn derives most of its business from an exceptionally busy pub. However, many appreciate the handful of antique bedrooms upstairs in the 15th-century building, with their old-world charm. Small but cozily comfortable in the best English pub tradition, each has a good bed with a firm mattress, plus a small, somewhat-cramped bath with a shower stall and thin towels. William and Mary, who later became king and queen of England, stopped here in 1679; you can follow their example, even going so far as to stay in the same room. The pub downstairs serves typical pub fare daily from 11am to 11pm. Crowds from the pub spill into a side room, the Chapel Restaurant, where illegal Catholic masses were held during the Civil War. It still has the entrance to a secret passageway that allowed celebrants to leave quickly in case of a raid.

WHERE TO DINE
MODERATE

Duck Inn. Pett Bottom, near Bridge. ☎ **01227/830354.** Reservations recommended. Main courses £7.45–£9.95 ($12.30–$16.40); fixed-price 2-course lunch (Mon–Fri) £9–£11 ($14.85–$18.15); fixed-price 3-course dinner £14–£20 ($23.10–$33). AE, DC, MC, V. Drive 5 miles outside Canterbury near the village of Bridge on the road to Dover. ENGLISH.

Once called the Woodsmen Arms, this restaurant became known as the Duck Inn because of its low door: The clientele would shout "duck!" when a new patron arrived. Set in the Pett Bottom valley, this 16th-century place keeps to English fare. During the summer season, waiters serve diners either indoors or out in the English country garden. The menu changes weekly, although there are a few standards. You can start with one of the homemade soups, such as country vegetable or celery and Stilton. For your main course, the menu may include game pies (in season) or mussels marinara; a duck preparation is always on the menu. For dessert, try a local favorite, the home-made date pudding with toffee sauce. Take note, Bond fans: According to the film *You Only Live Twice*, 007 grew up next door to the Duck Inn.

Old Well Restaurant. At Howfield Manor, Chartham Hatch. ☎ **01227/738294.** Reservations recommended. Main courses £9.95–£16.95 ($16.40–$27.95). AE, DC, MC, V. Daily noon–2pm and 7:30–9pm. CONTINENTAL/FRENCH.

At this country manor (see "Where to Stay," above), meals are served in the manor's chapel, dating back to 1181. Nearby, the old well where monks drew their water is still visible. Head chef, James Weaklands and his brigade, favor a market-fresh cuisine where each dish is prepared daily. Bolstered by a homelike atmosphere, friendly service, and a well-chosen wine list, Weaklands invites you to enjoy some of his culinary delights, such as open ravioli of prawns and scallops drizzled with lobster oil. Fine main courses abound, including grilled medaillons of venison set on braised red cabbage and juniper jus, or halibut steak baked with citrus and fresh herbs. Arrive early to enjoy a drink in the Priory Bar, with its trompe l'oeil murals and a real priesthole (the bar staff will be delighted to explain what that means, just to get the conversation rolling).

Sully's. In the County Hotel, High St. ☎ **01227/766266.** Reservations recommended. Fixed-price 2-course lunch EC$17 ($26.30), fixed-price 3-course lunch £19 ($31.35); fixed-price dinner £24.95 ($41.15). AE, DC, MC, V. Daily 12:30–2:30pm and 7–10pm. ENGLISH/CONTINENTAL.

The most distinguished restaurant in Canterbury is located in its most distinguished hotel (see "Where to Stay," above). Although the place is without windows and the decor is straight out of the 1960s, the seating and comfort level is first rate, and the menu offers good value. You can always count on a selection of plain, traditional English dishes, but try one of the more imaginatively conceived platters instead. Look for seasonal specialties as well. A typical menu might begin with leek-and-potato soup with chive cream or a warm rosette of smoked salmon on bitter leaves with a pimento-butter dressing, and follow with panfried breast of pheasant with caramelized apple and a mellow curry sauce or chargrilled Scottish eyesteak.

5 Shakespeare's Stratford-upon-Avon

91 miles NW of London, 40 miles NW of Oxford

Crowds of tourists overrun this market town on the Avon River during the summer months. In fact, Stratford so aggressively hustles its Shakespeare connection that it seems at times that everybody here is in business to make a buck off the Bard. If he could return today, Shakespeare would be faced with Bard T-shirts, china models of Anne Hathaway's cottage, and Big Macs, and might look for a less trampled town to live out his final days. He also might be surprised to find himself reinvented as the hero of a popular Oscar-winning film, *Shakespeare in Love*.

A magnet for visitors today is the Royal Shakespeare Theatre, where Britain's foremost actors perform. Other than the theater, Stratford is nearly devoid of any rich cultural life, and you may want to rush back to London after you've seen the literary pilgrimage sights and watched a production. If you can, visit in winter, when the throngs dwindle.

ESSENTIALS

GETTING THERE Amazingly, there are no direct trains from London. From London's Paddington Station, you can take a train to Leamington Spa, where you pick up a connection for Stratford-upon-Avon. The journey takes about 3 hours at a cost of £22.50 ($37.15) for a round-trip ticket. Call ☎ **0345/484950** or 01603/764776 for information and schedules. The train station at Stratford is on Alcester Road. It's closed on Sundays from October to May, so you'll have to rely on the bus.

Eight **National Express** buses (☎ **0990/808080**) leave daily from Victoria Station, with a trip time of 3¼ hours. A single-day round-trip ticket costs £11 ($18.15).

To drive from London, take the M40 toward Oxford and continue to Stratford-upon-Avon on A34.

VISITOR INFORMATION The **Tourist Information Centre,** Bridgefoot, Stratford-upon-Avon, Warwickshire CV37 6GW (☎ **01789/293127**), provides all the information you'll need. It's open March to October Monday to Saturday 9am to 6pm, Sunday 11am to 5pm. From November to February, the hours are Monday to Saturday 9am to 5pm.

To contact the **Shakespeare Birthplace Trust,** which administers many of the attractions, send a self-addressed envelope and International Reply Coupon to the Director, the Shakespeare Centre, Henley Street, Stratford-upon-Avon, Warwickshire CV37 6QW (☎ **01789/204016**).

VISITING THE SHRINES

Besides the attractions on Stratford's periphery, there are many Elizabethan and Jacobean buildings in town. One ticket—costing £11 ($18.15) for adults, £5.50 ($9.05) for children, or £26 ($42.90) family ticket (2 adults, 3 children)—will permit you to visit the five major Shakespeare Birthplace Trust sights: Shakespeare's Birthplace, Anne Hathaway's Cottage, New Place/Nash's House, Mary Arden's House, and Hall's Croft. Seniors and students pay £10 ($16.50). Pick up the ticket if you're planning to do much sightseeing (obtainable at your first stopover at any one of the Trust properties).

✪ **Shakespeare's Birthplace.** Henley St. ☎ **01789/204016.** Admission £4.90 ($8.10) adults, £2.20 ($3.65) children. Mar 20–Oct 19 Mon–Sat 9am–5pm, Sun 9:30am–5pm; off-season Mon–Sat 9:30am–4pm, Sun 10am–4pm. Closed Dec 23–26.

The son of a glover and whittawer (leather worker), the Bard was born on St. George's Day, April 23, 1564, and died on the same date 52 years later. Filled with Shakespeare memorabilia, this Trust property is a half-timbered structure, dating from the first part of the 16th century. It was bought by public donors in 1847 and preserved as a national shrine. You can visit the bedroom where Shakespeare was probably born, a fully equipped kitchen of the period (look for the "babyminder"), and a Shakespeare Museum, illustrating his life and times. Later, you can walk through the garden, planted with all the flowers mentioned in the plays. You won't be alone: It's estimated that some 660,000 visitors pass through the house annually.

Built next door to commemorate the 400th anniversary of the Bard's birth, the **Shakespeare Centre** serves both as the administrative headquarters of the Trust and as a library and study center. An extension houses a visitors' center, which acts as a reception area for all those coming to the birthplace. It's in the town center near the post office close to Union Street.

✪ **Anne Hathaway's Cottage.** Cottage Lane, Shottery. ☎ **01789/292100.** Admission £3.90 ($6.45) adults, £1.60 ($2.65) children. Mar 20–Oct 19 Mon–Sat 9:30am–5pm, Sun 9:30am–5pm; off-season Mon–Sat 9:30am–4pm, Sun 10am–4pm. Closed Dec 23–26. Take a bus from Bridge St. or walk via a marked pathway from Evesham Place in Stratford across the meadow to Shottery.

Before she married Shakespeare, Anne Hathaway lived in this thatched, wattle-and-daub cottage in the hamlet of Shottery, a mile from Stratford. It's the most interesting and the most photographed of the Trust properties. The Hathaways were yeoman farmers, and their descendents lived in the cottage until 1892. As a result, it was never renovated, and provides a rare insight into the life of a family in Shakespearean times. The Bard was only 18 when he married Anne, who was much older. Many of the original furnishings, including the courting settle and utensils, are preserved inside the house. After visiting the house, take time to linger in the garden and orchard.

New Place/Nash's House. Chapel St. ☎ **01789/204016.** Admission £3.30 ($5.45) adults, £1.60 ($2.65) children. Mar 20–Oct 19 Mon–Sat 9:30am–5pm, Sun 10am–5pm; off-season Mon–Sat 10am–4pm, Sun 10:30am–4pm. Closed Dec 23–26. Walk west down High St.; Chapel St. is a continuation of High St.

Shakespeare retired to New Place in 1610, a prosperous man by the standards of his day, and died here 6 years later. Regrettably, the house was torn down, so only the garden remains. A mulberry tree planted by the Bard was so popular with latter-day visitors to Stratford that the garden's cantankerous owner chopped it down. The mulberry tree that grows here today is said to have been planted from a cutting of the original tree. You enter the gardens through Nash's House (Thomas Nash married Elizabeth Hall, a granddaughter of Shakespeare). Nash's House has 16th-century period rooms and an exhibition illustrating the history of Stratford. The lovely **Knott Garden** adjoins the site and represents the style of a fashionable Elizabethan garden.

Mary Arden's House & the Shakespeare Countryside Museum. Wilmcote. ☎ **01789/ 204016.** Admission £4.40 ($7.25) adults, £2.20 ($3.65) children. Mar 20–Oct 19 Mon–Sat 9:30am–5pm, Sun 10am–5pm; off-season Mon–Sat 10am–4pm, Sun 10:30am–4pm. Closed Dec 23–26. Take the A34 (Birmingham) road for 3½ miles.

Reputedly this Tudor farmstead, with its old stone dovecote and various outbuildings, was the girlhood home of Shakespeare's mother—or so claimed an 18th-century entrepreneur. The house contains country furniture and domestic utensils, and in the barns, stable, cowshed, and farmyard you'll find an extensive collection of farming implements illustrating life and work in the local countryside from Shakespeare's time to the present.

Hall's Croft. Old Town. ☎ **01789/292107.** Admission £3.30 ($5.45) adults, £1.60 ($2.65) children, and £18 ($29.70) family ticket for the 3 houses in town. Mar 20–Oct 19 Mon–Sat 9:30am–5pm, Sun 10am–5pm; off-season Mon–Sat 10am–4pm, Sun 10:30am–4pm. Open at 1:30pm Jan 1 and closed Dec 24–26. Walk west from High St., which becomes Chapel St. and Church St. At the intersection with Old Town, go left.

This house is on Old Town Street, not far from the parish church, Holy Trinity. It was here that Shakespeare's daughter Susanna probably lived with her husband, Dr. John

Stratford-upon-Avon

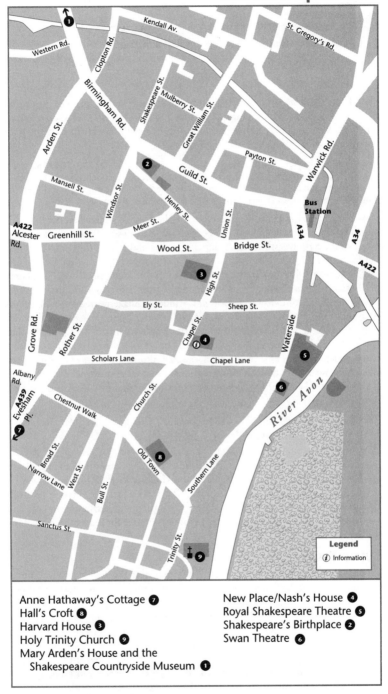

Anne Hathaway's Cottage ❼
Hall's Croft ❽
Harvard House ❸
Holy Trinity Church ❾
Mary Arden's House and the
    Shakespeare Countryside Museum ❶

New Place/Nash's House ❹
Royal Shakespeare Theatre ❺
Shakespeare's Birthplace ❷
Swan Theatre ❻

Impressions

It is something, I thought, to have seen the dust of Shakespeare.
　　　　　　　—Washington Irving, *The Sketch Book* (1820)

Hall. Hall's Croft is an outstanding Tudor house with a walled garden, furnished in the style of a middle-class home of the time. Dr. Hall was widely respected, and he built up a large medical practice in the area. Fascinating exhibits illustrate the theory and practice of medicine in Dr. Hall's time.

Holy Trinity Church (Shakespeare's Tomb). Old Town. ☎ **01789/266316.** Church, free; Shakespeare's tomb, donation 60p ($1) adults, 40p (65¢) students. Mar–Oct Mon–Sat 8:30am–6pm, Sun 2–5pm; Nov–Feb Mon–Sat 9am–4pm (Thurs until 5pm), Sun 2–5pm. Walk 4 minutes past the Royal Shakespeare Theatre with the river on your left.

In an attractive setting near the Avon River in the parish church where Shakespeare is buried (with the famous epitaph, "and curst be he who moves my bones"). The church is one of the most beautiful parish churches in England.

On the banks of the Avon, "whit gentle murmur glides," the church dates from the 13th century, its entrance framed by an avenue of lime trees. To see Will's grave, head for the chancel, which was reconstructed from 1465 to 1491 in the Perpendicular style, the tomb lit by stained-glass windows. Shakespeare's prominent burial position in the church was not because of his literary abilities. He earned this stellar tomb because he was a lay-rector in Stratford-upon-Avon. In 1623, Gerald Janse created a marble bust of Shakespeare that can be seen on the north wall of the sanctuary over the altar steps. In the chancel you'll also find the grave of Anne Hathaway, Shakespeare's wife, their daughter, Susanna, and her husband, John Hall. The Parish Register here displays the Bard's baptismal entry from 1564 and his burial notice from 1616.

Harvard House. High St. ☎ **01789/204507.** Free admission. Mar–Oct Tues–Sat 10am–4:30pm, Sun 10:30am–4pm. Closed Monday.

The most ornate home in Stratford, Harvard House is a fine example of an Elizabethan town house. Rebuilt in 1596, it was once the home of Katherine Rogers, mother of John Harvard, founder of Harvard College. In 1909, the house was purchased by a Chicago millionaire, Edward Morris, who presented it as a gift to the famous American university. The rooms are filled with period furniture, and the floors are made of local flagstone. Look for the Bible Chair, used for hiding the Bible during the days of Tudor persecution.

GUIDED TOURS

Guided tours of Stratford-upon-Avon leave from near the **Guide Friday Tourism Center,** Civic Hall, Rother Street (☎ 01789/294466). In summer, open-top double-decker buses depart every 15 minutes daily from 9am to 5:30pm (from 10am to 3pm in winter). You can take a 1-hour ride without stops, or you can get off at any or all of the town's five Shakespeare Properties. Although the bus stops are clearly marked along the historic route, the most logical starting point is on the sidewalk in front of the Pen & Parchment Pub, at Bridgefoot, at the bottom of Bridge Street. Tour tickets are valid all day, so you can hop on and off the buses wherever you want. The tours are £8 ($13.20) for adults, £6.50 ($10.75) for senior citizens or students, and £2.50 ($4.15) for children under 16. A family ticket sells for £18.50 ($30.55), and children under 5 go for free.

✪ GOING TO THE PLAYS

On the banks of the Avon, the **Royal Shakespeare Theatre,** Waterside, Stratford-upon-Avon CV37 6BB (☎ **01789/295623**), is a major showcase for the Royal Shakespeare Company. Seating 1,500 people, the theater's company includes some of the finest actors on the British stage. In an average season, five Shakespearean plays are staged. In 1999, the season will run through September; the season in 2000 will last from March 8 to October 5.

You'll usually need reservations. There are two successive booking periods, each one opening about 2 months in advance. You can make reservations with a North American or an English travel agent. A small number of tickets are always held for sale on the day of a performance, but it may be too late for a good seat if you wait until you arrive in Stratford. Tickets can be booked through New York agents **Edwards and Edwards** or **Keith Prowse** (who will add a service charge) or directly with the theater box office by major credit card. (For both U.K. and U.S. contact information for both agents, see p. 284 in chapter 9.) The box office is open Monday to Saturday from 9am to 8pm, but closes at 6pm on days when there are no performances. The price of seats ranges from £7 to £49 ($11.55 to $80.85). You can make a credit card reservation and pick up your tickets on the performance day, but you must cancel at least 2 full weeks in advance to get a refund.

Opened in 1986, the **Swan Theatre** is architecturally connected to the back of its older counterpart and shares the same box office, address, and phone number. It seats 430 on three sides of the stage, much as it would be in an Elizabethan playhouse. The Swan presents a repertoire of about five plays per season, with tickets ranging from £9 to £30 ($14.85 to $49.50).

The most recent addition to the Royal Shakespeare complex is **The Other Place,** a small, starkly minimalist theater located on Southern Lane, about 300 yards from its better-established counterparts. It was redesigned in 1996 as an experimental workshop theater without a permanent stage; seats can be radically repositioned (or removed completely) throughout the theater. Examples of recent presentations include a "promenade production" of *Julius Caesar,* in which the actors spent the whole play moving freely among a stand-up audience. Tickets are sold at the complex's main box office and generally range from £12 to £21 ($19.80 to $34.65), though this is subject to change.

The Swan Theatre has a **painting gallery** (☎ **01789/412602**) with a basic collection of portraits of famous actors and scenes from Shakespeare's plays by 18th- and 19th-century artists. The gallery also houses occasional small exhibitions. It also operates as a base for guided tours of both the Swan and Shakespeare theatres, with lively running commentary through the world-famous theaters. Guided tours are not conducted on a daily basis, but are subject to production schedules. Call beforehand to check times. Tours, which include stopovers at the souvenir shop, cost £4 ($6.60) for adults, £3 ($4.95) for students or senior citizens. Call ahead for tour times.

WHERE TO STAY

During the long theater season, it's best to reserve in advance. However, the **Tourist Information Center** (part of the national "Book-a-Bed-Ahead" service, which enables visitors to make reservations in advance) will help find accommodations in all ranges. The fee for room reservations made is 10% of the first night's stay (bed-and-breakfast rate only), deductible from the visitor's final bill.

VERY EXPENSIVE

✪ **Welcombe Hotel.** Warwick Rd., Stratford-upon-Avon, Warwickshire CV37 ONR. ☎ **01789/295252.** Fax 01789/414666. www.welcombe.co.uk. E-mail:sales@welcombe.

co.uk. 68 units. TV TEL. £175 ($288.75) double; £250–£295 ($412.50–$486.75) suite. Rates include English breakfast. DC, MC, V. Take A439 1½ miles northeast of the town center.

For a formal, historic hotel in Stratford, there's none better. One of England's great Jacobean country houses, this hotel is a 10-minute ride from the heart of Stratford-upon-Avon. Its keynote feature is an 18-hole golf course. It's surrounded by 157 acres of grounds and has a formal entrance on Warwick Road, a winding driveway leading to the main hall. Guests gather for afternoon tea or drinks on the rear terrace, with its Italian-style garden and steps leading down to flower beds. The public rooms are heroic in size, with high mullioned windows providing views of the park. Regular bedrooms—some seemingly big enough for tennis matches—are luxuriously furnished; those in the garden wing, although comfortable, are small. Some of the bedrooms are sumptuously furnished with elegant four-posters; all of them, however, have fine mattresses and deluxe linens. Each luxurious bathroom has monogrammed robes, a phone, fine toiletries, a hair dryer, and a rack of quality towels.

Dining: The hotel's restaurant offers a traditional mix of French and English dishes, although cuisine is not the major reason to check in here.

Amenities: 24-hour room service, laundry service and dry cleaning, baby-sitting, courtesy car, 18-hole 6,202-yard golf course, tennis courts, putting green.

EXPENSIVE

Alveston Manor Hotel. Clopton Bridge, Stratford-upon-Avon, Warwickshire CV37 7HP. ☎ **800/225-5843** or 01789/204581. Fax 01789/414095. www.stratforduponavon.co.uk/ alveston.htm. 114 units. TV TEL. £140–£160 ($231–$264) double; £180–£240 ($297–$396) suite. AE, DC, MC, V.

This Tudor manor is perfect for theatergoers—it's just a 2-minute walk from the Avon off B4066. The Alveston is one of the most atmospheric choices within the town itself. The hotel has a wealth of chimneys and gables, and everything from an Elizabethan gazebo to Queen Anne windows. Mentioned in the *Domesday Book,* the building predates the arrival of William the Conqueror. The rooms in the manor house will appeal to those who appreciate the old-world charm of slanted floors, overhead beams, and antique furnishings. Some triples or quads are available in the modern section, which is connected by a covered walk through the rear garden. The rooms here have built-in pieces and a color-coordinated decor; 15 are set aside for nonsmokers. Frankly, your opinion of this hotel will depend on your room assignment. You can live in luxury in the original rooms with imported walnut furniture, or else be assigned a rather routine standard twin which, though comfortable, will lack romance. Each room, however, is fitted with a quality mattress; and each has a combination bath (tub and shower), plus a set of medium-size towels. The lounges are in the manor; there's a view of the centuries-old tree at the top of the garden—said to have been the background for the first presentation of *A Midsummer Night's Dream.* Logs burn in the Tudor fireplace in the main living room, with its linen-fold paneling.

Dining: Meals are served amid oak beams and leaded-glass windows in the softly lit **Manor Grill.** This isn't, however, fine or intimate dining (bus tours stop here). But the bar, paneled in 16th-century oak, never closes, and is the best place in Stratford for a drink at any time.

Amenities: 24-hour room service, concierge, laundry service, conference room. A health club and massage service is nearby for an additional fee.

Stratford Moat House. Bridgefoot, Stratford-upon-Avon, Warwickshire CV37 6YR. ☎ **01789/279988.** Fax 01789/298589. 251 units. TV TEL. £140 ($231) double; £120 ($198) suite. AE, DC, MC, V.

Moat House stands on 5 acres of landscaped lawns on the banks of the River Avon near Clopton Bridge. Although lacking the charm of the Alveston Manor, as far as amenities go, this modern hotel is just as highly rated as the Welcombe. It's one of the flagships of Queens Moat Houses, a British hotel chain, and was built in the early 1970s and last renovated in 1995. The hotel hosts many conferences, so don't expect to have the place to yourself. Every medium-size bedroom has a high standard of comfort, especially the mattresses, with bathrooms with generous shelf space, good towels, large mirrors, coffeemakers, and hair dryers.

Dining: The restaurant features a standard British and continental menu, as well as a carvery of hot and cold roasts. You can drink in the **Tavern Pub** and in the **Terrace Nightspot,** a disco open Friday and Saturday from 10pm to 2am. Cover charge is £2.50 ($4.15) after 10:30pm.

Amenities: 24-hour room service, laundry service, and a leisure complex with a swimming pool.

MODERATE

The Arden Thistle Hotel. 44 Waterside, Stratford-upon-Avon, Warwickshire CV37 6BA. ☎ **01789/294949.** Fax 01789/415874. www.stratforduponavon.uk.ardenhtm. E-mail: stratford.uponavon@thistle.co.uk. 63 units. TV TEL. £122 ($201.30) double. AE, DC, MC, V.

Theatergoers flock to this hotel across the street from the main entrance of the Royal Shakespeare and Swan theatres. The Thistle chain completely refurbished the interior after buying the Arden in 1993. Its redbrick main section dates from the Regency period, although over the years a handful of adjacent buildings were included and an uninspired modern extension added. Today, the interior has a well-upholstered lounge and bar, a dining room with bay windows, a covered garden terrace, and comfortable but narrow bedrooms with trouser presses and hot-beverage facilities. Even though small, rooms have a sitting area with a couple of armchairs and round-side tables, plus twin beds (most often), each with a firm mattress. Sometimes a room is graced with a four-poster bed. The bathrooms are small but efficient, with a hair dryer and a combination shower and tub. The restaurant offers continental and English dishes, but don't expect much.

Dukes. Payton St., Stratford-upon-Avon, Warwickshire CV37 6UA. ☎ **01789/269300.** Fax 01789/414700. www.astanet.com/get/dukeshtl. 22 units. TV TEL. £69.50–£100 ($114.70–$165) double. Rates include English breakfast. AE, MC, V.

Located north of Guild Street in the center of Stratford, this little charmer was formed when two Georgian town houses were united and restored. It's a good place to escape the crowds that overrun such properties as the Falcon. The family-operated inn has a large garden and is close to Shakespeare's birthplace. The public areas and bedrooms are attractive, having been restored to an impressive degree of comfort and coziness. The furniture is tasteful, much of it antique. Bedrooms, ranging from small to medium, are constantly being renovated, so standards are high here. Rooms have firm mattresses and such extras as coffeemakers, and the small bathrooms are equipped with medium-size towels and a hair dryer. Dukes also serves a good English and continental cuisine. No children under 12 are accepted here. Despite the reasonable rates (for England, anyway), the hotel offers many amenities that you would find in a more expensive hotel: room service, concierge, and dry cleaning and laundry service.

Falcon. Chapel St., Stratford-upon-Avon, Warwickshire CV37 6HA. ☎ **01789/279953.** Fax 01789/414260. 84 units. TV TEL. £110 ($181.50) double; £130 ($214.50) suite. AE, DC, MC, V.

Falcon is a blend of the very old and the very new. The black-and-white timbered inn was licensed a quarter of a century after Shakespeare's death; connected to its rear by a glass passageway is a more sterile bedroom extension added in 1970. In the heart of Stratford, the inn faces the Guild Chapel and the New Place Gardens. You arrive at the rear portion to unload luggage, just as horse-drawn coaches once dispatched their passengers—except that today you might be jostled by a tour group checking in. The recently upgraded rooms in the mellow part have oak beams, diamond leaded-glass windows, some antiques, good reproductions, and such extras as radios, electric trouser presses, and coffeemakers, but not enough soundproofing to drown out the BBC on your next-door neighbor's telly. Carved headboards crown beds with firm mattresses. Bathrooms aren't special, some with brown linoleum floors and plastic tub enclosures. Each has a rack of medium-size towels.

The comfortable lounges, also recently upgraded, are some of the finest in the Midlands. In the intimate Merlin Lounge is an open copper-hooded fireplace where coal and log fires are kept burning under beams salvaged from old ships (the walls are a good example of wattle and daub, typical of Shakespeare's day). The Oak Bar is a forest of weathered beams, and on either side of the stone fireplace is paneling removed from the poet's last home, New Place. Most meals are à la carte, unless you prefer to eat in the bar, where platters are offered.

Grosvenor House Hotel. 12–14 Warwick Rd., Stratford-upon-Avon, Warwickshire CV37 6YT. ☎ **01789/269213.** Fax 01789/266087. 67 units. TV TEL. £85 ($140.25) double. AE, DC, MC, V.

A pair of Georgian town houses, built in 1832 and 1843, respectively, were joined together to form this hotel, which is one of the second-tier choices of Stratford on equal footing with Dukes or the Arden Thistle. Situated in the center of town, with lawns and gardens to the rear, it is a short stroll from the intersection of Bridge Street and Waterside, allowing easy access to the Avon River, Bancroft Gardens, and the Royal Shakespeare Theatre. All the small–to–medium-size bedrooms have trouser presses and firm mattresses, as well as tea- and coffeemakers. Bathrooms are small but well maintained, with medium-size towels and a hair dryer. The informal bar (open until midnight) and terrace offer relaxation before or after you lunch or dine in the large restaurant, whose floor-to-ceiling windows face the gardens.

White Swan. Rother St., Stratford-upon-Avon, Warwickshire CV37 6NH. ☎ **800/ 225-5843** in the U.S. and Canada, or 01789/297022. Fax 01789/268773. 41 units. TV TEL. £90 ($148.50) double; £110 ($181.50) suite. Children up to 16 stay free in parents' room. Rates include English breakfast. AE, DC, MC, V.

This cozy, intimate hotel is one of the most atmospheric in Stratford and is, in fact, its oldest building. In business for more than a century before Shakespeare appeared on the scene, it competes successfully with the Falcon in offering an ancient atmosphere. The gabled medieval front would present the Bard with no surprises, but the modern comforts inside would surely astonish him, even though many of the rooms have been preserved. Paintings dating from 1550 hang on the lounge walls. All bedrooms are well appointed; amenities include a radio, trouser press, a coffeemaker, and a firm mattress. Bathrooms are small but have a tub and shower combination, plus a hair dryer and a rack of medium-size towels. The hostelry has a spacious restaurant where good food is served. The oak-beamed bar is a popular meeting place (see "Pubs," below).

INEXPENSIVE

Sequoia House. 51–53 Shipston Rd., Stratford-upon-Avon, Warwickshire CV37 7LN. ☎ **01789/268852.** Fax 01789/414559. www.stratford-upon-avon.co.uk/sequoia.htm.

E-mail:info@sequoiahotel.co.uk. 24 units (20 with bath or shower). TV TEL. £65–£75 ($107.25–$123.75) double without bath, £75–£82.50 ($123.75–$136.15) double with bath. Rates include English breakfast. AE, DC, MC, V.

This privately run hotel has its own beautiful garden across the Avon opposite the theater, conveniently located for visiting the major Shakespeare sites. Renovation has vastly improved the house, which was created from two late-Victorian buildings. Bedrooms come in various shapes and sizes, and there is a constant program of refurbishment. Bedrooms have fine beds and are warmly decorated and color coordinated. Bathrooms are small, seven with a shower and tub combination, the others with a shower stall. Guests gather in a lounge that has a licensed bar and an open Victorian fireplace.

✪ **Stratheden Hotel.** 5 Chapel St., Stratford-upon-Avon, Warwickshire CV37 6EP. ☎ **01789/297119.** Fax 01789/297119. 9 units. TV TEL. £60–£66 ($99–$108.90) double. Rates include English breakfast. MC, V.

A short walk north of the Royal Shakespeare Theatre, this hotel is tucked away in a desirable position on a plot of land that was first mentioned in a property deed in 1333. Built in 1673 and today the oldest-remaining brick building in the town center, it has a tiny rear garden and top-floor rooms with slanted, beamed ceilings. Under the ownership of the Wells family for the past quarter century, it has improved again in both decor and comfort with the addition of fresh paint, new curtains, and good beds. Tea- and coffeemakers allow you to have a "cuppa" any time of the day or night. Units range in size from small to medium, but each comes with a good, comfortable bed, plus a small bath, with a hair dryer and a set of medium-size towels. Three units have only a tub, the rest showers. The dining room, with a bay window, has an overscale sideboard that once belonged to the "insanely vain" Marie Corelli, an eccentric novelist, poet, and mystic, and a favorite author of Queen Victoria. Corelli was noted for her passion for pastoral settings and objets d'art. You can see an example of her taste: a massive mahogany tester bed in Room 4.

WHERE TO DINE
MODERATE

The Box Tree Restaurant. In the Royal Shakespeare Theatre, Waterside. ☎ **01789/293226.** Reservations required. Matinee lunch £16.50 ($27.20); dinner £25.50–£28 ($42.05–$46.20). AE, MC, V. Thurs–Sat noon–2:30pm; Mon–Sat 5:45pm–midnight. FRENCH/ITALIAN/ENGLISH.

This restaurant enjoys the best location in town—in the theater itself—with its glass walls providing an unobstructed view of swans on the Avon. You can partake of an intermission snack of smoked salmon and champagne, or dine by flickering candlelight after the performance. Many dishes such as apple-and-parsnip soup are definitely old English; others reflect a continental touch, such as fried polenta with fillets of pigeon and bacon. For your main course, you might select Dover sole, salmi of wild boar, pheasant, or roast pork loin. Homemade desserts are likely to include crème brûlée, an old-time favorite at The Box Tree. There's a special phone for reservations in the theater lobby.

Greek Connection. 1 Shakespeare St. ☎ **01789/292214.** Reservations recommended. Main courses £8.50–£17.50 ($14–$28.90). MC, V. Daily 5:30–10:30pm. GREEK/INTERNATIONAL.

Situated in the heart of Stratford within a 3-minute walk of Shakespeare's birthplace, the Greek Connection occupies the vaulted premises of what was formerly a Methodist chapel built in 1854, which also put in service for a time as an automobile museum. The restaurant serves authentic Greek cuisine, accompanied by live Greek music and dancing nightly. Chefs Spiros and George serve a variety of Greek and international dishes from an à la carte menu. Their moussaka is especially inspiring; the chefs piquantly season freshly minced meat between layers of sliced eggplant, zucchini, and potato, crowning the layers with a creamy dome of béchamel and sprinkled Parmesan cheese, swelled like a soufflé through baking (they also offer a vegetarian version). The kebab charcoal grill holds a prime place in the kitchen, where lamb, pork, and chicken are barbecued over wood embers. Appetizers range from stuffed vine leaves to the famed *avgolemono* (chicken-and-rice soup creamed with beaten eggs and flavored with lemon). Many prefer the *mezedakia*, a sampling of Greek hors d'oeuvres. On Saturday nights, once dinner is over, the tables are swept away, and the restaurant turns into a disco.

INEXPENSIVE

✪ **Hussain's.** 6A Chapel St. (across from the Shakespeare Hotel and historic New Place). ☎ **01789/267506.** Reservations recommended. Main courses £5.95–£11.50 ($9.80–$18.95). AE, DC, MC, V. Daily 12:30–2:30pm and 5pm–midnight. INDIAN.

Similar to a private Indian home, this restaurant has many admirers—some consider it one of the brighter spots on the bleak culinary landscape hereabouts. The owner has chosen a well-trained, welcoming, alert staff. You can select from an array of northern Indian tandooris plus various curries with lamb or prawn. There is a three-course lunch from 12:30 to 2:30pm for £5.95 ($9.80). Fixed-price pre- and post-theater dinners are also available.

The Opposition. 13 Sheep St. ☎ **01789/269980.** Reservations recommended. Main courses £5.95–£19.95 ($9.80–$32.90). MC, V. Daily noon–2pm and 5:30–11pm. INTERNATIONAL.

Located in the heart of Stratford, in a 16th-century building, this is a refreshingly unpretentious restaurant with a high turnover of loyal clients drawn to the good bistro cookery at reasonable prices. Choices include chicken cooked with spinach, stuffed with mango and curry, or prepared Cajun-style; salmon either grilled or poached and served with hollandaise; and grilled sirloin or filet of beef. In case you wondered what Banoffi pie is (a specialty here), it's made with toffee, bananas, biscuits, and whipped cream.

PUBS

The Black Swan ("The Dirty Duck"). Waterside. ☎ **01789/297312.** Reservations required for dining. Main courses £7–£12 ($11.55–$19.80); bar snacks £3.50–£7.25 ($5.75–$11.95). AE, DC, MC, V (restaurant only). Pub Mon–Sat 11am–11pm; Sun noon–10:30pm. Restaurant Tues–Sun noon–2pm; Mon–Sat 6–11:30pm. ENGLISH.

Affectionately known as "The Dirty Duck," this has been a popular hangout for Stratford players since the 18th century. The wall is lined with autographed photos of its patrons such as Lord Olivier. The front lounge and bar crackles with intense conversation; in the spring and fall, an open fire blazes. Typical English grills are featured in the Grill Room, never accused of serving the best food in Stratford. You'll be faced with a choice of a dozen appetizers, most of which would make a meal in themselves. Main dishes include goose pie, roast chicken, or honey-roasted duck. In fair weather, you can have drinks in the front garden and watch the swans glide by on the Avon.

The Garrick Inn. 25 High St. ☎ **01789/292186.** Main courses £5–£10 ($8.25–$16.50). MC, V. Meals daily noon–8:30pm. Pub Mon–Sat 11am–11pm; Sun noon–10:30pm. ENGLISH.

Near Harvard House, this black-and-white timbered Elizabethan pub dating from 1595 has an unpretentious charm. The front bar is decorated with tapestry-covered settles, an old oak refectory table, and an open fireplace that attracts the locals. The black bar has a circular fireplace with a copper hood and mementos of the triumphs of the English stage. The specialty is homemade pies such as steak and ale, steak and kidney, or cottage pie.

White Swan. In the White Swan Hotel, Rother St. ☎ **01789/297022.** Dinner reservations recommended. Bar snacks £2–£6 ($3.30–$9.90); fixed-price 3-course dinner £16.95 ($27.95). AE, DC, MC, V. Morning coffee daily 10am–noon; self-service bar snacks daily 12:30–2pm; afternoon tea daily 2–5:30pm; dinner Mon–Thurs 6–9pm, Fri–Sat 6–9:30pm, Sun 7–9pm. ENGLISH.

Housed in the town's oldest building, this is one of the most atmospheric pubs in Stratford. Once you step inside, you're drawn into a world of cushioned leather armchairs, old oak settles, oak paneling, and fireplaces. You're likely to meet a worthy cross section of amiable drinkers in a setting once enjoyed by Shakespeare himself, when it was known as the Kings Head. At lunch you can partake of the hot dishes of the day, along with fresh salads and sandwiches.

6 Salisbury & Stonehenge

90 miles SW of London

Long before you've even entered Salisbury, the spire of Salisbury Cathedral will come into view—just as John Constable painted it so many times. The 404-foot pinnacle of the early English and Gothic cathedral is the tallest in England. Salisbury, or New Sarum, lies in the valley of the Avon River, and is a fine base for touring such sights as Stonehenge. Filled with Tudor inns and tearooms, it's known to readers of Thomas Hardy as Melchester and to fans of Anthony Trollope as Barchester.

Salisbury today is often viewed as only a "refueling stop" or overnight stopover for visitors anxious to explore Stonehenge. However, the old market town is an interesting destination in its own right. There's another reason some visitors like to drop off at Salisbury, the only true city in Wiltshire: Its pub-to-citizen ratio is said to be the highest in the country.

ESSENTIALS

GETTING THERE   A **Network Express** train departs hourly from Waterloo Station in London bound for Salisbury (trip time: 2 hours). For information, call ☎ **0345/484950** or 01603/764776.

Five **National Express** buses per day run from London Monday to Friday. On Saturday and Sunday, four buses depart Victoria Coach Station for Salisbury (trip time: 2¹/₂ hours). For information, call ☎ **0990/808080.**

To drive from London, head west on M3 to the end of the run, continuing the rest of the way on A30.

VISITOR INFORMATION   The **Tourist Information Centre** is at Fish Row (☎ **01722/334956,** fax 01722/422059). From October to April, it's open Monday to Saturday 9:30am to 5pm; in May, Monday to Saturday 9:30am to 5pm and Sunday 10:30am to 4:30pm; in June and September, Monday to Saturday 9:30am to 6pm and Sunday 10:30am to 4:30pm; and in July and August, Monday to Saturday 9:30am to 7pm and on Sunday from 10:30am to 5pm.

SEEING THE SIGHTS

✪ **Salisbury Cathedral.** The Close. ☎ **01722/555120.** Suggested donation £3 ($4.95). May–Aug daily 9am–8:15pm; Sept–Apr daily 9am–6:15pm.

You can search all of England, but you'll find no better example of the early-English or pointed style than Salisbury Cathedral. Construction began as early as 1220 and took 38 years to complete; this was considered rather fast in those days since it was customary for the building of a cathedral to last at least a century. In spite of an ill-conceived renovation in the 18th century, Salisbury Cathedral's architectural integrity remains.

The cathedral's especially attractive 13th-century octagonal chapter house possesses one of the four surviving original texts of the Magna Carta, along with treasures from the diocese of Salisbury and manuscripts and artifacts belonging to the cathedral. The cloisters enhance the beauty of the cathedral, and its exceptionally large close, comprising at least 75 buildings, sets off the cathedral effectively.

✪ **Wilton House.** 3 miles west of Salisbury on A30. ☎ **01722/746729.** Admission £6.75 ($11.15) adults, £4 ($6.60) children 5–15, free for children under 5. Easter–Oct daily 10:30am–5:30pm. Last admission at 4:30pm.

In the town of Wilton is one of England's great country estates, the home of the earls of Pembroke. Wilton House dates from the 16th century, but it's most noted for its 17th-century state rooms by the celebrated architect Inigo Jones. Many famous people have lived or visited here; it's believed that Shakespeare's troupe entertained at Wilton. Preparations for the D-day landings at Normandy were laid out here by Eisenhower and his advisers, with only the silent Van Dyck paintings in the Double Cube Room as witnesses.

The house is filled with beautifully maintained furnishings and world-class art, including paintings by Van Dyck, Rubens, Brueghel, and Reynolds. A dynamic film introduced and narrated by Anna Massey brings to life the history of the family since 1544, the year they were granted the land by Henry VIII. You can then visit a reconstructed Tudor kitchen and Victorian laundry plus "The Wareham Bears," a collection of some 200 miniature dressed teddy bears.

You'll find giant cedars of Lebanon growing on the 21-acre estate, the oldest of which were planted in 1630. The Palladian Bridge was built in 1737 by the ninth earl of Pembroke and Roger Morris. The grounds include rose and water gardens, riverside and woodland walks, and a huge adventure playground for children.

✪ **Stonehenge.** Junction of A303 and A344/A360. ☎ **01980/624715.** Admission £4 ($6.60) adults, £3 ($4.95) students and seniors, £2 ($3.30) children, family ticket £10 ($16.50). Mar 16–May and Sept–Oct 15 daily 9:30am–6pm; June–Aug daily 9am–7pm; Oct 16–Mar 15 daily 9:30am–4pm. Bus: Stonehenge.

Two miles west of Amesbury and about 9 miles north of Salisbury is the renowned Stonehenge stone circle, believed to be anywhere from 3,500 to 5,000 years old. This huge circle of lintels and megalithic pillars is the most important prehistoric monument in Britain. Some are disappointed when they see that Stonehenge is nothing more than concentric circles of stones surrounded by a fence. Keep in mind, however, that many of the boulders—the bluestones in particular—were quarried and moved from sites as far away as southern Wales in a time before forklifts, lorries, and dynamite.

The widely held view of 18th- and 19th-century romantics that Stonehenge was the work of the Druids is without foundation. The boulders, many weighing several tons, are believed to have predated the arrival in Britain of the Celtic cult. Recent excavations continue to bring new evidence to bear on the origin and purpose of Stonehenge. *Stonehenge Decoded,* by Gerald S. Hawkins and John B. White, maintains that the site was an astronomical observatory—that is, a Neolithic "computing machine" capable of predicting eclipses.

Your ticket permits you to go inside the fence surrounding the site that protects the stones from vandals and souvenir hunters and as far as a short rope barrier about 50 feet from the stones. A modular walkway has been introduced to cross the archaeologically important avenue, the area that runs between the Heel Stone and the main circle of stones. This enables visitors to complete a full circuit of the stones and to see

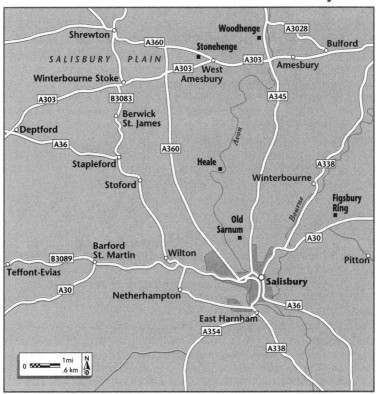

one of the best views of a completed section of Stonehenge as they pass by. This is an excellent addition to the well-received audio tour introduced in 1995.

WHERE TO STAY
MODERATE

✪ **Grasmere House.** 70 Harnham Rd., Salisbury, Wiltshire SP2 8JN. ☎ **01722/338388.** Fax 01722/333710. 20 units. TV TEL. £95–£125 ($156.75–$206.25) double. Rates include English breakfast. AE, DC, MC, V. Take A3094 1½ miles from the center of town.

Grasmere stands near the confluence of the Nadder and Avon rivers on 1½ acres of grounds. Constructed in 1896 for Salisbury merchants, the house still resembles a family home. Many old features were retained, including a "calling box" for servants in the dining room. Three luxurious bedrooms overlook the cathedral, as does a new conservatory bar. The original house holds four bedrooms; the rest are in the new wing. Most of the accommodations are quite roomy, and two are arranged for persons with disabilities. Each comes with a firm mattress, coffeemaker, and trouser press. The bathrooms are tidily arranged but small, but there is enough shelf space; each has medium-size towels and a hair dryer. The house operates a restaurant popular with locals and residents alike. Steaks are a specialty, ranging from flambéed to au poivre.

✪ **The Rose and Crown.** Harnham Rd., Salisbury, Wiltshire SP2 8JQ. ☎ **01722/399955.** Fax 01722/339816. 28 units. TV TEL. £135–£145 ($222.75–$239.25) double; £160–£165 ($264-$272.25) suite. AE, DC, MC, V. Take A3094 1½ miles from the center of town.

This half-timbered, 13th-century inn stands with its feet almost in the Avon River; beyond the water you can see the tall spire of the cathedral. Because of its more tranquil location, we prefer it to either the White Hart or the Red Lion; you can easily walk over the arched stone bridge to the center of Salisbury from here in 10 minutes or so. The lawns and gardens between the inn and the river are shaded by old trees, and chairs are set out so that you can enjoy the view and count the swans. The inn, part of the Queens Moat House Hotels chain, has both an old wing and a modern new one. The old wing has more appeal, with sloping ceilings and antique fireplaces and furniture. Each room has a radio, coffeemaker, firm mattress, and trouser press, sometimes a four-poster. The newer rooms have bland furnishings. Bathrooms are small, and contain a rack of medium-size towels and a hair dryer. You can dine on English fare while overlooking the river. Across the courtyard are two taverns; you can choose either of two bars with oak beams and log fires. Services include room service and laundry.

White Hart. 1 St. John St., Salisbury, Wiltshire SP1 2SD. ☎ **01722/327476.** Fax 01722/412761. 68 units. TV TEL. £107-£136 ($176.55-$224.40) double; £107-£124 ($176.55-$204.60) suite. AE, MC, V.

Combining the best of old and new, the White Hart has been a Salisbury landmark since Georgian times. Its classic facade is intact, with tall columns crowning a life-size effigy of a hart. The older accommodations are more traditional, and a new section with modern but blander appointments has been added in the rear, opening onto a large parking area—like a motel. Bedrooms range from small to large, and many are furnished in the English country house tradition as if Laura Ashley has swept through. The most desirable is a trio of rooms with old-fashioned four-poster beds. All, however, have firm mattresses and tasteful appointments. Bathrooms are small but neatly arranged, with a hair dryer, shelf space, and a rack of medium-size towels. The hotel was completely refurbished in 1995. You can enjoy a before-dinner drink in White Hart, followed by a meal in the White Hart Restaurant for £10 to £17 ($16.50 to $28.05).

INEXPENSIVE

✪ **The New Inn & Old House.** 39–47 New St., Salisbury, Wiltshire SP1 2PH. ☎ **01722/327679.** 7 units. TV. £49.50–£69.50 ($81.70–$114.70)double. Rates include continental breakfast. AE, MC, V. Free parking.

This upscale B&B is one of the finest in Salisbury but, despite its name, isn't new at all. It's a 15th-century building with a walled garden backing up to the Cathedral Close Wall. Its bedrooms are well appointed, oak beamed, and evocative of an earlier century. Rooms are small but cozy, each maintaining the standard of a "good pub hotel," with a comfortable bed and a small bath with old plumbing that still works beautifully. The inn's center is the serving bar, which adjoins onto three outer rooms: one, a tiny sitting area; another, a tavern with high-backed settles and a fireplace; and the third, a lounge. In the Inn, main courses are reasonably priced. Adjacent to the main building is a coffee house and gift shop. This was the first no-smoking facility in the U.K.

WHERE TO DINE

The best restaurants are found not in the core of Salisbury itself but on the outskirts— the Silver Plough at Pitton (see below) or Howard's House at Teffont Evias.

Harper's Restaurant. 7–9 Ox Row, Market Sq. ☎ **01722/333118.** Reservations recommended. Main courses £5.90–£12.50 ($9.75–$20.65); fixed-price 2-course meal £7 ($11.55) at lunch (and before 7pm), £8.50 ($14) at dinner. AE, DC, MC, V. Mon–Sat noon–2pm and 6–9:30pm (Sat until 10pm); Sun 6–9pm. Closed Sun Oct–May. ENGLISH/INTERNATIONAL.

The chef-owner of this place prides himself on specializing in "real food"—homemade, uncomplicated, and wholesome. The pleasantly decorated restaurant is on the second floor of a redbrick building at the backside of Salisbury's largest parking lot, in the center of town. Typical meals may include roast Barbary duck served on a red wine, plum, ginger-and–star anise confit, all-vegetarian pasta diavolo, or poached Scotch salmon with a lemon-and-chive hollandaise. Finish off with a chocolate mousse. In what has always been a gastronomic wasteland of England, food has exceptional flair and flavor.

Salisbury Haunch of Venison. 1 Minster St. ☎ **01722/322024.** Main courses £9–£12 ($14.85–$19.80); bar platters for lunches, light suppers, and snacks £4–£6 ($6.60–$9.90). AE, MC, V. Restaurant daily noon–2:30pm; Mon–Sat 7–9:30pm. Pub Mon–Sat 11am–11pm and Sun 7–11pm. Closed Christmas and Easter. ENGLISH.

Right in the heart of Salisbury, this creaky-timbered, 1320 chophouse serves excellent dishes, especially English roasts and grills. Stick to its specialties and you'll rarely go wrong. Begin perhaps with tasty warm salad of venison sausages with garlic croutons, and then follow with the house specialty: roast haunch of venison with garlic and juniper berries. Many other classic English dishes are served as well including a medley of fish and shellfish or else grilled Barnsley lamb chops with "bubble and squeak" (cabbage and potatoes).

The centuries have given a gleam to the oak furnishings, and years of polishing have worn down the brass. Tortuous steps lead to tiny, cozy rooms (there is one small room with space for about four to sit, where you can revel in England's past, present, and future). Two of the restaurant windows overlook St. Thomas's cloisters.

IN NEARBY PITTON

Silver Plough. White Hill, Pitton, near Salisbury. ☎ **01722/712266.** Reservations recommended. Main courses £6.95–£11.95 ($11.45–$19.70); bar platters £3.50–£8 ($5.75–$13.20). AE, DC, MC, V. Restaurant daily noon–2pm; Mon–Sat 7–10pm, Sun 7–10pm. Pub Mon–Sat 11am–3pm and 6–11pm; Sun noon–3pm and 7–10:30pm. Closed for some meals Dec 25–26 and Jan 1. Take A30 5 miles east of Salisbury; it's at the southern end of the hamlet of Pitton. ENGLISH.

Built as a stone-sided farmhouse 150 years ago, the Silver Plough is now a charming and accommodating country pub with a restaurant specializing in fish and game dishes. Its heavily beamed ceilings are hung with tankards, coach horns, and other country-inspired memorabilia. Snacks are available in the bar. In the somewhat more formal dining room, the chef prepares such dishes as king prawns cooked in garlic-and-lime butter, sliced breast of duck in cracked pepper or orange sauce, and roisettes of lamb, coated with a mint-and-honey sauce. The Silver Plough has known many famous visitors, but apart from displaying a signed letter from Queen Victoria thanking the women of England for their concern after the death of her husband, Albert, the management prefers to stick to its quiet, country atmosphere and to concentrate on making its guests feel at home.

Appendix:
London in Depth

More millions than ever before are preparing to descend on London and get a whiff of Blair's New Britain. With its projected new Millennium Dome at Greenwich, London may rival Rome in attracting end-of-the-century visitors. What is awaiting them is one of the world's truly vital cities, even if it's somewhat less English than ever before.

1 On the Cutting Edge: London Today

Like New York, London has become that most international of cities. As one observer on the scene told us, "Who in the world would want to live anywhere else? Possibly New York but that's it!"

The old Britishness—so lampooned by Americans—still exists. It's just harder to find. But it's there. Tune into a morning radio news show on the BBC and you can still hear 15 minutes of lecture on how to dunk a biscuit in a cup of tea, or how to achieve the best possible roses even when the weather doesn't cooperate.

Critics have suggested that the new cool Britain is public relations hype, superficial labeling, and cosmetic change. Naturally some of the change occurring is faddish and undoubtedly transitory, but much is real. As Britain's capital, London is still proud of its past (although it's got a lot to be ashamed of, too), but is no longer encumbered by its role as seat of an Empire.

Whatever his critics say, the young and charismatic prime minister, Tony Blair, no longer rules over "the sick man of Europe," as England was called when Margaret Thatcher took over in 1979. Today, he leads Europe's healthiest economy. Consumer-led industries such as music, design, entertainment, and cinema extend their cultural influence around the world. Yet for all the hype, London is presiding over one of the most volatile periods in British history. Britain is undergoing rapid change, moving from a social democracy into a market economy. Government-owned businesses have been privatized in one of the largest shifts in British property since the Reformation. Entire industries such as traditional coal and steel were allowed to wither and die before they blossomed again as well-run private businesses.

The city no longer speaks as much English as it did. A walk through London is like a visit to the Tower of Babel, as you hear Spanish, German, Italian, French, and most definitely Urdu.

Even the staid *New York Times Magazine*, on its front page, depicted Queen Victoria shedding a tear. The magazine headed a story by

Andrew Sullivan, provocatively called "The End of Britain." Sullivan, with some accuracy, warned that, "After four centuries, Great Britain is disappearing. Scotland and Wales are going their own ways, the House of Lords is under attack, the monarchy and the Constitution are being reinvented, and the currency could soon be abandoned."

It's hard to imagine a world without the British pound sterling. For the moment Britain has shunned the Euro, the new currency of the European Union that appears to be shaping up to give the dollar a fight for world supremacy. But one wonders as the Euro sweeps across the continent—can Britain survive as the financial center of the continent? Some are asking if Frankfurt might not become the capital of "Euroland," shutting London out or at least taking over a lot of its business in trading. That is, unless England agrees to abandon its beloved pound sterling and goes Euro crazy.

Incredible change is in the air. There's little doubt that "there will always be an England." The big question looming in the 21st century is, however, "Will there always be a Britain?" Will London indeed revert to becoming the capital of England, not of "Great Britain" or the "United Kingdom?"

Believe it or not, much of London, especially young London, seems to pay very little attention to these ponderous matters. "I don't ever plan to go to the Shetland Islands (Scottish islands to the north), so I don't bloody well care whether they're with us or not," one young Londoner told us.

As England's territory faces possible diminishment in the future, London remains the fun capital of Europe—even without the Euro. In fact, it's called the hottest, coolest city in the world.

The bundle of changes represent a restoration of confidence in London in the wake of 50 years of decline. London now accepts its position as the center of a diminished world power, though some conservative critics are aghast at the change. "Once," an irate MP said, "we ruled a great deal of the world. Now we are in danger of becoming a Disneyland for Americans who will no doubt demand that we parade the Queen out every day for their amusement."

Nothing gauges social change better than the monarchy itself. Following Diana's death, speculation raged that the queen would abdicate and that Prince Charles would never be king. Today Charles seems to be a liberated single parent and has even been getting good press for his charitable works. The queen's 50th wedding anniversary was called a "love-in" by the tabloids.

Comparisons to the Swinging '60s are everywhere—but there are differences, big and small, as noted by keen social critics. Although London is more open and dynamic than it's been since 1969, it's not just one giant house party this time. "The Swinging '60s were also the silly '60s," Conservative Member of Parliament Jonathan Aitken said in his book, *The Young Meteors*. "What's changed from last time is that [now] it's more hardheaded, less silly. There's a greater understanding that the world is a competitive place." Although seldom mentioned by the press, the awareness of AIDS also serves to keep today's London cooled down from a fever pitch.

It's the diversity of cultures and tastes that's really making the city so fascinating these days. It seems that half the world is flocking to London—currently one-fifth of London's population consists of ethnic minorities; based on present trends, those ethnic minorities are projected to rise to one-third of the city's population by the year 2010. The high-speed Eurostar rail link has brought the Continent to London's doorstep, but the invasion is of a kind Brits never expected: Many French (half of whom are under 25) now hop over for a bit of shopping and a good meal—almost unheard of until recently.

Impressions

And so the sun sets on the Thames, and all London's children, tucked in with bellies full of black puddings and bubble and squeak, dream dreams of a gleaming tomorrow . . . of a new Tate Gallery where the Bankside power station stands . . . of a new bridge from the Tate to St. Paul's Cathedral . . . of Sir Norman Foster's Millennium Tower pointing 76 stories into the glorious English sky. . . . Take care, Mum and Dad, to have smelling salts ready for the milkman—he won't believe his eyes when he makes his dawn round!

—David Kamp (1997)

There is some bad news. Traffic moves at exactly the same pace it did in the reign of Victoria. And pollution is still strong enough to have caused a rising rate of asthma in children. Unemployment remains at unacceptable rates, and racial tension is all too evident in London today, as is overcrowding.

But the Thames still flows through the city. The Queen is still on her throne (although her crown might be a bit shaky these days), and bobbies and Beefeaters are where you expect them to be. Playgoers flock to the latest productions; some 500,000 young clubgoers descend on London's clubland every Saturday night. Thousands of London pubs are as colorful as ever, and some are serving up better food than you can get at many restaurants. A born-and-bred Londoner recently said, with typical British understatement: "Even the sun itself shines on us now and again—if we're lucky."

2 History 101

Dateline

- **55 B.C.** Julius Caesar invades England; he lands just a short distance from present-day London.
- **A.D. 43** Roman armies defeat the Celts and establish a fortified camp called Londinium.
- **61** Celts from East Anglia burn and sack Londinium, but the settlement is repossessed by Romans.
- **410** Romans retreat from London and return to Europe.
- **886** King Alfred, a Saxon, conquers London but rules from his seat at Winchester.
- **1066** Norman invasion of England. William the Conqueror defeats Harold at the Battle of Hastings and is crowned in Westminster Abbey.

continues

The Celts, Romans & Early Middle Ages

London is a very old city by almost any standards. The oldest artifacts ever discovered in London and the first historical reference to the city date from the time of its occupation by the ancient Romans, who adapted a local Celtic name, "Lyn Din," into the Latinized form, Londinium.

Julius Caesar raided England in 55 and 54 B.C., fording the Thames with his armies somewhere downstream from today's London. By A.D. 61, Londinium had become a thriving port. That same year, a union of Celtic tribes, led by Queen Boadicea, attacked the unprotected rear flank of the Roman armies and burned the camp of Londinium to the ground. The Romans erected a much larger camp. Before they left, the Romans developed the city, but not to the status of a capital. While clearing World War II's rubble, a Roman temple and statues dedicated to various Greek deities were revealed. In the 2nd century, the Romans surrounded London with a massive wall; its remnants can still be seen.

The Romans advanced into northern England, as far as the site of Hadrian's Wall, but they faced continuous insurrection. By 410, Rome itself had come under siege, and the emperor

In the spring of 1997, Elizabeth II made history by launching the first official royal Web site. You can now find more than 150 pages of history, information, and trivia about the Windsors and the British monarchy online at **www.royal.gov.uk**.

Honorius ordered the Roman legions back home, leaving England isolated from the European mainland for some centuries.

By this time, the seeds of Christianity had been sown in England. In the 600s, London's first bishop, Mellitus, built a church in honor of St. Paul, but for the most part, London stagnated. A hodgepodge of medieval buildings arose, some in the middle of thoroughfares. The irregular medieval construction was continued by later generations of Londoners, who were usually required to respect the property lines of earlier owners and builders. As a result, independent neighborhoods and private enclaves developed.

The Saxons, Danes & Vikings   From about 449, Teutonic Saxons and Danes settled in England. Christianity was embraced or rejected according to who was in power. At one point, Mellitus, the reigning bishop, was banished, and London became rigidly and lustily pagan.

The Anglo-Saxons, as they were now known, were finally united under the first Saxon king, Alfred the Great, to oppose the constant threat of raids from the Norse Vikings. In 886, Alfred strengthened London's fortifications; he appointed his son-in-law as governor, while he continued to rule his growing kingdom from his capital at Winchester. For a century after Alfred's death (around 900), his heirs were occupied almost exclusively with securing and protecting their holdings against the Viking invaders.

Edward the Confessor (1003-66), who was later to be canonized, transferred his court and capital from Winchester to Westminster. He rebuilt Westminster Abbey, and Harold, the last of the Saxon rulers, was crowned there.

1066: The Normans Arrive   Harold ruled for only 9 months before the fateful Battle of Hastings in 1066. Here, with the victory of the Norman armies, led by William the Conqueror, the politics, bloodlines, language, and destiny of London and the Saxon kingdom were to change forever.

- **1100s** London asserts its right for some measure of self-government, establishing the office of Lord Mayor.
- **1400s** Trade flourishes in London.
- **1509–47** Reign of Henry VIII. His feud with Rome over his divorce leads to the English Reformation; church property is confiscated, and the English monarch is declared head of the new Church of England.
- **1558** Elizabeth I ascends throne, solidifying England's position as a Protestant country.
- **1586** William Shakespeare moves to London and buys part of the Globe Theatre.
- **1640s** The Civil War: Much fighting between Cromwellians and Royalists. King Charles I is beheaded at London's Whitehall (1649).
- **1660** Charles II restored to the throne.
- **1665** A plague decimates the population.
- **1666** Great Fire, started in a bakery in Pudding Lane, demolishes much of the city.
- **1710** Wren's St. Paul's Cathedral completed.
- **1710–1820** The arts thrive and London's population increases. Industrial Revolution begins.
- **1837–1901** Reign of Victoria, longest in English history.
- **1851** The Great Exhibition, the brainchild of Victoria's Prince Consort, Albert, is held at the Crystal Palace in

continues

Hyde Park to celebrate Britain's international dominance in trade, science, and industry.

- **1863** The Underground opens.
- **1888** "Jack the Ripper" terrorizes London's East End with the murders of six "women of ill repute."
- **1897** Queen Victoria's Diamond Jubilee. London described as the "centre of an empire on which the sun never sets."
- **1900–05** Four new electric Underground lines rapidly expand the city into sprawling suburbs.
- **1901** Edward VII ascends throne. The end of the Victorian age.
- **1914–18** The devastating Great War.
- **1920–30** Vast new housing estates, funded in part by the "Homes for Heroes" program, quadruple the size of London.
- **1940** The Blitz. London bombed, mainly in the City and East End. St. Paul's stands alone amid the rubble. The city's staunch resistance in the face of destruction is often remembered as London's "finest hour."
- **1945–55** Private and local government redevelopment results in fast modernization.
- **1951** The Festival of Britain celebrates the centennial of the Great Exhibition and gives birth to the South Bank Arts Centre.
- **1953** Elizabeth II ascends throne to begin long reign as head of the scandal-ridden House of Windsor.

continues

William was the first ruler to fully recognize the political importance of London. His coronation took place in Westminster Abbey, establishing a precedent that has been observed ever since. He recognized London as the capital and allowed the City of London to continue electing its own leaders—a decision that was to have far-reaching consequences. From that time on English monarchs, eager for the support of the country's wealthiest people, saw London as the key to controlling England.

By the 1400s, the banks of the Thames were lined with the warehouses and mansions of the wealthy London merchants. The population by this time had grown to 30,000. Ferryboats plied the waterway, and life burgeoned on both banks. Ecclesiastical establishments flourished. Many of their names—Blackfriars, Greyfriars, and Whitefriars—still remain part of contemporary London. The surbubs had by this time expanded beyond the City walls, but since there was no central planning, the roads developed haphazardly, creating the confusing street pattern that still exists today.

The Reformation & Elizabethan London
The modern history of London begins with the Tudors. Henry VIII built St. James's Palace and enclosed what is now Hyde Park and Green Park for his private grounds. Henry's Reformation (1530s), sparked by the Pope's refusal to grant him a divorce, made the English church independent of Rome. Unfortunately the Reformation and the dissolution of the monasteries led to the physical destruction of many medieval buildings. The wealth of the medieval Church was confiscated and redistributed to a newly appointed aristocracy willing to comply with Henry's wishes. London saw the executions of those who refused to acknowledge Henry's supremacy as head of the church. Among these were the humanist, Sir Thomas More, and Roman Catholic bishop John Fisher. Later, the city watched while two of Henry's wives, Anne Boleyn and Catherine Howard, were beheaded.

The convents, gardens, and priories of the Catholic church were divested and divided into narrow streets and overcrowded courtyards. The cripples and beggars who had been dependent on the church were unleashed, resourceless, on the population of London. Many recalcitrant nuns and monks, refusing to acknowledge the ecclesiastical leadership of the English monarch, were dragged through the streets to the scaffold, hanged by the neck, and disemboweled.

From the dissent, bloodshed, and strife of Reformation London sprang the creative juices of Elizabethan England, named for the great queen who reigned from 1558 to 1603. An era of peace and prosperity began under the tolerant queen. Poetry, theater, and spectacle flourished. William Shakespeare, arriving in London in 1586, bought part-ownership of the Globe Theatre, which was strategically located in Southwark, where the new Globe theater has been recreated today. (The puritanical City of London banned theaters, believing they attracted bad elements.) Plays by Shakespeare, Ben Jonson, and Christopher Marlowe were performed there. Along with the flowering of the arts, England, entered into a period of mercantile and colonial expansion in the Americas, Asia, and Africa, of which London was a prime beneficiary.

Plague, Fire & Revolution By the mid-1600s, London was crowded with half-timbered gabled houses topped by tile roofs. Streets were hopelessly narrow, especially those near the river, which London relied on for local transport and commerce as well as foreign trade.

In the 1640s, the conflict intensified between the Stuart monarch, Charles I, and the growing influence of the Puritans. But religion was not the only issue—Charles claimed the privileges of a king ruling by divine right against a Parliament that supported constitutional monarchy. The Puritan victory of 1649 culminated with Charles's execution in 1649 on the scaffold at Whitehall.

Under Oliver Cromwell's Protectorship, the arts were rigorously suppressed, and many of the important cathedrals were damaged—stained glass was smashed and altars destroyed. When the monarchy was restored in 1660 in the person of Charles II, everyone was relieved.

In 1665, the Great Plague swept through the city's overcrowded slums, claiming an estimated 75,000 lives. A year later, the Great Fire, which began in a bakery on Pudding Lane near London Bridge, destroyed much of the town, including 89 churches and 13,200 homes.

The 18th Century Urban planners, spearheaded by Sir Christopher Wren, used the tragedy of the fire as an opportunity to replan and rebuild London. The beauty of Wren's

- **1955–65** Boom years for property developers, who erect skyscrapers, while the state concentrates on suburban housing. Mass immigration from the Caribbean, India, Pakistan, and Hong Kong begins, continuing steadily for 15 years.
- **1960–70** "Swinging London." An economic and cultural boom, immigration, and changing values and wealth patterns make London more cosmopolitan.
- **1987** Conservatives under Margaret Thatcher win third term.
- **1990** John Major becomes prime minister.
- **1992** Royals jolted by fire at Windsor Castle and marital troubles of their two sons. Deep recession signals the end of the booming 1980s and the start of a more sober decade.
- **1994** For the first time since the Ice Age, England is linked to the Continent—this time by rail via the Channel Tunnel.
- **1996** The IRA breaks a 17-month cease-fire with a truck bomb at the Docklands that claims two lives. Her Majesty prompts Charles and Di's divorce after the affront of the Princess of Wales' latest tell-all biography; Prince Andrew and Sarah Ferguson's divorce finalized. The government concedes a possible link between "Mad Cow Disease" and a fatal brain ailment afflicting humans.
- **1997** World press hails British Renaissance, as London swings again. Upstart moderate Labour leader Tony Blair becomes the Prime Minister in a landslide, giving Britain its first Labour government in

continues

three decades. Death of Princess Di in a car crash in Paris sends Britain into national mourning.

- **1999** London readies the world's largest dome to welcome the millennium at Greenwich.

churches remains unequaled: They include St. Mary-le-Bow, one of the most famous, as well as St. Paul's Cathedral, both finished by 1710.

By this time, the aristocracy had begun migrating westward toward Covent Garden and Whitehall. The most convenient method of transportation was still via the Thames, while the sedan chair allowed aristocrats to be carried over the filthy streets, where dung, sewage, and refuse littered the undrained cobblestones.

Despite the hardships, the arts and sciences flourished in London. In the second half of the century, Joshua Reynolds painted his portraits, James Boswell wrote his reminiscences of lexicographer/critic/poet Samuel Johnson, David Garrick performed his famous Shakespearean roles, and some of the best landscape painting in the history of Europe was about to flower.

The spatial proportions of Georgian and (later) Regency architecture changed the facades of thousands of houses throughout London. For a limited number of citizens, the good life was bountiful, and London was the seat of all that was powerful, beautiful, desirable, intelligent, and witty.

The Victorian Age   The most visible industrial progress, as well as the greatest expansion of London, occurred during the Victorian era, when railroad lines and steam engines, sewage systems, cabs, underground trains, and new building techniques transformed London into a modern metropolis and hugely expanded its borders.

Victorian London was the center of the largest empire the world had ever seen. Londoners left their homes to fill military and administrative posts in such faraway dependencies as Calcutta, Kenya, Singapore, and Hong Kong. The art treasures of the world filled London's museums and private houses. In the poor neighborhood of east London, dyed-in-the-wool Londoners evolved the dialect and attitude later identified as Cockney; its accent and humor filled the city's music halls and vaudeville houses and influenced entertainment from Sydney to San Francisco. London thrived, burgeoning into one of the most complicated and diverse capitals of Europe. The population explosion in the 19th century meant that by 1902, London had almost 4½ million inhabitants.

The Dawn of the 20th Century   During the early 1900s, Victoria's successor, Edward VII, brought elaborate pageantry back to affairs of state (and a welcome laissez-faire attitude to affairs of the heart). Buckingham Palace was enlarged and sheathed in a honey-colored layer of stone, and a massive statue to Victoria was erected in front of its newly opened processional avenue leading to the Admiralty Arch. The controversial neo-Gothic grandeur of the Albert Memorial helped define the era's architectural style, which permeated vast neighborhoods of London with its eclecticism, ornateness, and high individualism.

The World Wars   World War I sent shock waves through Britain, although George V, who ascended the throne in 1910, ruled steadfastly from his London seat. Even if the damage was relatively minor compared to that later inflicted by World War II, 922 bombs fell on the financial district (the City), causing great damage as well as 2,500 casualties, and almost everyone lost someone near and dear to them at the front. Enraged Londoners poured a collective effort into a conflict that was to be idealistically defined as "the War to End All Wars."

During World War II, however, at least 30,000 people died, and vast tracts of London were destroyed by aerial bombing. Westminster Abbey (parts of which had stood unmolested since the 11th century) and the magnificent bulk of the Houses of Parliament were seriously damaged over two nights in May 1941. During a period remembered for the indomitable spirit of the people, thousands of Londoners systematically moved their mattresses every night to the Underground (the city's subway tunnels), considered safe from Nazi bombing. Amazingly, although the neighborhood that surrounded it was almost completely destroyed, St. Paul's Cathedral escaped with only minor damage, rising majestically above the rubble like a beacon of hope for the sorely tested people of London.

Following World War II, vast rebuilding projects replaced London's bombed-out rubble. The transportation system was improved. In 1953, the coronation of Elizabeth II sparked a period of beautification, with myriad houses painted and millions of flower beds planted.

Swinging London   *Time* magazine once wrote that, in every decade, the attention of the world often focuses on one city as the place to be—New York in the 1940s, Rome in the 1950s. In the 1960s, it was London. The pop-culture revolution that was sweeping the globe seemed to take root here more than anywhere else, with the possible exception of San Francisco. The sound of the Beatles having "A Hard Day's Night" was everywhere; no one remembered Elvis anymore. Mary Quant revolutionized fashion, and her Granny Takes a Trip boutiques sprouted up along King's Road. Young straight men—often wearing lipstick—flocked to Carnaby Street to don ruffled Edwardian blouses in brilliant chartreuse with orange pants and pink high heels. The air in the discos was laden with marijuana smoke inhaled by such icons as Mick Jagger, who, according to the musical *Hair,* every boy secretly wanted to sleep with. What had happened to staid old London? The horsey set was out, and rail-thin Twiggy was in. It was the psychedelic 1960s, and the mantra of the day was the late Timothy Leary's "tune in, turn on, drop out." London did just that, and even lived to recover from the era of rampant sex, heavy drugs, and rock 'n' roll—but it would never be the same again.

The 1970s & Beyond   In the 1970s and 1980s, a revitalized economy turned some run-down districts (Notting Hill, parts of Chelsea, the Docklands) into chic and desirable neighborhoods. English wits estimate that at one time or another since the end of World War II, virtually every corner of London has been covered with scaffolding, as builders, homeowners, and real-estate moguls added modern comforts and new life to virtually every building.

Prime Minister Margaret Thatcher's reforms of the 1980s created new and modernized financial institutions, including a computerized London Stock Exchange, whose presence has reinforced London's traditional role as a financial, shipping, and insurance center. In 1990, Thatcher was replaced as prime minister by another member of the Conservative party, the less flamboyant but also controversial John Major. In 1992, it wasn't the prime minister but the House of Windsor that got the boldest headlines. In a year that Elizabeth II labeled *annus horribilis,* a fire swept through Windsor Castle; the queen agreed to pay income taxes for the first time; and the marriages of two of her sons crumbled as Princes Charles and Andrew separated from their wives.

Although unemployment and terrorist bombings continued to dominate the headlines in 1993, the problems of the royal family captured the most media time. That year was launched by "Camillagate," the release of sexually

Britspeak

For many Americans, it's a shock to discover that the British speak a very different English language than we do. Believe it or not, there are enough differences between British English and American English to cause a total communication breakdown. Although the British use words and phrases you think you understand, they often have implications quite different from their U.S. equivalents.

When the British call someone "mean," they mean stingy. "Homely," meaning ugly or plain in America, becomes pleasant in England, meaning homey. "Calling" denotes a personal visit, not a phone call; however, a person-to-person phone call is a "personal call." To "queue up" means to form a line, which they do at every bus stop. And whereas a "subway" is an underground pedestrian passage, the actual subway system is called "the Underground" or "the Tube." The term "theatre" refers only to the live stage; movie theaters are "cinemas," and the films themselves are "the pictures." And a "bomb," which suggests a disaster in America, means a success in England.

In a grocery store, canned goods become "tins," rutabagas become "swedes," eggplants become "aubergines," and endive is "chicory" (while, conversely, chicory is "endive"). Both cookies and crackers become "biscuits," which can be either "dry" or "sweet"—that is, except for graham crackers, which are "digestives."

The going gets rougher when you're dealing with motor vehicles. When talking about the actual vehicle, very little means the same except for the word "car," unless you mean a truck, which is called a "lorry." In any case, gas is "petrol," the hood is the "bonnet," the windshield is the

explicit phone conversations between Prince Charles and his longtime companion, the then-married Camilla Parker-Bowles. British author Anthony Holden wrote that the Crown was dragged "as deep into the mud as at any time in the 500 years since Henry VII found it there at Bosworth Field."

In 1994, it was an engineering feat that captured London's attention. Queen Elizabeth II and François Mitterrand of France officially opened the Chunnel under the English Channel, the first link between Britain and France since the Ice Age. Pessimists predicted the "end of London as we know it before the foreign hordes descend."

The so-called fairy-tale marriage of Charles and Diana, which played out around the world, ended like a soap opera with a divorce in 1996. Prince Charles is a little poorer, having dug deep into his pockets for some $26 million in settlement (money now inherited by William and Harry).

In 1997, everyone's attention shifted to the parliamentary election. John Major's support had been steadily eroding since the early '90s, but the public's confidence in him seemed to hit an all-time low with his handling of the Mad-Cow Disease crisis. Although scientists now claim the epidemic will end naturally by 2001, many British voters blamed Major and the Tories for it.

The political limelight shifted to the young Labour leader Tony Blair. From his rock-star acquaintances to his "New Labour" rhetoric, which is chock-full of pop-culture buzzwords, he is a stark contrast to the staid Major. And his media-savvy personality obviously registered with the British electorate. On "windscreen," and bumpers are "fenders." The trunk is the "boot," and what you do on the horn is "hoot."

Most of us already know that an English apartment is a "flat" and that an elevator is a "lift." And you don't rent a room or an apartment, you "let" it. Although the ground floor is the ground floor, the second floor is the "first floor." And once you set up housekeeping, you don't vacuum, you "hoover."

Going clothes shopping? Then you should know that undershirts are called "vests" and undershorts are "pants," while long pants are called "trousers" and their cuffs are called "turn ups." Panties are "knickers" and panty hose are "tights." Pullover sweaters can be called "jumpers," with little girls' jumpers being "pinafores." If you're looking for diapers, ask for "nappies."

If you really want a challenge in this arena, you can always take on Cockney. The Cockneys are indigenous Londoners, although strictly speaking, the label refers only to people born within the sound of the bells of St. Mary-le-Bow in Cheapside. The exact derivation of the word "Cockney" is lost in the mist of antiquity, but it's supposed to have meant an "odd fellow." And the oddest feature about this fellow is undoubtedly the rhyming slang he has concocted over the centuries, based on the rhyme—or the rhyme of a rhyme—that goes with a particular word or phrase. So take my advice and don't try to delve further, unless you happen to be Professor Higgins—pardon me—"'iggins."

And the British spell many words slightly differently from Americans. Thus, British "colour" equals American "color," "cheque" equals "check," and "centre" equals "center."

May 1, 1997, the Labour Party ended 18 years of Conservative rule with a landslide election victory. Blair became Britain's youngest prime minister in 185 years, following in the wake of the largest Labour triumph since Winston Churchill was swept out of office at the end of World War II. At age 44 and newly installed at 10 Downing St., Blair is Britain's 50th prime minister.

Tony Blair is leading Britain on a program of constitutional reform without parallel in this century. Critics fear that Blair will one day preside over a "disunited" Britain, with Scotland breaking away and Northern Ireland forming a self-government.

Events took a shocking turn in August 1997 when Princess Diana was killed in a high-speed car crash in Paris, but in spite of wide criticism of the royal family in the wake of Diana's death, there is little support for doing away with the monarchy in Britain today. If polls are to be believed, some three-quarters of the British populace want the monarchy to continue. At the very least it's good for the tourist trade, on which Britain is increasingly dependent, and what would the tabloids do without it?

3 Pies, Puddings & Pints: The Lowdown on British Cuisine

You don't have to travel around England to experience regional English dishes; you'll find them all over London.

WHAT YOU'LL FIND ON THE MENU   On any pub menu you're likely to encounter such dishes as **Cornish pasty** and **shepherd's pie.** The first, traditionally made from Sunday-meal leftovers and taken by West Country fishers for Monday lunch, consists of chopped potatoes, carrots, and onions mixed together with seasoning and put into a pastry envelope. The second is a deep dish of chopped cooked beef mixed with onions and seasoning, covered with a layer of mashed potatoes, and served hot. Another version is **cottage pie,** which is minced beef covered with potatoes, also served hot.

The most common pub meal, though, is the **ploughman's lunch,** traditional farm-worker's fare, consisting of a good chunk of local cheese, a hunk of homemade crusty white or brown bread, butter, and a pickled onion or two, all washed down with ale. You'll now find such variations as pâté and chutney occasionally replacing the onions and cheese. Or you might find **Lancashire hot pot,** a stew of mutton, potatoes, kidneys, and onions (sometimes carrots). This concoction was originally put into a deep dish and set on the edge of the stove to cook slowly while the workers spent the day at the local mill.

Among the best-known traditional dishes is, of course, **roast beef and Yorkshire pudding**—the pudding made with a flour base and cooked under the joint, allowing the fat from the meat to drop onto it. The beef could easily be a large sirloin (rolled loin), which, so the story goes, was named by James I (not Henry VIII, as some claim) when he was a guest at Houghton Tower, Lancashire. "Arise, Sir Loin," he cried, as he knighted the joint with his dagger. Another dish that makes similar use of a flour base is toad-in-the-hole, in which sausages are cooked in batter. Game is also a staple on English tables, especially pheasant and grouse.

On any menu you'll find fresh **seafood**—cod, haddock, herring, plaice, or the aristocrat of flat fish, Dover sole. Cod and haddock are the most popular fish used in the traditional fish-and-chips (chips, of course, are fried potatoes or thick french fries), which the true Briton covers with salt and vinegar.

The East End of London has quite a few interesting old dishes, among them tripe and onions. Dr. Johnson's favorite tavern, Ye Olde Cheshire Cheese on Fleet Street, still (on most days) offers a beefsteak-kidney-mushroom-and-game pudding, in a suet case in winter and a pastry case in summer. East Enders can still be seen on Sunday at the Jellied Eel stall by Petticoat Lane, eating eel or cockles, mussels, whelks, and winkles—all consumed with a touch of vinegar.

The British call **desserts** "sweets" (although some people use the upper-class "pudding"), with trifle being the most famous. It consists of sponge cake soaked in brandy or sherry, coated with fruit or jam, and topped with a cream custard. A "fool," such as gooseberry fool, is a light cream dessert whipped up from seasonal fruits.

Cheese is traditionally served after dessert as a savory. There are many regional cheeses, the best known being Cheddar. A similar good, solid, mature cheese, is Cheshire, and from Wales comes the smooth-textured, crumbly Caerphilly. Stilton, a blue-veined cheese, is often enriched with a glass of port.

BRITISH CUISINE TODAY   The new obsession in England is not sex (that was the 1960s), but—amazingly, considering Britain's past reputation—food. Judge a country's interests by its newspapers: Some Sunday editions carry 20 pages dedicated to cuisine, with recipes, wine columns, and reviews of the latest trendy restaurant.

Under the rubric of "Modern British cuisine," young upstart chefs are giving traditional dishes unexpected twists. Parsnip soup is still served, but now it's likely to be with walnut salsa verde. The new buzzword for British cuisine is magpie—meaning borrowing ideas from global travels, taking them home, but improving on the original. If you want to see what Britain is eating today, just drop in at Harvey Nichols' Fifth Floor in London's Knightsbridge for its dazzling display of produce from all over the globe.

Even in British homes, instead of Sunday's leftover roast disguised as shepherd's pie, you're likely to encounter Indian, Chinese, Thai, or, most likely, Italian dishes. If you slip a look into the larder of your host, you might even find Mexican chiles, something almost unheard of a decade ago.

In contemporary London, the chef has taken on celebrity status. The cook creating breast of Gressingham duck topped with deep-fried seaweed and served with a passion-fruit sauce is honored the way the rock star was in the 1970s or the fashion designer in the 1980s. These days, some of the most celebrated chefs are getting so many offers for books, TV appearances, or whatever, that they're rarely around tending those pots 'n' pans; thus, it's the restaurant itself that is becoming celebrated, regardless of who's in the kitchen. Some restaurants are so popular that they are demanding reservations 2 weeks in advance, if not more.

WHAT TO WASH IT ALL DOWN WITH   London pubs serve a variety of cocktails, but their stock in trade is beer—brown beer, or bitter; blond beer, or lager; and very dark beer, or stout. The standard English draft beer is much stronger than American beer and is served "with the chill off" because it doesn't taste good cold. Lager is always chilled, whereas stout can be served either way. Beer is always served straight from the tap, in two sizes: half pint (8 oz.) and pint (16 oz.).

One of the most significant changes in English drinking habits can be seen in the growing popularity of wine bars. You will find many to patronize; some turn into dance clubs late at night. Britain isn't known for its wine, although it does produce some medium-sweet fruity whites. Its cider, though, is famous—and very potent in contrast to the American variety.

Whisky (spelled without the *e*) refers to scotch. Canadian and Irish whiskey (spelled with the *e*) are also available, but only the very best-stocked bars have American bourbon and rye. While you're in England, you may want to try the very English drink called Pimm's, a mixture developed by James Pimm, owner of a popular London oyster house in the 1840s. Although it can be consumed on the rocks, it's usually served as a Pimm's Cup—a drink that will have any variety of ingredients, depending on which part of the world (or empire) you're in. Here, just for fun, is a typical recipe: Take a very tall glass and fill it with ice. Add a thin slice of lemon (or orange), a cucumber spike (or a curl of cucumber rind), and 2 ounces of Pimm's liquor. Then finish with a splash of either lemon or club soda, 7-Up, or Tom Collins mix.

The English tend to drink everything at a warmer temperature than Americans are used to. So if you like ice in your Coke or Pepsi, be sure to ask for lots of it—or you're likely to end up with a measly melting cube or two.

Frommer's Online Directory: London

By Michael Shapiro

Michael Shapiro is the author of
Internet Travel Planning (Globe Pequot).

Frommer's Online Directory is a new feature designed to help you take advantage of the Internet to better plan your trip. Part I lists general Internet resources that can make any trip easier, such as sites for booking airline tickets. Please keep in mind that this is not a comprehensive list, but rather a discriminating selection of useful sites to get you started. In Part II you'll find some top online guides for London, including local lodging, top attractions, and getting around.

1 Top Travel Planning Web Sites

Among the most popular sites are online travel agencies. The top agencies, including Expedia, Preview Travel, and Travelocity, offer an array of tools that are valuable even if you don't book online. You can check flight schedules, hotel availability, car rental prices, or even get paged if your flight is delayed.

While online agencies have come a long way over the past few years, they don't always yield the best price. Unlike a travel agent, they're unlikely to tell you that you can save money by flying a day earlier or a day later. On the other hand, if you're looking for a bargain fare, you might find something online that an agent wouldn't dig up—a travel agent may not find it worthwhile spending half an hour trying to find you the best deal. On the Net you can be your own agent and take all the time you want.

Online booking sites aren't the only places to book airline tickets—all major airlines have their own Web sites and often offer incentives, such as bonus frequent flyer miles or Net-only discounts, for buying online. These incentives have helped airlines capture the majority of the online booking market. According to Jupiter Communications, online agencies such as Travelocity booked about 80 percent of tickets purchased online in 1996, but by 1999 airline sites (such as **www.ual.com**) were projected to own about 60 percent of the online market, with online agencies' share of the pie dwindling each year.

Below are the Web sites for the major airlines serving London's airports. These sites offer schedules, flight booking, and most have pages where you can sign up for email alerts on weekend deals.

Looking & Booking Online

Far more people look online than book online, partly due to fear of putting their credit cards through on the Net. Though secure encryption has made this fear less justified, there's no reason why you can't find a flight online and then book it by calling a toll-free number or contacting your travel agent. To be sure you're in secure mode when you book online, look for a little icon of a key (in Netscape) or a padlock (Internet Explorer) at the bottom of your Web browser.

Air Canada	www.aircanada.com
American Airlines	www.aa.com
British Airways	www.british-airways.com
Continental Airlines	www.flycontinental.com
Northwest Airlines	www.nwa.com
Qantas	www.qantas.com
United Airlines	www.ual.com
Virgin Atlantic	www.fly.virgin.com

WHEN SHOULD YOU BOOK ONLINE?

Online booking is not for everyone. If you prefer to let others handle your travel arrangements, one call to an experienced travel agent should suffice. But if you want to know as much as possible about your options, the Net is a good place to start, especially for bargain hunters.

The most compelling reason to use online booking is to take advantage of last-minute specials, such as American Airlines' weekend deals or other Internet-only fares that must be purchased online. Another advantage is that you can cash in on incentives for booking online, such as rebates or bonus frequent flyer miles.

Online booking works best for trips within North America—for international tickets, it's usually cheaper and easier to use a travel agent or consolidator.

Online booking is certainly not for those with a complex international itinerary. If you require follow-up services, such as itinerary changes, use a travel agent. Though Expedia and some other online agencies employ travel agents available by phone, these sites are geared primarily for self-service.

LEADING BOOKING SITES

Below are listings for the top travel booking sites. The starred selections are the most useful and best-designed sites.

Cheap Tickets. www.cheaptickets.com
Essentials: Discounted rates on domestic and international airline tickets and hotel rooms.

Sometimes discounters such as Cheap Tickets have exclusive deals that aren't available through more mainstream channels. Registration at Cheap Tickets requires inputting a credit card number before getting started, which is one reason many people elect to call the company's toll-free number rather than booking online. Cheap Tickets actually regards this policy as a selling point, arguing that "lookers" who don't intend to buy will be scared off by its "credit card first" approach and won't bog down the site with their queries. Despite its misguided credit card policy, Cheap Tickets is worth the effort because its fares can be lower than those offered by its competitors.

Take a Look at Frommer's Site

We highly recommend Arthur Frommer's Budget Travel Online (**www. frommers.com**) as an excellent travel planning resource. Of course, we're a little biased, but you will find indispensable travel tips, reviews, monthly vacation giveaways, and online booking.

Subscribe to Arthur Frommer's Daily Newsletter (**www.frommers.com/ newsletters**) to receive the latest travel bargains and inside travel secrets in your mailbox every day. You'll read daily headlines and articles from the dean of travel himself, highlighting last-minute deals on airfares, accommodations, cruises, and package vacations. You'll also find great travel advice by checking our Tip of the Day or Hot Spot of the Month.

Search our Destinations archive (**www.frommers.com/destinations**) of more than 200 domestic and international destinations for great places to stay, tips for traveling there, and what to do while you're there. Once you've researched your trip, you might try our online reservation system (**www.frommers.com/book-travelnow**) to book your dream vacation at affordable prices.

✪ Expedia. expedia.com

Essentials: Domestic and international flight, hotel, and rental car booking; late-breaking travel news, destination features and commentary from travel experts; deals on cruises and vacation packages. Free registration is required for booking.

Expedia makes it easy to handle flight, hotel, and car booking on one itinerary, so it's a good place for one-stop shopping. Expedia's hotel search offers crisp, zoomable maps to pinpoint most properties; click on the camera icon to see images of the rooms and facilities. But like many online databases, Expedia focuses on the major chains, such as Hilton and Hyatt, so don't expect to find too many one-of-a-kind resorts or B&Bs here.

Once you're registered (it's only necessary to do this once from each computer you use), you can start booking with the Roundtrip Fare Finder box on the home page, which expedites the process. After selecting a flight, you can hold it until midnight the following day or purchase online. If you think you might do better through a travel agent, you'll have time to try to get a lower price. And you may do better with a travel agent because Expedia's computer reservation system does not include all airlines.

Expedia's World Guide, offering destination information, has a glaring weakness—it takes a lot of page views to get very little information. However, Expedia compensates by linking to other Microsoft Network services, such as its Sidewalk city guides, which offer entertainment and dining advice for many of the cities it covers.

Preview Travel. www.previewtravel.com

Essentials: Domestic and international flight, hotel, and rental car booking; Travel Newswire lists fare sales and deals on cruises and vacation packages. Free (one-time) registration is required for booking. Preview offers express booking for members, but at press time this feature was buried below the fold on Preview's reservation page.

Preview features the most inviting interface for booking trips, though the wealth of graphics involved can make the site somewhat slow to load. Use Farefinder to quickly find the lowest current fares on flights to dozens of major cities. Carfinder offers a similar service for rental cars, but you can only search airport locations, not city pickup sites. To see the lowest fare for your itinerary, input the dates and times for your route and see what comes up.

Preview has a great feature called the "Best Fare Finder"—after a search for the best deal on your itinerary, it will check flights that are a bit later or earlier to see if it might be cheaper to fly at a different time. While these searches have become quite sophisticated, they still occasionally overlook deals that might be uncovered by a top-notch travel agent. It might be worthwhile, after searching online, to call an agent to see if you can get a better price.

With Preview's Fare Alert feature, you can set fares for up to three routes and you'll receive email notices when the fare drops below your target amount. For example, you could tell Preview to alert you when the fare from New York to London drops below $350. If it does, you'll get an email telling you the current fare.

Minor quibbles: When you search for a fare, hotel or car—at least when we went to press—Preview launches an annoying little "Please Wait" window that gets in the way of the main browser window even when your results begin to appear. The hotel search feature is intuitive, but the images and maps aren't as crisp as those at Expedia. Also: all sorts of extraneous information (such as NYC public school locations), irrelevant to most travelers, is on the maps.

Note to AOL Users: You can book flights, hotels, rental cars and cruises on AOL at keyword: Travel. The booking software is provided by Preview Travel and is similar to Preview on the Web. Use the AOL "Travelers Advantage" program to earn a 5% rebate on flights, hotel rooms, and car rentals.

Priceline.com. www.priceline.com

Launched in 1998 with a $10 million ad campaign, Priceline lets you "name your price" for domestic and international airline tickets. In other words, you select a route and dates, guarantee with a credit card, and make a bid for what you're willing to pay. If one of the airlines in Priceline's database has a fare that's lower than your bid, your credit card will automatically be charged for a ticket.

But you can't say *when* you want to fly—you have to accept any flight leaving between 6am and 10pm, and you may have to make a stopover. No frequent flyer miles are awarded, and tickets are nonrefundable and can't be exchanged for another flight. So if your plans change, you're out of luck. Priceline can be good for travelers who have to take off on short notice (and who are thus unable to qualify for advance purchase discounts). But be sure to shop around first—if you overbid, you'll be required to purchase the ticket and Priceline will pocket the difference.

Travelocity. www.travelocity.com

Essentials: Domestic and international flight, hotel, and rental car booking; deals on cruises and vacation packages. Travel Headlines spotlights latest bargain airfares. Free (one-time) registration is required for booking.

Travelocity almost got it right. Its Express Booking feature enables travelers to complete the booking process more quickly than they could at Expedia or Preview, but Travelocity gums up the works with a page called "Featured Airlines." Big placards of several featured airlines compete for your attention—if you want to see the fares for all available airlines, click the much smaller box at the bottom of the page labeled "Book a Flight."

Some have worried that Travelocity, which is owned by American Airlines' parent company AMR, directs bookings to American. This doesn't seem to be the case—I've booked there dozens of times and have always been directed to the cheapest listed flight, whatever the airline. But the "Featured Airlines" page does seem to be Travelocity's way of trying to cash in with ads and incentives for booking certain airlines.

There are rewards for choosing one of the featured airlines—you'll get 1,500 bonus frequent flyer miles if you book through United's site, for example, but the site doesn't tell you about other airlines that might be cheaper. If the United flight costs $150 more than the best deal on another airline, it's not worth spending the extra money.

On the plus side, Travelocity has some leading-edge techie tools for modern travelers. Exhibit A is Fare Watcher Email, an "intelligent agent" that keeps you informed of the best fares offered for the city pairs (round-trips) of your choice. Whenever the fare changes by $25 or more, Fare Watcher will alert you by email. Exhibit B is Flight Paging—if you own an alphanumeric pager with national access that can receive email, Travelocity's paging system can alert you if your flight is delayed. Finally, though Travelocity doesn't include every budget airline, it does include Southwest, the leading U.S. budget carrier.

FINDING LODGINGS ONLINE

While the services above offer hotel booking, on a site devoted primarily to lodging you may find properties that aren't listed on more general online travel agencies. You won't find some of the kinds of accommodations, such as bed-and-breakfast inns, which appear on the specialized sites on the more mainstream booking services. Other services, such as TravelWeb, offer weekend deals on major chain properties, which cater to business travelers and have more empty rooms on weekends.

All Hotels on the Web. www.all-hotels.com
Well, this site doesn't include all the hotels on the Web, but it does have tens of thousands of listings throughout the world. Bear in mind that each hotel listed has paid a small fee of ($25 and up) for placement, so it's not an objective list but more like a book of online brochures.

InnSite. www.innsite.com
B&B listings for inns in all 50 U.S. states and dozens of countries around the globe.

Find an inn at your destination, have a look at images of the rooms, check prices and availability, and then send email to the innkeeper if you have further questions. This is an extensive directory of bed-and-breakfast inns but only includes listings if the proprietor submitted one (note: it's free to get an inn listed). The descriptions are written by the innkeepers and many listings link to the inn's own Web sites, where you can find more information and images.

Places to Stay. www.placestostay.com
Mostly one-of-a-kind places in the U.S. and abroad that you might not find in other directories, with a focus on resort accommodations. Again, listing is selective—this isn't a comprehensive directory, but can give you a sense of what's available at different destinations.

✪ **TravelWeb. www.travelweb.com**
TravelWeb lists more than 16,000 hotels worldwide, focusing on chains such as Hyatt and Hilton, and you can book almost 90 percent of these online. TravelWeb's Click-It Weekends, updated each Monday, offers weekend deals at many leading hotel chains. TravelWeb is the online home for Pegasus Systems, which provides transaction processing systems for the hotel industry.

LAST-MINUTE DEALS AND OTHER ONLINE BARGAINS

There's nothing airlines hate more than flying with lots of empty seats. The Net has enabled airlines to offer last-minute bargains to entice travelers to fill those seats. Most of these are announced on Tuesday or Wednesday and are valid for travel the following

Atlanta Colts & Atlanta Mustangs
is proud to be sponsored by

theBESTeam

KEN BEST
404-873-1339
Fax – 404-873-1139

For all your
Real Estate Needs!

While most people learn about last-minute weekend deals from email, it can be best to find out precisely when these deals become available and check airlines' Web sites at this time. To find out when deals become available, check the pages devoted to these deals on airlines' Web pages. Because they are limited, these deals can vanish within hours, sometimes even minutes, so it pays to log on as soon as they're available.

weekend, but some can be booked weeks or months in advance. You can sign up for weekly email alerts at airlines' sites (For airlines' Web site addresses, see above) or check sites such as WebFlyer (see below) that compile lists of these bargains. To make it easier, visit a site (see below) that will round up all the deals and send them in one convenient weekly email. But last-minute deals aren't the only online bargains—other sites can help you find values even if you can't wait until the eleventh hour.

✪ 1travel.com. www.1travel.com
Deals on domestic and international flights, cruises, hotels, and all-inclusive resorts such as Club Med. 1travel.com's Saving Alert compiles last-minute air deals so you don't have to scroll through multiple email alerts. A feature called "Drive a little using low-fare airlines" helps map out strategies for using alternate airports to find lower fares. And Farebeater searches a database that includes published fares, consolidator bargains, and special deals exclusive to **1travel.com**. *Note:* The travel agencies listed by 1travel.com have paid for placement.

BestFares. www.bestfares.com
Bargain-seeker Tom Parsons lists some great deals on airfares, hotels, rental cars, and cruises, but the site is poorly organized. News Desk is a long list of hundreds of bargains, but they're not broken down into cities or even countries, so it's not easy to find what you're looking for. If you have time to wade through it, you might find a good deal. Some material is available only to paid subscribers.

Go4less.com. www.go4less.com
Specializing in last-minute cruise and package deals, Go4less has some eye-popping offers, such as off-peak Caribbean cruises for under $100 per day. The site has a clean design but the bargains aren't organized by destination. However you avoid sifting through all this material by using the Search box and entering vacation type, destination, month, and price.

Moment's Notice. www.moments-notice.com
As the name suggests, Moment's Notice specializes in last-minute vacation and cruise deals. You can browse for free, but if you want to purchase a trip, you have to join Moment's Notice, which costs $25.

Smarter Living. www.smarterliving.com
Best known for its email dispatch of weekend deals on 20 airlines, Smarter Living also keeps you posted about last-minute bargains on everything from Windjammer Cruises to flights to Iceland.

✪ WebFlyer. www.webflyer.com
WebFlyer is the ultimate online resource for frequent flyers and also has an excellent listing of last-minute air deals. Click on "Deal Watch" for a roundup of weekend deals on flights, hotels, and rental cars from domestic and international suppliers.

Check Email at Internet Cafes While Traveling

Until a few years ago, most travelers who checked their email while traveling carried a laptop, but this posed some problems. Not only are laptops expensive, but they can be difficult to configure, incur expensive connection charges, and are attractive to thieves. Thankfully, Web-based free email programs have made it much easier to check your mail.

Just open an account at a freemail provider, such as Hotmail (**hotmail.com**) or Yahoo! Mail (**mail.yahoo.com**) and all you'll need to check your mail is a Web connection, easily available at Net cafes and copy shops around the world. After logging on, just point the browser to **www.hotmail.com**, enter your username and password and you'll have access to your mail.

Internet cafes have become ubiquitous, so for a few dollars an hour you'll be able to check your mail and send messages back to colleagues, friends, and family. If you already have a primary email account, you can set it to forward mail to your freemail account while you're away. Freemail programs have become enormously popular (Hotmail claims more than 10 million members) because they enable everyone, even those who don't own a computer, to have an email address they can check wherever they log on to the Web.

TRAVELER'S TOOLKIT

Seasoned travelers usually carry some essential items to make their trips easier. Following is a selection of online tools to smooth your journey.

ATM LOCATORS:

Visa (**www.visa.com/pd/atm/**). MasterCard (**www.mastercard.com/atm**)
Find ATMs in hundreds of cities in the U.S. and around the world. Both include maps for some locations and list airport ATM locations, some with maps.

Intellicast. **www.intellicast.com**
Weather forecasts for all 50 states and cities around the world.

✪ MapQuest. **www.mapquest.com**
Specializing in U.S. maps, MapQuest enables you to zoom in on a destination, calculate step-by-step driving directions between any two U.S. points, and locate restaurants, hotels, and other attractions on maps.

✪ Net Café Guide. **www.netcafeguide.com**
Locate Internet cafes at hundreds of locations around the globe. Catch up on your email, log on to the Web and stay in touch with the home front, usually for just a few dollars per hour.

TheTrip: Airport Maps and Flight Status. **www.thetrip.com**
A business travel site where you can find out when an airborne flight is scheduled to arrive. Click on "Guides and Tools" to peruse airport maps for more than 40 domestic cities.

Universal Currency Converter. **www.xe.net/currency**
See what your dollar or pound is worth in more than a hundred other countries.

U.S. Customs Service Traveler Information. **www.customs.ustreas.gov/travel/index.htm**

Wondering what you're allowed to bring in to the U.S.? Check at this thorough site, which includes maximum allowance and duty fees.

2 The Top Web Sites for London

CITY & ENTERTAINMENT GUIDES
For AOL Members:

Digital City: London. Keyword: London
A vibrant city guide to London that enables you to get the skinny on arts, dining, nightlife, and more. For more on London's culture, try keyword: Londonleisure. You can also participate in AOL's active chat areas to see what others are saying, or pose a question of your own. Digital City: London is also available on the Web at (**london.digitalcity.com**).

Gay London. www.gaylondon.co.uk
A guide to gay-friendly clubs, restaurants, lodgings, shops, and fitness centers. The listings are quite extensive, but each is relatively bare bones, including just address, phone, hours, and nearest Underground stop.

Official London Theater Guide. www.officiallondontheatre.co.uk
An extensive theater guide with information on London's discount ticket booth. Search for plays by type of show, title, theater name, or date. Or simply view everything playing in London—listings include a brief summary, actors, times, prices, and the dates of a show's run. Remember if you see a date such as 03/10/00, that means it's playing until October 3, 2000, as the English place the day before the month.

This is London. www.thisislondon.com
This well-rounded site from the *Evening Standard* includes a dining guide with unbiased reviews and search capability, a guide to city attractions, and a Hot Tickets sections with insider advice on theater, music and comedy.

✪ Time Out London. www.timeout.com/london
A wide-ranging city guide that has extensive and honest information on sightseeing, dining, lodging, shopping, and entertainment. From theater to the club scene, it's all here. You'll also find sections for gays and lesbians, kids, and links to other Web sites of interest to visitors.

UK for Visitors (Mining Co.). gouk.miningco.com
Though the Mining Co. has an amateurish feel about it, this roundup of links does unearth some good Web sites. Clicking on London leads to sections on nightlife, shopping, dining, and lodging.

What's On Stage. www.whatsonstage.com
Theater listings and ticket information for London and the rest of the U.K. by day, week and month. This extensive site also includes recent reviews, theater news, and features on award winners. A separate section covers classical music. Submit your email address, if you like, for free weekly email updates on what's opening and closing.

LOCAL LODGING SITES
The sites below are specific to London or the U.K. For international guides that include listings for London, see the "Finding Lodgings Online" guide in section 1.

✪ Automobile Association—UK. www.theaa.co.uk
This outstanding guide includes extensive lodging listings, which are apparently objective. The hundreds of hotels, many of which accept online bookings, are ranked by

price and quality. You'll also find restaurant information with ratings based on food, service, atmosphere, and price. Most, but not all, restaurants list typical meal prices and which credit cards are accepted.

Hotels England. www.hotelsengland.com
Promising up to 50% off, this site has some reasonably good deals, but I checked a hotel where I paid about $120 for a room last year and the best Hotels England could do was $154. If you do find a good deal, you can book online.

London Holiday Accommodation Bureau. business.virgin.net/g.macnaughton/ index.htm
LHAB offers vacation rentals of apartments. Some are shared with your hosts; at others you'll have the place to yourself. A sample offering: shared accommodation near Church Street with separate kitchen, bathroom, and double-bed room for £120 per couple per week.

The National Trust: Travel. www.nationaltrust.org.uk/travel.htm
The National Trust maintains more than 200 cottages and other unusual lodgings throughout the U.K. The proceeds help support the work of this preservation organization. The more popular lodgings are typically reserved well in advance, so if you're interested, prepare to book early.

NEWSPAPERS

Electronic Telegraph. www.telegraph.co.uk
From the *London Telegraph* comes an elegant yet intuitive Web site, with news, sports, entertainment reviews, and lifestyle features.

Guardian Unlimited. www.guardian.co.uk
From the pages of the Guardian come news, sports, entertainment reviews, and lifestyle features.

Independent Online. www.independent.co.uk
Another rich source of information for visitors, the Independent is a deep resource for local news, sports, and opinionated views from columnists.

The Times of London. the-times.co.uk
This venerable newspaper may have slipped a bit in recent years, but it's still a good source for news, sports, and other London happenings. Free registration is required. The *Sunday Times* maintains a separate Web site at (**www.sunday-times.co.uk**).

ATTRACTIONS & SIGHTSEEING

The British Museum. www.british-museum.ac.uk
At press time, the first page of this site informed visitors, "There are currently no Egyptian mummies on display." Shame. Still, the British Museum is well worth visiting, and the Web sites can tell you what's on (and what's happening in the mummy-less Egyptian Galleries) during the dates of your visit.

Buckingham Palace. www.royal.gov.uk/palaces/bp.htm
The official site from the British monarchy offers history, images, and descriptions of the "working palace" and "visitors' palace."

Harrods. www.harrods.co.uk
The Web site includes a guide to the seemingly countless departments; you can download printable maps of each floor plan. You can also learn about sales and see images of the Egyptian escalator, antique department, food hall, and much more.

Houses of Parliament. www.parliament.uk
A matter-of-fact visitors' guide to the House of Commons and the House of Lords that includes tour times and a schedule of when Parliament is in session. See (**www. parliament.uk/parliament/TOURS.HTM**) for more about touring.

❂ **London Transport Museum. www.ltmuseum.co.uk**
An outstanding virtual tour of this fascinating museum, which chronicles the development of London's public transit system dating back to the early 1800s.

The National Gallery. www.nationalgallery.org.uk
At the Web site, you can browse through the permanent collection, see what's new, and find visitor information to help you plan when to go.

❂ **Natural History Museum. www.nhm.ac.uk/museum**
A remarkably lively and extensive site offering a preview of the exhibitions and special programs. Click on the gallery guide, where the sections include Dinosaurs, Creepy Crawlies, Wonders, and many more.

Shakespeare's Globe. www.rdg.ac.uk/AcaDepts/ln/Globe/Globe.html
The rebuilt Globe Theater was reopened in 1997 almost 400 years after the original Globe burned to the ground. This site offers program and ticket information, as well as Globe history and images of the rebuilt theater.

St. Paul's Cathedral. stpauls.london.anglican.org
Sightseeing details, a calendar of services and events, and the history of this remarkable landmark.

Tate Gallery. www.tate.org.uk
This visually arresting Web site shows off the Tate's broad range of modern art. See what's on at the Tate or browse through images from the permanent collection.

Tower Bridge. www.southwark.gov.uk/tourism/attractions/tower_bridge
History, trivia and a nice image of this stunning landmark.

❂ **Tower of London Tour. www.toweroflondontour.com**
An extensive and illuminating photographic tour. Click on Tower of London Tales for ghost stories or Site Map and Search for an index and maps from Queen Anne's time to the present. There's also a special tour for kids.

❂ **Westminister Abbey. www.westminster-abbey.org**
A superb historical tour with lots of photos of one of the world's most magnificent Gothic churches. Includes basic visitor information as tours of the nave, sanctuary, Henry VII Chapel, and a section on the coronations that have occurred at the abbey.

TOUR COMPANIES

The Big Bus Company. www.bigbus.co.uk
A city loop tour from atop an open-air, double-decker bus is a fine way to get an overview of London's leading attractions. The Web site includes route information, prices, and tour information. You can buy tickets online (and have them sent to your London hotel) for the Big Bus, as well as for Madame Tussaud's, the London Dungeon, and a couple of other attractions.

❂ **Original London Walks. www.walks.com**
London's most established walking tour company posts a schedule of walks by day of the week. Click on a day and get a list of more than a dozen distinct tours, such as "In the Footsteps of Sherlock Holmes" or "Jack the Ripper Haunts."

Rock Tours of London. **www.rocktourslondon.co.uk**
This tour claims to cover 101 rock music sites during a 2-hour jaunt around London.
The Web site includes a schedule and sampling of the attractions.

GETTING AROUND

BAA: London Airports. **www.heathrow.co.uk**
A guide and terminal maps for Heathrow, Gatwick, Stansted, and other lesser airports,
including flight arrival times, duty-free shops, airport restaurants, and information on
getting from airports to downtown London.

Eurostar. **www.eurostar.com**
Fares, timetables, and booking for this high-speed train, which shoots through the
Chunnel to Paris.

Heathrow Express. www.heathrowexpress.co.uk
Information and fares for the train that takes just 15 minutes to get from Heathrow
to Paddington Station in downtown London.

London Transport. www.londontransport.co.uk
London Transport is the agency that operates the Underground subway and city bus
systems. This extensive and well-designed site includes maps, fare information, and
advice to help you get around London as easily and cheaply as possible. You'll find
schedules for the last trains, which typically stop running about midnight, and for
night buses, which keep rolling till dawn.

○ Subway Navigator. **metro.ratp.fr:10001/bin/cities/english**
An amazing site with detailed subway route maps for London and more than 60 other
cities around the world. Select a city and enter your departure and arrival points.
Subway Navigator maps out your route and tells you how long the trip should take.

Both

Index

See also Accommodations and Restaurants indexes, below.
Page numbers in *italics* refer to maps.

General Index

FROMMER'S® COMPLETE TRAVEL GUIDES

Alaska
Amsterdam
Arizona
Atlanta
Australia
Austria
Bahamas
Barcelona, Madrid & Seville
Beijing
Belgium, Holland & Luxembourg
Bermuda
Boston
Budapest & the Best of Hungary
California
Canada
Cancún, Cozumel &
   the Yucatán
Cape Cod, Nantucket & Martha's Vineyard
Caribbean
Caribbean Cruises & Ports of Call
Caribbean Ports of Call
Carolinas & Georgia
Chicago
China
Colorado
Costa Rica
Denmark
Denver, Boulder & Colorado Springs
England
Europe
Florida
France
Germany
Greece
Greek Islands
Hawaii
Hong Kong
Honolulu, Waikiki & Oahu
Ireland
Israel
Italy
Jamaica & Barbados
Japan
Las Vegas
London
Los Angeles
Maryland & Delaware
Maui
Mexico
Miami & the Keys

Montana & Wyoming
Montréal & Québec City
Munich & the Bavarian Alps
Nashville & Memphis
Nepal
New England
New Mexico
New Orleans
New York City
Nova Scotia, New Brunswick &
   Prince Edward Island
Oregon
Paris
Philadelphia & the
   Amish Country
Portugal
Prague & the Best of the Czech Republic
Provence & the Riviera
Puerto Rico
Rome
San Antonio & Austin
San Diego
San Francisco
Santa Fe, Taos &
   Albuquerque
Scandinavia
Scotland
Seattle & Portland
Singapore & Malaysia
South Africa
Southeast Asia
South Pacific
Spain
Sweden
Switzerland
Thailand
Tokyo
Toronto
Tuscany & Umbria
USA
Utah
Vancouver & Victoria
Vermont, New Hampshire
   & Maine
Vienna & the Danube Valley
Virgin Islands
Virginia
Walt Disney World & Orlando
Washington, D.C.
Washington State

FROMMER'S® DOLLAR-A-DAY GUIDES

Australia from $50 a Day	Hawaii from $70 a Day	New Zealand from $50 a Day
California from $60 a Day	Ireland from $50 a Day	Paris from $85 a Day
Caribbean from $70 a Day	Israel from $45 a Day	San Francisco from $60 a Day
England from $70 a Day	Italy from $70 a Day	Washington, D.C.,
Europe from $60 a Day	London from $85 a Day	from $60 a Day
Florida from $60 a Day	New York from $80 a Day	

FROMMER'S® PORTABLE GUIDES

Acapulco, Ixtapa &	Dublin	Puerto Vallarta, Manzanillo
Zihuatanejo	Hawaii: The Big Island	& Guadalajara
Alaska Cruises & Ports of Call	Las Vegas	San Diego
Bahamas	London	San Francisco
Baja & Los Cabos	Maine Coast	Sydney
Berlin	Maui	Tampa & St. Petersburg
California Wine Country	New Orleans	Venice
Charleston & Savannah	New York City	Washington, D.C.
Chicago	Paris	

FROMMER'S® NATIONAL PARK GUIDES

Family Vacations in the	National Parks of the	Yellowstone & Grand Teton
National Parks	American West	Yosemite & Sequoia/
Grand Canyon	Rocky Mountain	Kings Canyon
		Zion & Bryce Canyon

FROMMER'S® GREAT OUTDOOR GUIDES

New England	Southern California & Baja
Northern California	Washington & Oregon

FROMMER'S® MEMORABLE WALKS

Chicago	New York	San Francisco
London	Paris	Washington D.C.

FROMMER'S® IRREVERENT GUIDES

Amsterdam	London	New Orleans	Seattle & Portland
Boston	Los Angeles	Paris	Vancouver
Chicago	Manhattan	San Francisco	Walt Disney World
Las Vegas			Washington, D.C.

FROMMER'S® BEST-LOVED DRIVING TOURS

America	Florida	Ireland	Scotland
Britain	France	Italy	Spain
California	Germany	New England	Western Europe

THE COMPLETE IDIOT'S TRAVEL GUIDES

Boston	Ireland	Paris
Chicago	Las Vegas	San Francisco
Cruise Vacations	London	Spain
Planning Your Trip to Europe	Mexico's Beach Resorts	Walt Disney World
Florida	New Orleans	Washington, D.C.
Hawaii	New York City	

THE UNOFFICIAL GUIDES®

Bed & Breakfast in
  New England
Bed & Breakfast in
  the Northwest
Beyond Disney
Branson, Missouri
California with Kids
Chicago

Cruises
Florida with Kids
The Great Smoky &
  Blue Ridge
  Mountains
Inside Disney
Las Vegas

London
Miami & the Keys
Mini Las Vegas
Mini-Mickey
New Orleans
New York City
Paris

San Francisco
Skiing in the West
Walt Disney World
Walt Disney World
  for Grown-ups
Walt Disney World
  for Kids
Washington, D.C.

SPECIAL-INTEREST TITLES

Born to Shop: France
Born to Shop: Hong Kong
Born to Shop: Italy
Born to Shop: New York
Born to Shop: Paris
Frommer's Britain's Best Bike Rides
The Civil War Trust's Official Guide
  to the Civil War Discovery Trail
Frommer's Caribbean Hideaways
Frommer's Europe's Greatest Driving Tours
Frommer's Food Lover's Companion to France
Frommer's Food Lover's Companion to Italy
Frommer's Gay & Lesbian Europe
Israel Past & Present
Monks' Guide to California

Monks' Guide to New York City
The Moon
New York City with Kids
Unforgettable Weekends
Outside Magazine's Guide
  to Family Vacations
Places Rated Almanac
Retirement Places Rated
Road Atlas Britain
Road Atlas Europe
Washington, D.C., with Kids
Wonderful Weekends from Boston
Wonderful Weekends from New York City
Wonderful Weekends from San Francisco
Wonderful Weekends from Los Angeles

WHEREVER YOU TRAVEL, $\mathcal{H}$ELP IS NEVER FAR AWAY.

From planning your trip to providing travel assistance along the way, American Express® Travel Service Offices are always there to help you do more.

London

ST MARTIN FAID

American Express Travel Service
78 Brompton Rd.
Knightsbridge
(44)(171) 584-6182

American Express Travel Service
111 Cheapside
(44)(171) 600-5522

American Express Travel Service
89 Mount St.
Mayfair
(44)(171) 499-4436

American Express Travel Service
102-104 Victoria St.
(44)(171) 828-7411

do more AMERICAN EXPRESS®

Travel

www.americanexpress.com/travel

American Express Travel Service Offices are found in central locations throughout London.